# MEDICAL SELF-REGULATION

# Medical Law and Ethics

*Series Editor*
Sheila McLean, Director of the Institute of Law and Ethics in Medicine, School of Law, University of Glasgow

The 21st century seems likely to witness some of the most major developments in medicine and healthcare ever seen. At the same time, the debate about the extent to which science and/or medicine should lead the moral agenda continues, as do questions about the appropriate role for law.

This series brings together some of the best contemporary academic commentators to tackle these dilemmas in a challenging, informed and inquiring manner. The scope of the series is purposely wide, including contributions from a variety of disciplines such as law, philosophy and social sciences.

*Forthcoming titles in the series*

Biotechnology and the Challenge of Property
Property Rights in Dead Bodies, Body Parts, and Genetic Information
*Remigius N. Nwabueze*
ISBN 978 0 7546 7168 8

The Jurisdiction of Medical Law
*Kenneth Veitch*
ISBN 978 0 7546 49441

Ethical and Regulatory Aspects of Human Genetic Databases
*Edited by Bernice Elger, Nikola Biller-Andorno, Alexandre Mauron and Alexander M. Capron*
ISBN 978 0 7546 7255 5

Altruism Reconsidered
Exploring New Approaches to Property in Human Tissue
*Edited by Michael Steinmann, Peter Sykora, and Urban Wiesing*
ISBN 978 0 7546 7270 8

Bioequity – Property and the Human Body
*Nils Hoppe*
ISBN 978 0 7546 7280 7

# Medical Self-Regulation

## Crisis and Change

MARK DAVIES
*University of Sussex*

ASHGATE

Published by
Ashgate Publishing Limited
Gower House
Croft Road
Aldershot
Hampshire GU11 3HR
England

Ashgate Publishing Company
Suite 420
101 Cherry Street
Burlington, VT 05401-4405
USA

Ashgate website: http://www.ashgate.com

**British Library Cataloguing in Publication Data**
Davies, Mark
Medical self-regulation : crisis and change
1. General Medical Council (Great Britain) 2. Physicians - Licenses - Great Britain 3. Physicians - Great Britain - Discipline 4. Physicians - Malpractice - Great Britain- Case studies 5. Physicians - Great Britain - Discipline - Case Studies
I. Title
344.4'104121

**Library of Congress Cataloging-in-Publication Data**
Davies, Mark, 1964-
Medical self-regulation : crisis and change / by Mark Davies.
p. cm.
Includes bibliographical references and index.
ISBN 978-0-7546-4459-0
1. Medical laws and legislation--Great Britain. 2. Physicians--Licenses--Great Britain. 3. Physicians--Malpractice--Great Britain. 4. Physicians--Discipline--Great Britain. 5. General Medical Council (Great Britain) I. Title.
[DNLM: 1. Malpractice--legislation & jurisprudence--Great Britain. 2. Legislation, Hospital--Great Britain. 3. Physicians--legislation & jurisprudence--Great Britain. 4. Professional Autonomy--Great Britain. W 44 FA1 D256m 2007]

KD2945.D38 2007
344.4104'1--dc22

2007002933

ISBN 978-0-7546-4459-0

Printed and bound in Great Britain by MPG Books Ltd, Bodmin, Cornwall.

# Contents

# Table of Cases and Legislation

Cases

Legislation

Statutes

Statutory Instruments



Health Service Circulars

# List of Abbreviations

| | |
|---|---|
| ARC | Assessment Referral Committee |
| AVSD | Atrio Ventricular Septal Defect |
| BMA | British Medical Association |
| BRI | Bristol Royal Infirmary |
| CHI | Commission for Health Improvement |
| CHRE | Council for Health Regulatory Excellence |
| CHRP | Council for the Regulation of Health Professions |
| CPD | Continuing Professional Development |
| CPP | Committee on Professional Performance |
| CRB | Criminal Records Bureau |
| CRHCP | Council for the Regulation of Healthcare Professionals |
| DHSS | Department of Health and Social Security |
| DoH | Department of Health |
| ECHR | European Court of Human Rights |
| EKHA | East Kent Health Authority |
| FHSA | Family Health Services Authority |
| FHSAU | Family Health Services Appeal Unit |
| FPC | Family Practitioner Committee |
| FSA | Financial Services Authority |
| FTP | Fitness to Practise |
| GMC | General Medical Council |
| GP | General Practitioner |
| HA | Health Authority |
| HC | Health Committee |
| HDU | High Dependency Unit |
| HRA | Human Rights Act 1998 |
| ICAS | Independent Complaints Advocacy Services |
| ICU | Intensive Care Unit |
| IOC | Interim Orders Committee |
| IOP | Interim Orders Panel |
| LMC | Local Medical Committee |
| LSA | Legal Services Authority |
| LSB | Legal Services Board |
| LSO | Legal Services Ombudsman |
| MCCD | Medical Certificate of Cause of Death |
| MDO | Medical Defence Organisation |
| MOT | Ministry of Transport |
| MSC | Medical Services Committee |
| NAO | National Audit Office |
| NCAA | National Clinical Assessment Authority |

| | |
|---|---|
| NCAS | National Clinical Assessment Service |
| NHS | National Health Service |
| NICE | National Institute for Clinical Excellence and subsequently the National Institute for Health and Clinical Excellence |
| NPSA | National Patient Safety Agency |
| NRLS | National Reporting and Learning System |
| NSF | National Service Framework |
| PALS | Patient Advice and Liaison Services |
| PCC | Professional Conduct Committee |
| PCS | Paediatric Cardiac Surgery |
| PCT | Primary Care Trust |
| PIDA | Public Interest Disclosure Act 1998 |
| PIWG | Performance Issues Working Group |
| PPC | Professional Proceedings Committee |
| PSI | Policy Studies Institute |
| RCGP | Royal College of General Practitioners |
| RCSE | Royal College of Surgeons of England |
| RDP | Registration Decisions Panel |
| RHA | Regional Health Authority |
| RMO | Regional Medical Officer |
| RMS | Regional Medical Services |
| SDP | Seriously Deficient Performance |
| SEADOC | South East Kent and East Sussex Doctors on Call Ltd |
| SHO | Senior House Officer |
| SPM | Serious Professional Misconduct |
| SRS | Supra Regional Services |
| UBHT | United Bristol NHS Trust |
| UKCC | United Kingdom Central Council for Nursing, Midwifery and Health Visiting |
| WHH | William Harvey Hospital |

# Preface

Self-regulation continues to play a central role in the legal framework governing the medical profession in Britain. When such regulation fails to operate effectively, the impact on individual lives and upon the wider community can be devastating. The object of the first part of this book is to consider the crisis in medical self-regulation, brought about by the numerous cases in recent years in which patients have been needlessly harmed or even killed at the hands of their doctor. From the murderous activities of Harold Shipman to the incompetence and arrogance of Rodney Ledward, these and other cases paint a picture of a self-regulatory process which had seriously lost direction. In the second part of the book I consider whether the changes and proposals for change have or are likely to result in change for the better. Will restructuring within the General Medical Council facilitate a sufficiently radical shift in day-to-day regulation? Can periodic revalidation of doctors ensure that they are all fit and competent? Or, does the profession continue to view the behaviour of its members through rose-tinted spectacles? That the latter may continue to present a significant obstacle to effective regulatory progress is of significant concern. In the final part of the book I consider the additional changes which might more effectively put medical self-regulation on the road to reform.

I am indebted to many people for their support in helping me complete this work. To colleagues in the Sussex Law School for providing me with research leave to finish the book in a timely manner and to Craig Barker, Jo Bridgeman, Peter De Cruz and Laurence Koffman for their constructive comments on earlier drafts. Also to the anonymous reviewers who made helpful comments about both the original book proposal and the first draft of the completed manuscript. Any omissions or errors do, of course, remain my own.

Mark Davies
July 2006

*For Chris*

# PART I
# Crisis

In the opening chapters of this book I consider the crisis which has confronted medical self-regulation in the United Kingdom in recent years. In particular, the role of the General Medical Council and, in general terms, the extent to which it has adequately performed this role.

# Chapter 1

# The Background to Medical Self-Regulation

## Introduction

In recent years the medical profession has come under intense scrutiny as a result of a number of scandals in both hospital medicine and general practice. These range from the unnecessary deaths of children at the Bristol Royal Infirmary, the improper retention of organs at Alder Hey, to the unlawful killing of over 200 patients by Harold Shipman. Clifford Ayling was imprisoned in 2000 for abusing female patients over a period of at least seven years, during which time he had been dismissed by a number of employers without action being taken against his registration. In addition to these high profile cases, over a four-year period at least seven GPs were reported to have been jailed for sexually assaulting patients.[1] The high profile cases have resulted in inquiries and reports, and the government and profession have responded by reviewing and changing aspects of the regulatory process. However, these cases are likely to be the tip of the iceberg. A former President of the GMC, Sir Donald Irvine has suggested that in excess of 11,000 doctors may be unfit to practise, 5 per cent of the total number of doctors on the medical register. Reasons include failing to keep up to date or other manifestations of incompetence, ill-health and deliberate wrongdoing. The Chief Medical Officer, Sir Liam Donaldson, said in 2001 that among hospital doctors the figure could be 6 per cent, while the Royal

1 For example, a number of incidents were reported by the BBC 1 programme, *Real Story*, Monday, 8 November 2005. This programme used a number of cases to illustrate problems with the current regulatory system. One case involved a doctor who had been using drugs and vaccines which were significantly out of date. Some patients had to be re-vaccinated and, presumably, were at risk of contracting serious illness in the interim. No effective action was taken after an initial report by the practice manager. Only after the third complaint did the GMC act, imposing restrictions on the doctor but not removing her from practice. Another pair of serious cases involved GPs using and profiting from patients as guinea pigs for clinical trials without their informed consent. Some of the patients involved suffered serious side effects. These doctors were suspended temporarily from practice, but not struck off. The case of a doctor who had restrictions placed on his practice (preventing him treating women alone) by the GMC after being found guilty, inter alia, of having asked a schoolgirl 'to touch his penis and guess its size', was also highlighted. The relatively lenient penalty was contrasted with the likely treatment by the criminal courts of a similar offender who was in a position of trust and responsibility over children.

College of General Practitioners has put it at 15 per cent of GPs. With respect to this latter figure, at least 3 million people in Britain could have a sub-standard GP.[2] Doctors in the United Kingdom have increasingly been subject to myriad forms of regulation. These include regulation as part of their employment (for the majority of doctors this will be within the National Health Service); civil action in negligence; criminal prosecution and 'self'-regulation by the General Medical Council. All but the GMC are limited in their scope. It has been relatively easy for a doctor to escape sanction in the employment context by either moving on before disciplinary action could be taken, or by being 'eased out' by the employer by way of voluntary severance to avoid expensive and often protracted disciplinary proceedings. Civil claims depend on the claimant being able to access the resources necessary to bring a claim. The latter are also predominantly compensatory and, because damages will usually be paid by an insurer or the doctor's employer, have little or no direct disciplinary effect. Criminal prosecutions against doctors will arise rarely and only in relatively extreme cases. This leaves the GMC as the only body which can remove a doctor's right to practise irrespective of his or her employment situation. The GMC is the only body which has responsibility for doctors from the stage of initial training through to retirement and beyond. It is the only body which can deal with doctors across a significant range of misconduct types – from relatively minor infractions on the one hand to the most serious criminal matters on the other. Unlike civil actions, the penalties imposed by the GMC apply directly against the doctor. In short, the GMC is absolutely central to the regulation of doctors.

In light of this importance, I consider the role of the GMC in both its historical and current context. My core argument is that the GMC has failed to perform the role expected of it in numerous and serious respects. In the first part of this book I consider the importance of medical self-regulation, including the historical development of the GMC's role. The second part consists of case studies used to illustrate the failings of the GMC. The third part considers recent reforms, other proposals for change and draws conclusions for the future.

## Contextual and Definitional Points

The GMC does have to operate within budgetary constraints and its powers are largely governed by a statutory framework. Both of these limitations may account for some of the failings identified in this book. However, the GMC should not be permitted to use these factors to more than a limited degree in its defence. As an influential body, the GMC has had the opportunity over many years, even decades, to seek to increase its statutory powers and to address areas of regulatory weakness. Until very recently it has been relatively inactive in this regard. Similarly, with respect to its funding for important investigatory and other regulatory tasks, the GMC appears to have been more or less content with the status quo. The Council is funded by the medical profession and during the period under discussion in this book has been dominated by a majority medical membership. In these circumstances, it is

2 Boseley, S., 'Doctors Failing 3m Patients', *The Guardian*, 18 December 2004, 1.

hardly surprising that the GMC has not sought significant extra funding from doctors for the purpose of imposing a more rigorous and possibly more intrusive regulatory regime on these same doctors.

Central to the thesis of this book is the argument that medical self-regulation has experienced a lengthy period of crisis. The word 'crisis' was chosen as the most descriptive shorthand for recent events in medical self-regulation. 'An unstable period; a crucial stage or turning point'[3]; 'a vitally important or decision stage; a state of affairs in which change for better or worse is imminent'.[4] As will be discussed in this book, all of these definitions aptly describe the recent history of medical self-regulation.

## Professions, Power and Regulation

Professions such as medicine involve the provision of services which are of high importance to clients and require high levels of expertise and judgement by the professional. The client is frequently unable to accurately assess the quality of service. External models of regulation, it is often argued, are unsuited to many issues arising within the field of regulating professionals. This is because the discretion much professional judgement entails is beyond the understanding of those outside of the profession, and is usually undertaken away from the visible aspects of professional practice. Self-regulation seeks to address these difficulties by having the expertise of others in the profession on hand, and by seeking to guarantee the quality and integrity of those entering and remaining in the profession. To achieve this, the state strikes a bargain with the profession, whereby the profession is granted a near monopoly over the provision of its services, and in return it provides rules of conduct and associated regulatory processes: 'Professions strike a bargain with society in which trust, autonomy from lay control, protection from lay competition, substantial remuneration and high status are exchanged for individual and collective self-control, designed to protect the interests of both clients and the public at large.'[5]

Maintaining quality of professional practice is therefore an important element in resisting external control. State-granted autonomy, a near monopoly of service provision and the right to control education, entry and to regulate members of the profession gives the profession a dominant position.[6] In return, registration as a

3 *Collins English Dictionary*, 1985, Collins, London.

4 *Oxford English Dictionary*, online edition. Accessed July 2006.

5 Rueschemeyer, D., *Lawyers and their Society: A Comparative Study of the Legal Profession in Germany and the United States*, 1973, Harvard University Press, Cambridge, Mass., 13. For further discussion, see, for example, Parsons, T., 'The Professions and the Social Structure', in *Essays in Sociological Theory*, 1954, Free Press, Glencoe, Illinois; and Larson, M.S., *The Rise of Professionalism*, 1977, University of California Press, Berkeley, CA.

6 See, for example, Secretary of State for Social Services, *Report of the Committee of Inquiry into the Regulation of the Medical Profession*, 1975, Cmnd 6018, HMSO, London; Stacey, M., 'The General Medical Council and Self-regulation', in Gladstone, D. (ed.), *Regulating Doctors*, 2000, Institute for the Study of Civil Society, London.

member of the profession should ensure both competence and appropriate standards of behaviour. Thus, *credat emptor* rather than *caveat emptor* should govern the professional–client relationship.[7]

Regulations imposed from outside may result in the alienation of the regulated. In this environment regulation may become inefficient and even unworkable. A significant advantage of professional self-regulation is the greater acceptability by the regulated, being controlled by 'one of us' rather than outsiders, who do not understand what it is like in the front line of professional practice. It has also been suggested that membership of a self-regulating profession is likely to enhance the sense of worth and from there enhance the standard of their work.[8]

In the 1970s, the Merrison Committee recognized the contractual nature of the relationship between profession and public in the context of self-regulation. Parliament was identified as the body charged with negotiating this contract on behalf of the public. The Committee warned of the need for the 'contract' to adapt to changing social circumstances.[9] It is of note that, once the general statutory structure is in place, Parliament historically has largely left the detail of the self-regulatory contract to the profession itself.

Durkheim identified professional ethics as a means of asserting moral standards in an industrial world, where the deregulation of society through the impact of individualism was leading to moral decline.[10] A core characteristic of professional power is the privilege the profession possesses to define both the content of its knowledge and the educated access to it.[11] Having largely defined the boundaries of their own knowledge base, this was subsequently institutionalized and taught by a 'professional school'.[12] In addition to legitimate distance between professional expertise and lay knowledge, the profession may also seek to 'mystify' this knowledge, adding further to lay uncertainty to the further advantage of professional power.[13] In return for monopoly power, the profession undertakes to use its expert knowledge to pursue the public good. Traditional models of professionalism therefore combined

---

7 See Hughes, E.C., 'Professions', in Callahan, J.C. (ed.), *Ethical Issues in Professional Life*, 1988, Oxford University Press, Oxford, 31.

8 Stacey, M., *Regulating British Medicine: the General Medical Council*, 1992, Wiley, Chichester, 219 and 251.

9 *Report of the Committee of Inquiry into the Regulation of the Medical Profession*, 1975, Cmnd 6018, HMSO, London.

10 For further discussion, see Parry, N. and Parry, J., *The Rise of the Medical Profession*, 1976, Croom Helm, London, 248.

11 For further discussion, see Larson, M., *The Rise of Professionalism*, 1977, University of California Press, Berkeley, CA, 48. Cited by Parker, Christine, 'Lawyer Deregulation via Business Deregulation: Compliance Professionalism and Legal Professionalism', *International Journal of the Legal Profession*, 1999, Vol. 6, No. 2, 175–96, 176.

12 See Freidson, E., *Professionalism: The Third Logic*, 2001, Polity Press, Cambridge; and Beck, J. and Young, M.F.D., 'The Assault on the Professions and the Restructuring of Academic and Professional Identities: a Bernsteinian Analysis', *British Journal of Sociology of Education*, April 2005, Vol. 26, No. 2, 183–97.

13 For further discussion, see Montgomery, J., 'Medicine, Accountability and Professionalism', *Journal of Law and Society*, Autumn 1989, Vol. 16, 319–39.

elements of what the profession expected from society – high status, generous rewards, restraints on competition and autonomy – in return for which the profession promised, inter alia, competence, an ethic of service and public protection.[14]

An important element of this public good is the assurance from the profession that its members will uphold the highest standards of conduct and use the power they command over the public responsibly. Regulation, and in particular self-regulation, of the profession is central to this concept and the means of maintaining public trust in the fact that the profession is upholding its side of the bargain. As Abel put it:

> …a profession is differentiated from other occupations by the privilege of self-governance…A governing body…represents a profession and is formally recognised as doing so, it has powers of control and discipline over its members. A profession is given a measure of self-regulation so that it may require its members to observe higher standards than could be successfully imposed from without.[15]

In terms of the application of self-regulation, dominant modes are self-assessment by each practitioner or assessment by other members of the profession. One unfortunate result of this is that practitioners may be motivated to be more concerned with the way in which their colleagues view them than the impression given to the public.[16] In the modern professional context, this has become less of a concern for clients of professional groups such as solicitors, who operate in a market environment, but remains of significant concern with regard to doctors practising within the monopoly environment of the NHS.

Professional self-regulation often takes two general forms – input and output. Whilst both seek ultimately to influence output (the quality of professional services), input operates by setting minimum standards of entry to the profession. Output, in contrast, focuses upon the quality of work produced.[17] The medical profession in England and Wales makes use of both approaches, but the primary focus tends to be on input – including recent revalidation initiatives – with limited concentration on outputs.

The public are frequently confused by the nature and various aspects of the regulatory process and it is often far from clear that the public appreciate or are encouraged to appreciate that professional regulation is ultimately a public gift which remains (or should remain) under democratic control.[18]

---

14 See, for example, Paterson, A., 'Professionalism and the Legal Services Market', 3 *International Journal of the Legal Profession*, 1996, 137, 145.

15 Abel, R., 'The Politics of the Market for Legal Services', 1982, in Disney, J., Basten, J., Redmond, P., Ross, S. and Bell, K., *Lawyers*, 2nd ed, 1986, The Law Book Co., Melbourne, 89.

16 Wasserstrom, R.A., 'Lawyers as Professionals: Some Moral Issues', in Callahan, J.C. (ed.), *Ethical Issues in Professional Life*, 1988, Oxford University Press, Oxford, 65.

17 See Trebilock, M.J., Tuohy, C.J. and Wolfson, A.D., 'Professional Regulation', 1979, 40–43, in Disney, J., Basten, J., Redmond, P., Ross, S. and Bell, K., *Lawyers*, 2nd ed, 1986, The Law Book Co., Melbourne, 209.

18 The professional bodies tend to highlight this aspect only when it suits their interests. For example, when the GMC were unable to discipline Harold Shipman prior to his conviction

Self-regulation is an important principle for the legal profession in a democratic society, as lawyers must be free to challenge with full rigour organs of the state. This argument has less power with regard to the medical profession. It is also arguable that the medical profession has already compromised its independence, in relation to the state, because of its position in the NHS. The creation of the NHS from 1948 has been described as the high watermark of security and status for the medical profession. Whilst doctors initially feared that provision on socialist lines would undermine their position, the reality was negotiation and the development of structures which strengthened the control exercised by the medical profession over the institutions providing medical care.[19] The profession, it has been suggested, recognized that state provision was the best means of ensuring that the necessary financial resources were available to maintain the standards of medical care 'appropriate to the degree of security and levels of remuneration the profession desired'.[20] In a predominantly state-funded service, the professional–state bargain takes on an even greater role. Whilst other professions such as lawyers and accountants promise high standards of expertise and behaviour in return for a near monopoly position in the market, the medical profession in the NHS does not even have to compete in this market environment.

The recent history of the medical profession illustrates a highly selfish approach in the face of public demands for an effective NHS. The profession has shown itself willing to exert undue pressure on the government, with consultants rejecting contracts which would limit their private practice in return for greater public pay. GPs look set to do the same, securing substantial pay rises in return for reduced working hours. If professionalism is viewed as an occupational strategy primarily directed at achieving and maintaining upward collective social mobility,[21] then professional sacrifice in terms of overzealous self-regulation should be the norm if the profession is to maintain the public confidence necessary to maintain this status. Analysed from an economic perspective, doctors have strong property rights holdings in the production and consumption processes, which are protected by self-regulation.[22]

Doctors' short-term technical emphasis and the element of uncertainty in medical practice has meant that medical ethics has become dominated by the individualistic aspects of virtue and duty. A third potential element, the 'common good', has generally been neglected. This in turn has resulted in the neglect of the possible clashes

for murder, they were quick to point out that this was because they lacked the statutory authority to do so.

19 For further discussion, see Parry, N. and Parry, J., *The Rise of the Medical Profession*, 1976, Croom Helm, London, 212.

20 See, for example, Parry, N. and Parry, J., *The Rise of the Medical Profession*, 1976, Croom Helm, London, 212.

21 Parry, N. and Parry, J., *The Rise of the Medical Profession*, 1976, Croom Helm, London, 79.

22 McGuire, A., 'Ethics and Resource Allocation: An Economist's View', in Dowie, J. and Elstein, A., *Professional Judgment*, 1988, Cambridge University Press, Cambridge, 492–507, 500–501.

between social values and individual values.[23] Self-regulation, therefore, remains focused upon individual conduct whilst modern medicine is dominated by complex structural issues. The ethical position is used to specify that the doctor will undertake all that is possible to fulfil the patient's needs. The strong ethical presumption is that the doctor is to be left alone to act in the best interests of the patient, isolated from wider structural issues.[24] The Bristol case, discussed in Chapter 7, is illustrative of this. The professional misconduct arose because the doctors in question did not try hard enough and were not honest with their patients, not because of the actual outcome. Also, whilst the report into the Bristol case recognized the importance of wider structural factors as well as professional conduct, disciplinary proceedings were concerned solely with the actions of doctors on an individual level.

## The Particular Importance of Medical Regulation

The circumstances and culture surrounding the foundation of the NHS in 1948 contributed to some of the cultural attitudes within the medical profession which have been subject to criticism. For example, consultants, as the elite within the new service, exerted their dominance over the science and technology of medicine as the means to reinforce their privileged position. In so doing, they neglected the 'soft' elements of practice, notably communication.[25] Compared with the position in many other countries, consultants in the UK are specialists who have to progress through a very competitive, narrow promotion filter. The reward was a very high degree of clinical autonomy and power and contributed to a closed, elitist culture at the top of the British medical hierarchy.[26] By being aloof and virtually unaccountable, consultants soon gained the image of near omnipotence, which in turn restricted their ability to admit fallibility and error. As the teachers and mentors of the next generation of doctors, this model became the self-perpetuating institutional norm. In addition, the 'command and control' producer-focused model of the NHS allowed for sloppy management and toleration of poor medical practice.[27]

Regulation of the medical profession in England is characterized by a complex web of structures. Much of the relevant law has been dominated by the acceptance of claims of medical professionalism, allowing the profession both to define the

---

23 Jonsen, A.R. and Hellegers, A.E., 'Conceptual Foundations for an Ethics of Medical Care', in Tancredi, L.R. (ed.), *Ethics of Medical Care*, 1974, Institute of Medicine, Washington. McGuire, A., 'Ethics and Resource Allocation: An Economist's View', in Dowie, J. and Elstein, A., *Professional Judgment*, 1988, Cambridge University Press, Cambridge, 492–507, 493 and 501.

24 McGuire, A., 'Ethics and Resource Allocation: An Economist's View', in Dowie, J. and Elstein, A., *Professional Judgment*, 1988, Cambridge University Press, Cambridge, 492–507, 501.

25 Irvine, D., 'The Changing Relationship Between the Public and Medical Profession', The Lloyd Roberts Lecture – Royal Society of Medicine, 16 January 2001.

26 Irvine, D., *The Doctors' Tale*, 2003, Radcliffe Medical Press, Oxford, 29.

27 Irvine, D., 'The Changing Relationship Between the Public and Medical Profession', The Lloyd Roberts Lecture – Royal Society of Medicine, 16 January 2001.

public need and how those needs are to be met. For example, in the context of medical negligence, not only have the courts been deferential to the profession, but the majority of cases are settled away from the public gaze of the courtroom.[28] Historically, this approach has been legitimized on the idealized grounds that the medical profession has brought a selfless, altruistic attitude to its practice and as a result needs to be protected from devious patients and the harshness of the free market. An alternative reality is that these traditional approaches obscure the reality that professional autonomy is actually an exercise of manipulative power.[29] Kennedy describes the inevitable nakedness, both physically and emotionally, experienced by the patient when he or she encounters the doctor. In turn 'it is hard to overstate the power which this vests in the doctor'.[30]

Brazier considers how medical misconduct compares with that of other professions:

> A solicitor who grossly overcharges, fails to keep proper records or conducts his client's business dilatorily will arouse public concern as well as private anger. But the outcry will not reach the same level of passion as that occasioned by reports of a doctor failing to visit a child when the child later dies…The cost of a medical error is such that doctors will always be expected to be better than others and the standards of the profession as a whole to be the highest.[31]

Historically, medical practitioners could offer very little in the way of effective treatments. As a result, the esteem afforded to doctors and the trust placed in them was naturally limited. In recent decades, relatively effective scientifically based medicine has become the norm. With this, the gap between specialist and lay understanding of the medical process has increased, as, arguably, has the respect from the public for mysterious but effective high tech treatments.[32] In these circumstances, medical regulation has also increased in importance, as the power of doctors has increased along with their capacity to do harm.

## The Regulation of Doctors

There are a number of ways in which doctors may be held to account for their shortcomings. Becher identifies three forms of accountability: contractual accountability – this occurs in organizational settings and calls for conformity with official requirements or legal regulations; professional accountability – which denotes collegial relationships within a professional community and requires members to avoid drawing the profession into disrepute; moral accountability – this

28 See Montgomery, J., 'Medicine, Accountability and Professionalism', *Journal of Law and Society*, Autumn 1989, Vol. 16, 319–39.

29 Montgomery, J., 'Medicine, Accountability and Professionalism', *Journal of Law and Society*, Autumn 1989, Vol. 16, 319–39, 328–36.

30 Kennedy, I., *The Unmasking of Medicine*, 1981, Allen & Unwin, London, 8.

31 Brazier, M., *Medicine, Patients and the Law*, 1992, Penguin, London, 8–9.

32 See Porter, R., *Blood and Guts: A Short History of Medicine*, 2002, Penguin, London, 153.

is owed to clients and others and derives directly from professionalism.[33] Doctors are subject to all three modes of accountability. The first two requirements will be imposed upon doctors externally, in the first case by employers or others and in the second by their own professional body in the form of codes and disciplinary sanctions. The final requirement is more subtle, deriving from deeper notions of professionalism. In practice, a patient may seek compensation in tort or, in the case of private healthcare, contract for harm suffered. In addition, the torts of assault and battery may also provide redress. For behaviour deemed to deserve punishment or other measures to address a doctor's behaviour or fitness to practise, local or national disciplinary procedures are available. In the most serious cases, the criminal law may also be invoked. In terms of these various accountability bodies, the courts have the disadvantage of lacking the technical expertise inherent within the other regulators. Regulators also have the advantage over the courts of being able to mix to optimum effect different regulatory approaches. However, these advantages come at the expense of the risk of 'capture' by regulated populations.[34]

## Arguments For and Against Self-Regulation

'Self-regulation' has been described as a 'normatively loaded term'. Supporters see it as responsive, flexible, well-informed and well-targeted, all of which encourage greater levels of compliance. This in turn makes use of the internal morality of the regulated group. The supporters therefore consider that professional self-regulation ensures that individual practitioners are accountable to their peers. Peer pressure, in theory, should ensure higher standards than could be enforced by an external regulator. It is also argued that governments in Western-style democracies could not regulate effectively without a self-governing element from the regulated population.[35] A further advantage is that the regulator and regulated should merge into one, and so the problem of influencing others in regulatory terms should not arise. However, this assumption is often not borne out in practice. In large professional groups the 'self' of the regulator and the 'self' of the regulated will usually be distinct. To the individual doctor, the General Medical Council may appear to be as distant and alien as any external regulator.

Opponents, in contrast, see self-regulation as self-serving and ineffective and therefore consider that it should not be used in areas which pose high risks or which are of significant public interest.[36] From this perspective, self-regulation may be

33 Becher, T., Eraut, M. and Knight, J., *Policies for Educational Accountability*, 1981, Heineman, London; Becher, T., *Professional Practices*, 1999, Transaction Publishers, New Brunswick, New Jersey, 208.

34 See Cane, P., 'Tort Law as Regulation', *Common Law World Review*, 2002, Vol. 31, 305–31, 313.

35 See, for example, Dunsire, A., 'Modes of Governance', in Kooiman, J. (ed.), *Modern Governance: New Government-Society Interactions*, 1993, Sage, London.

36 For further discussion of these and related ideas, see Black, J., 'Decentring Regulation: Understanding the Role of Regulation and Self-Regulation in a "Post-Regulatory" World', in Freeman, M.D.A., (ed.), *Current Legal Problems*, 2001, Vol. 54, Oxford University Press,

used to serve professional, as opposed to the public interests and professional codes may focus more towards benefiting members of the profession than the public. In the same way in which doctors are generally empowered by the state as the only group which can define health and illness, self-regulation tends to empower doctors as the only group which can define medical mishaps and even misconduct. This definitional power provides the medical profession with political power in debates about standards of practice and behaviour. For instance, as medical technology has advanced, the profession itself has played a dominant part in determining the levels of mishap deemed to be inevitable. This in turn has given rise to the tendency for the profession to seek to define untoward events as part of the inherent risk of practice, rather than as a mishap.[37]

## Information Economics and Self-Regulation

There are economic reasons for members of the medical profession to ensure that the regulatory process is effective. 'Information economics'[38] provides a basis for this argument. Problems arise in markets because information is asymmetric in the sense that sometimes sellers have information which buyers lack and vice versa. Cost of discovery by the deprived party is often prohibitive. A simple example is that of a poor quality car – a lemon. Often, a buyer lacks a ready means to determine whether a particular car is a lemon, but knows that some will be. At any given price, sellers of good quality cars are less willing to sell than those of poor quality cars. Knowing that some cars are lemons, buyers will be unwilling to pay a higher price for quality of which they cannot be sure. High quality products will gradually be withdrawn from the market, leaving only the lemons behind. Quality is therefore depressed and the market becomes dominated by low quality goods and services.[39] To counteract this, mechanisms can be developed to address the provision of otherwise expensive information. Typical examples include guarantees, brand names and other indicators of reputation.[40] In the context of professions, the 'brand name' value of the professional title is usually substantial and needs to be maintained by tight control

---

Oxford, 103–46; Baldwin, R. and Cave, M., *Understanding Regulation*, 1999, Oxford University Press, Oxford.

37 See Sharpe, V. and Faden, A., *Medical Harm: Historical, Conceptual and Ethical Dimensions of Iatrogenic Illness*, 1998, Cambridge University Press, Cambridge; Bosk, C., *Forgive and Remember: Managing Medical Failure*, 2nd ed., 1982, Chicago University Press, Chicago; and Mulcahy, L., *Disputing Doctors*, 2003, Open University Press, Maidenhead, 58.

38 This idea won the 2001 Nobel Prize for Economic Sciences. See Stiglitz, J.E., 'Contributions of the Economics of Information to Twentieth Century Economics', 2000, 115 *Quarterly J of Econ* 1441. Cited by Hon J J Spigelman AC, 'Are Lawyers Lemons?: Competition Principles and Professional Regulation', 2003, 77 *ALJ* 44–61, 49.

39 For full discussion, see Hon J J Spigelman AC, 'Are Lawyers Lemons?: Competition Principles and Professional Regulation', 2003, 77 *ALJ* 44–61, 44.

40 Akerlof, G.A., 'The Market for Lemons: Quality Uncertainty and the Market Mechanism', 1970, 84 *Quarterly J of Econ* 488. Cited by Hon J J Spigelman AC, 'Are Lawyers Lemons?: Competition Principles and Professional Regulation', 2003, 77 *ALJ* 44—61.

of entry standards and systems to ensure ethical conduct and maintain discipline.[41] The doctor whose own behaviour is exemplary risks allowing damage to occur to the 'brand name' of the profession as a whole if she or he turns a blind eye to misbehaviour of a colleague. There are numerous examples of this in recent years.

In this book I argue that the theoretical importance of effective self-regulation on the part of the medical profession has not been matched by practical implementation. In recent years there have been numerous examples of serious failures in the self-regulatory process. The medical profession has responded with proposals for change, but it remains open to question whether such changes are likely to be effective in genuinely improving the position.

The first part of the work considers the crisis facing the self-regulatory process operated on behalf of doctors in the United Kingdom. Recent case examples which illustrate this crisis are considered in detail in the second part. The third part of the work concentrates on potential changes and the likelihood that these will be effective.

41 Hon J J Spigelman AC, 'Are Lawyers Lemons?: Competition Principles and Professional Regulation', 2003, 77 *ALJ* 44–61, 44.

Chapter 2

# The General Medical Council – Powers and Failings

## Development of Medical Professionalism and Self-Regulation

The current representative, trades union, body for the medical profession, the British Medical Association, was created in 1832. The regulatory arm of the medical profession, the General Medical Council,[1] was established 26 years later by the Medical Regulation Act 1858. This Act has been described as 'a landmark in the development of the modern medical profession'[2] and crucial for the establishment of medicine as a single influential profession. It brought together previously diverse groups into a single formalized profession and focused its self-regulatory power through the General Medical Council.[3] From its inception, the GMC has been funded by its registered members. Prior to this there was no reliable means for the public to differentiate between trained doctors and 'quacks'. It has been estimated that almost one third of practitioners in the early 1840s had no medical qualifications.[4]

The GMC was empowered to control medical education and entry to the profession and to determine who should be removed from the profession.[5] These latter powers place the GMC in a fundamental position within the regulatory system, as it alone has the power to remove or restrict a doctor's registration, irrespective of the sector in which the doctor is employed. The extent of this latter power is

1 Originally known as a 'General Council' and acquiring the title 'General Medical Council' after the Medical Act 1950. Knight, B., *Legal Aspects of Medical Practice*, 1992, Churchill Livingstone, London.

2 Knight, B., *Legal Aspects of Medical Practice*, 1992, Churchill Livingstone, London; and Stacey, M., *Regulating British Medicine: the General Medical Council*, 1992, Wiley, Chichester.

3 Prior to 1858 there had been numerous separate licensing bodies, each with limited jurisdiction. Others had engaged in medical activity outside of the remit of any licensing body. For further discussion, see Porter, R., *Quacks*, 2000, Tempus Publishing Inc., Charleston, SC.

4 See Knight, B., *Legal Aspects of Medical Practice*, 1992, Churchill Livingstone, London; and Stacey, M., *Regulating British Medicine: the General Medical Council*, 1992, Wiley, Chichester.

5 The Act did not prevent unregistered practitioners from providing medical services, as long as they did not hold themselves out to be registered. The advantages which registration has brought have included: the right to hold appointment in the National Health Service and other public bodies, to prescribe restricted drugs and to give statutory certificates.

illustrated by the fact that historically only the Privy Council (replaced more recently by the High Court) could overturn regulatory decisions of the GMC.

The 1858 Act largely resulted from initiatives within the profession and, it has been suggested, the creation of the GMC was as much or even more in the interests of the profession than of the public – by controlling who could practise, competition was reduced.[6] Rigid admissions tests and adherence to strict professional codes would reserve professional status for only the most suitable, and in return those admitted to the profession would command the highest remuneration.[7] An essential feature, therefore, during the establishment of the modern medical profession was the desire of those who already had established status and market control, not to weaken their privileged position by permitting excessive expansion of the professional register.[8]

Some divisions did remain amongst registered practitioners – for instance in order to limit competition between hospital and general practitioners, physicians in hospitals were excluded from seeing patients directly without a GP referral, whilst general practitioners did not treat patients in hospital.[9] The general practitioner retained the patient, whilst physicians controlled the hospital.[10] This system evolved with the creation of the National Health Service in 1948. GPs retained the patient list and acted as gatekeeper to more specialist services. Therefore, although holding the status of independent contractor, GPs were and are important instruments of cost control for the state. Politicians manipulated the trust the public had in doctors by having doctors themselves undertake the rationing of healthcare. In return, the state conferred upon GPs a monopoly of primary care.[11]

From the sociological perspective, Macdonald describes the GMC as a curious mixture of self-regulation and state regulation, the Council having to make concessions to Parliament before a monopoly position would be allowed. However, since its creation, the GMC has been successful in developing effective tactics and administrative relationships with regard to its relationship with the state.[12]

## Powers and Functions of the GMC

As already discussed, the GMC controls entry to the medical profession and has the power to suspend or remove a doctor from the medical register. The quality of individual newly qualified doctors is not measured directly by the GMC, rather

6 See Stacey, M., *Regulating British Medicine: the General Medical Council*, 1992, Wiley, Chichester, 20; and Irvine, D., *The Doctors' Tale*, 2003, Radcliffe Medical Press, Oxford, 26 and 44.

7 See Newman, C., *The Evolution of Medical Education in the 19th Century*, 1957, Oxford University Press, Oxford, 112; and Parry, N. and Parry, J., *The Rise of the Medical Profession*, 1976, Croom Helm, London, 133.

8 Macdonald, K.M., *The Sociology of the Professions*, 1995, Sage, London, 106.

9 Irvine, D., *The Doctors' Tale*, 2003, Radcliffe Medical Press, Oxford, 27.

10 Stevens, R., *Medical Practice in Modern England: the Impact of Specialisation and State Medicine*, 1966, Yale University Press, London.

11 Irvine, D., *The Doctors' Tale*, 2003, Radcliffe Medical Press, Oxford, 29.

12 Macdonald, K.M., *The Sociology of the Professions*, 1995, Sage, London, 106.

the Council validates educational institutions which in turn ensure that individuals reach the appropriate standard. The GMC is the principal regulator, underpinned by statute, but it does operate alongside non-statutory institutions. For instance, the Royal Colleges determine and ensure compliance with professional standards within certain specialist branches of medicine. It also operates alongside local disciplinary systems and the civil and criminal law.

In the past, the powers of the GMC have been described as 'slender and vaguely expressed' and it was hard for it to exert authority over well-established bodies such as the Royal Colleges and the BMA. Voices of opposition also came from within the Council as well as from outside.[13] For instance, when, in 1982, the BMA accepted mandatory training for GPs, they were able to successfully resist any compulsory examination. Doctors entering general practice as principles were therefore still able to do so without any compulsory test of their competence.[14] This was not merely an academic issue. Information presented to the Merrison Committee in 1973 showed that of those practitioners who chose to take the examinations (one might reasonably assume these to be the practitioners most confident of their ability), only 65 per cent passed. The Royal College of General Practitioners (who had advocated compulsory testing) expressed concern that some of the failing doctors (all of whom were free to practise) demonstrated shortcomings so fundamental that patient safety was at issue. In terms of contractual negotiations with the state, doctors, through the BMA, have tended to dominate and the state, as employer, has shown insufficient interest in protecting patients against underperforming doctors. Similarly, until relatively recently the GMC showed little commitment to seriously addressing the issue of underperforming or misbehaving doctors. Only after the recent scandals, discussed later in this book, has the GMC appeared to grasp the true extent of its obligations to the public.[15]

Four key functions are central to the role of the GMC:

1. To set general standards of good practice for doctors, reflecting the expectations of the public and the profession.
2. To maintain a register of doctors.
3. To oversee the initial training of doctors in medical schools.
4. To deal with doctors whose conduct (and more recently health or performance) may bring their registration into question.[16]

The GMC's regulatory functions have been summarized in a number of recent cases. These require the balancing of three aims:

---

13 See Richardson, Lord, *The Council Transformed*, GMC Annual Report 1983, GMC, London. Cited by Irvine, D., *The Doctors' Tale*, 2003, Radcliffe Medical Press, Oxford, 44.

14 Irvine, D., *The Doctors' Tale*, 2003, Radcliffe Medical Press, Oxford, 53. The GMC had also neglected to sufficiently build primary care into the undergraduate curriculum, so could not even claim that it ensured this basic level of competence in general practice.

15 Irvine, D., *The Doctors' Tale*, 2003, Radcliffe Medical Press, Oxford, 43–4 and 55–6.

16 See GMC, *Acting Fairly to Protect Patients: Reform of the GMC's Fitness to Practise Procedures*, March 2001, 7.

1. To protect the public from doctors who are incompetent or unfit to practise.
2. To maintain the reputation of the medical profession and associated public confidence.
3. To ensure that doctors are provided with reasonable safeguards against unwarranted allegations.[17]

The GMC, in summarizing its overall purpose, has concentrated on serving the interests of patients and the 'protection, promotion and maintenance of health and safety of the community by ensuring proper standards in the practise of medicine'. Or, more succinctly, the GMC has described itself as the 'collective conscience of the medical profession'.[18]

Following the 1975 Merrison Report and the subsequent 1978 and 1983 Medical Acts, the GMC consisted of between 95 and 104 members. A significant majority of these members were doctors, most of whom were elected to the Council by the profession. Other medical members were appointed by universities with medical faculties, Royal Colleges and the Privy Council. Lay member numbers were between 11 and 13 from 1984 to 1996, rising to 25 in November 1996.[19]

Prior to 1950 the GMC exercised the disciplinary function directly and then after this date through its Disciplinary Committee. The 1978 Act replaced this with a number of formal disciplinary stages. The first stage was administrative, next came screening, and then the Preliminary Proceedings Committee (PPC) (until 1980, the Penal Cases Committee), and finally the Professional Conduct Committee (PCC) (previously the Disciplinary Committee). Only the PCC stage was held in public and a case could be closed at any stage before it reached the PCC.

Throughout the majority of its history, the regulatory powers of the GMC were disciplinary only. It was empowered by the 1858 Medical Act to erase the name of any doctor judged to have been guilty of 'infamous conduct in a professional respect'. In 1969 this was replaced by the term 'serious professional misconduct'.[20] As a result, the GMC has tended to focus primarily on the 'deviant fringe' of the profession, rather than regular inspection or monitoring of the competence and ongoing suitability of all medical practitioners. Parry observes that the focus of 'deviance' has changed over time. In the early years, the Council tended to focus on dealing with unqualified 'quacks' and maintaining the respectability of the profession, notably by seeking to control sexual misdemeanours. In the latter part of the nineteenth century the focus moved to controlling competition and self-promotion within the profession. By the time of the advent of the NHS in 1948, intra-professional competition was no longer of central concern to the profession and the focus moved to the inappropriate use of

---

17 See, for example, *Woods v General Medical Council* [2002] EWHC 1484, Admin; *R v General Medical Council ex parte Toth* [2000] 1 WLR 1290.

18 See Sir Graeme Catto, 'The GMC – Revalidation – What Are We Trying to Measure?', *Medico-Legal Journal*, 2003, 71(106), 2 October; and GMC, *Developing Medical Regulation: a Vision for the Future – the GMC's Response to the Call for Ideas by the Review of Clinical Performance and Medical Regulation*, April 2005.

19 See GMC, *The Draft Report of the Governance Working Group*, 18 September 2000, A31.

20 See Knight, B., *Legal Aspects of Medical Practice*, 1992, Churchill Livingstone, London, 27.

drink and drugs.[21] However, doctors who were physically or mentally ill, including those who were abusing drugs, were difficult to deal with within the disciplinary procedures. With the prospect of a public disciplinary hearing and punitive sanctions, doctors were reluctant to report colleagues who they considered to be ill. Irvine, for example, describes an occasion when he attempted to persuade a colleague whose illness was placing patients at risk to withdraw from practice. Irvine admits that had the persuasive approach failed, he would never have considered it appropriate to report the colleague to the GMC to face disciplinary charges.[22] Similarly, doctors within the GMC who were involved in the disciplinary process faced a conflict when having to choose whether to label a doctor as 'bad' when she or he was in reality ill.[23]

## Serious Professional Misconduct

The attempt to find a workable definition of 'serious professional misconduct', and its predecessor term 'infamous conduct', exercised the GMC and the courts for a considerable period of time. In 1894, Lopez LJ provided the following definition:

> If a medical man in pursuit of his profession has done something with regard to it which will be reasonably regarded as dishonourable by his brethren of good repute and competency, then it is open to the General Medical Council, if that be shown, to say that he has been guilty of infamous conduct in a professional sense.[24]

The term was described by Scruton LJ, in 1930, as meaning 'no more than serious misconduct according to the rules, written or unwritten, governing the profession'.[25]

In *Roylance v General Medical Council*[26] Lord Clyde said that misconduct consists of an act or omission which falls short of what would be proper in the circumstances. This is then qualified by the addition of the words 'professional', which links the misconduct to the profession of medicine, and 'serious'. Exactly what the 'link' to medicine might be will depend on the circumstances. The closest link will occur when the practitioner is directly engaged on his or her practice with a patient. These cases may involve a serious failure to meet the appropriate standards of practice, for example, 'gross neglect of patients or culpable carelessness in their treatment, or the taking advantage of a professional relationship for personal

---

21 Parry, N. and Parry, J., *The Rise of the Medical Profession*, 1976, Croom Helm, London, 245.

22 Irvine, D., *The Doctors' Tale*, 2003, Radcliffe Medical Press, Oxford, 57.

23 See, for example, discussion in the Fifth Report of the Shipman Inquiry, *Safeguarding Patients: Lessons from the Past – Proposals for the Future*, para 22.2 (www.the-shipman-inquiry.org.uk).

24 *Allinson v General Council of Medical Education and Registration* [1894] 1 QB 750.

25 *R v General Council of Medical Education and Registration of the United Kingdom* [1930] 1 KB 562.

26 [1999] Lloyd's Rep. Med. 139, at 149.

gratification'.[27] Their Lordships in *Roylance* emphasized that it was impractical to draw up an exhaustive definition of what should constitute misconduct. In *Preiss v General Dental Council*[28] Lord Cooke noted that serious professional misconduct did not require moral turpitude, but could include gross professional negligence. In *Rao v The General Medical Council*[29] the Privy Council concluded that negligent misconduct based on a single incident was not in itself sufficient. More was required to constitute serious professional misconduct.

Over the years, courts and regulatory committees have avoided establishing closed categories for SPM. The GMC made this clear in its guidance to the profession. For instance, the 1993 edition of the GMC's guide to the profession – *Professional Conduct and Discipline: Fitness to Practise* (usually referred to as the 'Blue Book') – emphasized that published categories of misconduct should not be seen as exhaustive, but that: 'Any abuse by doctors of any of the privileges and the opportunities afforded to them, or any grave dereliction of professional duty or serious breach of medical ethics, may give rise to a charge of serious professional misconduct.'[30]

Dishonesty on the part of a doctor could constitute SPM,[31] but the definition was not restricted to conduct which was morally blameworthy and so could include seriously negligent treatment or otherwise a failure to provide appropriate treatment. The GMC had formally recognized this for the first time in the 1985 edition of the Blue Book, which stated:

> The public are entitled to expect that a registered medical practitioner will afford and maintain a good standard of medical care. This includes:
> (a) conscientious assessment of the history, symptoms and signs of a patient's condition;
> (b) sufficiently thorough professional attention, examination and, where necessary, diagnostic investigation;
> (c) competent and considerate professional management;
> (d) appropriate and prompt action upon evidence suggesting the existence of a condition requiring urgent medical intervention; and
> (e) readiness, where the circumstances so warrant, to consult appropriate professional colleagues.[32]

In 1997, a GMC Working Group once again considered whether SPM should be defined more precisely. The Group acknowledged that the lack of a precise definition risked inconsistency in decision making, but felt that a significant balancing advantage was the flexibility of the existing approach. Not only would it be problematic to

---

27 See comments of Lord Mackay in *Doughty v General Dental Council* [1988] AC 164, at 173.

28 [2001] 1 WLR 1926, at page 1936C.

29 (2002) Lawtel transcript.

30 See the Fifth Report of the Shipman Inquiry, *Safeguarding Patients: Lessons from the Past – Proposals for the Future*, para 17.9 (www.the-shipman-inquiry.org.uk).

31 For recent discussion, see *Nandi v General Medical Council* [2004] EWHC 2317 (Admin) at paragraph 31.

32 See the Fifth Report of the Shipman Inquiry, *Safeguarding Patients: Lessons from the Past – Proposals for the Future*, para 17.10 (www.the-shipman-inquiry.org.uk).

attempt to draft a code which tried to anticipate every single disciplinary offence, but it would lead to 'interminable legal wrangling' about whether a particular case fell within the definition.[33] However, whilst these reasons against a definitive code are justifiable, the GMC has also resisted adopting any tested alternative approach – for instance, one based upon 'common law' case authority. From September 2004 the GMC did produce summary case reports, which were intended to provide useful examples of conduct which did and did not amount to SPM and examples of the penalties imposed. Whilst, in principle, this offered the potential for progress with regard to establishing a consistent approach to SPM, in practice the examples used gave little useful guidance about the threshold for SPM.[34]

In other documents from the late 1990s and again in 2000, the GMC attempted to provide the public with a straightforward workable definition of SPM. The two versions agreed upon were: 'conduct which makes us question whether a doctor should be allowed to practise medicine without restriction' and 'behaviour so serious it would justify restricting the doctor's right to hold registration'. Neither definition provides any useful advice about the type of behaviour considered serious enough to restrict a doctor's right to practise.[35] In a paper presented to the GMC in 1999, it was considered that a good starting definition of SPM was: 'A departure from the standards of conduct expected by the profession – whether or not covered by specific GMC guidance – sufficiently serious to call into question a doctor's registration.'[36]

Recent consideration by the Privy Council saw SPM described as 'a falling short by omission or commission of the standards of conduct expected among medical practitioners, and such falling short must be serious'.[37] 'Serious' must be given appropriate weight, and so whilst it is possible for negligent conduct to constitute SPM, it will only do so when the negligence is of a sufficiently high level.[38] This latter point reflects the fact that historically the GMC showed little or no interest in behaviour on the part of a doctor which fell within the definitions of negligence. The focus has been on deliberate misconduct rather than clinical practice – whether the doctor was fit to remain on the register – rather than whether he or she was competent to undertake particular treatment. As late as 1977, guidance to the profession specifically stated that the GMC was 'not concerned with errors in diagnosis or treatment'. By 1983, the provision had been modified to say:

---

33 Discussed in the Fifth Report of the Shipman Inquiry, *Safeguarding Patients: Lessons from the Past – Proposals for the Future*, paras 17.26–17.27 (www.the-shipman-inquiry.org.uk).

34 See the Fifth Report of the Shipman Inquiry, *Safeguarding Patients: Lessons from the Past – Proposals for the Future*, para 17.38 (www.the-shipman-inquiry.org.uk).

35 Contained in the GMC documents, *A Problem With Your Doctor*, 1997 and *The Conduct Procedures of the General Medical Council*, 2000.

36 See Allen, I., *The Handling of Complaints by the GMC: a Study of Decision-making and Outcomes*, 2000, Policy Studies Institute, London.

37 Per Lord Clyde in *Rylands v General Medical Council* [1999] Lloyd's Rep Med 139 at 149.

38 *Doughty v GDC* [1987] 3 All ER 843, *McCandles v GMC* [1996] 1 WLR 167, *Nandi v General Medical Council* [2004] EWHC 2317 (Admin) at paragraph 31.

> The Council is not ordinarily concerned with errors in diagnosis or treatment, or with the kind of matters which give rise to action in the civil courts for negligence, unless the doctor's conduct in the case has involved such a disregard of his professional responsibility to his patients or such a neglect of his professional duties as to raise a question of serious professional misconduct. A question of serious professional misconduct may also arise from a complaint or information about the conduct of a doctor which suggests that he has endangered the welfare of patients by persisting in independent practice of a branch of medicine in which he does not have the appropriate knowledge and skill and has not acquired the experience which is necessary.[39]

Even in 1994, an internal GMC Training Manual stated:

> We cannot investigate complaints of failure to diagnose, or failure to give what the complainant considers to be correct and appropriate treatment, or complaints about evident or alleged errors in treatment, which have allegedly resulted in damage to the patient. Such matters come into the category of medical negligence, which it is more appropriate for a patient to pursue in the civil courts…Those matters are not, however, regarded as serious misbehaviour by the doctor concerned, such as might justify action by the Council.
>
> …
>
> [F]ew complaints about treatment would actually be serious enough even if sustained to raise any question of serious professional misconduct.
>
> …
>
> The types of case relating to treatment which may…justify disciplinary procedures by the Council include cases where a doctor has allegedly failed to visit a patient when necessary, or failed to conduct an appropriate examination, or absented himself/herself from his/her practice or post when the doctor was supposed to be on duty, or has been drunk on duty, or has been guilty of some other culpable failure in relation to his or her responsibilities towards one or more patients.[40]

There has therefore been a persistent notion within the GMC that SPM must involve 'wilful' or at the very least 'reckless' behaviour. Falling below a reasonable standard, rather than wilfully refusing to give care, would not constitute SPM.[41]

With the exception of the occasional judicial attempt to define SPM, the courts have tended to defer to the profession itself to determine the boundary between acceptable and unacceptable conduct. In *Ghosh v GMC*[42] Lord Millett cited with approval the following:

> The principles upon which this Board acts in reviewing sentences passed by the Professional Conduct Committee are well settled. It has been said time and again that a disciplinary committee are the best possible people for weighing the seriousness of professional

39 For further discussion, see the Fifth Report of the Shipman Inquiry, *Safeguarding Patients: Lessons from the Past – Proposals for the Future*, paras 17.41–17.46 (www.the-shipman-inquiry.org.uk).

40 Cited in the Fifth Report of the Shipman Inquiry, *Safeguarding Patients: Lessons from the Past – Proposals for the Future*, para 17.47 (www.the-shipman-inquiry.org.uk).

41 See he Fifth Report of the Shipman Inquiry, *Safeguarding Patients: Lessons from the Past – Proposals for the Future*, para 17.48 (www.the-shipman-inquiry.org.uk).

42 [2001] UKPC 29, [2001] 1 WLR 1915.

> misconduct, and that the Board will be very slow to interfere with the exercise of the discretion of such a committee ...The committee are familiar with the whole gradation of seriousness of the cases of various types which come before them, and are peculiarly well qualified to say at what point on that gradation erasure becomes the appropriate sentence. This Board does not have that advantage nor can it have the same capacity for judging what measures are from time to time required for the purpose of maintaining professional standards.
> ...
> For these reasons the Board will accord an appropriate measure of respect to the judgment of the committee whether the practitioner's failings amount to serious professional misconduct and on the measures necessary to maintain professional standards and provide adequate protection to the public.

This approach has potentially serious implications. Research by the Policy Studies Institute found confusion and disagreement amongst decision makers within the GMC about what constituted SPM and the threshold at which it was reached. Some members considered 'recklessness' on the part of the doctor to be necessary. Others disagreed about whether particular behaviour was 'reasonable' and about acceptable margins of error within practice. This presented considerable scope for inconsistency in decision making, including the likelihood that unfit and even dangerous doctors have been allowed to remain in practice. The GMC had over-relied on the (erroneous) idea that as SPM decisions were being taken by experienced GMC members, the lack of agreed definitions were not of major consequence.[43]

Following the first PSI study, it was agreed that certain categories of case should be automatically referred by screeners as SPM 'by definition'. Cases in this category related to dishonesty, dysfunctional behaviour (for example, abusive behaviour, soliciting money from patients, persisting in practice when the carrier of an infectious disease), sexual assault, indecency and violence. Initially, this change saw a significant rise in the referral of cases – from 50 per cent or less, to 93 per cent. However, the PSI follow-up study in 2002 found that by 2000–2001 the figures had fallen back – for example, to a referral rate of 47 per cent of dishonesty cases in 2000 and 74 per cent in 2001. It appears that the GMC had backtracked with regard to the automatic referral procedures.[44]

Whatever definition of SPM individual disciplinary panels have used, it appears that the threshold for finding SPM has tended to be high, resulting in the acquittal of a significant majority of doctors about whom the GMC received complaints.[45] It has also been suggested that, in practice, neglect by a doctor of his or her duties to a patient has resulted in excessive leniency. Stacey found that in the 1980s the PCC demonstrated a reluctance to find serious professional misconduct in cases alleging disregard of professional responsibility, for instance, failure to visit, treat

43 See the Fifth Report of the Shipman Inquiry, *Safeguarding Patients: Lessons from the Past – Proposals for the Future*, paras 17.16, 20.94 and 27.214 (www.the-shipman-inquiry.org.uk).

44 See the Fifth Report of the Shipman Inquiry, *Safeguarding Patients: Lessons from the Past – Proposals for the Future*, paras 19.174–19.181 (www.the-shipman-inquiry.org.uk).

45 Smith, R., *Medical Discipline: The Professional Conduct of the GMC* 1858-1990, 1994, Oxford University Press, Oxford.

or refer. Thirty-six per cent of such cases resulted in not guilty findings, compared with between 4 and 13 per cent in cases of dishonesty, inappropriate prescribing and other types of offences against patients.[46] The penalties imposed against those found guilty also tended to be lower. For instance, between 1970 and the mid-1980s, no doctor found guilty of disregard of professional responsibility had his or her name erased from the medical register. In contrast, 40 per cent of doctors found guilty of sexual misconduct had their names erased. There were clear questions of appropriate prioritization when adulterous doctors were treated that much more severely than the uncaring or incompetent.[47] Other evidence from the 1980s also indicated that the GMC was more concerned with doctors who were seen to be undermining the status of the profession than those whose activities jeopardized patient care.[48]

## GMC Guidance to the Profession

The GMC traditionally provided guidance to the medical profession through its periodically updated guide to *Professional Conduct and Discipline: fitness to practise* (the 'Blue Book'). This was issued to doctors on qualification, although for much of its history the GMC considered it inappropriate to make the guide available to the wider public. Stacey analysed changes in Blue Book guidance between the 1970s and late 1980s. She found that the guidance in 1976 focused principally upon intra-professional matters, for example, regulation of competition and demeaning colleagues. Little guidance related to public protection. By 1987, whilst the intra-professional material was still present, the Blue Book had expanded to include more patient-focused material. The latter included guidance relating to standards of medical care and the handling of confidential patient information. External pressure, rather than proactive initiative by the GMC, appears to have been the primary motivator for these changes.[49]

In 1995 the Blue Book was replaced with *Good Medical Practice*. This new publication was intended to be more positive in tone than its predecessor – providing members of the profession with straightforward guidance about what it was to be a good doctor. As one President of the GMC described it:

> Instead of indicating all of those things that doctors shouldn't do, from 1995 onwards with Good Medical Practice, we indicate the positive aspects of medicine – what doctors

46 Stacey, M., *Regulating British Medicine: the General Medical Council*, 1992, Wiley, Chichester, 165.

47 Stacey, M., *Regulating British Medicine: the General Medical Council*, 1992, Wiley, Chichester, 159; Brazier, M., *Medicine, Patients and the Law*, 1992, Penguin, London, 14. Brazier notes that the case of *Rodgers v GMC* [1985] 1 PN 111 was the first in 15 years in which a doctor's name was erased for failing to visit.

48 Montgomery, J., 'Medicine, Accountability and Professionalism', *Journal of Law and Society*, Autumn 1989, Vol. 16, 319–39, 321.

49 Stacey, M., *Regulating British Medicine: the General Medical Council*, 1992, Wiley, Chichester, 150.

should do. We call it Good Medical Practice, not Excellent Medical Practice or First Class Medical Practice, because it is expected that all doctors will adhere to these precepts.[50]

The first edition of *Good Medical Practice* described its contents as 'guidance'. However, subsequent editions made it clear that the contents did constitute the standards against which a doctor would be judged if a fitness to practise issue arose. For example, the 2001 edition stated: 'Serious or persistent failures to meet the standards in this booklet may put your registration at risk.' However, *Good Medical Practice* is not suitable for determining in any simple way whether particular behaviour amounts to SPM, and could not in itself be relied upon by doctors or members of regulatory panels to determine different levels of misbehaviour. As the Shipman Inquiry was told:

> ... "Good Medical Practice" is a mixture of things which really must not be transgressed and which would be very serious, and other points which are, for example, being polite to your patients. This on its own could not raise an issue which ought to affect a doctor's registration presumably; so that you've within "Good Medical Practice" a lot of different things at different levels of seriousness.[51]

Guidance, however good, is only of use if the profession takes it to heart and acts upon it. The GMC encountered difficulties in getting doctors to take sufficiently seriously the requirements of the Blue Book and then *Good Medical Practice*. Doctors have demonstrated differing awareness and attitudes.[52]

## Screening

As previously noted, before a case could reach the stage of a public hearing before the PCC, it had to pass a number of preliminary stages – administrative filtering, initial screening and then screening by the PPC. For most of the GMC's history, the initial screening of complaints rested with the GMC President, who also chaired the key disciplinary committees. The power to decide what should happen to a complaint from the point it was received therefore rested with the President. From there, he[53] controlled which cases proceeded to committees he chaired and which were dismissed without a formal hearing. This gave rise to serious concerns that the President possessed far too much power and influence. These practices were modified in the 1970s, and after 1979 the offices of preliminary screener, deputy preliminary screener and preliminary screener for health were created.[54] However, even after these changes, the President (or a medical screener nominated by him) continued

50 Sir Graeme Catto, 'The GMC – Revalidation – What Are We Trying to Measure?', *Medico-Legal Journal*, 2003, 71(106), 2 October.

51 The Fifth Report of the Shipman Inquiry, *Safeguarding Patients: Lessons from the Past – Proposals for the Future*, para 17.19 (www.the-shipman-inquiry.org.uk).

52 See Irvine, D., *The Doctors' Tale*, 2003, Radcliffe Medical Press, Oxford, 139.

53 All GMC Presidents to date have been men.

54 See Stacey, M., *Regulating British Medicine: the General Medical Council*, 1992, Wiley, Chichester, 93.

to chair the PPC. Also, the President retained the power to nominate screeners and chairmen of other committees 'and so could wield his influence vicariously'.[55] These changes did not remove the possibility that a screener could also be a member of the PPC, effectively having two bites at deciding whether a case should progress to the public arena of the PCC. The chairman of the PPC was also principal medical screener, and two other medical screeners and one lay screener were also members of the committee. This position was only changed in 1999.[56]

Historically, screening was an opaque process undertaken behind closed doors. There was no screening database, nor an effective means to track cases.[57] Whether or not a complaint progressed rested with the individual screener before whom the case happened to come. There were no set standards, no monitoring or audit to ensure consistency of decision making. There were also difficulties with the interaction between the conduct, health and performance procedures. For instance, it was possible at any stage to refer a case from the conduct or performance procedures into the health procedures, but not from health or conduct into performance. The health procedures therefore took centre stage, perhaps reflecting a preoccupation of the medical profession but not necessarily meeting public expectations in terms of priorities. Significant power was therefore in the hands of the screener, both with respect to whether a case should progress and, if so, through which route.[58]

A screener might dismiss a complaint based upon the conclusion that even if all facts alleged were true, it could not amount to SPM or that it fell outside of the jurisdiction of the Council. An alternative to complete dismissal was the issuing of a warning letter to the doctor. These were used extensively. Warning letters were, from the GMC's perspective, an easy means of disposing of some cases where the doctor had admitted allegations or the facts had been proved or were beyond dispute.[59]

Where there was no admission or proof of misconduct and the case was not considered sufficiently serious for the PCC, but the PPC remained concerned about the doctor's behaviour, it adopted the practice of sending a 'cautionary letter' or 'letter of advice'. The former notified the doctor that the case would be filed and looked at again if a subsequent similar complaint was received. The latter advised the doctor regarding future conduct. The Shipman Inquiry heard that cautionary letters had ceased to be used, but letters of advice remained widely used – for example, in 2002 and 2003 the PPC dealt with over 40 per cent of its cases in that way. There are obvious concerns that so many cases were dealt with in this way, without any thorough investigation to determine whether the doctor presented a continuing risk

55 See the Fifth Report of the Shipman Inquiry, *Safeguarding Patients: Lessons from the Past – Proposals for the Future*, para 19.260 (www.the-shipman-inquiry.org.uk).

56 Allen, I., *The Handling of Complaints by the GMC: a Study of Decision-making and Outcomes*, 2000, Policy Studies Institute, London. See also The General Medical Council (Fitness to Practise Committees) Rules 2000.

57 See Allen, I., Perkins, E. and Witherspoon, S., *The Handling of Complaints Against Doctors*, 1996, Policy Studies Institute for the Racial Equality Group of the GMC, London.

58 For further discussion, see GMC, *Acting Fairly to Protect Patients: Reform of the GMC's Fitness to Practise Procedures*, March 2001, 15.

59 See the Fifth Report of the Shipman Inquiry, *Safeguarding Patients: Lessons from the Past – Proposals for the Future*, para 20.32 (www.the-shipman-inquiry.org.uk).

to the public.[60] It is also difficult to see how letters of advice, given that the doctor has admitted the offence, constitute an appropriate penalty and deterrent.[61]

Stacey notes that in the 1970s, when she was a lay member of the GMC, the screening processes were shrouded in mystery. She was, however, able to identify a very high proportion of cases which did not proceed to a formal hearing. For instance, in 1974, of 847 complaints or convictions, less than one quarter were progressed to the stage of a formal committee.[62] The position was equally, if not more, extreme in the 1980s and 1990s. Between 1987 and 1998, between 82 and 89 per cent of cases were closed at the screening stage. There was no mechanism to appeal against a screening decision other than by way of judicial review, although no such review was undertaken until 1997.[63] Robinson, another lay member, noted that the screening process was not even subject to oversight by other GMC members:

> From the time I was appointed to the GMC, and was elected to the Preliminary Proceedings Committee, I was asking for further details of rejected cases. I seemed to be the only member of Council who wanted to know. My request for basic information about the majority of complaints the Council received was sometimes interpreted as distrust of the Screener, who is always an eminent and respected doctor. My view is that I do not care if the Angel Gabriel is Preliminary Screener. Members of the Council and the public have a right to know what kind of complaints the Council receives, whether some kinds are increasing or decreasing, and which get further investigation and which do not.[64]

Screening remained dominated by medical members of the GMC until 1990, when the Professional Conduct Rules[65] were amended to provide for the appointment of a lay screener, who would consider those conduct cases (although not criminal conviction cases) which the medical screener had determined should be closed. If agreement could not be reached between the medical and lay screeners, the lay screener's view prevailed. Whilst this did provide a useful additional safeguard, its limitations were of concern. Not only were conviction cases excluded, but so were decisions by the medical screener to refer a case to the health or performance

---

60 See the Fifth Report of the Shipman Inquiry, *Safeguarding Patients: Lessons from the Past – Proposals for the Future*, paras 20.33–20.34 (www.the-shipman-inquiry.org.uk).

61 This was the view taken by Jean Robinson. Robinson, J., *A Patient Voice at the GMC: a Lay Member's View of the GMC*, Report 1, Health Rights, London.

62 Stacey, M., *Regulating British Medicine: the General Medical Council*, 1992, Wiley, Chichester, 152. On questioning the large proportion of complaints which were dismissed, Stacey recalls the only answer she received was that 'most of them came from deranged persons'.

63 See the Fifth Report of the Shipman Inquiry, *Safeguarding Patients: Lessons from the Past – Proposals for the Future*, paras 19.5 and 19.40 (www.the-shipman-inquiry.org.uk).

64 See Robinson, Jean, *A Patient Voice at the GMC: a Lay Member's View of the GMC*, Report 1, Health Rights, London; and the Fifth Report of the Shipman Inquiry, *Safeguarding Patients: Lessons from the Past – Proposals for the Future*, para 19.37 (www.the-shipman-inquiry.org.uk).

65 General Medical Council Preliminary Proceedings Committee and Professional Conduct Committee (Procedure) (Amendment) Rules 1990, rule 10(2) of the Professional Conduct Rules 1988.

procedures. The latter had a significant impact on the manner in which the doctor was dealt with and the maximum penalties available. Similarly, lay screeners had no involvement in cases where administrative staff or the medical screener determined that the complainant should pursue the matter through local procedures.[66]

Research in 1993 and 1994 by the Policy Studies Institute considered the work of the, then, three medical screeners. The research found that the screeners did most of their work away from GMC premises and fitted it in around other GMC commitments and their usual work as practising doctors. Perhaps reflecting the substantial nature of each screener's workload, in a significant proportion of cases the screener followed the advice which administrative staff provided with the case paperwork. This raised issues about who the real decision makers were at this stage of the process.[67] An example of a failure in the screening process was highlighted by the Shipman case (discussed in Chapter 12). In 1990 Shipman was found to be in breach of his terms of service as a result of prescribing an excessive drug dose to a patient with epilepsy. In 1993, a similar finding was made after Shipman had failed to visit a patient. After this second case, the Family Health Services Appeal Unit reported Shipman to the GMC. A GMC caseworker produced a memorandum for screening purposes, including details of Shipman's convictions in 1976. The caseworker expressed strong reservations about the evidential strength of the case and whether the facts could give rise to misconduct of relevance to the GMC. The medical screener expressed the view that the first case was too old for the GMC to act and the second involved 'evidence which is now obscured by time' and had been sufficiently dealt with locally. Despite concluding that the second matter was 'borderline' in terms of possible SPM, the case was closed – without, apparently, the requisite referral to a lay screener.[68] Not only do these facts illustrate a highly favourable stance towards the doctor, when there is any element of doubt, but also that screeners were engaging in substantive weighing up of evidence and decision making. Only with the introduction of the Handbook for Screeners in 1997 was it expressly stated that screeners should not engage in weighing up the strength of the evidence.[69]

66 For further discussion, see the Fifth Report of the Shipman Inquiry, *Safeguarding Patients: Lessons from the Past – Proposals for the Future*, paras 19.31 and 19.248–19.249 (www.the-shipman-inquiry.org.uk).

67 See the Fifth Report of the Shipman Inquiry, *Safeguarding Patients: Lessons from the Past – Proposals for the Future*, paras 19.53–19.55 (www.the-shipman-inquiry.org.uk).

68 See the Fifth Report of the Shipman Inquiry, *Safeguarding Patients: Lessons from the Past – Proposals for the Future*, paras 19.44–19.49 (www.the-shipman-inquiry.org.uk).

69 See the Fifth Report of the Shipman Inquiry, *Safeguarding Patients: Lessons from the Past – Proposals for the Future*, paras 19.78 and 19.81 (www.the-shipman-inquiry.org.uk). The Inquiry does note that whilst the handbook 'represented a real attempt to change that culture', some aspects of the advice were ignored by screeners or soon fell into disuse. There was also no effort made to update the contents or systematically remind screeners of the key principles.

The GMC did not seek to maintain oversight of the screening process by means of audit or other review.[70] The 2000 PSI Report considered the degree of consistency in decision making between the, then, seven screeners. Very significant variations were found between different screener's assessments of levels of seriousness with regard to behaviour they considered would place the public at risk.[71] The PSI recommended that all participants in the GMC's fitness to practise procedures should have a common shared understanding of key principles relating to public risk and other measures of seriousness.[72] Judicial review case examples also illustrate these problems. For example, in *R v GMC, ex parte Holmes*[73] two GPs, Dr A and Dr B, were reported to the GMC after they failed to diagnose a colloid cyst on the brain. At local level, the GPs had been found to be in breach of their terms of service with respect to the incident. In early 1999, Dr A's case was considered by two medical and one lay screeners, all of whom dismissed the complaint. In Dr B's case, the medical screeners decided to dismiss the case but the lay screener determined that it should proceed to the PPC. In September 1999, the PPC dismissed the case. Documents disclosed as part of the judicial review proceedings revealed that administrative advice to the screeners was that the actions were thought not to constitute SPM. Written comment from one of the medical screeners was that, due in part to the three-year delay in the case reaching the GMC, 'I am inclined to no action'. Most of this delay was due to the case needing to progress through the NHS complaints procedures. Not only should the time lapse have been irrelevant to the screening decision, but the GMC would typically insist upon local procedures having been exhausted, so were to a significant degree responsible for the delay. Of similar, if not greater, concern were comments from the other medical screener (the principal GMC medical screener at the time) which expressly stated that there was no SPM because of the difficulty with the particular diagnosis. This screener also noted that Dr A was a member of the Royal College of Physicians. The judicial review court noted that this screener fell into the trap of considering whether the behaviour *did* amount to SPM, rather than whether it *could* have. Membership of the Royal College of Physicians should have had no bearing on the decision. The Shipman Inquiry expressed concern that 'errors as fundamental as this' were still being made in 1999, that screeners habitually applied the wrong test and took into account entirely irrelevant information.[74]

---

70 See the Fifth Report of the Shipman Inquiry, *Safeguarding Patients: Lessons from the Past – Proposals for the Future*, para 19.38 (www.the-shipman-inquiry.org.uk).

71 See the Fifth Report of the Shipman Inquiry, *Safeguarding Patients: Lessons from the Past – Proposals for the Future*, paras 19.99–19.101 and 19.143 (www.the-shipman-inquiry.org.uk). No simple conclusions could be drawn from these findings, as cases were not distributed randomly to screeners. However, following this report, the GMC introduced a randomized system of distributing cases, yet the PSI in a 2003 follow-up study found that this did not remove variation between screeners.

72 See the Fifth Report of the Shipman Inquiry, *Safeguarding Patients: Lessons from the Past – Proposals for the Future*, paras 19.104–19.105 (www.the-shipman-inquiry.org.uk).

73 [2001] EWHC 321 (Admin).

74 See the Fifth Report of the Shipman Inquiry, *Safeguarding Patients: Lessons from the Past – Proposals for the Future*, paras 19.122–19.136 (www.the-shipman-inquiry.org.uk).

*R on the Application of Toth v GMC*[75] provides judicial analysis of the role of screeners, and in doing so demonstrates that for many years screeners had been exceeding their powers. In *Toth*, the screener had written to the complainant explaining that the case had been dismissed because there was a 'clear conflict of evidence' between the accounts given by the doctor and that of the complainant. In the absence of further evidence from the complainant, the screener had concluded that the case could not reach the requisite 'beyond reasonable doubt' standard and so there was 'no prospect of [the] allegations being proved'.

It was observed by Lightman J in *R v General Medical Council ex parte Toth*[76] that:

> The general principles underlying the Act and Rules are that (a) the public have an interest in the maintenance of standards and the investigation of complaints of serious professional misconduct against practitioners; (b) public confidence in the GMC and the medical profession requires, and complainants have a legitimate expectation, that such complaints…will be publicly investigated by the PCC; and (c) justice should in such cases be seen to be done.
>
> The screener's role was therefore to determine a negative, whether the complaint need not proceed further. The only question for the screener in resolving this question was whether the allegations appear to raise the question whether the practitioner has committed serious professional misconduct. It was not for the screener to arrogate to himself the role of the PPC and decide whether the complaint ought to proceed further, still less to arrogate to himself the role of the PCC and weigh up conflicting evidence or judge the prospects of success.

Complaints with any prospect of success should not, therefore, be routinely screened out. That this was happening was especially concerning where protection of the public necessitated full investigation. In this latter respect, this was particularly important where the complaint involved a doctor who continued to practise, rather than one who had retired.[77] *Toth*, the facts of which occurred in 1998, also illustrates that the 1997 Screener's Handbook, which reminded screeners that their role was not to weigh evidence, was being ignored very soon after its publication. The case also illustrates that the earlier introduction of the requirement for the final decision to screen out a complaint to rest with a lay screener, was not working as an effective check on medical screeners. Even when the procedures worked as they were required to in a systems context, there was evidence that lay screeners were being persuaded to favour the view of their medical colleagues instead of allowing the case to progress if there was any doubt. Research by the PSI found that in 1999 lay screeners had agreed with the determination of their medical colleagues in 98 per cent of cases.

75 (2002) Lawtel transcript.

76 [2000] 1 WLR 1290 at paragraph 14.

77 Although it might be added that a factor not mentioned by Lightman J is that 'retirement' for doctors need not be an end to their contact with patients. Examples of doctors in their 60s and 70s who continue to practise in some capacity are not uncommon.

Four years later, the GMC's own research found a slightly lower, but still very high, incidence of agreement, at around 93 per cent.[78]

The GMC's response to *Toth* was to change the screening test, although this change was not highlighted in the Screeners' Handbook. Practice on the ground was also little affected. The proportion of complaints referred to the PPC in the year immediately preceding the *Toth* decision had been 30 per cent, yet by 2001 and 2002 this had *fallen* to between 25 and 27 per cent (after a brief increase to 39 per cent in 2000) and rose slightly to 33 per cent by 2003.[79]

A case example illustrating this lack of real change derives from Alder Hey, where a number of doctors who had been criticized by the Alder Hey Inquiry were reported to the GMC. Two of these cases were dismissed at the screening stage, whilst nine others were dismissed by the PPC. These decisions were challenged by way of judicial review in *Woods v General Medical Council.*[80] The two cases which were screened out were assessed by the medical screener as not giving rise to SPM or Seriously Deficient Performance. The lay screener had initially disagreed, but had been persuaded by the medical screener that, 'on balance', the complaints should be dismissed. Both screeners had applied the incorrect, pre-2000, test of whether the complaint 'need not proceed further', rather than the appropriate one of 'whether there is no arguable case'. Not only was it of significant concern that screeners were still applying the wrong test so long after the change, but the court noted that the medical screener had screened in excess of 400 cases during that time – presumably all with the application of the wrong test. Commenting on this case, it was observed in the Shipman Inquiry that it was unlikely that this problem was restricted to these two screeners:

> One might have expected that having had to concede the errors made in Toth and Holmes would have been a chastening experience for the GMC. One might have thought that, having sought and obtained an amendment of the Rules to effect a change in the test to be applied by screeners, the GMC would have given a high priority to the education and training of screeners so as to enable them to apply the test correctly and consistently. Yet it appears that this was not done.[81]

---

78 The Fifth Report of the Shipman Inquiry, *Safeguarding Patients: Lessons from the Past – Proposals for the Future*, paras 19.250 and 19.256 (www.the-shipman-inquiry.org.uk). See also *Woods v General Medical Council* [2002] EWHC 1484.

79 See the Fifth Report of the Shipman Inquiry, *Safeguarding Patients: Lessons from the Past – Proposals for the Future*, paras 19.90 and 19.92 (www.the-shipman-inquiry.org.uk). The statistical position has to be treated with some caution, as it contains elements of subtle complexity. For instance, the late 1990s had seen a significant increase in the number of cases referred by screeners to the PPC – from 11 and 12 per cent in 1997 and 1998 to percentages in the mid 20s and higher a year or so later. However, prior to *Toth*, this was attributed to changes in practice which had seen cases dismissed before the screening stage, by administrative staff, if they were considered to fall clearly outside the remit of the GMC. Prior to this change, the majority of these cases would have appeared in the 'screened out' statistics.

80 [2002] EWHC 1484 Admin.

81 The Fifth Report of the Shipman Inquiry, *Safeguarding Patients: Lessons from the Past – Proposals for the Future*, para 19.142 (www.the-shipman-inquiry.org.uk). See also paras 19.137–19.141 for further discussion.

Following *Woods*, the screening test was changed again to require a case to be referred to the PPC if the screener was satisfied that it was 'properly arguable that the practitioner's conduct constitutes serious professional misconduct'.[82]

The 2002 Screeners' Handbook clarified the position by confirming that the screening threshold was very low. The screener was to assume, inter alia, that the allegation was true, and assess seriousness not credibility. Screeners were expressly told not to attempt to resolve conflicts of evidence and that the evidential burden for progression was 'minimal'. However, in this regard the advice had the potential to be contradictory, as later in the Handbook it also said:

> Screeners should bear in mind that if they determine that a doctor deviated from best practice, as set out in our guidance, but not by so much as to call his or her registration into question, a closing letter containing advice to the doctor may be the logical outcome.

As recognized by the Shipman Inquiry, this came very close to inviting the screener to reach evidential conclusions.[83]

## The Role of the Preliminary Proceedings Committee

The functions of the PPC were set out in the Medical Act 1978:

> It shall be the duty of the Committee to decide whether any case referred to them for consideration in which a practitioner is alleged to be liable to have his name erased...or his registration suspended or made subject to conditions...ought to be referred for inquiry by the Professional Conduct Committee or the Health Committee.[84]

No guidance was provided regarding the 'ought to be referred' element of this legislation. There were also close similarities between the test to be applied by screeners, 'need not proceed further', raising the question of whether the two distinct stages were both necessary.[85]

After the decision in *Toth*, the GMC commissioned senior counsel to produce an aide-memoire to be used by the PPC. This described the task of the PPC to determine whether 'there is a real prospect of serious professional misconduct being established before the PCC'. This 'real prospect' applied both to the factual aspects of the case and also the question of whether the facts, if proved, would amount to SPM. The approach required a 'genuine (not remote or fanciful) possibility', rather than a mere probability. In considering these factors the PPC would consider, inter alia, the

82 Rule 6(3) of the Professional Conduct Rules 1988 was amended in November 2002. See the Fifth Report of the Shipman Inquiry, *Safeguarding Patients: Lessons from the Past – Proposals for the Future*, para 19.146 (www.the-shipman-inquiry.org.uk).

83 See the Fifth Report of the Shipman Inquiry, *Safeguarding Patients: Lessons from the Past – Proposals for the Future*, paras 19.148–19.152 (www.the-shipman-inquiry.org.uk).

84 Section 13(2), coming into force in August 1980 and subsequently repeated in the Medical Act 1983, section 42(2).

85 See the Fifth Report of the Shipman Inquiry, *Safeguarding Patients: Lessons from the Past – Proposals for the Future*, paras 20.20–20.21 (www.the-shipman-inquiry.org.uk).

weight of evidence and the need for the PCC to be satisfied to the criminal standard of proof. In doing this, however, the PPC's role was not to resolve substantial evidential conflicts, in particular because it worked only with documentary evidence. The PPC should also be cautious about dismissing complaints where another body having considered the same case, for instance, NHS organization or coroner, has found the doctor to have acted improperly in some respect. In overview, if in doubt, the PPC should err in favour of public protection and refer the case to the PCC.[86]

After the detailed review of the screening and PPC stages of the disciplinary process in the *Toth* and *Richards*[87] cases and the research by the PSI, the conclusion of the Shipman Inquiry was that the errors in decision making were not isolated, rather it was 'evident that decision-making in the PPC must have been defective for years, if not always'. Furthermore, these failings were not limited to less serious cases or those involving no risk to the public. For instance, as recently as the early 2000s, the PPC had referred a mere 28–39 per cent of sexual assault and indecency allegations to the PCC. A significant number (up to 45 per cent) of the non-referrals were dealt with by means of letters of warning or advice, meaning that the allegations were admitted or proved. Similarly, only 45–55 per cent of dishonesty cases (excluding those where criminal convictions had resulted, which were recorded separately) were referred to the PCC. Again, in terms of evidence, 22–43 per cent must have been admitted or proved, because warning letters had been sent.[88]

In terms of specific case examples, the Shipman Inquiry considered a number which gave rise to significant concerns yet had not been referred to the PCC; for instance, a doctor who had been abusing drugs in such a way that patients had been put at risk both by being treated by a doctor under the influence of drugs and (because of the doctor's method by which he obtained his supplies) by receiving 'watered down' medication. In both this and other similar cases the PPC tended to ignore the associated dishonesty and risk to patients, in favour of considering the doctor's health needs.[89]

Prior to 1999 the vast majority of cases were dealt with very briefly by the PPC. Fifty per cent of cases were concluded in two minutes or less and 76 per cent in five minutes or less. Changes in 1999 saw these figures falling to 8 per cent and 50 per cent. Average measurements of this type are, of course, highly simplistic. More complex cases are likely to take longer, whilst very straightforward cases will bring the average time down. Also, papers were available in advance to committee

---

86 See comments of Burton J. in *Woods v General Medical Council* [2002] EWHC 1484.

87 (2000) QBD, Lawtel transcript.

88 See the Fifth Report of the Shipman Inquiry, *Safeguarding Patients: Lessons from the Past – Proposals for the Future*, paras 20.143 and 20.192–20.193 (www.the-shipman-inquiry.org.uk).

89 See the Fifth Report of the Shipman Inquiry, *Safeguarding Patients: Lessons from the Past – Proposals for the Future*, paras 20.212–20.214 (www.the-shipman-inquiry.org.uk). US data has suggested that 25 per cent of drug abusing doctors returned to drug taking within eight years of being drug free. On the basis of this, the Shipman Inquiry recommended the commissioning of research into drug-abusing doctors and the outcomes of their cases under the fitness to practise procedures.

members. However, even longer than average PPC hearings could not substitute for the days of oral proceedings which could result if a case reached the PCC. After the changes, rates of referral to the PCC rose from 35 per cent to 47 per cent. Of course, even at the higher level, a majority of cases were not progressed to the PCC. The absence of contemporaneous record-keeping by the PPC and its practice of not giving reasons for its decisions also meant that transparency was lacking.[90]

## The Professional Conduct Committee

The PCC came into being in 1980 and was initially composed of 20 members (a Chairman, Deputy Chairman, 16 medical and two lay members). The quorum per sitting was five, with a maximum of ten (including one lay member). By 1994, membership of the PCC had risen to 34 (26 medical and eight lay), although it fell back to 30 in 1996. The maximum size of a sitting panel had been reduced to eight, with at least two lay members (with a quorum of five, including at least one lay member). The quorum fell to three (including one lay member) in 2000. Until 2003, members of the GMC Council were also permitted to sit on the PCC.[91]

The PCC's procedures were adversarial, with the prosecution usually presented by a GMC-appointed lawyer. In theory, an individual complainant could present his or her own case, but the GMC taking over the prosecution was the norm. Doctors were typically defended by a lawyer provided by their medical defence organization. Although not compelled to do so, the PCC adopted the practice of using the criminal standard of proof in all cases. Review by the Privy Council in *McAllister v General Medical Council* recognized that this was appropriate when allegations amounted to a serious criminal charge, but saw it as 'neither necessary nor desirable' in other cases:

> In charges brought against a doctor where the events giving rise to the charges would also found serious criminal charges it may be appropriate that the onus and standards of proof should be those applicable to a criminal trial. However there will be many cases, where the charges which a doctor has to face before the committee could not be the subject of serious or any criminal charges at all. The committee is composed entirely of medical men and women learned in their profession and to require that every charge of professional misconduct has to be proved to them just as though they were a jury of laymen is, in their Lordships' view, neither necessary nor desirable. What is of prime importance is that the charge and the conduct of the proceedings should be fair to the doctor in question in all respects.[92]

90 Allen, I., *The Handling of Complaints by the GMC: a Study of Decision-making and Outcomes*, 2000, Policy Studies Institute, London.

91 See the Fifth Report of the Shipman Inquiry, *Safeguarding Patients: Lessons from the Past – Proposals for the Future*, paras 21.3–21.7 4.41 (www.the-shipman-inquiry.org.uk).

92 [1993] AC 388. See also discussion in the Fifth Report of the Shipman Inquiry, *Safeguarding Patients: Lessons from the Past – Proposals for the Future*, paras 21.13, 21.26 and 24.150 (www.the-shipman-inquiry.org.uk). It will be noted that the requirement of a lay minority on PCC panels is ignored in this quotation, although this omission does not detract from the general message.

Post the Human Rights Act, it has been suggested that the criminal standard would need to be retained for the most serious allegations heard by the PCC – certainly those which were tantamount to a criminal offence. However, less serious matters might be suitable for a sliding civil standard.[93]

Section 36 of the Medical Act 1983 set out the sanctions available to the PCC:

> (1) Where a fully registered person --
> (a) is found by the Professional Conduct Committee to have been convicted in the British Islands of a criminal offence, or to have been convicted elsewhere of an offence which, if committed in England and Wales, would constitute a criminal offence, whether while so registered or not; or
> (b) is judged by the Professional Conduct Committee to have been guilty of serious professional misconduct, whether while so registered or not;
> the Committee may, if they think fit, direct --
> (i) that his name shall be erased from the register;
> (ii) that his registration in the register shall be suspended…during such period not exceeding twelve months…; or
> (iii) that his registration shall be conditional on his compliance, during such period not exceeding three years…with such requirements so specified as the committee think fit to impose for the protection of members of the public or in his interests.

Where concerns relate to health rather than misconduct, the Health Committee would address these, in accordance with section 37 of the Act.[94] The powers of the Health Committee were similar to those of the PCC, with the exception of the power to erase a practitioner's name from the register. The Professional Conduct Rules 1980 provided that the PPC could refer a case to the Health Committee. This was a one way process: if the referral turned out to be inappropriate, the Health Committee could not refer it back to the PPC. In such circumstances, the ability for the GMC to deal with the doctor was lost.[95] Where it was considered appropriate, the PCC could also transfer a case to the Health Committee.[96] If the Health Committee certified that the fitness of the practitioner to practise was seriously impaired, then the PCC would cease to act. If, however, it certified that the practitioner's health was not seriously impaired, the PCC would resume its inquiry.

## Sanctions

Erasure of a doctor's name from the medical register is the most severe sanction at the GMC's disposal and is key to protecting the public against unsuitable doctors.

93 See GMC, *Acting Fairly to Protect Patients: Reform of the GMC's Fitness to Practise Procedures*, March 2001, 18. This view derived from an experts' conference commissioned by the GMC, hosted by the King's Fund and chaired by Lord Lester QC.

94 The health procedures were first introduced by the Medical Act 1978, coming into effect on 1 August 1980.

95 See the Fifth Report of the Shipman Inquiry, *Safeguarding Patients: Lessons from the Past – Proposals for the Future*, para 20.25 (www.the-shipman-inquiry.org.uk).

96 The power was contained in rule 51 of the General Medical Council Preliminary Proceedings Committee and Professional Conduct Committee (Procedure) Rules 1988.

However, the GMC's use of this sanction has been problematic. Not only have there been inconsistencies in the imposition of erasure, but also examples of erased doctors being readmitted, only to proceed to further misconduct. For example, in *Prasad v GMC*[97] the doctor had his name erased from the register, later successfully applied for restoration, went on to re-offend and was admonished, and subsequently offended again to a degree that his name was once again erased. It has been suggested that both the GMC and the wider profession have lacked a consensus view about the primary purpose of erasure – the extent to which it is there to punish, rehabilitate or protect the public.[98] Originally, the Medical Act 1983 allowed a doctor to apply for readmission after only ten months, and there are case examples of readmission within relatively short periods after the erasure.[99] In total, between 1988 and 1998, 39 of the 153 doctors whose names were erased, approximately 25 per cent, were restored to the register.[100] The offences leading to the erasure of these doctors had included fraud, indecent behaviour and 'the manslaughter of a husband's mistress'.[101] It has been suggested that this position not only undermined public trust in the system, but also influenced the rigour with which some cases were pursued: 'The practitioner's ability both to appeal and to apply for restoration…may make the daunting task of preparing a case for the GMC seem to be hardly worth the effort.'[102]

This also raises questions regarding the deterrence value of GMC sanctions. It has been suggested that the value of deterrence lies principally with the potential offender's perception, rather than with the actual certainty or severity of punishment. Gibbs talks about 'perceived normative scope' – the deterrence effect depending on what potential offenders believe the punishment for a crime *could* be. The actual punishments imposed are, in turn, important for offender perceptions. The principle extends to include both general deterrence, deterring those who have never committed an offence when they hear about the punishment of others, and specific deterrence – applying to the person who has offended and been punished with regard to their risk of re-offending.[103]

Only in 2000 was the Medical Act amended to prohibit restoration within five years after the erasure.[104] Irvine argues that it was not only the government which

---

97 [1987] 1 WLR 1697.

98 Irvine, D., *The Doctors' Tale*, 2003, Radcliffe Medical Press, Oxford, 162.

99 Even when a doctor was not actually readmitted in such a short time, the very fact that this could occur undermined the disciplinary process. For instance, a number of Rodney Ledward's former patients were reported as being shocked that he could apply for readmission 'after such a short space of time'. *The Ledward Report*, Part VII.

100 Beecham, L., 'GMC Wants a Tougher Restoration Procedure', *BMJ*, 1999, 319, 1319, 20 November.

101 News, *Health Service Journal*, August 2000, Vol. 110, No. 5667.

102 Carrier, J. and Kendall, I., *Medical Negligence: Complaints and Compensation*, 1990, Avebury, Aldershot, 39.

103 For further discussion, see Gibbs, J.P., 'Deterrence Theory and Research', in Melton, G.B. (ed.), *The Law as a Behavioural Instrument*, 1985, University of Nebraska Press, Lincoln, 87–130, 87—8.

104 The GMC was also empowered to direct that after a second unsuccessful application for restoration, further applications should be refused.

came to recognize these issues as a problem, but that the GMC itself had been pressing for a change in the law.[105] However, the fact that readmission could be applied for soon after erasure should not be allowed to disguise the fact that the power rested with the GMC to refuse readmission in particular cases. It was also illustrative of confused thinking that the GMC had recommended a shorter minimum period of erasure – three years. The reasoning behind this was that if the minimum was too long, PCC panels might be reluctant to impose the ultimate sanction. The reality, of course, should be that doctors whose names are erased from the register should have no expectation of return, the sanction reflecting the fact that the doctor is unfit to be a member of the medical profession.[106]

## When is a Complaint not a Complaint?

When a matter reaches the GMC from an official source, 'from a person acting in a public capacity', '*there is no complainant* in the eyes of the GMC'. This was so, even if the official source had acted as a result of a complaint from a patient or other member of the public. In the eyes of the GMC this original complainant became a 'mere' witness if the case reached the PCC. For example, Robinson discusses the case of a complainant whose wife died of cancer in 1986. Her GP failed to act upon suspicious cervical smears, even after the patient became ill. The GP was fined £500 by the local FPC (increased to £1,000 by the Secretary of State). When the DHSS passed the case to the GMC, the husband became a potential witness rather than a complainant. In the event, the GP admitted to the facts, so no witnesses were called. The PCC concluded that the facts were insufficient to constitute serious professional misconduct. As he was not the complainant, the husband was not entitled to see a transcript of the hearing nor the speeches of the counsel involved. In Robinson's contention, this situation could not easily have been avoided by the husband:

If he had complained first to the GMC he would have been told to complain to the NHS and the GMC would not have looked at his case (though if they had, he would have counted officially as the 'complainant'). When his complaint did reach the Preliminary Screener it did so because it came via the DHSS so he was not the complainant and had no right to a transcript. A better case of Catch 22 would be hard to find.

The solution, she suggests, was that of the husband sending the report from the FPC hearing directly to the GMC. He would then have counted as 'the complainant'. This would have conferred him not only with the right to see documents and transcripts, but also to have his own legal representation.[107]

---

105 Irvine, D., *The Doctors' Tale*, 2003, Radcliffe Medical Press, Oxford, 162.

106 For further discussion and response from the then Secretary of State for Health, see Irvine, D., *The Doctors' Tale*, 2003, Radcliffe Medical Press, Oxford, 170–71.

107 Robinson, J., *A Patient Voice at the GMC: a Lay Member's View of the GMC*, Report 1, Health Rights, London.

## Extent of GMC Disciplinary Action

In 2003 the President of the GMC estimated that there were in the region of 200,000 doctors on the medical register, about 120,000 of whom were in active practice.[108] In recent years the numbers of complaints made annually against doctors has been in the region of 4,000–5,000, a significant rise from the 1,500 or so in the early to mid-1990s. In 1990, 147 cases were referred to the PPC, 46 of which progressed to the PCC.[109] By the early 2000s action was still typically taken against fewer than 1,000 doctors per year.[110] Historical analysis by Stacey, Robinson and others of the functioning of the GMC lead to the conclusion that these low numbers derive less from an extremely low level of misbehaviour within the profession, and more from structural and attitudinal failings within the Council.

The GMC has also been criticized for delays in dealing with fitness to practise cases. The GMC's target to deal with conduct cases within 12 months was only met in 35 per cent of cases, with some complaints taking over two years to resolve.[111] In the case of the health procedures, between 1989 and 1996 the average delay was 50 weeks.[112] This was of particular concern in cases where the doctor presented a potential continuing risk to patients. For example, in *Omar v GMC*[113] the doctor was convicted of indecent assault against a patient and sentenced to six months' imprisonment. The case took over two years from the date of conviction to reach the PCC, at this point the offence being considered to be sufficiently serious to warrant erasure.

There have been some positive developments in recent years. For example, the GMC obtained additional legislative powers in August 2000 to allow recruitment of additional medical and lay members to serve on the PCC. By November of that year 73 additional panel members had been appointed, allowing the GMC to plan to almost 600 hearing days in 2001, twice the total for 2000 and four times that for 1995.[114]

## The Health Procedures

Only in 1978, following recommendations in the 1975 Merrison Report, were the health procedures introduced.[115] The Health Committee of the GMC was empowered to deal with health issues and could:

---

108 Precise numbers on the Register of Medical Practitioners on 1 January 2000 were put at 193,266. See GMC, *The Draft Report of the Governance Working Group*, 18 September 2000, A31.

109 Knight, B., *Legal Aspects of Medical Practice*, 1992, Churchill Livingstone, London, 30.

110 Sir Graeme Catto, 'The GMC – Revalidation – What Are We Trying to Measure?', *Medico-Legal Journal*, 2003, 71(106), 2 October.

111 See, for instance, Burke, K., 'Trust Chiefs Cause Flood of Serious Cases to GMC', *BMJ*, 2002, Vol. 321, 1177, 18 May.

112 The Fifth Report of the Shipman Inquiry, *Safeguarding Patients: Lessons from the Past – Proposals for the Future*, para 22.83 (www.the-shipman-inquiry.org.uk).

113 (1999) Lexis transcript.

114 See GMC, *Acting Fairly to Protect Patients: Reform of the GMC's Fitness to Practise Procedures*, March 2001, 5.

115 By the Medical Act 1978, carried through to the Medical Act 1983.

> Where the fitness to practise of a fully registered person is judged by the Health Committee to be seriously impaired by reason of his physical or mental condition, the Committee may…direct –
> (a) that his registration…shall be suspended…during such a period not exceeding twelve months…; or
> (b) that his registration shall be conditional on his compliance, during such a period not exceeding three years…[116]

The purpose of the HC was therefore to protect patients whilst also allowing the doctor the opportunity to return to practice when his or her health improved. The HC sat in private. The Committee was advised by a legal assessor and two medical assessors, chosen with regard to the alleged health condition and the doctor's practice area. Only after 1987 could a complainant appear before the HC – although only to give evidence and to hear the HC's decision.[117]

In 2001, the majority of health cases dealt with involved the misuse of alcohol or drugs.[118] Only a small proportion of cases were typically referred by medical screeners to the health screener – 31 out of 2,235 cases in 2001, 13 out of 2,239 in 2002, and 7 out of 1,304 in 2003.[119]

The circumstances in which the PCC might properly refer a case to the Health Committee were addressed in *Crabbie v General Medical Council.*[120] In that case the doctor was convicted of causing death by dangerous driving and driving with excess alcohol, and sentenced to five years' imprisonment. Medical evidence submitted to the PCC suggested that the doctor's fitness may have been affected by alcohol dependency. The PCC declined to refer the case to the Health Committee, concluding that the offence was so serious that public interest would not be adequately protected by suspension or conditional registration, the determinations available to the Health Committee. The conclusion of the Privy Council, dismissing the doctor's appeal, was that the power of referral to the Health Committee was discretionary. Account should be taken of all the circumstances of the case, including the scope of the powers available to the Health Committee. The PCC should not refer a case to the Health Committee unless it is sure that erasure from the medical register would not be appropriate. The Privy Council in *Sreenath v General Medical Council*[121] adopted a similar approach. The doctor was found guilty of serious professional misconduct, having been found to have behaved inappropriately and indecently with two female patients. The PCC adjourned the case for the doctor to be medically examined, prior to considering the penalty. A provisional conclusion was that he might be

---

116 Section 37, Medical Act 1983 (previous, section 8 of the 1978 Act).

117 For further discussion, see the Fifth Report of the Shipman Inquiry, *Safeguarding Patients: Lessons from the Past – Proposals for the Future*, para 22.130 (www.the-shipman-inquiry.org.uk).

118 See Burke, K., 'Trust Chiefs Cause Flood of Serious Cases to GMC', *BMJ*, 2002, Vol. 321, 1177, 18 May.

119 See the Fifth Report of the Shipman Inquiry, *Safeguarding Patients: Lessons from the Past – Proposals for the Future*, para 19.164 (www.the-shipman-inquiry.org.uk).

120 (2002) Lawtel transcript.

121 (2002) Lawtel transcript.

suffering from organic brain damage. The PCC refused to refer the case to the Health Committee or to adjourn for further medical evidence, directing that the doctor's name be erased from the medical register. Rejecting the appeal against this decision, the Privy Council emphasized that the functions of the PCC and the Health Committee were distinct, albeit complementary. The approach taken in *Crabbie* was confirmed as correct.

In *R on the Application of Toth v GMC*,[122] Elias J reviewed both of these decisions and added that even where the PCC did not consider erasure as a possible sanction, it may still choose not to refer a case to the Health Committee if the public interest warranted that it be determined in public arena of the PCC.

## Poorly Performing Doctors

For much of the history of the GMC, an incompetent doctor may have been able to practise for years without regulatory interference. As long as he or she managed to avoid an error of such magnitude that it fell within the remit of the misconduct procedures, such a doctor could operate below the GMC radar. The lack of GMC powers were exacerbated by the fact that the multitude of employing bodies within the NHS provided no sufficient regulatory substitute.[123]

In 1983 the GMC Professional Conduct Committee heard the case of a general practitioner who had been called to attend one of his patients Alfie Winn, a young child, who had a high temperature and vomiting. The doctor attended three hours after the call and found the boy in an unconscious state. The doctor asked the child to open his mouth, but he was unresponsive. The doctor is reported to have said: 'If he can't be bothered to open his bloody mouth, I shall not bloody well look at him.' The doctor prescribed an antibiotic and left. Two hours later the family called an ambulance; the child died in hospital four days later. The PCC expressed concern at the doctor's low level of courtesy and failure to arrange specialist care. However, whilst such behaviour was below the standard expected from a member of the profession, the PCC found that it did not constitute serious professional misconduct.[124] In the words of the committee chairman to the doctor:

> The committee are seriously concerned by the evidence which has been adduced before them in this case. They are disturbed not only by your failure to arrange appropriate specialist treatment for a seriously ill boy...but also by the poor standard of courtesy which you extended towards the patient's parents. The committee regard such behaviour as below the standard which can be regarded as acceptable in a medical man.
>
> They have nevertheless felt able to take account of your expression of regret. The committee have accordingly determined that in all the circumstances you are not guilty of serious professional misconduct in relation to the facts proved against you in the charge.[125]

---

122 (2002).

123 For further discussion, see Scally, G., 'Tackling Deficient Doctors', *BMJ*, 1997, 314: 1568, 31 May.

124 Irvine, D., *The Doctors' Tale*, 2003, Radcliffe Medical Press, Oxford, 75.

125 *GMC Minutes, CXX*, 1983, 95–6, cited by Stacey, M., *Regulating British Medicine: the General Medical Council*, 1992, Wiley, Chichester, 183.

The same doctor was found guilty of SPM in a different case the following year, but had remained in practise during the intervening period.[126]

The Winn case gave rise to criticism and questions regarding the threshold for serious professional misconduct. Nigel Spearing MP, in whose constituency the patient had lived, took the matter up with the GMC. Spearing called for the introduction of a lesser charge of unacceptable medical conduct. Examples of this two-tier approach could be found in other jurisdictions, for instance, New Zealand.[127] The GMC reviewed the position but concluded that it could find insufficient evidence to lower that threshold. The GMC also contended that had the change been implemented, there might arise a tendency to play safe and use the lesser charge of unacceptable conduct when SPM was actually more appropriate and would better protect the public. The GMC also argued that they already had the lower level option, that of the 'warning letter'. However, as Robinson pointed out, warning letters were without power to compel a doctor to change and also were unlikely to reassure complainants that the doctor had been appropriately disciplined. Robinson suggests that the GMC objected because the change would have diluted their powers, by giving the Preliminary Screener less chance to screen out cases and increasing the number which have to be considered by the Preliminary Proceedings Committee.[128] It took another six years before a GMC working party recommended that the GMC give further consideration to establishing procedures to deal with incompetent doctors whose behaviour did not reach levels determined to constitute SPM. It was a further year before the GMC decided to establish a working party to consider arrangements for identifying and dealing with deficient performance. This protracted timescale illustrates that, far from being strongly motivated, proactive advocates of change, it appears that the GMC had to be dragged in that direction.[129]

The artificial distinction between 'incompetence' and 'misconduct' is not unique to medical regulation. Writing in 1998, the Legal Services Ombudsman observed that the legal professions practised in an environment which included a 'collective act of amnesia'. They worked as if there was an absolute distinction between incompetence and misconduct – the former being tolerated, the latter not, as if performing badly had no ethical impact.[130] The medical profession moved to address this issue much earlier than lawyers, although not necessarily as enthusiastically as some members of the medical profession would now wish it to be believed. This was recognized by Irvine, who noted that government pressure was such that had the GMC not acted, legislative change would have been imposed:

126 See the Fifth Report of the Shipman Inquiry, *Safeguarding Patients: Lessons from the Past – Proposals for the Future*, para 17.11 (www.the-shipman-inquiry.org.uk).

127 See Stacey, M., *Regulating British Medicine: the General Medical Council*, 1992, Wiley, Chichester, 183.

128 See General Medical Council, *Questions Concerning Serious Professional Misconduct – Working Party Report*. Council minutes, November 1984. Appendix XIX. Cited by Irvine, D., *The Doctors' Tale*, 2003, Radcliffe Medical Press, Oxford, 75 and 221.

129 See Irvine, D., *The Doctors' Tale*, 2003, Radcliffe Medical Press, Oxford, 79—80.

130 Abraham, A., 'Legal Ethics and the Legal Services Ombudsman', *Legal Ethics*, Summer 1998, Vol. 1, Part 1, 23–4.

> ...the received wisdom today is that the GMC's decision to go with what was to become the performance procedures in the 1990s was as a result of strongly pro-active action. It was not. Such action had to be dragged out of the Council, as many of the medical members glanced over their shoulders, perhaps quite understandably, at what their colleagues might say in other places, such as the craft committees of the BMA.[131]

The position was changed by the Medical (Professional Performance) Act 1995, which amended the Medical Act 1983 to empower the GMC to deal with incompetent doctors. The new procedures came into force on 1 July 1997 and permitted the GMC to act when the professional performance of a doctor was 'seriously deficient'.[132] The definition of 'seriously deficient performance' was far from clear. The GMC's own, not particularly helpful, circular definition was: '...a departure from good professional practice...sufficiently serious to call into question the doctor's registration.'[133]

The changes resulted in the establishment of two new committees of the GMC, the Committee on Professional Performance and the Assessment Referral Committee. Section 36A provided that the CPP was under a duty, where the standard of professional performance of a registered medical practitioner was found to have been seriously deficient, to direct:

> (a) that his registration...shall be suspended...during such period not exceeding twelve months...; or
> (b) that his registration shall be conditional on his compliance, during such period not exceeding three years...with the requirements so specified.[134]

Suspensions could be extended, but there was no power under the performance procedures to erase a doctor's name from the medical register.

It is of note that the procedures deal with 'performance' as opposed to 'competence'. The latter relates to a doctor's knowledge and skills in abstract, what the doctor *can* do. The former looks at what the doctor actually does. A doctor can therefore be competent yet still perform inadequately, whilst an incompetent doctor cannot perform adequately, however much he or she wishes to. The distinction can be of particular relevance when a doctor who has given rise to concern is not currently practising. In these circumstances, whilst competence could be assessed by means of examination, performance could only be determined historically. Similar problems arise when a doctor has changed specialism and the alleged poor performance relates to a previous area of practice.[135]

---

131 Irvine, D., *The Doctors' Tale*, 2003, Radcliffe Medical Press, Oxford.

132 See Section 36A of the Medical Act 1983 and the General Medical Council (Professional Performance) Rules 1997. The first reported suspension under the new procedures occurred in December 1998, some 13 months after the doctor in question, a GP registrar, had been dismissed by his employer for inadequate performance and inadequate response to additional training. See Kirwin, S., 'First Doctor Suspended under GMC Performance Procedures', *BMJ*, 1999, 318: 10, 2 January.

133 GMC, *Performance Procedures Position Paper No 2*, June 1996.

134 Section 36A(1).

135 See the Fifth Report of the Shipman Inquiry, *Safeguarding Patients: Lessons from the Past – Proposals for the Future*, paras 24.9–24.11 (www.the-shipman-inquiry.org.uk).

The Rules made provision for three key elements: screening; assessment; and adjudication by the CPP. The new provisions envisaged that action by the CPP would be a matter of last resort. The Rules aim first to facilitate the voluntary rehabilitation of a practitioner by means of mentoring and retraining. Screening was undertaken by both medical and lay members of the GMC. If they considered that an assessment was needed, the medical screener initiated the assessment process. Otherwise the medical screener referred the case to the ARC, which decided whether there should be an assessment. Evidence to the Shipman Inquiry suggested that the original purpose of the ARC had been to provide an additional safeguard against excessive numbers of doctors being sent for assessment. The test to be applied by the screener was whether the complaint suggested that the doctor's performance might have been seriously deficient and 'it is appropriate to take action'. The ARC had the task of deciding whether the standard of performance 'may have been seriously deficient' and whether an assessment 'needs to be carried out'.[136] These two tests appear to be very similar, although the latter can be interpreted as being slightly higher. The screening and ARC procedures took place in private and whilst the complainant (or representative) could address the ARC, this did not extend to hearing other evidence. This was particularly unfortunate when the complainant was an employer, who was likely to be in a good position to confirm or refute the account given by the doctor.[137]

## Performance Assessment

The assessment process was supervised by a case co-ordinator, until July 2003 a medical member of the GMC, and conducted by an assessment panel. This panel included a doctor (from the same speciality as the doctor being assessed) as lead assessor, another doctor and a lay person, none of whom were members of the GMC.

The assessment consisted of interviews with interested parties, including the complainant, the practitioner and up to five persons nominated by the practitioner. The panel was also free to obtain advice or assistance from anyone else whom they considered might assist them. If appropriate, the panel would inspect a sample of the medical records produced by the doctor, and could also observe the doctor practising. If the first phase gave rise to concerns, the matter would be progressed to a second stage. This second stage of the assessment procedures involved tests of competence, focusing on the doctor's area of practice. The doctor's scores were compared with those of a control group, with the minimum satisfactory score being set deliberately low.[138]

---

136 The Fifth Report of the Shipman Inquiry, *Safeguarding Patients: Lessons from the Past – Proposals for the Future*, para 24.52 (www.the-shipman-inquiry.org.uk).

137 The Fifth Report of the Shipman Inquiry, *Safeguarding Patients: Lessons from the Past – Proposals for the Future*, para 25.24 (www.the-shipman-inquiry.org.uk).

138 Southgate, L., Campbell, M., Cox, J., Foulkes, J., Jolly, B., McCrorie, P. and Tombleson, P., 'The General Medical Council's Performance Procedures: the Development and Implementation of Tests of Competence with Examples from General Practice', *Medical*

The panel's report was required to include, inter alia, its opinions (with reasons) regarding whether:

> (a) the standard of the practitioner's professional performance has been seriously deficient;
> (b) the standard of the practitioner's professional performance is likely to be improved by remedial action;
> (c) the practitioner should limit his professional practice, or cease professional practice...[139]

Following the assessment panel's report, the case co-ordinator (acting in consultation with a lay adviser) could refer the case immediately to the CPP, decide to take no further action or prepare a statement of requirements for the doctor.[140] The latter could include reference to: aspects of the practitioner's professional performance which required improvement; the standard of professional performance to be achieved; improvements required to the running of the practitioner's professional practice; restrictions which should be imposed on the practitioner's professional practice. The statement of requirements also set the time period within which the requirements are to be fulfilled and provision for further assessment.[141]

If the case co-ordinator considered that public protection or the best interests of the practitioner require suspension or conditional registration, the matter could be referred to the CPP. Similar referral may be made if the practitioner fails to comply with the statement of requirements; is not benefiting from education or training being undertaken in accordance with a statement of requirements; or the practitioner's fitness to practise may be seriously impaired by reason of his physical or mental condition.[142] If the CPP formed the opinion that the doctor's behaviour was more likely to have given rise to SPM than SDP it could not, under the original procedures, refer the case to the PCC. This was a problem addressed by the new fitness to practise procedures (discussed in Chapter 16), which do provide for erasure if this is considered appropriate.

Somewhat illogically, greater levels of supervision were initiated against doctors subject to voluntary statements of requirements than against those suspended or made subject to conditional registration by the CPP. In the latter cases, it was left to the doctor to make arrangements for appropriate retraining without monitoring to ensure that it was done.[143]

---

*Education*, 2001, Vol 35 (Suppl. 1): 20–28, cited in the Fifth Report of the Shipman Inquiry, *Safeguarding Patients: Lessons from the Past – Proposals for the Future*, para 24.65 (www.the-shipman-inquiry.org.uk).

139 Rule 13(2).

140 Rule 17.

141 Rule 18.

142 Rule 25.

143 The Fifth Report of the Shipman Inquiry, *Safeguarding Patients: Lessons from the Past – Proposals for the Future*, para 24.103 (www.the-shipman-inquiry.org.uk).

A practitioner had a right of appeal from a decision of the CPP on questions of law only.[144] The latter was to be interpreted widely, in the interests of justice.[145]

Consideration was given to the performance procedures by the Privy Council in *Krippendorf v General Medical Council.*[146] In 1997 the doctor, a specialist in child health, was employed as a locum consultant. In 1998 a complaint was made about her injection technique in the immunization of over 200 children, and also a complaint about her performance in two potential child protection cases. The performance procedures were implemented. In June 1999 the assessment panel reported, expressing the opinion that the doctor's professional performance had been seriously defective, and that she required full retraining in general paediatrics. In July 1999 the CPP held a 'performance hearing'. The CPP decided that the doctor's professional performance was seriously deficient,[147] and suspended her registration with immediate effect. On appeal, the Privy Council concluded that the assessment panel had erred in assessing the doctor's current competence rather than her actual past performance:

> ...everything in the Rules suggests that it is the duty of the CPP and the Panel to have regard to the track record of the practitioner in the work which he has actually been doing. It is not their function to conduct an examination equivalent to that of a student's examination board. Theoretical questions are relevant only insofar as the answers may throw light on the practitioner's professional performance in the specific areas of work which he has actually been doing.

In December 2002 the Medical Act 1983 (Amendment) Order 2002 introduced the provision that 'professional performance' includes a medical practitioner's professional competence. In the following year, in the case of *Sadler v The General Medical Council*[148] the Privy Council revisited the distinction between competence and performance, concluding that the approach in *Krippendorf* should not be taken too far:

In most cases there is an obvious correlation between competence and performance. Moreover the assessment panel is concerned, not only with assessing past professional performance, but also with what needs to be done to improve a practitioner's performance, both in the public interest and in the practitioner's own best interests...The purpose of assessment is not to punish a practitioner whose standards of professional performance have been seriously defective, but to improve those standards, if possible, by a process of supervision and retraining, for the

144 Section 40.

145 *Stefan v General Medical Council* [2002] UKPC 10.

146 [2001] 1 WLR 1054.

147 The guidance from the GMC at the time was that 'seriously deficient performance' is a: '"[D]eparture from good professional practice, whether or not it is covered by specific GMC guidance, sufficiently serious to call into question a doctor's registration". This means that we will question your registration if we believe that you are, repeatedly or persistently, not meeting the professional standards appropriate to the work you are doing – especially if you might be putting patients at risk. This could include failure to follow the guidance in our booklet Good Medical Practice.'

148 (2003) unreported.

protection and benefit of the public. The process of assessment must include forming a view as to the standard of past performance, but if it is to achieve its objectives the process must not be restricted to that sort of backward-looking exercise.

*Sadler* also addressed the standard of proof to be adopted by the CPP. It was noted that the function of the CPP was not penal, rather it was to protect the public and to attempt to rehabilitate doctors whose professional standards have fallen too low. In determining whether performance has been seriously deficient, the CPP had to ascertain the primary facts. This would normally be subject to the civil standard of proof.[149]

The GMC performance procedures take on added significance when it is considered that complaints typically come from employers who have exhausted all local routes of action, and who consider the matters to be so serious that action against the doctor's registration is needed. Other, private, complainants had more difficulty in being heard. On receipt of such a complaint, the GMC did not automatically contact the doctor's employer so did not know whether the matter complained about was part of a pattern of behaviour. It is likely that a number of cases were screened out because the complaint alone was not considered sufficient to constitute SPM and inadequate steps were taken to determine whether, together with other problems, there was SDP.[150] A different problem arose with regard to doctors working in the private sector. It has been suggested that private hospitals are very unlikely to report a doctor because of the negative commercial affect this might have if the hospital becomes associated with the doctor's SDP.[151] In their early years the performance procedures were used infrequently. In 1998 action was initiated in only ten cases. In 1999 this had risen, but only to 26. Common reasons for the low numbers of referrals by screeners were that the case showed no pattern of poor performance or involved a single incident only. There appears to have been little recognition that in some (perhaps many) cases this would have been because no investigation was undertaken to ascertain whether there was evidence of other incidents. This was recognized by the PSI in its 2000 Report:

> ...screeners...clearly felt restricted by the requirement for a case to show a pattern of poor performance before it could be referred under the performance procedures. Since most of the cases they saw related to single incidents, and no investigation had taken place to establish whether there was a pattern of poor performance, it was not surprising that this was the conclusion they came to.[152]

Only from 2000 did a significant rise in activity occur, with 126 cases in that year, 70 in 2001 and 80 in 2002.[153]

---

149 Paragraph 73.

150 Rule 5(2) of the 1997 Performance Rules empowered the medical screener to seek additional information of this type.

151 See the Fifth Report of the Shipman Inquiry, *Safeguarding Patients: Lessons from the Past – Proposals for the Future*, paras 24.24–24.26 and 24.34 (www.the-shipman-inquiry.org.uk).

152 See the Fifth Report of the Shipman Inquiry, *Safeguarding Patients: Lessons from the Past – Proposals for the Future*, paras 24.111–24.112 (www.the-shipman-inquiry.org.uk).

153 The Fifth Report of the Shipman Inquiry, *Safeguarding Patients: Lessons from the Past – Proposals for the Future*, para 24.114 (www.the-shipman-inquiry.org.uk).

Matters were progressed very slowly through the performance procedures because they were unnecessarily complicated. It was recommended by the Ledward Inquiry that the situation would be improved by the introduction of a national Assessment and Support Centre, to act instead of the GMC in assessing the performance of doctors. Such an approach would have the advantage of independence and objectivity. Duplication of effort with NHS procedures would also be avoided, and most importantly the procedure could be implemented much more promptly. Referral should occur as soon as shortcomings with a doctor's performance were observed, without the need to wait for evidence of 'seriously deficient performance'. If this was followed, the GMC would be freed to concentrate on its proper role, to consider whether doctors are fit to practise and therefore entitled to remain on the medical register.[154]

## Health and Performance – Public Protection or Professional Protectionism?

The health and performance procedures filled the gaps in regulatory cover which could not meaningfully or appropriately be addressed by conduct procedures alone. However, the mechanisms for dealing with issues of poor performance and ill health place even greater control in the hands of the profession than do the conduct procedures. The latter are very far from perfect, but at least the lay members hearing such cases are able to adopt a similar independent stance to a jury or lay magistrates hearing criminal cases. In contrast, both the health and performance procedures were dominated by medical experts. In these circumstances, lay members were unlikely to have any significant say in decision making. There was also a risk within these procedures that technical and ethical issues would become blurred. The health procedures in particular offered a convenient alternative, often more palatable to the profession, than misconduct proceedings.[155]

## Future Directions

In late 2002 a Performance Procedures Review Group[156] was established. The Group noted that the GMC had made a number of key assumptions which had subsequently proven to be wrong. Amongst these were the expectations that most doctors would be capable of remediation and of returning to practice without restriction, and that most cases would relate to hospital doctors failing to keep up with latest practices. It is telling that the GMC appear to have had very little in-depth knowledge of the

154 *An Inquiry into Quality and Practice within the National Health Service Arising from the Actions of Rodney Ledward – The Report*, 1 June 2000, Part VII, paras 3.3–3.7.

155 For further discussion, see the Fifth Report of the Shipman Inquiry, *Safeguarding Patients: Lessons from the Past – Proposals for the Future*, chapter 24 (www.the-shipman-inquiry.org.uk).

156 Chaired by Dame Deirdre Hine, former Chairman of the Commission for Health Improvement, with a membership including Professor Alastair Scotland and Dame Lesley Southgate.

nature of underlying problems within the profession. It was also noted that the GMC's performance procedures were not as well integrated into the wider patient protection framework as they could have been, and there was inadequate feedback between the GMC and local employers. Performance assessment reports were not made available to doctors' employers. When the ARC or CPP found no inadequate performance, its reasons tended to be too inadequate to be of value. As the Group noted: '...it is essential that the GMC gives reasons for every decision it makes on fitness to practise, including decisions not to take any action. An employer's role is made harder if no information is available to explain why apparently serious concerns have not been taken forward.'

The Review Group also considered that the private nature of the performance procedures were incompatible with 'openness, transparency and accountability'. Overall, the focus should always be on patient protection. If remediation via voluntary procedures is not successful or has been ruled out, the implication from the Review Group's report was that further action should be directed at removing the doctor from practice.[157]

The GMC's response was to acknowledge that remediation was important for local procedures, but should not be its focus. By the time cases reach the GMC, its powers to suspend or impose conditions should be used to force cooperation on the part of the doctor, with the ultimate threat of erasure. There should be a move away from previous attitudes, where the GMC had made great efforts to save a doctor's career, even when a public protection focus would have been more appropriate.[158]

## Interaction with Other Procedures – the National Clinical Assessment Service

In September 1999 the government published a consultation paper, *Supporting Doctors, Protecting Patients*, which proposed the establishment of a new body, originally called the National Clinical Assessment Authority, subsequently renamed the National Clinical Assessment Service, which would have the role of assessing doctors who were alleged to be performing poorly. This task would be performed by local centres, with the GMC becoming involved only if a doctor's registration became an issue. The centres would advise NHS organizations about dealing with concerns about doctors and undertake assessments to determine the nature of problems. The local employer would then implement the recommendations.

The NCAS was created in 2001. It can be called upon when an NHS employer is faced with a poorly performing doctor. It can offer assessments and provide advice regarding appropriate and systematic ways to deal with the doctor, as an alternative to disciplinary proceedings. In the end the NCAS did not adopt the local centre idea – having faced opposition from the profession on the basis that they would

157 See the Fifth Report of the Shipman Inquiry, *Safeguarding Patients: Lessons from the Past – Proposals for the Future*, paras 24.182–24.198 (www.the-shipman-inquiry.org.uk).

158 See evidence of Sir Donald Irvine and Mr Finlay Scott, Chief Executive of the GMC to the Shipman Inquiry. The Fifth Report of the Shipman Inquiry, *Safeguarding Patients: Lessons from the Past – Proposals for the Future*, para 24.208 (www.the-shipman-inquiry.org.uk).

resemble 'boot camps'. Instead an administrative centre was to be established in London.[159] The aim of assessment is formative rather than summative; is the doctor suitable for the work currently being undertaken? If not, this does not inevitably mean that the doctor is not fit for an alternative type of medical work. Compliance with recommendations can only be enforced by the doctor's employer or, if patients are at risk, by the GMC.[160]

The Shipman Inquiry noted with some concern that it was possible for a GP whose performance gave rise to concern to be separately assessed up to three times – locally, then by the NCAS, and finally by the GMC. This was wasteful in resource terms and also could result in 'very substantial delays, during which the doctor may continue to practice, with consequent risk to patient safety'. Even when a matter did reach the GMC performance procedures, the risk of delay was far from over. For example, in one illustrative case a GP whose drug prescribing habits gave rise to concerns about patient safety was able to practise virtually unchecked for over three years whilst the performance procedures were progressing. In another case, a doctor whose performance had been found seriously deficient by the CPP, including the finding that patients were at risk, was able to practise unsupervised as he had moved to another specialism.[161]

## Previous Criticisms of the GMC Regulatory Processes

To the casual observer, some of the responses of the GMC to the recent crisis in medical regulation give the impression that it had been taken almost completely by surprise. However, even a brief historical review reveals that this should have been far from the case. In the early 1980s, Ian Kennedy raised doubts about the continued viability of the existing self-regulatory process. He argued that the GMC had no effective mechanism for identifying the public interest which it was ultimately charged to protect. Too many complaints were dealt with and dismissed at preliminary stages without any lay involvement or scrutiny within a public environment. It was also suggested that the numbers of doctors disciplined was limited because the GMC lacked resources to do more. Kennedy also concluded that the appeal process to (at that time) the Privy Council was an ineffective control mechanism over the GMC. Kennedy's proposed solutions included more proactive inspection and investigation of medical practice and the introduction of periodic re-registration.[162]

Criticism was aired more publicly when, in 1983, the BBC *That's Life* TV programme reported that a UK registered doctor was undertaking laser surgery to remove tattoos without the necessary competence. When the GMC was challenged

159 See the Fifth Report of the Shipman Inquiry, *Safeguarding Patients: Lessons from the Past – Proposals for the Future*, para 5.84 (www.the-shipman-inquiry.org.uk).

160 See the Fifth Report of the Shipman Inquiry, *Safeguarding Patients: Lessons from the Past – Proposals for the Future*, paras 5.85–5.87 (www.the-shipman-inquiry.org.uk).

161 The Fifth Report of the Shipman Inquiry, *Safeguarding Patients: Lessons from the Past – Proposals for the Future*, paras 5.95, 24.153–24.170 (www.the-shipman-inquiry.org.uk).

162 Kennedy, I., The *Unmasking of Medicine*, 1981, Allen & Unwin, London.

for failing to take any action, it accepted the criticism that in failing to be concerned with errors of diagnosis or treatment, it was neglecting its responsibility to ensure that a doctor is fit to practise. The GMC was also challenged on the basis that fellow doctors were aware of the poor practice but did not report it, fearing that they would be subject to disciplinary action for 'disparaging' a fellow doctor. The Council quickly modified its guidance to the profession with regard to both of these areas[163], although, as I discuss later, with little apparent effect given the events which were later to come to light regarding, inter alia, the Bristol Royal Infirmary and Harold Shipman.

In 1988, Jean Robinson published a critical account of the Council.[164] Robinson was highly critical of the GMC for referring, as standard, complaints about NHS treatment back to the NHS. Over one five-month period, 43 per cent of complaints to the GMC were dealt with in this way. The GMC knew, or should have known, that many complainants slipped through the net because of this approach. Similarly, those who did use the NHS complaints system were often far from well served by it. Robinson attributed the relative lack of hospital doctors referred to the PCC as being due, in part at least, to the weaknesses within the NHS procedures. The combination of referrals to the NHS and other complaints dismissed at the early stages of the GMC's procedures meant that between 1983 and 1987, only 22 per cent of complaints received by the GMC reached a stage where there was lay involvement in the decision making process.[165]

Criticisms of the GMC also came from within the profession. For example, Richard Smith in 1989, at the time deputy editor of the *British Medical Journal*, described the GMC as essentially an outdated institution which was progressively losing touch with modern regulatory requirements. The Council had become bogged down with its own internal concerns at the expense of addressing more important concerns regarding the competence and conduct of doctors.[166] Notwithstanding these comments, and the renewed expression of concerns by Stacey in the 1990s,[167] the GMC continued to move slowly and without obvious commitment to its core function of protecting the public.

Notwithstanding some progressive developments in the 1990s, the Council remained committed to its traditional piecemeal approach to regulation. The GMC retained the atmosphere of a closed club and continued to struggle in coming to

---

163 See Stacey, M., *Regulating British Medicine: the General Medical Council*, 1992, Wiley, Chichester, 186.

164 Robinson, J., *A Patient Voice at the GMC: a Lay Member's View of the GMC*, Report 1, Health Rights, London.

165 See Carrier, J. and Kendall, I., *Medical Negligence: Complaints and Compensation*, 1990, Avebury, Aldershot, 35. The GMC did address this in the late 1980s and the procedures were modified to prevent a complaint being screened out without the final say by a lay member of the GMC. See *GMC Annual Report 1989*.

166 Smith, R., 'The Day of Judgement Comes Closer', *BMJ*, 1989, 298, 1241–4; Lock, S., 'Regulating Doctors: a Good Case for the Profession to Set Up New Inquiry', *BMJ*, 1989, 299: 137–8.

167 Stacey, M., *Regulating British Medicine: the General Medical Council*, 1992, Wiley, Chichester.

terms with wider social changes. The consumer revolution had largely passed the GMC by.[168] As Irvine put it:

> The GMC of that time did not see itself…as a mainstream player in medical care. It did not look at the big picture of developing quality and the nature of medical practice, and ask itself what as the regulator it could and should contribute to that…It did not automatically think 'patients'. In business terms it did not really know what business it was in…[169]

In 1999, *Health Which?*[170] magazine surveyed 264 patients who had complained to the GMC. In only six cases was action ultimately taken against the doctor. Dissatisfaction with the GMC's handling of these complaints was found to be very high. Eighty-two per cent of complainants expressed dissatisfaction with the fairness of the process, 79 per cent were dissatisfied with the handling of their complaint, 77 per cent felt that the level of support they were given was inadequate and 63 per cent were unhappy that they had not been kept adequately informed. Seventy-eight per cent did not feel that the GMC was impartial and, overall, 85 per cent said that they were left with a negative view of the GMC following their encounter. The perception from complainants was that the GMC was far more anxious to protect doctors, rather than do justice regarding patients.

By 2000, Smith, then editor of the *British Medical Journal*, noted that to work effectively the GMC needed the trust of the public, the government and doctors. In reality, the Council had descended to a level that it was trusted by none of these. For example, the Kerr/Haslam Inquiry heard from healthcare professionals that they saw no point in passing on disclosures to the GMC because it was believed that no action would be taken.[171] Within the medical profession, leading candidates were running for election to the GMC on an anti-GMC platform, and one member was elected by the profession even though she had a disciplinary record with the GMC. Within some quarters of the profession, the belief persisted that what was in the interests of doctors must also be in the interests of patients.[172] It has also been suggested that fundamental conflicts of interest can arise when elected members also have roles in trade union-style bodies, such as the British Medical Association. This is particularly noticeable when elected members play a key role in delaying, blocking or watering down regulatory reforms which have a strong public interest element.[173]

---

168 One simple example highlighted by Irvine was the response by the Council to complaints in the 1980s that the GMC's telephone system was antiquated and it was problematic to get through. The GMC responded by improving access to GMC members but apparently gave no thought to the centrally important issue – the need for the complainant to be able to readily make contact. Irvine, D., *The Doctors' Tale*, 2003, Radcliffe Medical Press, Oxford, 95.

169 Irvine, D., *The Doctors' Tale*, 2003, Radcliffe Medical Press, Oxford, 95.

170 *Health Which*, 12 October 1999.

171 See *The Kerr/Haslam Inquiry Report*, July 2005, Cm 6640-1, 724.

172 Smith, R., 'The GMC: Where Now?', *BMJ*, 2000, 320: 1356, 20 May.

173 See Walshe, K., *Regulating Healthcare: a Prescription for Improvement?*, 2003, Open University Press, Buckingham; and Walshe, K. and Benson, L., 'GMC and the Future of Revalidation – Time for Radical Reform', *BMJ*, 2005, 330: 1504–1506, 25 June.

## Procedural Obstacles

Up until November 2002, ostensibly to discourage frivolous or unfounded allegations against doctors, the GMC had required lay complainants to present their complaint in the form of a sworn statement. This presented an obvious obstacle to complainants. As recently as 2000, for instance, the guidance to prospective complaints on the GMC's website had emphasized that the complainant would need to consult a solicitor or other appropriate organization to obtain a sworn statement. Even though it was suggested that the cost was likely to be low, the prospect of a complainant who already feels let down by a professional having to consult and pay another professional was likely to be a significant disincentive for some. Tellingly, it demonstrates a naivety on the part of the GMC with respect to the discomfort many people feel when having to enter the alien professional realms occupied by doctors and lawyers. The same website also listed types of complaint which the GMC was unlikely to take forward. Amongst these were 'complaints which are not related to a doctor's medical work'. This is an unfortunate choice of wording, as it may have deterred some complaints which would or should have been of interest to the GMC. Similarly, the GMC's choice to emphasize that the complainant will have to consent to the doctor being shown the complaint: 'We will need your permission to show the doctor your complaint. If you do not give your permission, we will probably not be able to take your complaint any further.'[174]

That this will form part of the process is to be expected, but what is problematic is the choice by the GMC to emphasize the point before a complaint has been made, possibly acting as a further deterrent to some complainants. The approach adopted by the GMC appears to have been to limit its own workload by discouraging potential complainants very early in the process. Out of sight, out of mind, seems to have been the GMC's preferred mantra.[175]

## Criticism Generated by the GMC's Own Research

In August 2000 research commissioned by the GMC was published. This was undertaken by Professor Isobel Allen and based on a two-year investigation of the GMC's disciplinary procedures.[176] This study followed up a 1996 research project, *The Handling of Complaints against Doctors*.[177] The 1996 report had highlighted

174 www.gmc-uk.org, 7 November 2000.

175 As part of the same section, the guidance does go on to say that if the potential complainant is worried about the prospect of the doctor seeing their complaint, they might 'find it helpful to talk to anyone advising you, or you can talk to us about it'. The latter wording does have a half-hearted feel to it, and is certainly not taking the more appropriate public protection stance that if someone has concerns about a doctor, it would be best to let the GMC know.

176 Allen, I., *The Handling of Complaints by the GMC: a Study of Decision-making and Outcomes*, 2000, Policy Studies Institute, London.

177 Allen, I., Perkins, E. and Witherspoon, S., *The Handling of Complaints against Doctors*, 1996, Policy Studies Institute, London.

that the GMC's conduct procedures lacked transparency, making it difficult to assess whether they were fair and objective. The initial screening stages, in particular, lacked information regarding how decisions were made. As discussed above, it was recognized that even in the late 1990s, there was no commonly accepted definition of 'serious professional misconduct'. This in turn resulted in a lack of clarity and consistency in applying this concept within different GMC committees. In a 1998 follow-up to its 1996 study, the PSI identified the extent to which the categorization of complaints was inadequately recorded, adding to the risk that cases which did raise issues of SPM were not reaching the PPC.

Allen found that between 1996 and 1999, 70 per cent of complaints to the GMC related to sub-standard treatment/clinical practice (80 per cent of those from members of the public), but only 10–15 per cent of these were referred to the PPC or to the performance procedures. It was also found that complaints from public bodies tended to be considered by the GMC screeners as far more serious than those from lay complainants. For example, in 1997 and 1998 only 5 per cent of complaints from the public were referred to the PPC, compared with 40 per cent from public bodies. A key reason identified for this was the greater amounts of evidence typically supplied by institutional complainants and also the fact that doctors in these cases may already have been found guilty in another disciplinary forum. It was also found that there was wide variation between screeners with regard to cases which they considered to be serious and to pose a risk to the public. At the extreme, screeners differed between 10 and 36 per cent in the number of cases they categorized as raising issues of SPM.[178]

Key recommendations from the study included:

- Development of an agreed definition of 'serious professional misconduct'
- Increased efficiency in resolving disciplinary cases which, inter alia, constitute a risk to the public, involve dishonesty, dysfunctional behaviour, sexual assault and criminal convictions
- Increased communication between the GMC and other bodies to agree the most appropriate organization to deal with particular types of complaints against doctors
- The establishment of appropriate protocols for addressing complaints which involve poor treatment or sub-standard clinical practice.

A screening decision form was also designed to divide complaints into three principal categories: (i) convictions, all of which, with the exception of minor motoring offences, would be referred to the PPC; (ii) complaints which by definition raised issues of serious professional misconduct, for example, those involving dishonesty, indecency and violence, which should be referred automatically to the PPC unless the screener considered there to be overwhelming reasons against this; (iii) those complaints, for instance, alleging sub-standard clinical practice, where it was appropriate for the screener to use discretion regarding referral to the PPC.

---

178 Allen, I., *The Handling of Complaints by the GMC: a Study of Decision-making and Outcomes*, 2000, Policy Studies Institute, London.

The effect of this was that 'referral' rates to the PPC rose from around 50 per cent of doctors accused of criminality or dishonesty (less in the case of those accused of other types of misconduct) in 1997 and 1998, to 93 per cent between July and December 1999.[179]

## Problems with the Health Procedures

A key problem with the operation of the health procedures was delay in the submission of supervisor reports – these being central to the oversight of doctors subject to the procedures. Delay typically resulted from missed appointments by the supervised doctor or problems in obtaining information from other sources. Even when reports were submitted, significant information regarding fitness to practise was missing in a number of cases. In cases involving addiction, supervisors were often reluctant to conduct random tests. Supervisors were also often reluctant to ensure that doctors complied with restrictions on their right to practise. Where information was available, over 50 per cent of doctors had breached undertakings. Some cases had been concluded even though there was insufficient evidence that the doctor had improved sufficiently to be fit to practise safely.[180]

Once the health procedures had been initiated, it seems that the GMC was at risk of losing 'sight of its role as regulator [and assuming]...the role of treating doctor at one remove'. The focus was on rehabilitation and there tended to be the assumption that any further misconduct was a result of the health problems. This is particularly telling when the problem related to the misuse of drugs. As Dame Janet Smith observed:

> [I]t seems to me that there must be a number of cases where there is no satisfactory explanation for the doctor beginning to take drugs. Nowadays, quite a lot of people take drugs for recreation. In those cases, there must be a 'lead-in' period where the doctor is exercising 'free will' in deciding to 'experiment' with drugs. His or her judgement is not at that time overborne by craving. It seems to me that a doctor, who should know of the dangers of taking addictive drugs, should not simply be regarded as an innocent 'victim' of the drug. I would have thought it unwise to assume that doctors who were prepared to obtain drugs by dishonest means at a time when they were not yet dependent would necessarily revert to honest behaviour when cured of their dependence.[181]

Some cases of this type had been progressed down the health route, when the disciplinary route would have been more appropriate. What should have been the GMC's central focus, that of protecting the public, was therefore undermined.

---

179 Allen, I., *The Handling of Complaints by the GMC: a Study of Decision-making and Outcomes*, 2000, Policy Studies Institute, London.

180 For further discussion, see the Fifth Report of the Shipman Inquiry, *Safeguarding Patients: Lessons from the Past – Proposals for the Future*, paras 22.99–22.110, 22.117 and 22.171 (www.the-shipman-inquiry.org.uk).

181 The Fifth Report of the Shipman Inquiry, *Safeguarding Patients: Lessons from the Past – Proposals for the Future*, para 23.50 (www.the-shipman-inquiry.org.uk).

**Appeals and Accountability**

Historically, the accountability of the GMC has been unclear. Lay membership of the Council has been intended to provide an oversight function independent of the profession. However, there has been an absence of an explicit mechanism to hold the GMC accountable for its performance.[182]

A statutory right of appeal to the Privy Council against first instance GMC disciplinary decisions was introduced by the Medical Act 1950. Prior to that, appeals against erasure were to the High Court, but only on questions of law or alleged disregard to natural justice.[183] Appeal to the Privy Council was by way of complete rehearing and was available only to the doctor, not to the complainant. More recently, the High Court replaced the Privy Council as the tribunal for first instance appeals.

Historically, there has been a reluctance on the part of the courts to interfere with decisions by regulatory committees of the GMC. This approach was expressed clearly by Lord Hoffman in *Bijl v General Medical Council*:

> Although the Board has full jurisdiction under section 40 of the Medical Act 1983 to entertain an appeal by way of rehearing…it has traditionally and rightly exercised that jurisdiction with circumspection. As the Board said in Evans v. General Medical Council (unreported) Appeal No. 40 of 1984 at p. 3:
>
> > '...a disciplinary committee are the best possible people for weighing the seriousness of professional misconduct and...the Board will be very slow to interfere with the exercise of discretion of such a committee...The Committee are familiar with the whole gradation of seriousness of the cases of various types which come before them and are peculiarly well qualified to say at what point on that gradation erasure becomes the appropriate sentence. This Board does not have that advantage nor can it have the same capacity for judging what measures are from time to time required for the purpose of maintaining professional standards.'[184]

In order to terminate a direction by the PCC it would be necessary to show that it was 'manifestly wrong'.[185]

Brazier suggests that this reluctance also originates from a 'fraternal respect' which exists between the senior members of the legal and medical professions. Judges show a hesitance to criticize doctors, to an extent not typically shown to other professions.[186]

---

182 The GMC itself has acknowledged this. See GMC, *Effective, Inclusive and Accountable Reform of the GMC's Structure, Constitution and Governance*, March 2001, 23. In this report, the GMC sees Parliament as the most appropriate point of accountability.

183 See Carrier, J. and Kendall, I., *Medical Negligence: Complaints and Compensation*, 1990, Avebury, Aldershot, 36.

184 [2001] UKPC 42, paragraph 2.

185 See, for example, *Prasad v GMC* (1987), *Salvi v GMC* (1993) and *R v GMC, ex parte Omar* (1998).

186 Brazier, M., *Medicine, Patients and the Law*, 1992, Penguin, London, 25.

## Self-Imposed Limitations

The GMC has been described as bureaucratic, deadly slow and biased against complainants.[187] In response to some of the high profile cases discussed in this book, the GMC has argued that its statutory powers have restricted the action available to it. It is correct that the powers of the GMC have been in the past more restricted than perhaps they should have been, but the GMC is far from blameless in this regard. Not only has the GMC been slow, even inactive, in seeking the additional powers, but it has also failed to use the powers it did have sufficiently creatively to protect the public. The Council's preferred stance has been that it was not there to deal with patients' complaints, nor to punish doctors. Instead, it limited its functions to maintaining standards amongst members of the profession. It is difficult to imagine how the latter could be achieved without appropriate engagement with the former.[188] Irvine acknowledges that the GMC adopted a very legalistic attitude, retreating to the statutory basis for its activities in a manner which narrowed its operations and generated an inward-looking perspective towards regulation.[189] Stacey suggested that the Council was afraid of taking a harsher regulatory stance, lest it lose legitimacy with the profession. Prosecuting a few exemplary cases was preferred, rather than seeking out all miscreants.[190] Similarly, it has been suggested that the GMC was reluctant to open what it knew was a 'Pandora's box' of poorly performing doctors.[191]

The GMC also tended to adopt an excessively deferential approach to the Royal Colleges, with their hold over specialist medicine, as well as to government. For instance, the Colleges successfully resisted attempts by the GMC to coordinate control of all stages of medical education. The Merrison Committee noted that significant numbers of overseas doctors whose skills fell below acceptable standards were admitted to the medical register to meet government manpower requirements for the NHS.[192]

Historically, the GMC has also shown only limited interest in allegations which, if proven, are not of sufficient seriousness to result in the removal of the doctor from the medical register. Examples include a professor of cardiology who had misstated his qualifications. The case was dismissed at the screening stage, even though the doctor in question continued to hold an influential position in the education and examining of future doctors. Another case involved the early dismissal of a complaint alleging the use of experimental treatment without ethics committee approval or

---

187 Irvine, D., *The Doctors' Tale*, 2003, Radcliffe Medical Press, Oxford, 105.

188 See Stacey, M., *Regulating British Medicine: the General Medical Council*, 1992, Wiley, Chichester; Irvine, D., *The Doctors' Tale*, 2003, Radcliffe Medical Press, Oxford.

189 Irvine, D., *The Doctors' Tale*, 2003, Radcliffe Medical Press, Oxford, 68.

190 Stacey, M., *Regulating British Medicine: the General Medical Council*, 1992, Wiley, Chichester, 221.

191 Irvine, D., *The Doctors' Tale*, 2003, Radcliffe Medical Press, Oxford, 68.

192 *Report of the Committee of Inquiry into the Regulation of the Medical Profession*, 1975, Cmnd 6018, HMSO, London, paragraphs 185–7. See also Stacey, M., *Regulating British Medicine: the General Medical Council*, 1992, Wiley, Chichester, 54; Irvine, D., *The Doctors' Tale*, 2003, Radcliffe Medical Press, Oxford.

the consent of the patients.[193] Surprisingly, given its orientation towards protecting doctors, it has also been observed that the GMC has been reluctant to prosecute unregistered practitioners.[194]

It has also been suggested that doctors have been able to escape self-regulatory sanction by applying for voluntary removal from the medical register. This was of concern to the Inquiry which investigated the behaviour of Michael Haslam.[195]

## Lack of Proactive Investigation

The GMC has been categorized as stubbornly reactive, exhibiting a continuing reluctance to initiate investigations. Reliance upon matters being brought to it by way of complaint has resulted in ad hoc rather than systematic and comprehensive regulation.[196] The approach taken by the GMC was opposite to that normally taken by the criminal justice process, where charges are brought only after completion of the police investigation. A complaint received by the GMC which progressed to the stage of the PCC was filtered administratively, screened, referred to the PPC and then to the PCC.[197] In many cases, only at this final stage did the Council make any meaningful attempt to find evidence to support the charges.[198] These limitations have been acknowledged from within the GMC. For instance, Mr Finlay Scott, Chief Executive of the GMC, gave evidence to the Kerr/Haslam Inquiry that the Council had not seen itself as an investigatory body: 'We saw ourselves as reacting to complaints. In the absence of a complaint, because there was no complainant, there was no basis for taking something forward.'[199]

---

193 Wilmshurst, P., 'The GMC is Too Lenient', *BMJ*, 2002, 325: 397, 17 August. See also Templeton, S., 'Doctors Face Charges after 12-year Fight', *The Sunday Herald*, 25 August 2002.

194 Stacey, M., *Regulating British Medicine: the General Medical Council*, 1992, Wiley, Chichester, 57 and 63.

195 *The Kerr/Haslam Inquiry Report*, July 2005, Cm 6640-1. For further examples, see 'Inquiry into Blunders by Doctor, 78', *The Guardian*, 13 June 2000 (web edition). For alternative discussion, see Smith, R.G., *Medical Discipline: The Professional Jurisdiction of the General Medical Council, 1858-1990*, 1994, Clarendon Press, Oxford.

196 Irvine, D., *The Doctors' Tale*, 2003, Radcliffe Medical Press, Oxford, 105.

197 Latterly, the GMC itself acknowledged this weakness. See GMC, *Acting Fairly to Protect Patients: Reform of the GMC's Fitness to Practise Procedures*, March 2001, 9. It was not until 2000 that the GMC obtained powers to compel the production of documents and other information prior to referral to the PPC or PCC. See the Fifth Report of the Shipman Inquiry, *Safeguarding Patients: Lessons from the Past – Proposals for the Future*, para 18.115 (www.the-shipman-inquiry.org.uk). The GMC's own slowness in seeking such power indicates its reluctance to address the historical need for it to take responsibility for all necessary stages of the disciplinary process.

198 The Shipman Inquiry heard evidence that the paradoxical nature of this approach had been recognized within the GMC. The Fifth Report of the Shipman Inquiry, *Safeguarding Patients: Lessons from the Past – Proposals for the Future*, para 18.133 (www.the-shipman-inquiry.org.uk).

199 *The Kerr/Haslam Inquiry Report*, July 2005, Cm 6640-1, 426.

Criticisms of this type are not new. Thirty years ago, the Merrison Committee identified problems about the manner in which the GMC found out about potential problem doctors and its dependency on matters being brought to its attention. Merrison had recommended the establishment of a GMC investigation unit, staffed with appropriate specialists. The GMC was opposed to this proposal and successfully resisted its implementation.[200] Merrison had anticipated concern from the profession, predicting that some doctors would view an investigatory unit as an unwelcome addition to the scrutiny they were already subject to. [201] Similar observations were made by Parry in 1976:

> The [GMC] cannot act as a police force and seek out cases, nor was it intended to do so. It has no inspectorate as does the Pharmaceutical Society; it must rely on such outside sources as the police, who may report convictions of doctors in the Courts or upon reports from professional colleagues, executive councils, government departments, patients or their aggrieved friends or relatives.[202]

Robinson, writing in 1988, also expressed concern that the GMC lacked its own investigatory capacity and was therefore heavily reliant on the Department of Health and the Home Office.[203]

When it has chosen to, the GMC has proven itself capable of thorough and comprehensive investigations, through appointed firms of solicitors. However, this requires a willingness to invest sufficient resources, and has proven to be a rare occurrence. [204]

The impact of the GMC's approach was illustrated by research undertaken by the Policy Studies Institute in 1996. The PSI found that in 22 per cent of cases where the GMC had taken no action, it had requested further evidence from the complainant. Notwithstanding the fact that a lay complainant was likely to be daunted by such a request, if a response was not forthcoming there was usually no follow-up. It was not even the GMC's standard practice to make enquiries of the doctor's employer or even its own records to determine whether there had been other complaints or expressions of concern. The Shipman Inquiry identified a number of cases in which a complaint had been dismissed, notwithstanding the doctor in question having a disciplinary history. For example, in one case the Medical Adviser in a particular

200 See Stacey, M., *Regulating British Medicine: the General Medical Council*, 1992, Wiley, Chichester, 57, 62 and 239.

201 Merrison Report, 1975, paragraph 258. Cited by Stacey, M., *Regulating British Medicine: the General Medical Council*, 1992, Wiley, Chichester, 239.

202 Parry, N. and Parry, J., *The Rise of the Medical Profession*, 1976, Croom Helm, London, 244.

203 Robinson, J., *A Patient Voice at the GMC: a Lay Member's View of the GMC*, Report 1, Health Rights, London. The Shipman Inquiry heard evidence that, unlike the Home Office, the GMC did not have the power to enter doctors' surgeries and inspect records. The GMC's powers were described as being limited to its 'solicitors knocking politely on people's doors and seeing how far they could get'. However, it was acknowledged that 'We have no formal investigative powers' tended to drift erroneously into 'We cannot investigate'.

204 See the Fifth Report of the Shipman Inquiry, *Safeguarding Patients: Lessons from the Past – Proposals for the Future*, para 18.113 (www.the-shipman-inquiry.org.uk).

area had, following Shipman's conviction, undertaken an analysis of GP prescribing and found that one particular doctor had been prescribing over ten times the amount of morphine compared with other doctors in the area. Despite the outcry after Shipman, it took the GMC almost two years to write substantively to the Health Authority, asking for any additional documentation. When the HA responded saying that it did not have any, the case was closed. As the Shipman Inquiry noted: 'The fact that a member of the GMC staff considered that there was "no other reason for proceeding" in a case involving the possible unlawful supply of controlled drugs is extremely worrying.'

It was also of concern that when a subsequent complaint was made against the same doctor, this earlier closed complaint was not considered. Indeed, for a brief period in the 1990s, the GMC appears to have placed so little value on background information of this type that it went through a phase of disposing of files relating to complaints which had been closed. In another case, a doctor accused of being drunk at work was referred to the GMC health procedures when, unknown to the screener, the GMC had been informed that the doctor had recently been convicted of unlawful possession of class A and class B drugs.[205] As expressed by the Shipman Inquiry:

> It is disappointing that the GMC, which has the protection of patients as its declared objective, has been content for so long to look at individual complaints in isolation. There seems to have been a failure fully to appreciate the effect that knowledge about a previous complaint might have on the evaluation of a later complaint. It also seems that there has been a view…that it would be 'unfair to doctors' to seek background information which might, in some circumstances, be unfavourable to them. From the viewpoint of patient safety, it seems to me essential that, when a decision is being taken whether or not to institute disciplinary action, the person making the decision should have a full picture of all issues which may affect the doctor's fitness to practise.[206]

The handbook for screeners, introduced in 1997, expressly stated that previous complaints should not be taken into account if they could not be substantiated. This ignored the fact that a lack of substantiation (for example, due to insufficient evidence) did not inevitably mean that the allegation had been untrue, and a subsequent similar complaint might indicate a pattern of misbehaviour on the part of the doctor.[207]

The absence of effective investigation by the GMC meant that around 65 per cent of complaints were rejected at a very early stage by administrative staff, without reference to a medical screener. This was still the case as late as 2003, notwithstanding the various scandals which had come to the knowledge of the GMC by that stage. The PSI in 1996, and in its follow-up report in 2000, found that the most important factor influencing whether the GMC took action was the origin of the complaint. A

205 The Fifth Report of the Shipman Inquiry, *Safeguarding Patients: Lessons from the Past – Proposals for the Future*, paras 18.185–18.192 (www.the-shipman-inquiry.org.uk). As with many other examples of past problematic behaviour, evidence on behalf of the GMC assured the Inquiry that practices had been modified to prevent a repetition.

206 The Fifth Report of the Shipman Inquiry, *Safeguarding Patients: Lessons from the Past – Proposals for the Future*, para 18.177 (www.the-shipman-inquiry.org.uk).

207 See the Fifth Report of the Shipman Inquiry, *Safeguarding Patients: Lessons from the Past – Proposals for the Future*, para 19.75 (www.the-shipman-inquiry.org.uk).

significant majority of doctors referred to the PPC, and from there to the PCC, had been complained about by public bodies, which typically provided well-presented cases complete with evidence. In contrast, as many as 95 per cent of complaints from members of the public, which typically were not presented virtually ready made and complete with evidence, were rejected prior to the PPC stage.[208]

The Shipman Inquiry expressed concern that the GMC had been unwilling to undertake preliminary investigations of complaints from private individuals:

> I recognise that to undertake such investigations would have been a costly exercise for the GMC. However, I have the clear impression that cost was not the only reason why such investigations were not undertaken. The impression I received was that complaints from individuals were suspected of being, in some way, unreliable, at least unless and until the complainant could produce sufficient evidence to amount to a *prima facie* case of SPM, backed – until November 2002 – by a statutory declaration. Also, there was resistance to any action which might be seen as 'assisting complainants' and, therefore, as 'unfair to doctors'.[209]

Case examples were also found where the GMC exhibited stereotypical attitudes towards certain types of complainant. For instance, when a complaint was received from an ex-spouse, it was often assumed that this was driven by malice. For example, the GMC was notified that a doctor had received a police caution for being in unlawful possession of class A and class B drugs. Subsequently, a letter was received from a woman who had been in a long-term relationship with the doctor. This alleged that he had abused drugs for a number of years and that this was continuing. In determining how to proceed, the caseworker completely ignored the letter, without any attempt to check the truth of any of the allegations. It subsequently transpired, by his own admission, that the doctor had been abusing at least one type of class A drug for seven years. As observed by the Shipman Inquiry: '[T]he GMC must not be surprised that the public does not have confidence in it if it sweeps aside allegations such as those made in this case without making any attempt to discover the truth.'[210]

With regard to statutory declarations, these were required from private (but not institutional) complainants and their witnesses before a matter could progress beyond the screening stage. Ostensibly to deter bogus or trivial complaints, some genuine complainants are highly likely to have also been deterred by this additional hurdle. Within the GMC, there appears to have been little recognition that this and other hurdles resulted in the loss to the regulatory process of cases which might have revealed doctors who presented a serious risk to the public.[211]

---

208 See the Fifth Report of the Shipman Inquiry, *Safeguarding Patients: Lessons from the Past – Proposals for the Future*, paras 18.2, 18.124–18.125, 18.150 and 18.179 (www.the-shipman-inquiry.org.uk).

209 The Fifth Report of the Shipman Inquiry, *Safeguarding Patients: Lessons from the Past – Proposals for the Future*, para 18.128 (www.the-shipman-inquiry.org.uk).

210 The Fifth Report of the Shipman Inquiry, *Safeguarding Patients: Lessons from the Past – Proposals for the Future*, para 22.185, and paras 22.181–22.184 (www.the-shipman-inquiry.org.uk).

211 The Fifth Report of the Shipman Inquiry, *Safeguarding Patients: Lessons from the Past – Proposals for the Future*, para 18.136 and 18.144 (www.the-shipman-inquiry.org.uk).

In the case of criminal convictions, the police or Home Office are required to notify the GMC when a registered medical practitioner is convicted of a criminal offence. In the past, the Council have complained about long delays in receiving such notification.[212] However, the Council seem to have made little attempt to compensate for failings by other agencies by enhancing their own investigatory capacity.

Evidence of the continuing lack of investigation on the part of the GMC is provided by a recent case pursued before the High Court and then the Court of Appeal.[213] A registered medical practitioner, Dr C, appeared before the PCC on 20 October 2003. Dr C was charged with engaging in an emotional and sexual relationship with a patient (Mrs A), who was also possibly psychiatrically vulnerable. The relevance of this case from the investigatory point of view is that the chairman of the PCC announced the decision as follows:

> The only information provided to us is that contained within the charge itself. We have received no evidence as to the circumstances or context of any relationship with Mrs A, nor of any treatment you provided to her…[T]he Committee are acutely aware of the dangers of making unsupported assumptions to fill the void resulting from a lack of evidence and we have therefore not done so. Having in mind that the standard of proof required is that we should be sure, the Committee have determined that such facts as have been found proved are insufficient to support a finding of serious professional misconduct.

Shortly after the PCC decision, on 28 October 2003, Dr C's Primary Care NHS Trust wrote to the Council for the Regulation of Healthcare Professionals, saying that medical records were available to establish those elements of the charge which had not been pursued or found not proved. Also, the partners of Dr C had been prepared to give evidence before the PCC, but had not been called. The Chief Executive of the Primary Care Trust wrote to the GMC on 5 November 2003, enclosing what purported to be a record of a meeting that he had conducted with Mrs A. For the GMC to have inquired of the PCT and Dr C's partners would hardly have presented a challenging investigatory task. Yet this was not done. Only recently, with the advent of the CRHCP, has a clear mechanism for challenging laxity on the part of the GMC been available. However, the courts have made it clear that this is to be used sparingly and only when it is necessary for the protection of the public.[214] This is a far from ideal approach to address what should be an essential first instance issue.

---

212 Stacey, M., *Regulating British Medicine: the General Medical Council*, 1992, Wiley, Chichester, 57 and 150.

213 *Council for the Regulation of Healthcare Professionals v General Medical Council and another -- Council for the Regulation of Healthcare Professionals v Nursing and Midwifery Council and another* [2004] EWCA CIV 1356, [2004] All ER (D) 272 (Oct); and *Council for the Regulation of Health Care Professionals v General Medical Council and another* [2004] EWHC 527 (ADMIN), [2004] All ER (D) 541 (Mar).

214 See *Council for the Regulation of Healthcare Professionals v General Medical Council and another -- Council for the Regulation of Healthcare Professionals v Nursing and Midwifery Council and another* [2004] EWCA CIV 1356, [2004] All ER (D) 272 (Oct) at 42.

## Efforts at Identification

In some cases, investigation by the GMC did not even extend to attempting to identify the doctor being complained about. For instance, a patient who is ill in hospital may be unable to readily recall the name or other details regarding a doctor they wish to report. Alternatively, even if the complainant can provide a correct name, there may be numerous registered doctors with this name. The Policy Studies Institute found that the identification problem had worsened between 1997 and 2003. In 1997, the GMC failed to identify the doctor in 15 per cent of cases. By 2003, this had risen to 25 per cent. Even though the GMC's explanation for this increase was that the cases were ones which could never give rise to SPM or seriously deficient performance, the PSI noted that 22 per cent of cases in which the doctor was unidentified involved allegations of dishonesty or other criminality. Also, it appeared not to have occurred to the GMC that without knowing the doctor's identity, it was not possible to ascertain whether he or she had a disciplinary history. A previous disciplinary record could influence whether the current complaint might represent a pattern of behaviour, or otherwise influence whether it could constitute SPM or SDP. Similarly, the current complaint will not become part of the doctor's record. Finally, by not taking steps to identify the subject of the complaint, the GMC cannot be sure that he or she is not an unregistered person masquerading as a doctor.[215] This latter point was illustrated by a case example considered by the Shipman Inquiry. The complaint related to laser eye treatment. GMC staff closed the case on the basis that the local complaints procedures had not been used. The GMC had no idea whether the person in question was actually registered as a doctor, or was an impostor. Nor did it know whether, if the person was a doctor, there was a disciplinary history. The complainant had supplied the address of the clinic, so making inquiries should have been straightforward. A final issue of seriousness with this case was that the complaint related to a private clinic, to which members of the public could turn without a referral from their GP. The GMC was therefore a, probably *the*, key body in terms of public protection. Advising the complainant to refer to the clinic's own complaints procedures, of which the GMC knew nothing, which the complainant had said had already failed to respond satisfactorily, appears to have fallen far short of meeting the level of protection required.[216]

## Importance of Investigation – Failures Elsewhere

The significance of the GMC's failure to develop an appropriate investigatory capacity is exacerbated by similar failures elsewhere in the system. Failure by

215 See the Fifth Report of the Shipman Inquiry, *Safeguarding Patients: Lessons from the Past – Proposals for the Future*, paras 18.204–18.208 (www.the-shipman-inquiry.org.uk). The serious implications of unregistered and registered but unqualified 'doctors' are discussed by Lister, S., 'How a Fake Doctor Took £1½m and Helped 1,000 People to get Asylum', *The Times*, 18 January 2005, 3.

216 See the Fifth Report of the Shipman Inquiry, *Safeguarding Patients: Lessons from the Past – Proposals for the Future*, paras 18.213–18.221 (www.the-shipman-inquiry.org.uk).

employers to investigate emerged as a common problem in numerous recent cases. For example, the Ayling report concluded that: 'It was not until 1998 that complaints about Ayling were investigated and taken seriously. From 1971 until 1998, we have identified a number of missed opportunities when concerns and complaints about Ayling might have been acted on.'[217]

In the Richard Neale case: 'The inability of [Richard Neale's] employers to provide sufficient control and monitoring procedures only made matters worse.'[218]

The Kerr/Haslam Inquiry identified similar problems, and concluded that the common themes which emerged from these reports were that 'too little monitoring, with too loose control leading to a freedom for the clinicians in question to deal with some of their patients in an allegedly damaging and unacceptable way'.[219]

The initial response which prospective complainants receive from the GMC is likely to determine how many of those complainants persist with their concerns. One of the victims of Clifford Ayling recalled that, having plucked up the courage to contact the GMC, she was told that there was no one to speak to her and that she should phone again later.[220] For complainants who believe that they have suffered at the hands of their doctor and who are already intimidated by the prospect of complaining, this is likely to be a good way to frighten them away entirely.

## The Gentleman's Club

At its foundation in 1858, the GMC was little different to a gentleman's club. Membership of the club was intended to guarantee that registered doctors would not engage in ungentlemanly behaviour. It was this approach which placed adultery and inappropriate sexual advances at the forefront of outlawed behaviour.[221] For example, a former medical member of the GMC gave evidence to the Shipman Inquiry that in 1976, around the time Shipman had been allowed to remain in practice despite convictions for drug offences, liaison between a doctor and a patient was still regarded as one of the most serious issues of misconduct. For example, he recounted a case of adultery between a doctor and patient, where the patient's only contact with the surgery was a vaccination by the practice nurse. The doctor had met the patient outside of his professional environment and the relationship was 'totally consensual'.[222] Stacey describes the white male-dominated club atmosphere as still present in the 1970s. She attributed to the club ethos the reluctance of practitioner members of the GMC to erase the names of colleagues from the register. The good

217 The Honourable Mrs Justice Pauffley, Committee of Inquiry – Independent Investigation into how the NHS Handled Allegations about the Conduct of Clifford Ayling, 15 July 2004, Cm 6298, para 4.1.

218 Committee of Inquiry – Independent Investigation into how the NHS Handled Allegations about the Conduct of Richard Neale, Cm 6315, 2004.

219 *The Kerr/Haslam Inquiry Report*, July 2005, Cm 6640-1, 467.

220 *Real Story*, broadcast on BBC 1, 7.30pm, 8 November 2004.

221 Stacey, M., *Regulating British Medicine: the General Medical Council*, 1992, Wiley, Chichester, 204.

222 Evidence to the Shipman Inquiry in November 2003 (Day 200).

name of the profession demands that doctors who behave outrageously are removed from the profession, but in medical eyes few cases are outrageous. The 'there but for the grace of God' and 'it could happen to any of us' approach tended to dominate.[223] The club ethos was so strong that, even though members are aware that some registered doctors should never have been admitted to the profession, once they are on the register every effort is made to keep them there.[224]

## Reforms

Writing in the early 1990s, Stacey concluded that the GMC was in need of reform because it was not fulfilling the promise made to the state, to ensure that registered practitioners are worthy of the trust the public places in them. The register had never genuinely reflected only the competent and trustworthy.[225] Where the GMC has innovated and moved forwards, this has tended to favour the profession rather than the public. To this end, lay representation was kept low and greater voice given to doctors. It was important that the GMC changed this attitude, as reform should come from within – without ownership of the process, there was a serious risk that the subjects of regulation would fail to cooperate with initiatives, or even derail them.[226] Once agreed, standards should be embedded within medical education and underpinned by 'robust arrangements to secure full and willing compliance'.[227] There is clearly scope for conflict between seeking 'willing compliance' whilst also ensuring that procedures remain robust.

The GMC has argued that it moved from reactive to proactive mode with the publication of *Good Medical Practice* in 1997. It was said that the Council had made 'a determined attempt to forge an explicit view of how doctors should practise to the highest standards'. The Council has also sought to make clear that its central function is to protect patients, not to represent doctors. Professionally led regulation in partnership with the public has become the new mantra.[228]

It has also been argued that the centrally organized, complaints-led GMC system is no longer appropriate. Accountability must be incorporated into systems at all levels – from hospitals and general practices to clinical teams and individual doctors. Local detection of dysfunctional practice is the way forward. The new system of licensing, and reinforcing the idea that self-regulation must happen amongst groups

---

223 Stacey, M., *Regulating British Medicine: the General Medical Council*, 1992, Wiley, Chichester, 205.

224 Stacey, M., *Regulating British Medicine: the General Medical Council*, 1992, Wiley, Chichester, 206.

225 Stacey, M., *Regulating British Medicine: the General Medical Council*, 1992, Wiley, Chichester, 57 and 203.

226 Stacey, M., *Regulating British Medicine: the General Medical Council*, 1992, Wiley, Chichester, 57 and 203.

227 Irvine, D., *The Doctors' Tale*, 2003, Radcliffe Medical Press, Oxford, 106.

228 Irvine, D.H., 'The Performance of Doctors I: Professionalism and Self-Regulation in a Changing World', *BMJ*, 1997, 314: 1540–2 and 196.

of doctors and clinical teams at local level, are seen as the way to ensure that all practising doctors are fit to do so.[229]

## Intermingling Evidence and Mitigation

One of the issues of concern with the operation of the GMC disciplinary process was the tendency to intermingle issues of evidence and issues of mitigation – taking into account a doctor's past professional history and character when determining whether he or she was guilty of serious professional misconduct. Dame Janet Smith noted that it was 'very common for the doctor to produce testimonials from patients and colleagues about his/her general abilities and character', potentially relevant to sanctions, but generally irrelevant to the decision as to whether the doctor is guilty of serious professional misconduct. It was similarly considered inappropriate that the PPC should take such factors into account when deciding whether a complaint should progress to the PCC. This problem was further exacerbated by the fact that there was usually no balance, in that there was no ready source of information about a doctor's full career history, and even his or her disciplinary history was often incomplete. Research by the PSI also found that members of the PPC might speculate why a doctor had acted in a particular way or consider possible mitigation (such as systems failures or particular practice pressures) for which they had no evidence. Similarly, contrition and an apology by the doctor could influence PPC decision making. Doctors were far more likely to seek to rationalize and excuse the behaviour of colleagues who appeared before them. Medical members of the PPC took a very different approach to their judicial role, compared with the way in which a lawyer would approach a similar situation.[230]

However, it also has to be recognized that doctors are not lawyers, and in some appealed cases the Privy Council failed to make the position absolutely clear. One leading example is *Preiss v General Dental Council.*[231] However, in *R (on the application of Campbell) v General Medical Council*[232] the previous interpretations of *Preiss* were questioned. In *Campbell* the Court of Appeal held that the PCC should not take into account the personal mitigation advanced by a doctor when deciding whether he or she was guilty of serious professional misconduct. It was recognized that there may be occasions when determinations of guilt and background overlap. For example, the professional history of the practitioner may support a finding of serious professional misconduct on the basis that he has been reported previously for the same type of activity. The previous allegation may not have resulted in a finding of serious professional misconduct, but the 'history' may result in a finding of guilt because of the repetition. The Court of Appeal considered that *Preiss* had been misinterpreted in earlier cases. The oft-quoted passage by Lord Cooke relating

229 Irvine, D., *The Doctors' Tale*, 2003, Radcliffe Medical Press, Oxford, 107.

230 See the Fifth Report of the Shipman Inquiry, *Safeguarding Patients: Lessons from the Past – Proposals for the Future*, paras 20.65–20.66, 20.94–20.98 and 20.107 (www.the-shipman-inquiry.org.uk)

231 [2001] 1 WLR 1926.

232 [2005] EWCA CIV 250, [2005] All ER (D) 193 (Mar).

to the 'unblemished record' of the appellant appeared in a paragraph which related exclusively to the issue of penalty and had no relevance to the issue whether the appellant was guilty of serious professional misconduct. This supported the contention that culpability and personal mitigation should be considered separately.[233] The cases of *Rao v GMC*[234] and *Silver v GMC*,[235] both of which had interpreted *Preiss* as authority for the possible relevance of a practitioner's unblemished record to a finding of guilty, were disapproved. A similarly disapproving stance was taken by the Shipman Inquiry:

> Taking into account material which was irrelevant to the issue 'muddied the waters' and inevitably resulted in cases of serious misconduct being excused because the doctor had a good past record. This must have resulted in some doctors who were in fact guilty of SPM avoiding a finding to that effect, with obvious implications for patient safety. It must also have caused great distress to patients and families who will have had the impression that the misconduct which had been demonstrated was somehow acceptable to the GMC.[236]

*Campbell* and the Shipman Inquiry address problems which were present under the 'old' GMC disciplinary procedures. The new rules introduced from November 2004[237] no longer anticipate that personal mitigation be taken into account when considering 'impairment' of a doctor's 'fitness to practise' (the terminology which replaced 'serious professional misconduct'). Instead, the panel will consider whether the doctor's fitness to practise is impaired to such a degree that it justifies action on registration. The reality, however, may prove to be somewhat different. It will be just as problematic for a fitness to practise panel to determine whether a single serious lapse on the part of a doctor justifies action on registration, as it was for the PCC to decide whether an equivalent lapse constituted SPM. In these circumstances, mitigation which should be irrelevant to guilt may continue to creep in.

## Interim Orders Committee

One serious problem highlighted by the Shipman case was the limited powers possessed by the GMC to restrict the right to practise of doctors before misconduct was proved against them. When, during the police investigation, it became clear that Shipman may have killed a number of patients, there was great concern that neither NHS nor GMC procedures provided for his prompt suspension.[238] As a result, the

---

233 [2005] EWCA CIV 250, [2005] All ER (D) 193 (Mar), para 38.

234 [2003] Lloyd's Med 62.

235 [2003] Lloyd's Med 333.

236 See the Fifth Report of the Shipman Inquiry, *Safeguarding Patients: Lessons from the Past – Proposals for the Future*, para 21.46 (www.the-shipman-inquiry.org.uk).

237 Discussed later.

238 The NHS Tribunal had the power to suspend him, and on 18 August, the West Pennine Health Authority contacted Tribunal, but the earliest date for a hearing was 29 September. The Tribunal agreed to the suspension, but this was only communicated to the Health Authority on 15 October. The Health Authority then had to wait 14 days, until the expiration of the period for an appeal, before being able to take control of the practice. See The Honourable

police decided to arrest Shipman and seek his remand in custody at an earlier point in their investigation than they would have wished.[239] The PPC had the power to make an interim order imposing conditions on or suspending a doctor's registration if the interests of the public or those of the doctor warranted this.[240] This could only be done when the PCC had concluded that the case should progress to the PCC or Health Committee and, initially, for a maximum (non-renewable) period of two months. In practice, extremely limited use was made of these powers, only four interim orders being made between 1980 and 1996. Rule changes in 1996 increased the maximum period of the order to six months, with power to renew for up to three months. This saw some increase in use of the power, five interim orders being made in 1997, ten in 1998, 13 in 1999 and 32 in the first seven months of 2000.[241]

The GMC had been aware of the limitations for some time, although does not appear to have taken it particularly seriously. For example, it did not seek to increase its powers in this respect when the rules were changed in 1996. The issue was addressed in a paper considered by the GMC Fitness to Practise Policy Committee in November 1998. At this time the GMC were aware of six ongoing cases, two involving murder charges (including Shipman), three involving serious sexual offences and one involving serious sexual offences with offences of violence. Four of the six doctors were remanded on bail and remained free to practise without restriction. The focus of the 1998 discussions strongly favoured the doctor's position, noting that if a doctor were to be suspended but ultimately acquitted, he or she would have suffered an injustice. Concerns about the risk to the public from a doctor who was ultimately convicted appears to have taken second place.[242]

The government questioned whether the GMC was as restricted as it said it was, but expressed a willingness to legislate to remove any ambiguity.[243] Section 41A of the Medical Act 1983 (as amended) was enacted and introduced new powers to be exercised by the Interim Orders Committee of the General Medical Council. This section empowered the IOC to impose an interim suspension in the public interest or in the interest of the doctor. Generally, the role of the IOC was not to make findings of fact in relation to the pending disciplinary charges, rather it worked on the assumption that the charges may be proved in due course.[244] Over the years, there

---

Mrs Justice Pauffley, Committee of Inquiry – Independent Investigation into how the NHS Handled Allegations about the Conduct of Clifford Ayling, 15 July 2004, Cm 6298, para 4.74.

239 See the Fifth Report of the Shipman Inquiry, *Safeguarding Patients: Lessons from the Past – Proposals for the Future*, para 20.44 (www.the-shipman-inquiry.org.uk).

240 Medical Act 1978, section 13 and Professional Conduct Rules 1980, rule 12.

241 See the Fifth Report of the Shipman Inquiry, *Safeguarding Patients: Lessons from the Past – Proposals for the Future*, paras 20.38–20.40 (www.the-shipman-inquiry.org.uk).

242 See the Fifth Report of the Shipman Inquiry, *Safeguarding Patients: Lessons from the Past – Proposals for the Future*, paras 20.46–20.55 (www.the-shipman-inquiry.org.uk).

243 See NHS Executive, Modernising Medical Regulation: Interim Strengthening of the GMC's Fitness to Practise Procedures, March 2000, 7.

244 See Rule 14 of the General Medical Council Procedure Rules Orders of Council 2000 and, for example, the comments of Burnton J in *The Queen on the Application of Steven James Walker v General Medical Council* (1993) QBD, unreported.

have been many cases where doctors charged with serious criminal offences have remained registered to practise until convicted. It is of concern that it took crimes of the magnitude committed by Harold Shipman before the GMC committed itself to seeking a change in this position.[245]

## A Step Backwards? GMC Reverts to Reliance on Local Procedures

Historically, the GMC has been criticized for being too willing to reject complaints on the basis that local complaints procedures had not been exhausted. Where a complainant had not made use of local procedures, the case would be closed unless there was cause to suspect that the doctor presented a danger to patients. In a typical year, up to 20 per cent of complaints were dealt with in this way.[246] Writing in 1988, Robinson argued that this 'hidden policy' meant that a significant number of complaints would be considered by the GMC only if they had been investigated and found proved by NHS complaints procedures. Even then, the Council relied upon the NHS body to deem the matter sufficiently serious that it should be referred back. In practice, this rarely happened.[247] The result of this was that serious allegations might not be properly considered by the GMC, or even those which did make it back might have done so only after a delay of two or three years – during which time the doctor remained free to practise. Of particular concern were those cases where the doctor already had a disciplinary history. For example, the Shipman Inquiry identified such a case where the doctor had a previous finding of SPM for perverting the course of justice, yet a subsequent complaint a few years later was simply referred back for local resolution, without any apparent follow up.[248] It is of note that this practice was occurring even though, for instance, the 1988 Professional Conduct Rules stated that where it appeared to the Registrar that the complaint raised the question 'whether the conduct of a practitioner constitutes serious professional misconduct' it should be submitted for screening. The Shipman Inquiry concluded that, by ignoring this mandatory wording and increasing the threshold to require a suspicion that the doctor was 'dangerous', the GMC was acting unlawfully.[249] The issue of

245 See comments in the Fifth Report of the Shipman Inquiry, *Safeguarding Patients: Lessons from the Past – Proposals for the Future*, para 18.42 (www.the-shipman-inquiry.org.uk).

246 For example, in 2000 and 2001, the figures were 20 and 18.7 per cent respectively. The Fifth Report of the Shipman Inquiry, *Safeguarding Patients: Lessons from the Past – Proposals for the Future*, para 18.83 (www.the-shipman-inquiry.org.uk).

247 Robinson, J., *A Patient Voice at the GMC: a Lay Member's View of the GMC*, Report 1, Health Rights, London. See also the Fifth Report of the Shipman Inquiry, *Safeguarding Patients: Lessons from the Past – Proposals for the Future*, paras 18.48–18.52 and 18.64 (www.the-shipman-inquiry.org.uk). Robinson also notes that, prior to her intervention, the standard letters written by the GMC to complainants had not informed them that they could renew their complaint with the GMC after the NHS process.

248 The Fifth Report of the Shipman Inquiry, *Safeguarding Patients: Lessons from the Past – Proposals for the Future*, para 18.66 (www.the-shipman-inquiry.org.uk).

249 The Fifth Report of the Shipman Inquiry, *Safeguarding Patients: Lessons from the Past – Proposals for the Future*, paras 18.28–18.29 and 18.53 (www.the-shipman-inquiry.

referring back to local resolution became even more pointed from 1996 when NHS complaints and discipline were separated. Local resolution therefore increased its focus on 'remediation rather than disciplinary action'. The Shipman Inquiry noted that 'the illogicality of that situation…does not appear to have been appreciated by the GMC'.[250]

In September 2005 the GMC announced[251] that from 17 October 2005 it would refer significant numbers of complaints directly to NHS Trusts or Primary Care Trusts, to be addressed under their local complaints procedures. The reasoning behind this was that, of the 5,000 or so complaints about doctors received by the GMC each year, many did not warrant action against the doctor's fitness to practise and registration. The formal and often protracted procedures of the GMC disciplinary system were said to have caused undue anxiety for both complainants and the doctor complained about.[252] Local procedures are seen as more appropriate to deal with these and, in addition, may be able to identify any systemic problems. A distinction is drawn between complaints which clearly require immediate GMC investigation – 'Stream 1' complaints – and complaints which could justify action by the GMC if they were part of a wider pattern of concern about a doctor, but would not justify GMC action on their own. These are referred to as 'Stream 2' complaints. Around one third of the annual complaints received by the Council are said to be Stream 2, another third Stream 1 and the remainder 'frivolous'.[253] The GMC indicated that it would continue to investigate all Stream 1 complaints. Furthermore, only those Stream 2 complaints involving a doctor's work within the NHS would be referred back to the employer. The GMC will retain Stream 2 cases involving a doctor's private practice or where the doctor is a peripatetic locum. The employer will be at liberty to refer the matter back to the GMC if further information reveals that the doctor's fitness to practise and continued registration needs to be drawn into question. The GMC have also said that it expects to be kept informed of the progress of the local procedures and recognizes that some 'local complaints systems can leave a lot to be desired'.[254] The process will involve the GMC requesting consent from the complainant to disclose the complaint to the doctor and to refer it on to the appropriate NHS Trust or PCT. The doctor will then be asked for details of his or her employer and the complaint

org.uk). This latter point had been raised over a decade earlier by Robinson. Robinson, J., *A Patient Voice at the GMC: a Lay Member's View of the GMC*, Report 1, Health Rights, London.

250 The Fifth Report of the Shipman Inquiry, *Safeguarding Patients: Lessons from the Past – Proposals for the Future*, para 18.77 (www.the-shipman-inquiry.org.uk).

251 General Medical Council – Fitness to Practise Procedures Referring Complaints to Local NHS Procedures, GMC website, 25 September 2005.

252 See comments of the GMC President, Graeme Catto, reported in Kmietowicz, Z., 'Trusts to Handle Minor Complaints against Doctors, Says GMC', *BMJ*, 2005, 331: 178, 23 July.

253 Kmietowicz, Z., 'Trusts to Handle Minor Complaints against Doctors, Says GMC', *BMJ*, 2005, 331: 178, 23 July.

254 See comments of the GMC President, Graeme Catto, reported in Kmietowicz, Z., 'Trusts to Handle Minor Complaints against Doctors, Says GMC', *BMJ*, 2005, 331: 178, 23 July.

then referred on. The employer will be asked to keep the Council updated regarding the progress of any investigation, although the GMC emphasizes that it will not retain overall responsibility for referred cases. In terms of information availability, a doctor's name will no longer be removed from the GMC's online database if the complaint is categorized as Stream 2. Previously, all complaints, whichever stream, resulted in the removal of the doctor's name from the online search database, to prompt any potential employers to contact the GMC.[255]

## The New GMC – Stakeholder Views

Following a number of its reforms, the GMC commissioned a qualitative survey to assess the views of key stakeholders. Overall, many respondents confirmed that the GMC has improved in many important ways in recent years. However, patient interest groups still perceived the GMC to be a 'doctors club', protective of the medical profession rather than protective of the public. Similarly, it was felt that there was little real patient or public input into the GMC. In contrast, a number of doctors considered the GMC to be far too patient-focused – willing to give excessive credence to some allegations, often at the expense of a doctor's reputation.

The image of a slow bureaucratic, organizationally incompetent GMC also continued to prevail. Slowness of the disciplinary processes impact significantly on the doctor's ability to practise and is also stressful for complainants faced with a 'laborious and gruelling process'. The GMC was also seen to be excessively dominated by inappropriate traditions, to retreat behind closed doors and to use obscure legalistic language to further undermine confidence.

Concern was also expressed about the significant majority of complaints to the GMC which were rejected, by a process that lacked transparency. Specifically, it was felt that, whilst *Good Medical Practice* provides for minimum standards on matters such as behaviour and politeness, the GMC lacks procedures for actually dealing with these issues. Such absence of redress for patients was considered to run against modern perceptions of regulation.

In short, the GMC's regulatory processes remain dominated by doctors. It has worked hard to be, and to be seen to be, properly independent and effective. Furthermore, it must address those issues which are of concern to the public interest, rather than becoming embroiled with the parochial interests of its various stakeholders.

---

255 See GMC Online Update, July 2005.

## Chapter 3

# Criminal Convictions and the General Medical Council

Before the GMC can act with regard to a doctor who has been convicted of a criminal offence, the fact of the conviction must come to its notice. This may occur in one of a number of ways. For example, reports may be made by the police or the Home Office, or the GMC may find out about it from its press cuttings agency. However, in practice the GMC has not always found out about a conviction in a timely manner, or sometimes at all. In a paper considered by the GMC Fitness to Practise Policy Committee in November 1998, it was acknowledged that the Council would not necessarily be aware of cases where doctors were facing serious criminal charges.

There are concerns about the limited effort the GMC itself puts into trying to find out about convictions, rather than simply relying upon other bodies. Not until 2004 did the GMC see fit to take steps to require doctors to report information themselves about criminal convictions or impending criminal proceedings.[1] Notwithstanding these limitations, the number of convictions reported annually to the GMC increased threefold between 1996 and 2001, from around 1,500 to 4,500. This placed significant pressure on the GMC and increased the delays in dealing with cases. The Shipman Inquiry was told that 'by 2000, it had been recognised that the GMC had no effective way of managing cases'.[2]

The approach of the GMC regulatory process to doctors who have been convicted of criminal offences gives rise to concern. In high profile cases, such as that involving Harold Shipman, a criminal conviction for an offence related to practice as a doctor did not result in sanctions or monitoring which might have prevented, or at least discouraged, subsequent criminal behaviour. One explanation for this put forward by the GMC was that this approach prevailed in the 1970s, but that a very different stance had been taken more recently. However, the evidence does not entirely support this assertion. For example, between 1997 and 1999 only between 13 and 29 per cent of criminal conviction cases were referred to the PCC. Even when the non-referrals which related to drink-driving cases were excluded from the statistics, the referral rate was still only between 28 and 58 per cent. In 2001, in only 50 per cent of those cases which did reach the PCC was the doctor's name erased from the

1 See the Fifth Report of the Shipman Inquiry, *Safeguarding Patients: Lessons from the Past – Proposals for the Future*, paras 18.7–18.8 and 20.46–20.47 (www.the-shipman-inquiry.org.uk).

2 See the Fifth Report of the Shipman Inquiry, *Safeguarding Patients: Lessons from the Past – Proposals for the Future*, para 18.43 (www.the-shipman-inquiry.org.uk).

medical register (down from 73 per cent in 1999).[3] A study by the Policy Studies Institute found that in a number of serious conviction cases, inappropriate disposal had occurred because the PPC had paid undue attention to the doctor's personal and professional circumstances, rather than the seriousness of the offence. An example given by the Shipman Inquiry is that of a hospital doctor convicted of stealing money. Instead of restricting itself to the task of deciding whether the offence was serious enough to warrant referral to the PCC, the PPC focused on mitigation – that the doctor was under stress, had personal problems or had submitted testimonials to his skills as a doctor. The PSI recommended that virtually all types of conviction should be considered by the PCC, without involvement of screeners or the PPC. This was not adopted. A more limited change was introduced, permitting convictions resulting in an immediate custodial sentence to progress directly to the PCC.[4] As is illustrated by the manslaughter cases discussed below, even very serious offences committed by doctors have often resulted in a suspended custodial sentence. The change to the rules was therefore of very limited consequence.

Only in 1991 had the GMC included in its definition of 'criminal offence' a finding of guilt which resulted in an absolute or conditional discharge, or probation.[5] The latter was of particular concern, given that in criminal law terms, a community penalty such as probation was only a step away from custody and could be imposed for relatively serious offences.

## Unlawful Killing by Doctors

The most serious criminal charge a doctor is likely to face is that of unlawfully killing a patient. Harold Shipman demonstrated that this could amount to murder, but manslaughter is more common. The current legal position was established in *R v Adomako*.[6] The defendant doctor, an anaesthetist, either failed to notice that his patient was in serious distress when this should have been obvious, or may even have been absent inappropriately from the operating theatre at the time. The test which the court established for manslaughter by gross negligence contains three components: the defendant was in breach of a duty of care towards the victim; the breach of duty caused the victim's death; the breach of duty should be characterized as gross negligence and therefore as a crime. With regard to the requisite seriousness of the

3 See the Fifth Report of the Shipman Inquiry, *Safeguarding Patients: Lessons from the Past – Proposals for the Future*, para 21.136 (www.the-shipman-inquiry.org.uk).

4 See the Fifth Report of the Shipman Inquiry, *Safeguarding Patients: Lessons from the Past – Proposals for the Future*, paras 20.76–20.80, 20.185 and 20.188 (www.the-shipman-inquiry.org.uk). Some of the non-referred cases were dealt with by the health procedures, but a high proportion, between 35 and 65 per cent, were dealt with by way of cautionary letter – that is, received no sanction or other effective disposal.

5 The most recent fitness to practise procedures treat police cautions in the same way as convictions, although discharges were still differentiated from other convictions. See the Fifth Report of the Shipman Inquiry, *Safeguarding Patients: Lessons from the Past – Proposals for the Future*, para 18.10 (www.the-shipman-inquiry.org.uk).

6 [1991] 5 Med LR 277, first instance, [1995] 1 AC 171 HL.

breach of duty, the question for the jury to ask themselves was whether 'the conduct of the defendant was so bad in all the circumstances as to amount…to a criminal act or omission'.[7] Emphasis was further placed on the point that this 'is supremely a jury question'. The appropriateness of criminal liability in these circumstances has been questioned on the basis, for example, that to warrant criminal punishment, conduct requires recklessness rather than mere negligence, however gross.[8] For example, if the defendant had left the operating theatre without ensuring appropriate cover, this may have amounted to recklessness. However, remaining in the operating theatre and doing his best, albeit not good enough in the circumstances, is more appropriately described as incompetence which, however gross, lacks the element of subjective wrongdoing.[9] The House of Lords acknowledged that the test contained an element of circularity – to constitute a criminal offence the defendant's conduct must be so bad as to be criminal. Ultimately, the test lacks any clear determination of how bad the conduct must be and so the jury is in effect left to determine a question of law.

The issue of circularity was more recently considered by the Court of Appeal in *R v Misra and another.*[10] It was submitted on behalf of one defendant that manslaughter by gross negligence is an offence which lacks certainty, requiring the trial judge to direct the jury that the defendant should be convicted if they are satisfied that his conduct was 'criminal'. It was argued that the circularity of this approach leads to uncertainty. Article 7 of the European Convention of Human Rights provides:

> 7(1) No-one shall be held guilty of any criminal offence on account of any act or omission which did not constitute a criminal offence under national or international law at the time when it was committed nor shall a heavier penalty be imposed than the one that was applicable at the time the criminal offence was committed.

The Court of Appeal identified this as meaning that an individual must be able to foresee the consequences of his or her actions, and in particular to be able to avoid incurring the sanction of the criminal law. This was a principle which was not novel to the ECHR; it had long roots in English law. However, the requirement is for 'sufficient rather than absolute certainty'. Indeed, excessive certainty may entail undue rigidity, which would prevent the law from keeping pace with changing circumstances.[11] The fact that, even when applying the same laws to the same facts, different courts or tribunals may reach different conclusions, did not inevitably make these laws insufficiently certain.[12] It was also submitted that, with the exception of causing death by dangerous driving, no serious criminal offence could be committed without mens rea. Conviction of

---

7 Lord Mackay, *R v Adomako* [1995] 1 AC 171.

8 Mason, J.K., McCall Smith, R.A. and Laurie, G.T., *Law and Medical Ethics*, 2002, Butterworths, London, 306.

9 Mason, J.K., McCall Smith, R.A. and Laurie, G.T., *Law and Medical Ethics*, 2002, Butterworths, London, 306–7; and McCall Smith, A., 'Criminal Negligence and the Incompetent Doctor', 1 *Medical Law Review* 336, 1993.

10 [2004] EWCA CRIM 2375, [2004] All ER (D) 107 (Oct).

11 *Sunday Times v United Kingdom* [1979] 2 EHRR 245.

12 *Wingrove v United Kingdom* [1996] 24 EHRR 1.

serious crime should not rely simply on proving that the defendant caused a harmful outcome by act or omission, but also that his or her state of mind was culpable. The Court of Appeal responded by noting that involuntary manslaughter encapsulates homicides in which the perpetrator lacked the specific intention to cause death or serious bodily harm. Gross negligence manslaughter requires gross negligence in circumstances where the risk is to the life of an individual to whom the defendant owes a duty of care. It therefore protects his or her right to life.

Notwithstanding these concerns, in the context of medical regulation, such jury decisions are one of the few areas where a completely lay body is given the opportunity to determine the seriousness with which they view a doctor's conduct. Juries will reach their decision having heard all of the evidence and knowing the seriousness of a guilty verdict. Given this grass roots societal involvement in judging a doctor's behaviour, the public might reasonably expect that convicted doctors will be removed from practice in all but the most exceptional circumstances. If the profession is to sustain the trust of society, then it has to treat seriously society's concerns as demonstrated by a criminal conviction for a serious offence. However, in practice the GMC does not appear to have consistently taken this view on board. This can be illustrated by recent cases. For example, in *R v Misra and another*[13] the two defendants, Dr D and Dr E, were senior house officers convicted of manslaughter of a patient. Each was sentenced to 18 months' imprisonment, suspended for two years. The essence of the gross negligence was the failure by both doctors to diagnose and treat a staphylococcus aureus infection in a post-operative patient. The prosecution case was not related to the failure to diagnose the precise condition, which was rare. Instead, the prosecution relied on the failure to appreciate that the patient was seriously ill, showing severe and persistent signs of infection. Errors included the misreading by Dr E of the patient's fluid chart and failure at one point to read the observation chart. The defendants also failed to obtain the results of blood tests and ignored expressions of concern by nursing staff. Blood cultures were not taken. Expert evidence for the prosecution concluded that 'the observations of the patient showed "severe sepsis", to be treated with broad spectrum antibiotics until a clear alternative diagnosis was available'.[14] Professor Forrest, forensic toxicologist at Sheffield University, concluded that the failure by the defendants to react to the severity of the deceased's illness fell below the standard he would expect from a final-year medical student.[15] Dr Wilcox, consultant and head of medico-microbiology at Leeds Training Hospitals, concluded that if he were examining a third- or fourth-year medical student, and postulated the observations of the deceased's condition, and the student failed to diagnose infection, he might have failed the student on that basis alone. The jury were directed that they must be sure of something much more serious than the carelessness required to establish civil negligence. Even very serious mistakes and very serious errors of judgement are nowhere near enough for a crime as serious as manslaughter to be committed. The conduct has to be gross, falling

13 [2004] EWCA CRIM 2375, [2004] All ER (D) 107 (Oct).

14 Dr Lowes, microbiologist in the public health laboratory used by Southampton General Hospital. Para 17.

15 Para 18.

so far below the standard to be expected of a reasonably competent and careful senior house officer that it was something which the jury considered to be 'truly exceptionally bad, and which showed such an indifference to an obviously serious risk to the life of [the patient] and such a departure from the standard to be expected as to amount…to a criminal act or omission, and so to be the very serious crime of manslaughter'.[16] Gross negligence itself provides the necessary mental element, and therefore provides the necessary element of culpability. The defendants were found guilty. On appeal, the Court of Appeal concluded that the law is clear. If a hypothetical person is able to establish that if she or he owed a duty of care to the deceased, which had been negligently broken, and that death resulted, she or he would be guilty of manslaughter if the jury was satisfied that the negligence was gross. Doctors should therefore be aware that grossly negligent treatment which exposes a patient to the risk of death, and causes death, constitutes manslaughter.

When the GMC considered the behaviour of doctors D and E, it concluded that neither warranted the erasure of their names from the medical register.

## The GMC's Attitude towards Criminal Convictions

The GMC and commentators from within the profession appear to take the view that the determinations and penalties of the criminal courts are secondary to the profession's own character judgement of its members. The GMC's starting point appears to be the assumption that, having been admitted to the profession, a doctor's character should place him or her in a different position to other people. There is evidence that the medical profession is out of touch with public perception, or in some instances may see itself as somehow detached from the legal norms applied to the rest of society. An example of this is provided by an editorial in the *British Medical Journal*, which took issue with a newspaper article critical that a doctor found guilty of manslaughter had been allowed to return to practice. The newspaper reported the father of the deceased patient, responding to this news, as saying: 'I don't think there is any normal human being in this country who would say this is right.' And: '[the doctors] were only spared jail by the judge because their barristers told the court their careers were over and that was punishment enough. Now they are both working as doctors again. How can that be justified? It's wrong. It's an insult to my son's memory that they can be let anywhere near patients again. How can doctors found guilty of manslaughter be allowed to keep working?'[17] The editorial found the father's distress understandable, but not the insinuation that the GMC and employing authorities are not 'normal human beings'.[18] Notwithstanding the sensationalist headline of the newspaper report in question, it is telling that even after the cumulative effect of the Bristol, Shipman, Ledward and other medical scandals, the editor of one of the leading journals for the medical profession fails to acknowledge the public disquiet when a doctor convicted of an offence as serious

16 Para 25.

17 Armstrong, S., 'Dad Fights for Death Case Doc to be Fired', *Newcastle Evening Chronicle*, 6 January 2004, 2.

18 Smith, R., 'Doctors Mangled by "Justice"', *BMJ*, 2004, Volume 328, 17 January.

as manslaughter is allowed to return to work in medicine. This is no reflection upon the particular doctor in question and the possibility of his professional rehabilitation. Rather, it is a reflection on the medical establishment which apparently still cannot even contemplate taking a subordinate stance to the public. A jury decision appears to command little respect from within the profession.

The summing up to the jury in *Misra* had emphasized that they should not take their decision lightly:

> Mistakes, even very serious mistakes, and errors of judgment, even very serious errors of judgment, and the like, are nowhere near enough for a crime as serious as manslaughter to be committed…
>
> Over the years, the courts have used a number of expressions to describe this vital element of the crime, but the key is that it must be gross in the perhaps slightly old-fashioned sense now of the use of that word. So in this case, when you are considering the conduct of each doctor, I think you will find it most helpful to concentrate on whether or not the prosecution has made you sure that the conduct of whichever one you are considering in all the circumstances you have heard about and as you find them to be, fell so far below the standard to be expected of a reasonably competent and careful senior house officer that it was something, in your assessment, truly exceptionally bad, and which showed such an indifference to an obviously serious risk to the life of Sean Phillips and such a departure from the standard to be expected as to amount, in your judgment, to a criminal act or omission, and so to be the very serious crime of manslaughter.

Why should the medical profession claim the right to undermine this very public input into the regulation of doctors? It is also of note that *Misra* is not an isolated example. Other cases include *R v Becker*[19] in which a GP was convicted of manslaughter after injecting a patient with three times the maximum safe dose of diamorphine. In *R v Sinha*[20] the doctor was convicted of doing acts tending and intended to pervert the course of public justice, falsifying patient records following the death of a patient, and sentenced to six months' imprisonment. In both cases, a search of the medical register showed that the doctors apparently remained free to practise.[21]

Similar levels of relative leniency can also be seen in some cases involving dishonesty. For instance, in *Singh v GMC*[22] the doctor, a sole practising GP, was convicted of numerous counts of dishonesty and sentenced to two years' imprisonment. A number of the offences related directly to medical practice. Despite noting that the offences had occurred over a number of years and concluding that there was no room in the profession for dishonest doctors, the PCC considered a twelve-month suspension to be sufficient. In *Trivedi v GMC*[23] the defendant was convicted of ten charges of false accounting. When the matter reached the PCC, the Committee considered that a three-month suspension was sufficient, even though it had commented that: 'Doctors who behave dishonestly

19 (2000) Lexis transcript.

20 [1995] Crim LR 68.

21 Medical register searched using GMC website in July 2002.

22 (1998) Lawtel transcript.

23 (1996) Lexis transcript.

undermine the trust which is central to the practice of medicine...The convictions proved against you...demonstrate systematic dishonesty in the course of your medical practice...'

There are also concerns that the GMC has been over reliant on the sentence imposed by the criminal court as a measure of seriousness, especially when the court has been relatively lenient. The problem with this is that courts are often persuaded towards leniency because of strong mitigation regarding the impact the conviction will have on the doctor's career. As Dame Janet Smith put it:

> When sitting as a judge...I have heard pleas in mitigation made on behalf of doctors convicted of criminal offences, in which the court has been urged to treat the doctor leniently because his/her career – or even life – is said to be in ruins as a result of the action that will inevitably be taken by the GMC as a result of his/her conviction. The implication is that the doctor will lose his/her livelihood and will face professional disgrace. Faced with that kind of plea in mitigation, it is not surprising if a court feels constrained to impose a more lenient sentence than might otherwise be thought appropriate.[24]

This results in a circularity whereby neither the court nor the GMC appropriately sanction the doctor. The Council's focus is fitness to practise; this is not the focus of the court. Ultimately, therefore, the court's penalty should be virtually irrelevant to the GMC's decision.[25]

These cases reflect the very small number of instances where the actions or omissions of a doctor are considered so serious that they warrant the moral blame associated with a serious criminal conviction, and usually a custodial sentence (whether or not suspended). That doctors in such circumstances are allowed to remain in practice or return to practice after a relatively short period of suspension does give rise to concerns that the GMC still fails to recognize the importance of its role in ensuring that the public are protected and trust is maintained in the profession. However great the sympathy those involved in the GMC disciplinary process may have for individual doctors and however much concern those members might generally have about the appropriateness of the application of the criminal law to certain behaviour, it remains the case that the doctor has been found guilty of the unlawful killing of a patient and found deserving of a custodial sentence. For the GMC not to recognize the likely public outrage at allowing a doctor convicted of a very serious offence to remain in practice suggests that the lessons of Alder Hey, Shipman and similar cases have not been learned. The GMC should return to first principles and remember that professional status is a privilege and not a right.

A further matter of concern arising from serious conduct cases of this type is the lack of publicly available, or at least readily available, information from the GMC about its dealings with doctors. One newspaper reported that the GMC was less than

---

24 See the Fifth Report of the Shipman Inquiry, *Safeguarding Patients: Lessons from the Past – Proposals for the Future*, para 20.184 (www.the-shipman-inquiry.org.uk).

25 See the Fifth Report of the Shipman Inquiry, *Safeguarding Patients: Lessons from the Past – Proposals for the Future*, paras 20.184 and 23.34 (www.the-shipman-inquiry.org.uk).

forthcoming when asked about the disciplinary position of a doctor who is on public record as having been convicted of manslaughter.[26]

That the GMC has failed to adequately address key issues relating to doctors convicted of criminal offences further supports the thesis that the Council has failed in its self-regulatory responsibilities. Criminal convictions provide the GMC with ready-made cases, which have already been the subject of public scrutiny by either a jury or a bench of magistrates.[27] Only a minority of doctors in those cases at the most serious end of the scale, notably charges of manslaughter, are convicted.[28] This reinforces the view that juries take their responsibilities very seriously and, as should be the case, convict only when the evidence is overwhelming. Notwithstanding this, the GMC appears to have given very little weight to some of these decisions, or has even failed to detect some convictions at all.

26 McLeod, N., 'Sickening. This Bungling Doctor was Convicted of Killing a Patient. 8 Months Later He's Back at Work', *News of the World*, 4 January 2004, Lexis-Nexis transcript.

27 The only exceptions are those cases which happen to have been heard in the magistrates' court by a District Judge.

28 See, for example, 'Doctors Accused', *The Times*, 1 June 2006, 4.

# Chapter 4

# Doctors' Attitudes to Self-Regulation

## Medical Socialization and Public Protection

The professional socialization of medical students has the potential to undermine attempts to ensure that doctor-led regulation acts in the public interest. Historically, this has manifested itself in numerous ways. For instance, students have reported how anatomy led them to see people differently. The human body takes on new meaning and a new manner of interacting with the body becomes the norm. 'Students…describe increasingly experiencing the body as "machinelike"'.[1] The invasion of privacy, both physical and mental, which is typical of most doctor–patient encounters, influences fundamentally the way in which the future doctor comes to view the patient. As one doctor has described it:

> The first patient I met was a dead man whom I chopped up into increasingly smaller pieces. I had no preparation for what lay behind the dissection room door – the God-awful smell, the sound of the saw slicing off the top of the skull or the sight of genitals swollen in the preservation process. When Ian Kennedy spoke of the tribalism and emotional indifference of doctors in his interim report on organ retention, I tried to take myself back to the dissection room. We didn't care that much about dead peoples' parts, because we never met anyone else who did. We were learning to be callous. This attitude remains prevalent. The worse thing anyone can accuse you of as a young doctor is becoming 'emotionally involved'. Small wonder we can view suffering with such brutal detachment.[2]

May argues that practitioners are loath to regulate each other, loyalty to colleagues tending to take precedence over obligations to the wider public.[3] This is illustrated by the finding that only a small minority of complaints or reports to the GMC come from other doctors. Students have described the experience of being swallowed up by medicine, losing their personal lives to their professional identity and the

---

1 Good, B.J. and Good, M.D., '"Learning Medicine" – The Construction of Medical Knowledge at Harvard Medical School', in Lindenbaum, S. and Lock, M., *Knowledge, Power and Practice – The Anthropology of Medicine and Everyday Life*, 1993, University of California Press, Berkley, 96.

2 Hammond, P., 'Bristol Inquiry: Medical Training Means Learning How to be Callous; a Physician's View', *Independent on Sunday*, 22 July 2001, 6.

3 May, W.F., Professional Virtue and Self-Regulation. Cited by Parker, J., 'Moral Philosophy – Another Disabling Profession?', Chapter 3, in Allsop, J. and Mulcaly, L., *Maintaining Professional Identity: Doctors' Responses to Complaints*, 1998, Blackwell, Oxford.

'medical machine'.[4] These observations have important implications with regard to both the behaviour of doctors towards their patients, and towards the willingness of doctors to 'betray' their colleagues, especially to those outside of the 'medical machine'. Within the network of friends which develops during the socialization process, loyalty to colleagues tends to take precedence over the obligations to the wider public. Professional colleagues come to rely upon one another for favours, information and other services whilst, in contrast, patient encounters are relatively transient. 'In the language of the sociologist: Every *Gesellschaft* (organization) tends to become a *Gemeinschaft* (community).'[5] Overall, an inherent aspect of this professional socialization tends to have the practical effect that doctors are reluctant to regulate each other. As observed following the Bristol case: 'Traditionally, the medical profession has been too eager to close ranks against criticism, and to go into denial about colleagues' professional failures. "Never mind the patients; it's our colleagues who count," has, in effect, been the motto.'[6]

## Professional Attitudes

Historically, members of the medical profession have tended to react defensively to criticism and complaints, perceiving these as an attack on professional identity.[7] Complaints undermine the assumption that technical expertise and professional status should result in unquestioning acceptance by the patient and others. A complaint or allegation of incompetence by a lay person, someone deemed incapable of judging medical work, constitutes in the doctors' minds a breach of the basic trust to which they consider themselves entitled. The complaint is therefore often perceived to constitute a personal attack, challenging the doctor's authority and going to the heart of his or her sense of identity.[8] Indeed, there has been a tendency for the GMC and the medical press to categorize most complainants as obsessive and their complaints as unjustified.[9]

Further evidence of the lack of awareness within the profession of the power imbalance in favour of doctors and against patients is provided by accounts of other

---

4 Good, B.J. and Good, M.D., '"Learning Medicine" – The Construction of Medical Knowledge at Harvard Medical School', in Lindenbaum, S. and Lock, M., *Knowledge, Power and Practice – The Anthropology of Medicine and Everyday Life*, 1993, University of California Press, Berkley, 96–100.

5 May, W.F., 'Professional Virtue and Self-regulation', in Callahan, J.C. (ed.), *Ethical Issues in Professional Life*, 1988, Oxford University Press, Oxford, 410.

6 'The Bristol Report Must Mark the End of Doctors' Lack of Accountability – Incompetence and Arrogance Make a Lethal Combination', *The Independent*, 19 July 2001, 3.

7 See Allsop, J., 'Two Sides to Every Story: Complainants' and Doctors' Perspectives in Disputes about Medical Care in a General Practice Setting', *Law & Policy*, April 1994, Vol. 16, No. 2, 149–83, 160. See also Freidson, E., 'A Theory of Professions: State of the Art', in Dingwall, R. and Lewis, P. (eds), *The Sociology of the Professions: Lawyers, Doctors and Others*, 1983, London, Macmillan.

8 Allsop, J. and Mulcahy, L., 'Maintaining Professional Identity: Doctors' Responses to Complaints', *Sociology of Health & Illness*, 1998, Vol. 20, No. 6, 802–24.

9 The Fifth Report of the Shipman Inquiry, *Safeguarding Patients: Lessons from the Past – Proposals for the Future*, para 7.71 (www.the-shipman-inquiry.org.uk).

aspects of doctors' responses to complaints. Mulcahy reports doctors as expressing dissatisfaction at a lack of redress against complainants when a complaint proves to be unjustified.[10] In one respect, it is understandable that the subject of a complaint will feel aggrieved. However, at a deeper level this indicates a lack of self-awareness within the profession of the responsibilities which accompany self-regulation. A healthy and robust regulatory process will inevitably result in a proportion of acquittals.

Attitudes of this type also found their way into the GMC. One of the arguments presented to justify the GMC's historical reluctance to investigate complaints is that the Council is a neutral arbiter. If it were seen to assist complainants, then doctors would lose confidence in the fairness of the process. Whilst investigation by the GMC need not be partisan, and many complainants will experience a severe imbalance of power when faced with a doctor supported by a medical defence organization, there have been vested interests within the GMC to retain this position. In particular, with a predominance of elected medical members on the Council, prospective candidates would do little to encourage their election if they rejected this approach.[11]

Distribution of responsibilities within the GMC has also been the subject of criticism. Stacey recalls that members who were elected to committees always seemed to include those whom the 'establishment' thought appropriate. 'Appropriate' included those with 'a particular point of view'. She also reports that the business of meetings was controlled to a high degree, with some members commenting that everything, even the decision, seemed to be rearranged.[12]

## The Profession's Attitude to Self-Regulation

It has already been noted that professional self-regulation is a privilege. In return for high status, power and significant autonomy, the profession promises that it will police its members with a level of expertise and a degree of rigour which would be beyond the capacity of an external regulator. However, to have any chance of being effective, all (or at least a very substantial proportion) of the individual members of the profession must have a clear understanding and commitment to their obligations within the self-regulatory framework. For individual members of the medical profession, this requires an ongoing focus on their duty not only to their own patients but to members of the wider community. This requires ongoing vigilance of professional colleagues and a willingness to institute formal action against colleagues who they suspect of inappropriate behaviour.

Evidence from the Shipman Inquiry suggests that the profession has been failing in this regard. For instance, speaking in January 2004, Professor Richard Baker said:

> Since beginning to investigate Shipman in 2000, I have been trying to understand how it was that he could kill so many patients without detection. There were, of course, some

---

10 Mulcahy, L., *Disputing Doctors*, 2003, Open University Press, Maidenhead, 107—8.

11 See the Fifth Report of the Shipman Inquiry, *Safeguarding Patients: Lessons from the Past – Proposals for the Future*, para 18.145 (www.the-shipman-inquiry.org.uk).

12 Stacey, M., *Regulating British Medicine: the General Medical Council*, 1992, Wiley, Chichester, 97.

> system failures, but it has been impossible to avoid the question as to why the system weaknesses were tolerated to the extent that Shipman was able to murder not merely one or two patients, but over 200. The conclusion I have come to is that all doctors, and not general practitioners alone, share responsibility for creating the circumstances that enabled Shipman to be so successful a killer.

Drawing from this, Dame Janet Smith reached the conclusion that the culture within the profession was one of mutual self-protection, and paternalism towards patients and other non-doctors.[13]

Irvine identifies medical culture[14] as more important than anything else in dictating the profession's behaviour and response to outside pressures. Relations with patients, colleagues and the regulatory process are all dictated by this culture. Some of the problems in recent years have arisen because professional culture has failed to keep pace with wider social changes.[15] Lacking from professional culture for some doctors in recent years has been a true sense of professional values. They appear to have been happy to shelter under the umbrella of professional privilege, but spend too little time reflecting on the responsibilities which should accompany such privilege. A simple illustration can be drawn from the Shipman case. During the period of Shipman's crimes, a number of murdered patients were cremated – thus destroying evidence. The Shipman Inquiry revealed that fellow GPs and other 'safeguard' doctors in the cremation process had little awareness that they were supposed to be policing their colleagues. The so-called 'ash cash' for counter-signing cremation forms had lost any real connection with professional values. Furthermore, when the *British Medical Journal* reported that the GMC was to bring disciplinary proceedings against seven doctors who had been involved in signing cremation certificates of patients whom Harold Shipman had killed, a number of the published responses from members of the profession were highly critical that this action was being taken.[16] The overall impression is that within at least some parts of the profession, individual doctors consider that they should be under no obligation to police their colleagues.

## Professional Power

In 1969 the GMC received statutory authority to charge doctors an annual fee to remain on the register. Even though the charge was not particularly high and was subject to tax relief, the profession was highly vocal in its opposition. Several thousand doctors refused to pay the fee and were faced with the prospect of having their names erased from the medical register. Had this happened, the NHS would

13 The Fifth Report of the Shipman Inquiry, *Safeguarding Patients: Lessons from the Past – Proposals for the Future*, para 1.10 (www.the-shipman-inquiry.org.uk).

14 Irvine defines professional culture as expressing and reflecting professional values and standards as well as social expectations which exist at any particular time.

15 Irvine, D., *The Doctors' Tale*, 2003, Radcliffe Medical Press, Oxford, 198–9.

16 Dyer, C., 'Seven Doctors to Face GMC over Shipman Inquiry Findings', *BMJ*, 2004, 329: 591, 11 September (online edition).

have been plunged into crisis. The dispute was only resolved when the government intervened.[17] Junior hospital doctors and GPs in particular are reported to have resented the fact that they were funding a body where elected members were in a minority. Both junior doctors and GPs were outside of the senior ranks in universities and the Royal Colleges – from where appointed members were drawn. This was considered by the Merrison Committee and addressed by the subsequent 1978 Medical Act and an order of the Privy Council.[18] Whilst, in principle, there can be few objections to a 'self'-regulatory body being elected, the power to elect brings with it significant responsibility. This series of events illustrates the extraordinary power the medical profession can wield, but without illustrating a corresponding degree of responsibility. The majority-elected GMC, which won after threats by some within the profession to plunge the NHS into chaos, is the GMC which has presided over the regulatory crisis described in this book. In essence, the profession has failed over a lengthy period to use its democratic powers to ensure that the GMC favours public safety, commands public confidence and places the public interest ahead of the interests of doctors. One illustrative example occurred in 2000. The profession elected to the GMC a doctor whose name had previously been erased from the medical register. Her name had been erased in 1987[19] for, inter alia, failing to provide adequate treatment to patients, being convicted for driving whilst four times over the alcohol limit and driving whilst disqualified.[20]

## Professional Arrogance and Rationalizing Uncertainty

A significant majority of doctors, 88 per cent of hospital consultants and 75 per cent of GPs, are reported as considering that complaints made against them were unjustified.[21] Sociological studies suggest that clinical identity may be the dominant criteria for self-identification amongst doctors. Criticism of a doctor's work, therefore, becomes a criticism of the doctor him or herself, calling into question the doctor's technical and moral authority over medical knowledge.[22] To address this, blame avoidance strategies have become common within the medical profession. Key amongst these are references to the uncertainty inherent in much medical practice.

---

17 See Stacey, M., *Regulating British Medicine: the General Medical Council*, 1992, Wiley, Chichester, 34.

18 Stacey, M., *Regulating British Medicine: the General Medical Council*, 1992, Wiley, Chichester, 30 and 71.

19 She was restored to the medical register in 1989.

20 Dyer, C., 'GMC Member Forced to Stand Down from Disciplinary Panel', *BMJ*, 2000, 320: 822, 25 March.

21 Allsop, J. and Mulcahy, L., 'Maintaining Professional Identity: Doctors' Responses to Complaints', *Sociology of Health & Illness*, 1998, Vol. 20, No. 6, 802–24, 809. This did not simply reflect doctors denying responsibility for technical legal reasons, as 98 per cent of GPs denied the allegations against them.

22 See Allsop, J. and Mulcahy, L., 'Maintaining Professional Identity: Doctors' Responses to Complaints', *Sociology of Health & Illness*, 1998, Vol. 20, No. 6, 802–24, 809; Giddens, A., *Modernity and Self Identity: Self and Society in the Late Modern Age*, 1991, Polity Press, Cambridge.

For instance, the technique of 'denial' sees alleged mistakes being redefined within the sphere of unavoidable risks inherent within the particular procedure or due to some other external factor.[23] In her study of complaints against GPs, Allsop found that 80 per cent of doctors used this approach, or a variation of it, in their defence. In some of these cases the doctor attempted to shift blame to patients themselves, for failing to give adequate information on which to base an accurate diagnosis. In a mere 8 per cent of cases did the doctors actually admit error.[24] It has also been found that doctors subject to criticism or complaints are most likely to turn to medical colleagues within the same organization or unit for support, often strengthening group identity and reiterating understanding of who was inside and who was outside the group. This was the case, even where colleagues were higher up in the medical and managerial hierarchy.[25] The risks with this are illustrated by the Bristol Royal Infirmary case, where the close, even cosy, relationships between senior doctors prevented any effective managerial control.

It has also been argued that a certain level of arrogance on the part of doctors is necessary:

> It would be deadly for us, the individual actors, to give up our belief in human perfectibility. The statistics may say that someday I will sever someone's main bile duct, but each time I go into a gallbladder operation I believe that with enough will and effort I can beat the odds. This isn't just professional vanity. It's a necessary part of good medicine, even in a superbly 'optimized' system.
>
> This may explain why many doctors take exception to talk of 'systems problems', 'continuous quality improvement', and 'process re-engineering.' It is the dry language of structures, not people. I'm no exception: something in me, too, demands an acknowledgment of my autonomy, which is also to say my ultimate culpability.[26]

Findings of this type raise important issues regarding the medical majority in the GMC regulatory process and the risks to public safety associated with the, conscious or unconscious, 'there but for the grace of god go I' attitude.

Some doctors argue that they are significantly over-regulated. As Tallis describes it:

> ...our consultant is accountable in at least five different kinds of ways: to the court of her conscience...; to her peers...; to the evidence-base and adherence to guidelines and protocols; to professional regulatory bodies...; and to the law. Every aspect of her work... is recorded, monitored and to a greater or lesser degree regulated.[27]

---

23 See Mizrahi, T., 'Managing Medical Mistakes: Ideology, Insularity and Accountability Among Internists-in-Training', *Social Science and Medicine*, 1984, 19, 135–46; and Allsop, J., 'Two Sides to Every Story: Complainants' and Doctors' Perspectives in Disputes about Medical Care in a General Practice Setting', *Law & Policy*, April 1994, Vol. 16, No. 2, 149–83, at 167.

24 See Allsop, J., 'Two Sides to Every Story: Complainants' and Doctors' Perspectives in Disputes about Medical Care in a General Practice Setting', *Law & Policy*, April 1994, Vol. 16, No. 2, 149–83, at 169–75.

25 Mulcahy, L., *Disputing Doctors*, 2003, Open University Press, Maidenhead, 117.

26 Gawande, A., *Complications*, 2003, Profile Books, London, 73.

27 Tallis, R., *Hippocratic Oaths*, 2004, Atlantic, London, 87.

Regulation has increased, it is suggested, because medical power has come to be seen as malign. Without closer and closer regulation, practitioners will misbehave. 'Left to themselves [doctors] will be negligent, blundering, idle, uncaring, ignorant, fraudulent scoundrels who will damage patients by acts of commission or omission.'[28]

In common with Tallis, Dalrymple reacts with outrage to what he sees as excessive regulatory interference. Recent developments, he concludes, reflect 'a sinister manifestation of a society that tolerates no error, and therefore no thought; that is in constant need of scapegoats; and that offers vanishingly little resistance to the centralisation of authority'.[29]

Dalrymple and Tallis both take a stance from within the profession which ignores the power accumulated by the medical profession; power which, in some instances, has been seriously abused.

## Changing Professional Culture – Myth or Reality?

Irvine describes the rise of a new professionalism within medicine. Patients, he argues, have become autonomous participants in a partnership with their doctors. In addition, team-based practice and associated collective responsibility have largely replaced individualism. A strong commitment to quality improvement and transparency of practice is essential.[30] From outside, it is difficult to find sustained evidence that this so-called new professionalism is really taking hold in the medical profession. Or, if it is taking hold, that progress is sufficiently swift. Junior doctors may be increasingly trained in the new ways, but they are unlikely to be in a position to force change upon their senior colleagues and the public cannot wait for the old guard to all retire. Anecdotal evidence from lay commentators continues to find some in the profession significantly wanting in terms of behaviour. For example, John Diamond, writing shortly before his death and no stranger to the medical world in his last few years, had the following to say:

> Parts of that [the medical] establishment still have the mindset of Sir Lancelot Spratt in Richard Gordon's *Doctor in the House* novels of half a century ago: patients are little more than an encumbrance upon the doctors who treat them; knowledge is something better kept from the patients…; consultation is strictly a one way process.[31]

Similarly, individual accounts of doctors performing intimate examinations without adequate explanation, or briskly telling a tearful patient – whilst in a hospital corridor – about the outcome of a painful outpatient investigatory procedure, suggest a less than reformed profession.

---

28 Tallis, R., *Hippocratic Oaths*, 2004, Atlantic, London, 89.

29 Dalrymple, T., 'Useful Scapegoat Struck Off', *The Times*, 21 July 2005, 20.

30 Irvine, D., *The Doctors' Tale*, 2003, Radcliffe Medical Press, Oxford, 206.

31 Diamond, J., *Snake Oil*, 2001, Vintage, London, 46.

## Doctor as Both Consumer and Supposed Consumer Champion

Some within the medical profession have argued that consumerism puts pressure on them to act against their better judgement. For instance, Tallis refers to findings in the United States that doctors were undertaking cardiopulmonary resuscitation in circumstances when it was obviously futile and undignified for the dying patient. This approach resulted from fear of criticism and even litigation, if relatives did not see that doctors had taken the steps they, the relatives, expected.[32]

Consumerism may also be viewed in a different way. Entrants to the medical profession may be less interested in traditional ideas of vocation and themselves be consumers of career opportunities: 'As we see the rise in consumerism, one of the problems is the fall in vocationalism. People no longer go into the profession out of a sense of public service duty and vocation; they go in because it is another career option…'[33]

In this new consumerist environment, patients may demand the consumer power they have become used to when they shop at a supermarket, but combined with traditional characteristics from their doctor of compassion and empathy. Consumerist doctors are likely to lack these traditional characteristics, but may derive personal benefits if they successfully feign them. At its core: 'The…relationship between patient and doctor will be a meeting of the naked consumerism of the patient and the consumerism of the doctor concealed under a thick carapace woven out of the verbal (and, it mustn't be forgotten, non-verbal) signals of "caring for the person beneath the consumer".'[34]

## The Voice of the Medical Establishment

Following the events at the Bristol Royal Infirmary, the President of the Royal College of Surgeons, when asked why the public should trust surgeons, simply replied that surgeons relied on trust and were an 'ancient profession' with an 'extremely good' record. When questioned about moves in some US states to publish the records of individual surgeons, with a corresponding drop in cardiac mortality of 40 per cent in one state, the response was that '…there is still a little way to go [but]…can't change overnight'.[35] This response, to an audience of millions on national television, is, to say the least, underwhelming. It demonstrates little recognition of the massive undermining of trust caused by Bristol. Talking of an 'extremely good' record and 'a little way to go' when other cases were also making headlines smacks of professional arrogance at the potential scale of the problem. This is reflected in feedback from

32 Marco, C.A. and Bessman, E.S. et al, 'Ethical Issues of Cardiopulmonary Resuscitation: Current Practice among Emergency Physicians', Academic Emergency Medicine, 1997, 4: 898–904, cited by Tallis, R., *Hippocratic Oaths*, 2004, Atlantic, London, 244.

33 Bull, A., *Risk and Trust in the NHS*, Foxwood, H. (ed.), 2002, The Smith Institute, London, cited by Tallis, R., *Hippocratic Oaths*, 2004, Atlantic, London, 247.

34 Tallis, R., *Hippocratic Oaths*, 2004, Atlantic, London, 247.

35 BBC, *Panorama*, broadcast 24 June 2001.

patient organizations: 'The one thing that comes through all the time from patients who are complaining is the arrogance of doctors.'[36]

The reactions from the established medical press to apparent attempts by the GMC to toughen up its regulatory stance further illustrate a deep lack of understanding by the profession to the public concerns raised by recent medical scandals. For example, Richard Horton, in an editorial in the *Lancet*, sees the Council as simply adopting a draconian stance in an attempt to shore up and retain its regulatory status in the light of damning criticisms in recent years. What the GMC forgets, he argues, is that whilst the public must have confidence that the statutory medical regulator will act in the public interest, the profession must also have confidence that the regulator is acting fairly and proportionately towards them. It is impossible, he says, to put into words the low esteem with which the GMC is currently held by many among the rank and file of medicine in the UK today.[37]

In similar vein, Fiona Godlee, in an editorial in the *British Medical Journal*, recounts the views of doctors as describing the GMC engaging in the 'prolonged and painful pursuit of cases that are subsequently found to have no grounds' and a more general loss of faith in the ability of the GMC to fairly regulate the profession.

> Should we now be talking about the problem of over investigation of doctors?... The sheer number of doctors who have been referred to the GMC is surprising. I had thought this was a rare event… Making examples of people who come before its fitness to practise panels is more likely to continue the downward spiral of loss of public confidence in the profession and loss of professional and government confidence in the GMC.[38]

Appropriate attitudes by doctors to self-regulation are essential if the process is to be effective and robust. This requires each member of the profession to be willing to fully support the principles and necessary practice of such regulation – both financially in terms of the resources needed by the regulatory body, and more directly when they are needed to personally step forwards when a colleague raises cause for concern. As discussed in this and subsequent chapters, many members of the medical profession have failed to demonstrate these attitudes. Indeed, from within the profession the approach is often one of accepting the privileges of professional status whilst conveniently neglecting the associated obligations.

---

36 Joyce Robins speaking on behalf of the pressure group, 'Patient Concern', reported in Boseley, S., 'Doctors' Caring Image Struggles to Survive', *The Guardian*, 13 May 2000.

37 Horton, R., *The Lancet*, 2005, Vol. 366, 23 July.

38 Godlee, F., 'The GMC: Out of its Depth?', *BMJ*, 2005, 331, 30 July.

## Chapter 5

# Trust and the Medical Profession

### Introduction

Social scientists have variously identified trust as a 'public good' necessary for the smooth running of many transactions,[1] an essential requirement for stable social relationships[2] and a way for social actors to cope with uncertainty and vulnerability.[3] Trust, at its best, assumes that promises will be kept, that relationships will be dependable and that neither sanctions nor rewards are necessary for it to be exercised.[4] O'Neill emphasizes that every profession needs trust. Without it, there can be no reliance that others will act as they say that they will. In turn, loss of trust is of considerable significance:

> Since trust has to be placed without guarantees, it is inevitably sometimes misplaced: others let us down and we let others down. When this happens trust and relationships based on trust are both damaged. Trust, it is constantly observed, is hard earned and easily dissipated. It is valuable social capital and not to be squandered.[5]

Risk and trust are interrelated as, inevitably, to place trust in someone is to take a risk.[6] Other commentators have gone even further, some identifying professions as supposedly representing 'the height of trustworthiness'.[7] This sentiment has been fostered internally by professions themselves, as well as externally. In large complex professions it is not always easy for outsiders to assess the trustworthiness of individuals, which makes it vitally important that trust can be placed in the profession

1 Hirsch, F., *Social Limits to Growth*, 1978, Harvard University Press, Cambridge, Mass, 78–9.

2 Blau, P., *Exchange and Power in Social Life*, 1964, Wiley, New York, 99.

3 Heimer, C., 'Uncertainty and Vulnerability in Social Relations', 1976, cited by, and see for further discussion, Barber, B., *The Logic and Limits of Trust*, 1983, Rutgers, New York, 8.

4 Groundwater-Smith, S. and Sachs, J., 'The Activist Professional and the Reinstatement of Trust', *Cambridge Journal of Education*, 2002, Vol. 32, No. 3, 342.

5 O'Neill, O., *Reith Lectures 2002*, Radio 4 (http://www.bbc.co.uk/radio4/reith2002/ONora O'Neill).

6 Earle, T.C. and Cvetkovich, G.T., *Social Trust: Toward a Cosmopolitan Society*, 1995, Praeger, Westport, CT.

7 Barber, B., *The Logic and Limits of Trust*, 1983, Rutgers, New York, 131.

as a whole.[8] Trust takes on added significance for the practice of professionals such as doctors and lawyers, because very often they cannot guarantee success. The most they can promise is to do their best. Clients will often have a great deal at stake, so must be in no doubt about a professional's motivation.[9] It is for this reason that moral errors have been treated more seriously than technical errors. It also provides an additional reason why a 'no blame' culture, discussed later, should not be taken too far.

Trust may be seen as a means of dealing with complexity. However, trust is not always desirable, for instance, if it is 'foolish', 'naïve', 'gullible' or 'blind'. Trust necessitates a lack of control, but in the trust relationship control should no longer be an issue. Trust can be based on erroneous factors, notably familiarity – placing trust in someone because he or she feels familiar. There may also be a tendency to mechanize trust – confusing trust 'with *reliance* and *dependability*'.[10] Handy argues that 'it is unwise to trust people whom you do not know well [and] whom you have not observed in action over time…'. Once established, trust should not be taken for granted.[11] If distrust emerges, those who are the subjects will find it difficult to get sufficiently close to others to demonstrate that they have changed – 'trust is like glass: once broken it can never be the same again'. If trust is missing, far more time and effort have to be invested in checking systems of control. To avoid this, the maintenance of trust must be ruthless.[12]

## Trust and the Medical Profession

Historically, doctors have been trusted because of a recognition of the value of their knowledge and their concern for the well-being of patients. This has been referred to as 'status trust' – deference being shown to expertise and social standing. Such trust inevitably requires an act of faith in the usual absence of personal knowledge of the individual member of the profession being trusted. For the profession as a whole, trustworthiness can be equated with the sum of the trustworthiness of each member of the profession.[13] Furthermore, the power of doctors is reinforced by the nature of trust: 'when we trust people, we look hard for further reasons to trust

---

8 See, for example, Sztompka, P., 'Trust, Distrust and Two Paradoxes of Democracy', *European Journal of Social Theory*, 1998, 1, 19.

9 Bosk, C.L., 'Forgive and Remember: Managing Medical Failure', in Dowie, J. and Elstein, A., *Professional Judgment*, 1988, Cambridge University Press, Cambridge, 525.

10 Solomon, R.C. and Flores, F., *Building Trust*, 2001, Oxford University Press, Oxford, 45 and 55–6.

11 See Solomon, R.C. and Flores, F., *Building Trust*, 2001, Oxford University Press, Oxford, 5; and Luhmann, N., Trust and Power, 1980, Wiley, New York.

12 Handy, C., *The Hungry Spirit*, 1998, Arrow, London, 187 and 191.

13 For discussion in the context of lawyers, see Webb, J. and Nicolson, D., 'Institutionalising Trust: Ethics and the Responsive Regulation of the Legal Profession', *Legal Ethics*, Winter 1999, Vol. 2, No. 2, 148–68. See also *Bolton v Law Society* [1994] 1 WLR 512 [1994] 2 All ER 486.

them…'[14] This latter principle may be observed within the judicial as well as the public environment. As the longstanding principle adopted in *Bolam*[15] demonstrates, in most circumstances the courts have trusted doctors to determine the standards to be met by their colleagues. With respect to the possible loss of trust, *the Kerr/Haslam Inquiry Report*[16] noted that:

> The trust that exists, or at least should exist, between a patient and their doctor is fundamental. That trust is inevitably damaged by allegations of wrongdoing…The early restoration of trust is vital – so that all patients can be at ease when being treated and cared for, whether alone with their doctor, with other in attendance, at hospital or at home. Trust must be restored so that doctors, and other medical professionals, can carry out their work without unnecessary levels of intrusive regulation…[17]

Self-regulation reflects the trust which the state places in the medical profession, the assumption being that individual members of the profession can be trusted to bring a selfless approach to unsupervised practice. The expectation is that members each have a highly developed sense of moral responsibility. The practitioner must, of course, be competent, but competence without trust is worthless. In its determination of the hearing against the three doctors in the Bristol Royal Infirmary case,[18] the PCC began by emphasizing that the trust patients place in their doctors lay at the centre of the matter. It was hard to envisage a situation where trust was more important than when parents were placing the care of their seriously ill child in the medical profession. They must be confident that the doctors will put the best interests of the child before anything else. A failure by doctors to meet these expectations will undermine the confidence the public has in the whole medical profession. This corresponds with Irvine's argument, that public confidence in the medical profession is sustained when expectations are in harmony with professional culture and performance. Conversely, public trust and confidence is undermined by an environment in which the medical profession retains an outdated concept of professional culture in a wider society which has moved on.[19]

Significant elements of doctors' day-to-day practice are beyond regulation. The highly individualistic nature of clinical decision making and the myriad individual decisions taken by doctors are beyond direct, ongoing supervision. Highly developed personal self-discipline resulting in effective personal self-regulation is therefore vital.[20] The effective functioning of the profession's self-regulatory processes are therefore central to underpinning trust in the whole profession. Any misconduct on the part of a doctor which may draw into doubt his or her personal integrity and

---

14 Solomon, R.C. and Flores, F., *Building Trust*, 2001, Oxford University Press, Oxford, 25 and 32.

15 *Bolam v Friern Hospital Management Committee* [1957] 1 WLR 582.

16 Discussed in Chapter 9.

17 *The Kerr/Haslam Inquiry Report*, July 2005, Cm 6640-1, 611.

18 Discussed in Chapter 7.

19 Irvine, D., *The Doctors' Tale*, 2003, Radcliffe Medical Press, Oxford, 6.

20 See, for example, Irvine, D., *The Doctors' Tale*, 2003, Radcliffe Medical Press, Oxford, 40.

ability to 'self-regulate' must be treated with the greatest seriousness. Trust also demands transparency – effective trust relationships are more likely to be built with organizations which make their operations and functions easy to understand, visible and open to scrutiny.[21] The GMC appears to have lost sight of these factors. This is perhaps a reflection of one of the well-chronicled potential weaknesses of professional self-regulation – self-interest and inappropriate levels of solidarity and collegiality can undermine trust and effective regulation. Members of the medical profession have been complicit in manipulating the trust placed in them. Errors and other problems may be filtered or even concealed, thereby inappropriately retaining trust.[22]

From the perspective of economics, asymmetric information, deriving from specialized knowledge possessed by the doctor, means that a patient has little choice but to enter into an agency relationship with the doctor. In economic terms, the doctor identifies the treatment required (the necessary level of production) and simultaneously specifies to the patient the amount of consumption needed to improve his or her health status.[23] Viewed in this way, recent moves by government and the GMC have limited meaning unless accompanied by appropriate trust relationships. Consent to treatment, for instance, has been a focus of attention. Kennedy, in his report following the Bristol Inquiry, noted that informing patients about treatment and its risks must become a process, rather than a one-off event. Similarly, the GMC has increased the requirements that registered doctors obtain genuine consent, based upon appropriate information about the proposed treatment and relative risks and benefits. Notwithstanding the practical implication of doctors complying with these requirements, even if they were rigorously followed, they offer artificial certainty. In the case of all but the simplest of treatments, meaningful risk-benefit information may be difficult enough for doctors to access and understand, and extremely difficult for the doctor to explain to the patient.[24] Inevitably, doctors will be selective in the research findings they choose to incorporate into their explanations, and selective again in translating this research into language accessible to the lay person. Only trust in the doctor to act in the patient's best interests can be relied upon in these circumstances. As described from within the profession:

> In the end, given that understanding the nature of disease and its treatment, and the rationale for treatments, requires quite a bit of training, and given, too, that the rational assessment of risk is not very well developed in many of us, there will be an irreducible

---

21 Sztompka, P., 'Trust, Distrust and Two Paradoxes of Democracy', *European Journal of Social Theory*, 1998, 1, 19, 23.

22 See Giddens, A., *The Consequences of Modernity*, 1990, Polity Press, Cambridge; and Quick, O., 'Outing Medical Errors: Questions of Trust and Responsibility', *Medical Law Review*, Spring 2006, 14, 22–43.

23 McGuire, A., 'Ethics and Resource Allocation: An Economist's View', in Dowie, J. and Elstein, A., *Professional Judgment*, 1988, Cambridge University Press, Cambidge, 492–507, 498.

24 The recent controversy surrounding the safety of the MMR vaccine illustrates the issues surrounding differing opinions within the medical and scientific community, and the difficulty in conveying such technical debate to the lay public.

element of trust in agreeing to a treatment. …[Communication] will probably remain the source of most complaints, not because things cannot be improved but because they will never reach the ideal envisaged, or assumed, by medical ethicists for whom the notion of the autonomous (that is fully informed) patient is taken for granted.[25]

## Evidence of Public Trust in the Profession

Despite the various crises which have hit the medical profession in recent years, there is little evidence that public trust has waned significantly. For instance, a 1998 survey of over 100,000 patients found that 83 per cent trusted and had confidence in their doctors. Even after the highly newsworthy scandals surrounding the events at Alder Hey and the Bristol Royal Infirmary, a MORI poll commissioned by the BMA found 89 per cent of respondents trusted the medical profession.[26] Tallis sees as even more encouraging a 2004 MORI poll which found that 92 per cent of respondents trusted doctors to tell the truth, the best result for any professional group and the highest finding since polling began in 1983.[27]

From the perspective of my discussion, these findings are only encouraging if they are actually deserved. There is evidence that public faith in the medical profession may be built upon fundamental misapprehensions. For example, a survey in July 2005 found that almost 50 per cent of those members of the public surveyed believed that doctors were already subject to regular reappraisal.[28] Tallis compares doctors with those groups towards the bottom of the ladder of trust, notably politicians and government ministers, with a 22–23 per cent trust rating. However, scepticism and a relative lack of trust can be healthy if it facilitates the public in critically assessing what is offered or presented to them. In the case of politicians, it should encourage those who wish to be re-elected to be ever mindful of the need to convince the public of the appropriateness of their actions. In the case of doctors, a continuingly high trust rating, in the face of scandals which might be expected to dent trust, is actually of concern. Indeed, high levels of trust have quite possibly facilitated continuing failings on the part of the medical profession to adequately self-regulate. Rather than viewing popular trust in a positive light, the profession should see this trust as potentially misplaced and, therefore, as a cue for far greater self-reflection. Members of the public have a vested interest in convincing themselves that they trust their doctors. From swallowing a prescribed drug, agreeing to an injection, to consenting to surgery, the patient is obliged to place faith in the competence and best intentions of the doctor. The profession knows, or should know, that this trust is not always deserved, and it has been privileged by society in the guise of self-

25 Tallis, R., *Hippocratic Oaths*, 2004, Atlantic, London, 55–6.

26 Figures cited by Tallis, R., *Hippocratic Oaths*, 2004, Atlantic, London, at 102 and 296.

27 Tallis, R., *Hippocratic Oaths*, 2004, Atlantic, London, 296.

28 See Department of Health, *Good Doctors, Safer Patients – Proposals to Strengthen the System to Assure and Improve the Performance of Doctors and to Protect the Safety of Patients: A Report by the Chief Medical Officer*, July 2006, Chapter 8, paragraphs 2, 8 and 9.

regulation to protect unsuspecting patients against doctors in whom their trust would be misplaced.

Competence of the person trusted is a typical condition of trust and is central to the trust placed in professionals. As areas of professional expertise increase in complexity, often beyond even the basic grasp of the lay person, trust in the professional and the professional's competence becomes unavoidable. However, it has been emphasized that competence does not lie at the heart of trust, rather it is simply a precondition.[29] 'Good will' or 'caring' are vital additions to competence in the professional relationship; for example, doctors are trusted not only to know what they are doing, but also to take into account the feelings of their patients. We want to trust our doctor's knowledge and skills, but now our primary concern is whether we can trust them (or their organization) to provide us with the best care. An additional level of complexity arises because in practice it is often a matter of trust to rely on the person trusted to be accurate and honest about their competence. This includes honesty with themselves.[30] For example, the surgeons in the Bristol case appear, in part at least, to have misled themselves that some of the procedures they performed were within their ability. This should not be a problem with a well-regulated profession, ensuring that those who enter and remain within the profession are competent. The GMC has failed in this regard.

## Alternatives to Trust

O'Neill argues that the alternatives to trust – namely transparency, regulation and accountability – will not deal with the true enemy of trust, deception. These alternatives can also have a negative impact. For instance, as transparency increases, information overload often increases – reducing the ability of people to understand what is going on, or to place various items of information in context. Ultimately, frustration at this state of affairs may actually decrease trust in those institutions which provide, process and contextualize the information upon which transparency relies.[31] Similar arguments can be applied to replacing trust with more and more regulation. One obvious and well-rehearsed question is 'who regulates the regulators?' For an already highly trusted profession, such as doctors, this simply shifts the need for trust away from the regulated and towards the regulators. Some in the profession also argue that shifting the balance further towards regulation and away from trust will simply result in doctors viewing every patient as a potential complainant or litigant. The doctor–patient relationship will be damaged, defensive medicine will increase and 'The primary duty to protect the patient is overridden by the doctor's

29 See Solomon, R.C. and Flores, F., *Building Trust*, 2001, Oxford University Press, Oxford, 83–4.

30 Solomon, R.C. and Flores, F., *Building Trust*, 2001, Oxford University Press, Oxford, 84–5.

31 O'Neill, O., *Reith Lectures 2002*, Radio 4 (http://www.bbc.co.uk/radio4/reith2002/). See also Tallis, R., *Hippocratic Oaths*, 2004, Atlantic, London, 103.

concern to protect himself'. This is not cost-free for patients, who may be subjected to ultimately unnecessary tests and procedures.[32]

An audit culture also erodes trust, distorting the 'proper aims of professional practice' and harming professional pride and integrity. Traditional ideals of professional practice focus upon the personal interaction between professionals and 'those whom they serve'.[33] Rules may be seen as 'surrogates for trust', thereby weakening the moral conditions for trust.[34] By seeking to achieve measurable, pre-determined outcomes, audit may erode professional judgement and as a result the trust placed in the moral competence of practitioners is reduced. This in turn can result in the development of compliance strategies and verification rituals.[35] As already noted, deception – contrasted with honest mistakes, 'merely' getting things wrong – it has been argued, is the real enemy of trust. The increased transparency sought by audit is unlikely to reduce deception. Knowing that information may be disclosed will encourage massaging of the truth by those who generate information. Furthermore, seeking to increase trust by increasing transparency simply shifts the necessity for trust to those who determine what information should be released and how.[36] These are valid concerns. However, one major difficulty with this approach is the notion that the medical profession in recent years has had at its core a service ethos. The crisis and whistleblowing failures recorded in this work repeatedly illustrate a strong self-serving and self-protective streak within the medical profession. To the extent that mistrust is instilled by modern audit cultures, this is a penalty being paid by the profession for previous failures to live up to the trust placed in it.

## Educational and Regulatory Underpinnings of Trust

If trust is the means by which we deal with situations of risk,[37] there can be no greater risk than that to the bodily integrity which the patient entrusts to the doctor. The parents of the Bristol babies trusted the doctors to do their best, but also to honestly assess their own competence and success rate. Shipman's victims placed their trust

32 Tallis, R., *Hippocratic Oaths*, 2004, Atlantic, London, 107–8.

33 O'Neill, O., *Reith Lectures 2002*, Radio 4 (http://www.bbc.co.uk/radio4/reith2002/ONora O'Neill).

34 Harre, R., 'Trust and its Surrogates', in Warren, M. (ed.), *Democracy and Trust*, 1999, Cambridge University Press, Cambridge, 249–72. Cited by Groundwater-Smith, S. and Sachs, J., 'The Activist Professional and the Reinstatement of Trust', *Cambridge Journal of Education*, 2002, Vol. 32, No. 3, 345.

35 See, for example, Groundwater-Smith, S. and Sachs, J., 'The Activist Professional and the Reinstatement of Trust', *Cambridge Journal of Education*, 2002, Vol. 32, No. 3, 341; Power, M., *The Audit Society: Rituals of Verification*, 1999, Oxford University Press, Oxford.

36 O'Neill, O., *Reith Lectures 2002*, Radio 4 (http://www.bbc.co.uk/radio4/reith2002/ONora O'Neill).

37 See, for example, Luhmann, N., 'Familiarity, Confidence, Trust: Problems and Alternatives', in Gambetta, D. (ed.), *Trust: Making and Breaking Cooperative Relations*, 1988, Blackwell, Oxford.

in him that the injections he gave were therapeutic, or at least harmless. Mulcahy neatly sums up the position:

> Recent investigations have shown that the presumption of trust is strongly embedded in people's perceptions of clinical acts. As a result, it can take a considerable time for a person to interpret the behaviour of a health professional as potentially injurious…One of the most haunting aspects of the Shipman Inquiry has been the revelation that so many of his patients had continued to place trust in him despite his homicidal activities.[38]

Trust is a mechanism for attempting to control risk, but trust relationships are themselves risky because they require an act of faith, and in the professional–client context usually involve power and knowledge asymmetries.[39] Professional trust relationships usually derive from an act of faith in the status of the professional rather than on personal knowledge. The challenge to the medical profession is to ensure that each of its members is trustworthy, and from this the profession as a whole retains and maximizes the trust of the public. The building of this trust must begin at medical school and continuously develop from there. Dame Janet Smith has called for the teaching of ethical issues to medical students from the start of their time at medical school. She also emphasized the importance of ensuring that students have the right characteristics to become fit and proper doctors:

> [The]…profession…should be pretty tough on students who present with a history of past misconduct or, indeed, those who get into trouble while on the course. That may sound harsh, but I think it is generally accepted that past behaviour is the best predictor of future behaviour and that the main objective must always be the protection of the public.[40]

It has been acknowledged on behalf of the GMC that its lack of statutory or other legal powers over the behaviour of medical students is a limitation which should be addressed.[41]

One example of concern, which suggests that medical schools may have some way to go, is illustrated by an editorial discussion in the *British Medical Journal.* This involved an allegation that a student who cheated in an exam at a major medical school was nevertheless allowed to graduate. This, it was suggested, had the potential to undermine the credibility of medical education and broader issues of self-regulation.[42] A structured research project by Rennie and Crosby also identified a small, but concerning, minority of medical students who had either engaged in academic misconduct or did not consider it wrong for others to do so. Three per cent of respondents considered that it was not wrong to forge a doctor's signature

---

38 Mulcahy, L., *Disputing Doctors*, 2003, Open University Press, Maidenhead, 60.

39 Webb, J. and Nicolson, D., 'Institutionalising Trust: Ethics and the Responsive Regulation of the Legal Profession', *Legal Ethics*, Winter 1999, Vol. 2, No. 2, 148–68, 150.

40 Cohen, D., 'Medical Students should be Added to GMC Register, Says Judge', *BMJ*, 2005, 330: 1104, 14 May.

41 See comments attributed to Peter Rubin, chairman of the GMC's education committee, in Cohen, D., 'Medical Students should be Added to GMC Register, Says Judge', *BMJ*, 2005, 330: 1104, 14 May.

42 Smith, R., 'Cheating at Medical School', *BMJ*, 2000, Vol. 321, 398, 12 August.

on a piece of work (a further 4 per cent were 'not sure'). Nine per cent had done or would consider taking such a step. Two per cent of students did not consider it wrong to copy answers in a degree examination and 2 per cent had done or would consider taking such a step. Six per cent did not consider it wrong to copy another student's work (with a further 3 per cent 'not sure') and 6 per cent had done or would consider taking such a step. Twenty-four per cent did not consider it wrong to lend work to another student to copy (with a further 15 per cent 'not sure') and the same percentage had done or would consider taking such a step. Twelve per cent did not consider it wrong to write work for another student (with a further 6 per cent 'not sure') and 9 per cent had done or would consider taking such a step. Five per cent did not consider it wrong to submit another student's work as their own (with a further 2 per cent 'not sure') and 4 per cent had done or would consider taking such a step. Fourteen per cent did not consider it wrong to record that the result of a clinical examination was normal when the exam had not been done (with a further 11 per cent 'not sure') and 32 per cent had done or would consider taking such a step.[43]

Once an appropriate educational model is established, disciplinary and regulatory mechanisms must rigorously address individual failures of trust, in the interests of the wider profession as well as the public. This latter requirement must, however, be approached in the appropriate manner. The form, focus and enforcement of professional rules of conduct can, in principle, substantially undermine institutional trust in a profession.[44] Disciplinary codes which attempt to set minimum standards by means of detailed legalistic regulations often fail on both their own terms – it is difficult, even impossible, to draft rules which anticipate in full the potential complexity of the professional–client relationship – and in terms of more aspirational approaches to seeking to ensure that members of a profession seek to improve ethical awareness and trust-fostering behaviour. Webb and Nicolson argue that aspirational codes can more easily accommodate broad ethical principles, such as trust, and that reflexivity within these codes can best ensure that such trust is enhanced. Prescriptive codes, in contrast, are reductive in that they tend to reduce trust to a contractual principle, denying genuine trust relationships and the need for confidence which underpins them. Such codes also tend to conflate loyalty with trust. Loyalty can arise for reasons which have little or nothing to do with genuine trust, for example, career ambition or fear of disciplinary consequences.[45] Traditional approaches to professional codes and professional regulation also undermine the more recent reality of team-based professional practice, by focusing upon individual responsibility only. This tends to ignore important features of team-based practice, which can result in practitioners adopting double standards in terms of their individual ethical perspective compared

43 Rennie, S.C. and Crosby, J.R., 'Are "Tomorrow's Doctors" Honest? Questionnaire Study Exploring Medical Students' Attitudes and Reported Behaviour on Academic Misconduct', *BMJ*, 2001, 322: 274–5, 3 February.

44 For discussion in relation to the legal profession, see Webb, J. and Nicolson, D., 'Institutionalising Trust: Ethics and the Responsive Regulation of the Legal Profession', *Legal Ethics*, Winter 1999, Vol. 2, No. 2, 148–68, 150.

45 Webb, J. and Nicolson, D., 'Institutionalising Trust: Ethics and the Responsive Regulation of the Legal Profession', *Legal Ethics*, Winter 1999, Vol. 2, No. 2, 148–68, 156.

with that relating to their membership of the team. For example, it has been suggested that senior practitioners in their role as team managers are likely to participate in complex patronage relationships with their teams.[46] Members of the team will face potentially conflicting ethical loyalty between the client on the one hand and the team and the interests of personal advancement on the other. Team-based working also increases the likelihood that individual practitioners will be less likely to consider themselves individually ethically responsible. 'Problems of 'floating responsibility'[47] may arise, whereby ethical responsibility for a specific act becomes too diffuse, so that it is simultaneously everyone's, but ultimately no one's'.[48] Even those aspects of codes which require practitioners to report incompetence or misbehaviour by colleagues frequently ignore the challenges which this poses to a practitioner locked into the complex interpersonal and patronage structures of a team.

## Reducing Trust and Empowering Society

So far in this chapter I have talked about the importance for the medical profession to work to ensure that the public trust placed in its members is well-founded. However, there is a converse to this line of argument – the importance of mistrust. Put at its simplest, recent crises in professional regulation have highlighted examples of misplaced trust which the public have placed in the medical profession. The reluctance of parents to challenge the doctors at Bristol, and the willingness of many of Shipman's victims to be 'treated' alone in their own homes, illustrates that the medical profession has been exceptionally successful in establishing its position of trust. If any positive outcomes can be derived from these and other cases, it is a gradual erosion in the public mind of this trust. Whilst the medical profession must work hard internally to ensure that it is truly worthy of a high degree of trust, this trust in practice must not be forthcoming. Society must maintain a sufficient element of mistrust to ensure that individual patients and others are alive to the possibility of incompetence or misbehaviour, and have the confidence to react appropriately. From the simplest case of the patient challenging the doctor to wash his or her hands between examinations, to a willingness to challenge more complex concerns arising from cases such as those at Bristol. Sztompka talks about the institutionalization of distrust, requiring institutions (or in the context of this discussion, professions and professional regulatory bodies) to have, amongst other things, limited competence within a system of checks and balances to avoid abuses of power, to be committed to

46 For discussion in the context of the legal profession, see Flood, J., 'Doing Business: The Management of Uncertainty in Lawyers' Work', *Law & Society Review*, 1991, 25; and Webb, J. and Nicolson, D., 'Institutionalising Trust: Ethics and the Responsive Regulation of the Legal Profession', *Legal Ethics*, Winter 1999, Vol. 2, No. 2, 148–68, 157.

47 Bauman, Z., *Alone Again: Ethics After Certainty*, 1994, Demos, London, 8; Luban, D., *Lawyers and Justice: An Ethical Study*, 1988, Princeton University Press, Princeton, NJ, 123–4.

48 Webb, J. and Nicolson, D., 'Institutionalising Trust: Ethics and the Responsive Regulation of the Legal Profession', *Legal Ethics*, Winter 1999, Vol. 2, No. 2, 148–68, 157.

open communication and to ensure that citizens have an adequate means of redress.[49] Scott describes the notion of 'wary trust'. Where the environment has been volatile, hostile and uncertain, trust will be difficult to establish and a healthy mistrust may be the better option.[50]

## GMC Failures to Address Key Trust Issues

All of the case examples discussed in this work demonstrate failures of trust on the part of medical practitioners and corresponding failures by the GMC. However, there are also other case examples where the GMC's failure to address the significance of trust has the potential to place the public at risk not individually, but in hundreds, even thousands. In such cases, whilst the rhetoric from the GMC has been strong, the penalties imposed have tended to be towards the middle or lower ends of the scale. For example, in December 2000 a doctor engaged in medical research appeared before the PCC for publishing fraudulent research in December 1990. The PCC commented that:

> Medical research is central to the advance of medical practice and must always be conducted with scrupulous honesty and integrity. It is highly irresponsible, and potentially dangerous for patients, for a doctor to falsify research…The committee consider that these events illustrate seriously irresponsible and dishonest behaviour on your part.[51]

Notwithstanding this strong condemnation, a twelve-month suspension was considered to be sufficient. In March 2001, the doctor's supervisor at the time of the fraud was found guilty of serious professional misconduct. The supervisor had been warned by colleagues from November 1988 about concerns with the doctor's research, but failed to take sufficient action. Once the fabrication came to light, he also took insufficient steps to ensure that retractions were published or to notify the appropriate authorities, including the GMC. A severe reprimand was deemed to be a sufficient penalty.[52] It was also suggested that pressure was brought to bear on potential whistleblowers at the university in question, resulting in a six- or seven-year delay before the matter came to the attention of the GMC. It then took a further three years for the GMC to investigate and bring an action against the doctor. In part, the GMC were hindered because key documents had been shredded by the employing university. There was also evidence that the doctor had been awarded a

---

49 Sztompka, P., 'Trust, Distrust and Two Paradoxes of Democracy', *European Journal of Social Theory*, 1998, 1, 25–7. Cited by Webb, J. and Nicolson, D., 'Institutionalising Trust: Ethics and the Responsive Regulation of the Legal Profession', *Legal Ethics*, Winter 1999, Vol. 2, No. 2, 148–68, 158.

50 Cited by Groundwater-Smith, S. and Sachs, J., 'The Activist Professional and the Reinstatement of Trust', *Cambridge Journal of Education*, 2002, Vol. 32, No. 3, 342.

51 Ferriman, A., 'Consultant Suspended for Research Fraud', *BMJ*, 2000, 321: 1429, 9 December.

52 Ferriman, A., 'Professor Faces GMC for Failure to Prevent and Report Fraud', *BMJ*, 2001, 322: 508, 3 March; and Dyer, C., 'Professor Reprimanded for Failing to Act over Fraud', *BMJ*, 2001, 322: 573, 10 March.

postgraduate degree, even though the university was aware that research in his thesis was fraudulent.[53] There is no indication that the GMC attempted to pursue those behind the scenes who ignored concerns, or even blocked investigations.

A second example of inadequate GMC action relates to the issue of hand-washing. It has been suggested that 9 per cent of patients will acquire an infection during their stay in hospital, 15 per cent of which are preventable.[54] The failure by medical staff to wash their hands between patients has been attributed to contributing to the spread of hospital-acquired infections.[55] This has been the subject of news reporting for a number of years, with accounts of deaths and serious illness as a result. Notwithstanding this, members of the medical profession continued to put their patients at risk. For example, in late 2005 the Patients Association found that doctors were still neglecting basic hygiene procedures, with under 50 per cent always washing their hands with antiseptic gels between patients.[56] Notwithstanding the starkness of these statistics and the publicity surrounding them, they seem to have pricked neither the consciences of many individual members of the profession nor spurred the GMC into taking effective action. Trust on the part of patients, that doctors will observe necessary hygiene standards and that this will be underpinned by the self-regulatory process, appears to have been misplaced. Furthermore, whilst doctors are not the only participants in the healthcare process who must observe appropriate standards of hygiene, they stand at the apex of the professional hierarchy and so act as role models for others.

53 Ferriman, A., 'Consultant Suspended for Research Fraud', *BMJ*, 2000, 321: 1429, 9 December.

54 See National Audit Office, *A Safer Place for Patients: Learning to Improve Patient Safety*, 31 October 2005, page 56, www.nao.org.uk.

55 See Eaton, L., 'Hand Washing is More Important than Cleaner Wards in Controlling MRSA', *BMJ*, 2005, 330: 922, 23 April.

56 See Templeton, S., 'Babies Fall Sick as Doctors Ignore Superbug Hygiene', *The Sunday Times*, 16 October 2005, 2.

## Chapter 6

# The NHS Complaints and Disciplinary Processes

### Introduction

It has been argued from within the GMC that the onus cannot only be on the Council to ensure that doctors are behaving and performing appropriately. Employers must also play a central part. As Irvine puts it: 'The GMC does not, cannot, and should not manage the detail of doctors in their everyday work. That is and always has been the responsibility of employers.'[1]

The GMC itself has argued that many of the complaints it receives are serious, but not so serious as to call into question the doctor's registration or continuation in practice unrestricted. In these circumstances, local NHS procedures were seen to be more appropriate. 'The GMC should not be seen as another general complaints body or a substitute for the NHS complaints system.'[2] In this chapter I consider the place of the NHS complaints procedures within the wider disciplinary context and whether the GMC's attitude can be substantiated.

### NHS Complaints Procedures

The history of complaints handling in the NHS is marked by fragmentation between procedures developed for primary care, secondary care and public health. This resulted in what has been described as a confusing web of systems for addressing complaints and disciplining doctors.[3] The overall effectiveness of the system has also been questioned because of the positions of power and influence doctors acquired within the health service. In developing complaints handling within the NHS, medical discourse has been privileged over that of other participants in the process.[4] Acquisition by the profession of both power and significant medical

---

1 Cited by Boseley, S.and Wintour, P., 'New Checks will Rule Out "Dodgy Doctors"', *The Guardian*, 23 June 2000 (web edition).

2 GMC, *Acting Fairly to Protect Patients: Reform of the GMC's Fitness to Practise Procedures*, March 2001, 8.

3 See, for example, Mulcahy, L., *Disputing Doctors*, 2003, Open University Press, Maidenhead, 16.

4 See, for example, *Health Memorandum* (HM (66) 15) (DHSS 1966), which allowed for complaints handling about doctors to be dealt with almost exclusively by doctors, free of

autonomy during the early years of the NHS has significantly restricted more recent attempts to rein in its power.[5]

Until 1990 disciplinary procedures for hospital medical staff derived from national guidance in the 1961 Circular HM (61) 112, *Disciplinary Proceedings in Cases Relating to Hospital Medical and Dental Staff*. This guidance distinguished between 'personal' and 'professional' misconduct. 'Personal' misconduct was addressed using internal disciplinary procedures which the NHS employer could use for any grade of staff. 'Professional' misconduct, however, required a 'special procedure' which protected doctors against dismissal on all but the most serious grounds.

For the purposes of this work, the 1970s provides an appropriate starting point for consideration of NHS complaints systems. There had been criticisms that complaints had been suppressed and staff who had attempted to support patients were victimized. Investigation of complaints was informal and undertaken by those who were responsible for the treatment or other service complained about. Hospitals were also largely free to develop their own complaints investigation and handling procedures and lacked clear guidance regarding dissatisfied complainants. Defensiveness often involved a 'sue or shut up' attitude, hospitals fearing that complainants would use the system to gain evidence for civil proceedings.[6] Indeed at levels of both primary and secondary care there has been a reluctance towards, even a prohibition against, investigating or otherwise pursuing a complaint when civil action was threatened or underway. Given the extensive time which can elapse before a civil claim is resolved, there were obvious concerns that a complaint which might reveal a dysfunctional, possibly dangerous, doctor might go unheeded. By the mid-1970s, it was evident that a thorough review of hospital complaints procedures was needed.

The DHSS set up an investigatory committee, chaired by Sir Michael Davies. The Davies Committee identified four major criticisms of the then existing procedure:

1. A failure by practitioners to take seriously the issue of complaints.
2. A defensive attitude to complaints. Hospital staff tended to operate the system in a manner which insulated them from criticism.
3. Inadequate information for complainants and staff about complaints procedures, nor was there an effective system of external checks on the management of complaints.
4. Insufficient attention paid to encouraging complaints.

Even though non-medical staff were often formally in charge of the complaints procedures, hospital consultants retained significant control over the actual investigation of complaints. Furthermore, the Davies Committee considered that

---

outside interference. Discussed by Mulcahy, L., *Disputing Doctors*, 2003, Open University Press, Maidenhead, 31.

5 See Allsop, J., *Health Policy and the NHS: Towards 2000*, 1995, Longman, London; Perkin, E., *The Rise of Professional Society – England Since 1880*, 1996, Routledge, London; Mulcahy, L., *Disputing Doctors*, 2003, Open University Press, Maidenhead.

6 See Carrier, J. and Kendall, I., *Medical Negligence: Complaints and Compensation*, 1990, Avebury, Aldershot, 46–7.

there was no effective external system for monitoring the management and progress of complaints handling. This had particular pertinence to the de facto self-regulatory nature of complaints handling, as consultants were perceived to be reluctant to evaluate or question the clinical judgement of a colleague.[7]

The Davies Committee made 82 recommendations. Key amongst these were that a proper system of investigation should be implemented, with investigation panels consisting of both medical and lay members and legally qualified chairmen. The members of the committee also accepted the need for a division between clinical and non-clinical complaints. The former were considered to be more complex and problematic.[8]

The ultimate recommendations of the Davies Committee have been described as a compromise which satisfied virtually none of the interested parties. Stacey, a lay member of the committee, later expressed regret at having signed up to the report. She also reported that a medical member of the committee, a member of the Royal College of Physicians, was 'relegated...to a backwater [by his professional colleagues] for signing the report'.[9] This latter assertion illustrates the reluctance by the medical profession to accept any outside interference with regulation and discipline, however watered down this might be.

The Department of Health and Social Security issued a draft code of practice for complaint handling in June 1976. This accepted the separation of clinical and non-clinical complaints, largely ignoring the former and dismissing the appropriateness of managerial oversight. The key feature of the procedure for clinical complaints was that it was almost exclusively overseen by clinicians.[10]

## The 1980s

In April 1981 the Department of Health published its Health Complaints Procedure for hospitals in a memorandum annexed to Circular HC(81)5. Complaints not involving clinical judgement (Part II) and those which did involve clinical judgement (Part III) were addressed separately. The initial stage of the Part III procedure encouraged

7 Department of Health and Social Security, *Report of the Committee on Hospital Complaints Procedure*, HMSO, London. See also The Honourable Mrs Justice Pauffley, *Committee of Inquiry – Independent Investigation into how the NHS Handled Allegations about the Conduct of Clifford Ayling*, 15 July 2004, Cm 6298, paras 5.4–5.9; and Mulcahy, L., *Disputing Doctors*, 2003, Open University Press, Maidenhead, 36.

8 The Neale Inquiry noted that consultants rejected outright the need for management input into complaint handling. Managers were seen as 'outsiders' who lacked the necessary medical knowledge required to construct a response to a complaint about medical care. See Matthews, J., *Committee of Inquiry to Investigate how the NHS Handled Allegations about the Performance and Conduct of Richard Neale*, August 2004, Cm 6315, para 20.8.

9 Stacey, M., Opening Address, the Public Law Project Complaints Forum, New Connaught Rooms, London, 25 March, 1999. Cited by Mulcahy, L., *Disputing Doctors*, 2003, Open University Press, Maidenhead, 38.

10 For further discussion, see Matthews, J., *Committee of Inquiry to Investigate how the NHS Handled Allegations about the Performance and Conduct of Richard Neale*, August 2004, Cm 6315, para 20.1.

the consultant complained about to meet with the patient. If the patient was still dissatisfied, matters could be taken to a second stage. The Regional Medical Officer would discuss the complaint with the consultant, following which a meeting might be held again with the complainant to resolve the complaint. If matters remained unresolved, the RMO could use the third stage – an 'independent' review by two consultants. This was not available if the complainant was likely to bring legal proceedings. The Ledward Inquiry concluded that these procedures were complex, unwieldy and difficult for staff and patients to follow.11

The Hospital Complaints (Procedure) Act 1985 made it compulsory for all hospitals to institute a complaints system. HC(88)37 was similar to earlier guidance on complaints, except that a designated officer should be appointed to handle complaints. The Unit General Manager was likely to be most suitable for this role. The designated officer would investigate all complaints, other than those involving, inter alia, clinical judgement, disciplinary proceedings, physical abuse of patients and criminal offences. Investigation of these latter matters would include other senior officers – notably the Regional Medical Officer or District General Manager.[12]

Despite the Davies recommendations, during the 1980s and 1990s there was little evidence of good practice within NHS complaints handling. Complacency was common, as was the assumption that the absence of complaints meant that all was well.[13] Complaints procedures were characterized by delay and excessive bureaucracy, as well as being weighted in favour of the practitioner. The complaints system at the time was described by the Kerr/Haslam Inquiry as:

> [D]ifficult and obstructive. It was neither 'user friendly' nor designed to ensure that patient safety was paramount. Those who came through it did so in spite of it, and were left damaged and disillusioned by it. Most never made it through the labyrinth of artificial barriers, unnecessary formalities and plain obstruction to any kind of resolution of issues. Patient complainants largely got nowhere; professional complainants often fared worse, attracting blame, criticism and a degree of professional ostracism that deterred others from following their lead.[14]

It was also suggested that some doctors regarded complaints as a challenge to their professional status and that overall, the complaints system adopted a defensive stance.[15] Fear of medical negligence litigation amongst the medical profession and the 'ideal of self-regulation' resulted in the creation of a separate complaints

---

11 See *The Ledward Report*, paras 18.21–18.25. Only in 1996 did complaints about clinical judgement come under the auspices of the Health Service Ombudsman.

12 For further discussion, see *The Kerr/Haslam Inquiry Report*, July 2005, Cm 6640-1, 869–72.

13 See Matthews, J., *Committee of Inquiry to Investigate how the NHS Handled Allegations about the Performance and Conduct of Richard Neale*, August 2004, Cm 6315, Chapter 4.

14 *The Kerr/Haslam Inquiry Report*, July 2005, Cm 6640-1, 11.

15 Association of Community Health Councils for England and Wales, The NHS Complaint Procedure: ACHCEW's Memorandum to the Public Administration Committee, 1990; Ackroyd, E., 'The Patient's Complaint', British Journal of Hospital Medicine, December 1986; and Donaldson, L. and Cavanagh, J., 'Clinical Complaints and their Handling: a Time

procedure for clinical complaints. During its period of operation, between 1981 and 1996, the medical profession was able to exercise considerable discretion over the handling of 'professional' complaints.[16] In 1990, further guidance was issued in Circular HC (90) 9, *Disciplinary Procedures in Cases Relating to Senior Medical and Dental Staff*. The central features of the earlier system remained, but two additional elements were introduced: Professional Review machinery – a professional panel could review the behaviour of hospital consultants relating to allegations of failure to meet contractual obligations; an Intermediate Procedure – to address allegations of professional misconduct and incompetence which, if proved, would result in action short of dismissal. Circular HC(90)9 resulted from a working party report published in August 1988 entitled 'Disciplinary Procedures for Hospital and Community Doctors and Dentists'. The working party recognized that a specialist dismissed from an NHS post on professional grounds would probably not find alternative employment and might become virtually unemployable. With this level of seriousness, the grounds for dismissal needed to be fully justified. The procedures for reaching such conclusions should be of sufficient gravity to reflect the long training and competitive selection procedures necessary before a doctor could reach senior status.[17]

## The 'Personal' and 'Professional' Distinction

Circular HC(90)9 was incorporated into the employment contracts of most hospital doctors. The 'professional conduct' route was governed by a formal procedure, whilst 'personal conduct' was dealt with more informally without, for example, the right of legal representation. In terms of the procedure to be adopted in particular cases, professional conduct was defined as 'performance or behaviour of practitioners arising from the exercise of medical or dental skills'. Personal conduct was 'performance or behaviour of practitioners due to factors other than those associated with the exercise of medical or dental skills'. The 'professional conduct' route was clearly more doctor-friendly. The choice of route rested with the employer, subject to challenge before the court. The House of Lords has indicated that the disciplinary code set out in Circular HC(90)9 required a broad and purposive interpretation. For instance, a case where a doctor intimately examined a patient when this was wholly unnecessary was likely to fall within the scope of professional misconduct. The doctor is only able to perpetrate the misconduct because of his professional position.[18]

Only in 2005, with the introduction of a new framework by the Department of Health, Maintaining High Professional Standards in the Modern NHS, was the

---

for Change?', Quality and Regulation in Healthcare, 1992, 1(1), 21–5. Cited by Mulcahy, L., *Disputing Doctors*, 2003, Open University Press, Maidenhead, 43.

16 Matthews, J., *Committee of Inquiry to Investigate how the NHS Handled Allegations about the Performance and Conduct of Richard Neale*, August 2004, Cm 6315, Chapter 4.

17 See *Skidmore v Dartford & Gravesham NHS Trust* [2003] UKHL 27, [2003] 3 All ER 292, [2003] IRLR 445, paragraph 13.

18 *Skidmore v Dartford & Gravesham NHS Trust* [2003] UKHL 27, [2003] 3 All ER 292, [2003] IRLR 445.

distinction between personal and professional misconduct removed, and so the difference in approach to doctors compared with other healthcare professionals.[19] The central focus of the framework was on capability and clinical performance, although conduct remains within the remit of local procedures. Notwithstanding these changes, a significant risk remains that the voices of patients and staff who wish to raise concerns will not be adequately listened to.[20]

## Special Professional Panels – the 'Three Wise Men'

Circular HC(82)13,[21] issued in 1982, suggested that health authorities institute committees whose aim would be to prevent harm to patients resulting from physical or mental disability, including addiction, of medical staff. A pool of four or five consultants should be appointed to form a Special Professional Panel, which would sit in threes – commonly known as the 'three wise men' (re-named in some hospitals the Professional Standards Advisory Group or Committee). Reflecting the dominance of self-regulation, the circular stated: 'The medical and dental professions fully agree that a collective responsibility for the safety of patients rests upon the professional staff as a whole...'[22]

The panel would consider concerns reported to it and, if necessary, interview the practitioner concerned. If patients were considered to be at risk, the panel could attempt to influence the behaviour of the practitioner. If unsuccessful, the matter should be referred to the Regional Medical Officer or, if fitness to practise was in doubt, the GMC. The Kerr/Haslam Inquiry concluded that the 'three wise men' system was far from effective. The Shipman Inquiry heard that the 'three wise men procedure' was 'very patchy'. From within the profession, Hammond and Mosley cite the example of a hospital consultant struggling to deal with an alcoholic colleague:

---

19 NHS bodies, with the exception of Foundation Trusts, were expected to implement the recommendations by June 2005. Foundation Trusts were only 'advised' to implement them. Such a distinction is difficult to justify if patient safety is the central priority across the NHS. For further discussion, see *The Kerr/Haslam Inquiry Report*, July 2005, Cm 6640-1, 738–9.

20 Department of Health. *Maintaining High Professional Standards in the Modern NHS: Directions on Disciplinary Procedures*. Department of Health, Crown, London, 2005. See also *The Kerr/Haslam Inquiry Report*, July 2005, Cm 6640-1, 811; and Department of Health, *Good Doctors, Safer Patients – Proposals to Strengthen the System to Assure and Improve the Performance of Doctors and to Protect the Safety of Patients. A Report by the Chief Medical Officer*, July 2006.

21 'Prevention of Harm to Patients Resulting from Physical or Mental Disability of Hospital or Community Medical or Dental Staff'. The procedure had been first conceived under HM(60)45: 'Prevention of Harm to Patients Resulting from Physical or Mental Disability of Hospital Medical or Dental Staff'. See *Ayling Inquiry Report*, 15 July 2004, Annex 4 and *The Ledward Report*, Part III, para 5.3.

22 See *Ayling Inquiry Report*, 15 July 2004, Annex 4.

> We knew that he had a problem and for a while we covered up for him until the workload got too much. Then we insisted he get help through the 'three wise men' system…He was allowed to carry on operating with psychiatric support and supervision of his work.
>
> Some months later, I discovered that I was the one who was supposed to be supervising the work but no one had told me. In any case, I was too busy doing his work for him and undoing his mistakes to monitor him. We kept trying to get him to stop operating because he was a risk to patients but it took ten years, from start to finish, before he agreed to stop and then only because he'd started to have fits.[23]

The system has also been criticized for its relative obscurity within hospitals and secrecy surrounding deliberations.[24] This was the situation at the William Harvey Hospital where Rodney Ledward worked. Few witnesses to the Ledward Inquiry knew the identities of the three wise men, and as a result the committee met rarely.[25] Notwithstanding the myriad problems, by the late 1980s no one had raised any concerns about Ledward to the three wise men.[26]

In September 2003 the Department of Health and the BMA jointly issued a statement of principles, which replaced previous guidance on discipline and the 'three wise men' procedure. The statement contained 11 principles, including the focus on helping doctors to keep their skills and knowledge up to date and a resistance to an ethos of punishment for problems with clinical performance. All issues relating to conduct were to be dealt with by local Trust procedures.[27]

## The Wilson Committee

In 1994 the Department of Health responded to renewed criticism of the NHS procedures by instigating its own inquiry – chaired by Professor Alan Wilson. The subsequent report, *Being Heard*, acknowledged that the existing systems favoured the interests of staff over complainants. One of the most significant conclusions was that the distinction between clinical and non-clinical complaints was artificial. The resulting recommendation was that the two types of complaint, in both primary and secondary care, should fall within the same procedure. The committee's recommendations also included the replacement of the medical-dominated appeals procedure with a lay panel to be advised by medics.[28] In April 1996, the government introduced proposals for new complaints handling processes and procedures.

The Professional Conduct Committee of the GMC expressed concern to the Wilson Committee that NHS bodies were failing to refer cases to the GMC. This

---

23 Hammond, P. and Mosley, M., *Trust Me I'm A Doctor*, 2002, Metro Publishing, London, 38.

24 See, for example, the comments of Sir Liam Donaldson, referred to in *Sick Doctors*, Editorial, *BMJ*, 1994, 309, 557–8, 3 September.

25 *The Ledward Report*, paras 18.3.1–18.3.3.

26 *The Ledward Report*, Part IV, para 10.7.

27 For further discussion, see *The Kerr/Haslam Inquiry Report*, July 2005, Cm 6640-1, 732.

28 NHS Executive, *Being Heard: Report of the Review Committee on NHS Complaint Procedures*, 1994.

included cases where doctors were dismissed for misconduct, but no steps taken to ensure that appropriate action was taken regarding their registration.[29] Of course, the GMC's expressions of concern have to be viewed in the light of the fact that the GMC itself had for many years been rejecting complaints which had not already been through NHS procedures – without mechanisms in place to ensure that these matters were followed up.

After the Wilson Report, new complaints processes for the NHS were implemented in April 1996. A key feature was that grievances should be resolved at local level by the service provider. Underpinning this was the idea that this should provide speedy and personal resolution to complaints. The new procedure also focused on the separation between complaint handling and disciplinary processes, the new guidelines relating only to the former.

Primary and secondary care providers were required to implement a two-stage structure for complaint handling. The first stage required those being complained about to seek early resolution. In primary care, coordination was to be undertaken by the practice manager. The new guidelines also emphasized flexibility, with principles being more important than procedure and the avoidance of bureaucratic and legalistic approaches. The second stage should provide that if complainants were dissatisfied with the outcome of the first stage, they could refer their grievance to a 'convener'. The role of the convener, in conjunction with a lay chairperson (and a clinician if the complaint involved clinical issues) was to decide whether an Independent Review Panel should be established.[30] Alternatively, the convenor might consider that the stage one procedures had not been exhausted and refer the matter back.

Notwithstanding the various attempts at change, the Select Committee on Health noted in 1998–99 that the NHS complaints process remained complex, with a 'myriad of pathways'.[31]

In September 2003, the Department of Health and the BMA's Central Consultants and Specialists Committee jointly issued a framework which replaced all previous guidance on discipline and the 'three wise men' system. The focus was on helping practitioners practise safely and to keep up to date, rather than to impose punitive sanctions for problems with clinical performance. All issues of conduct were to be addressed using local Trust procedures.[32]

---

29 See the Fifth Report of the Shipman Inquiry, *Safeguarding Patients: Lessons from the Past – Proposals for the Future*, para 18.58 (www.the-shipman-inquiry.org.uk).

30 The Review Panel is chaired by an independent chair nominated from a regional list. Complaints involving clinical care also required the appointment of two independent clinical assessors.

31 For full discussion, see Matthews, J., *Committee of Inquiry to Investigate how the NHS Handled Allegations about the Performance and Conduct of Richard Neale*, August 2004, Cm 6315, Chapter 4.

32 For further discussion, see Matthews, J., *Committee of Inquiry to Investigate how the NHS Handled Allegations about the Performance and Conduct of Richard Neale*, August 2004, Cm 6315, para 4.2.

## General Practitioners

General practitioners are independent contractors providing services to the NHS. The complaints process applicable to GPs has tended to focus on breaches of contractual terms of service. Family Health Services Authorities (Family Practitioner Committees[33] prior to the National Health Service and Community Care Act 1990) have been responsible for managing the contracts of GPs and for dealing with complaints. In addition, Local Medical Committees are elected by GPs. Primarily, LMCs are political groupings representing the interests of GPs and providing support to individual practitioners. Originally, LMCs were intended to give GPs a voice in the administration of general practice. However, the role of LMCs has extended beyond this and have acquired a formal statutory role in disciplinary and complaints procedures involving GPs.[34] FPCs (and their successors) were required to consult the LMC on matters affecting the terms of service, complaints and aspects of professional conduct. This duality of roles was not always easy to reconcile; on the one hand the LMC is there to support GPs (the GMC had even recommended that GPs see the LMC as a source of advice), on the other it has a role to ensure that problems with GPs are addressed.[35] One witness who gave evidence to the Ayling Inquiry observed that:

> …from the GP's point of view [LMCs] were almost their friend and counsel in helping them with problems. So in that sense, the Local Medical Committee – you could never be quite sure whether they were thinking of more of the GP's needs or whether the organisational needs were more important.[36]

FPCs were described by one witness to the Shipman Inquiry as 'really just pay and rations organisations'. They lacked responsibility for professional competence or quality of care and had no access to independent medical expertise. There were limited circumstances in which a GP could be removed from the FPC list, when the

---

33 Prior to 1989 FPCs were governed by a 30-member executive board, half of which was drawn from the contractor professions (GPs, dentists, opticians and pharmacists) and the other half were lay members. The GP members were nominated by the LMC. A 1989 White Paper proposed a reduction in FPC membership to 11 and a reduction in the proportion of professional members. In order to distance the FPC from the practitioners for whom it was responsible, the remaining professional members were to be appointed by regional health authorities to act in a personal, rather than a representative, capacity. See the Fifth Report of the Shipman Inquiry, *Safeguarding Patients: Lessons from the Past – Proposals for the Future* (www.the-shipman-inquiry.org.uk).

34 For further discussion, see the Fifth Report of the Shipman Inquiry, *Safeguarding Patients: Lessons from the Past – Proposals for the Future* (www.the-shipman-inquiry.org.uk).

35 The Honourable Mrs Justice Pauffley, *Committee of Inquiry – Independent Investigation into how the NHS Handled Allegations about the Conduct of Clifford Ayling*, 15 July 2004, Cm 6298, paras 4.98–4.102.

36 The Honourable Mrs Justice Pauffley, *Committee of Inquiry – Independent Investigation into how the NHS Handled Allegations about the Conduct of Clifford Ayling*, 15 July 2004, Cm 6298, para 4.101.

GP posed a threat to patients or where standard of practice fell below that which patients could reasonably expect. However, the procedures for implementing such actions were cumbersome and so rarely used. Where an FPC was concerned about a doctor's ability to meet his or her contractual obligations because of physical or mental illness, it could require the doctor to supply a medical report to the LMC. However, it was the LMC which selected the doctor to prepare the report and determine the extent of the investigation. If the report indicated that the doctor was unfit to practise, the LMC had to be further involved before action could be taken. Therefore, in practice it was the LMCs locally and the GMC nationally which assumed responsibility for maintaining professional standards.[37]

The Shipman Inquiry also noted that during much of the period of Shipman's crimes, any (limited) monitoring of GPs was undertaken by the Regional Medical Service. The RMS included medical and administrative staff, headed by divisional medical officers who in turn were supported by regional medical officers. RMOs visited GPs, usually on an annual or bi-annual basis. Such visits tended to be pastoral in nature, although could include elements of inspection, for example, with regard to prescribing. However, that latter element tended to be concerned with cost rather than clinical quality. For instance, RMOs visiting Shipman are unlikely to have detected that he was improperly obtaining opiates. RMOs were also responsible for checking controlled drugs registers and stocks of these drugs. However, if, as in the Shipman case, the GP told the RMO that he did not keep controlled drugs, this was unlikely to be challenged. After changes in 1991, inspection of controlled drugs registers became even less frequent. The Shipman Inquiry reported that in January 2002, from a sample of 59 GP practices that kept stocks of controlled drugs, 31 had not been inspected in the past ten years.[38]

Prior to the 1970s, RMOs would examine clinical records, but this function had ceased by the mid-1960s. The reasons for this are not clear, but the Shipman Inquiry heard evidence which suggested that the most likely reasons included resistance from within the profession to inspection of its records. This is supported by the observation that even though GPs' terms of service have required them to keep adequate medical records and to provide them to the FHSA (later the HA) on request, attempts to apply this met resistance from the profession. As the Shipman Inquiry was told: '[I]f the [Health Authority] had attempted to carry out random inspections of records, the BMA…would have been on our backs immediately.'[39]

If an RMO was concerned about some element of a GP's practice, for instance, inappropriate prescribing or the failure to keep proper medical records, this would be reported to the LMC rather than the FPC. This further reflects the deep-seated

37 The Fifth Report of the Shipman Inquiry, *Safeguarding Patients: Lessons from the Past – Proposals for the Future*, chapter 3 (www.the-shipman-inquiry.org.uk).

38 The Fifth Report of the Shipman Inquiry, *Safeguarding Patients: Lessons from the Past – Proposals for the Future*, para 4.59 (www.the-shipman-inquiry.org.uk).

39 The Fifth Report of the Shipman Inquiry, *Safeguarding Patients: Lessons from the Past – Proposals for the Future*, chapter 3 and paras 4.55 and 4.87 (www.the-shipman-inquiry.org.uk).

assumptions that medical issues should be regulated by the profession itself. In any event, these procedures were infrequently used and when they were used, the ultimate sanction tended to be limited to the withholding of remuneration from the doctor.[40]

Where governments have attempted to improve primary healthcare, for instance, following the 'Promoting Better Health' White Paper in November 1987, this has been done by means of financial incentives, for example, for vaccination and screening, to secure the cooperation of independent contractor GPs.[41] In this respect, it seems that in many ways GPs within the NHS have been seen as any other business, with elements of the *caveat emptor* philosophy which would apply to other consumer services.

In April 1996 new procedures were introduced, following recommendations in the Wilson Report. Complaints and discipline were divided so that a patient complaint against a GP no longer led automatically to the possibility of disciplinary proceedings. The underlying philosophy was that complaints should be treated as opportunities for learning, rather than punishment. The Wilson Report had recommended that all complaints should be handled first by the organization being complained about. All organizations, including GP practices, should have someone who acts as a complaints manager.[42] The second stage would involve, if necessary, an external complaints body and independent review. Such reviews were intended to be informal and non-confrontational. In practice, only a small proportion of requests for independent review were granted, for example, around 22 per cent in the years 1996–2001. Evidence to the Shipman Inquiry suggested that the criteria for allowing progress to stage two were too restricted – including a prohibition on progress if the complainant intended to bring civil proceedings. In terms of those complaints which did reach the second stage, there was a very low satisfaction rating from complainants, around 25 per cent. In contrast, a very high proportion of the staff who were the subject of complaints were very satisfied by the procedures – suggesting a system biased in their favour.[43] If a complainant remained dissatisfied, the third stage of the process offered the potential to refer the matter to the Health Service Ombudsman.[44] These procedures remained in place until the National Health Service (Complaints) Regulations 2004 came into force in July of that year.

---

40 The Fifth Report of the Shipman Inquiry, *Safeguarding Patients: Lessons from the Past – Proposals for the Future*, chapter 3 and paras 4.52–4.53 (www.the-shipman-inquiry.org.uk).

41 The Fifth Report of the Shipman Inquiry, *Safeguarding Patients: Lessons from the Past – Proposals for the Future*, paras 4.28–4.33 (www.the-shipman-inquiry.org.uk).

42 The requirements for GPs to operate these procedures at practice level were implemented by amendment of the GP terms of service in the National Health Service (General Medical Services)

Amendment Regulations 1996.

43 The Fifth Report of the Shipman Inquiry, *Safeguarding Patients: Lessons from the Past – Proposals for the Future*, para 7.27 and 7.54–7.55 (www.the-shipman-inquiry.org.uk).

44 The Ombudsman's powers were extended to cover GPs in 1996.

Experience from both the medical and the solicitors' professions demonstrate that devolving complaints to a local level is frequently ineffective.[45] For example, with respect to the second stage procedures, neither the Independent Review Panel nor the HA had powers to compel compliance by the GP. It is of note that Shipman appointed himself as complaints manager, with his practice nurse as deputy.[46] He was therefore in an ideal position to ensure that complaints which might have unearthed his criminal activities did not progress beyond the first stage. Also, by appointing himself to this role, Shipman no doubt exacerbated the reluctance of patients to complain, for fear that they would undermine their relationship with him or even be removed from the practice list.[47] An additional side effect of the procedures was that the basis of complaints only rarely came to the notice of HAs. GP practices were required to notify the HA annually of the number of complaints, but not their nature. This approach was based upon trust. Shipman, for instance, over a two-year period, appears to have disclosed only one of the three complaints made against him.[48] Only after the coming into force of the National Health Service (Complaints) Regulations 2004 was the position changed, so that the complainant had the option of going direct to the PCT, instead of the practice. The new regulations also extended the categories of potential complainant to include anyone who is affected or likely to be affected by the actions or omissions of the NHS body being complained about.[49] The Shipman Inquiry also received evidence that if individual patient medical records were examined as part of the investigation of a complaint, and these records were found to be inadequate, this would not lead to any wider inspection of the GP's records. GPs' clinical competence continued to be seen as the responsibility of the GMC, rather than being for local resolution:

> [T]he profession provided the best (indeed the only) means of imposing high standards of clinical care and professional conduct on doctors and of monitoring those standards. It was believed that it would do so rigorously. Hence, matters of professional concern arising locally were left to be determined by LMCs with the GMC as the ultimate arbiter of fitness to practise. This belief, which was fostered by the profession, was difficult to challenge in an area involving the need for professional expertise.[50]

---

45 See, for example, Davies, M., 'Regulatory Crisis in the Solicitors' Profession', *Legal Ethics*, 2003, Vol. 6, No. 2, 185—216.

46 The Fifth Report of the Shipman Inquiry, *Safeguarding Patients: Lessons from the Past – Proposals for the Future*, para 7.12 (www.the-shipman-inquiry.org.uk).

47 The Fifth Report of the Shipman Inquiry, *Safeguarding Patients: Lessons from the Past – Proposals for the Future*, para 7.24 (www.the-shipman-inquiry.org.uk).

48 The Fifth Report of the Shipman Inquiry, *Safeguarding Patients: Lessons from the Past – Proposals for the Future*, paras 7.34 (www.the-shipman-inquiry.org.uk).

49 See the Fifth Report of the Shipman Inquiry, *Safeguarding Patients: Lessons from the Past – Proposals for the Future*, paras 7.84–7.87 (www.the-shipman-inquiry.org.uk).

50 The Fifth Report of the Shipman Inquiry, *Safeguarding Patients: Lessons from the Past – Proposals for the Future*, para 4.110 (www.the-shipman-inquiry.org.uk). There was a GP equivalent of the 'three wise men', appointed by the LMC. However, this procedure was informal, lacked a basis in statute and could not enforce compliance by a GP. See para 4.35.

The period in which the Bristol, Ledward and Shipman cases were coming to prominence coincided with the publication in 1997 of the White Paper, 'The New NHS'. This sought major reorganization, with an increased focus on quality of care. Responsibility for ensuring that standards of care were met was to be devolved to professionals and managers at local level. In July 2001 the government announced that responsibility for primary care services, including general practice, was to transfer from health authorities to primary care trusts. The latter came into being in April 2002.[51] The Health Act 1999 required, inter alia, health authorities and PCTs: '...to put and keep in place arrangements for the purpose of monitoring and improving the quality of health care which it provides to individuals.'[52]

Clinical governance, the creation of systems and structures for ensuring quality of care, was to be central to achieving these goals.[53] Each Trust must develop policies for managing risk, improving quality and procedures for staff to report poorly performing colleagues. All hospital doctors will be required to participate in clinical audit, in which his or her performance is reviewed by other doctors.[54] Perhaps the most striking change from the perspective of professional control and self-regulation is the involvement of managers in clinical quality issues. Responsibility for the statutory duty of quality assurance lies ultimately with the chief executive of the relevant NHS body. Other elements of the reforms which threaten the traditional dominance of the medical profession are government setting of *National Service Frameworks* to set standards for particular areas of practice.[55] By setting national standards for best practice, *National Service Frameworks* are likely to lead to uniformity in the care outside of the control of the medical profession. Overall, therefore, legislative changes since 1999 have introduced a notable shift in the focus and source of regulation. Power has been shifted from the professional self-regulatory position to more directly controlled government regulation.[56]

One of the suggested strengths of the new PCTs was local professional leadership. However, the counter argument was that there is likely to be overlap between membership of LMCs and PCTs. This in turn provides the potential for conflict of interest when PCTs are required to consult with LMCs and, in particular, when these bodies are dealing with a complaint about a GP who is a close professional colleague

---

51 At the same time, the 95 existing health authorities were replaced with 28 new health authorities. The latter were subsequently renamed 'Strategic Health Authorities'. See the Fifth Report of the Shipman Inquiry, *Safeguarding Patients: Lessons from the Past – Proposals for the Future*, para 5.8 (www.the-shipman-inquiry.org.uk).

52 Section 18.

53 See the Fifth Report of the Shipman Inquiry, *Safeguarding Patients: Lessons from the Past – Proposals for the Future*, paras 5.5–5.13 (www.the-shipman-inquiry.org.uk).

54 See Department of Health, *A First Class Service*, 1998, HSC 1998/113 3.2–3.27. For further discussion, see Davies, A.C.L., 'Don't Trust Me, I'm a Doctor – Medical Regulation and the 1999 NHS Reforms', *Oxford Journal of Legal Studies*, September 2000, 20(437); and Kennedy, I. and Grubb, A., *Medical Law*, 2000, Butterworths, London, 114–20.

55 Department of Health, *National Service Frameworks*, 1998, HSC 1998/074.

56 Section 18, Health Act 1999.

of a PCT and/or LMC member.[57] It is of note that during his long reign of murderous behaviour, Harold Shipman had been secretary of the LMC and also a member of the Family Practitioner Committee for around seven years. Even after his resignation from these positions in 1988, he would have remained well known to continuing members. It was also recognized that Shipman was able to use these positions to enhance his reputation in the locality and further remove suspicion that he might be anything other than a caring, hardworking GP.[58]

## Alert Letters

An 'alert letter' could be used within the NHS procedures when there was reason to believe a doctor would attempt to find work elsewhere following dismissal or suspension by his or her employer. The letter notified prospective employers to contact the previous employer. However, evidence suggests that these letters were not always used as consistently or as widely as might have been appropriate. For example, when Ledward was suspended in February 1996, the South Kent Hospitals NHS Trust notified local private hospitals and GPs, but no general alert letter was issued – the Trust having received legal advice that this could prejudice the disciplinary proceedings.[59]

## Local versus National

Over-reliance on local procedures, focused in the early stages around the service provider, have the potential to undermine the detection of more serious misconduct. This was illustrated by the evidence to the Shipman Inquiry from Mr John Shaw. Mr Shaw was a self-employed taxi driver, who had previously been a member of the police service. Mr Shaw had become concerned about the deaths of a number of his clients, 19 of whom (out of 21 identified by Mr Shaw), the Shipman Inquiry concluded, Shipman had killed. However, Mr Shaw realized that his suspicions were so incredible that he was unlikely to be believed, especially within the local NHS where Shipman was held in high regard. Mr Shaw also felt unable to go to the police because he had no substantive evidence, and lacked confidence that the GMC (of which it appeared he had a basic knowledge) would take his concerns seriously. Mr Shaw's evidence was that he would have felt able to report his concerns had there been an independent, non-local organization which was unconnected to the medical profession. Such an organization would need to be well-publicized and available for sympathetic advice. This was supported by the conclusions of the Shipman Inquiry:

> Mr Shaw…had valuable information to give – information which, if properly considered and investigated, could have led to Shipman's early detection. It is important that persons

---

57 See the Fifth Report of the Shipman Inquiry, *Safeguarding Patients: Lessons from the Past – Proposals for the Future*, para 5.27 (www.the-shipman-inquiry.org.uk).

58 See the Fifth Report of the Shipman Inquiry, *Safeguarding Patients: Lessons from the Past – Proposals for the Future*, para 6.66 (www.the-shipman-inquiry.org.uk).

59 *The Ledward Report*, Part VII.

such as Mr Shaw should feel able to bring forward any genuine and serious concerns which they may have, secure in the knowledge that those concerns will be objectively and independently examined and that persons airing concerns will not be penalised as a result of their action in voicing them.[60]

A similar desire was expressed by another witness at the Shipman Inquiry, Mrs Dorothy Foley, a home help who was concerned about some of her clients who died at the hands of Shipman. Mrs Foley had not felt able to report her concerns to her manager or otherwise locally. Other witnesses also gave evidence that they would have been unwilling to report concerns locally, but would have welcomed an independent, non-local, well-publicized agency to which they could have expressed concerns.[61]

Such an agency should, of course, already exist in the guise of the GMC. However, as will be illustrated in the subsequent case examples, the Council repeatedly failed to meet these expectations.

## The NHS Complaints Processes – a Viable Competitor of the GMC?

There are a number of reasons why the NHS complaints procedures do not provide an effective alternative to a rigorous self-regulatory system. For instance, the changes introduced in 1996 lacked sufficient independence from the NHS and also were insufficiently integrated when, as often happened, a complaint ranged across more than one healthcare sector.[62] As already noted, there was also significant trust placed in front line providers to operate the first stage of the disciplinary process. Research by the Public Law Project, published in 1999, found that many local procedures were not operated fairly, with inadequate investigations and failure to properly consider the imbalance of power inherent in the doctor–patient relationship. It was also suggested that complaints managers were often defensive with a tendency towards 'collective back-covering'. There was also concern that the separation of complaints and discipline, and the resulting decline in disciplinary proceedings in favour of retraining and other non-punitive measures, gave the impression that doctors were not accountable at local level.[63]

It has also been recognized that the complexity of the complaints process has also deterred their use:

Present NHS procedures for detecting and dealing with poor clinical performance are fragmented and inflexible. There is a strong impression that some doctors who are

60 The Fifth Report of the Shipman Inquiry, *Safeguarding Patients: Lessons from the Past – Proposals for the Future*, para 8.76 (www.the-shipman-inquiry.org.uk). For full discussion of Mr Shaw's evidence, see paras 8.68–8.76.

61 The Fifth Report of the Shipman Inquiry, *Safeguarding Patients: Lessons from the Past – Proposals for the Future*, paras 8.77–8.92 (www.the-shipman-inquiry.org.uk).

62 See Longley, D., 'Complaints after Wilson; Another Case of Too Little Too Late?', *Medical Law Review*, Summer 1997, 5, 172–92.

63 See the Fifth Report of the Shipman Inquiry, *Safeguarding Patients: Lessons from the Past – Proposals for the Future*, paras 7.45–7.50 (www.the-shipman-inquiry.org.uk).

performing poorly are slipping through the net because employers are not willing to use daunting disciplinary procedures, because it is difficult to hold the employee to account or because no adequate procedures exist, because other health professionals are reluctant to report a colleague's problems, or because the systems to detect poor performance or underlying ill health are just not adequate. Nor does it seem that referral to the GMC's new performance procedures has always been made on occasions when perhaps it should have been.[64]

There was also concern that notwithstanding changes to the complaints system, it remained complainant-driven. The onus remained on complainants to pursue their concerns beyond the first stage if they remained dissatisfied, yet evidence to the Shipman Inquiry suggested that many did not do this, even when their allegations raised serious concerns about the doctor.[65] The events leading to complaints tend to be viewed as discrete occurrences. The opportunity to spot early problem doctors or systems failures was therefore lost.[66] Another case which illustrated the failings was that of GP, Dr F. In July 2000, Dr F was convicted of sexual assaults against patients. In August 2001 the Commission for Health Improvement reported the results of its investigation. The CHI found that the NHS complaints system operated in a culture which was insufficiently inquisitive, did not listen to complainants and as a result did not detect misconduct or criminal activity. Concerns about Dr F had been raised 23 times over a 12-year period (1985–1997), both within the NHS and externally to the police and GMC. No effective action had been taken and no cross referencing undertaken or patterns noticed.[67]

The Neale Inquiry Report also recognized that complaints constitute only one, limited, part of the wider quality and risk management matrix. It was noted that relatively few complaints were made against Neale. In light of what became known about Neale, these figures illustrated the restrictions in placing too much significance on complaints statistics as an early warning of poor performance or other problems.[68] These limitations are supported by those sociological studies which have found that patients are reticent regarding making formal complaints about doctors, and that they are more likely to address dissatisfaction 'through gossip and story telling'. Patients who do complain often need to find justification and validation for making a complaint against a doctor. 'It is as if making a complaint at all is breaking a norm of social behaviour and requires a demonstration of moral worth.'[69] This problem is

64 *Supporting Doctors, Protecting Patients*, NHS Consultation Paper, 1999.

65 The Fifth Report of the Shipman Inquiry, *Safeguarding Patients: Lessons from the Past – Proposals for the Future*, para 7.25 (www.the-shipman-inquiry.org.uk).

66 Mulcahy, L., *Disputing Doctors*, 2003, Open University Press, Maidenhead, 135.

67 See the Fifth Report of the Shipman Inquiry, *Safeguarding Patients: Lessons from the Past – Proposals for the Future*, para 7.59–7.60 (www.the-shipman-inquiry.org.uk).

68 Matthews, J., *Committee of Inquiry to Investigate how the NHS Handled Allegations about the Performance and Conduct of Richard Neale*, August 2004, Cm 6315, paras 20.1–20.2.

69 See Allsop, J., 'Two Sides to Every Story: Complainants' and Doctors' Perspectives in Disputes about Medical Care in a General Practice Setting', *Law & Policy*, April 1994, Vol. 16, No. 2, 149–83, at 159 and 162; Stimson, G. and Webb, B., *Going to See the Doctor: The Consultation Process in General Practice*, 1975, Routledge & Kegan Paul, London; Black,

exacerbated when complaints are not always taken seriously, with NHS organizations lacking a proactive approach, neither encouraging nor facilitating complaints.[70] When complainants were willing to take their concerns forward, they could often find that they were poorly served. NHS Trusts often delegated the complaints handling role to junior, administrative, employees, who lacked the status and authority to challenge senior doctors. This was illustrated by the Neale case. The Neale Inquiry suggested that Neale's 'formidable personality' and his 'forceful and overarching control of the department' would have made it difficult for both patients and complaints handling staff to raise concerns about or with him.[71] The Shipman Inquiry recommended that complaints handlers be drawn from at least middle management to ensure that they possessed sufficient authority to undertake the role effectively.

Circular HSG 95(25) allowed an NHS Trust to retire a doctor prematurely on grounds of 'efficiency of the service', where a doctor's performance had declined to unacceptable levels and remedial action was unlikely to be effective.[72] The risk of a problem doctor being quietly removed from his or her employment via the back door, but being free to obtain alternative employment, is ever present with this provision.

## Continuing Failings with the NHS Complaints Process

Nine per cent of NHS investigations were not progressed to conclusion because the staff member dealing with the case left. This, it has been said, is symptomatic of the wider failings of clinical governance. Furthermore, even when cases were pursued to conclusion, there were inadequate mechanisms for sharing information in order to protect patients. In some instances, disciplined doctors were simply able to move area and change employer.[73] Even within a single employing organization, information was not always shared – for instance, a line manager might deal with a complaint locally without involving central management structures or considering the broader implications of a complaint. Similarly, as previously discussed, GP practices have not been obliged to report complaints to their PCT.

Delay in the process was also found to be a problem. The average time for resolution was found to be in the region of seven to eight months, rising to an average

---

D., *The Behavior of Law*, 1976, Academic Press, New York; Lloyd-Bostock, S., 'Attributions and Apologies in Letters of Complaint to Hospitals and Letters of Response', in Harvey, J.H., Orbuch, T.L. and Weber, A.L. (eds), *Attributions, Accounts and Close Relationships*, 1992, Springer-Verlag, New York.

70 Matthews, J., *Committee of Inquiry to Investigate how the NHS Handled Allegations about the Performance and Conduct of Richard Neale*, August 2004, Cm 6315, para 20.4.

71 Matthews, J., *Committee of Inquiry to Investigate how the NHS Handled Allegations about the Performance and Conduct of Richard Neale*, August 2004, Cm 6315, para 20.8.

72 See *Supporting Doctors, Protecting Patients*, NHS Consultation Paper, 1999.

73 In this respect, the use of 'Alert Letters' was found to be inconsistent and so ineffective in many cases. *The Kerr/Haslam Inquiry Report*, July 2005, Cm 6640-1, 631.

17 months when the GMC became involved. In some cases, resolution took up to four years.[74]

The process has also been found to be unnecessarily restrictive about who can complain. The emphasis is upon the complainant having a direct link with the challenged behaviour, rather than the more wide-ranging issue of patient safety. Status takes precedence over knowledge and as a result the message becomes less important than the messenger.[75]

Complaints about primary care pose additional problems. The relative smallness of GP practices means that there will almost inevitably be a limited distance between the member of staff complained about and the person handling the complaint. The recommendation of the Shipman Inquiry was that if the complainant was unhappy about this, she or he should have the choice to refer the matter direct to the PCT. Furthermore, even if the complaint was made to the GP practice, there should be an obligation on the practice to report all complaints to the local PCT. This would enable PCTs to identify trends and take steps to promptly deal with potential risks to patient safety. The Shipman Inquiry also envisaged that PCTs would 'call in' and handle complaints which involved patient safety or quality issues – leaving GPs to handle only those complaints which related to private low level grievances. These proposals were also supported in principle by the Kerr/Haslam Inquiry, although there was concern that the de facto creation of a dual system would undermine the redress function which requires users of the NHS to be able to call staff to account. It was also felt that the distinction made in the Shipman Report between private grievances and clinical government concerns would be far harder to apply in practice than the principle anticipated. For instance, is a complaint about a dusty consultation room a minor private grievance or an indication of wider concerns about hygiene? Is a complaint about rudeness a minor issue, or an indication that a doctor has potentially serious communication problems? In the absence of detailed understanding of the technical aspects of treatment, complainants will often raise issues in areas of familiarity, for instance, 'housekeeping' issues such as cleanliness. Investigations may, however, reveal that the 'real' issues actually relate to clinical concerns.[76]

## The NHS Complaints Process – a Sufficient Alternative to the GMC?

The NHS complaints system has been simplified in recent years, for example, the extension of the role of the Health Service Commissioner to cover both clinical and non-clinical complaints. Similarly, the transfer of procedures for the second stage of the complaints procedure for both primary and secondary care to the Healthcare Commission.[77] However, the NHS system still remains only one part of a complex array of procedures – the approach of a potential complainant differs depending

74 *The Kerr/Haslam Inquiry Report*, July 2005, Cm 6640-1, 632.

75 See, for example, *The Kerr/Haslam Inquiry Report*, July 2005, Cm 6640-1, 661–2.

76 *The Kerr/Haslam Inquiry Report*, July 2005, Cm 6640-1, 712–15.

77 For further discussion, see *The Kerr/Haslam Inquiry Report*, July 2005, Cm 6640-1, 698.

upon whether treatment was NHS or privately funded; the type of practitioner to be complained about; whether the complaint involves allegations of criminal behaviour and the remedy sought. Whilst local NHS procedures are appropriate for minor complaints, the history of these procedures demonstrates that they offer no substitute for an effective, rigorous, proactive self-regulator, when concerns go to the heart of a doctor's suitability to practise. Furthermore, even when evidence came before the NHS procedures that concerns were such that a doctor's registration would be open to question, communication between NHS bodies and the GMC has proven to be poor.[78] Examples of these failings are illustrated in the subsequent case study chapters. In this context, the GMC remains a fundamentally important body as the central registrant of all practising doctors.

78 See, for example, *Report of the Committee of Inquiry into the Regulation of the Medical Profession*, 1975, Cmnd 6018, HMSO, London, Paragraph 230.

# PART II
# Cases

The following chapters discuss case studies which demonstrate that the GMC's failings have been widespread. In each case misconduct was ongoing for many years without any meaningful action on the part of the GMC. The first case relates to the Bristol Royal Infirmary, an account of predominantly well-intentioned but ultimately ineffective doctors. The next case considers Rodney Ledward, a hospital consultant who showed a reckless disregard for the well-being of his patients. The cases of William Kerr and Michael Haslam, two senior consultant psychiatrists, provide examples of serious abuse against patients perpetrated over many years. The Clifford Ayling case also involved prolonged abuse of patients, from both a general practice and a hospital setting. In all three of the Kerr, Haslam and Ayling cases, the GMC only took an interest after criminal charges were brought. The Richard Neale case involved a hospital consultant who was appointed to a senior NHS post, despite having been disciplined and his name erased from the medical register in Canada. The final case, that of Harold Shipman, demonstrates that a general practitioner was able to murder over 200 patients during the course of his practice over a period of 20 years or more. During this time no suspicions appear to have been aroused on the part of the GMC.

# Chapter 7

# The Bristol Royal Infirmary

## Introduction

Past President of the GMC, Sir Donald Irvine, described the events at Bristol as triggering huge changes in the regulation of doctors, and provoking significant development of a new professionalism for medicine.[1] The Bristol case demonstrates that NHS procedures were wholly inadequate to deal with senior consultants, some of whom were also holders of senior managerial office. The GMC should have been the significant external power, able to deal with the doctors free from any inhibiting issues arising from seniority or status. However, during the critical period the Council failed in this respect – it was either unwilling or incapable of acting to protect the public.

The Bristol Inquiry was established in 1996 following concerns about paediatric cardiac surgery at the Bristol Royal Infirmary in the period 1984 to 1995. The Inquiry found that in 30 per cent of cases children received 'less than adequate' care and in around 9 per cent of cases this may have affected the outcome. Between 160 and 170 children suffered because of this. Between 1991 and 1995, between 30 and 35 children died. Others were left with brain damage or permanent health problems. Between 1988 and 1995, the mortality rate at Bristol was double that of other hospitals performing paediatric cardiac surgery. The Inquiry was unable, largely because of the unreliability of hospital records, to determine how many of the children who died at Bristol would have survived had they been operated on elsewhere.

The Inquiry was critical of a wide range of participants: surgeons, hospital managers and a former President of the Royal College of Surgeons. The report also condemned the club culture and an unwillingness to accept criticism – if a member of staff was not in the club, it was very difficult to air concerns and to be heard. These factors allowed poor surgical standards to go unchecked for many years.

## Key Participants in the Bristol Case

Mr James Wisheart was a senior cardiac surgeon and also Medical Director from 1992 to 1995. He was also at times the Associate Clinical Director for Cardiac Surgery

---

1 Irvine, D., *The Doctors' Tale*, 2003, Radcliffe Medical Press, Oxford, 2.

and Chair of the Clinical Audit Committee. Mr Janardan Dhasmana was a cardiac surgeon and Associate Clinical Director from 1992 to 1995. Dr John Roylance was Chief Executive of the NHS Trust.

## The Background to the Bristol Case

In the early 1980s, the Department of Health and Social Security decided to create Supra Regional Services, concentrating resources and expertise. Paediatric cardiac surgery was one of the services so categorized and in 1984 the Bristol Royal Infirmary was made one of the nine designated centres.[2]

There were early warning signs about potential problems. For instance, in October 1986, Professor Andrew Henderson, from the University of Wales, distributed a letter at a meeting of the South Glamorgan Health Authority which stated: '[I]t is no secret that…[the Bristol paediatric cardiac] surgical service is regarded as being at the bottom of the UK league for quality.'[3]

By the late 1980s, concerns were being increasingly expressed about the Bristol Unit from a range of sources. But only in 1995, after an operation performed on Joshua Loveday, was action finally taken. In 1998 two cardiac surgeons, Mr James Wisheart and Mr Janardan Dhasmana, and the Chief Executive of the Trust, Dr John Roylance were found guilty by the GMC of serious professional misconduct. Dr Roylance and Mr Wisheart had their names erased from the medical register. Mr Dhasmana was allowed to remain in practice, but the condition that he should not operate on children was imposed on his registration for a period of three years.

In June 1998 the Secretary of State for Health announced the establishment of an Inquiry. The Terms of Reference were:

> To inquire into the management of the care of children receiving complex cardiac surgical services at the Bristol Royal Infirmary between 1984 and 1995 and relevant related issues; to make findings as to the adequacy of the services provided; to establish what action was taken both within and outside the hospital to deal with concerns raised about the surgery and to identify any failure to take appropriate action promptly; to reach conclusions from these events and to make recommendations which could help to secure high quality care across the NHS.[4]

The Inquiry was, therefore, wide-ranging in its remit. The following discussion considers those aspects of the events at Bristol which have relevance to the work of the GMC.

---

2 Kennedy, I.M., *The Inquiry into the Management of Care of Children Receiving Complex Heart Surgery at The Bristol Royal Infirmary* (www.bristol-inquiry.org.uk), (hereafter 'The Bristol Report'), para 24.

3 The Bristol Report, para 134.

4 The Bristol Report, para 26.

## The Introduction of General Management

In February 1983 the Secretary of State for Health and Social Security set up an inquiry into management in the NHS. The inquiry team, headed by Roy Griffiths, concluded that the NHS had no coherent system of local management. Clinical practice and the effectiveness of clinical interventions were not subject to effective evaluation. The Griffiths Inquiry determined that a crucial element was the need to involve doctors, particularly senior doctors, in day-to-day management. After a number of unsuccessful models were tried, clinical services were organized into directorates, each having a clinical director or lead consultant. The relationship between the clinical director and medical colleagues was one which involved negotiation and persuasion, rather than line management. In turn, the clinical director had a similar relationship with the unit general manager.[5]

Dr John Roylance was appointed as District General Manager of the Bristol & Weston District Health Authority with effect from 1 April 1985.[6] Dr Roylance had significant influence on the delivery of health services in the region, being budget-holder and bearing responsibility for the development of policies and for monitoring their implementation. There were also four advisory committees to support the general managers at both unit and district level.

In 1989 clinical directorates began to be introduced, semi-autonomous units based on a medical specialty or group of specialties. Each was managed by a clinical director, a consultant and a general manager. Clinical directors were responsible for formulating policy and general managers for implementing it. As the system evolved, the clinical directors reported to the district general manager (the chief executive after the adoption of Trust status).

On 1 April 1991 the UBHT came into existence, with Dr Roylance as Chief Executive. The clinical directorates remained in place. The approach taken by Dr Roylance was that clinical directors would be in charge of the doctors and the general manager would be responsible for ensuring that support services were in place to allow the directorate to run effectively. The Bristol Inquiry was told that Dr Roylance was known for saying 'don't give me your problems, give me your solutions' and that responsibility for issues was pushed back to the directorates. Furthermore, it was said that the management style of Dr Roylance tended towards what was described as a 'club culture', 'to which you either belonged or not'. Dr Roylance, it was said, also believed that healthcare in the hospital was led by consultants and that they were 'self-teaching' and 'self-correcting'. Managers should not interfere with this, indeed he said that this was 'impossible'. Only clinicians were equipped to recognize defects in the performance of other clinicians. Excessive delegation was in itself problematic, but was compounded by the significant concentration of power amongst a few managers at Bristol. Dr Roylance was said to have used his power to appoint other managers in accordance with whether someone would 'fit' within

5 The Bristol Report, paras 52–3.

6 At the time, the appointment of a doctor to this role was unusual, only 15 out of 188 District General Managers in 1986 having a medical background.

the 'club', rather than performance. Reflexivity and honest self-assessment were unlikely to be fostered within this climate.[7]

James Wisheart was a consultant in cardiac and thoracic surgery at the United Bristol NHS Trust. He was also Chair of the Hospital Medical Committee between 1992 and 1994, Associate Clinical Director of Cardiothoracic Surgery between October 1990 and December 1993 and Medical Director between April 1992 and 1996. The Bristol Inquiry observed that Mr Wisheart carried out a range of procedures on babies, with a mortality rate of between 45 and 100 per cent.

As well as his clinical duties, Mr Wisheart held the position of Medical Director of the UBHT from 1992 to 1995. This involved advising the Chief Executive and Trust Board on medical issues. One of the effects of this was that Mr Wisheart was one, (even two)[8] of the 'three wise men'. Mr Wisheart was also the Associate Clinical Director for Cardiac Surgery from 1990 to 1992 and Chair of the Clinical Audit Committee for six months from July 1994. Mr Dhasmana succeeded as Associate Clinical Director from 1992 to 1995.

Janardan Dhasmana was appointed as a consultant cardiothoracic surgeon in 1986 and worked in the unit led by James Wisheart. He undertook various surgical procedures on babies. It is of note that with respect to one such procedure, the atrio ventricular septal defect correction operation, his mortality rate of 10 per cent was better than the national average. However, he also undertook operations on babies with transposition of the great vessel, requiring an arterial switch operation. The Bristol Inquiry noted that Mr Dhasmana's mortality rate for this procedure was over 50 per cent. Of the 38 operations he carried out between 1988 and 1995, 20 patients died. Nationally, the mortality rate was in the region of 10–20 per cent.

## Responsibility for the Quality of Clinical Care

In the period 1984–1995, responsibility for the quality of clinical care was seen as lying with healthcare professionals. Professional status, education and training were the most important criteria for determining standards. There were no set standards beyond this, applying to healthcare professionals as a team or within the NHS as a whole. At the national level, the focus was upon the effective use of resources and numbers of patients treated. Quality of care was low on the political agenda – it was simply assumed that care would be good.[9]

There was no requirement that hospital consultants kept their skills and knowledge up to date, and surgeons could introduce new techniques without any system of permission or even notification. Management within the NHS reflected this prevailing attitude – managers ventured very reluctantly into issues of clinical care. Even within government, clinical performance was traditionally thought of as

---

7 The Bristol Report, para 201. For instance, in 1992 Mr Wisheart was simultaneously Medical Director, a Clinical Director and Chair of the Hospital Medical Committee.

8 Two, because for a period of time the positions of Medical Director and Chair of the HMC were held by the same person. It was eventually recognized that this was too much for one person, so Mr Wisheart relinquished the HMC role in 1994.

9 The Bristol Report, paras 74–7.

being within the exclusive domain of the medical profession. The Inquiry concluded that clinical audit, the periodic review of practice to consider what worked well and what did not, had a long informal history as a means to improve the care of patients. However, it was voluntary, unstructured and was confined within professional boundaries – doctors only being audited by fellow doctors.

Detailed plans for a system of medical audit were included in the Government White Paper *Working for Patients: Medical Audit Working Paper No. 6*. Regional and district health authorities were asked to develop audit strategies. However, the presumption remained that audit should remain within the preserve of healthcare professionals, insulated from management, and should be voluntary and confidential within the professional group. Audit was to be educational, rather than a systematic mechanism for identifying problems and for ensuring professional accountability.[10] Managers were often careful to ensure that doctors understood this, fearing a backlash if doctors believed that audit was going to be used as a management tool. This was reflected in the 1992 Annual Report of audit activity at the UBHT, which stated that medical audit: '…must continue to be seen to be a confidential and independent educational process…'. Between 1991 and 1995, funds for audit activities were allocated directly from the Region to the consultant medical staff. It was, therefore, for each medical specialty to determine audit topics and the arrangement of audits. Managers had no control over the funds, nor were they able to monitor how they were used. The Inquiry heard from the Regional General Manager, South West Regional Health Authority (SWRHA), that in the late 1980s there was no reliable information regarding clinical outcomes for patients. As she put it: '…at that time, you did not know when people left hospital whether they were dead or alive.'[11]

Therefore, notwithstanding the growth of audit and other initiatives directed at improving quality, the Bristol Inquiry concluded that the dominant paradigm remained one in which each individual medical professional was left to determine what was an acceptable standard of clinical care. Sir Alan Langlands, Chief Executive of the NHS Executive between 1994 and 2000, described the position after the establishment of Trusts as one which relied upon a combination of professional self-regulation, audit and a 'rudimentary' internal market. There was no guarantee that any of these elements would identify or respond to issues of clinical performance.[12]

The recommendation of the Bristol Inquiry was that, in future, all healthcare professionals should have a contractual duty to undergo appraisal, continuing professional development and revalidation to ensure that they remain competent.

## Bristol Clinicians' Self-Monitoring of Paediatric Cardiac Surgery

Mr Wisheart gave evidence that, in order to monitor his own performance, he kept a record, including the procedure and outcome, of the open-heart operations he performed from 1975 until the end of his career. Similarly, Mr Dhasmana said that he kept a log which allowed him to undertake a personal audit and to recognize any

10 The Bristol Report, paras 74–7.

11 The Bristol Report, para 80.

12 The Bristol Report, para 78.

problems at an early stage.[13] The surgeons also had access to statistics relating to paediatric cardiac surgery at other centres, which allowed them to compare their own performance.[14]

Mr Wisheart also told the Inquiry that an audit of cardiac surgery was instituted formally in 1990–91, with reviews focusing on individual cases. Regular departmental audit meetings also began in 1990. These built upon informal meetings which were held at the homes of consultants from the early to mid-1980s. These were described as 'multi-disciplinary' in nature, including cardiologists, surgeons, anaesthetists, radiologists and pathologists.[15]

The Inquiry recognized that paediatric cardiac surgery involved more than just the consultants undertaking the operation. A bed in the Intensive Care Unit, nursing staff, theatre technicians and a paediatric cardiac anaesthetist all had to be coordinated. At Bristol, paediatric cardiac surgery and aftercare was provided on two sites. The operation would be carried out in an operating theatre and then the child was transferred to the ICU two floors above, and often after this was returned to a ward in a different building.[16]

## The Raising of Concerns

The Bristol Inquiry emphasized that 'concerns' were more than expressions of opinion that the provision of care could be improved. Rather, in common with the approach taken by the courts in clinical negligence cases, a practice was only to be considered unacceptable 'when reasonably competent practitioners in this specialist area would advise that it exposes the patient to risks beyond those ordinarily to be expected…'.[17]

Dr Stephen Bolsin, a consultant anaesthetist appointed to Bristol in September 1988, became concerned about the performance of open-heart surgery. In particular, operations seemed to take significantly longer than they should have done, and as a result the children were on bypass for longer. Soon after his appointment, Dr Bolsin raised the matter as a clinical problem, speaking first with senior anaesthetist colleagues, Professor B1 and then the Chairman of the Division of Anaesthesia, Dr B2. Dr Bolsin first began to collect data about the performance of paediatric cardiac surgery in 1989.[18] Dr Bolsin told the Inquiry that in August 1990 he wrote to Dr Roylance expressing concerns about what, in his interpretation, was a misleading

13 The Bristol Report, paras 90—91.

14 The Bristol Report, para 93.

15 The Bristol Report, para 96.

16 The Bristol Report, paras 115–18.

17 The Bristol Report, para 131.

18 The mortality rate for PCS in the under-1s in Bristol for 1988 was 37.9 per cent, and 27 per cent for the period 1984–87. National figures for 1984–87 were 22 per cent. For 1989–90 the mortality rate at Bristol was 37.5 per cent, whilst the UK figure was 18.8 per cent. Even though annual figures might not be reflective, because of the small numbers involved, a consistent pattern of poor outcome emerges, when compared with the national average when figures covering a number of years were aggregated.

entry in the application for Trust status. In this letter, he also referred to mortality for open-heart surgery for under-1s as: 'one of the highest in the country' and said that he considered that this needed to be addressed.[19] In 1991 he discussed his findings with Professor B1 and was advised to collect more data before drawing conclusions.[20] Professor B1 did agree to speak informally with Dr Roylance. Also in 1991, Dr Bolsin produced minutes of a meeting held jointly between the cardiologists, cardiac surgeons and anaesthetists on 28 July 1991. He described the mortality rate as 'reaching crisis proportions'. Dr Bolsin said that he was rebuked and told that the minutes were unrepresentative, would not be circulated and that he should not keep minutes again.[21] In 1992 Dr Bolsin again saw Professor B1 with further data, but was advised to continue collecting. During this time, Dr Bolsin was making his concerns known to a widening group of colleagues, including the production in spring 1993 of a report, *Analysis of Paediatric Cardiac Mortality Data from UBHT 1990–92.*[22]

Dr Bolsin gave evidence that Mr Wisheart had rebuked him for raising issues with 'outsiders', a category within which he included Dr Roylance. In his evidence to the Bristol Inquiry, Mr Wisheart denied that this meeting took place. Another colleague, Dr B2, confirmed that Mr Wisheart had been annoyed by the letter distributed by Dr Bolsin and Dr B2 also confirmed that: 'No one supported the way in which Steve Bolsin had raised the issue but all were fully supportive of his efforts to obtain appropriate data…in an endeavour to improve results.'[23] 'Improve results' is the key term – that fellow doctors appeared to be trying their best was more important than the actual outcomes.

Towards the end of 1991, Dr Bolsin's views came to the attention of colleagues in anaesthesia outside of the UBHT (notably in Southampton and the Frenchay Hospital in Bristol). In spring 1992, Dr Bolsin spoke with the General Manager of the Directorate of Surgery. In April 1992, Dr Bolsin expressed concerns to a trainee GP who had also worked as a junior doctor at Bristol, Dr Phil Hammond. Dr Hammond subsequently wrote articles in the magazine *Private Eye*, raising his concerns. He wrote in 1992 of the unusually high mortality rate at Bristol, and that within the profession, from as early as 1988, the paediatric cardiac unit was dubbed 'The Killing Fields'. Neither the Department of Health nor the GMC took any action. He wrote a further article in the same year, highlighting that a mortality rate of 30 per cent at Bristol compared with 3 per cent elsewhere.[24] Hammond recorded that he was

---

19 The Bristol Report, para 137. Whilst Dr Bolsin was clear in his evidence to the Inquiry that he intended in this letter to raise concerns about paediatric cardiac surgery with the expectation of action being taken, Dr Roylance said that he had not interpreted the letter in this way. A similar response was received from Mr Dean Hart, Chair of the Hospital Medical Committee (HMC), to whom a copy of the letter was also sent.

20 In 1991 Dr Bolsin was elected the first National Audit Co-ordinator for the Association of Cardiothoracic Anaesthetists of Great Britain. His responsibilities included the collation of data on outcomes in cardiac surgery on adults.

21 The Bristol Report, paras 138–9.

22 The Bristol Report, paras 94–5, 136 and 140.

23 The Bristol Report, para 138.

24 Actual figures cited by the Bristol Report were a mortality rate for open heart surgery on the under-1s of 30 per cent at Bristol in 1991, compared with a national average in 1990 of

later told by a manager at Bristol that the articles were dismissed as scandal and that Wisheart's account was believed.[25] These articles did bring to a head concerns on the part of the President of the Royal College of Surgeons for England, who decided to reconsider the Bristol mortality data. This data showed that performance at Bristol was worse than that of any other centre.[26] However, a distinction was drawn between the role of the Royal Colleges in assessing suitability for training, and any role in assessing quality of care. The Royal Colleges were therefore seen as very poorly equipped to identify areas of concern or to respond to concerns brought to their attention.[27] It appears that only after Bristol were the Royal Colleges motivated to act with any vigour, focusing on clinical governance and the defining and assessing of core areas of practice.[28]

In 1993 Dr Bolsin repeated his concerns to other cardiac surgeons at Bristol, including Professor B3, head of the new Directorate of Cardiac Services. Later in1993, Dr Bolsin showed statistics on outcomes in open-heart PCS to Mr B4, a senior lecturer in Cardiac Surgery and consultant cardiothoracic surgeon. Mr B4 said that he found this information 'disturbing' and was also aware that concerns were shared by senior colleagues such as Professor B5, Professor B1, Professor B6 and Dr B7. Dr B7, the anaesthetists' clinical director, told the Inquiry that he saw the data, but did not follow it up at the time with Mr Wisheart or Mr Dhasmana because the statistics 'were not verified'.[29] Later, Dr B7 did make attempts to bring concerns to the attention of Dr Roylance and Mr Wisheart, without success. In March 1994, Dr B7 and Professor B5 invited Mr Wisheart and Dr Bolsin to an informal dinner, to facilitate an open discussion. The Inquiry noted that the dinner represented 'in microcosm the inability of these colleagues to communicate on the questions at issue, and the conversation turned to football'.[30]

After the problems at Bristol were eventually acted upon, Dr Bolsin noted that: 'My problem was that the person I was complaining about, James Wisheart, was medical director and chair of the hospital medical committee, which meant he himself was two of the three wise men. It was completely inappropriate.'[31]

Two operating theatre sisters, Ms B8 and Mrs B9, also gave evidence that by 1992 they had concerns about mortality rates and discussed the matter with Dr Bolsin. However, the Inquiry concluded that the hierarchical system within medical practice made it difficult for the nursing staff to raise concerns and to be heard if they did try to do this. Ultimately, the two theatre sisters refused to scrub in for neonatal Switch operations performed by Mr Dhasmana.[32]

---

under 16 per cent. The Bristol Report, para 140.

25 See *Private Eye*, issue 793, 8 May 1992; *Private Eye*, issue 797, 3 July 1992; Hammond, P. and Mosley, M., *Trust Me I'm A Doctor*, 2002, Metro Publishing, London, 56.

26 The Bristol Report, paras 141–2.

27 The Bristol Report, paras 158–9.

28 Irvine, D., *The Doctors' Tale*, 2003, Radcliffe Medical Press, Oxford, 200.

29 The Bristol Report, para 144.

30 The Bristol Report, para 173.

31 See *Health Service Journal*, 27 August 1998, Features; and Hammond, P. and Mosley, M., *Trust Me I'm A Doctor*, 2002, Metro Publishing, London, 54–7.

32 The Bristol Report, paras 143, 175 and 214.

On 19 July 1994, Dr B10, Senior Medical Officer at the DoH, was present at an audit meeting at the BRI. As he left, Dr Bolsin gave him an envelope containing data about PCS. Dr B10 gave evidence to the Inquiry that he did not look at the data, but wrote to Professor B5 notifying him that concerns had been expressed about mortality rates in PCS and requesting confirmation that action was being taken to deal with the problem.[33] The Inquiry were critical that Dr B10 did not look at the data himself:

> Dr [B10] was inappropriately reluctant to get engaged in what he saw as a dispute between doctors. It is true that, ordinarily, the DoH sought not to become involved in local clinical issues, taking the view that such matters are best dealt with locally. But this situation was different. Dr [B10], by not looking at Dr Bolsin's data, simply chose not to have to make a decision.[34]

The Inquiry noted that the difficulties Dr Bolsin encountered revealed both the territorial loyalties and boundaries within medical practice, and also the power and influence of senior practitioners. Dr Bolsin's efforts were criticized by his colleagues, and appear to have antagonized senior managers and clinicians. The Inquiry also noted that Dr Bolsin was not alone in encountering difficulty in approaching senior colleagues. For example, it was suggested that when Professors B5 and B6 attempted to raise concerns with Mr Wisheart in December 1993, the latter spoke to them 'like a couple of schoolboys'.[35] Inappropriate hierarchies, it seems, were able to inhibit action at any appropriate level.

## The Final Crisis

In early 1995 Mr Dhasmana was due to perform a Switch operation on 18-month-old Joshua Loveday. On 6 January, Professor B5 sought to persuade Mr Wisheart that it would be unwise to proceed. After consulting Dr Roylance, Dr B10, Dr B11 and Professor B6, Professor B5 put this advice in writing to Mr Wisheart on 10 January.

At a clinical meeting on 11 January, Dr B12, Dr B13, Dr B14, Mr Dhasmana, Mr Wisheart, Dr B15, Dr B7, Dr Bolsin and Dr B16 all considered whether to proceed with the operation on Joshua Loveday. All agreed that there were no clinical obstacles to the operation, as Mr Dhasmana's non-neonatal Switch results were within the acceptable range. Dr Bolsin dissented on non-clinical grounds. Joshua Loveday died following surgery and Dr B10 wrote to Dr Roylance stating that 'it would be extremely inadvisable to undertake any further neonatal or infant cardiac surgery'.[36]

33 The Bristol Report, para 148.

34 The Bristol Report, para 157.

35 The Bristol Report, para 161.

36 The Bristol Report, para 150.

## The Three Wise Men

External bodies such as the Royal Colleges said that they considered that responsibility for monitoring quality of care rested locally in Bristol or centrally in the DoH. An obvious potential local step would have been to engage the 'three wise men' procedures. Dr Bolsin did not follow this route. The Inquiry did not find this surprising, noting that this approach was perceived as being directed principally at individual clinicians who were experiencing problems, such as ill health. As already noted, an issue of even greater significance at Bristol was that one of the senior surgeons giving rise to concerns, Mr Wisheart, at times held two of the three management positions from which the 'wise men' were drawn.

## Self-Delusion?

Mr Wisheart consistently explained away poor results as being due to the poor condition of the patients. Mr B4 gave evidence that the culture was one:

> of explaining or justifying...mediocre or poor results on the basis of case severity rather than directing attention to producing better results…[I]f you are confronted with a result which is not very good, then there are two responses...either...'the results are not very good and they should be better, we must be doing something wrong, we have to get this right and improve things', or...'actually the results are not very good but it is because they are bad patients...and we are doing our best'.[37]

The lack of appropriate discussion was exacerbated by medical hierarchies, notably an uncomfortable relationship between anaesthetists and surgeons. A senior surgeon such as Mr Wisheart would not readily accept criticism from an anaesthetist. Senior clinicians appeared to adopt the view that the behaviour of younger consultants in anaesthetics and cardiology was not always 'appropriate' – they were insufficiently deferential and unduly willing to question senior colleagues. The mindset among senior managers was that clinicians such as Mr Wisheart could be trusted to get on with things without oversight, and could be trusted to inform other senior managers if they encountered problems. The Inquiry described the relationship amongst senior managers as having the nature of a 'club culture', 'to which one belonged or from which one was excluded'.[38] As a result, legitimate concerns from those outside of the 'club' could easily go unheard. Bristol lacked effective systems for addressing concerns and the management environment inhibited 'speaking out'.

Only Mr Dhasmana showed willingness to seek training and to withdraw from a procedure until his skills improved. Mr Dhasmana recognized that there were problems with the neonatal Switch procedure, after the deaths of five babies. He stopped using the procedure in September 1992 and sought advice from a senior consultant paediatric cardiac surgeon at Birmingham Children's Hospital. Dhasmana

37 The Inquiry noted that its Clinical Case Note Review carried out in 1999 did not reveal serious problems in surgical technique, rather the problems were due to the overall organization of care. Mr Wisheart should have realized this. The Bristol Report, para 164.

38 The Bristol Report, paras 164–5.

discussed and observed an operation and took away the video for further study. He went to Birmingham again for training in July 1993.[39] However, the Inquiry concluded that when matters had not improved sufficiently, Mr Dhasmana should have demonstrated greater foresight, and realized that Joshua's parents would have wished to know the full picture, including details of the meeting between the senior clinicians.

## The Actions of Dr Roylance

The Inquiry heard that Dr Roylance relied on Mr Wisheart to advise him whenever an issue regarding paediatric cardiac surgery arose. Dr Roylance did not obtain a second opinion, notwithstanding Mr Wisheart's obvious potential for conflict of interest. As the Inquiry noted: 'Dr Roylance did not agree to a review of the PCS service until December 1994...[T]his was excessively late. Furthermore, it was not appropriate in the circumstances to ask Mr Wisheart to organise the review.'[40]

Dr Roylance adopted a management style which the Inquiry categorized as 'wilful blindness', insisting that clinicians solved problems for themselves. This management style was inflexible, even when patient safety was drawn into question. He lacked awareness of the potential problems this created, notably with respect to effective communication. One result of this stance was that he refused to engage with the issues raised by the anaesthetists. Dr Roylance was also blind to the problems generated by the concentration of power in the hands of a small elite group within the hospital.[41]

Notwithstanding the criticism of Dr Roylance, the Bristol Inquiry concluded that a doctor in a senior management position should not automatically assume responsibility for the care individually of each patient admitted to the Hospital Trust. Becoming involved in senior management, to the exclusion of clinical practice, should allow the medical practitioner to put aside his or her duty to any particular patient and take up managerial responsibility on behalf of the collective patient body. In this respect, the opinion of the Inquiry differed from that eventually taken by the GMC and the Privy Council in *Roylance v GMC*.[42]

## Mr Wisheart as Medical and Clinical Director

The Bristol Inquiry concluded that as a senior member of the surgical team, Mr Wisheart was too close to be an objective manager and director. It was unsurprising that his reactions were ones of denial and inaction. The Inquiry concluded that he lacked the insight to appreciate the inherent conflicts of interest he faced. He preferred to believe that things were improving. He combined this with the self-persuasion that plausible explanations existed for the poor results, to the limited extent that he

39 The Bristol Report, para 144.

40 The Bristol Report, para 166.

41 The Bristol Report, paras 167–8.

42 [1999] 3 WLR 541.

accepted that the results were in fact poor.[43] Mr Wisheart's management style, it was said, lacked leadership and a team-based approach. The view of some colleagues was that his style of management was 'autocratic' and that he was part of the 'club culture' which fostered a sense of 'them and us'. As a result, junior colleagues in particular were unlikely to feel able to approach Mr Wisheart with concerns.[44] The Inquiry was critical of Wisheart for apparently misleading the Trust Board about the outcomes in paediatric cardiac surgery. It was also a serious error of judgement not to inform the extraordinary meeting, called to discuss the care of Joshua Loveday, that Dr Roylance had considered commissioning an independent review of the PCS service. Had he done so, the clinicians at the meeting would almost certainly have had to postpone the surgery.

## Clinicians in Managerial Positions

The Bristol Inquiry noted that insufficient thought had been given to the skills and training needed for senior clinicians to be effective managers. Traditions within medicine, clinical protocols and loyalties may all have impinged on effective management. Mr Wisheart may have thought it inappropriate to intervene in Mr Dhasmana's decision to operate on Joshua Loveday, because of the tradition that one consultant should not interfere in the clinical judgement of another. However, as Medical Director, Mr Wisheart had a duty to interfere.[45] Overall, too much power was concentrated in the hands of too few people. There was an absence of agreement about what was meant by 'high-quality care', or who held responsibility for ensuring that it was provided. If concerns arose about the competence of a consultant, the systems to address this, such as they were, relied upon insight and cooperation from the person involved.[46] The GMC was notable by its absence. Having permitted, even fostered, loyalty within the profession to the exclusion of the wider public, the Council had taken no steps through its education or disciplinary functions to ensure that attitudes within the profession met the requirements of modern management within complex organizations.

## Adequacy of Care

The Inquiry conclusions emphasized that the events at Bristol did not involve bad or uncaring people, let alone people who wilfully harmed patients. Rather, the problems arose because people failed to work together effectively, lacked insight, were poor leaders or were poorly led. An imbalance of power, with too much control in the hands of a few individuals, added to the problems. Care was further compromised because PCS was split between two sites, had no dedicated specialist nurses, no dedicated paediatric intensive care beds and had no full-time paediatric cardiac

43 The Bristol Report, para 168.
44 The Bristol Report, para 169.
45 The Bristol Report, para 171.
46 The Bristol Report, para 176.

surgeon.[47] However, inadequacies in resources was shared elsewhere within the NHS, at centres which did not experience the high complication and mortality rates seen at Bristol. For example, shortages of nurses and cardiologists was identified as a national problem. In this respect, what went wrong at Bristol was not *caused* by an absence of resources.

The Bristol Inquiry was critical of the traditional ideas which assumed that when something goes wrong, this is caused by the people directly involved. Thus, if a patient suffers harm during surgery, the likely presumption is that the surgeon is at fault. This approach ignores the fact that individuals work within systems. Simply seeking to blame and punish individuals, without addressing any systemic issues, 'virtually guarantees that the error will be repeated'. 'Learning from error, rather than seeking someone to blame, must be the priority in order to improve safety and quality.' The Inquiry adopted what it called the 'human factors' approach – the study of the interrelationships between people, their environment and the tools they use. Errors and poor performance are seen as resulting from systems which are not operating well. This was seen as offering a more sophisticated and comprehensive approach to causation than the 'person-focused' approach. The performance of individuals is not ignored, but is included within a much wider contextual setting.

Systems analysis divides failure into two types: active and latent. Active failures, for example, lapses and mistakes, are the obvious types of event which are closely and directly connected to the error. A typical example would be leaving a surgical instrument in a patient during an operation. Systems analysis would see the active failure as needing to be combined with latent factors to ensure a full picture of causation. For example, what effect might communication systems within the operating theatre, working hours of staff or the overall morale of the team have had on the likelihood of a surgical instrument being left in the patient?[48] However, for the purposes of the Bristol case, it is important not to lose sight of the fact that the systems in question were operated by powerful, highly educated people with the capacity to change things, or at least to forcefully raise objections. For example, a sales rep may feel the need to exceed the speed limit when driving between appointments in order to meet demanding targets. It may be argued that the 'system' is compelling this dangerous behaviour, yet this is only likely to change if individuals – from the rep through to his employers – face the prospect of individual blame.

## A Lack of Interest by the Department of Health in the Monitoring of Quality

The Department of Health regarded issues of quality and performance of clinical services as matters to be addressed locally. Sir Alan Langlands, Chief Executive, NHS Executive between 1994 and 2000, gave evidence to the Bristol Inquiry that the DoH relied on professional self-regulation, audit and an internal market where contractual obligations could provide some control. Thus in the Bristol case, the DoH failed to respond when an issue regarding quality of care was brought to its

47 The Bristol Report, paras 178–9.

48 The Bristol Report, para 183.

attention. The assumption was that the problem would be addressed elsewhere, an assumption which, unfortunately, was shared by others who also could have acted but did not.[49] The Bristol Inquiry summarized the problem as a lack of 'any real system whereby any organisation took responsibility for what a layperson would describe as "keeping an eye on things"...We cannot say that the external system for assuring and monitoring the quality of care was inadequate. There was, in truth, no such system.'[50]

For instance, the Royal College of Surgeons of England inspected the training of potential surgeons working in teaching hospitals. These visits were intended to confirm the adequacy of training and the ongoing suitability of the hospital. The RCSE was 'anxious to make it clear that they did not have responsibility for assessing or monitoring the quality of the care provided at the hospitals which were visited'. After the events at Bristol it was recognized that the quality of surgery would affect the quality of training, but it seems that this was not apparent at the time. Similar sentiments were expressed by Professor David Baum, then President of the Royal College of Paediatrics and Child Health, who told the Inquiry: 'It was not a part of the mindset of the time to inquire into the quality of surgical outcomes.'[51]

It was of particular concern that on two separate occasions when the BRI was inspected by representatives of the Royal College of Surgeons of England as a centre suitable for training surgeons, no adverse comment was made about the inadequacy of the lifts used to transfer children between the operating theatres and ICU. These were cramped, lacked resuscitation and monitoring equipment and were even at risk of being summoned and stopped, or sent to another floor, if the lift button was pressed while in transit. One lift was so cramped that sometimes staff 'accompanying' a child had to run up the two flights of stairs to meet it.[52] Until October 1995, the PCS services were provided on two sites. Very sick children had to be transported up to 200 metres, up a steep hill, between the Children's Hospital and the BRI.[53] The Inquiry noted that it was not only a problem of a split site, but more fundamentally a split service. The Bristol surgeons lacked cardiological support when operating, and sometimes in the ICU, communication between cardiologists and surgeons was also impaired. There was even evidence of separate sets of medical notes being prepared and, on occasions, the notes from one site would not accompany the child on transfer to the other. The Inquiry concluded that, of all the factors adversely affecting the adequacy of the PCS service, the split service was probably the most serious and was 'actually dangerous'.[54] Time pressures could also result in children not being assessed fully by a cardiologist before surgery. The Inquiry heard expert

49 The Bristol Report, paras 185–7.

50 The Bristol Report, para 192.

51 The Bristol Report, para 208.

52 The Bristol Report, para 214.

53 Expert evidence to the Inquiry noted that the process of preparing and stabilizing a child for a short journey was as demanding as for a journey of hundreds of miles. The need to transfer patients between the two sites was described as a factor giving rise to a risk to the child. The Bristol Report, para 211.

54 The Bristol Report, paras 206–10.

evidence 'that it was *imperative* for the cardiologists and surgeons to meet before an operation to review the notes and examine the test results together'.[55] In the opinion of the Inquiry, 'if ever there were an environment conducive to error and danger this was it'. Yet on both visits, the Royal College inspectors appeared to have completely missed the issue – an extremely worrying oversight, which cast serious doubt on the rigour of the inspection process.[56] Similarly, prior to the coming to light of the crisis, the GMC showed no interest in the potential disciplinary issue arising from this scenario.

## Ongoing Quality Assurance

Once hospital consultants had completed their training, there was no formal procedure to ensure continuing competence. The senior clinicians in Bristol had no one to satisfy but themselves about the quality of the service they provided. There were no systematic mechanisms for monitoring clinical performance, consultants were answerable to no one and effectively had a job for life. Only when misconduct could be proved, a complex, time-consuming and problematic process, was it potentially possible for an employer to remove a consultant. In essence, there was no effective local mechanism for ensuring that patients were receiving adequate care from consultants.[57]

This contrasted with the position relating to nurses, who were subject to an ongoing process of quality assurance and periodic re-registration. In addition, both employers and the nursing professional bodies had significant powers to address poor performance by nurses. Nurses were therefore subject to far greater control than consultants, even though the former had far less capacity to harm patients as part of their day-to-day work.

## Teamwork

Consultants at Bristol saw themselves as leading their medical teams, but the Inquiry concluded that they did not necessarily see themselves as part of the team. Also, teams were not multi-disciplinary – being focused primarily around the needs of the patient – but rather tended to consist of similar professionals: consultant surgeon leading surgeons, and so on. Mr Wisheart, the Bristol Inquiry heard, had a tendency to arrive late for surgery and Mr Dhasmana was reported as becoming impatient with staff in the theatre, indicating an inappropriate approach to team working.[58]

55 The Bristol Report, para 212.
56 The Bristol Report, para 214.
57 The Bristol Report, para 193.
58 The Bristol Report, para 213.

### Inappropriate Delegation

Care in the ICU was mainly provided by junior doctors undergoing training in general surgery. They were unlikely to have high levels of expertise in cardiac care, paediatrics or intensive care. The Bristol Inquiry heard that: '[ICU] was a unit run by trainees...quite familiar with the cardio-vascular system...but relatively poor at integrating that with other systems, for instance the respiratory system.' This approach was particularly unsatisfactory because elsewhere in the NHS, intensive care had developed substantially as a specialism. These developments were not embraced at Bristol.[59]

The obtaining of consent from parents was also something which tended to be delegated to junior doctors. Mr Dhasmana indicated that 'traditionally' getting parents to sign the consent form after the admission of their child was 'part of their [junior doctor's] clerking procedure in routine cases'. It was acknowledged by the Inquiry that this would have been common practice elsewhere in the NHS.[60]

### Ignoring Evidence

By around 1990, basic statistical data for 1988–90 was available which should have given rise to the clinicians in the Bristol Unit questioning their performance in open-heart surgery on the under-1s. Such an analysis would have provided evidence of less than adequate performance. Indeed, for five of the seven years between 1988 and 1994, complication rates at Bristol from open-heart surgery on children aged under one was roughly double the national average. Mortality rates nationally were falling substantially, but not at Bristol.[61] The internal failures at Bristol were not compensated for by any external body. The GMC had no interest in proactively considering statistical data. Nor, at the time, did the Society of Cardiothoracic Surgeons perceive that it had any responsibility in this area.[62]

### GMC Involvement

The GMC were late in becoming involved in the events at Bristol. The revelations in *Private Eye* appear to have been ignored. The story was exposed again in March 1996, by a Channel 4 *Dispatches* programme and an article in *The Times* on 1 April 1996. The GMC only began to investigate when Dr Bolsin, and a little later bereaved parents, submitted complaints. Preliminary investigations began, and a

59 The Bristol Report, paras 215–16 and 230.

60 The Bristol Report, para 219.

61 The Bristol Report, paras 240–41.

62 This changed from April 1997, when 'surgeon-specific outcome data' would be collected and the President of the Society would seek clarification from any surgeon whose performance fell outside pre-defined limits. If this did not resolve matters, the Medical Director of the Trust would be contacted and 'the Society will provide, in conjunction with the Royal College of Surgeons, a discrete and supportive external review'. The Bristol Report, para 242.

more substantial inquiry – described by Irvine as 'the largest that the GMC had undertaken' – was started in June 1996. The Preliminary Proceedings Committee concluded that there was sufficient evidence to charge Dr Roylance, Mr Wisheart and Mr Dhasmana with serious professional misconduct.[63] Irvine, then President of the GMC, chaired the disciplinary inquiry and it is worth quoting in full the basis upon which the investigation was founded:

> Doctors have an ethical duty to practise within the limits of their professional competence. Moreover, they have an ethical duty to report poor practice where it may endanger patients. In a landmark case in 1994, an anaesthetist…was found guilty of SPM when he failed to act properly after being told by colleagues about the practice of a locum that was giving cause for great concern. In the determination, which was widely publicised, the Conduct Committee said, 'Doctors who have reason to believe that a colleague's conduct or professional performance poses a danger to patients must act to ensure patient safety. Before taking action in such a situation doctors should do their best to establish the facts…At all times patient safety must take precedence over all other concerns, including understandable reticence to bring a colleague's career into question.'[64]

The case against the Bristol surgeons was essentially that they failed critically to analyse their own performance, and to recognize that they should stop operating until the cause of their poor results was established. This failure had resulted in potentially avoidable patient deaths. The failures by Dr Roylance resulted from his unwillingness to respond to warnings by Dr Bolsin and to investigate paediatric surgery within the hospital. Tellingly, Irvine states that he had 'never witnessed such a detailed scrutiny of clinical cases before…Many distinguished experts were called by all parties to contribute to that examination.'[65] With respect to thorough investigation, it took a media and public outcry for the GMC to do what it should have been doing on a regular basis, although it is open to question whether the GMC is actually equipped and has sufficient resources to do this.

All three surgeons were found guilty of serious professional misconduct. Wisheart and Roylance had their names erased from the medical register. In the case of Dhasmana, the PCC felt that because he had taken some steps to confront the problems and been denied some information by the other two respondents, it could step back from the ultimate sanction of erasure. Mr Dhasmana was subject to conditional registration which prohibited him from undertaking paediatric cardiac surgery for a period of three years.

The disciplining by the GMC of John Roylance broke new ground with regard to the professional responsibilities of doctors who were also managers. The PCC, with subsequent confirmation by the Privy Council,[66] recognized that the general obligations of a registered medical practitioner to care for the sick did not disappear with senior managerial appointment. Indeed, it was concluded that any attempt to

---

63 See Irvine, D., *The Doctors' Tale*, 2003, Radcliffe Medical Press, Oxford, 123–4.

64 Cited by Irvine, D., *The Doctors' Tale*, 2003, Radcliffe Medical Press, Oxford, 125.

65 Irvine, D., *The Doctors' Tale*, 2003, Radcliffe Medical Press, Oxford, 125–6.

66 *Roylance v GMC* [1999] 3 WLR 541.

divorce administration from medical care, in such a manner that the administrator was freed from professional responsibilities, must inevitably be unsound.

In addition to the findings specific to the three doctors, the PCC also highlighted issues of concern which needed to be addressed by the whole profession. These included: a means for evaluating clinical competence; clearly presented clinical standards; a clearly identified basis for attributing responsibility in team-based medical practice; communication with patients about risks; the need to take prompt action when concerns about colleagues arise and the means available to communicate these concerns.[67] It is arguable that all of these issues should have been addressed by the GMC long before the Bristol case. For example, almost a decade earlier, Alderson had discussed the complexities of ensuring informed parental consent to proposed cardiac surgery on a child.[68] Similarly, Stacey, writing in 1992, observed that at least some members of the medical profession (including some within the GMC) downplayed the importance of informed consent and did not view it as an issue which should give rise to misconduct proceedings.[69]

## General Recommendations from the Bristol Inquiry

The 'job for life' environment enjoyed by consultants made it extremely difficult for employers to introduce changes. The Bristol Inquiry concluded that employees from different medical fields – doctors and nurses as well as managers – should be treated more or less equally. There should be clear lines of accountability and comparable terms of employment. Furthermore, whilst it does exist, the 'job for life' culture increases the importance of the disciplinary functions of the GMC. In the absence of effective power in the hands of the employer, the focus of responsibility turns to the GMC – as the only body with the power to effectively control consultants.

The Bristol Inquiry also recommended the creation of two independent, overarching organizations to bring together the bodies which regulate healthcare. One, a Council for the Quality of Healthcare, should bring together those bodies such as the Commission for Health Improvement and the National Institute for Clinical Excellence, which regulate health standards. The second, a Council for the Regulation of Healthcare Professionals,[70] should bring together individual professional regulatory bodies, such as the GMC and Nursing and Midwifery Council. Both organizations would ensure that the approach to setting standards was integrated and, subsequently, appropriately monitored. They would also seek to identify and address any gaps in coverage between bodies. The Bristol Inquiry also recommended that the principles set out in the GMC's guide, *Good Medical*

---

67 For further discussion, see Irvine, D., *The Doctors' Tale*, 2003, Radcliffe Medical Press, Oxford.

68 Alderson, P., *Choosing for Children: Parent's Consent to Surgery*, 1989, Oxford University Press, Oxford. See also Stacey, M., *Regulating British Medicine: the General Medical Council*, 1992, Wiley, Chichester, 223.

69 Stacey, M., *Regulating British Medicine: the General Medical Council*, 1992, Wiley, Chichester, 223.

70 This body was referred to in *The NHS Plan* as the 'Council of Health Regulators'.

*Practice*, should be incorporated into the contracts of employment of hospital doctors and into GPs' terms of service. Employers would then be able to deal directly with breaches of the professional code, independently of action by the GMC. The Bristol Inquiry also recommended that revalidation should be compulsory for all healthcare professionals, to ensure that they remained fit to practise. This requirement should also be included in doctors' contracts of employment.

## Reporting of Sentinel Events

The Bristol Report recommended the creation of a single, accessible system for reporting and analysing sentinel events. Public confidence should be enhanced by placing responsibility for managing the database of reports in the hands of the National Patient Safety Agency. All reports should be analysed locally, at Trust level, with reference to both the conduct of individuals and wider organizational factors.

Mechanisms to enable sentinel events to be reported should be as straightforward as possible, with all necessary means of communication – for instance, confidential telephone lines – being used. Staff members who reported within agreed timescales (the Bristol Inquiry recommended 48 hours) would be immune from disciplinary action, as long as they have not committed a criminal offence as part of any involvement. In contrast, a failure to report would itself be a disciplinary offence. All staff would receive training regarding the systems for reporting and the consequences for failing to report. In addition to the reporting requirements, attention should be paid to redesigning systems so as to remove, as far as is possible and practical, those risk factors most likely to give rise to sentinel events.

## Scapegoats or Evidence of a Widespread Problem?

Hammond, who drew attention to the events at Bristol in *Private Eye*, questions elsewhere whether there was an element of scapegoating in the treatment of the Bristol surgeons. Hammond cites examples of institutionalized poor practice throughout the medical establishment. For example, he reports that virtually all paediatric senior house officers were found to lack advanced training in paediatric resuscitation techniques. In over 75 per cent of cases involving the deaths of babies under one month old, different care 'would' (over 50 per cent) or 'might' (25 per cent) have made a difference, and particular concern was expressed regarding the errors of more junior doctors.[71] In 1996 it was found that 25 per cent of weekend and night operations, usually emergencies, were undertaken by unsupervised junior doctors. Only 25 per cent of consultants always supervised their senior house officers. Twenty per cent of house officers and 10 per cent of senior house officers undertook at least one activity weekly which they felt was beyond their competence. These activities included operations. Other studies showed that SHOs were often left to

---

71 See Hope, B., 'Half the Deaths of Young Infants may be Avoidable', *BMJ*, 1997, 315: 143–8, 19 July; and Hammond, P. and Mosley, M., *Trust Me I'm A Doctor*, 2002, Metro Publishing, London, 32.

undertake their first attempts at a range of operations without senior support present in theatre, or sometimes even in the hospital.[72]

## Recommendations after Bristol

The Bristol Report recommended that any doctor undertaking any clinical procedure for the first time must be directly supervised by colleagues who possess the requisite skill. This supervision should continue until the necessary expertise has been acquired. Approval of local ethics committees should also be required for hitherto untried invasive procedures.

The GMC, with its responsibility for medical education and appropriate behaviour in practice, should have been aware of and taking steps to address these issues long before the events at Bristol. Indeed it had provided for some of these contingencies in the February 1991 edition of the Blue Book, under the heading 'Delegation of medical duties to professional colleagues':

> ...consultants in hospital practice, and doctors engaged in private practice...should seek to ensure that proper arrangements are put in hand to cover their own duties...during any period of absence...Consultants and other senior hospital staff should delegate to junior colleagues only those duties which are within their capabilities.

What was absent was investigation and enforcement of these requirements. Instead, it has been reported that when, very late in the day, some within the GMC did attempt to become involved, they came under pressure to prevent them from taking effective action. According to Hammond, a long-serving member of the GMC, who had been chairman of the Professional Standards Committee, had attempted to raise the issues at Bristol at a Council meeting, only to be reassured that 'Wisheart was a good chap'. He also recounted contacts from doctors outside of the GMC, who were asking if he could get the charges dropped on the basis that Wisheart was a 'good chap'.

## Organ Retention

### *Public Concern – an Example of Professional Detachment from Lay Sensibilities*

In 1996 the mother of a child who had died at the Bristol Royal Infirmary requested a copy of the medical records. She discovered that her child's heart had been retained. Following the subsequent formation of the Bristol Heart Children's Action Group, it was discovered that retention of tissue was routine – not only at Bristol but elsewhere. It then came to light that the largest collection of retained organs and

72 See Hammond, P. and Mosley, M., *Trust Me I'm A Doctor*, 2002, Metro Publishing, London, 33.

tissue from children was at the Royal Liverpool Children's Hospital (Alder Hey) in Liverpool.[73]

In 1999, one of the witnesses at the Bristol Inquiry revealed that doctors frequently removed and retained organs from children following post-mortem examinations, without the knowledge and consent of the parents. This ultimately resulted in a further Inquiry, into activities at the Alder Hey hospital.[74]

The Inquiry Report focused on malpractice by one particular pathologist, Professor B17, who, it was said, removed and retained thousands of organs without consent.[75] However, the wider findings, those of particular relevance to this study, relate to patronizing, paternalistic and evasive attitudes by the medical establishment towards the bereaved parents. This attitude prevailed at the time of the original organ retention, and was still prevalent at the time the scandal broke.[76]

### *The Coroner's Compared with Hospital Post-mortems*

At the time, the legal position relating to the retention of organs and tissues after death divided into two categories: following a coroner's post-mortem or a hospital post-mortem. A coroner could direct a post-mortem examination where there was reasonable cause to suspect that the person had died a sudden death of unknown cause. Consent from next of kin was not required. A coroner's post-mortem was restricted to establishing the identity of the deceased, and how, when and where the deceased died. Retention of organs or tissues was only permitted for the time necessary to establish the above.

The removal and retention of organs or tissues for hospital post-mortems for teaching, therapeutic or research purposes was governed by the Human Tissue Act 1961. Permission could be given by the patient prior to death, or by the person lawfully in possession of the body after death. In the latter instance the person in possession must, inter alia, seek to ensure that relatives of the deceased do not object. The Alder Hey Inquiry found that frequently the medical profession did not consider the Human Tissue Act at all, and there were numerous instances of failure by doctors to make the requisite enquiries of parents.

73 The full extent of the scandal was revealed in January 2001 with the publication of the report of the Alder Hey inquiry, chaired by Michael Redfern QC. For further academic discussion, see, for example, Maclean, M., 'Doctors, Parents and the Law – Organ Retention after Paediatric Cardiac Surgery at the Bristol Royal Infirmary', *Child and Family Law Quarterly*, December 2001, 13.4 (399). For an example of medical reaction, see Tallis, R., *Hippocratic Oaths*, 2004, Atlantic, London, 188.

74 Royal Liverpool Children's Inquiry, *Report*, 2001, Stationery Office, London (www.rlcinquiry.org.uk/).

75 It was also found that he falsified records, statistical analysis and post-mortem reports. He also lied to parents about the way post-mortem examinations were conducted and about the findings.

76 For discussion of the Inquiry Report, see Hunter, M., 'Alder Hey Condemns Doctors, Management, and Coroner', *BMJ*, 2001, 322: 255; and Bauchner, H. and Vinci, R., 'What Have We Learnt from the Alder Hey Affair?', *BMJ*, 2001, 322: 309–10.

The Bristol doctors were identified as being confused about the differences between hospital and coroner post-mortems. It appears that the confusion about the legal position, coupled with the desire to use retained materials for scientific research, facilitated doctors in continuing with inappropriate practices. During the Bristol Inquiry, it emerged that children's hearts removed during post-mortem examination had frequently been retained. In some cases no consent had been obtained, in others consent forms had been signed, but the relatives had not fully understood what they were agreeing to. Professor Ian Kennedy, Chairman of the Bristol Inquiry, described the approach of the medical profession as one of 'professional arrogance', underpinned by medical paternalism. This had created a 'social and ethical time bomb'.

*Parents' Evidence*

The evidence of parents in the Alder Hey case is powerful and instructive of the mismatch between medical and lay understanding of important ethical issues. From the perspective of the thesis of this work, this mismatch is of value in understanding failures of self-regulation. The GMC cannot realistically place public protection at the centre of its activities if it and members of the profession lack insight into public concerns and expectations.

Amongst the findings from the Alder Hey Inquiry were that the collection of children's hearts had begun in 1948, retention usually occurring without parental knowledge. The final collection of over 2,000 hearts was one of the largest in the world. Other body parts, including a number of children's heads and intact bodies were kept. The 'most disturbing' specimen was said to be the head of a boy aged 11 years. These findings, together with evidence given by the parents, demonstrate a systematic lack of respect by doctors. Chapter 14 of the Alder Hey Inquiry Report records the oral evidence given by the parents, outlining their recollections and feelings. A selection of cases are summarized in the following paragraphs.

The Alder Hey Inquiry found that inappropriate attitudes from doctors had a long history. Marie died in hospital in 1962. Her parents were not properly informed about the death, seeing the death certificate whilst waiting for someone to tell them what had happened. They did not sign a post-mortem consent form, nor did they consent to organs being removed. When they discovered, in 2000, that organs had been retained and that Marie had not been buried 'in tact', the parents were described as being 'physically and mentally devastated'. The medical profession was described by them as 'walking over the rights of patients and their families'.

More recently, Craig, born with congenital heart disease, died in 1986 whilst undergoing heart surgery. Only in 1999 did his parents discover that a post-mortem examination had been carried out and that organs had been retained. They described themselves as devastated to learn about the retained organs and the thought that they had not 'buried their son intact'.

Sean was born in 1997 with congenital heart disease and died during surgery. The parents indicated that they had felt pressured into consenting to a hospital post-mortem examination. They had no idea that the heart and lungs would be removed at post-mortem and retained, and would not have consented to this. They described a sense of revulsion and betrayal on discovering that Sean's heart had been retained. They were also concerned that when they eventually secured the release of the retained heart and lungs, the hospital carried out last-minute sampling without permission.

Heather was born with congenital heart disease and died during surgery in 1984. Heather's parents described feeling that the treatment at the hands of the doctors was as if 'they did not exist'. Only in 1999 did they find out that Heather's heart had been retained.

Kathryn died at Alder Hey Hospital in 1993, having developed Hodgkin's disease. Very soon after her death, less than one hour, her parents were asked for consent to a post-mortem examination. They were assured that only small tissue samples would be removed through a restricted incision. In 1999, the parents were informed that Kathryn's heart, chest and abdomen had been retained. Shortly afterwards, this list was expanded to include lung, liver, spleen and kidneys. The post-mortem report had merely recorded a small mid-sternal incision, with only organ biopsies taken. This was effectively a fiction; the parents, it appeared, had been lied to on several occasions.

Gareth died at Alder Hey in 1993, following major heart surgery. After his death, the surgeon was said to have been 'angry, incredulous, blunt and insensitive'. The paediatric cardiologist was said to have been insensitive, telling the parents that they could always 'have another baby'. In 1999, the parents found out that a post-mortem examination had been carried out within ten minutes of Gareth's death and that his heart and lungs had been retained. This had never been raised with them and they had not signed a consent form. The parents described feeling that they had 'been treated with complete lack of respect'.

Thomas was born with a congenital cardiac defect and died following heart surgery in 1992. The parents, although reluctant, were persuaded by a cardiac surgeon to agree to a post-mortem examination to 'help other children in similar cases'. They categorically refused to consent to organ retention. In 1999 they contacted Alder Hey, and organ retention was eventually admitted. They also discovered that the consent form had been altered after they had signed it. The parents described their treatment as 'very bad, dishonest and patronising'. They considered that they had been lied to on several occasions, leaving them feeling 'betrayed, let down and angry'.

Sarah was born in 1992 with congenital heart disease and died shortly after major cardiac surgery at Alder Hey. A hospital post-mortem was undertaken. Her parents only found out in 1999 that there had been a full retention of Sarah's organs. The parents described having lost their faith in the medical profession. Having thought that Sarah had been buried intact, they described their lives as 'devastated by the disclosure of organ retention'.

Laura was stillborn in 1993. 'Three minutes' after the birth, Laura's mother was asked to sign a consent form. She was in no position to know what she was signing. She discovered in 1999 that a post-mortem had been undertaken and numerous organs retained. She described herself as feeling sick that the organs were kept for no purpose.

Jordan was stillborn in 1994. His parents initially refused to consent to a post-mortem, but were persuaded to change their minds. They were reassured that organs would not be retained. They discovered in 1999 that every organ had in fact been kept. They described feeling 'despair and anguish' at not having put their whole child to rest. They felt that they had signed the consent following pressure and lies. Jordan 'lost his dignity and was treated like a piece of meat in a butcher's shop'.

Claire died in 1988, aged 14, from a paracetamol overdose. A coroner's post-mortem and inquest were held. Claire's parents were not told that organs would be retained. They described anger: '…at the deceit, grotesqueness and obscenity of removing without their knowledge or consent their daughter's brain, heart and lungs'. The Inquiry noted the inapplicability of the usual attempt at justification for organ retention – to assist research into infant mortality.

Christopher was stillborn in 1987. Despite parental protests, the hospital insisted that it was best that the body be buried in the hospital grounds. They were not allowed to attend, but were told that the ceremony would be dignified. As a Catholic family, burial was important to them and to bury their child intact was part of their religious belief. In 1999 the parents found out that Christopher had been sent to the University from Alder Hey without their consent and had never been buried.

Christopher died aged five in 1988 whilst undergoing heart surgery. His parents were reassured by clinicians that, whilst a post-mortem examination would have to be done, all organs would be returned to the body. Organs, including Christopher's brain, were removed and retained. His parents described feeling 'extremely let down' and 'totally betrayed' by the clinician, who had not been honest with them.

Brazier summarizes the feelings expressed by the Alder Hey parents as follows:

> (1) the child is 'theirs'. She belongs to them. Her body belongs to them. They are still parents, albeit bereaved parents; (2) they are the guardians of the family's values, be they religious or cultural imperatives, or simply personal convictions; (3) robbed of their child, parents need the means to come to terms with the loss of all the joys of parenthood. They need some means of regaining control; (4) the parents' own mental health and emotional wellbeing are at stake; and (5) the physical body of a beloved child remains fixed in the mind. Rationally parents know the child does not suffer or bleed. In the imagination, nightmares haunt their sleep.[77]

Medical evidence given to the Alder Hey Inquiry confirmed that training in recent decades reflected a prevailing medical culture which shied away from going into details with next of kin about what a post-mortem involved, in order to minimize distress. The fear was that upset relatives might refuse consent.

Also from within the profession, Tallis describes the position at Alder Hey as far from exceptional: 'While the scale of [B17's] collection was far beyond anything

77 Brazier, M., 'Organ Retention and Return: Problems of Consent', 29 *J.M.E.*, 2002, 30–33, at 31. See also McLean, M., 'Letting Go…Parents, Professionals and the Law in the Retention of Human Material after Post Mortem', in Bainham, A., Day Sclater, S. and Richards, M. (eds), *Body Lore and Laws*, 2002, Hart Publishing, Oxford; and Liddell, K. and Hall, A., 'Beyond Bristol and Alder Hey: The Future Regulation of Human Tissue', *Medical Law Review*, Summer 2005, 13, 170–223.

either he or anyone else could justify, the collection of organs was not in itself aberrant.'[78]

*Appropriateness of Lay/Parental Responses*

Once parents were aware that they had buried their children 'incomplete', some felt the need to hold second, third even fourth funerals.[79] It has been suggested from within the profession that the preoccupation with retained organs forced parents to engage with the reality of the post-death fate of the body. However, the focus of press and public was still to avoid these post-death realities – stigmatizing the medical profession instead.[80] As Tallis put it:

> It would be tactless and cruel to spell out the fact that dead bodies cannot suffer and that if they could suffer they would suffer no more from an autopsy than from burial or cremation. Yet superstition about the suffering of dead bodies combined with guilt at failure to protect one's child can make the discovery of an autopsy one does not recall authorizing a real shock.
>
> ...However, the transformation of grief into grievance makes grief only temporarily bearable. This became evident when a few parents started to arrange funerals for slides containing microscopic slivers of tissue.[81]

Dr Phil Hammond expresses similar views:

> On one level, however, the organ retention hysteria simply amounted to a realisation that pathologists collect pathology specimens. Big deal, maybe this year we'll discover that surgeons cut you up with knives, bodies are left to rot underground and it gets pretty hot in the crematorium.[82]

Tallis and Hammond are apparently frustrated that the public do not universally share the profession's view about death and the objectification of the body after death. It is outside of the scope of this book to engage in the complex discussion regarding post-death rituals and belief systems relating to the sanctity (or otherwise) of the body after death. What is within the scope of this book is a consideration of why the GMC was apparently not in tune with the range of public opinions on the subject and, in this context, ensured that doctors behaved appropriately. Alder Hey appears to have caught the GMC and the profession by surprise, in challenging, or even simply questioning, the longstanding 'right' doctors had claimed for themselves to make use of bodies post-mortem.

---

78 Tallis, R., *Hippocratic Oaths*, 2004, Atlantic, London, 189.

79 Fifty-eight sets of parents who had already had second funerals were subsequently told that there were cerebella still awaiting burial. Other parents were informed that remains had been disposed of by incineration as clinical waste.

80 Tallis, R., *Hippocratic Oaths*, 2004, Atlantic, London, 191.

81 Tallis, R., *Hippocratic Oaths*, 2004, Atlantic, London, 191.

82 Hammond, P., 'The Death of the Autopsy', *NHS Magazine*, June 2002 (online edition).

## The Cost to the Medical Profession

A subsequent census by the Chief Medical Officer for England (2000) and the Isaacs Report (2003) confirmed what some of the witnesses at the Alder Hey Inquiry had revealed, that there was widespread storage and use of organs and tissue without appropriate consent. The Chief Medical Officer recommended fundamental revisions to the law,[83] resulting in the enactment of the Human Tissue Act 2004. The new Act replaces, inter alia, the Human Tissue Act 1961, the Anatomy Act 1984 and the Human Organ Transplants Act 1989.[84] The new legislation introduces mandatory 'informed consent' as the more demanding requirement for doctors to comply with before undertaking most activities that use cells, tissues or organs. The Act also makes radical changes to the law governing the use of tissues obtained from living persons. Criminal sanctions[85] may be imposed if consent is not obtained when required.[86] The implications of the new legislation are that even tissue left over after surgery or diagnostic tests cannot be stored or used for research without consent. This has been described as 'a disproportionate response to the issues raised by Alder Hey'.[87] However, it is difficult to resist the conclusion that the medical establishment, including the GMC, has brought this on itself. Lack of proactive involvement on the part of the GMC illustrates a failure of the Council over a long period to set an appropriate ethical tone within the profession. It would be surprising if, over time, at least some of the medical members of the GMC were not aware that human tissue was being retained and used without regard for patients or next of kin. If the GMC were to argue otherwise, they undermine their own case for self-regulation – the idea that this is needed because of the complexity of medical practice and the need for insider knowledge. Such an argument can hardly be sustained if such knowledge has gaping holes of this type. Also, the tissue retention scandals draw into question the strength of the arguments put forward by the advocates of no fault regulation. The sanction-less 1961 legislation was, to a greater or lesser extent, largely ignored by the medical profession, predominantly through convenience and general thoughtlessness towards the feelings of others. It is naïve to presume that in other areas of professional behaviour and practice, medical practitioners will embrace cooperation without sanction when they may have motivating pressures not to cooperate.

---

83 *The Removal, Retention and Use of Human Organs and Tissue from Post Mortem Examination*, 2001.

84 Explanatory Notes to the Human Tissue Act 2004, www.opsi.gov.uk/acts/en2004/2004en30.htm.

85 A fine or up to three years' imprisonment.

86 The medical community has expressed concern at uncertainties within the legislation, notably the absence of a definition of 'consent' and the failure to specify the essential criteria for criminal offences punishable by up to three years' imprisonment. See Liddell, K. and Hall, A., 'Beyond Bristol and Alder Hey: The Future Regulation of Human Tissue', Medical Law Review, Summer 2005, 13, 170–223, 218; and Royal College of Physicians, 'Response to the Human Tissue Bill', 14 May 2004.

87 Liddell, K. and Hall, A., 'Beyond Bristol and Alder Hey: The Future Regulation of Human Tissue', Medical Law Review, Summer 2005, 13, 170–223, 182–3.

After the publication of the Inquiry Report in January 2001, it appears that the Chief Medical Officer referred it to the GMC for consideration of disciplinary proceedings against doctors considered by the Alder Hey Inquiry. In all, cases against 13 doctors were initially brought, but all were dismissed prior to reaching the PCC (two were dismissed at the screening stage and the remainder by the PPC).[88]

88 See *Woods v General Medical Council* [2002] EWHC 1484, Admin.

# Chapter 8

# Rodney Ledward

## Introduction

The Ledward case provides an example of an influential hospital consultant who committed serious professional misconduct whilst practising both in the NHS and privately. In common with the other case examples discussed, the GMC took no action for most of the period of misconduct. On 30 September 1998, Rodney Ledward's name was eventually erased from the medical register by the GMC and on 17 March 1999 the Secretary of State for Health set up an Inquiry into his actions. The terms of reference of the Inquiry were:

> To consider why the serious failures in the NHS clinical practice of Mr Rodney Ledward at South Kent Hospitals NHS Trust were not identified and acted upon earlier and to consider the action taken when those failures came to light. In doing so, to review the role of the management and staff of the Trust (and its predecessor body) and other external bodies concerned with the quality of patient care and to consider the adequacy of systems, including clinical audit, to ensure quality…

The Inquiry, chaired by Jean Ritchie QC, published its report on 1 June 2000.[1] The principal findings were that Ledward was able to harm patients, over at least a 16-year period, because of a culture where hospital consultants received god-like treatment and other staff feared retribution if they reported concerns. Colleagues should have known that his performance was significantly below standard and his attitude towards patients inappropriate. A number of victims described a culture where their concerns were ignored, or they were simply disbelieved. When concerns did eventually come to light, senior managers failed to investigate.

Key recommendations by the Inquiry which have relevance to the GMC and the self-regulatory process included: screening to filter out candidates for the medical profession who were psychologically unsuitable; national benchmarking against which the performance of doctors could be measured; and an open culture to encourage whistleblowing. The Inquiry also recommended that independent judicial members should chair GMC fitness to practise hearings and the civil standard of proof should be used.

---

1 *An Inquiry into Quality and Practice within the National Health Service Arising from the Actions of Rodney Ledward – The Report*, 1 June 2000, para 1.2 (hereafter referred to as 'The Ledward Report'), para 1.1.

In addition to its own investigation, the Inquiry was also able to draw upon the 'Report of the Inquiry held into the Professional Competence and Conduct of Mr Rodney Ledward for South Kent Hospitals NHS Trust' – the Disciplinary Inquiry which resulted in Ledward being dismissed from his NHS post. This Inquiry had adopted the highest civil standard of proof (a strong balance of probabilities). It was also able to draw upon the transcript of the hearing before the General Medical Council, which had adopted the criminal standard of proof.[2]

The evidence from the Ledward Inquiry is discussed in some detail in this chapter in order to demonstrate the full extent of Ledward's misconduct. This is necessary because, viewed alone, many of the instances of misconduct might be mistaken for negligence. Only when the cumulative picture is considered does the full extent of Ledward's misconduct become clear.

## Ledward's Career

Ledward originally obtained a degree in Pharmacy in 1959 and then transferred to medicine. After House Officer, Senior House Officer and Registrar jobs in hospitals throughout the country, in 1975 he was appointed Senior Registrar at the City and Women's Hospital in Nottingham and Clinical Teacher at the University of Nottingham. Ledward had become a Member of the Royal College of Obstetricians and Gynaecologists in 1971 and became a Fellow of the Royal College of Surgeons in 1976. On 1 January 1980, at the age of 41, he was appointed as a Consultant Gynaecologist and Obstetrician by the South Thames Regional Health Authority. Between 1 January 1981 and 31 December 1982, Ledward was Chairman of the Obstetrics and Gynaecology Division. Ledward was recognized as a 'flamboyant…colourful character', but with an impressive academic curriculum vitae. In addition to his NHS practice, he acquired admitting rights to a number of private hospitals.[3]

By February 1996 Ledward had been suspended by the Trust and shortly afterwards dismissed from his consultant post. In erasing his name from the medical register in September 1998, the Professional Conduct Committee of the General Medical Council described the position as follows:

> During the course of this inquiry the Committee has heard evidence of your lack of care and judgment pre-operatively, failings in your surgical skills, inappropriate delegation and your poor post operative care and judgment. The standard of care which you provided fell lamentably below that which the public requires and which the medical profession expects of its members.[4]

Both the NHS Trust and GMC actions faced significant professional support for Ledward. The Ledward Inquiry referred to a number of supporting letters written by fellow Consultant Gynaecologists, and other doctors from the UK and abroad. Many

2 *The Ledward Report*, paras 3.1–3.2.

3 *The Ledward Report*, para 6.1 and Part III, para 4.1.

4 *The Ledward Report*, para 6.2.

of these doctors, it was said, wrote in support despite having no recent first-hand experience of Ledward's practice or skills.[5]

## Pre-Consultant Years

There were signs during Ledward's early career that his practice might give rise to concerns. As the Inquiry observed, '...even in the days when Rodney Ledward was a Senior Registrar, there was something slapdash and unmethodical in his character; an element of seeing what he could get away with.'[6] Two Consultant Gynaecologists, who were Senior Registrars in the 1970s when Ledward was a Senior House Officer, told the Inquiry that Ledward 'seemed to be a man on the make whom it was difficult to trust'. He would 'try to skate across the surface of things, the quickest and shortest way of getting things done seemed to be what he achieved. It did not matter about quality.'[7]

## Selected Evidence of Ledward's Incompetence

Within six months of Ledward's appointment as a consultant, serious surgical mishaps began to emerge. These were of a type and number which should have given rise to concerns. The failure to explain the position to patients or their GPs indicated that Ledward either ignored the problems or attempted to hide them.[8] The following constitute a selection of examples of these incidents.

In July 1980, Ledward performed a total abdominal hysterectomy on an NHS patient during which he tied both ureters. The following day, he attempted a repair, without assistance from a urologist. The patient went on to develop a vesicovaginal fistula and was eventually referred to a Consultant General Surgeon, Mr L1. Mr L1's evidence was that it was rare for a gynaecologist to damage a ureter, and that this case caused him concern. Other Consultant Gynaecologists confirmed that the cutting or tying off of a ureter is a rare and serious surgical mishap. To tie two in the same patient was particularly serious, especially as this was not recognized at the time. In October 1980, a private patient developed a pelvic abscess following a vaginal hysterectomy performed by Ledward. This was an uncommon, serious complication of such surgery. In January 1981, an NHS patient suffered a post-operative wound haematoma. This was an uncommon complication of such surgery. The patient's evidence was that she suffered continuing bladder problems, but that Ledward had told her that the haematoma was 'normal'. In 1982 Ledward performed a hysterectomy on a private patient, who suffered a primary haemorrhage and had to be returned to theatre for surgery and a blood transfusion. This was an uncommon complication. Ledward failed to mention this in the discharge letter to the patient's GP. During an operation in July 1983, Ledward made a hole in an NHS patient's

5 *The Ledward Report*, para 6.5.

6 *The Ledward Report*, paras 4.1–4.4.

7 *The Ledward Report*, para 5.1.

8 *The Ledward Report*, paras 22.1–22.2.

bladder, which he attempted to repair. The patient suffered permanent incontinence. She was not told by Ledward about the damage, nor was there any mention of this in the discharge letter to her GP. In January 1985, Ledward made a hole in a patient's bladder during a vaginal hysterectomy. He attempted a repair himself. A vesicovaginal fistula developed and Ledward twice attempted to repair this before eventually asking for specialist assistance. He should have asked for specialist assistance immediately.[9]

## Excessive Speed

During the period 1985–90, a number of Ledward's patients suffered ureteric damage, urinary tract damage, bowel damage and other surgical complications. In a number of cases he followed unacceptable medical practice and worked too quickly.[10] Case examples include the following. In February 1986, Ledward carried out a total abdominal hysterectomy on a private patient when she had only requested sterilization. This operation lasted for less than 15 minutes. It was subsequently found that the patient's left ureter was obstructed. The patient suffered permanent incontinence. The patient was erroneously told by Ledward that her incontinence was a normal consequence of the procedure. The complications were omitted in Ledward's letter to the patient's GP. Another private patient was subjected in May 1986 to a total abdominal hysterectomy which took less than 30 minutes. A number of complications occurred. In evidence to the Inquiry, the patient said that she had intended to bring legal proceedings against Ledward, but was prohibited for financial reasons. The latter point reinforces the importance of effective and 'free' complaints and disciplinary procedures, especially those operated by the GMC. The Inquiry heard that Mr L2, the surgeon who had attempted a repair in this case, had spoken to Mr L1, Consultant General Surgeon and Unit General Manager of the WHH, and a member of the District Management Team. Mr L1 had indicated that he had also seen a patient of Ledward's, also with a cut ureter. They proceeded to discuss other cases, but Mr L1 was reported as saying that there was little he could do about Ledward's surgical abilities.[11]

In 1993, an initiative was launched to cut back surgical waiting lists. Over a four-hour period on one Saturday morning, Ledward undertook seven major operations when, the Ledward Inquiry concluded, a competent and careful surgeon would have been able to complete three. Three of these patients experienced complications and subsequently initiated negligence actions, all of which were settled.[12]

9 *The Ledward Report*, Part III, paras 3.1.1–4.2, 4.8, 5.4, 6.3 and 8.1.

10 *The Ledward Report*, Part IV, para 21.1.

11 *The Ledward Report*, Part IV, paras 3.2 and 3.3.1–3.3.2.

12 *The Ledward Report*, Part V, paras 5.3.1–5.3.4.

## Evidence of Ledward's Uncaring Attitude and Manner

Ledward displayed arrogance and an uncaring attitude towards a number of patients. This could manifest physically in rough internal examinations or by speaking to patients in a patronizing and belittling way.[13] Examples include the following. An NHS patient who lost her child as a premature delivery told the Inquiry that Ledward had been arrogant and uninterested in her distress. Another patient was very distressed after her baby died in utero. At a subsequent examination, Ledward had asked her how her baby was. In March 1984 Ledward undertook 'a deforming surgical procedure' on a private patient without obtaining consent. The patient also complained that Ledward had attended her whilst he was wearing 'a dusty sweater and jodhpurs'. His manner, she said, had been uncaring and inappropriate. In September 1984, Ledward operated on a private patient for fibroids, but in fact no fibroids were shown on histology. The patient suffered a primary haemorrhage and told the Inquiry that Ledward had been patronizing and treated her as if the post-operative complications were her own fault. No reference was made to the post-operative complications when Ledward wrote to the patient's GP. The patient was also unhappy that he attended her in riding clothes. An NHS patient gave evidence that in November 1984, Ledward had subjected her to a very rough vaginal examination. She found him unpleasant and lacking compassion, especially as he had told her to 'stop being so stupid' when she had complained.[14]

## Unnecessary Private Surgery

There was significant evidence that Ledward went beyond the limits of acceptable practice in persuading or pressurizing patients to pay for private treatment. Tactics included telling a patient that she had a risk of cancer, when there was no evidence for this other than the risk applicable to the population at large. Other examples include the following. Between 1981 and 1983, Ledward carried out a ventrosuspension and five additional surgical procedures on a private patient. Another private patient had an abdominal hysterectomy in 1981, a laparoscopy and then the removal of an ovary in July 1982, and an appendicectomy in 1983. The Inquiry was concerned as to whether all of these procedures were necessary. In 1982, Ledward persuaded an NHS patient to pay privately for a hysterectomy, claiming that the NHS waiting list was around two years and that there might be an underlying malignancy. There was no evidence to support the latter statement. In July 1983, Ledward performed a total abdominal hysterectomy and two further surgical procedures on a private patient, the need for which the Inquiry strongly questioned. Another private patient had surgery every year from 1985 to 1990; the Inquiry seriously doubted whether all of these procedures were medically necessary. During the 18 months from June 1984, Ledward carried out six surgical procedures on one of his private patients. The Inquiry expressed concern about whether these were necessary. After one procedure, a hysterectomy, the patient suffered a haemorrhage. Ledward could not be contacted

13 *The Ledward Report*, Part IV, paras 23.1–24.1.

14 *The Ledward Report*, Part III, paras 3.3, 4.6, 7.1, 7.9 and 7.11.

and another doctor had to attend the patient as an emergency.[15] The patient also gave evidence that he examined her in his riding clothes, which she felt was inappropriate. When the patient's funds ran out and she had to resort to NHS treatment, she said that Ledward's attitude changed completely; he became abrupt and offensive. By way of final example, an NHS patient gave evidence to the Inquiry that in 1981, she and her husband were unduly pressurized by Ledward to have a Caesarean section at 38 weeks of gestation, because he was to be away for two weeks.[16]

## Evidence from Doctors, Nurses and Managers

### *Consultants*

The Inquiry received evidence from other consultants in obstetrics and gynaecology and from other specialties. Some acknowledged that they knew of problems with Ledward's practice going back over a number of years. However, others denied any knowledge of the problems, claims which the Inquiry found 'incredible' within the close-knit atmosphere of the hospital.[17]

Mr L3, a Consultant Gynaecologist, told the Inquiry that in the late 1980s he attended one of Ledward's private patients with a pelvic abscess. Mr L3 was concerned that Ledward had gone to London, leaving his patient with no proper cover. Mr L3 also commented that Ledward could be 'arrogant and overbearing'. He also knew that Ledward pushed patients towards private practice and 'tried to obtain a financial advantage whenever he could do so'. For instance, Ledward had suggested to Mr L3 that they each turn down patients for NHS terminations, and should then refer the patients to the other for private care. Mr L3 described his horror at the proposal, but 'did not feel able to tell anyone because it would have simply been one consultant's word against the other'. Another Senior Consultant Gynaecologist, Mr L4, recalled warning Ledward that it was 'extremely foolish' to persuade NHS patients to be treated privately. This was reinforced by another fellow Consultant Gynaecologist, Mr L5, who gave evidence that he had noticed over time that Ledward had pursued various money-making schemes, including fostering his private practice, at the expense of devoting sufficient time to his clinical work. Mr L3 also observed that during this period of time, whilst Ledward was Director of Medical Audit for the Obstetric and Gynaecology Directorate, there was no audit of the division as a whole and Ledward had only audited the occasional case for teaching purposes.[18]

---

15 The Inquiry heard other evidence regarding other cases where Ledward carried out operations in private practice without making appropriate arrangements for their continuing care. *The Ledward Report*, Part III, para 7.6.

16 *The Ledward Report*, paras 23.1–23.2, Part III, paras 4.3–4.4, 4.9, 6.2, 7.3–7.5 and 7.14.

17 *The Ledward Report*, para 9.1.

18 *The Ledward Report*, Part V, paras 13.2.1–13.3.3 and Part IV, paras 9.2.1–9.2.2 and 9.3.

Mr L2, Consultant General Surgeon, gave evidence that he saw a number of Ledward's patients after complications had arisen. His impression was that problems increased in frequency over time. He noted two particular cases during the 1990s; both patients unnecessarily suffered damaged ureters. Mr L2 said that he was very concerned that nothing was being done about Ledward and had suggested to the two patients that they obtain legal advice. Even though these patients told him that they were unable to pursue this option, he had not felt able to act further. He was unaware of any system to report or investigate colleagues and said that he had been reluctant to 'stick my neck out and find myself sacked'. One of the two patients was eventually the basis of a finding of SPM against Ledward before the GMC.[19]

A number of general surgeons had ongoing concerns from around 1985 about Ledward's care of his patients. Gossip amongst surgeons recognized that Ledward was always 'supremely confident and never acknowledged that there was anything wrong with his practice'. One surgeon said that Ledward was regarded as being 'not frightfully good', but it was difficult to take action because his complications could usually be explained. However, the number of complications made Ledward's practice stand out. A Consultant Anaesthetist and a Consultant Pathologist told the Inquiry that the District General Manager was aware of the concerns about Ledward but no action was taken. The anaesthetist also recalled being given cash by Ledward for anaesthetizing a private patient, even though the patient was on an NHS list. He said he was highly critical of this, said so to Ledward and stopped anaesthetizing for Ledward's private practice. Ledward, he said, also made facetious remarks about patients in the operating theatre. Dr L6's evidence was that 'everybody thought everybody else was going to do something about it' and that at the time '…there was no real mechanism for getting to grips with this [a problem doctor] and no person who really was interested in keeping consultants in line...'. Similar views were voiced by GPs, who noted the absence of any easy mechanism for GPs to make complaints about a consultant.[20]

Mr L1, a Consultant General Surgeon at the William Harvey Hospital since the 1960s, gave evidence to the Inquiry that there had been a growing sense of unease about Ledward as the 1980s progressed. Mr L7, another Consultant General Surgeon, acknowledged that Ledward was known to be 'quick and rough', and generally there had been concerns about his surgical technique almost from the beginning. A third general surgeon, Mr L8, also considered Ledward to be rough and was concerned about his complication rate. Mr L8 was also aware that Ledward put his patients under pressure to pay for private treatment. He did not raise any of this formally, but simply stopped referring patients to Ledward. Similar observations were made by a Consultant Anaesthetist, Dr L6, who noted that Ledward's skills and commitment deteriorated over a period of time. Ledward began to attend operations late, relying on junior staff to start procedures, and surgical mishaps occurred. Concerns about Ledward were widespread by about 1983 or 1984. Notwithstanding this, one

---

19 *The Ledward Report*, Part V, para 14.2.1.

20 *The Ledward Report*, Part IV, paras 10.1–10.2 and 10.5.1–10.5.2 and 10.6.

consultant, Dr L9 – one of the hospital's 'three wise men', gave evidence that he had been unaware of any problem until Ledward's suspension in 1996.[21]

A Consultant General Surgeon, Mr L10, gave evidence that he had become very concerned about Ledward's patients by early 1991. Mr L10 said that he had spoken to Mr L20, then Unit General Manager of the William Harvey Hospital, in mid 1991 but no action had been taken as a result. His concerns were so great that he also spoke with Dr L11, Regional Director of Public Health, but was told that unless he 'was able to prove chapter and verse he could do nothing'. Dr L11's evidence was that he had told Mr L10 that he would need to collect evidence, to determine whether there was a prima facie case against Ledward. At the time, a pattern of poor performance was considered insufficient to justify disciplinary action – rather, evidence of serious incompetence was required.[22]

A Consultant Urologist, Mr L12, had become concerned about Ledward's practice in the early 1990s. Nursing staff and fellow consultants had spoken to him about Ledward. Nurses' concerns were that he operated too quickly and had too many complications. Mr L12 repeated the observations of other witnesses, that Ledward was frightening and intimidating, and that 'people did feel physically threatened by him and would not stand up against him because of that'. He had eventually reported Ledward in 1996, but had found this very distressing.[23]

### *Junior Doctors*

In contrast to the views of consultants, a number of junior doctors were complimentary about Ledward. For instance, Dr L13 had said that as a junior doctor between 1985 and 1986, he had found Ledward to be an 'exemplary' and committed teacher. Dr L14, a Senior House Officer and locum Registrar between 1985 and 1987, wrote: 'I can honestly say that the largest contribution I had to my career development has been through Mr Ledward. He is the single greatest contributor to my success in becoming a Member of The Royal College of Obstetricians and Gynaecologists.'[24] It was of note that there was a culture amongst junior doctors of reluctance to criticize their seniors, because of the perceived threat that this would pose to their careers.[25] Therefore, it was unclear how representative these positive comments were and if other doctors had resisted coming forwards to give evidence.

### *Nursing Staff*

A number of nursing staff commented that Ledward could have a poor manner with patients and that whilst he had started well, problems emerged gradually during the early 1980s. Some nurses were reluctant to speak out against Ledward. Some took

---

21 *The Ledward Report*, Part III, paras 11.1–11.3, 11.6 and 11.8.

22 *The Ledward Report*, Part V, paras 3.11.1–3.11.3.

23 *The Ledward Report*, Part V, paras 14.3.1–14.3.2.

24 *The Ledward Report*, Part III, paras 12.1–12.2.

25 *The Ledward Report*, paras 8.1–8.2 and 13.5.

the view that it was not for them to criticize a consultant, whilst others feared being criticized themselves.[26]

An outpatient sister gave evidence about Ledward's poor hygiene standards and failure to adequately explain procedures to patients. Ledward also 'appeared to be rough' when undertaking vaginal examinations. She had also heard Ledward incorrectly advise some patients that the treatment they required was not available on the NHS. Another sister, who had worked with Ledward in the Obstetric and Gynaecology theatre from 1993–1994, also criticized his hygiene – saying that he was 'perfunctory' when scrubbing for operations and failed to change his gown when moving from one operation to another. She also said that he did not change gloves between patients and sometimes omitted gloves altogether. The same sister also expressed concerns at the speed of Ledward's operations and an associated lack of care. She described his style as 'extremely quick and slap dash'; his speed prevented both nursing staff and the anaesthetist from doing their jobs properly. Ledward would also leave the operating theatre during operating lists, and could be difficult to find. These concerns were widely shared by both nurses and doctors.[27]

An operating theatre sister who had worked with Ledward for around five years gave evidence that he often did not remain in theatre, but would return to his office, leaving a junior doctor to finish the operation and sometimes to start the next. Other consultants did not behave in the same way. She also considered Ledward's surgery to be too fast to be safe. There were also occasions when Ledward had removed ovaries without explicit consent. The sister told the Inquiry that there was no means to indicate on the theatre record that a procedure was being carried out without the patient's consent. Post-operatively, Ledward often failed to attend if there was a problem. The sister also described problems with Ledward's hygiene. He had to be pressured to wash his hands and did not always wear surgical gloves when examining patients. The sister said that she had raised these matters with her line manager and with two other consultants.[28]

A ward sister observed that his visits to patients were far less frequent than those of other consultants. She had also noted that Ledward's operations appeared to be rushed, and therefore his patients needed more careful observation afterwards. Concerns were further increased because Ledward was often difficult to contact if there was a problem with one of his patients. The sister had felt unable to raise concerns, saying: '…as a nurse, "you did not complain to another consultant or question that consultant's ability. You did not do it. It just was not done."'[29]

A staff nurse who had worked on the gynaecology ward noted that during ward rounds, Ledward's examinations of patients were very quick, nurses were not given time to cover patients, and he would move on before the patient had time to ask questions. Even if a patient had suffered complications, Ledward did not visit

26 Others, in contrast, were complimentary about Ledward, saying, for example, that he was 'superb with his patients', 'enjoyed a very good reputation and that a lot of people thought the world of him'. *The Ledward Report*, Part III, paras 13.1–13.2, 13.4 and 13.6.

27 *The Ledward Report*, Part V, paras 16.1.2 and 16.3.1–16.3.5.

28 *The Ledward Report*, Part IV, paras 12.1.1–12.1.5.

29 *The Ledward Report*, Part IV, paras 12.2.1–12.2.3.

until his scheduled weekly ward round. The sister in charge of outpatients described how patients complained that Ledward 'treated them like slabs of meat and taught his students over them'. He often left patients in tears. She also gave evidence about Ledward's unsubtle attempts to persuade patients to become private patients, sometimes exaggerating the NHS waiting list times. It was said that other consultants knew what was happening. A midwifery sister gave evidence of an occasion when, during the delivery of a baby, Ledward 'appeared to be worse the wear for drink'. She described the delivery as 'brutal', and although the baby was in good health, the mother was very traumatized. The sister reported the matter the next morning, but no action was taken. The Nursing Officer for Midwifery gave evidence that Ledward was rough when examining patients and his attitude flippant. She said that it was difficult to raise concerns about a consultant at the time because 'they were treated as gods'.[30]

A staff nurse gave evidence that around 1993, a patient came to the WHH with serious post-partum bleeding. A junior doctor attended and then Ledward. She said that Ledward was 'obviously drunk'. An altercation had occurred between the junior doctor and Ledward regarding the most appropriate treatment. As Ledward had been the Clinical Director at the time, the nursing staff had felt helpless to intervene.[31] A staff nurse also gave evidence that the nursing staff thought that Ledward had significant power with the Royal College of Obstetricians and Gynaecologists and he spoke about 'knowing people in the GMC'. This, coupled with his reputation as a bully, prevented them from acting.[32]

### *General Practitioners*

Some general practitioners had developed concerns about Ledward's practice and manner. For example, one general practitioner gave evidence that initially he was happy to refer patients to Ledward, but this view changed within 2–3 years as patients increasingly suffered complications. The GP was also concerned that Ledward put inappropriate pressure on patients to go privately. The GP and his senior partner 'even discussed reporting…[their concerns] to the General Medical Council. However, they felt that the GMC would probably do nothing and so no referral was made.' Instead, the GP stopped referring his patients to Ledward. Another GP, who had observed that Ledward's patients suffered more complications than he would have expected, and private patients were undergoing excessive procedures, said that he lacked the authority to challenge Ledward. Instead, he reduced referrals to him. Other GPs reinforced the feeling that it was difficult for a GP to criticize a specialist. Of those GPs who professed to be unaware of problems, the Inquiry concluded that they were 'those who tended to bury their heads in the sand, who did not listen to patients' concerns or who felt that any Consultant must…be good at his job and beyond challenge'.[33]

---

30 *The Ledward Report*, Part IV, paras 14.1.1–14.1.3.

31 *The Ledward Report*, Part V, para 5.31.

32 *The Ledward Report*, Part V, para 16.5.2.

33 *The Ledward Report*, paras 11.1, Part III, paras 12.3–14.2 and Part IV, paras 13.2–13.3.

On 5 June 1995 there was a meeting of the South East Kent General Practitioner Committee, at which it was said that there was a frank discussion about Ledward and a general consensus by the GPs that they did not wish to refer patients to him.[34] A number of patients had asked for a referral to an alternative consultant, but some GPs had been unwilling to do this, considering it to be somehow unethical. Similarly, some GPs were unwilling to accede to patients' wishes for a second opinion, possibly because of the criticism of Ledward this might imply.[35] An example of this occurred in September 1984, when a private patient suffered a primary haemorrhage after hysterectomy. Ledward was contacted during the following night by the Consultant Anaesthetist, but did not attend. The patient also gave evidence that during a follow-up appointment, Ledward had subjected her to a 'brutal internal examination'. When she made a complaint to the private hospital, this was simply passed on to Ledward. When the patient asked her GP to refer her to another gynaecologist, she was told that it would be unethical do this.[36]

The Inquiry recommended that all NHS Trusts should monitor, at a senior level, patterns in GP referrals. This should be accompanied by Clinical Liaison Groups, which should include consultants and GPs. This group would implement procedures for detecting and acting upon problems. GPs and others primary care providers should also be told how to raise concerns with the Medical Director of an NHS Trust.[37]

### *Managers*

Ledward worked within a local management structure, but was employed by the South East Thames Regional Health Authority.[38] Mr L1 was the General Manager of the William Harvey Hospital and a member of the District Management Team between 1986 and 1989. He confirmed that some of the concerns about Ledward were known by the Management Team, and he accepted that management should have taken action. Similarly, the Chief Nursing Officer and member of the District Management Team from 1982 to 1994 also confirmed that she had become aware of concerns. She could not recall any formal management discussion about Ledward during the early to mid 1980s.[39] Overall, evidence from management acknowledged awareness of far fewer problems than those revealed by medical colleagues. This suggests that fellow doctors and other medical staff were in a stronger position

34 *The Ledward Report*, Part V, para 11.2.

35 *The Ledward Report*, Part VII.

36 *The Ledward Report*, Part III, para 7.8. Another NHS patient had a similar experience in 1991. Having found Ledward to be arrogant, patronizing and intimidating, she had asked her GP to refer her to another consultant. She was told by the GP that this 'was not the done thing'. Part V, para 3.4.

37 *The Ledward Report*, Part VII.

38 All consultants, senior and junior registrars and doctors of other training grades were employed by the Regional Health Authority. *The Ledward Report*, Part III, para 16.1.

39 *The Ledward Report*, Part III, para 14.1. Similar sentiments were expressed by another GP, who also stopped referring patients to Ledward; see paras 15.4–15.5.

than managers to monitor colleagues.[40] This was the position adopted by Mr L15, District General Manager until March 1994, who gave evidence to the Inquiry that he saw his responsibility for the quality of medical care as minor. He always worked on the assumption that it was the job of the GMC to deal with matters of clinical competence. The GMC should act first, following which the employer could take any appropriate steps from its perspective. Mr L16, Chief Executive of the East Kent Health Authority, gave evidence that before clinical governance was introduced, there was no clear agreement about who was responsible for quality of patient care. The Inquiry disagreed with these assumptions, concluding that by the summer of 1995, at the latest, the Trust management[41] should have been alerted to the fact that there might be significant problems with Ledward's practice. Instead of taking appropriate action, the management 'abdicated responsibility' by referring this back to the GPs, for them to speak to Ledward. The management should have fully investigated the concerns raised by the GPs by undertaking a proper audit. For management to simply rely on mutual monitoring by the surgeons was inappropriate. When they did act, the managers tried to address each problem separately, rather than looking at the whole situation. As a result, the full extent of the problems was not appreciated.[42] As the Inquiry put it: 'We accept that investigation would have been demanding of time and energy by management. It would have been a difficult and unpleasant task. However in our view managers are appointed to manage and if they shrink from that responsibility, the NHS is poorly served.'[43]

Disciplinary action was eventually taken in August 1995, after Ledward had treated a private patient whilst signed off sick from the WHH. However, as previously noted, this was dealt with in isolation, rather than a full investigation being initiated. Ledward was suspended in January 1996 and disciplinary proceedings instituted. However, it had taken 16 years to reach that point. The Inquiry concluded that for at least ten of those years there was evidence which should have alerted management to serious concerns about Ledward.[44]

## Post-Suspension Activities

For a period of time after his suspension, Ledward continued to undertake private work. At the conclusion of disciplinary action, he was dismissed from his NHS consultant post and a report was made to the GMC. On 16 February 1997, Ledward commenced employment as a Consultant Gynaecologist and Obstetrician for the Ministry of Defence, working in Cyprus. As the Ministry of Defence viewed the position as short-term and casual, Ledward was not interviewed, nor was his last employer contacted. He was appointed on the strength of the recommendation of

40 *The Ledward Report*, Part IV, para 14.6.1.

41 From April 1994, consultants were employed by the Trust and no longer by the Region.

42 *The Ledward Report*, Part V, paras 18.8.1, 21.1.1–21.1.4, 27.5–27.6, 27.9 and 31.2–31.12.

43 *The Ledward Report*, Part V, para 31.2.

44 *The Ledward Report*, Part V, paras 31.13–31.15.

the outgoing (retiring) post-holder and two personal references. It appears that the outgoing post-holder took the view that Ledward had been unfairly dismissed – illustrating the influence of informal friendship networks as a means of undermining formal regulatory systems.[45]

It is of note that in the following year, in *Good Medical Practice*, the GMC described the duty of a doctor in relation to references as follows:

> Patients may be put at risk if you confirm the competence of someone who has not reached or maintained a satisfactory standard of practice. When providing references for colleagues your comments must be honest and justifiable; you must include all relevant information which has a bearing on the colleague's competence, performance, reliability and conduct.

The Ledward Inquiry concluded that, if a doctor fails to comply with these requirements, this should constitute serious professional misconduct.

**Evidence from the Private Sector**

Mr L17, Chief Executive of the Chaucer Hospital from October 1990, gave evidence that when he joined the hospital, there was already concern from operating theatre and nursing staff about Ledward's lack of skill in operating. Anaesthetists in particular were very unhappy about working with Ledward. Similar evidence was given by Mr L18, General Manager at St Saviour's Hospital. However, Mr L18 also confirmed that there was an ingrained culture amongst the nursing staff that they did not challenge or question the judgement of consultants. Legal actions would be handled by the consultant's defence union, and the hospital would not generally be notified.[46]

In December 1993 a number of consultant surgeons from the WHH, who also had admitting rights at St Saviour's Hospital, informed the General Manager of their concerns about Ledward's surgical complication rate. An investigation was initiated, but this did not involve contacting Ledward's NHS employers. Even though the investigations revealed that Ledward's complication rate was higher than those of his colleagues, no action was taken.[47] The Inquiry concluded that it could not criticize the private hospital managers for failing to act in the climate that existed at the time.[48] Future changes were, however, needed. The Chief Executive or General Manager of each private hospital should be responsible for the quality of care. The Clinical Governance procedures applicable to the NHS should also be implemented in the private sector. Although, in contrast to the Fifth Report of the Health Committee published in July 1999, which recommended a separate Private Sector Ombudsman, the Ledward Inquiry favoured the use of a single Ombudsman for all health matters.[49]

---

45 *The Ledward Report*, Part VI, paras 1.1–1.2 and 2.1–2.8.

46 *The Ledward Report*, Part IV, paras 16.2.1 and 26.1, and Part V, paras 22.1.1–22.2.5.

47 *The Ledward Report*, Part V, paras 32.2–32.3.

48 *The Ledward Report*, Part IV, paras 16.2.1 and 26.1, and Part V, paras 22.1.1–22.2.5.

49 *The Ledward Report*, Part VII, paras (ii)–(iv).

## GMC Professional Conduct and Discipline Pamphlets – the 'Blue Books'

The May 1977 edition of the 'Blue Book' was operational when Ledward became a consultant. Under the heading 'Failure to treat or visit patients', the Book stated that:

> The Council in pursuance of its primary duty to protect the public institutes disciplinary proceedings when a doctor appears seriously to have disregarded or neglected his professional duties to his patients, for example by failing to visit or to provide or arrange treatment for a patient when necessary.

It also stated that the GMC was 'not concerned with errors in diagnosis or treatment'.[50]

Under the subheading 'Delegation of medical duties', the Blue Book stated: '...a doctor who delegates treatment or other procedures must be satisfied that the person to whom they are delegated is competent to carry them out. It is also important that the doctor should retain ultimate responsibility for the management of his patients…'

This edition of the Blue Book also contained a warning that deprecation by a doctor of another doctor's professional skill, knowledge, qualifications or services could constitute serious professional misconduct.[51]

The 1981 edition of the Blue Book modified the guidance regarding diagnostic and treatment errors:

> In considering complaints...about the conduct of a doctor, the Council is not ordinarily concerned with errors in diagnosis or treatment. But in pursuance of its primary duty to protect the public the Council may institute disciplinary proceedings when a doctor appears to have disregarded or neglected his professional duties to his patients, for example by failing to visit or to provide or arrange treatment for a patient when necessary.[52]

The 1983 edition of the Blue Book dealt with the issue in the following terms:

> The Council is not ordinarily concerned with errors in diagnosis or treatment, or with the kind of matters which give rise to action in the civil courts for negligence, unless the doctor's conduct in the case has involved such a disregard of his professional responsibility to his patients or such a neglect of his professional duties as to raise a question of serious professional misconduct.[53]

Under the heading 'Personal behaviour: Conduct derogatory to the reputation of the profession', the Blue Book also introduced the provision that: 'A doctor who treats patients or performs other professional duties while he is under the influence of drink…is liable to disciplinary proceedings.'[54]

---

50 Discussed in *The Ledward Report*, para 19.1.3.

51 Discussed in *The Ledward Report*, paras 19.1.4–19.1.5. The difficulties with these provisions in successive editions of the Blue Book are discussed in greater detail later.

52 Discussed in *The Ledward Report*, para 19.3.1.

53 Discussed in *The Ledward Report*, para 19.4.1.

54 Discussed in *The Ledward Report*, para 19.4.2.

The focus of this heading, on the reputation of the profession rather than the specific protection of patients, is notable as a reflection of the focus of the GMC at this time.

By April 1985, the Blue Book stated that:

> The public are entitled to expect that a registered medical practitioner will afford and maintain a good standard of medical care. This includes:
> (a) conscientious assessment of the history, symptoms and signs of a patient's condition;
> (b) sufficiently thorough professional attention, examination and, where necessary, diagnostic investigation;
> (c) competent and considerate professional management;
> (d) appropriate and prompt action upon evidence suggesting the existence of a condition requiring urgent medical intervention; and
> (e) readiness, where the circumstances so warrant, to consult appropriate professional colleagues…
>
> The Council is concerned with errors in diagnosis or treatment, and with the kind of matters which give rise to action in the civil courts for negligence, only when the doctor's conduct in the case has involved such a disregard of his professional responsibility to patients or such a neglect of his professional duties as to raise a question of serious professional misconduct…[55]

Whilst there was a gradual development from edition to edition of the Blue Book, these changes were not highlighted. For the message to get through to doctors, the GMC was relying upon every doctor to read each edition, compare it with the last and thereby identify changes.[56] This reliance appears to have been misplaced.

Even by the mid 1980s, negligence by a doctor in the care and treatment of a patient did not, from the perspective of the GMC, warrant disciplinary action. Only a serious dereliction of a doctor's duties to patients would suffice.[57] Presumably, one very serious act or a pattern of errors would have been needed to satisfy this requirement.

The June 1990 edition of the Blue Book repeated significant aspects of previous editions, but also envisaged that disciplinary action could result from 'improper arrangements calculated to extend or benefit a doctor's practice'. This could include putting pressure on a patient to undergo private treatment, for instance, by making unfavourable comparisons with NHS treatment or waiting times. This edition also made clear that doctors were under a duty to report a colleague whose behaviour raised a potential question of serious professional misconduct, or whose fitness to practise might be seriously impaired.[58]

The February 1991 Blue Book, under the heading 'Delegation of medical duties to professional colleagues', stated:

55 Discussed in *The Ledward Report*, para 19.5.1.

56 Discussed in *The Ledward Report*, para 19.6.

57 Discussed in *The Ledward Report*, para 19.6.

58 *The Ledward Report*, Part IV, paras 19.1.1–19.1.2.

> ...consultants in hospital practice, and doctors engaged in private practice...should seek to ensure that proper arrangements are put in hand to cover their own duties...during any period of absence...Consultants and other senior hospital staff should delegate to junior colleagues only those duties which are within their capabilities.

Under a new heading, 'Comments about professional colleagues', it was acknowledged that certain situations might require a doctor to comment on another's practice:

> Doctors are frequently called upon to express a view about a colleague's professional practice. This may, for example, happen in the course of a medical audit or peer review procedure, or when a doctor is asked to give a reference about a colleague...Honest comment is entirely acceptable in such circumstances, provided that it is carefully considered and can be justified, that it is offered in good faith and that it is intended to promote the best interests of patients...
>
> Further it is any doctor's duty, where the circumstances so warrant, to inform an appropriate person or body about a colleague whose professional conduct or fitness to practise may be called in question or whose professional performance appears to be in some way deficient...However, gratuitous and unsustainable comment which...sets out to undermine trust in a professional colleague's knowledge or skills is unethical.

Thus, after February 1991, there was a positive duty to report imposed upon any doctor who was concerned about another doctor's conduct, fitness or competence.[59] As illustrated, the changes to the Blue Book from the mid 1980s onwards provided appropriate provisions to allow the GMC to bring action against Ledward. However, as discussed in Chapter 2, the lack of investigatory provision or motivation towards being proactive within the GMC meant that nothing was done.

## Good Medical Practice

When *Good Medical Practice* replaced the Blue Book in October 1995, the new booklet began with the provision that: 'Patients are entitled to good standards of practice and care from their doctors. Essential elements of this are professional competence, good relationships with patients and colleagues and observance of professional ethical obligations.'

This clear focus on patient care in a new form was a positive advance on the creeping change in the Blue Book, although the message did not necessarily make its way through to all those doctors who needed to heed it.[60]

*Good Medical Practice* also required doctors to, inter alia: listen to patients and respect their views; treat patients considerately and politely; respect the dignity and privacy of patients; allow patients to be fully involved in decisions about their care; respect the rights of patients to refuse to participate in teaching or research. It was also emphasized that a doctor must not abuse the trust of a patient by, for example,

59 *The Ledward Report*, Part V, paras 25.1.3–25.1.5.

60 *The Ledward Report*, Part V, para 25.6.

putting pressure on the patient to pay for treatment or recommending treatment which was not in the patients' best interests. Doctors also had to ensure that, when they were unavailable, appropriate arrangements were made for the medical care of their patients. Doctors were also required to act in the best interest of patients when a colleague's behaviour, performance or health might be a threat to them. However, this had to be reconciled with the obligation not to make any patient doubt a colleague's knowledge or skills by making unnecessary or unsustainable comments about them.[61]

## Complaints

There was little or no evidence of formal complaints against Ledward in the early to mid 1980s. This might have been attributable to a combination of factors, in particular a scarcity of information about how to complain, a complex complaints system and the sensitive nature of the medical problems concerned. There also remained the prevailing culture, shared by staff and patients, that a consultant could not be questioned or criticized. Some patients were also afraid that if they complained, this would affect their future treatment and care.[62]

In August 1992, a patient did complain formally about Ledward, alleging that he had roughly inserted an instrument into her vagina without prior explanation. Students also examined her without permission. The response to the complaint was to arrange a meeting between Ledward and the patient. Ledward had apologized that he had 'not lived up to the patient's expectation' and had been 'less than perfect on this occasion'.

In another case, a patient had complained about the quality of care received from Ledward. Ledward's written responses were accepted at face value by senior NHS managers, and so no investigation was undertaken. In October 1995, the mother of a patient wrote to complain about Ledward's treatment of her daughter. Ledward failed to diagnose an ectopic pregnancy, which required emergency surgery the next day. The complainant wrote:

> ...we were both shocked by his manner and professional conduct. Apart from being late for the appointment, he did not, we believe, pay sufficient attention to [her] presenting symptoms and medical history, preferring instead to concentrate on her responsibility regarding birth control and making inaccurate and offensive social judgements.

Senior managers met with the patient and her mother, and also spoke with Ledward. Ledward's response was that his treatment had been appropriate. The patient's mother was informed of Ledward's response and the complaint was closed. These cases indicate that, notwithstanding a decade of problems with his practice, it remained relatively easy for Ledward to fob off both his patients and his employers.[63]

61 *The Ledward Report*, Part V, para 25.5.3.

62 *The Ledward Report*, paras 25.4–25.6 and Part V, para 7.22.

63 *The Ledward Report*, Part V, paras 4.4, 6.8.6 and 7.21.1–7.21.3.

## Fear of Initiating Formal Procedures

In January 1996, Ledward performed a total abdominal hysterectomy; during the surgery the patient's bladder and ureter were damaged. After the surgery, Ledward could not be contacted. Another consultant had to attend and it was subsequently found that the patient was suffering from peritonitis and two urinary tract injuries. Ledward, it was said, had performed the procedure far too quickly and should have recognized the damage at the time he was operating. Dr L19, Medical Director, was informed about this patient and spoke to her. The patient had explained her medical experience and also complained that Ledward had pressured her to pay for private treatment. Dr L19 concluded that the allegations were sufficiently serious that Ledward should be prevented from operating until investigations were complete. Mr L20, then Unit General Manager of the William Harvey Hospital, agreed that Ledward should be immediately suspended and disciplinary action begun.[64] Mrs L21, Business Manager, told the Inquiry: '[T]hat she had thought it was very brave of Dr L19 and Mr L20 to suspend Rodney Ledward since if it had gone wrong it would have been disastrous for the Trust and for them.'

Other witnesses echoed these concerns, considering that bringing disciplinary action against Ledward 'was a momentous step, because he was powerful and intimidating' and there was fear that he might 'harm or destroy the careers of those who spoke against him'.[65]

It was estimated that because the disciplinary procedures were 'outmoded' and 'cumbersome', the cost of bringing action against Ledward was in the region of £500,000. The Inquiry heard from a number of witnesses that:

> it would be a brave Chief Executive and Medical Director who began such a procedure without being very sure of the outcome…[H]ad such expenditure been incurred and the disciplinary panel not found the cases against Rodney Ledward proved, the Chief Executive and the Medical Director would have had to resign.[66]

## Misplaced Loyalty

As already discussed, some witnesses believed that 'Ledward had friends in high places, including within the GMC'. This added to reservations about reporting him or agreeing to give evidence. Whilst this fear was not specifically substantiated, the Inquiry did note that some eminent doctors who knew Ledward socially, or from academic encounters, 'wrote in strident terms in his support although they had little or no first hand knowledge of his skills as a Gynaecologist'. Further, some consultants who gave evidence against Ledward in the NHS disciplinary proceedings or the GMC, or both, reported that they 'were left in no doubt by some of their eminent colleagues that if the case against Rodney Ledward did not succeed they would find themselves ostracised'. This would have significantly impinged upon their continued

---

64 *The Ledward Report*, Part V, paras 8.2.1–8.2.7.

65 *The Ledward Report*, Part V, para 8.2.13.

66 *The Ledward Report*, Part VII, paras 2 and 6.

and future employment.[67] Such a climate of fear and intimidation within the senior ranks of the profession gives serious cause for concern.

## Should Fellow Doctors be Criticised for Failing to Act?

The Inquiry concluded that the consultants who had concerns about Ledward were aware that the District Management team knew of these concerns, and considered that it was up to management to act. It is possible that they considered that, since management was aware, they had complied with any Blue Book duty to inform an 'appropriate body'. The Inquiry acknowledged that, at the time, it would have been a very significant step for a doctor to report a colleague to the GMC. The focus in the 'Blue Book' warnings against disparaging colleagues, and that negligence alone was not a disciplinary matter, would have also dissuaded these colleagues from reporting any concerns to the GMC.[68] However, the question remains – if members of the medical profession believe and/or benefit from the rhetoric associated with self-regulation, why did they fail to do more? Management (some of the most senior managers also being senior doctors) were eventually made aware, but it should have become clear relatively quickly that no action was being taken. The profession has been vocal in its opposition to external interference when this approach has served its interests. To justify self-regulation, doctors must be equally vociferous in seeking to ensure that the GMC takes action when one of their number presents a risk to patients.

## GMC Action against Ledward

Ledward was dismissed by the South Kent Hospitals NHS Trust in December 1996, and the GMC informed on 12 December 1996. On 22 January 1997, the GMC asked the Trust for information about the patients whose cases had formed the basis of the Disciplinary Inquiry. Medical records were sent to the GMC after consent was obtained from the patients. Five months later, at the end of May 1997, the GMC screener referred the case to the Preliminary Proceedings Committee. Ten months after the initial notification to the GMC, at a meeting on 10 October 1997, the PPC decided to refer Ledward to the Professional Conduct Committee and imposed an interim suspension on him. It was almost a year later, on 14 September 1998, that the PCC met. On 30 September 1998, Ledward's name was erased from the medical register.[69]

It is of considerable concern that the GMC process took almost two years to reach a conclusion, and almost a year to impose an interim suspension. It is also of concern that witnesses at the GMC hearing told the Ledward Inquiry that they found giving evidence 'stressful and emotionally draining' and were concerned that they themselves came under attack. A number of consultants went so far as to say

67 *The Ledward Report*, Part VII, paras 1.9–1.10.

68 *The Ledward Report*, Part IV, paras 25.5–25.7.

69 *The Ledward Report*, Part VII, paras 1.1–1.6.

that 'had they known what it would be like they would not have given evidence and would never subject themselves to a similar experience again'.[70] Clearly, this is of significant concern in terms of the reporting/whistleblowing process.

The basis of the GMC action included examples of incompetent treatment, inadequate record-keeping, operating without consent, failing to arrange adequate cover and inappropriate delegation to junior staff. The Inquiry recommended that the feeling of attack on the part of witnesses would be reduced if the Professional Conduct Committee of the GMC adopted the civil, rather than the criminal, standard of proof – on the strong balance of probabilities.[71] Furthermore, hearings should be chaired by an experienced judge who would ensure that proceedings were conducted fairly in the appropriate interests of all participants. In 2001, the GMC rejected the proposition that the civil standard should be used by the PCC, but saw its possible use should the Council come to deal with allegations of misconduct which fall short of serious professional misconduct. The GMC also expressed concern about any move towards a legally qualified chair for the PCC, in particular, the perceived danger that a lawyer might take an overly legalistic approach, as well as the broader risk of weakening the link between the medical profession and the regulatory process.[72] This argument would have carried more weight if the performance of the GMC had not been so problematic. For an organization faced with regulatory problems on a range of fronts, criticism that a more legalistic approach would worsen the position even further requires far more convincing substantiation than was actually put forward by the GMC.

The Ledward Inquiry also expressed concern that there was significant duplication between the Trust and GMC disciplinary procedures. This was particularly onerous for those witnesses who had to give evidence twice. The Inquiry's conclusion was that the introduction of an Assessment and Support Centre and associated disciplinary system should be sufficient to meet both aspects.[73]

## Incident Reporting

Prior to Ledward's suspension, there was no system of clinical incident reporting in place. When reporting systems were introduced, the stated aim was to ensure that untoward events were identified and lessons learned. A Clinical or Critical Incident Report Form should be completed when anything untoward occurs, including any complications which vary from the norm, and unusual event. An example of the latter would be the absence of a chaperone during an intimate examination. Anyone who is aware of an event should complete a form. The Inquiry heard that the system was very variable in its effectiveness across the NHS, and that nurses tended to be better than doctors in completing forms. The Inquiry concluded that an effective

---

70 *The Ledward Report*, Part VII, para 1.6.

71 The government, in its *NHS Plan for England*, also recommended consideration of the civil standard.

72 See GMC, *Acting Fairly to Protect Patients: Reform of the GMC's Fitness to Practise Procedures*, March 2001, 19—20; and *The Ledward Report*, Part VII.

73 *The Ledward Report*, Part VII, paras 1.7–1.12.

reporting system is dependent on the presence of an effective and respected person in charge, who should be directly answerable to the Chief Executive of the NHS Trust and should be a member of the Clinical Governance Committee of the Trust. Had an effective system and appropriate Clinical Risk Manager been present during Ledward's misconduct, it is likely that he would have been detected far earlier.[74]

The Ledward Inquiry recommended that clinical or critical incident forms should be renamed 'Incident Report', and should cover all aspects of medical care, including matters of conduct. Each Royal College should draw up a list of untoward clinical events which should trigger an incident report. Trusts should draw up a list of non-clinical events, conduct in the widest sense, which should trigger an incident report. Thus, *any NHS employee should complete an incident report for any untoward event.* For example, support staff would fill in a form when an item of equipment is broken, a surgeon would complete a form when unexpected harm occurs to a patient.[75]

---

74 *The Ledward Report*, Part VII, paras 1—5.

75 *The Ledward Report*, Part VII, paras (i)–(iii) and (v).

## Chapter 9

# William Kerr and Michael Haslam

### Introduction

In 2000 and 2003 two senior consultant psychiatrists, William Kerr and Michael Haslam, were convicted of offences involving the sexual abuse of patients. Both consultants had worked in the same hospital in the 1970s and 1980s. Kerr was convicted (in absence, on a trial of facts[1]) of one count of indecent assault. Haslam was convicted of four counts of indecent assault. The victims were 'vulnerable female psychiatric patients' who were being treated by the respective consultant. The outcome of the breach of trust this involved was described as 'devastating'. It was also said that Kerr played on this vulnerability by threatening some of his victims with forcible detention under mental health legislation or the removal of their children.[2]

In July 2001 the Secretary of State for Health announced the setting up of an independent Inquiry to consider the activities of Kerr and Haslam.[3] The subsequent Inquiry Report identified 59 former patients of William Kerr who alleged sexual assault or inappropriate sexualized behaviour. In the period 1965–1983, at least 30 of these patients raised concerns with at least 11 different GPs. Only one GP attempted to take the matter forward – unfortunately, as it transpired, to the other consultant subject to the Inquiry, Michael Haslam. In the same period, complaints or disclosures were also made to 11 hospital staff and the Secretary of the Leeds Regional Hospital Board and the Health Service Commissioner. No investigation resulted. One of these disclosures was even referred to William Kerr himself by a more junior colleague. Kerr dismissed the complaint as 'malicious'.[4] Only in 1997, almost ten years after Kerr had retired and 30 years after concerns were first raised, was an appropriate investigation undertaken and criminal prosecutions eventually initiated.

The questions which the subsequent Inquiry posed were: why were patients not listened to effectively, and why were many opportunities to investigate missed so that

---

1 Kerr was not fit to plead and so was not able to be tried by a jury in the usual way. Instead, the prosecution was permitted to place the evidence before the jury, the defence was allowed to challenge this evidence and the jury was asked to decide whether the alleged 'facts' had been proved beyond reasonable doubt. *The Kerr/Haslam Inquiry Report*, July 2005, Cm 6640-1, 270.

2 *The Kerr/Haslam Inquiry Report*, July 2005, Cm 6640-1, 4 and 247.

3 This was one of three Inquiries announced together. The other two were to be set up to consider the activities of Clifford Ayling and Richard Neale.

4 *The Kerr/Haslam Inquiry Report*, July 2005, Cm 6640-1, 170.

abuse went undetected for very significant periods of time?[5] Many fellow doctors and other medical professionals ignored warning signs or chose to remain silent when they should have spoken out, in a culture where consultants were 'all powerful'. This was exacerbated by management failures and poor systems for communication.

### William Kerr

The first allegation of sexual assault against Kerr was made in 1964 when he was working in Northern Ireland. The complaint was taken before a medical disciplinary committee and it appears that Kerr was found guilty of professional misconduct and advised to leave Northern Ireland if he wished to continue in practice. In December 1964 Kerr applied for a Registrar post in Leeds. References were not taken up from his previous employer and the interview panel appear to have offered Kerr the job without knowledge of the circumstances which had resulted in him leaving Northern Ireland. The Inquiry noted that the failure to take up references was not limited to the 1960s. When Haslam was appointed to the post of Medical Director in 1993 (after concerns about him had come to light, see later) no references were taken up. Within the first year of Kerr taking up his new post, the first allegation of sexual misconduct arose, this being made to a GP, who did not pursue the matter. Rumours also began to spread about Kerr's 'reputation'. These continued throughout his career.[6]

Kerr became a consultant in 1967 and remained at this grade until his retirement in 1988. During this time, 38 patients had made disclosures to NHS staff of sexualized behaviour by Kerr. None of these resulted in appropriate investigations. Following the establishing of the Inquiry, at least 29 further patients came forward with similar allegations. Allegations involved indecent exposure by Kerr, invitations to patients to perform sexual acts and in some cases sexual intercourse. Kerr would seek to explain his actions as being part of the patient's psychiatric treatment and generally leave them confused as to whether they were at fault. Virtually none of the complaints made whilst Kerr was in practice were acted upon. An exception was Patient A22, who in 1979 complained about Kerr to her GP, Dr KH1. Unfortunately (as it turned out), Dr KH1 raised the matter with Michael Haslam. Another exception arose in 1983 when Patient A17 gave an account of an alleged sexual relationship with Kerr to Deputy Nursing Sister Linda Bigwood. Unlike many of her colleagues, Linda Bigwood tried to act. She attempted to raise her concerns about this and other patients, who had alleged abuse by both Kerr and Haslam, with the District and Regional Health Authorities. Attempts, both in writing and face to face, to raise concerns with senior NHS managers over a period of four years resulted in no investigation into

5 *The Kerr/Haslam Inquiry Report*, July 2005, Cm 6640-1, 5.

6 The rumours ranged from gossip that he was a 'flirt' with female members of staff to more serious suggestions that he made sexual advances towards female patients. The Inquiry recognized that acting merely on rumour and gossip was dangerous because of the risk, for example, that such were malicious or unfounded. However, rumours could not be dismissed as absolutely without value. Consistent rumours from different sources could represent a valuable warning that things were amiss. *The Kerr/Haslam Inquiry Report*, July 2005, Cm 6640-1, 84–9.

Kerr's practice. One patient, in 1983, was reported to have offered to help Deputy Sister Bigwood. However, as the health authority ignored calls to investigate Kerr's practice, statements were never obtained from this or other patients. The Inquiry concluded that, had the health authority sought evidence from patients such as this, it would have led them in turn to at least one GP surgery, the partners of which were in receipt of complaints from at least five patients.[7] Whilst Kerr retired from the NHS with a positive record, Linda Bigwood suffered 'professional detriment' as a result of her attempts to blow the whistle.

Kerr was only formally investigated by the police in 1997, almost ten years after his retirement and over 30 years after concerns had first been raised.

## Michael Haslam

Michael Haslam was a consultant psychiatrist from 1970. From this time, at least eight patients had raised concerns about alleged sexual advances. The first complaint was made in 1974 by a patient to her GP. The GP did not pursue this. In three other cases written complaints, including in one case a letter from a solicitor, were made. However, when the complainants refused to pursue matters through the formal complaints procedure, no investigations were undertaken. Two further complainants came forward once the Inquiry was established.[8]

Examples of complaints included that from Patient B5 who, in 1987, complained to her GP about Haslam. The GP, Dr KH2, raised the issue with a member of the hospital management team, Dr KH3, but when it emerged that the patient did not wish to pursue a formal complaint, no investigation was undertaken.

The Inquiry found that only in 1988 was any real attempt made to consider the collective complaints against Haslam. However, Haslam was allowed (or even encouraged) to retire, rather than an investigation being undertaken.[9] In the cases of both Haslam and Kerr, retirement appears to have been seen as a convenient solution to what otherwise would have been a difficult and time-consuming problem. After his retirement, Haslam moved into private practice, from which at least one further allegation emerged. Haslam also continued to enjoy high status in retirement, being appointed an honorary NHS consultant in 1989 and later a non-clinical Medical Director. Haslam was only formally investigated in 1997 (by means of an internal NHS inquiry, the 'Manzoor Inquiry') when he was implicated in the police investigations into Kerr. Haslam was granted voluntary erasure from the medical register in 1999.

## The Response of Local GPs and Other Health Professionals

The Inquiry found that there was a general concern amongst the GP community about Kerr, to the extent that some GPs avoided referring female patients to him. Between

7 *The Kerr/Haslam Inquiry Report*, July 2005, Cm 6640-1, 109.

8 *The Kerr/Haslam Inquiry Report*, July 2005, Cm 6640-1, 8–9.

9 *The Kerr/Haslam Inquiry Report*, July 2005, Cm 6640-1, 10.

1965 and 1988, the majority of those patients who made allegations about Kerr raised their concerns first, and usually only, to their GP. Disclosures of inappropriate sexual behaviour were raised with at least 11 different GPs. However, with the exception of one, Dr KH1, none took any active steps to pursue concerns or complaints about Kerr.[10] For example, one patient, A9, said that she had complained to her GP that Kerr had made sexual advances and had exposed himself to her. The account of the GP's response was that Kerr was a senior figure, that it would be inappropriate to complain against him, and that she would not be believed. Another example was that of Patient A20 who, in 1979, informed her GP of sexualized behaviour by Kerr. The GP, she alleged, told her that he 'could not or would not do anything, as William Kerr was a friend of his'. In the early years, at least, there appears to have been institutionalized support for the lack of a proactive stance by GPs. In the case of the very first complainant, Patient A1 in 1965, the patient alleged to her GP that Kerr had made sexual suggestions to her. The GP contacted the Medical Defence Union and reported that he was advised only to tell the patient to report the matter, but to take no action himself.[11] In the case of some patients, allegations were made to the same GP each time without success. The GP in question either dismissed allegations or even attempted to persuade the patient to withdraw the complaint. In one instance, it was said that he 'made obscene jokes and informed [the patient's] husband that his wife was fantasising'.[12] Patient A37 said that in 1985, she had told her GP that Kerr had sexually assaulted her during a hospital consultation. Unusually, in comparison with the other GPs, the doctor recorded the detail of the allegation in the patient's notes. The GP discussed the allegation with his partners, but no further action was taken. The reasoning behind this reflected the confused attitudes within the GP community. In evidence to the Inquiry, the GP in question explained the difficulty in knowing where to take the allegation. He did not think that the GMC would have been interested unless the patient had provided a sworn statement. Questioning from the Inquiry Chairman took the following form:

> [Question] Your evidence is that...[Patient A37] may have been telling the truth?
> [Answer] Yes.
> [Question] The allegations she made, whether they be of rape or of oral sex, were of the most serious kind?
> [Answer] Right.
> [Question] You continued...to refer patients to William Kerr, even though the allegations may have been true and they were of the most serious kind?...
> [Answer] That is true.
> [Question] When it came to doing anything about what you had been told, you spoke to your partners...You did not do anything else; is that right?...
> [Answer] That is right.[13]

---

10 *The Kerr/Haslam Inquiry Report*, July 2005, Cm 6640-1, 12 and 89.

11 *The Kerr/Haslam Inquiry Report*, July 2005, Cm 6640-1, 91, 98 and 170.

12 *The Kerr/Haslam Inquiry Report*, July 2005, Cm 6640-1, 106—107.

13 *The Kerr/Haslam Inquiry Report*, July 2005, Cm 6640-1, 154.

The Inquiry concluded that GPs were aware of complaints regarding allegations of sexual misconduct against Haslam by 1974 and Kerr by 1979. The Inquiry described itself as being struck by the 'paralysis that had taken hold of some members of the local GP community when it came to complaints of sexual misbehaviour'. Inaction resulted from the combination of a lack of training and 'cultural and professional impediments'. It was also suggested that, even though GPs were not dependent upon consultants for professional advancement, the perception remained that consultants occupied a higher status within the medical hierarchy.[14] A common response from GPs to the widely held view that Haslam had sex with his patients was that such behaviour was not illegal, so there was nothing they could do. Overall, inappropriate intra-professional loyalty and the 'old boy network' inhibited appropriate action. Factors such as a perceived lack of 'hard evidence'; the perceived threat of disciplinary action; having to endure protracted disciplinary proceedings; fear of defamation proceedings; and the general threat of being branded as disloyal or a troublemaker all served as excuses which GPs used for a failure to report concerns.[15] Even those GPs who appeared to be more understanding still failed to act. For example, one GP recalled discussing with partners a number of allegations made by different patients. Their conclusions were that, as the patients did not wish to make formal complaints, nothing could be done. In these circumstances, the GP would not even have made notes about the allegations.[16]

Additional factors present in North Yorkshire were a low turnover of GPs and a close combination of professional and social roles. Examples were identified of related GPs, for instance, husband and wife, and GPs who had trained as junior doctors alongside consultants in the area. This made for a cohesive medical community with implicit pressure not to cause trouble or to 'rock the boat'. Close relationships between GPs may have restricted the availability of genuinely independent advice when a GP was faced with a difficult allegation. Close professional ties also resulted in close social encounters. The Kerrs, for example, were said to hold an annual summer social gathering which many local doctors attended. In addition, GPs were often isolated in the sense that there was no coordinated system to ensure exchange of information between partners within a practice, let alone between practices. There was no systematic recording of complaints within practices; knowledge therefore resided with individuals and retired or left with them.[17] The Inquiry summarized the position:

> Without any unifying structure, a complaint that crossed sectors was difficult to navigate and individual GPs, from their isolated position, had to have specific time and motivation to handle such matters. Some GPs had limited knowledge of how the complaints system within a hospital operated or to whom complaints should be forwarded. Further, large

---

14 *The Kerr/Haslam Inquiry Report*, July 2005, Cm 6640-1, 429 and 434. Dr KH1, the GP who took limited steps to report Kerr, confirmed that the attitude that GPs were inferior to consultants was one fostered and encouraged during his medical student days.

15 *The Kerr/Haslam Inquiry Report*, July 2005, Cm 6640-1, 419.

16 *The Kerr/Haslam Inquiry Report*, July 2005, Cm 6640-1, 109 and 416–17.

17 *The Kerr/Haslam Inquiry Report*, July 2005, Cm 6640-1, 420–21 and 423.

> hospitals...were seen as fairly closed systems – this acted as an additional inhibiting factor.[18]

What this ignores is the fact that all GPs should have known how to make a complaint to the GMC. The evidence to the Inquiry was that this was not the case, many GPs being unaware of the procedures for reporting to the GMC.[19] Little can be said about this state of affairs other than doctors are happy to enjoy the benefits of self-regulation. There can be little or no excuse for members of the profession, both individually and collectively, ensuring that they know how this system works. From the perspective of the GMC, doctors should be more fearful of not reporting concerns than they are of reporting them.

Lack of action also extended to the Local Medical Committee. Patient A37 made a specific allegation of rape by Kerr to a second GP. This GP informed the Secretary of the Local Medical Committee, but no action was taken. The Secretary confirmed that he had been told of this allegation and was aware of others. However, as the information was second- or even third-hand, he considered it inappropriate to take the matter further.[20]

The first account of a GP taking steps to deal with allegations about Kerr occurred in 1979 with GP Dr KH1. In evidence to the Inquiry, Patient A22 said that when she told Dr KH1 about Kerr's sexualized behaviour, Dr KH1's response was 'Oh no, it has happened before'. The patient's expectation was that Dr KH1 would know what to do to protect other patients: 'If you told a member of the [medical] profession, you would expect them to know the ropes, what to do to protect other people.' Dr KH1's evidence was that by 1979, he and his partners were aware of Kerr's reputation for flirting with patients. Dr KH1 referred the complaint of Patient A22 to Kerr's fellow consultant psychiatrist, Michael Haslam, and also spoke to Haslam personally. Unfortunately, but with the benefit of hindsight unsurprisingly, Haslam took no action. It is also of note that even after this incident, Dr KH1 and his partners continued to refer female patients to Kerr.[21] Dr KH1 said that he felt unable to report the situation to the District or Regional Health Authority: 'It was just incomprehensible that someone could behave in this way and one would never have imagined that this behaviour would have been from a professional colleague, particularly a consultant professional colleague.'[22] Dr KH1 also recounted the stern warning he remembered from his training: 'You would never criticise a colleague, whether they be a GP or a consultant.'[23]

Patient A50 alleged that Kerr had required her to perform oral sex upon him, claiming that this was part of her treatment. During her final consultation, a home visit, the patient alleged that Kerr raped her. Patient A50 made no complaint at the time, but in 1989 informed her GP. The GP's evidence was that the patient did not wish to make a formal complaint. The GP claimed that he had no suspicions

18 *The Kerr/Haslam Inquiry Report*, July 2005, Cm 6640-1, 422.
19 *The Kerr/Haslam Inquiry Report*, July 2005, Cm 6640-1, 426.
20 *The Kerr/Haslam Inquiry Report*, July 2005, Cm 6640-1, 158.
21 *The Kerr/Haslam Inquiry Report*, July 2005, Cm 6640-1, 136–9.
22 *The Kerr/Haslam Inquiry Report*, July 2005, Cm 6640-1, 432.
23 *The Kerr/Haslam Inquiry Report*, July 2005, Cm 6640-1, 434.

about Kerr until Patient A50's allegations. The GP was in partnership with Dr KH1, suggesting in the Inquiry's opinion 'a concerning lack of communication between partners'. The GP also gave evidence that he had 'counselled' Patient A50 over a long period of time regarding the allegations, yet the Inquiry noted 'a concerning lack of any notes recording the "counselling" sessions'. In his evidence to the Inquiry, the GP recognized that he should have contacted the GMC. He should have recognized his obligations to protect the public and also that, notwithstanding the fact that Kerr had retired, he remained registered and free to practice.[24]

In the case of Haslam, only in 1987 and 1988 did two relatively new GPs, Drs KH2 and KH4, respond positively to allegations from their patients. The Inquiry suggested that this may have reflected a gradual change of culture within the medical profession and a willingness of younger GPs to challenge the status quo.

The Inquiry concluded that doctors did not generally see their role as pursuing complaints on behalf of patients unless the evidence was 'unequivocal and incontrovertible'. The tendency was to assume explanations which did not involve misconduct, and to adopt a belief that doctors would not deliberately harm their patients. Avoiding confrontation with other professionals appeared to be preferable to the initiation of action to ensure patient safety.[25]

## Complaints to Nurses

Prior to 1983, complaints were raised with at least 11 hospital staff, plus the Secretary of the Regional Health Board and the Health Service Commissioner. None led to any investigation and in one of the few instances where the recipient, a nursing sister, did take action, she referred the matter to Kerr himself.[26] In 1978 Patient A17 said that she made an allegation to a nurse and later to a nursing sister, that she had been involved in a sexual relationship with Kerr. The nurse, it was said, told the patient to 'keep quiet'. Another patient, A19, alleged that Kerr forced her to perform oral sex on him at a time when she was an inpatient. She made a complaint via her solicitor, as a result of which she was transferred from the care of Kerr to Haslam. However, the Inquiry found no evidence that the complaint was otherwise investigated. Patient A26 complained to hospital staff, including a nurse, about sexual behaviour on the part of Kerr. The nurse passed the complaint along to his nursing sister, who informed Kerr. Unsurprisingly, Kerr dismissed the allegation as false and no investigation was undertaken. In 1968 Patient A3 made an allegation to a nurse that she had been raped by Kerr. The nurse told no one, her reasoning being that to take the matter further 'would bring nothing but trouble and further harm to the patient…'.[27] One of the patients, a student nurse, whose allegations resulted in a criminal charge against Kerr, had also attempted to report the matter to her matron. Her account was that the matron had accused her of lying and 'would cause both herself and William Kerr a great deal of trouble by saying such things', and that she was a 'nasty, dirty

24 *The Kerr/Haslam Inquiry Report*, July 2005, Cm 6640-1, 167.

25 *The Kerr/Haslam Inquiry Report*, July 2005, Cm 6640-1, 15.

26 *The Kerr/Haslam Inquiry Report*, July 2005, Cm 6640-1, 170.

27 *The Kerr/Haslam Inquiry Report*, July 2005, Cm 6640-1, 94 and 99.

girl…'. In a similar case, another patient, who was also a student nurse, claimed that she had informed her home sister and (it appears, the same) matron that Kerr had persuaded her to have sexual intercourse with him. The patient said that she was disbelieved and subsequently asked to leave her nursing course on the grounds that she 'did not fit in'.[28] Patient A26 expressed concern to a psychiatric nurse that Kerr had propositioned her. The nurse was sufficiently concerned to contact his line manager, a nursing sister, at home. The sister called the nurse back to say that she had raised the matter directly with Kerr and that the allegation was unfounded and malicious. Various similar accounts were received from other patients who had communicated allegations to nursing staff. The Inquiry concluded that these responses were indicative of the culture at the time, where patient safety was not central.[29] One nurse summarized the position:

> Nursing staff simply did not raise issues…If you attempted to raise issues, it was not looked upon favourably by your colleagues. The advice given to staff was to report anything untoward up through line management. However, it seemed that if you reported anything up the line you were quickly moved on to a different position…There was a culture amongst staff that you did not complain about colleagues. Anyone who had attempted to make a complaint would have felt very vulnerable.[30]

The first communication to management appears to have occurred in 1972. A patient wrote to the hospital board alleging that Kerr had made sexual advances towards her and sexually assaulted another patient. The Inquiry could find no evidence that action was taken nor a reply received.[31] In 1986, Patient A37 made a telephone inquiry to the Yorkshire Health Authority regarding the process for making a complaint against a psychiatrist. The patient explained the sexual nature of the allegation but did not name the psychiatrist. By the time of this communication, the hospital authorities should have been aware of the similar allegations from Deputy Sister Bigwood and could have identified Kerr from the patient's medical notes. No further action was taken by the health authority.[32]

## Complaints to Consultants and Other Doctors

In October 1975, a 23-year-old patient told her GP that Kerr had made sexual advances towards her. Her evidence was that the GP did not believe her account. Two years later the patient sought a further psychiatric referral and was referred (unbeknown to her at the time) to the wife of Kerr. When the patient recounted the allegation of sexual assault, she was listened to sympathetically but given no encouragement or assistance to bring a formal complaint. Patient A37 told her consultant cardiologist that she had a sexual relationship with Kerr. The cardiologist, she said, did not believe her. He found it 'inconceivable' that a consultant would act in such a manner.

---

28 *The Kerr/Haslam Inquiry Report*, July 2005, Cm 6640-1, 100–101.

29 *The Kerr/Haslam Inquiry Report*, July 2005, Cm 6640-1, 143–4.

30 *The Kerr/Haslam Inquiry Report*, July 2005, Cm 6640-1, 244.

31 *The Kerr/Haslam Inquiry Report*, July 2005, Cm 6640-1, 90–91.

32 *The Kerr/Haslam Inquiry Report*, July 2005, Cm 6640-1, 97.

The Inquiry found it disturbing that the consultant would filter disclosures if he did not believe the patients. Patient A44 alleged that Kerr had made her perform oral sex acts on him. This occurred between 1985 and 1988, although the patient did not feel able to express concern until around 1992. She informed a consultant psychiatrist who, in turn, informed the patient's then treating psychiatrist. The first psychiatrist expressed the view that he had done all that he felt was needed in the circumstances. Some time later, in 1996, Patient A44 also informed a hospital registrar about her previous psychiatrist's sexual demands. The registrar established from the patient's notes that the psychiatrist in question was William Kerr, and accordingly wrote to the patient's GP and her consultant. As Kerr had retired, the registrar took the view that he had done all that was required.[33] Patient A17 told a very junior doctor that she had had a long-term sexual relationship with Kerr. The doctor made no note of this and took no steps to pass on the complaint. Her reasons to the Inquiry were that the prevailing culture of the time required loyalty to fellow doctors, coupled with the fact that junior doctors relied heavily on good references from consultants if they were to progress in their careers.[34] In 1987 Patient B6 reported to Dr KH5, Haslam's Senior House Officer, that Haslam had propositioned her. The patient was very upset and Dr KH5 advised her to make a formal complaint. She did not do this and Dr KH5 took no steps to pursue the matter. Dr KH5's justifications were (mistakenly) that the facts were not substantial (the patient was clearly distraught) and that to report the matter would be a breach of patient confidentiality (this was both erroneous and, in any event, did not prevent Dr KH5 from disclosing concerns to another doctor at a later date). The Inquiry's conclusion was that even though these reasons were erroneous, they probably continued to prevail today.[35]

When Dr KH6 took over as consultant from Haslam in 1987, he said that within a month he met a group of local GPs who expressed relief that they could 'now start referring young female patients back to psychiatry'. They went on to recount some of Haslam's sexual relationships with patients. Dr KH6 described his shock at these revelations and said that he passed on this information to senior health authority doctors.[36]

## Cumulative Complaints to Medical Professionals

One case, that of Patient A19, is particularly illustrative of the failings of numerous health professionals to take action. This patient, a nurse, communicated to her GP that she had been the victim of sexual assault by Kerr. She also told nursing colleagues, a locum accident and emergency doctor, and a clinical psychologist. The Inquiry noted that her attempts to complain were variously met with inaction, derision and even obstruction. No investigation was undertaken, even though the patient's allegations were supported by others – notably her husband, a friend and a solicitor.

33 *The Kerr/Haslam Inquiry Report*, July 2005, Cm 6640-1, 114–16, 156 and 163–4.

34 *The Kerr/Haslam Inquiry Report*, July 2005, Cm 6640-1, 183.

35 *The Kerr/Haslam Inquiry Report*, July 2005, Cm 6640-1, 338–9.

36 *The Kerr/Haslam Inquiry Report*, July 2005, Cm 6640-1, 336 and 417.

If a complainant with this level of support could make no progress, there was little prospect that less well-supported complainants would receive serious attention.[37]

## Other Monitoring Failures

Haslam had used unrecognized 'innovative' treatments in quiet parts of the hospital, without a chaperone and without wider monitoring or other forms of control. The treatments in question were implicated in three of the sexual assault convictions. The system present in the 1980s was summarized as one that was not open to challenge and involved consultant psychiatrists working in isolation.[38]

## A Summary of the Reasons for Inaction

The Inquiry concluded that those who could and should have undertaken investigations failed to do so for a range of reasons. These included, inter alia:

- Excessive respect and even fear of senior consultants
- A lack of leadership and associated communication at district and regional levels
- A focus on protecting health practitioners rather than removing risks to patient safety
- Exaggerated loyalty by more junior doctors to their senior colleagues.[39]

## Other Failures to Respond to Complaints

In November 1973, a patient whose complaint at local level had been ignored wrote directly to the Health Service Commissioner, repeating allegations of sexual assault by Kerr. The response was that such complaint fell outside of the Commissioner's remit. Following this, the patient's mother also wrote to the Commissioner asking for the result of enquiries made of the hospital authorities. The Inquiry noted that there was no evidence of any such enquiries being made and went on to comment that, had the response been more sympathetic and understanding, 'it might not have been necessary for there to have been a delay of another 24 years' before investigations into Kerr's activities were eventually investigated.[40]

In 1976, solicitors instructed to act for Patient B2 wrote to the District Administrator of the York Health District alleging that Michael Haslam had instigated a sexual relationship with B2. This relationship was said to have lasted for almost two years, during which time B2 was a patient of Haslam. Haslam was immediately notified of the complaint. He denied the allegation. There was no evidence that the

37 *The Kerr/Haslam Inquiry Report*, July 2005, Cm 6640-1, 133–5.

38 *The Kerr/Haslam Inquiry Report*, July 2005, Cm 6640-1, 279 and 282.

39 *The Kerr/Haslam Inquiry Report*, July 2005, Cm 6640-1, 235.

40 *The Kerr/Haslam Inquiry Report*, July 2005, Cm 6640-1, 105.

complaint had been investigated, nor were records kept of this or other complaints, so no pattern could emerge. Such a pattern should have been easy to spot, as it was generally accepted by witnesses to the Inquiry that complaints of sexual misconduct against consultants were rare.[41]

In common with Harold Shipman,[42] Kerr and Haslam were able to alter patient records or write self-serving letters to protect themselves and to put patient complaints in an unfavourable light. In one case, the husband of a patient who had an inappropriate sexual relationship with Haslam confronted Haslam. One of the responses by Haslam was to write a letter to the patient's GP, which went on to become part of her medical notes. The letter suggested an extramarital affair with an unnamed partner, and went on to explain that any allegations the patient might make against Haslam were a result of 'transference' and 'counter-transference', and that such allegations may be forthcoming because of feelings of rejection. Other examples involved contact with GPs to pre-emptively undermine a potential complaint from the patient.

## Eventual Action

The only action taken against Haslam by his employer was the attempt to secure his resignation. The Inquiry suggested that the principal explanation for this ineffectual approach was the preference for senior NHS managers to enjoy a quiet life. Haslam was therefore allowed to retire in 1989, aged 55, without any negative inference on his professional status. He had been allowed to see female patients alone right up to the point of his retirement, was given the position of Honorary Consultant when he left, and references were provided. The Inquiry noted that, at the time Haslam was being given his honorary consultancy, at least one senior doctor confirmed in evidence that he considered him to be an 'abuser of patients'.[43] Counsel for the health authority accepted that: 'There is no doubt that by the time Drs Kerr and Haslam left the health service alarm bells were ringing in every direction from hospital to region.'[44]

A short time before Haslam 'retired', a request was made for a reference in relation to the proposed appointment of Haslam as 'Medical Director and Person in Charge' of the Harrogate Clinic. Following legal advice, the reference played down the complaints against Haslam, emphasizing that they remained unsubstantiated.[45] A further reference was also supplied from a former (very senior) colleague, the key part of which read: '…I have a high opinion of Dr Haslam's professional skill as a psychiatrist, his administrative ability and his personal qualities. He is a man of high intelligence and unquestionable integrity…' The colleague in question had not worked with Haslam for around 20 years.[46]

The Inquiry concluded that:

41 *The Kerr/Haslam Inquiry Report*, July 2005, Cm 6640-1, 305–11.

42 Discussed in Chapter 12.

43 *The Kerr/Haslam Inquiry Report*, July 2005, Cm 6640-1, 353–7 and 365–8.

44 *The Kerr/Haslam Inquiry Report*, July 2005, Cm 6640-1, 368.

45 *The Kerr/Haslam Inquiry Report*, July 2005, Cm 6640-1, 371.

46 *The Kerr/Haslam Inquiry Report*, July 2005, Cm 6640-1, 375–6.

> The North Yorkshire NHS not only failed to take any steps to prevent Michael Haslam taking up [the Harrogate] appointment, but it went further, and allowed Michael Haslam to leave the NHS not under a cloud, but with all the indicators of a perfectly normal departure…being allowed to remain on ethics committees, remaining as one of the 'Three Wise Men', and finally, being granted an honorary consultancy…What is striking is that even in 1988, when senior NHS managers had very real concerns about Michael Haslam, not one of them considered it appropriate to mention their concerns to the GMC.[47]

It was against this background that Haslam returned to the NHS in 1993, when he was appointed to the position of Medical Director of the South Durham NHS Trust. He remained in post until his eventual suspension in 1997, following police investigations into the activities of William Kerr.[48]

## Investigations

By the end of 1997, Professor Sir Liam Donaldson, then Regional Director NHS Executive Northern and Yorkshire, convened an independent review (chaired by Mrs Zahida Manzoor, Regional Chair, NHS Executive Northern and Yorkshire) to consider the allegations of sexual misconduct against Haslam between 1984 and 1988. The panel concluded that Haslam had taken advantage of his position to sexually exploit vulnerable patients. Senior managers had been too ready to find reasons to avoid investigating allegations against Haslam and there had been a failure to support complainants. After the conclusion of the Manzoor review, Haslam was dismissed in September 1998 from his post in Durham.[49]

## GMC Involvement

In March 1996, Dr KH7 wrote to the GMC to inform them of allegations made to him by Patient B10 about a sexual relationship with Haslam. The GMC instructed solicitors to take a statement from Dr KH7. In September 1996, Patient B11 wrote to the GMC alleging a physical relationship with Haslam. When the GMC responded, stating that solicitors would be in touch to obtain a statement, B11 withdrew her complaint, stating that 'any publicity of her allegations would have disastrous repercussions upon her current family life'.[50]

In June 1997, the GMC wrote to the Chief Executive of the Harrogate NHS Trust regarding newspaper articles about police investigations into a consultant psychiatrist. The GMC wanted to know whether this related to Haslam. After receiving details of the allegations made against Haslam at local level, it was decided that the GMC investigation should be suspended until the NHS review was completed. In January 1998, the GMC were informed of the increased concerns which the health authority had about Haslam following the investigation by the Manzoor panel. In February

47 *The Kerr/Haslam Inquiry Report*, July 2005, Cm 6640-1, 380.

48 *The Kerr/Haslam Inquiry Report*, July 2005, Cm 6640-1, 382.

49 *The Kerr/Haslam Inquiry Report*, July 2005, Cm 6640-1, 382–92.

50 *The Kerr/Haslam Inquiry Report*, July 2005, Cm 6640-1, 393.

1998, two consultant psychiatrists, Drs KH8 and KH6, wrote to the GMC. Dr KH8 detailed allegations made to him by Patient B12. Dr KH6 had received no complaints directly, but had heard from a number of GPs about allegations of sexual impropriety by Haslam. In April 1998, a GP wrote to the GMC regarding a patient who had recounted a sexual relationship with Haslam over a nine-year period between 1985 and 1994.[51]

In April 1998, Dr KH7 wrote to the GMC to query whether any progress had been made following his letter of March 1996. He was particularly concerned that Haslam continued to treat private patients. The GMC replied two months later, explaining that it would await the results of the NHS investigations.[52] In evidence to the Inquiry, Dr KH7 said:

> I have found the GMC to be opaque and uninterested. I think it is worth stating that apart from one rather anodyne press release, I have seen nothing in which anyone has actually said the word sorry for this. It is also worth stating that if Haslam had not sued the *Sunday Times*,[53] he would have got away with it.[54]

In June 1998, the GMC was sent a copy of the final Manzoor Report. The GMC concluded, following legal advice, that the absence of certain evidence prevented the report itself from forming the basis of a case before the PPC. The GMC therefore instructed its solicitors to recommence investigations into Haslam.[55] In April 1999, charges against Haslam were referred to the PCC; however, this included an offer of voluntary erasure, which Haslam accepted. The latter involved the Assistant Registrar of the GMC writing to Haslam in the following terms: '…[if] you do not wish to undergo a public hearing…[the PPC] would instead accept an application from you to remove your name from the Register. The voluntary removal of a doctor's name carries no stigma…'[56]

In evidence to the Inquiry, the Chief Executive of the GMC accepted that this was 'an unfortunate form of words'. When challenged about this by the York HA, the GMC justified its decision on the basis that this approach was 'a speedy way to make sure that doctors do not practice…[or] where there is a risk that a case against a doctor might not be found proven...'[57]

Concerns about this approach also came from former patients. For instance, Patient B12 wrote to the GMC as follows:

---

51 *The Kerr/Haslam Inquiry Report*, July 2005, Cm 6640-1, 394.

52 *The Kerr/Haslam Inquiry Report*, July 2005, Cm 6640-1, 396.

53 On 24 January 1999, the *Sunday Times* had published an article which reported that two senior psychiatrists were being investigated regarding suspicions of sexual assaults against numerous female patients. In January 2000, Haslam commenced libel proceedings. These were eventually settled, with Haslam agreeing not to pursue the matter and to pay a substantial sum towards the defence costs. *The Kerr/Haslam Inquiry Report*, July 2005, Cm 6640-1, 411–12.

54 *The Kerr/Haslam Inquiry Report*, July 2005, Cm 6640-1, 403.

55 *The Kerr/Haslam Inquiry Report*, July 2005, Cm 6640-1, 396.

56 *The Kerr/Haslam Inquiry Report*, July 2005, Cm 6640-1, 399.

57 *The Kerr/Haslam Inquiry Report*, July 2005, Cm 6640-1, 400–401.

> Whilst I appreciate that he is no longer able to practise, he is still carrying out the posturing role of pillar of the community…It would appear that the matter has been conveniently swept under the carpet and a man who used his position to systematically abuse vulnerable patients has once again got away scot-free and failed to have been called to public account…I feel personally cheated of any justice and feel that once again there has been a cynical disregard for the suffering of the patient.[58]

Overall, it had taken the GMC three years to investigate complaints, during which time Haslam was free to practise.[59] Patients had very little emotional or physical strength with which to fight against an abusive psychiatrist. They were let down by the complacency of other medical staff and the GMC in their failure to protect them against abuse.[60]

There is some evidence of a continuing disparity between medical and public attitudes towards sexual misconduct by doctors. For example, in a GMC case from July 2004, the doctor was found guilty of SPM for carrying out inappropriate and largely clinically unjustified intimate examinations on five female patients. The PCC concluded that the doctor did not constitute a danger to patients and restricted its penalty to a reprimand.[61]

## The Position and Power of Consultants

The Kerr/Haslam Inquiry noted that, until very recently, consultants' contracts of employment were managed at regional level, a significant distance from their practice. This and other beneficial contractual provisions was the price paid by government to ensure that consultants cooperated with the foundation of the NHS. Once appointed, a consultant might be in post for 20 years or more, becoming so much part of the local establishment as to be virtually immune from criticism. The central assumption was that consultants were answerable to no one but themselves for clinical matters.[62] The power and autonomy of consultants created an impediment to patient complaints. The consultant was described as 'the most revered and autonomous practitioner within the system'. As one doctor described the position when he arrived in North Yorkshire in 1989: '…I felt the culture was that nothing would be done if there were concerns about a consultant's behaviour. At best the consultant would be asked to go elsewhere and matters would be swept under the carpet.'[63]

Other professional witnesses such as nurses, social workers and counsellors also gave evidence that they viewed consultants as 'untouchable'. Administrators described a sense of powerlessness and fear of challenging consultants. Junior doctors and nurses said that they considered that consultants could adversely affect their future employment prospects.[64]

---

58 *The Kerr/Haslam Inquiry Report*, July 2005, Cm 6640-1, 402.
59 *The Kerr/Haslam Inquiry Report*, July 2005, Cm 6640-1, 406.
60 *The Kerr/Haslam Inquiry Report*, July 2005, Cm 6640-1, 511.
61 Discussed in *The Kerr/Haslam Inquiry Report*, July 2005, Cm 6640-1, 897.
62 *The Kerr/Haslam Inquiry Report*, July 2005, Cm 6640-1, 480–81.
63 *The Kerr/Haslam Inquiry Report*, July 2005, Cm 6640-1, 481.
64 *The Kerr/Haslam Inquiry Report*, July 2005, Cm 6640-1, 482–4, 486–7.

There were also significant obstacles to employers controlling the work of consultants. '[N]othing short of an admission by the consultant, or clear and compelling written evidence, would suffice before any direct action would be taken.' Similarly, no action was taken by the Royal College of Psychiatrists, whose President described their role as 'primarily educational rather than regulatory'. The disciplinary procedures possessed by the College were rarely used.[65]

All of these findings reinforce the vital importance of the role that the GMC should have played. All doctors, including the 'god-like' consultant, should have feared GMC investigation and discipline if they overstepped the mark or failed to report misconduct by colleagues. The added difficulty inherent within psychiatric practice, that some patients might make unfounded accusation, further reinforces the importance of effective self-regulation. The medical profession, through the agency of the GMC, should have been in the best position to bring forward the necessary expertise to appropriately investigate the allegations against Kerr and Haslam.

## Confidentiality

The principle of patient confidentiality, prima facie a protective force for patients, was used by some in the medical profession as an excuse for not reporting misconduct. The Inquiry Report noted that: 'We were struck by the evidence to the Inquiry that it is only those who did nothing, or not enough, who relied on patient confidentiality to justify their lack of action.'[66]

Whilst both the courts and the GMC have remained protective of the principle of patient confidentiality,[67] it has also been recognized that the principle has its limits. In *W v Edgell*,[68] the Court of Appeal recognized that a doctor was entitled to communicate otherwise confidential information to the appropriate authorities when there was the fear of a real risk to public safety. In part, this clarified GMC guidance of the time which stated that in rare cases, a breach of confidentiality would be justified in the public interest, for example, when a failure to disclose would expose the patient or a third party to a risk of death or serious harm.[69] Sexual abuse by a psychiatrist should fall within the exceptional category, with details of the patient(s) being anonymized if necessary. Even if such disclosure is of limited direct use for disciplinary proceedings, it may prove invaluable in identifying a pattern of misconduct. As one witness told the Inquiry: 'A feature of every one of

65 For instance, in the case of Haslam, they were only employed after his criminal conviction in 2003, four years after his voluntary erasure by the GMC. *The Kerr/Haslam Inquiry Report*, July 2005, Cm 6640-1, 725.

66 *The Kerr/Haslam Inquiry Report*, July 2005, Cm 6640-1, 527.

67 See, for example, *Hunter v Mann* [1974] QB 767, [1974] 2 All ER 414; and A-*G v Guardian Newspapers Ltd (No. 2)* [1990] AC 109, [1988] 3 All ER 545.

68 [1990] Ch 359, [1990] 1 All ER 835.

69 For further discussion, see Mason, J.K., McCall Smith, R.A. and Laurie, G.T., *Law and Medical Ethics*, 2002, Butterworths, London; and *The Kerr/Haslam Inquiry Report*, July 2005, Cm 6640-1, 528.

the scandals…over the past 10 years is that patients felt for a long time that there is no one else suffering as they had…'[70]

In the view of the Inquiry, no significant or effective changes had been made to address the reluctance of doctors to act when important information which revealed a risk to other patients was received in confidence. It was felt that determining appropriate future action to redress this was 'a perfect area for the Council for Healthcare Regulatory Excellence', which could ensure that common provisions were introduced for all healthcare professionals.[71]

## Reluctance to Use the NHS Disciplinary Procedures

As previously discussed, the older NHS disciplinary procedures were based upon national guidance dating from a 1961 Health Circular.[72] This circular made the distinction between 'personal' and 'professional' misconduct. 'Professional' misconduct was the more problematic of the two, requiring the implementation of special procedures which protected doctors against dismissal in all but the most serious circumstances. These provisions were modified in 1990 by circular HC(90)9 – *Disciplinary Procedures in Cases Relating to Senior Medical and Dental Staff*, although the essential elements of the previous provisions were retained.[73]

The Kerr/Haslam Report draws particular attention to the legal advice attached to both HM(61)112 and HC(90)9 by Regional and District legal officers. The Inquiry heard of the lack of enthusiasm for bringing proceedings against consultants, which were almost invariably time-consuming (in some instances taking years to reach final conclusion), difficult (operating on the criminal standard of proof) and often unsuccessful. The privileged position occupied by consultants in relation to 'professional conduct' applied in the early 2000s in much the same way as it had in the 1960s.[74]

It might reasonably have been expected that the lengthy, problematic proceedings associated with 'professional conduct' would have been avoided in cases involving allegations of serious sexual misconduct. Behaviour of this type, especially when involving criminal proceedings, could properly be said to fall within the more straightforward 'personal conduct' category. However, the Inquiry found that when a doctor denied such allegations, the alleged behaviour would be defined as 'professional conduct', irrespective of how outrageous and extraneous to the expected professional standard it could be said to have been. It therefore remained extremely problematic for employers to deal with doctors in a prompt and effective manner. As a result, a doctor who was shown to have more likely than not committed a serious offence (satisfying the civil standard of proof) would be free to continue

70 *The Kerr/Haslam Inquiry Report*, July 2005, Cm 6640-1, 531.

71 *The Kerr/Haslam Inquiry Report*, July 2005, Cm 6640-1, 527–8.

72 HM(61)112 – *Disciplinary Proceedings in Cases Relating to Hospital Medical and Dental Staff.*

73 For further discussion, see *The Kerr/Haslam Inquiry Report*, July 2005, Cm 6640-1, 732.

74 For further discussion, see *The Kerr/Haslam Inquiry Report*, July 2005, Cm 6640-1, 734–5.

treating patients, in the absence of proof to the criminal standard. This protection was specific to doctors; it was not shared by other healthcare professionals.[75]

## Final Thoughts

The Kerr and Haslam cases raise significant concerns regarding abuse of trust by the doctors concerned, but also with respect to the regulatory failures and the lack of earlier detection. Kerr and Haslam were also not isolated examples. For instance, in 1990 and in 1993, a doctor was convicted of exposing himself to teenage girls. The GMC, it was reported, did not take action either time. In 1999 he opened his own practice, but shortly afterwards was convicted of possessing child pornography. Only after that conviction was his name erased from the medical register.[76] In 2002, a consultant gynaecologist was convicted on two counts of indecent assault against patients (26 other counts were left on the court file, the jury having failed to reach verdicts) and sentenced to a period of 18 months' imprisonment (suspended). It was also reported that the consultant had been subject to four earlier complaints of a similar nature in the 18 months before the police were called in to investigate.[77] Also in 2002, a psychiatrist was convicted of indecent assault and sentenced to a term of imprisonment. The psychiatrist was reported to have previously had his name erased from the medical register following sexual assaults against patients, first in New Zealand in 1988, and then in the UK in 1989. He was readmitted by the GMC in 1996.[78] A general practitioner was convicted on nine counts of indecent assault against patients and sentenced to eight years' imprisonment. The assaults, it was reported, were committed over a 12-year period, and after the conviction, criticism was directed at the NHS and the medical profession for failing to act earlier.[79] Another GP was convicted in 2004 on seven counts of sexual assault committed over a 21-year period.[80] One national newspaper reported that the GP had received a police caution for indecent behaviour three years before these convictions, but 'the GMC has no record of disciplining him'.[81]

75 For further discussion, see *The Kerr/Haslam Inquiry Report*, July 2005, Cm 6640-1, 736–7.

76 Waterston, C., 'Dirty Docs Carry on Working; Perverts a Danger to Women Patients', *The People*, 5 December 2004.

77 Bruce, D., 'Vinall Faced 4 Previous Complaints', *Yorkshire Evening Post*, 11 March 2002 (Lexis transcript).

78 'Struck Off; Dr Kolathur Unni', *The Times*, 12 July 1989; and Lawrence, L., 'Sex Predator Doctor Had Been Struck Off Twice Before I Was Victim No. 3; Patient's Fury over GMC Scandal', *Sunday Mirror*, 14 July 2002, 27.

79 See, for example, Hall, C., 'NHS at Fault for Failing to Stop Sex Assault GP', *The Daily Telegraph*, 31 August 2001, 9; Laurance, J., 'GPs Face Inquiry for Failing to Stop Colleague Abusing Patients', *The Independent*, 31 August 2001.

80 See *The Kerr/Haslam Inquiry Report*, July 2005, Cm 6640-1, 613; Jenkins, R., 'Doctor Jailed for Indecent Acts on Women Patients', *The Times*, 20 March 2004, 9; and 'Five Years for GP in Sex Assaults', *Daily Mail*, 20 March 2004, 5.

81 Waterston, C., 'Dirty Docs Carry on Working; Perverts a Danger to Women Patients', *The People*, 5 December 2004.

Between 1970 and 2003 there were 79 cases heard by the GMC involving allegations of improper sexual and emotional relationships between doctors and patients.[82] Of concern, there were cases involving inappropriate sexual contact with patients which were found not to amount to serious professional misconduct; for example, a doctor who admitted to a sexual relationship with a vulnerable patient with a history of psychiatric problems; the behaviour was not considered inappropriate.[83] Even when SPM was established, in 38 per cent of cases the doctor's name was not erased from the medical register. For example, in two separate cases, doctors who carried out intimate, unchaperoned examinations on four and five patients respectively, without consent and with little or no medical justification, were reprimanded. Three cases, each involving sexual relationships with vulnerable psychiatric patients, resulted in conditional registration and short suspensions respectively. Conditional registration was also considered sufficient sanction for a doctor who engaged in indecent behaviour towards two patients, one of whom was a 14-year-old girl.[84] Even when more severe sanctions were imposed, the final effect was sometimes diluted. For example, a doctor convicted of indecent assault of a patient was sentenced to nine months' imprisonment in 1997 and subsequently had his name erased from the medical register. However, he was restored to the register only four years later and allowed to practise free of conditions approximately a year after that.[85]

The Inquiry's conclusion was that Kerr and Haslam were able to continue to practise and to assault patients due to the combination of flawed structures, poor procedures, systems failures and individual failures. These all came together in an environment and time when 'the idea that patients might need protection from doctors was unthinkable'. Changes have been made, but barriers to complaining remain a significant obstacle. The onus should be on all healthcare staff to adopt the attitude that complaints or revelations should in the first instance always be accepted at face value. Encouragement should be given for concerns to be articulated and then diligently pursued by the staff member.[86]

The focus had been on the need for a cooperative complainant with the strength and resolve to pursue matters to conclusion. In evidence to the Inquiry, Sir Liam Donaldson accepted that the absence of a committed complainant should not be seen as justification for failure at both NHS and GMC levels to undertake any investigation.

There had to be a move away from seeing complaints as merely a time-consuming distraction. Equally, it is important to move away from the culture where medical personnel who support a complaint may themselves put their career progression at risk – the focus must be on the message rather than the messenger.[87]

---

82 *The Kerr/Haslam Inquiry Report*, July 2005, Cm 6640-1, 623.
83 *The Kerr/Haslam Inquiry Report*, July 2005, Cm 6640-1, 624.
84 *The Kerr/Haslam Inquiry Report*, July 2005, Cm 6640-1, 625–6.
85 *The Kerr/Haslam Inquiry Report*, July 2005, Cm 6640-1, 625–6.
86 *The Kerr/Haslam Inquiry Report*, July 2005, Cm 6640-1, 801 and 804.
87 See *The Kerr/Haslam Inquiry Report*, July 2005, Cm 6640-1, 805 and 810.

# Chapter 10

# Clifford Ayling

## Introduction

In September 2002 Mrs Justice Pauffley was appointed to chair an investigation into how the NHS handled allegations about the conduct of Clifford Ayling. She submitted her report in July 2004.[1]

The Secretary of State for Health had first announced the setting up of the Inquiry in July 2001 (along with Inquiries into the activities of Richard Neale, and William Kerr and Michael Haslam). The overall purpose of the Inquiry was:

> To assess the appropriateness and effectiveness of the procedures operated in the local health services (a) for enabling health service users to raise issues of legitimate concern relating to the conduct of health service employees; (b) for ensuring that such complaints are effectively considered; and (c) for ensuring that appropriate remedial action is taken in the particular case and generally.[2]

The remit of the Inquiry did not extend to inquiring into non-NHS bodies such as the GMC, although the Chief Executive of the GMC did voluntarily provide evidence.[3]

---

1 The Honourable Mrs Justice Pauffley, Committee of Inquiry – Independent Investigation into how the NHS Handled Allegations about the Conduct of Clifford Ayling, 15 July 2004, Cm 6298.

2 The Honourable Mrs Justice Pauffley, Committee of Inquiry – Independent Investigation into how the NHS Handled Allegations about the Conduct of Clifford Ayling, 15 July 2004, Cm 6298, paras 1.5 and 1.9–1.12. The Inquiry was to be held in private. This was challenged on behalf of a number of women, including some who had been indecently assaulted by Ayling, initially before the Secretary of State and subsequently by means of judicial review (the latter action also being based around the Neale Inquiry). These challenges failed, so the media and public would continue to be excluded from the Inquiry hearings. The Secretary of State did make some concessions regarding the attendance of interested parties or their representatives at the Inquiry hearings. Also, a Queen's Counsel or other demonstrably independent person would be appointed to head the Inquiry in place of the original appointee, Dame Yvonne Moores.

3 The Honourable Mrs Justice Pauffley, Committee of Inquiry – Independent Investigation into how the NHS Handled Allegations about the Conduct of Clifford Ayling, 15 July 2004, Cm 6298, para 1.23.

The Ayling case provides an example of a doctor able to commit serious misconduct over a number of years whilst practising both as a GP and in a hospital setting.

## The Background to the Ayling Case

In November 1998, Clifford Ayling was arrested and charged with indecently assaulting former patients. On 20 December 2000, Ayling was convicted on 12 counts of indecent assault, relating to ten female patients. He was sentenced to four years' imprisonment and his name was placed on the sex offender's register. In July 2001, Ayling's name was erased from the medical register by the GMC.[4]

Ayling had qualified in 1963 and had worked in a number of hospitals. In 1981 he had entered general practice in Folkestone, initially with a partner, but from 1983–98 as a sole practitioner. In 1998 he rejoined a partnership. During his time as a GP, Ayling also undertook locum medical sessions in family planning clinics in east Kent and was a member of the local GP deputizing service co-operative, SEADOC. From 1974–88 he also worked part-time as a clinical assistant[5] in obstetrics and gynaecology at the Kent and Canterbury Hospital in Canterbury and the Isle of Thanet Hospital. This appointment was reviewed annually. In 1982, Ayling became a full-time general practitioner, but he retained his clinical assistant role until 1988. From 1984–94, he was also employed as a part-time clinical assistant in colposcopy at the William Harvey Hospital. Many of these areas of practice, as a single-handed GP, working unsupervised as a clinical assistant covering weekend emergencies and working in outpatient clinics away from main hospital sites, allowed Ayling to undertake much of his work in relative professional isolation.[6]

The facts which led to the convictions for sexual assault related to inappropriate touching of women's breasts or gynaecological organs. Most incidents occurred when Ayling was acting as a GP and the earliest incident considered by the court dated back to 1991. The Ayling Inquiry's remit was significantly longer, dating back to complaints from 1971. The Inquiry observed that medical practice was not static.

4 The Honourable Mrs Justice Pauffley, Committee of Inquiry – Independent Investigation into how the NHS Handled Allegations about the Conduct of Clifford Ayling, 15 July 2004, Cm 6298, paras 1.1.4 and 3.402–3.403.

5 The status of clinical assistants within the medical hierarchy was considered to be roughly the same level as a registrar. A clinical assistant was usually under the supervision of a consultant. However, the Inquiry heard evidence that consultants often considered such assistants to have the professional capability of working independently, calling for help from the supervising consultant only when it was needed. The term 'Clinical Assistant' is not found in the hospital medical staff terms and conditions of service, but is covered by the appointments procedure specified at paragraph 94, and by the NHS General Whitley Council agreements. See The Honourable Mrs Justice Pauffley, Committee of Inquiry – Independent Investigation into how the NHS Handled Allegations about the Conduct of Clifford Ayling, 15 July 2004, Cm 6298, paras 4.83–4.84 and Annex 3.

6 The Honourable Mrs Justice Pauffley, Committee of Inquiry – Independent Investigation into how the NHS Handled Allegations about the Conduct of Clifford Ayling, 15 July 2004, Cm 6298, paras 2.1–2.4 and 2.13.

During the period under consideration, the practice of obstetrics and gynaecology moved in the direction of fewer intimate examinations, and those which remained tended to be less invasive. Ayling's unsuccessful defence at the criminal trial was that he was just an 'old fashioned' practitioner, who continued to carry out examinations when many of his peers had moved away from them.[7] Whilst the jury rejected this explanation, a number of fellow doctors had initially been unwilling to judge Ayling's behaviour as outside the sphere of that which could be justified. When the evidence began to mount, medical colleagues recast what they heard to explain away the allegations as unfounded.[8]

The Inquiry concluded that appropriate guidance for dealing with this type of behaviour was not available within the regulatory process, and that this was in urgent need of a remedy. Of particular relevance and concern to the historical effectiveness of the GMC, the Inquiry was unable to identify any single organization or body which tracked repeated concerns or complaints about an individual doctor. No body had an overview of a pattern of concerns which might arise throughout the career of a doctor. The Inquiry recommendations that records of complaints and outcomes should be kept on the practitioner's personnel file for the length of their employment[9] is a poor substitute for action by the GMC.[10] Had the GMC been serious about its role as maintainer of the integrity of the medical register, it would have sought to obtain and keep all records of concerns and complaints about a registered practitioner.

## Sole Practitioners and Multi-Disciplinary Teams

The Ayling Inquiry concluded that in today's NHS the predominance of multi-disciplinary teams provides an integral self-regulating benefit.[11] However, some doctors continue to practise in relative isolation, and for these specific support programmes are necessary. These programmes should focus upon managing the risks of professional isolation. Trusts should also seek to develop the independence of

7 The Honourable Mrs Justice Pauffley, Committee of Inquiry – Independent Investigation into how the NHS Handled Allegations about the Conduct of Clifford Ayling, 15 July 2004, Cm 6298, paras 2.7 and 2.10.

8 The Honourable Mrs Justice Pauffley, Committee of Inquiry – Independent Investigation into how the NHS Handled Allegations about the Conduct of Clifford Ayling, 15 July 2004, Cm 6298, paras 2.11 and 2.27.

9 The Honourable Mrs Justice Pauffley, Committee of Inquiry – Independent Investigation into how the NHS Handled Allegations about the Conduct of Clifford Ayling, 15 July 2004, Cm 6298, para 2.44. It was also recommended that the employing organization should use the information for the purpose of identifying patterns of complaints against a practitioner, see para 2.45.

10 The Honourable Mrs Justice Pauffley, Committee of Inquiry – Independent Investigation into how the NHS Handled Allegations about the Conduct of Clifford Ayling, 15 July 2004, Cm 6298, paras 2.26–2.27 and 2.41.

11 This does overlook, or at least downplay, cases such as Bristol where multi-disciplinary and multi-profession teams were singularly ineffective in terms of self-regulation. However, it remains possible that were similar concerns to arise today, greater notice would be taken of whistleblowers and at a much earlier stage.

practice managers in single-handed GP practices, including addressing the potential for conflicts of interest when the manager is the spouse or other close relative of the practitioner.[12] It is open to question whether closeness of professional and personal relationships should be permitted. Following both the Ayling and Shipman cases and the need to protect the public, one cost of remaining a sole practitioner could be the requirement to employ an independent practice manager.[13]

## Ayling's Career[14]

As previously noted, after qualifying in 1963, Ayling was initially employed in a range of surgical training posts at Senior House Officer and Registrar grades in hospitals in London and Kent. He also held part-time clinical assistant posts in obstetrics and gynaecology.[15] Clinical assistant posts were not subject to formal supervision, although in principle Ayling was accountable to up to four consultants in his areas of practice (Mr A1, Mr A2, Mr A3 and Mr A4). However, Ayling also acted as a locum consultant when these consultants were on leave, and so at times stood in for those who were supposed to be overseeing his practice. This was reflective of a more general difficulty at the time, with a lack of effective audit and supervision amongst all grades of doctor. Ayling's autonomy as a specialist practitioner was such that the consultants formally responsible for his work gained little direct experience of his competence. They were reliant on nursing staff and patients to identify and report concerns. Yet, as discussed below, the reality was that these more junior medical and lay voices were rarely listened to.

There were concerns about Ayling throughout his career, but on very few occasions were these investigated. During his time as a clinical assistant, a number of nurses and midwives developed serious concerns about Ayling's behaviour and clinical management. Some of these came to light contemporaneously, but others were only aired in evidence before the Inquiry. For example, in 1971 Ayling delivered Patient A's first child at the North Middlesex Hospital. The delivery was traumatic. Patient A gave evidence to the Inquiry, recounting that her physical difficulties were exacerbated by Ayling's manner. Patient A also told the Inquiry that Ayling had an erection during the course of a pre-natal examination. Patient A did complain at the time to her consultant, but she was unaware of the procedures for raising a more

12 The Honourable Mrs Justice Pauffley, Committee of Inquiry – Independent Investigation into how the NHS Handled Allegations about the Conduct of Clifford Ayling, 15 July 2004, Cm 6298, paras 2.48–2.49.

13 Whilst appearing draconian at first sight, there is no difference in principle between this restriction and restrictions faced by lawyers when they encounter conflict of interest situations.

14 The information contained in the following discussion is largely drawn from The Honourable Mrs Justice Pauffley, Committee of Inquiry – Independent Investigation into how the NHS Handled Allegations about the Conduct of Clifford Ayling, 15 July 2004, Cm 6298, Chapter 3.

15 Ayling became a Diplomate of the Royal College of Obstetricians & Gynaecologists in 1967, a Member in 1970 and a Fellow in 1985.

formal complaint. In 1987, a serious incident resulted in the hospital deciding not to renew Ayling's contract as a clinical assistant in obstetrics and gynaecology. He was re-employed as a clinical assistant in colposcopy, but this was terminated in 1988, following a patient complaint. The fact and circumstances of these terminations were not communicated to Ayling's Family Practitioner Committee.

## Staff Complaints

Midwives at Thanet had widespread concerns about Ayling's obstetric practice and conduct to A3's female patients. However, the Inquiry had difficulty identifying specific occasions, by means of written records, on which such concerns had been translated into a complaint to a senior manager or clinician. The culture of the time supported informal mechanisms for raising concerns about a colleague. One exception involved Delphine Bentley, a midwife at Thanet, who made a formal complaint about Ayling's behaviour during the delivery of a baby. Even though this complaint was in writing, no action was taken.[16] The perception was also that doctors would close ranks in support of Ayling. As a result, there was a lack of accumulated information about Ayling's behaviour such that might have led to an earlier formal investigation.[17]

The evidence highlighted a number of persistent themes. The length and frequency of internal and breast examinations and excessive roughness when performing internal examinations or delivering babies.[18] Some witnesses also recalled that Ayling made inappropriate personal remarks, containing sexual innuendo, to patients whilst undertaking intimate examinations. One midwife recalled challenging Ayling about this, but subsequently observed no change in his practice. This was one of a number of factors which illustrated the significant power imbalance between nursing staff and patients on one side, and doctors on the other. A number of patients as well as some female staff made it clear that they did not wish to be treated by Ayling. Avoidance appears to have been the only effective weapon they could employ.

## The Knowledge of the 'Supervising" Consultants

In evidence to the Inquiry, Mr A1 accepted that he was aware of Ayling's reputation for heavy handedness, including frequent occasions of high levels of blood loss during his procedures. Mr A1 acknowledged that the accounts given by nursing staff of Ayling's inappropriate comments and approach to female patients related to the

16 The Honourable Mrs Justice Pauffley, Committee of Inquiry – Independent Investigation into how the NHS Handled Allegations about the Conduct of Clifford Ayling, 15 July 2004, Cm 6298, paras 3.78–3.79.

17 The Honourable Mrs Justice Pauffley, Committee of Inquiry – Independent Investigation into how the NHS Handled Allegations about the Conduct of Clifford Ayling, 15 July 2004, Cm 6298, para 3.47.

18 The Honourable Mrs Justice Pauffley, Committee of Inquiry – Independent Investigation into how the NHS Handled Allegations about the Conduct of Clifford Ayling, 15 July 2004, Cm 6298, para 3.48.

types of incident which should have come to his attention. However, Mr A1 did not accept that he had received any specific complaints about sexualized conduct by Ayling. There had been something of a 'conspiracy of silence' regarding sexual issues, which had inhibited communication between nursing staff and doctors.[19] Mr A2's evidence was that he had not been aware of complaints. Nor did he agree that there were cultural factors preventing nursing staff from complaining to consultants about other doctors.[20]

## The Incident at Thanet Antenatal Clinic in 1980

Nursing Sister, A5, told the Inquiry that in 1980 she was directly involved in a serious incident involving Ayling at the Antenatal Clinic at Thanet. She was summoned urgently by a nurse chaperone at a post-natal examination and she found Ayling masturbating during a vaginal examination on a young woman. She said that she pulled Ayling away from the patient and told him to leave the clinic. Subsequently, she tracked down the patient's consultant, Mr A2, and asked him to attend immediately. She said that when Mr A2 attended he was understanding and sympathetic, and indicated that Ayling would be referred to a psychiatrist. Because of the speed of this reaction, Sister A5 felt that this was something Mr A2 already had in mind. The possibility of police involvement was not raised. Sister A5 heard nothing further about the matter, but presumed Ayling was receiving psychiatric help. As her primary concern was to keep Ayling away from her patients, and this had been achieved, she did not personally take any further action.[21]

An incident of this type should have been immediately investigated at the most senior level, with possible referral to the police and the GMC.[22] As with other case examples discussed in this book, the opportunity was missed to cut short what turned out to be a sustained period of misconduct. This case also illustrates the numerous ways in which rigid hierarchies within medicine can contribute unnecessarily to risks faced by patients. For example, the junior nurse chaperone was clearly ineffective in a direct sense, neither deterring Ayling's behaviour nor being able to address and stop it personally. Whilst Sister A5 was able to take control of the immediate crisis situation, subsequent developments saw the medical hierarchy reassert itself at the cost of appropriate action.

---

19 The Honourable Mrs Justice Pauffley, Committee of Inquiry – Independent Investigation into how the NHS Handled Allegations about the Conduct of Clifford Ayling, 15 July 2004, Cm 6298, paras 3.60 and 3.82.

20 The Honourable Mrs Justice Pauffley, Committee of Inquiry – Independent Investigation into how the NHS Handled Allegations about the Conduct of Clifford Ayling, 15 July 2004, Cm 6298, para 3.81.

21 The Honourable Mrs Justice Pauffley, Committee of Inquiry – Independent Investigation into how the NHS Handled Allegations about the Conduct of Clifford Ayling, 15 July 2004, Cm 6298, paras 3.63–3.67.

22 The Honourable Mrs Justice Pauffley, Committee of Inquiry – Independent Investigation into how the NHS Handled Allegations about the Conduct of Clifford Ayling, 15 July 2004, Cm 6298, para 3.75.

Some time after the incident, Sister A5 had discovered that another of the consultants, Mr A1, was planning to re-introduce Ayling to the antenatal clinic. She said that she challenged Mr A1 about this in Ayling's presence, but was told 'not to question a Fellow of the Royal College of Gynaecologists'.[23]

## Examples of Patient Complaints

In 1977, a baby died during Ayling's attempt at a forceps delivery. The circumstances were such that they should have raised serious issues about Ayling's ability to make appropriate clinical decisions in the course of difficult deliveries. In conjunction with other concerns, this may be seen as the beginning of a pattern of behaviour from a doctor who lacked the skills to perform his obstetric duties. However, there was no systematic audit of Ayling's practice, either at the time or subsequently. In another case, the husband of Patient C wrote to Mr A2 complaining about Ayling's clinical judgement and describing his behaviour as 'callous' and 'brutal, if not actually bordering on the sadistic'. Mr A2 suggested two possible routes of action, an administrative inquiry initiated by the hospital secretary, or a referral to the 'three wise men'. Mr A2 recommended the second, less formal, procedure as in his view it would more appropriately deal with Ayling if he was suffering from a psychiatric illness.[24] Ayling was interviewed by the 'three wise men' and referred to a consultant psychiatrist, who concluded that he was not suffering from any mental illness. In evidence to the Inquiry, Mr A2 claimed to have been unaware of the outcome of the 'three wise men' investigation or the psychiatric referral. The Inquiry found this level of ignorance 'lamentable', given the seriousness of the matter. This was exacerbated by the fact that, having encouraged the patient to opt for the less formal procedure, he failed to follow this through.[25]

Patient D alleged that in July 1981 Ayling had made sexualized comments about her during an examination. Later she came around after an operation and found herself naked, with Ayling standing next to her bed, looking at her. When a complaint was made to Mr A1, he was defensive of Ayling. In evidence to the Inquiry, Mr A1 acknowledged that there had been no clinical justification for Ayling's behaviour and it had been inappropriate to dismiss the complaint.[26]

---

23 The Honourable Mrs Justice Pauffley, Committee of Inquiry – Independent Investigation into how the NHS Handled Allegations about the Conduct of Clifford Ayling, 15 July 2004, Cm 6298, para 3.68.

24 The Honourable Mrs Justice Pauffley, Committee of Inquiry – Independent Investigation into how the NHS Handled Allegations about the Conduct of Clifford Ayling, 15 July 2004, Cm 6298, paras 3.85–3.91.

25 The Honourable Mrs Justice Pauffley, Committee of Inquiry – Independent Investigation into how the NHS Handled Allegations about the Conduct of Clifford Ayling, 15 July 2004, Cm 6298, paras 3.93–3.95.

26 The Honourable Mrs Justice Pauffley, Committee of Inquiry – Independent Investigation into how the NHS Handled Allegations about the Conduct of Clifford Ayling, 15 July 2004, Cm 6298, paras 3.98–3.100.

### The Caesarean Section – 1987

Early in 1987, Ayling was responsible for a Caesarean section. Ayling cut into the baby's abdomen so severely that it had to be repaired surgically. Notwithstanding the seriousness of this event, it was several weeks before a meeting of senior clinicians and management was convened, during which time Ayling continued to practise in the field of obstetrics. The decision to terminate Ayling's employment was taken on the basis of a history of problems, culminating in this event.[27] However, only a few months later Ayling was re-employed in the colposcopy clinic. Mr A1 was of the opinion that the reasons for Ayling's termination as a clinical assistant in obstetrics and gynaecology had no relevance to his competence as a colposcopist. This appears to have been seriously misjudged. In 1988, the mother of one of Ayling's patients said that she had accompanied her 18-year-old daughter to the colposcopy clinic. Ayling had been sexually aroused and had rubbed himself against her daughter. The complainant insisted on remaining anonymous and explained that her daughter was unaware of the incident. Was her daughter to find out, she would lose all trust in the medical profession. After discussion within the hospital, it was decided that the circumstances prevented any action being taken, including referral to the police or the GMC. Instead, Ayling's contract of employment was not renewed. The reason given to him did not relate to the complaint, but was that clinical assistant posts were intended to be training positions, and that Ayling no longer fell within that definition. No enquiries were made to discover whether Ayling was employed elsewhere – he had also been working at the colposcopy clinic at the William Harvey Hospital. To compound the problem, Mr A1 was also not told the true reasons for the non-renewal.[28]

### General Practice

Ayling was a general practitioner between 1981 and 2000 and for much of this time, worked as a sole practitioner. Ayling's staff included a senior receptionist, who in 1984 became his wife. In 1985, Mrs Ayling became the practice administrator. In the mid 1980s a practice nurse also joined the surgery.[29]

Ayling routinely required patients to remove all clothing for breast and vaginal examinations, which were unduly prolonged and patients were not offered any covering. As one former patient explained to the Inquiry: 'I knew that it was perfectly

---

27 The Honourable Mrs Justice Pauffley, Committee of Inquiry – Independent Investigation into how the NHS Handled Allegations about the Conduct of Clifford Ayling, 15 July 2004, Cm 6298, paras 3.105—3.108. In contrast, Mr A2 continued to maintain that he was unaware of any cumulative problems regarding Ayling, and that the discussion involved only the one incident. The Inquiry preferred Mr A1's account. Paras 3.108–3.109.

28 The Honourable Mrs Justice Pauffley, Committee of Inquiry – Independent Investigation into how the NHS Handled Allegations about the Conduct of Clifford Ayling, 15 July 2004, Cm 6298, paras 3.112–3.121.

29 The Honourable Mrs Justice Pauffley, Committee of Inquiry – Independent Investigation into how the NHS Handled Allegations about the Conduct of Clifford Ayling, 15 July 2004, Cm 6298, paras 3.146–3.149.

possible to listen to a woman's chest without her having to remove her bra. However, I didn't feel that I had much choice. He was the doctor after all.' Such examinations were also undertaken when patients considered there to be no reason for them and without the presence of a chaperone.[30]

The Inquiry concluded that there was an awareness amongst other local GPs of the distress caused to patients by Ayling's conduct of examinations. A number of patients transferred from Ayling's practice to another practice in the area, Surgery A6. That practice interviewed all new patients, keeping notes of each interview. In addition, the Kent Family Practitioner Committee and its successor, the Kent Family Health Services Authority, were made aware of specific incidents involving Ayling in 1985 and 1991. The latter was the subject of one of the criminal convictions in 2000.[31]

## The Concerns Raised by Patient F – March 1985

In March 1985, Patient F experienced an extremely distressing examination by Ayling. She wrote to the FPC requesting the removal of her and her family from Ayling's list. Patient F said that she did not specifically request an investigation, but hoped that the FPC would 'be professional and instigate such an investigation into Ayling's treatment of [her]'. What actually happened was that she merely received a pro forma letter acknowledging receipt of her communication. Even though the letter from Patient F was a complaint, which raised serious concerns about Ayling, it was simply treated as a request to transfer.[32]

## Complaint to the Police – 1991

On 9 January 1991, a young patient of Ayling complained to the Kent Police about the way she had been examined. Her statement ended with the description that she had felt 'dirty and abused', as if she had been 'sexually abused and defiled'. Ayling was convicted in 2000 of indecent assault against this patient. However, in 1991 the Crown Prosecution Service had decided not to prosecute. Kent Police did write to the FHSA in May 1991, describing the patient's account as follows:

> The allegation was that Dr Ayling had carried out an internal examination without any consent, that he had prolonged the examination unnecessarily and had made suggestive

30 The Honourable Mrs Justice Pauffley, Committee of Inquiry – Independent Investigation into how the NHS Handled Allegations about the Conduct of Clifford Ayling, 15 July 2004, Cm 6298, paras 3.132–3.136.

31 The Honourable Mrs Justice Pauffley, Committee of Inquiry – Independent Investigation into how the NHS Handled Allegations about the Conduct of Clifford Ayling, 15 July 2004, Cm 6298, paras 3.125–3.130.

32 The Honourable Mrs Justice Pauffley, Committee of Inquiry – Independent Investigation into how the NHS Handled Allegations about the Conduct of Clifford Ayling, 15 July 2004, Cm 6298, paras 3.158–3.162.

comments during it. It was also alleged that he had insisted she strip naked and had 'fondled' her breasts, and pushed his leg against her naked thigh.[33]

In response, the local district manager of the FHSA wrote a memo to Dr A7, Medical Director of the Kent FPC and FHSA, on 6 June 1991, requesting that he undertake the 'advisor's role' with regard to Ayling's future conduct. Dr A7 gave evidence that he discussed the matter with Mr A8, Chief Officer of the Kent FPC and later the FHSA, and it was agreed that Mr A8 would speak to Ayling. This approach was also discussed with Chairman of the FHSA, Professor A9. Dr A7 wrote to Ayling on 11 June 1991 offering to discuss the complaint and stating that his major concern related to the absence of a chaperone, with the hope that Ayling had already addressed this omission. Neither Dr A7 nor Mr A8 actually met with Ayling to discuss the matter.[34]

The FHSA senior management placed far too little weight on the seriousness of this alleged incident, and therefore failed to appropriately investigative. For instance, no attempt was made to contact the patient to ascertain whether she wished to make a formal complaint, or even to determine whether she needed support.[35]

## The White House Surgery

The White House surgery was only a few hundred metres from Ayling's surgery. The relationship between the two practices had been strained since the 1960s when Ayling's former partner had complained to the GMC that the White House was 'poaching' his patients. It was for this reason that the partners at the White House had adopted the practice of interviewing all transferring patients to discover the reasons for their wish to do so. At such interviews, many female patients talked about apparent misconduct by Ayling when undertaking intimate examinations. There were at least 32 cases, between 1985 and 1995, where concerns were raised by transferring patients. These included comments about excessively painful vaginal examinations; being required to strip completely naked; repeated breast examinations; and intrusive questioning of a crude or sexual nature. A further 12 interviews between 1995 and 1998 also revealed such incidents.[36]

Dr A10, who had practised from the White House surgery between 1961 and 1995, was responsible for entry interviews between 1985 and 1995. He gave various

33 The Honourable Mrs Justice Pauffley, Committee of Inquiry – Independent Investigation into how the NHS Handled Allegations about the Conduct of Clifford Ayling, 15 July 2004, Cm 6298, paras 3.167–3.168.

34 The Honourable Mrs Justice Pauffley, Committee of Inquiry – Independent Investigation into how the NHS Handled Allegations about the Conduct of Clifford Ayling, 15 July 2004, Cm 6298, paras 3.170–3.173.

35 The Honourable Mrs Justice Pauffley, Committee of Inquiry – Independent Investigation into how the NHS Handled Allegations about the Conduct of Clifford Ayling, 15 July 2004, Cm 6298, paras 3.174 and 3.177.

36 The Honourable Mrs Justice Pauffley, Committee of Inquiry – Independent Investigation into how the NHS Handled Allegations about the Conduct of Clifford Ayling, 15 July 2004, Cm 6298, paras 3.182–3.188.

reasons why it took a number of years after the first report of misconduct before he took any action. First, he identified each issue as an individual one which, even if constituting deplorable action on behalf of Ayling, did not alone warrant action. Even when patterns emerged, he hoped that things would put themselves right. Dr A10 also felt that there would be little point raising the issue formally, on the basis of relatively little evidence. It did not occur to him to consult patients themselves about pursuing the matter formally. Dr A10 also reinforced the presumption that 'you must never denigrate a fellow practitioner', saying that this had been 'drilled into him' from qualification. He saw the Hippocratic Oath as saying the same – a doctor must never defame a colleague's character, especially where there was a risk of retaliation by counter allegations.[37]

By 1987, Dr A10 had some concerns, which led him to discuss this with his partners. It was decided that he would speak to one of the most senior GPs in the area, Dr A11. Dr A11 agreed to speak with Ayling, but later reported back that Ayling had denied any inappropriate behaviour. By 1988, five further examples had come to Dr A10's attention, two of these related to allegations of inappropriate sexualized behaviour, of a type which should have been reported to the GMC. Notwithstanding this, Dr A10 had not considered himself to be under a duty to do this. His response to the Inquiry was described as 'forceful':

> There are occasions when I have to override this advice from the GMC. This is overridden by my fear of retaliation, of being accused of defamation of character. So serious might the consequences be to me, personally, that I might have to leave the town. I couldn't risk my good reputation in the town by making a complaint unless it was of a more serious nature.[38]

This provides further evidence to support the assertion that if the GMC is to gain the information it needs to properly regulate the profession, the fear on the part of doctors of not reporting must be greater than the fear of the possible consequences of reporting.

In late 1993, Dr A10 had a further discussion with his partners and it was decided that he should contact the Kent Local Medical Committee.[39] Dr A10 spoke with Dr A12 (now deceased), then Secretary of the LMC. However, Dr A10's evidence was that Dr A12 did not treat the matters as particularly serious. About three to four months later, Dr A12 informed Dr A10 that there was no need for any action by the LMC because the William Harvey Hospital was taking steps, after receiving complaints of a similar nature. Dr A10 accepted that it did not occur to him to

---

37 The Honourable Mrs Justice Pauffley, Committee of Inquiry – Independent Investigation into how the NHS Handled Allegations about the Conduct of Clifford Ayling, 15 July 2004, Cm 6298, paras 3.190–3.197.

38 The Honourable Mrs Justice Pauffley, Committee of Inquiry – Independent Investigation into how the NHS Handled Allegations about the Conduct of Clifford Ayling, 15 July 2004, Cm 6298, paras 3.198–3.199.

39 The Local Medical Committee is the professional organization which represents GPs to the FPC and its successors. LMCs also provide advice to local practitioners on issues relating to general practice such as fees, partnership disputes or occupational health matters.

question how any action taken by the hospital would affect Ayling's practice as a GP. He seems to have assumed that if Ayling had been convicted of indecent assault as a result of the hospital complaints, his name would be erased from the medical register. However, Dr A10 did not see fit to make it known that he had additional evidence which might have strengthened such an investigation. It was of concern that the perceived risk of damage to reputation outweighed considerations of the harm that might come to patients.[40]

When Dr A10 retired in 1995, the job of interviewing new patients passed to Dr A13, who had joined the practice in 1993. There was no formal handover and Dr A10 retained his notebooks. Dr A13, therefore, had to start from scratch. Dr A13 began receiving disturbing information almost immediately and by late 1996 he had reached the conclusion that there was 'sexual deviation'. He did not suspect sexual assault until some time later. Dr A13 attributed his early lack of action to the culture of the time. For a doctor to even suggest to a patient that they had grounds for complaint was not the done thing. Only in 1998 had Dr A13 become sufficiently concerned that he contacted his Medical Defence Organisation for advice. He was told that, unless a patient complained, there was little he could do. As troubling information was still coming to his attention, Dr A13 decided to contact the Medical Adviser to the East Kent Health Authority (EKHA). He played a role in the police investigation.[41]

Overall, the Inquiry concluded that the failure of the White House practice to promptly report the litany of complaints to any relevant bodies was significant in enabling Ayling to continue to practise as a GP over such a long period. Of particular note was the inappropriate preference for informal approaches, rather than direct reporting to the FHSA or GMC. The White House partners had considered GMC requirements and guidance as secondary to their own self-interest.[42]

## Hospital Practice 1984–1994

### *William Harvey Hospital, Ashford*

Ayling was appointed to the position of Clinical Assistant in Obstetrics & Gynaecology at the William Harvey Hospital (WHH) in Ashford in March 1984, under the supervision of Rodney Ledward (although as at Thanet and KCH, actual supervision appears to have been largely illusory). The William Harvey Hospital was unaware of certain aspects of Ayling's other contemporaneous employment and

40 The Honourable Mrs Justice Pauffley, Committee of Inquiry – Independent Investigation into how the NHS Handled Allegations about the Conduct of Clifford Ayling, 15 July 2004, Cm 6298, paras 3.202–3.205 and 3.213.

41 The Honourable Mrs Justice Pauffley, Committee of Inquiry – Independent Investigation into how the NHS Handled Allegations about the Conduct of Clifford Ayling, 15 July 2004, Cm 6298, paras 3.206–3.212.

42 The Honourable Mrs Justice Pauffley, Committee of Inquiry – Independent Investigation into how the NHS Handled Allegations about the Conduct of Clifford Ayling, 15 July 2004, Cm 6298, paras 3.219–3.220.

about the concerns and complaints about him elsewhere. The Inquiry heard evidence from four nurses who had worked with Ayling at the William Harvey. One described cruel and brutal treatment by Ayling. Another two reported making their concerns known to senior management, but no action was taken.[43]

*Examples of Specific Complaints*

In April 1992, a student midwife at the WHH alleged that Ayling had 'grabbed her by the waist and then the buttocks' to move her closer to him and to the teaching microscope. This had been witnessed by a nurse, Nurse A14.[44] The incident was brought to the attention of the Director of Nursing Services, Ms A15.[45] Ms A15 told the Inquiry that she had kept the Unit General Manager, Mr L20,[46] fully informed. It was agreed that Mr L20 would speak to Ayling. It was almost two months later when he did speak with Ayling, by which time Ayling claimed to be unable to remember the incident. Mr L20 ultimately attributed a complaint which, if proved, constituted an indecent assault, to the student's misinterpretation of the encounter. He appears to have reached this conclusion without having spoken directly to the complainant.[47]

In June 1993, Patient I, a patient at Ayling's Antenatal Clinic, wrote to Ms A15 complaining that Ayling had made inappropriate sexual comments and pressured her to undergo an inappropriate internal examination. This episode eventually led to one of Ayling's criminal convictions. Mr L20 wrote an apologetic letter, assuring the patient that Ayling would not conduct clinics in future. Notwithstanding this, Ayling conducted clinics on at least four further occasions. In September 1993, Mr L20 wrote to Ayling informing him that his contract would not be renewed.[48] Four complaints within two years should have given rise to concerns at WHH about Ayling's activity, with a more proactive stance than merely the non-renewal of his contract.[49]

---

43 The Honourable Mrs Justice Pauffley, Committee of Inquiry – Independent Investigation into how the NHS Handled Allegations about the Conduct of Clifford Ayling, 15 July 2004, Cm 6298, paras 3.222–3.234.

44 Nurse A14 confirmed the basis of the allegation in a statement to the police in 1999 and again to the Inquiry. She also said that her recollection was that she had made a statement to the hospital authorities at the time of the incident.

45 Director of Nursing Services and Quality Assurance at the South East Kent Health Authority. Responsibilities included addressing concerns and complaints raised by patients and staff. Inquiry Report paragraph 3.240.

46 Unit General Manager of the Hospitals Unit of the South East Kent Health Authority from April 1991.

until April 1994, and then Chief Executive of the South Kent Hospitals NHS Trust. Inquiry Report paragraph 3.238.

47 The Honourable Mrs Justice Pauffley, Committee of Inquiry – Independent Investigation into how the NHS Handled Allegations about the Conduct of Clifford Ayling, 15 July 2004, Cm 6298, paras 3.241–3.242.

48 The Honourable Mrs Justice Pauffley, Committee of Inquiry – Independent Investigation into how the NHS Handled Allegations about the Conduct of Clifford Ayling, 15 July 2004, Cm 6298, paras 3.253–3.260.

49 The Honourable Mrs Justice Pauffley, Committee of Inquiry – Independent Investigation into how the NHS Handled Allegations about the Conduct of Clifford Ayling,

## Ayling's General Practice between 1992 and 1998

The first 'joined-up' examination of concerns about Ayling took place in 1993.[50] Dr A17 was Director of Public Health for the South East Kent District Health Authority between May 1990 and March 1994. She managed doctors working in family planning clinics. GPs working in the clinics were accountable to the Family Planning Service, which was led by a consultant, Dr A18. Dr A18 told the Inquiry that he believed that disciplinary and employment issues were the responsibility of the Director of Public Health.[51]

*Ayling's Activities in the Family Planning Clinics*

A nurse, A19, gave evidence of an incident at the family planning clinic, concerning a young female patient attending for a cervical smear. She had passed the patient's notes to Ayling and had waited to be present as a chaperone. She was not called in, so entered and found the patient distressed, completely naked, without the usual blanket. Ayling had performed a full physical examination. The patient was offered the opportunity to make a formal complaint with the nurse's support, but declined. In these circumstances, many patients would not have been sure that anything untoward had taken place. Also, some patients may have been embarrassed to admit that they were attending a family planning clinic. A19 provided a written record of the incident to her superior, A20, but was not aware of any action having been taken. A20 gave evidence about another incident which had been reported to her. This involved Ayling undertaking an unchaperoned vaginal examination on a young woman visiting the clinic for the first time. In addition to the absence of a chaperone, he had ignored a policy decision that these examinations should normally not be performed at the first visit. It was not considered necessary to document or pursue this incident, as the patient was not complaining. The Inquiry was also told that a number of Ayling's GP patients came to the clinic and complained to the nurses about Ayling performing unnecessary or unnecessarily frequent breast and vaginal examinations. When these concerns were passed on to more senior staff, the nurses were told that nothing could be done unless complaints were made in writing by the patients.[52]

---

15 July 2004, Cm 6298, para 3.269.

50 This came about when the FHSA's Medical Director was made aware of concerns about Ayling by the Director of Public Health for the SE Kent DHA (in respect of her responsibilities for the family planning clinics) and the Medical Director of the William Harvey Hospital. See The Honourable Mrs Justice Pauffley, Committee of Inquiry – Independent Investigation into how the NHS Handled Allegations about the Conduct of Clifford Ayling, 15 July 2004, Cm 6298, para 3.272.

51 The Honourable Mrs Justice Pauffley, Committee of Inquiry – Independent Investigation into how the NHS Handled Allegations about the Conduct of Clifford Ayling, 15 July 2004, Cm 6298, paras 3.275–3.276.

52 The Honourable Mrs Justice Pauffley, Committee of Inquiry – Independent Investigation into how the NHS Handled Allegations about the Conduct of Clifford Ayling, 15 July 2004, Cm 6298, paras 3.280–3.289.

Dr A17's response to the concerns raised about Ayling was to take what she acknowledged was the 'easy way out', removing Ayling's name from the list of locums and issuing the instruction that he should not be allowed to take family planning clinics again. Dr A17 did not speak to or otherwise communicate her decision directly to Ayling, acknowledging that she was embarrassed to do so. She did speak to Dr A7, the Medical Director of Kent FHSA. Dr A7 had gone on to warn Ayling that his approach to intimate examinations was unacceptable, but Dr A17's account was that it was considered that patients were overreacting to Ayling's behaviour and that the situation was not particularly serious. Dr A17 had never considered that Ayling's behaviour might be criminal in nature; she had not, therefore, undertaken any investigations. Nor did she seek advice from the GMC. The Inquiry was critical of the professional preference for informal discussion rather than instigating a formal process of investigation, and of 'convenient' partial solutions such as removing a doctor from employment without further steps.[53]

*Complaints to Other Doctors*

Dr A21 was a GP in Folkestone, and also worked part-time in family planning clinics. During the course of the latter work, Dr A21 received several complaints about Ayling. His evidence was that he advised patients to complain to the FPC/FHSA or to the police if they were alleging sexual assault. Dr A21 explained that he felt precluded from taking steps himself to bring matters to the attention of the FPC/FHSA or Dr A18, consultant at the family planning clinic, because of the absence of written consent from patients. A similar explanation was given for the failure to contact the GMC. Dr A21 had spoken to Dr A18 in the mid 1980s about Ayling's failure to use a chaperone. Dr A18 had subsequently issued a general letter reminding medical staff of the chaperone procedures. However, no action was taken to deal directly with Ayling.[54]

Overall, the absence of contemporaneous documentation of patient or staff concerns resulted in the absence of records from which a pattern of behaviour by Ayling could have been identified. The over-reliance on informal mechanisms to respond to complaints coincided with a lack of consideration that concerns should be reported in accordance with wider professional responsibilities. It was also unfortunate that a number of doctors wrongly concluded that unless a complaint was made in writing, no action could be taken.[55]

---

53 The Honourable Mrs Justice Pauffley, Committee of Inquiry – Independent Investigation into how the NHS Handled Allegations about the Conduct of Clifford Ayling, 15 July 2004, Cm 6298, paras 3.293–3.296.

54 The Honourable Mrs Justice Pauffley, Committee of Inquiry – Independent Investigation into how the NHS Handled Allegations about the Conduct of Clifford Ayling, 15 July 2004, Cm 6298, paras 3.297–3.299.

55 The Honourable Mrs Justice Pauffley, Committee of Inquiry – Independent Investigation into how the NHS Handled Allegations about the Conduct of Clifford Ayling, 15 July 2004, Cm 6298, paras 3.304–3.306.

## Managerial Action

On 29 October 1993, Dr L19, Medical Director at the William Harvey Hospital, telephoned Dr A7 notifying him of three serious complaints about Ayling. The Inquiry concluded that there was a total failure of understanding between Dr L19 and Dr A7 as to who would refer Ayling's alleged conduct to the GMC. No referral was made. Instead, Dr A7 wrote to Ayling on 3 November 1993. In this letter Dr A7 actually reassured Ayling that he did not expect any official complaint to be made to the GMC, the FHSA or the police. He simply offered to speak with Ayling. When this meeting took place in November 1993, it appears that Dr A7 was relatively easily placated by Ayling, who was able to demonstrate that he understood how to carry out a properly chaperoned intimate examination and the importance of such proper procedures. He also explained away the 'erect penis' incident as a bunch of keys in his pocket. Had Dr A7 further investigated this explanation, he may have discovered that Ayling had given an identical excuse to Mr L20 in June 1992.[56] The letter suggests that Dr A7 was aware of multiple incidents. It also suggested, by the reference to the police and GMC, that the subject matter of the complaints might have constituted criminal offences and/or serious professional misconduct.[57]

*Community Midwives*

A number of community nursing staff, such as health visitors and midwives, provided care to Ayling's patients. A number of former patients provided evidence to the Inquiry that they had made their concerns about Ayling known to these staff. One community midwife, A22, was named by six patients in this respect.[58] Ms A22 and another midwife, A23, had passed on concerns to their line manager, A24.[59] These concerns included inappropriate breast examinations. However, A22 denied any awareness at that time of sexualized behaviour by Ayling. She claimed that she only became aware of the latter in 1997 when a patient told her about a vaginal examination during which she had felt Ayling's erect penis against her thigh. The patient had been very clear that she did not want the matter to be reported. Ms A22 had sought advice from the Royal College of Midwives, after consulting the head of midwifery, and had been told that without the cooperation of the patient, there was nothing that she could do.[60]

---

56 The Honourable Mrs Justice Pauffley, Committee of Inquiry – Independent Investigation into how the NHS Handled Allegations about the Conduct of Clifford Ayling, 15 July 2004, Cm 6298, paras 3.307–3.312.

57 The Honourable Mrs Justice Pauffley, Committee of Inquiry – Independent Investigation into how the NHS Handled Allegations about the Conduct of Clifford Ayling, 15 July 2004, Cm 6298, paras 3.310 and 3.315.

58 The Honourable Mrs Justice Pauffley, Committee of Inquiry – Independent Investigation into how the NHS Handled Allegations about the Conduct of Clifford Ayling, 15 July 2004, Cm 6298, paras 3.318–3.320.

59 Supervisor of Midwives working in the community in Folkstone from 1989 to 1995.

60 The Honourable Mrs Justice Pauffley, Committee of Inquiry – Independent Investigation into how the NHS Handled Allegations about the Conduct of Clifford Ayling,

*South East Kent and East Sussex Doctors on Call Ltd (SEADOC)*

In 1992, GPs in Kent and Sussex set up a co-operative deputizing service, SEADOC. SEADOC had a complaints procedure, but no consistent mechanism for keeping a record of complaints about particular doctors. This informal approach was adopted notwithstanding the serious nature of some complaints. When a complaint was made, there was no automatic procedure to look back for previous complaints, and so no patterns were likely to emerge. In the period 1993 to 2000, there were ten recorded complaints about Ayling, none relating to sexual impropriety.[61] There was some doubt about the completeness of this record. For instance, one witness gave evidence to the Inquiry about an examination conducted by Ayling in July 1998. She had complained to SEADOC, but received no follow up and SEADOC had no record. In 1996, two doctors reported concerns about inappropriate examinations, but the patients involved did not want to complain formally. One notable figure was that Ayling was subject on average to 13 times more complaints than other SEADOC doctors.[62]

**1998 to 2000**

Between 1998 and 2000, the EKHA and the GMC received increasing numbers of complaints about Ayling. The investigations which followed led to reports to the police and ultimately to Ayling's criminal trial in 2000. The first detailed investigation was instigated after a complaint was sent to the EKHA on 23 February 1998. It detailed two consultations with Ayling at his surgery, during which he undertook what were described as humiliating internal examinations and unnecessary breast examinations. During one of these, Ayling was said to have been sexually aroused. A second letter of complaint was received on 12 March 1998. The patient complained that Ayling had undertaken repeated internal examinations and had asked inappropriate questions. Both complaints resulted in convictions for indecent assault and were also referred to the GMC. On 1 June 1998, a further complaint, alleging that Ayling had prescribed inappropriate drugs to a patient, was received. The EKHA initiated the procedures of the Poorly Performing Doctors Panel.[63] Advisers to the panel met with Ayling on 14 July 1998. Ayling was strongly advised to use chaperones and to avoid placing his patients in embarrassing positions. The panel decided in late September to refer Ayling to the GMC on the grounds of professional misconduct

15 July 2004, Cm 6298, paras 3.325–3.330.

61 Instead, they related to alleged delay or failure to visit. Some raised concerns about Ayling's manner or clinical management of a case.

62 The Honourable Mrs Justice Pauffley, Committee of Inquiry – Independent Investigation into how the NHS Handled Allegations about the Conduct of Clifford Ayling, 15 July 2004, Cm 6298, paras 3.331–3.351.

63 The panel was established in 1997 (following the introduction of new performance procedures by the GMC) and was a sub-committee of the EKHA. The role of the panel was to ensure that patients were protected, but also to support doctors and encourage remedial action.

and poor practice. They indicated in their report to the GMC that educational input was unlikely to improve Ayling's practice. A fourth complaint was received on the 11 September 1998, alleging an inappropriate and intrusive breast examination without the presence of a chaperone. This had taken place only two months after Ayling had been given a strong warning. The patient was advised to report the matter to the GMC and the police.[64]

## Referrals to the General Medical Council

The first two complaints to the EKHA had also been sent directly to the GMC by the patients concerned. It was not until 16 June 1998, almost two months later, that the GMC wrote to the EKHA indicating possible grounds for action under the fitness to practise procedures, but requiring further details from the complainants. In September 1998, after the third complaint about Ayling's sexual conduct, Mark Outhwaite[65] wrote to the GMC expressing concern about their slow pace. Cathy Bolton[66] contacted the GMC again in November to check progress. The GMC's response was that they were intending to await the outcome of criminal proceedings, although it was acknowledged in evidence to the Inquiry that there had been undue delay. This was attributed to a very heavy workload at the time because of events at the Bristol Royal Infirmary, plus the number of referrals having doubled since 1995.[67] This explanation falls somewhat flat when it is considered that problems of this type can be identified as spanning decades, rather than the relatively short period during which events at Bristol were being considered.

## Arrest and Bail

Ayling was arrested on 10 November 1998 and he was subsequently released on bail, subject to the condition that he could not practise as a GP. However, on appeal the High Court allowed Ayling to practise, provided that a chaperone was present during the examination of female patients and that he did not undertake any home visits. His access to medical records was to be limited to that appropriate to the medical practice he was allowed to undertake. No breach of these bail conditions came to light at the time, but two patients informed the Inquiry that they thought that the conditions had been breached. One said that she was subjected to intimate examinations on three occasions without a chaperone. The second patient talked of

---

64 The Honourable Mrs Justice Pauffley, Committee of Inquiry – Independent Investigation into how the NHS Handled Allegations about the Conduct of Clifford Ayling, 15 July 2004, Cm 6298, paras 3.354–3.365.

65 Chief Executive of the EKHA.

66 Secretary to the EKHA Board.

67 The Honourable Mrs Justice Pauffley, Committee of Inquiry – Independent Investigation into how the NHS Handled Allegations about the Conduct of Clifford Ayling, 15 July 2004, Cm 6298, paras 3.370–3.373.

an examination where a nurse had been present initially, but was sent out of the room from time to time.[68]

## Obstacles to Complaining

The Ayling case provides a useful insight into the failings of the NHS complaints system. Three principal barriers emerged to patients complaining about Ayling's activity in general practice:

1. Until 1996, the narrow definition of a complaint – the GP had to have breached the terms and conditions of the national contract. Furthermore, the requirement that the complaint be made in writing and within 13 weeks of the events complained about.
2. The requirement that patients present their complaint in person to the Medical Services Committee and be prepared to face challenges by the practitioner or their representative. This would have been daunting at the best of times, but especially when the subject matter of the complaint was as intensely personal.
3. The system was reactive; no attempts were made to seek out complaints or concerns.[69]

In addition, the misconceptions that complaints had to be in writing, and could not be taken forward if the complainant wished to remain anonymous, provided further restrictions.[70]

As described at various points in this chapter, and in common with the other case examples, the GMC failed to fill the gaps or to provide the overarching regulation necessary for public protection. In particular, the various instances of doctors inappropriately protecting their own positions and covering up for misbehaving colleagues demonstrates a lack of recognition of one of the fundamental aspects necessary for effective self-regulation.

68 The Honourable Mrs Justice Pauffley, Committee of Inquiry – Independent Investigation into how the NHS Handled Allegations about the Conduct of Clifford Ayling, 15 July 2004, Cm 6298, paras 1.1–1.2, 3.374–3.375 and 3.388.

69 The Honourable Mrs Justice Pauffley, Committee of Inquiry – Independent Investigation into how the NHS Handled Allegations about the Conduct of Clifford Ayling, 15 July 2004, Cm 6298, paras 5.30–5.35.

70 The Honourable Mrs Justice Pauffley, Committee of Inquiry – Independent Investigation into how the NHS Handled Allegations about the Conduct of Clifford Ayling, 15 July 2004, Cm 6298, paras 5.36–5.37. The Inquiry considered that there was some justification for this belief in the GP context, but less so in the hospital setting. The latter appeared to originate from confusion about the 1976 complaints procedure, not clarified until 1981.

# Chapter 11

# Richard Neale

## Introduction[1]

Richard Neale was a UK graduate gynaecologist with dual Canadian and British nationality. He qualified in London in 1970 and obtained full registration with the GMC in 1971. He was admitted as a member of the Royal College of Obstetricians & Gynaecologists in July 1975. He worked as a GP in the UK between 1972 and 1974 and then mainly in Canada, having emigrated there in 1977. He obtained a certificate in obstetrics and gynaecology from the Royal College of Physicians and Surgeons of Canada in 1978 and became a Fellow of the Royal College of Physicians and Surgeons of Canada (in the Division of Surgery) in the same year. In 1978, he undertook a high-risk operation, against the advice of a more senior colleague, and the patient died. As a result of this he lost his hospital privileges and was required to retrain or cease practice. In 1981, he was practising in Ontario, Canada, when another patient died following treatment. In June 1982, the College of Physicians and Surgeons of Ontario (CPSO) began an investigation into Neale. In June 1985, the Discipline Committee of the College found Neale guilty of incompetence, having displayed 'a lack of knowledge, skill or judgment or disregard for the welfare of the patient of a nature or to an extent that demonstrates he is unfit to continue in practice'. The professional misconduct was said to be of a most serious nature and Neale's name was erased from the Canadian medical register. An application in 1987 for readmission was unsuccessful.

In 1984 Neale sought a post with the NHS in Britain. He applied for and was offered employment by the Yorkshire Regional Health Authority, working at the Friarage Hospital and Darlington Memorial Hospital (the latter until 1990). By May 1985 Neale had become Chairman of the Surgical Division. This was notwithstanding the fact that the GMC had been informed on two occasions by the Canadian authorities about his disciplinary record in that country. In 1992 he moved to the Northallerton Health Services NHS Trust and was appointed as Clinical Director of Obstetrics and Gynaecology. Shortly afterwards, in 1993, media revelations broke about Neale's striking off in Canada.

Neale was able to practise for a significant number of years in the UK before finally appearing before the GMC in 2000. He was found guilty of 34 charges of

---

1 Unless referenced otherwise, the factual details in this chapter are taken from the Neale Inquiry Report, Matthews, J., *Committee of Inquiry to Investigate how the NHS Handled Allegations about the Performance and Conduct of Richard Neale*, August 2004, Cm 6315.

misconduct and his name erased from the medical register. His failings included undertaking surgery without consent, undertaking unnecessary procedures, improper surgical technique, failure to monitor the condition of patients post-operatively and failing to inform the patients' general practitioners of complications caused by his failures. The subsequent Inquiry[2] concluded that between 1985 and 1997 there had been systems failures both within the NHS and professional regulators. As the Chairman of the Inquiry expressed it in her introduction:

> I believed that the most perplexing aspect was how Richard Neale could be struck off in Canada, but able to retain his licence to practise medicine in the United Kingdom. Explanations given to the Inquiry in the summer of 2003 though honestly given, lacked conviction. Between January and the end of March 2004 significant evidence was finally obtained that confirmed not only had the General Medical Council been fully aware of his history in Canada, but had chosen deliberately not to act on this in 1986 and subsequently. The GMC Disciplinary Committee [sic] finally sat in judgment on him in 2000.

The Inquiry also concluded that Neale was able to practise in an environment in which his arrogant and overbearing manner was able to stifle criticism from colleagues and complaints by patients. He was in a position to endanger patients by overreaching himself in undertaking certain procedures. Peer-based monitoring of clinical practice was inadequate, the peers in question often lacking the expertise needed for this purpose, and clinical audit was underdeveloped.

## The GMC's Response to the Inquiry

Information initially came to the attention of the GMC about Neale's disciplinary history in Canada by means of two independent routes. Firstly, on 10 July 1985, the Registrar of the Medical Council of Canada wrote to the GMC informing it of the erasure from the Canadian medical register on 2 July 1985. Secondly, in 1985 or 1986, a colleague of Neale, Dr Andrew Sear, telephoned the GMC in an attempt to report the fact that the disciplinary history had come to his attention. His evidence to the Inquiry was that he was told that a doctor's standing in an overseas jurisdiction was of no concern to the GMC. The Neale Inquiry heard from other witnesses that the GMC were only concerned with professional matters arising in the UK, and lacked procedures for dealing with overseas issues. There was no evidence that the GMC had responded or sought further information following the report from Canada. The GMC's action appears to have been limited to placing Neale's name on a 'stop list', so that an alert would be raised if he applied for registration. However,

---

2 Matthews, J., *Committee of Inquiry to Investigate how the NHS Handled Allegations about the Performance and Conduct of Richard Neale*, August 2004, Cm 6315. The jurisdiction of the Inquiry did not extend to the consideration of the actions of the GMC. However, the GMC did offer some voluntary cooperation regarding its involvement in the history of the Neale affair.

Neale was already registered and working in the UK.[3] Evidence to the Inquiry from the Chief Executive of the GMC rejected the idea that the GMC lacked interest in the behaviour of a doctor undertaken outside of the UK. However, the Council could not take action based upon a regulatory finding outside of the UK. Instead, the GMC had to initiate its own investigation and bring its own proceedings. In relation to Dr Sear's evidence, the GMC had no records. The best guess was that Dr Sear had spoken to a clerk in what at the time was the Overseas Registration Division.

The GMC received a further reminder of Neale's history a couple of years later. In January 1986, Neale applied to become a police surgeon. At the time there were no vacancies, so his letter remained on file. In 1986 or 1987, Neale's first wife told Detective Superintendent Robin Cooper (as he then was) that Neale had been struck off the medical register in Canada. As this had relevance to Neale as an expert witness,[4] Mr Cooper wrote in May 1988 to the College in Canada. The College replied with details of Neale's striking off. Following discussion with the Head of CID and the Chief Constable, it was agreed that Mr Cooper would notify the GMC and the health authority. He did this, but his evidence was that the GMC's response was that they would not be taking action because Neale had not committed any offence in the UK. Detective Chief Superintendent Anthony Fitzgerald also contacted the GMC. He was informed that the GMC knew of Neale's history, but were satisfied that he was competent and did not intend to institute proceedings in the UK. In 1997, Neale applied to become a medical assessor for the GMC's professional performance procedures. He was provisionally appointed in October 1997, but was invited to withdraw his application when the appointment was criticized in a BBC regional programme in January 1998.

The view of the GMC in 2004 was that this response to the police communication was 'inexplicable' and that the approach today would be 'quite different'.[5] However, it remains of concern that callers could be given such inaccurate information and 'sent away' by the GMC. That this happened to a doctor and senior police officers attempting to make contact provides little scope for optimism that a lay complainant would be heard.

## The Appointment in 1984

The Inquiry concluded that the Yorkshire and Northern Regional Health Authorities obtained appropriate references before employing Neale. No statement of good standing was sought from Canada because Neale was fully registered with the GMC and usual practice would have been to rely on this. This further emphasizes the importance that the GMC gets it right, as reliance is rightly placed upon it by various bodies.

---

3 See Dyer, O., 'GMC Regrets Failure to Act on Police Warning about Gynaecologist', *BMJ*, 2004, 328: 1035, 1 May.

4 For instance, in September 1985, he had examined two young girls who were the subject of sexual abuse.

5 GMC Statement dated 26 March 2004, cited by the Neale Inquiry.

## Concerns at the Friarage

There appear to have been no concerns about Neale's competence, although the District General Manager of Northallerton District Health Authority from 1985–90 did refer to occasional concerns about his behaviour. Similarly, Neale's colleague, Mr N1, was very positive about Neale's clinical skills, but did develop some concerns about Neale's availability whilst on-call and other aspects of his behaviour. The latter involved allegations of inappropriate shouting and swearing. There was also an incident in 1988 when Neale applied to live outside of the area required for on-call duties. Mr. N1's evidence was that Neale had said that he (N1) had agreed to this, when this was not the case. Concerns therefore arose about Neale's honesty.

## Initial NHS Investigation in 1988

The Yorkshire RHA appear to have become aware of the events in Canada around June 1988. This information came from a local MP, from Neale's ex-wife and also from her parents. In addition, the local police also passed on the information they had obtained. DCS Fitzgerald spoke directly to the 'Chief Executive' and was assured that the hospital knew of the events in Canada and had no concerns about Neale's competency. In August 1988, the Yorkshire RHA contacted the Canadian medical authorities and in December 1988 received an account of the events in Canada.

When officers from the health authority discussed these reports with the GMC, they were told that the licensing arrangements in Canada were very different and so they could not take any steps in relation to Neale.[6] Overall, the Neale Inquiry concluded that the local investigation was inadequate, with insufficient regard being shown for patient safety.

## Criminal Behaviour

In April 1991, Neale was arrested and subsequently accepted a police caution following a 'sexual' incident in a public toilet. The Inquiry found that when arrested, Neale initially misled the police about his date of birth, address and occupation. A senior police officer formally notified the 'Personnel Manager' of Northallerton District Health Authority of the circumstances of the arrest and caution. In January 1992, Neale was given a formal 'final' warning by the Yorkshire RHA, requiring him to ensure that his future public behaviour did not cast aspersions on his professional standing. In dealing with this as an isolated, 'out of character', incident, account was not taken of the fact that Neale had been struck off in Canada; had failed to disclose this when he applied for the Northallerton post; and had made a misleading statement to the Yorkshire RHA when applying for reinstatement in Canada. It should have been of added concern that Neale had again lied, this time to the police.

6 An expert witness to the Neale Inquiry was of the opinion that Neale's behaviour in Canada constituted 'reckless management', and considered that a similar case before the GMC would probably have led to a period of suspension.

In September 1991 the Assistant Chief Constable wrote to the Registrar of the GMC notifying the Council of the caution, in accordance with Home Office guidance of the time, which provided that: 'The police are asked to report convictions in relation to all groups listed in Schedule 2, particularly for offences involving violence, indecency, dishonesty, drink or drugs, because they may reflect on a person's suitability to continue in a profession or office.'[7]

The police were able to provide to the Neale Inquiry written evidence of this communication. The GMC, in contrast, could find no record and so there was no evidence that they had followed the matter up, nor even kept the report on file for reconsideration, should further issues of misconduct have come to light.

## Neale's Career Progression

Notwithstanding his disciplinary record, Neale was appointed Clinical Director of Obstetrics & Gynaecology, the most senior member of that department, in late 1992. Neale was also responsible for the audit programme and controlled complaints handling. He represented the hospital on the Regional Medical Audit Committee and was Chairman of the District Medical Audit Committee. These positions of power and influence were held even though at least one senior colleague of Neale's had also become increasingly concerned about his poor time-keeping, his inadequate commitment when on-call and his questionable truthfulness. However, these concerns were not disclosed at the time.

## Initial Investigations

In autumn 1993, press reports appeared regarding Neale's striking off in Canada and the incident in the public toilet. Faced with this challenge to its public image, the Trust Board convened an Investigation Panel, chaired by Dr Richard Peterson, and in December 1993 an investigation was begun. The Peterson Investigation found that, depending upon the medical procedure in question, between 18 and 29 per cent of GPs had stopped referring patients to Neale, and some GPs even questioned Neale's fitness to practise, although, in common with some other case studies in this book, some other GPs appeared to close ranks in defence of Neale. Of even greater concern, in terms of doctors protecting their own, the Northallerton Consultants' Association wrote to Dr Peterson objecting to the collecting of such information from GPs and expressing the opinion that 'internal disciplinary matters should not be influenced…by external agencies'. Whilst some in the profession were complaining about the Peterson Investigation exceeding acceptable boundaries in terms of its scope, the Neale Inquiry expressed the opinion that the investigation had been restrained in its approach and as such had omitted to follow up important leads or avenues of enquiry.

In January 1994 the Peterson Panel reported to the Trust Board with the conclusion that the Canadian events and the public toilet incident had already been adequately

7 Circular No. 45/1986, paragraph 11.

dealt with. The panel's conclusions were, inter alia, that Neale should remain in post, but should cease to be Clinical Director. Training should be offered to improve his communication skills and there should be no intra-departmental referrals of patients to Neale without the express permission of the initial referring GP. The Trust Board accepted most of these recommendations and Neale was demoted from his post as Clinical Director.

The Peterson Investigation was seen by the Inquiry as a welcome attempt to address the problems, but ultimately the terms of reference and lack of arms-length independence resulted in a flawed exercise. Patient safety was not, therefore, assured.

## 1995 Investigation

By July 1995, the Medical Director was informed that difficulties were continuing. Key amongst these problems were inappropriate leave and a failure to adequately supervise junior staff. Neale, it was said, would absent himself from duties frequently, often at the last minute, and on occasions was unavailable when on-call. A number of incidents had occurred where Neale had refused to attend to supervise junior colleagues when he was on-call. In some of these cases, patients came to harm. There were also allegations of theft of trust property and inappropriate expenses claims.

A disciplinary hearing was called for 30 August 1995. Neale denied the allegations and emphasized that he was actively seeking an alternative post. In light of this, the Trust Board decided that the best way forwards was to agree a negotiated severance agreement. As an alternative to disciplinary action, this agreement was seen as a means to relieve staff of the risk of being faced with a long period of uncertainty and associated stress. The matter would probably have dragged on for two years or more – with no guarantee of success, so the cost of settlement was seen to be reasonable compared with the salary which would have been payable to Neale during this time.

The agreement provided Neale with a 12-month period of paid leave. Unless Neale had accepted alternative employment by the end of this period, the Trust would pay him a £50,000 lump sum and his employment would terminate. A reference, the content of which was to be agreed with Neale, would be supplied. Neale spent a year on sabbatical leave, but was employed at Leicester Royal Infirmary NHS Trust from November 1995 to March 1996 and periodically on the Isle of Wight between April and July 1996.

## References

In the early 1990s, the GMC had provided very little guidance regarding the providing of references by doctors for their colleagues. In the case of Dunn in March 1994, the Professional Conduct Committee of the GMC provided limited guidance:

> Doctors who have reason to believe that a colleague's conduct or professional performance poses a danger to patients must act to ensure patients' safety. Before taking action in such

a situation, doctors should do their best to establish the facts. Where there is doubt, it is unethical for any doctor to give references about a colleague, particularly if it may result in the employment of that doctor elsewhere. References about colleagues must be carefully considered. Comments in them must be justifiable, offered in good faith and intended to promote the best interests of patients.

The 1998 edition of *Good Medical Practice* provided the following guidance: 'When providing references…your comments must be honest and justifiable; you must include all relevant information which has a bearing on the colleague's competence, performance, reliability and conduct.'[8]

By the time of the 2001 edition, the guidance was framed as follows: 'You must provide only honest and justifiable comments when giving references for, or writing reports about, colleagues. When providing references you must include all relevant information which has any bearing on your colleague's competence, performance and conduct.'[9] The agreement to provide a wholly positive reference for Neale meant that a future employer would not be aware of the problems he had presented.

The GMC did belatedly take action against one of the doctors who provided references for Neale, Professor N2. N2 twice provided a reference without mentioning that Neale had been cautioned by the police. N2 had also been a screener for the GMC and had decided that a complaint in 2000 against Neale from the North Yorkshire Police should not proceed. N2 had not informed the GMC's registrar of his connections to Neale. In December 2005, a GMC fitness to practise panel found that N2's errors of judgement impaired his fitness to practise and excluded him from acting in a judicial or administrative capacity with the GMC for three years. He was also prohibited from providing any professional references for the same period.[10]

## Complaints from Patients

By the mid-1990s, there had been seven complaints against Neale, mainly concerning issues of clinical care. Three of these had been found to be unsubstantiated, one was dealt with by means of an apology and the remaining three proceeded to litigation. Complaint numbers increased significantly after March 1999, when Neale's activities were featured in a BBC *Panorama* programme, and again after the media coverage accompanying his erasure in July 2000. During the period March 1999 to July 2001, 82 complaints were made. Almost all of Neale's patients who provided evidence to the Inquiry explained that little or no information was provided about the possibility of post-operative complications. Consent to surgery was probably not, therefore, 'informed'.

Neale's manner was described by a number of patients as 'arrogant, rude, abrupt and dismissive'. Patients described occasions when Neale had made wholly inappropriate remarks during consultations, in at least one example 'loudly' in the

8 Paragraph 11.

9 Paragraph 14.

10 See Dyer, O., 'GMC Censures Professor for Not Disclosing Conflict of Interest', *BMJ*, 2005, 331: 1358, 10 December.

hearing of others. One patient described attending as an outpatient in 1992 with a growth at the neck of the womb into the vagina. She described Neale as almost immediately beginning 'tugging away at the growth'; this was without explanation and caused her extreme pain. She described feeling 'vulnerable and violated'.

Many patients said that they were reluctant to complain – fearing that this might prejudice future treatment. Others simply did not have access to the necessary information about how to make a complaint. In common with other cases, notably that of Ledward, some patients (as well as nursing and other staff) viewed hospital consultants as powerful and beyond criticism.

## Staff Concerns

Evidence to the Inquiry from nursing staff was mixed. For example, Neale's main theatre sister at the Friarage Hospital did not recall him being rude, nor did she notice Neale making any obvious errors or become aware of any problems with his clinical skills. She considered him to be a good surgeon. A theatre nurse also gave evidence that she considered Neale to be a good surgeon and had allowed him to perform her hysterectomy. Another staff nurse was also positive, although she did recall occasions when Neale was not readily available when needed. A senior midwife and Head of Midwifery at the Friarage from 1993 had told the Peterson Investigation that Neale had always been caring and she respected his clinical abilities.

The sister in charge of the gynaecology ward throughout Neale's time at the Friarage observed that Neale could be more irritable and brusque than other consultants, which sometimes upset patients. His pre-operative discussions with patients also tended to be shorter. He was also less consistent about making post-operative visits to his patients after surgery. He could also be rude to junior colleagues. However, she was not concerned about Neale's clinical competence, and her concerns about his manner did not reach a degree of seriousness that she felt the need to raise them with anyone else.

The Deputy Head and then Head of Midwifery gave evidence that Neale's manner was inconsistent; he could be charming but also angry and abusive to staff. Her greatest concerns related to Neale's inconsistent availability on-call, to such an extent that 'the majority of staff would dread him being the Consultant on-call'.

A staff midwife gave evidence that Neale's poor availability when on-call became 'a real source of anxiety' from the early 1990s. She was also unhappy about his hygiene standards. For instance, he did not always put scrubs on for procedures and on occasions walked down the corridors in blood-stained theatre greens. The most serious incident she recalled occurred in May 1993 and involved a difficult labour. Neale had been reluctant to attend when called, and when he did arrive undertook a rough vaginal examination, catheterized the patient without explanation and without appropriate aseptic technique. He was so rough with forceps that the patient cried out in pain and was pulled down the bed. He repaired a vaginal tear and left. The repair subsequently failed. In a follow-up communication to the patient's GP, Neale had attributed her problems to failures in midwifery care.

## Other Doctors

A senior colleague provided a positive account of Neale's practice when he wrote to the Royal College of Physicians of Ontario in March 1989. However, by 1992 he had increasing concerns about Neale's manner, his honesty and on-call availability. However, under-staffing had prevented him from stirring matters up with Neale. This latter point is of obvious concern and illustrates that local interests may pull in opposing directions. Once again, this emphasizes the vital role to be played by the GMC in providing an arms-length, objective process which should always concentrate on patient safety.

A consultant anaesthetist at the Friarage had not been concerned about Neale's clinical competence, although found Neale to be arrogant at times. At a much later stage, he realized that some patients had suffered complications which had not been recorded in the medical notes or about which the patient had not been given sufficient explanation.

The Clinical Director became aware, from the spring of 1995 onwards, that Neale was not undertaking all of his outpatient clinics, theatre lists were being cancelled, and he was taking leave without informing anyone. He also became aware that Neale was not always available when on call. In July 1995, he communicated his concerns to the Medical Director.

The conclusions drawn by the Inquiry were that staff were to a significant extent 'in awe of…Neale and felt unable to challenge his clinical competence…'. His character also made it difficult to express concerns. Neale was also free from peer monitoring of his clinical work. Indeed, it was said that his peers lacked the expertise to monitor his highly specialist area of surgery, urogynaecology.

## Appointments after the Friarage

Neale obtained locum positions at the Leicester Royal Infirmary NHS Trust and subsequently St Mary's Hospital, Isle of Wight. In the case of both appointments, the references were incomplete with regard to the negative aspects of Neale's career. The Inquiry observed that employers also failed to follow up gaps in the references.

During the latter appointment, in April 1996, a complaint arose following the treatment by Neale of Mrs K. Neale had performed a vaginal hysterectomy when consent had been given for an abdominal hysterectomy. He had nicked the bladder during the operation and had failed to call for urological assistance, nor otherwise taken steps to repair the damage. The error was not properly recorded in the medical notes, nor was any problem highlighted in the discharge letter to Mrs K's GP.

These events eventually gave rise to four of the disciplinary charges found proved by the GMC. The Inquiry was critical of the lack of a clinical incident report and the failure by the Trust to promptly report Neale to the GMC.

## The GMC Proceedings

Following media coverage about Neale, the GMC began investigations in January 1998. By November 1998, the GMC's solicitors had enough information to refer the case to the PPC. It was considered that the events in Canada were by then too old to form the basis of proceedings. It was also considered that the police caution should not be proceeded on. In January and April 1999, the PPC concluded that charges should be brought before the PCC. In September 1999, Neale was subjected to an interim suspension. Ultimately, in April 2000, charges relating to 14 patients were brought and PCC hearings took place between 12 June 2000 and 25 July 2000. Neale was found guilty of serious professional misconduct and his name erased from the medical register. Specific matters constituting SPM included: unacceptably low diagnostic skills and clinical management of patients;[11] failure to seek timely help from more experienced colleagues; failure to obtain appropriate informed consent and failure to give appropriate information either before or after an operation; failure to communicate appropriately with professional colleagues, including failing to give GPs full and accurate information about their patients' operations; misleading a patient to encourage her to undergo private treatment; rude and aggressive communication with one patient; and falsification of his curriculum vitae when applying to become a medical assessor with the GMC. The latter is of particular concern, as it would have been expected that at the time of Neale's application, the GMC would have accessed previous disciplinary concerns about Neale, as he was applying to become part of the GMC's own regulatory system.

## Conclusions

It was known, or should have been known, from 1986 that Neale was 'at the least dangerously incompetent and possibly worse'. The Canadian regulatory system acted with speed and efficiency, in significant contrast to the subsequent inaction in Britain. As the position was summed up judicially: 'Even when limited steps were taken in 1995 [Neale] continued to cause mayhem.'[12]

The Neale Inquiry recommended that the Secretary of State for Health consider establishing a new organization, or extending the powers of the Council for Health Regulatory Excellence, to adopt an overarching view of the appointment and employment of doctors. This organization would have the power to investigate issues in the wider interests of patient safety. This raises the issue of whether such a new body should, in effect, replace the GMC, as the proposed functions include those which, arguably, the GMC should be doing already.

---

11 The Neale Inquiry found that, unlike Ledward, Neale did not exhibit systematic substandard care. Rather, his failings were cumulative, as demonstrated by the GMC's findings.

12 See *Howard and Wright-Hogeland v Secretary of State for Health* [2002] EWHC 396, para 65.

# Chapter 12

# Harold Shipman

## Introduction

In July 2002, the report of the first stage of the Inquiry into the activities of Harold Shipman was published. This was followed by five further reports. The Inquiry, chaired by Dame Janet Smith, followed the conviction of Shipman for the murder of 15 of his patients. The Shipman Inquiry reports chart a history of unlawful killing spanning more than 20 years and involving at least 215 victims.

## Shipman's Professional Career

Shipman first entered general practice in 1974, securing a position in Todmorden and, after a short period of probation, became a junior partner. One of his responsibilities was disposal of out-of-date controlled drugs and ordering new stocks for use by practice members. In February 1975, the Home Office Drugs Inspectorate and the local police drugs squad became aware that Shipman was obtaining abnormally large amounts of pethidine. However, initial enquiries concluded that there was no cause for concern. Later in 1975, the Home Office Inspectorate advised the practice in relation to its poor record-keeping regarding the supply and destruction of controlled drugs. During 1975, Shipman also experienced health problems, suffering 'blackouts' or 'seizures'. By September 1975, Shipman's partners discovered that he had been abusing pethidine, having obtained large quantities improperly, ostensibly for practice use. Ultimately Shipman was dismissed from the Todmorden practice and underwent voluntary treatment at a private hospital. Both psychiatrists responsible for Shipman's care notified the Home Office that Shipman should be registered as a drug addict.

Shipman admitted during the course of police investigations that he had been abusing pethidine for 18 months. In February 1976, he was convicted on specimen charges of obtaining controlled drugs by deception, possession of controlled drugs and forging prescriptions. A large number of further offences were taken into consideration. During the course of the investigation, Shipman had stated: 'I have no further intention to return to General Practice or work in a situation where I could obtain supplies of pethidine'.[1] By the time of his conviction, Shipman had started a new job as a clinical medical officer. He had been open with his new employers about his past and had no access to controlled drugs.

1 Smith, J., *The Shipman Inquiry*, First Report, Volume One, Death Disguised, July 2002, HMSO, para 1.15.

Shipman's convictions were reported to the GMC. The GMC had psychiatric reports and a letter of support from Shipman's new employer. The relevant GMC committee[2] concluded that the matter need not be referred for possible disciplinary action. The GMC informed the Home Office of its decision. The Home Office, apparently influenced by the GMC decision not to discipline Shipman, decided not to restrict Shipman's access to controlled drugs in the course of his medical practice.[3]

Notwithstanding his earlier assurances, Shipman did return to general practice in 1977, joining a partnership (the 'S1 Practice'). He admitted his previous drug problems to the members of the practice who made inquiries of the GMC and the Home Office and were told (correctly) that there were no restrictions on Shipman's right to practise. When interviewed for the partnership position, Shipman underplayed and gave a self-serving account of the events in Todmorden. In confirming that Shipman was registered, with no restrictions on his practice, it seems that the GMC would not have volunteered the fact that Shipman had a fitness to practise history and would have treated the warning issued to Shipman as confidential. The Home Office confirmed that it would have informed an inquirer that Shipman's ability to prescribe was not restricted. Further information would not have been volunteered, even if it was already in the public domain, for fear of damaging Shipman's employment prospects. In evidence to the Inquiry, partners at S1 expressed concern that they had been unaware that Shipman had forged prescriptions, and would have been uncomfortable appointing a partner convicted of offences involving dishonesty. The S1 partners took their lead from the GMC, 'which they believed would have had knowledge of all the facts relating to Shipman's drug taking activities, [and] had found that Shipman was fit to practise. It was not for the practice to go behind that finding.' In terms of Shipman's application to join the medical list, the FPC simply checked that he was registered by the GMC. The assumption was that 'it was the GMC's task, not that of the FPC, to decide whether a doctor was fit to treat patients'.[4] Shipman stayed with this practice for 14 years, leaving in 1991 to practise alone. In 1992 Shipman set up a sole practice from a surgery in Market Street, Hyde.

## Shipman's Criminal Activities

Shipman was popular and well respected, although described as arrogant and overbearing by some.[5] However, by March 1998, some people had become concerned that a number of Shipman's patients were dying in curiously similar circumstances.

---

2 The procedure at the time was for the Penal Cases Committee to consider, on the basis of written evidence and submissions, whether the matter should be referred for Inquiry to the GMC Disciplinary Committee. Smith, J., *The Shipman Inquiry*, First Report, Volume One, Death Disguised, July 2002, HMSO, para 1.19.

3 Smith, J., *The Shipman Inquiry*, First Report, Volume One, Death Disguised, July 2002, HMSO, para 1.21.

4 The Fifth Report of the Shipman Inquiry, *Safeguarding Patients: Lessons from the Past – Proposals for the Future*, paras 3.39–3.54 (www.the-shipman-inquiry.org.uk).

5 Smith, J., *The Shipman Inquiry*, First Report, Volume One, Death Disguised, July 2002, HMSO, para 1.30.

Initial police investigations concluded that there were no grounds for concern. Shipman's activities only came to light following the sudden and unexpected death on 24 June 1998 of Kathleen Grundy. Mrs Grundy's daughter, a solicitor, reported her concerns to the police when it emerged that what purported to be Mrs Grundy's last will left her entire estate to Shipman. Police investigations revealed a crude attempt at forging the will by Shipman. Exhumation of Mrs Grundy's body revealed levels of morphine sufficient to have caused her death. Police investigations then extended to look at the deaths of other Shipman patients.

## Report to the GMC

The police informed the GMC in 1998 that Shipman was under investigation, and in October of that year that he had been charged with murder. At the time, the GMC considered that its statutory powers were not such that it could suspend Shipman from the register prior to his conviction. Shipman was remanded in custody at the time, but in principle remained free to practise. On 31 January 2000, Shipman was convicted on 15 counts of murder and one of forging Mrs Grundy's will. He was sentenced to 15 terms of life imprisonment and a concurrent term of four years for forgery. On 11 February 2000, the GMC erased Shipman's name from the medical register.

## Investigations Following Conviction

In September 2000, the Secretary of State announced that a public Inquiry would be held into the issues surrounding the Shipman case.[6] In January 2001, the Chief Medical Officer commissioned Professor Richard Baker to review Shipman's practice.[7]

### *The Baker Review*

Professor Baker, having undertaken a statistical analysis of the number of deaths certified by Shipman during his general practice career, concluded that there were 236[8] excess deaths about which there should be cause for concern. Unusual features

6 In February 2000, an Inquiry under the provisions of the National Health Service Act 1977 had been announced. However, once members of the families of deceased former patients and others discovered that this Inquiry was to be held in private, they successfully brought a judicial review action which set aside the decision and required the Secretary of State to reconsider the matter; *R v Secretary of State for Health, ex parte Wagstaff and others; R v Secretary of State for Health, ex p Associated Newspapers Ltd and others* [2001] 1 WLR 292, 56 BMLR 199.

7 Department of Health, *Harold Shipman's Clinical Practice 1974-1998*(http://www.doh.gov.uk/hshipmanpractice/shipman.pdf), undertaken by Professor Richard Baker of the Clinical Governance Research and Development Unit, Department of General Practice and Primary Health Care, University of Leicester.

8 Based upon a 95 per cent confidence interval 198 to 277.

about the deaths of Shipman's patients included the proportion of older females who died suddenly at home, in the afternoon, with Shipman present.[9] Shipman was over 24 times more likely to be present at the death of one of his patients than other general practitioners were with theirs.[10] Shipman's patients were also certified as having died quickly[11] and there was a weak association between the clinical history and the certified cause of death.[12] Shipman was also over six times more likely than other general practitioners to certify two or more deaths on the same day.[13] Baker concluded that a system for monitoring the mortality rates of patients of general practitioners should have detected these unusual patterns in Shipman's practice. However, Frankel et al cast doubt upon the effectiveness of routine statistical monitoring. In the case of a general practitioner such as Shipman, with a patient list of around 3,000, up to 18 excess deaths per annum would not be statistically noticeable. The same would be true for 30–40 excess deaths in larger practices.[14] Routine statistical monitoring could therefore only detect a doctor who killed on a very large scale and who did not modify his or her behaviour to defeat statistical analysis. On this basis, Shipman would have escaped detection for at least 14 years. In resource terms, intensive annual investigation of around 0.5 per cent of the 9,000 general practices in England, 45 in all, would be required.[15] Overall, Frankel et al

---

9 Fifty-five per cent of Shipman's patients died in the afternoon compared with 25 per cent of patients of other general practitioners.

10 Nineteen point five per cent in the case of Shipman, 0.8 per cent in the case of comparison practitioners. Department of Health, *Harold Shipman's Clinical Practice 1974-1998* (http://www.doh.gov.uk/hshipmanpractice/shipman.pdf); see also Smith, J., *The Shipman Inquiry*, First Report, Volume One, Death Disguised, July 2002, HMSO, Appendix A, 205. If Shipman did not admit to being present at death, it was more likely that the patient died alone. Forty point four per cent of Shipman's patients were said to have died alone, compared with 19.0 per cent for other general practitioners. The implication from the report's findings are that unsuspicious deaths at home generally occur with relatives or carers present.

11 Sixty point four per cent of Shipman's patients were said by him to have died in 29 minutes or less, compared with 22.7 per cent for other general practitioners.

12 Department of Health, *Harold Shipman's Clinical Practice 1974-1998* (http://www.doh.gov.uk/hshipmanpractice/shipman.pdf); see also Smith, J., *The Shipman Inquiry*, First Report, Volume One, Death Disguised, July 2002, HMSO, Appendix A, 204.

13 Sixty-two Shipman deaths (11.8 per cent) occurred on the same day as another death, compared with 1.9 per cent for comparison practitioners. On two occasions, Shipman certified three deaths on the same day, an occurrence encountered by no comparison general practitioner. Department of Health, *Harold Shipman's Clinical Practice 1974-1998* (http://www.doh.gov.uk/hshipmanpractice/shipman.pdf).; see also Smith, J., *The Shipman Inquiry*, First Report, Volume One, Death Disguised, July 2002, HMSO, Appendix A, 229.

14 Frankel, S., Sterne, J. and Smith, C.D., 'Mortality Variations as a Measure of General Practitioner Performance: Implications of the Shipman Case', *British Medical Journal*, 2000, 320: 489, 19 February.

15 This estimate is based upon 99 per cent confidence intervals. It does not take into account complicating factors such as changes in average death rate due to particular local factors, deprivation and an elderly population. It is suggested that an annual investigation rate of more than 0.5 per cent would be required to account for these. Frankel, S., Sterne, J.

conclude that routine monitoring would be of limited benefit in detecting future 'Shipmans', and the process would perhaps create a false sense of security.

## Work Commissioned by the Shipman Inquiry

The Shipman Inquiry commissioned Dr Paul Aylin to consider the prospect of routine monitoring of death rates for detecting misconduct in general practice.[16] Dr Aylin undertook a pilot exercise using national data from 1993 to 1999. For the period up to 1997, the success rate in linking death registration records to GP lists was relatively low (under 60 per cent) due to gaps in data records. However, the position improved significantly in the later years, reaching 98–99 per cent in 2000. Since this date, the Department of Health has been moving towards a single national database which links every diseased person and their cause of death with the GP or practice. Dr Aylin developed a system which could be used, it was said, with over 96 per cent accuracy, to screen for excessively high mortality rates. The system could be tuned to identify different thresholds of alarm with, for example, a lighter touch investigation at the lower threshold and a more intensive investigation at the higher level.[17] The process would be ongoing, rather than operating simply on the basis of an occasional snapshot of death rates. The system would be set up specifically for the purpose desired, for example, excess deaths caused by criminal activity or, alternatively, those due to incompetence. Once the alarm was raised, it would remain to be decided what subsequent action should be taken.[18]

Dr Aylin observed that if monitoring was undertaken at practice level, it would be difficult to detect excess deaths caused by a single doctor. For example, in a practice of six GPs, the system might be able to detect an excess of 25 deaths caused annually by a single doctor. Even a killer as prolific as Shipman would only have satisfied this during three of his years in practice. It should be possible to devise a system whereby a patient's contact with individual GPs in a practice is recorded so that the predominant treating doctor can be identified. This, however, would probably slow down the monitoring process.[19]

---

and Smith, C.D., 'Mortality Variations as a Measure of General Practitioner Performance: Implications of the Shipman Case', *British Medical Journal*, 2000, 320: 489, 19 February.

16 Aylin, P., Best, N., Bottle, A. and Marshall, C., 'Following Shipman: a Pilot System for Monitoring Mortality Rates in Primary Care', *The Lancet*, 2003, Vol 362: 485–91.

17 Each threshold would offer particular advantages and disadvantages. For example, operating at a lower threshold would detect a greater proportion of problem doctors but would also give higher numbers of false positives – doctors whose data raised concerns but were actually innocent. This would waste investigatory resources and possibly cause unnecessary stress to those innocent doctors. In contrast, a higher threshold would result in far fewer false alarms but might also miss some doctors who should be investigated.

18 See the Fifth Report of the Shipman Inquiry, *Safeguarding Patients: Lessons from the Past – Proposals for the Future*, paras 14.23–14.64 and 14.71 (www.the-shipman-inquiry.org.uk).

19 See the Fifth Report of the Shipman Inquiry, *Safeguarding Patients: Lessons from the Past – Proposals for the Future*, paras 14.105–14.111 (www.the-shipman-inquiry.org.uk).

Based upon the available historical data, Shipman would only have given rise to concern in 1997. However, with improved data collection processes, concerns about Shipman would have come to light much earlier in his career. However, the system would not detect a doctor who killed infrequently or who hastened the death of a terminally ill patient by only a short period of time.[20]

Whilst routine monitoring of death rates would not guarantee detection of a future Shipman-type killer, it offers the potential to deter both wilful misconduct and to detect incompetent doctors.[21]

## Initial Findings of the Shipman Inquiry

The initial findings of the Shipman Inquiry were that over a period of 23 years, 1975 to 1998, Shipman killed 215 of his patients, usually by the administration of a lethal dose of an opiate.[22] The initial 71 killings were committed whilst Shipman was in partnership, but the majority, 143, occurred from 1991 onwards, whilst he was a sole practitioner. Most of Shipman's victims were elderly, but not all. The youngest victim was 41 years old and in the advanced stages of terminal illness. The youngest whose death was unexpected was 47 years old.

## Drug Misuse

As already noted, following his criminal convictions in 1976, Shipman was not disciplined by the GMC and he was therefore able to continue in general practice without restriction. This was so even though, apparently as a result of drug misuse, he had suffered sudden blackouts which in themselves may have presented some risk to patients. He also declared his intention never to carry controlled drugs again and, accordingly, he was not obliged to keep a controlled drugs register. Nevertheless, he was able to obtain large quantities of controlled drugs which he used to kill his victims. Shipman was able to prescribe and collect large quantities of diamorphine in the names of patients who had no medical need for the drugs. He was also able to take possession of large quantities of 'left over' opiates after the deaths of cancer patients.[23] On one single occasion in 1996, he prescribed and collected 12,000mg of diamorphine, sufficient to kill up to 360 people, in the name of a terminally ill

---

20 See the Fifth Report of the Shipman Inquiry, *Safeguarding Patients: Lessons from the Past – Proposals for the Future*, paras 14.118–14.119 (www.the-shipman-inquiry.org.uk).

21 See the Fifth Report of the Shipman Inquiry, *Safeguarding Patients: Lessons from the Past – Proposals for the Future*, para 14.153 (www.the-shipman-inquiry.org.uk).

22 Smith, J., *The Shipman Inquiry*, First Report, Volume One, Death Disguised, July 2002, HMSO, 2–3. The deaths of a further 45 patients gave rise to suspicions that Shipman may have been responsible, but the evidence was inconclusive. Unlike the Baker review, which reached its conclusions by means of statistical analysis, Smith approached her task by investigating the circumstances surrounding all of the deaths which Shipman had certified.

23 Smith, J., *The Shipman Inquiry*, First Report, Volume One, Death Disguised, July 2002, HMSO, 105.

patient who had already died.[24] In this respect, the Inquiry concluded that Shipman was able to obtain very large quantities of controlled drugs illegally by means of deception and forgery, and without complying with any of the statutory requirements of record-keeping. Furthermore, he must have committed drugs offences virtually every day that he was in general practice, by being in possession of controlled drugs without lawful authority.[25] The extent to which Shipman was able to kill his patients was inextricably linked to his ability to obtain quantities of controlled drugs, yet no element of the self-regulatory process was able to detect this. Another example of slowness of action by the GMC with regard to drug misuse is provided by *Finegan v GMC*.[26] Over a nine-year period (1976–85), a GP frequently and inappropriately prescribed controlled drugs for his wife. His wife also stole drugs from his medical bag and forged prescriptions. For three of the years (1977–80) the doctor also failed to complete a controlled drugs register. The doctor's misconduct was known for much of the nine years in question, but he gave repeated, unfulfilled assurances that the practice would stop. As a result the GMC delayed taking action. In fact, the misuse was continuing up to the month of the GMC hearing. Whilst very different in substance from Shipman, this case reinforces the view that an apparently lax approach by the GMC to the misuse of controlled drugs by general practitioners was not a one-off slip in the Shipman case.[27]

## False Certification

### *Death Certificates*

The requirement for a doctor to complete the Medical Certificate of Cause of Death is intended to ensure that unexplained or suspicious deaths are investigated by the coroner. The certificate should only be completed if the doctor has attended the patient during the previous 14 days and is able to state with some precision the cause of death. Expert evidence presented to the Shipman Inquiry was that it was never appropriate simply to certify the cause of death as being due to 'natural causes', as that would signify that the doctor does not know what the cause of death was – such a decision was for the coroner. It might be permissible for a doctor to certify that death was due to 'old age', but only when the patient had been ill for a significant period – weeks or months – and death was expected. 'Old age' would not

24 Smith, J., *The Shipman Inquiry*, First Report, Volume One, Death Disguised, July 2002, HMSO, 168.

25 Smith, J., *The Shipman Inquiry*, First Report, Volume One, Death Disguised, July 2002, HMSO, 107 and 168.

26 [1987] 1 WLR 121.

27 In contrast to the approach taken by the GMC to Shipman's drug-related offending, it did discipline the doctor – imposing a three-year ban on his prescribing controlled or prescription-only drugs. In the context of a general practitioner, this was a severe sanction as it would effectively prevent him undertaking many of the usual aspects of general practice for this period. However, this eventual action by the GMC cannot excuse the fact that the doctor was able to behave as he did, unchecked, for a significant period of time.

be appropriate if the deceased had been active up to the day of death.[28] In 15 cases in which Shipman was found to have unlawfully killed the patient, he certified the cause of death as 'old age', even though the patient had not met the above criteria. Shipman would also certify that he had seen the deceased legitimately in the 14 days before death, when this was not true. In other cases, Shipman certified as causes of sudden and unexpected death, medical conditions which would not usually be expected to develop without prior symptoms or warning.[29]

### *Cremation Forms*

Six of the 15 cases for which Shipman was convicted had been certificated for cremation. One hundred and sixty-six of the 200 additional cases where the Inquiry gave a finding of unlawful killing had also been certificated for cremation, and so had 36 of the 45 cases where there was a real suspicion of Shipman being responsible for the deaths. Because cremation of a body destroys evidence and removes the possibility of further direct investigation into the cause of death, additional safeguards are supposedly in place before cremation can be authorized. In addition to the usual MCCD process, the doctor who completed the MCCD also completes a second, more detailed certificate (Form B). A second doctor must confirm the cause of death and a third (the medical referee) must check the paperwork. The procedure therefore required Form B to be completed by the doctor who attended the deceased before death, had seen the body and identified the cause of death. The second doctor completes Form C.[30] The second doctor is required to 'carefully examine' the body and 'see and question' the doctor who completed Form B. The Form C doctor should also say whether he or she has made further inquiries, for example, of relatives or carers of the deceased. The final authorization to cremate is given by the medical referee, who completes Form F after scrutinizing Forms B and C. Form F included the declaration: '…I have satisfied myself…that the cause of death has been definitely ascertained and that there exists no reason for any further inquiry or examination…'[31] The medical referee may refuse to allow a cremation without the need to give reasons.

### *Examples of Cremation Certification Failure*

The Inquiry found that Shipman was careless in a number of cases when it came to completing cremation forms.[32] In the case of Miss Ada Warburton, Shipman recorded

---

28 Smith, J., *The Shipman Inquiry*, First Report, Volume One, Death Disguised, July 2002, HMSO, 51 and 52.

29 Smith, J., *The Shipman Inquiry*, First Report, Volume One, Death Disguised, July 2002, HMSO, 146.

30 The Form C doctor must have been registered for at least five years and not be in practice with the doctor who completed Form B or related to the deceased.

31 Smith, J., *The Shipman Inquiry*, First Report, Volume One, Death Disguised, July 2002, HMSO, 55–60.

32 See Smith, J., *The Shipman Inquiry*, First Report, Volume One, Death Disguised, July 2002, HMSO, 55–8.

on Form B that he had last seen her alive at 5.30pm and that she had died at 'about 17.30'. However, he went on to record that he was not present at the time of death and that he had seen the body 'about 45 minutes after death'. In the case of Mrs Deborah Middleton, Shipman recorded the time of death as around 5pm and said that he had seen the deceased about two hours before death. However, on the same form he said that Mrs Middleton had been found by her daughter at 2.30pm, an ambulance had arrived and she was found to have died by 3.00pm. Shipman also erroneously declared on Form Bs that other persons were present at the time of death. The most striking example of this was that of Mrs Dorothy Long, where Shipman claimed that paramedics were present at the moment of death. Yet in an alternative account, he said that the patient had been dead for 36 hours before paramedics attended.

Shipman would also frequently declare on Form B that he had performed complete and, by implication, comprehensive external examinations to ascertain the fact and cause of death. However, relatives of the deceased told the Inquiry that he often never even touched the bodies. The expert witness to the Inquiry also said that Shipman's descriptions of the modes and duration of death on Form B were such as to give cause for concern, as were his answers to the question on the form which asked about nursing care. In this latter respect, Shipman often said that the deceased had been in receipt of no nursing care, yet he went on to certify the cause of death as 'old age', which in the opinion of the expert, as already noted, implies a high level of frailty. That a patient should have died in these circumstances should itself have given rise to concerns about possible neglect.

Doctors who agreed to complete death certificates and cremation forms did so under a statutory duty, and not as a part of their employment, for example, with the NHS. They are not, therefore, answerable to their employers, but the matter does fall within the regulation of their professional conduct by the GMC. It is of significant concern that the cremation certification process is one of the few direct 'on the ground' applications of self-regulation, and in the case of Shipman it clearly failed repeatedly. Furthermore, the scale of Shipman's crimes would suggest that this failure was not isolated to this case, but evidence of a much more widespread problem. This is not only of concern should there be other doctors who are unlawfully killing their patients, but also because it is very likely that there are doctors who, through neglect or incompetence, are harming their patients yet remaining undetected.

It might reasonably have been expected that the GMC would have seen the cremation certification process as an ideal vehicle to enhance mutual monitoring by doctors in the interests of self-regulation. In reality, the Shipman case supports the critical interpretation that self-regulation provides a shell around the profession, protecting members from external scrutiny, without the promised reciprocal obligation that members of the profession will appropriately monitor each other in the interests of the public.

### Falsification of Patient Records

Shipman falsified records and lied about his patients' medical histories in order to avert suspicion about their sudden deaths. In some cases he entered fictional serious medical conditions. In other cases medical records would show a dramatic shift in narrative, for example, a patient in Shipman's surgery would be giving an account of elbow pain and the record would suddenly change to record coronary thrombosis and death. In some instances, Shipman apparently became confused about his own fabrications, leading to inconsistencies within the records. For example, in the case of Mrs Elsie Barker, whom the Inquiry determined Shipman killed in July 1996, Shipman's entry in the medical records showed that he had visited her on the day she died, yet on cremation Form B he stated that he had last seen her five days before.[33] From 1993, when another general practice, the S2 practice, moved into premises close to Shipman's surgery, Shipman had an arrangement whereby doctors from that practice would sign cremation Form Cs. The Inquiry was told that Shipman would bring patient records with him and give a very full account of the history leading up to death. However, he would not show the records to the Form C doctor. For example, in the case of Mrs Norah Nuttall, the doctor who signed Form C, confirming the cause of death as left ventricular failure, said that he would have relied entirely on what Shipman told him. According to the Inquiry expert, Shipman's description of the death was not typical of ventricular heart failure, nor was the description by Mrs Nuttall's son, of his mother's condition shortly before her death.[34] The S2 doctors became used to large numbers of deaths amongst Shipman's patients, but attributed this to the age profile of his patients. Only in 1998 did an S2 practice doctor report to the coroner her concerns about signing 16 cremation forms for Shipman in a three-month period. In comparison, the S2 practice, with three times the number of patients, had only 14 deaths in the same period.[35]

Fabrication of records by Shipman was only discovered because an audit trail had been installed on his computer in October 1996. From then, the dates on which records had actually been produced and when changes had been made could be ascertained.

## Inadequate Medical Care

It appears odd to have a sub-heading *Inadequate Medical Care* when discussing a doctor who has been found to have murdered over 200 patients. However, it is pertinent to ask the question whether the evidence surrounding Shipman's practice should at least have led to concerns and investigation regarding his competence as a doctor. Poor medical practice, inadequate attempts at resuscitation, confirming death without proper examination and the circumstances surrounding deaths of patients at his surgery, all provide evidence that Shipman should have come to the attention of a properly functioning GMC.

---

33 Smith, J., *The Shipman Inquiry*, First Report, Volume One, Death Disguised, July 2002, HMSO, 170.

34 Smith, J., *The Shipman Inquiry*, First Report, Volume One, Death Disguised, July 2002, HMSO, 275–6.

35 Smith, J., *The Shipman Inquiry*, First Report, Volume One, Death Disguised, July 2002, HMSO, 174.

### *Poor Medical Practice*

The Inquiry revealed numerous examples of behaviour on the part of Shipman which should have given rise to concerns about his competence. Shipman frequently certified bronchopneumonia and other respiratory conditions as a cause of death, often describing the onset from reasonably good health to illness and death in a matter of minutes. The expert view given to the Inquiry was that patients with pneumonia may become ill rapidly, but this would occur over a few hours, not minutes, and the deterioration would be evident to family and friends. Furthermore, in the view of the expert, death from pneumonia of otherwise healthy patients should be very rare in modern medicine, because of the availability of antibiotics and, if necessary, prompt admission to hospital.[36]

In seven of the cases for which Shipman was convicted and numerous others identified by the Inquiry, the patient was found dead at home shortly after Shipman had left. At no time during Shipman's career did the self-regulatory process identify that, on the basis of his own accounts, he left patients who were so ill as to be at risk of imminent death, without arranging for their admission to hospital or other appropriate care.[37] A variation on this theme was Shipman's explanation that he had identified the urgent need for hospital admission, but the patient had refused to go. The expert view presented to the Inquiry was that, not only was it rare for a general practitioner to encounter a seriously ill patient who refused hospital admission, but also a competent doctor in these circumstances would make far greater efforts to persuade the patient of the need to go to hospital, enlisting the help of friends and family if possible. If the patient was beyond persuasion, a detailed note of the efforts made would be usual.[38] A competent doctor would not, as Shipman apparently claimed he did, have left a seriously ill patient alone to die, having not contacted friends or family. For example, in the case of Mrs Irene Turner, the conclusion of the Inquiry's expert was that:

> …if the [medical] note was accurate, it showed a woman in urgent need of hospital admission for intravenous re-hydration and control of the diabetes. She was a medical emergency. There should have been no delay…
>
> Shipman's account of his treatment of Mrs Turner was inappropriate. In order to explain the course of events, he was driven to give an account of his actions which, if true, would have shown him to be seriously incompetent. This was a common feature of Shipman killings…records of the events preceding the death were woefully inadequate and mutually inconsistent…Shipman was a poor record keeper and this is amply demonstrated in very many cases.[39]

---

36 Smith, J., *The Shipman Inquiry*, First Report, Volume One, Death Disguised, July 2002, HMSO, 71–2.

37 Smith, J., *The Shipman Inquiry*, First Report, Volume One, Death Disguised, July 2002, HMSO, 111–12.

38 Smith, J., *The Shipman Inquiry*, First Report, Volume One, Death Disguised, July 2002, HMSO, 84.

39 Smith, J., *The Shipman Inquiry*, First Report, Volume One, Death Disguised, July 2002, HMSO, 285–6.

A further variation involved Shipman visiting a patient and (having killed them) then leaving. A neighbour, on seeing Shipman leave, would go over to see the patient and discover them dead. On being called back, Shipman's explanation was that he had left to fetch something from the surgery and had been on his way back. Again, Shipman's own account is one of a doctor whose competence is such that he either failed to diagnose the severity of a patient's condition or, having diagnosed it, nevertheless left the patient alone.[40]

Some of Shipman's accounts in medical records and on death certification were described by the Inquiry expert as 'breathtaking'. For example, 'I turned round to get my stethoscope out of my bag and she just collapsed and died'.[41] In the case of one victim, Mrs Cox, Shipman's account was that he left the patient, who, he said, had a history of angina and was complaining of chest pain, alone without calling an ambulance or even contacting Mrs Cox's daughter. This account was described by the expert witness to the Inquiry as 'incredible' and descriptive of a practice which no doctor should adopt. The Inquiry's conclusion was that: '[Shipman] was becoming quite confident in giving an explanation which, on rational consideration, can be seen to be quite implausible. Shipman seems to have realised that even a highly implausible explanation would not be questioned.'[42]

In the case of Mr Frank Halliday, Shipman's records indicated that the patient had been complaining of chest pains for two days. On the cremation Form B, Shipman said that he had been with Mr Halliday for an hour before his death. A competent doctor would have been expected to refer Mr Halliday urgently to hospital. In the case of Miss Mona White, Shipman told relatives that he had arrived to find Miss White having a massive heart attack. He had known that she was going to die so he had not bothered to call an ambulance.[43] On numerous occasions Shipman was present at the time a patient died or had visited the patient a few hours before.[44] Expert evidence suggested that even with a patient list with the age profile of Shipman's, a doctor would be expected to be present at the death of a patient at home on average only once per annum. Many of the deaths were sudden and unexpected, and even if Shipman had not been intentionally killing his patients, there should have been significant cause for concern about the quality of medical care these patients had received leading up to their deaths. Furthermore, Shipman's notes regarding the

40 Smith, J., *The Shipman Inquiry*, First Report, Volume One, Death Disguised, July 2002, HMSO, 114

41 Smith, J., *The Shipman Inquiry*, First Report, Volume One, Death Disguised, July 2002, HMSO, 113.

42 Smith, J., *The Shipman Inquiry*, First Report, Volume One, Death Disguised, July 2002, HMSO, 145.

43 Smith, J., *The Shipman Inquiry*, First Report, Volume One, Death Disguised, July 2002, HMSO, 148–50.

44 For example, in 1989 Shipman had visited 16 patients within four hours or less of their deaths at home. In 1993 he was present at the time of six out of 28 home deaths which he certified and had visited within a few hours of six others. In a six-month period up to March 1998, Shipman admitted to having been present at the time of seven out of 31 deaths at home. Smith, J., *The Shipman Inquiry*, First Report, Volume One, Death Disguised, July 2002, HMSO, 75.

home deaths at which he was present were unsatisfactorily brief, or non-existent.[45] One of the complicating factors was that evidence to the Shipman Inquiry suggested that 'the records of all the doctors at the [S1] practice…were "fairly terrible, if not pathetic" at the time Shipman left'. The poor quality of Shipman's notes may not, therefore, have stood out.[46]

### *Attempts at Resuscitation*

In many cases, Shipman claimed that, having attended a patient whose condition suddenly deteriorated, he had attempted resuscitation. The Inquiry concluded that this could not have been true because, for example, the patients had not been placed on an appropriate surface to allow the proper resuscitation procedures to be followed, or witnesses claimed that the victim was fully dressed with no evidence that clothing had been loosened or other steps taken to allow attempted resuscitation.[47] Furthermore, in the opinion of the expert to the Inquiry, resuscitation by a lone doctor was very difficult. The appropriate procedure would be to call an ambulance, and then to attempt resuscitation until it arrived.[48] Shipman either did not call an ambulance, or lied and said that he had, but had cancelled the call when the patient died. In the case of Mrs Harding, whom Shipman killed in his surgery, it appears that Shipman called (or claimed to have called) an ambulance and then began resuscitation attempts along with his practice nurse. He ceased these attempts before the ambulance arrived and cancelled the ambulance. The expert to the Inquiry said that it made no sense to start resuscitation but stop before the ambulance arrived. It is of note that the practice nurse did not consider it unusual for resuscitation to be stopped. This was so, even though Shipman had not made use of the resuscitation equipment available on the practice premises.[49]

### *Confirming Death*

Shipman rarely carried out appropriate examinations to ascertain the fact of death. In some cases he never even approached the body and in at least one case, he purported to confirm death by merely looking through the patient's window.[50] The findings of

---

45 Smith, J., *The Shipman Inquiry*, First Report, Volume One, Death Disguised, July 2002, HMSO, 75–6.

46 The Fifth Report of the Shipman Inquiry, *Safeguarding Patients: Lessons from the Past – Proposals for the Future*, para 4.56 (www.the-shipman-inquiry.org.uk).

47 Smith, J., *The Shipman Inquiry*, First Report, Volume One, Death Disguised, July 2002, HMSO, 143.

48 Smith, J., *The Shipman Inquiry*, First Report, Volume One, Death Disguised, July 2002, HMSO, 80.

49 The Fifth Report of the Shipman Inquiry, *Safeguarding Patients: Lessons from the Past – Proposals for the Future*, paras 9.58 and 9.93 (www.the-shipman-inquiry.org.uk).

50 In the case of Mrs Olive Heginbotham, Shipman, on looking through her window, claimed to be able to tell that she had died. He then departed, leaving a neighbour to deal with the situation. Smith, J., *The Shipman Inquiry*, First Report, Volume One, Death Disguised, July 2002, HMSO, 161.

the Inquiry were that Shipman need not examine the bodies, he knew exactly when the patient had died because he had killed them. What should have raised concerns within the self-regulatory process is that without properly ascertaining death, a doctor could not be sure that the patient was beyond help and so could not be acting with an appropriate degree of professional competence.

### *Surgery Deaths*

The Inquiry concluded that Shipman killed six patients in his surgery, five of these whilst he was a sole practitioner. No investigations occurred at the time and the coroner was not informed. Expert evidence suggested that it is very unusual for a patient to die in a general practitioner's surgery.[51] Shipman's explanations for the deaths were far from convincing. For example, in the case of Mrs Bertha Moss, the patient had been chatting to a friend in the waiting room and appeared well. Shortly afterwards she died alone with Shipman. Shipman's explanation was that he had taken an electrocardiograph and, whilst he was putting the equipment away, Mrs Moss had suffered a heart attack. He claimed to have attempted resuscitation, without success. Shipman's account does not accord with that of appropriate medical practice. He did not call an ambulance nor enlist the help of surgery employees.[52] In the case of Mrs Dora Ashton, Shipman's account was that the patient had fallen to the floor as she was walking into his consulting room. He diagnosed a minor stroke and managed to sit her down, but she had a second stroke and died. Again, no attempt was made to seek help or call an ambulance. From the case of his very first surgery victim, Mrs Mary Hamer, Shipman's accounts contained inconsistencies. Shipman told his receptionist that Mrs Hamer had died in the examination room whilst he was seeing another patient. He told the victim's family that when she came into his consulting room, Mrs Hamer had chest pain which Shipman diagnosed as coronary thrombosis. He said that he had given a small dose of morphine and telephoned the hospital. When he returned, Mrs Hamer had died.[53] Again, there was no evidence of the full-scale emergency response which appropriate medical practice would dictate in a crisis of this type.

## A Gap in GMC Powers?

One argument advanced by the GMC for its historical failure to deal with underperforming doctors was that, prior to the introduction of the performance procedures, it lacked adequate statutory powers. Applied to Shipman, the conclusion

---

51 Smith, J., *The Shipman Inquiry*, First Report, Volume One, Death Disguised, July 2002, HMSO, 166–7.

52 Expert evidence indicated that a collapse on surgery premises would be expected to result in an emergency response in which virtually all members of the practice are called to assist. Smith, J., *The Shipman Inquiry*, First Report, Volume One, Death Disguised, July 2002, HMSO, 166–9.

53 Smith, J., *The Shipman Inquiry*, First Report, Volume One, Death Disguised, July 2002, HMSO, 155.

might have been that his apparent poor medical practice would not have been worth investigating because no regulatory powers existed to deal with it. For example, the 1979 professional conduct guide stated that the GMC was 'not concerned with errors of diagnosis or treatment'. By 1985, the wording had been relaxed to the extent that the GMC was concerned with errors in diagnosis or treatment, but only when the doctor's conduct had involved such a disregard of professional responsibility or such neglect of professional duties as to raise a question of serious professional misconduct. The 1985 guide does go on to say that patients are entitled to expect appropriate examination, diagnosis, management and action when the condition requires urgent attention.[54] However, the question remains whether the GMC could have done more. The wording of the 1985 guide appears to cover Shipman's activities. In covering up his crimes, Shipman created records and other evidence which painted a clear picture that he failed to 'examine', correctly 'diagnose' and provide appropriate 'urgent action'. It is difficult to envisage more serious disregard of professional responsibility than that which results in the death of a patient. Decisions of the Professional Conduct Committee of the GMC and the Privy Council also support the proposition that the GMC had, and knew it had, power to act prior to 1997. For example, in *Ramdence v GMC*,[55] the PCC had suspended a general practitioner for poor record-keeping and failing to admit a patient to hospital. In reaching this decision, the PCC stated:

> ...the committee take a serious view of...the shortcomings in your clinical management of this patient's case and the inadequacy of your record keeping concerning your treatment of his condition...in both respects you failed to provide the patient with the competent and considerate professional attention which he had a right to expect of his general practitioner.

Similarly, with regard to a general practitioner in *Jones v GMC*,[56] they said: '... the committee take a very serious view...of your defective clinical methods and, in particular, your repeated failure to carry out a proper examination of the patient... and your failure to secure his prompt admission to hospital.'

In *McCandles v GMC*,[57] the Privy Council confirmed that serious professional misconduct could include seriously negligent treatment. The GMC was under a duty to protect the public against incompetent practitioners as well as deliberate wrongdoers, and in this respect it had significant independence to deal with poor practice and to develop a jurisprudence accordingly.

Shipman overtly committed acts of the type addressed in *Jones* and *Ramdence* over many years and, whilst these cases show that the GMC had precedents allowing them to take action, they lacked the investigatory capacity and the willingness to actually operate in a manner which might have detected Shipman.

---

54 Bolt, D., 'Dealing with Errors of Clinical Judgment', 54 *Medico-Legal Journal*, 1986, 220.

55 (1995) 24 BMLR 1.

56 (1992) Lexis transcript.

57 [1996] 1 WLR 167.

## Restrictions at Local Level

The terms of service expected from a GP at the time of Shipman's criminal behaviour required the doctor to exercise the skill, knowledge and care of a reasonable GP. The doctor was also required to refer patients to other NHS services where appropriate. Furthermore, the GP was required to keep appropriate records. The Shipman Inquiry heard evidence that in the mid 1990s there was an expansion in the categories of cases in which the circumstances leading to a GP's breach of terms of service would also be reported to the GMC. This would include, inter alia, a wider range of cases involving clinical shortcomings and record-keeping failures.[58] Some complaints were made against Shipman during his career. One in particular, from 1992, included the allegation that Shipman had failed to visit and possibly falsified the patient record. After local deliberations, the matter was referred to the GMC. However, the latter decided to take no action – on the basis that the case was too old to reopen and would be difficult to investigate because Shipman had made no admissions. It was noted with concern by the Shipman Inquiry that the local procedures did not provide for an independent investigation – leaving this to the parties – and the GMC declined to investigate. The Inquiry did conclude that the three local complaints identified as having been made against Shipman during his career are unlikely to have revealed his criminal activities, even if fully investigated. However, the number of murders committed by Shipman fell dramatically during those periods when local complaints were being considered, suggesting a deterrent effect. It is also of note that in accordance with the complaints procedures in place between 1996 and 2004, the first stage for any complainant was Shipman himself – as self-appointed complaints manager within his own practice.[59] There may have been complaints which Shipman successfully diverted from reaching any of the external procedural stages.

## Inquiry Conclusions

The Inquiry concluded that it was deeply disturbing that Shipman's killing of his patients did not arouse suspicion for so many years. The systems which should have detected misconduct and safeguarded his patients failed to operate satisfactorily. It appears that relatives and friends of patients, and other professionals who harboured suspicions, felt unable to report their concerns. It was not until 1998 that another general practitioner reported suspicions to the coroner. That investigation amounted to nothing. If it had not been for Shipman's gross incompetence in forging the

58 See the Fifth Report of the Shipman Inquiry, *Safeguarding Patients: Lessons from the Past – Proposals for the Future*, paras 6.3–6.5 and 6.26 (www.the-shipman-inquiry.org.uk). It is of note that Shipman had been Secretary of the LMC and also a member of the Family Practitioner Committee for around seven years in the 1980s. This placed him in a position of influence and enhanced his reputation in the locality.

59 The Fifth Report of the Shipman Inquiry, *Safeguarding Patients: Lessons from the Past – Proposals for the Future*, paras 6.79–6.88 and 7.12 (www.the-shipman-inquiry.org.uk).

will of Mrs Grundy, it is by no means clear that his crimes would ever have been detected.[60]

There were numerous sources of information which provided evidence that, at the very least, Shipman was not acting with an appropriate degree of professional competence. These sources included the accounts given by relatives, friends and neighbours; Shipman's own account in medical records, death and cremation certificates; and even in the account given in response to a formal complaint.[61] It might reasonably be expected that had an effective self-regulatory process existed, some of this information would have come to the attention of the GMC and would have been acted upon. Self-regulation remains of central importance – it is clear from the Shipman Inquiry itself that expert evidence was necessary to identify the more subtle aspects of Shipman's misconduct. In this respect, one traditional justification for professional self-regulation – that only members of the profession have the expertise to detect and judge misconduct by their colleagues – is supported. What the Shipman case reveals is a significant failure in the operation of medical self-regulation, rather than a failure of the concept. In simple terms, the GMC were not alerted to Shipman's misconduct by other members of the medical profession and made no effort to look for it. They simply waited passively for complaints to be brought to them and, as I illustrate later, even then they were often unwilling to act.

## Would GMC Action Have Made a Difference?

It remains open to question whether, had the GMC acted with regard to Shipman's apparent incompetence, it would have made any notable difference. The Shipman Inquiry identified cases from the 1990s where doctors had administered drug overdoses with fatal consequences. One such example involved the doctor administering ten times the appropriate dose of fentanyl. An Inquest verdict of unlawful killing was

---

60 Smith, J., *The Shipman Inquiry*, First Report, Volume One, Death Disguised, July 2002, HMSO, 200.

61 The Inquiry concluded that in late 1979, Shipman killed Mr Jack Skelmerline who had chronic bronchitis and suffered an episode of heart failure. Shipman gave an injection of opiate, the patient went into a deep sleep and never awoke. Mr Skelmerline's son complained to the regional health authority, not about Shipman but because Shipman had promised a visit from a geriatrician which did not materialize. In response, Shipman confirmed that he had given a 10mg injection of morphine. The Inquiry report concluded that Shipman had in fact given more and intended to kill Mr Skelmerline, but even the 10mg would have been excessive for someone in Mr Skelmerline's condition. In another case, that of Mrs Renate Overton, Shipman was called to see the patient who was suffering an asthma attack. Mrs Overton's daughter was also in the house. Shipman stabilized the asthma, but then claimed that Mrs Overton had suffered a heart attack. Mrs Overton's daughter called an ambulance and paramedics managed to restart Mrs Overton's heart. Mrs Overton remained in a coma and died 14 months later. The Inquiry concluded that Shipman had intended to kill Mrs Overton but perhaps miscalculated the dose. Shipman admitted to hospital staff and paramedics that he had given Mrs Overton 10mg of diamorphine. This itself was a high dose and inappropriate for an asthmatic patient. Smith, J., *The Shipman Inquiry*, First Report, Volume One, Death Disguised, July 2002, HMSO, 136 and 164.

recorded. The doctor's explanation was that she had used unfamiliar specialist equipment, in a situation where its use was not necessary. She had also failed to seek advice from more senior colleagues, and had not consulted the instruction manual. The doctor admitted that she had been 'reckless and irresponsible' and was found by the GMC to have committed SPM. However, in light of various personal mitigating factors, the PCC considered a 'severe reprimand' to be a sufficient penalty.[62] It seems likely that had an isolated example of a Shipman murder come before the GMC in the guise of an erroneous overdose, Shipman too may have escaped with a low-level penalty. This might have given rise to some self-restraint on his behalf for a time, but would have fallen far short of the GMC taking decisive steps to protect patients.

Similarly, based upon its past record, it is unlikely that the GMC would have dealt harshly with Shipman, had it determined that inadequate clinical skills had resulted in harm to patients. This is illustrated by a case from the mid 1990s in which the doctor had prescribed a contra-indicative drug to a patient with asthma, resulting in her death. The doctor subsequently falsified the patient's records, was convicted for perverting the course of justice and was sentenced to six months' imprisonment. When the GMC investigated this case it discovered that the doctor had falsified patient records on a previous occasion, to cover up another mistake. The PCC found the doctor guilty of SPM, but limited the penalty to conditional registration for 12 months. The significance of the doctor's dishonesty and the seriousness with which the court viewed this appeared to have been downplayed or ignored by the PCC. Even with this record, when, seven years later, the doctor was the subject of a complaint relating to the alleged failure to diagnose meningitis in a child, the case was closed because the complainant had not exhausted local procedures. In another case, the doctor had committed offences of dishonesty, indecency and the inappropriate prescribing of controlled drugs, and had been sentenced to a term of imprisonment (suspended). The PCC saw fit to allow the doctor to remain on the register – imposing a 12-month suspension.[63] A further case illustrates that Shipman may have been able to use manipulation and dishonesty to minimize a GMC sanction. In the case in question, two GPs were able to escape erasure, in part by producing large numbers of supportive testimonials from patients. It subsequently transpired that some of these had been obtained in 'dubious circumstances', yet the original lenient penalty was allowed to stand. The conclusion of the Shipman Inquiry was that 'these two dishonest doctors ran rings around the GMC'.[64]

The Shipman Inquiry considered what would have happened to Shipman had Dr S3 reported concerns to the GMC regarding Mrs Overton. The conclusion was that the matter would have reached at least the screening stage and that documentation would have been sent to Shipman for comment. However, there would have been no further investigation by the GMC, the onus to produce evidence being almost entirely

62 The Fifth Report of the Shipman Inquiry, *Safeguarding Patients: Lessons from the Past – Proposals for the Future*, paras 21.57–21.59 (www.the-shipman-inquiry.org.uk).

63 See the Fifth Report of the Shipman Inquiry, *Safeguarding Patients: Lessons from the Past – Proposals for the Future*, paras 21.73–21.98 (www.the-shipman-inquiry.org.uk).

64 See the Fifth Report of the Shipman Inquiry, *Safeguarding Patients: Lessons from the Past – Proposals for the Future*, para 21.112 (www.the-shipman-inquiry.org.uk).

on the complainant. With the available evidence being Dr S3's statement, Shipman's response and possibly the medical records, the screener might have referred the case to the PPC, but it was far from certain that it would have progressed to the PCC. The Inquiry had come across cases which on the face of things were just as serious as what appeared to have happened to Mrs Overton, but had not reached the PCC. In one such case, considered in the late 1990s, there was evidence that the doctor had injected a fatal overdose of local anaesthetic into a young patient. Notwithstanding evidence from an eminent professor confirming that the dose was 'unacceptably large and suggested that the doctor had been guilty of SPM', the matter was not referred to the PCC but, instead, was dealt with by way of a warning as to future practice. Even if Shipman's case had reached the PCC, erasure or other severe sanction was unlikely. For example, in a case from the early 1990s, a GP who had given a patient 100mg of diamorphine, which led to a respiratory arrest, was found guilty of SPM and made subject to conditional registration for a period of six months, with the requirement to undergo a structured programme of retraining.[65]

**Particular Issues with Sole Practitioners**

In 2003, sole practising GPs accounted for less than 10 per cent of total GP numbers. One of the questions arising from Shipman's case was whether his practice as sole practitioner facilitated his criminal activity. It has been argued that doctors who practise with colleagues provide an element of mutual monitoring, whilst sole practitioners lack such informal accountability and are at risk of professional isolation.[66] Indeed, the absence of such accountability may tempt doctors who wish to engage in misconduct, or those whose competence is suspect, to enter sole practice to avoid prying eyes. For instance, in 1998 Shipman attempted to assuage suspicion by claiming that he had undertaken an audit of deaths occurring in his practice. He had not in fact done this, but without partners there was no check on such lies. There is also a risk that some patients of sole practitioners will lack experience of consulting other doctors and so have no means to compare the quality of service they receive. They may also place excessive and unwarranted trust in their doctor. For instance, during the years that Shipman was murdering patients, others greatly admired, respected and trusted him. As a result, the threshold at which these patients (and their families) would have been willing to challenge Shipman's actions was extremely high.[67] As previously discussed, similar issues were encountered

65 The Fifth Report of the Shipman Inquiry, *Safeguarding Patients: Lessons from the Past – Proposals for the Future*, paras 10.91–10.98 (www.the-shipman-inquiry.org.uk).

66 See *The Future of Professionally Led Regulation for General Practice – a Discussion Document Issued in Conjunction with and on Behalf of The Royal College of General Practitioners, The General Practitioners Committee of the British Medical Association and the Joint Committee on Postgraduate Training for General Practice.* Cited in the Fifth Report of the Shipman Inquiry, *Safeguarding Patients: Lessons from the Past – Proposals for the Future*, para 13.2 (www.the-shipman-inquiry.org.uk).

67 The Fifth Report of the Shipman Inquiry, *Safeguarding Patients: Lessons from the Past – Proposals for the Future*, paras 13.32–13.33 and 13.42 (www.the-shipman-inquiry.org.uk).

with Clifford Ayling who was able to sexually abuse some of his general practice patients in part because these patients had not experienced intimate examinations from any other doctor. However, the risks associated with sole practice should not be overstated. Although Shipman committed many of his murders whilst he was a sole practitioner, he nevertheless killed between 78 and 108 patients whilst practising in partnership. His partners during this period suspected nothing.[68]

## Self-Regulation – Failure at the Ground Floor

It is a reasonable expectation that, in return for the privilege of self-regulation, a profession will ensure that a primary expectation is that each member would see it as a fundamental individual duty to take steps to deal with or report colleagues about whom they had concerns or suspicions. Collectively, the profession should support regulatory structures which foster this aim. As with the other case examples discussed in this work, the reality evidenced in the Shipman case is very different. Individual members of the profession had become detached from *their* regulatory process. Individual doctors did not see themselves as the first line of detection for self-regulation and, historically, the GMC has encouraged this with prohibitions against the 'deprecation' of a fellow doctor.

However, it should have been the case that by 1991, if not 1987, the wording of professional guidance was such that there was an obligation within the profession to require fellow doctors to report concerns about Shipman. By 1987, the requirement was as follows: '…a doctor has a duty, where the circumstances so warrant, to inform an appropriate body about a professional colleague whose behaviour may have raised a question of serious professional misconduct, or whose fitness to practise may be seriously impaired…[69] However, as was also recognized by the Ledward Inquiry, not all members of the profession will have maintained a watchful eye on the, often subtle, changes in the regulatory provisions relating to whistleblowing.

## Failures by the GMC

### *Previous Misconduct*

It might be expected that a key indicator of a doctor's instability might be prior professional misconduct or criminal activity. It came as a surprise to many that Shipman had neither been subject to professional discipline for his drugs offences in 1976, nor had any follow up or monitoring been undertaken. The incident appears to have been effectively expunged from his curriculum vitae shortly after its conclusion.

---

68 For further discussion, see the Fifth Report of the Shipman Inquiry, *Safeguarding Patients: Lessons from the Past – Proposals for the Future*, paras 13.3–13.25 and 13.50 (www.the-shipman-inquiry.org.uk).

69 General Medical Council, *Professional Conduct and Discipline: Fitness to Practise* (1987), cited by Kennedy, I. and Grubb, A., *Medical Law*, 3rd ed, 2000, Butterworths, London, 165–6.

The GMC response following Shipman's convictions for murder was to place the 1976 events in an historical context, emphasizing that their approach had changed significantly in the intervening years. The evidence, however, presents a rather different picture. For example, by way of a small test, I made inquiries of the GMC regarding three medical practitioners convicted of serious criminal offences related to their medical practice, one a hospital physician convicted in the late 1980s of manslaughter and the other two (both general practitioners) convicted in the 1990s, one for manslaughter and the other for doing acts intending to pervert the course of justice (falsification of patient records). In only one of the cases (the GP manslaughter in the late 1990s) was the GMC able to confirm that the doctor in question had been subject to a disciplinary hearing before the Professional Conduct Committee. He had been subject to a period of conditional registration before returning to fully registered status. In the other manslaughter case, the GMC had no doctor of the name in question registered and could provide no information regarding a previous disciplinary history. The final, attempting to pervert the course of justice, case is perhaps of greatest concern. Initial enquiries of the GMC revealed three registered practitioners with the name in question but, without further information, the GMC was unable to identify which, if any, was the subject of the conviction. Further enquiries of the fitness to practise directorate led to the conclusion that the GMC had no record of any doctor of that name with a conviction against them.[70] There were strong indications from the law report that the practitioner in question was registered at the time of the offence (the report states that he set up in sole practice as a GP after its discovery and up to the trial) and the fact of the conviction and subsequent unsuccessful appeal became a matter of public record. In two out of three cases, chosen because reports of them were readily available,[71] the GMC apparently had no record of the doctors in question having come to their notice and no clearly articulated means of detecting potential professional misconduct, even when the doctor had been subject to a public criminal trial. It is likely that other lower profile cases, for example, those which do not go beyond the first instance court, will fall into the same category.[72]

## Significant Event Reviews/Audits

A group of doctors, usually within a practice, may discuss significant events which have occurred in the course of practice, primarily as a learning process. The recent GP contract provides financial incentives for practices to undertake minimum numbers

70 Information obtained by means of correspondence between the author and the GMC in July and August 2002.

71 All three were obtained from Lexis-Nexis, but two were reported elsewhere also.

72 One example is the case of a doctor who was severely reprimanded by the GMC in 2002 for terminating a pregnancy without the patient's consent. The misconduct had occurred in 1993 and the doctor had been subject to criminal proceedings, charged with illegally procuring a miscarriage. He was acquitted of these charges in 1995. Despite the public trial, the GMC only became aware of the matter in 1998 when a private complaint was lodged. See *British Medical Journal*, 2002, 334: 1354, 8 June.

of such reviews. Had Shipman been required to discuss with a fellow doctor some of the deaths of his patients, it should have become clear that many were different to those experienced by the average GP.[73] However, Shipman may have been able to select for review genuine natural deaths in order to divert suspicion. During his years as a sole practitioner, he may also have been able to make selective contact with particular GPs whom he judged would be less likely to stand up to and challenge him. Shipman's ability to deceive those doctors who signed cremation Form Cs for him illustrates the potential for such manipulation. Significant event review, therefore, lacks the capacity to be an effective monitoring tool for doctors who may intentionally be setting out to cause harm.[74]

## Conclusions

There are those who argue that no system of regulation can be 100 per cent effective against a determined criminal.[75] However, even if these views are correct, they do not explain why Shipman was not caught out by more mundane but also more common examples of inadequate practice. These, as Shipman himself explained them, were serious – his patients died. It has also been argued in some quarters that the Shipman case involved the 'mere' coincidence of a serial killer who just happened to be a doctor. Or, from the more theoretical perspective, the notion that if a doctor works to undermine health, she does not work as a doctor but as an impostor, a charlatan.[76] However, this line of argument does not withstand scrutiny. It was only because of his particular professional status that Shipman had the means and the opportunity to commit his crimes. Furthermore, it has been noted by a former BMA chairman that medicine arguably accounts for more serial killers than any other profession. In part this is because they may have the means and opportunity to kill undetected. However, it was also suggested that the medical profession may attract a disproportionate number of people with a pathological interest in commanding the power of life and death.[77] These matters certainly should have been a focus of self-regulation, and the GMC should have been in a position to act far sooner than it actually did.

---

73 The Fifth Report of the Shipman Inquiry, *Safeguarding Patients: Lessons from the Past – Proposals for the Future*, paras 12.59–12.63 (www.the-shipman-inquiry.org.uk).

74 The Fifth Report of the Shipman Inquiry, *Safeguarding Patients: Lessons from the Past – Proposals for the Future*, para 12.65 (www.the-shipman-inquiry.org.uk).

75 See, for example, comments of this type from the GMC, reported in 'Shipman: the NHS's Response', *Health Service Journal*, 2000, Vol. 110, No. 5460, 3 February.

76 Airaksinen, T., 'Service and Science in Professional Life', in Chadwick, R.F. (ed.), *Ethics and the Professions*, 1994, Avebury, Aldershot, 8.

77 Kinnell, H.G., 'Serial Homicide by Doctors: Shipman in Perspective', *BMJ*, 2000, Vol. 321, 1594, 30 December.

# PART III
# Change

So far I have concentrated upon the crises facing medical self-regulation, brought about by the GMC and the profession as a whole failing to rise sufficiently to their responsibilities. In this final part I consider the responses to the crises and proposals for change.

# Chapter 13

# Whistleblowing

## Introduction

Research from the US has found that a significant improvement in the overall quality of medical practice is marred by a small percentage of repeat defaulters. In asking why self-regulatory mechanisms fail to satisfactorily deal with this minority, one conclusion is that social and peer control mechanisms are relatively ineffective. Efficient collegial influence relies on a sufficient depth of identification by individual practitioners with the professional group, the degree of solidarity of that group and the capacity of the group to provide meaningful guidance regarding standards of conduct. However, with increasing group identification and solidarity comes an increasing likelihood that group members will protect one another from outside scrutiny. In essence, there is an inherent tension between bonds of professional collegiality and peer enforcement of rules.[1] Close proximity in working relationships between members of professions is therefore more likely to breed consensus which discourages whistleblowing.[2] Doctors are likely to avoid confronting or reporting colleagues in all but the most exceptional circumstances.[3] They might attempt to avoid working with such colleagues, but often no action was taken to prevent them moving elsewhere. If a doctor, nurse or other practitioner did formally report a colleague, it was often the whistleblower themselves who found themselves ostracized or punished in some way.[4]

---

1 See Maiman, R.J., McEwen, C.A. and Mather, L., 'The Future of Legal Professionalism in Practice', *Legal Ethics*, 1999, Vol. 2, No. 1, 71–85, 83; and Abel, R.L., *American Lawyers*, 1989, Oxford University Press, New York, 144–5.

2 The term 'whistleblow' is often used as convenient shorthand to extend to any situation where a professional raises concerns about the performance of a colleague, whether internally or externally and through appropriate channels or otherwise. See Burrows, J., 'Telling Tales and Saving Lives: Whistleblowing – The Role of Professional Colleagues in Protecting Patients from Dangerous Doctors', *Medical Law Review*, Summer 2001, 9, 110–29, 111. For historical discussion with respect to lawyers, see Rhode, D.L., 'Ethical Perspectives on Legal Practice', *Stanford Law Review*, 1985, Vol. 37: 589, 629; Luban, D. (ed.), *The Ethics of Lawyers*, Dartmouth, Aldershot, 437.

3 See, for example, Freidson, E., *Professional Dominance: The Social Structure of Medical Care*, 1970, Atherton Press, New York. Cited by Rhode, D.L., 'Ethical Perspectives on Legal Practice', *Stanford Law Review*, 1985, Vol. 37: 589, 638; Luban, D. (ed.), *The Ethics of Lawyers*, 1994, Dartmouth, Aldershot, 446.

4 See, for example, Freidson, E., *Professional Dominance: The Social Structure of Medical Care*, 1970, Atherton Press, New York; Freidson, E., *Profession of Medicine: A Study*

Patient safety demands that doctors and other medical staff are willing to report concerns about colleagues. As the Shipman and other cases illustrate, patients are not always in a good position to assess the appropriateness of a doctor's behaviour. For example, it is not uncommon for the GMC to receive testimonials from patients about a doctor who is found to be guilty of serious professional misconduct, seriously deficient performance or to have other fitness to practise issues.[5] The profession, however, has not addressed this with the openness it requires. As one commentator put it:

> [No] profession has made such a fetish of professional secrecy as has the medical. Where lawyers, accountants and, above all, architects…expect the outcomes of their endeavours to be openly subject to public scrutiny, doctors have hitherto avoided it, hiding behind a melange of reasons – patient confidentiality, the mysteries of their art and, let it be said, the adulation of a public which seemed to put them beyond the reach of any scheming government. [Y]ou have all the ingredients necessary for lethal incompetence that will remain unseen, undetected and uncorrected.[6]

Notwithstanding the reluctance of individual members of the profession to police each other, it is suggested that workplace communities offer greater potential for control than professional bodies. These bodies should therefore seek ways to mobilize these influences.[7] As Dame Janet Smith put it:

> [T]he willingness of one healthcare professional to take responsibility for raising concerns about the conduct, performance or health of another could make a greater potential contribution to the safety of patients than any other single factor. I consider that very few unsafe doctors would escape notice by a fellow professional…[8]

To the extent, therefore, that whistleblowing by members of the medical profession is essential for effective self-regulation, the ethos instilled by the GMC plays a vital role. Professional training involves more than just the transmission of technical knowledge, it also entails significant socialization into the values of the profession, including standards of professional integrity. As Beck and Young described it: 'the creation of a professional habitus'.[9] In addition, broader ethical

---

*of the Sociology of Applied Knowledge*, 1970, Dodd, Mead and Co., New York; Freidson, E., *Doctoring Together*, 1975, Elsevier, New York; Barber, B., *The Logic and Limits of Trust*, 1983, Rutgers, New York, 144.

5 See, for example, the Fifth Report of the Shipman Inquiry, *Safeguarding Patients: Lessons from the Past – Proposals for the Future*, para 24.163 (www.the-shipman-inquiry.org.uk).

6 Mahendra, B., 'Bristol and Beyond', *New Law Journal*, 2001, Vol. 151, No. 6995, 1149.

7 In the context of lawyers, see Maiman, R.J., McEwen, C.A. and Mather, L., 'The Future of Legal Professionalism in Practice', *Legal Ethics*, 1999, Vol. 2, No. 1, 71–85, 83.

8 The Fifth Report of the Shipman Inquiry, *Safeguarding Patients: Lessons from the Past – Proposals for the Future* (www.the-shipman-inquiry.org.uk).

9 Beck, J. and Young, M.F.D., 'The Assault on the Professions and the Restructuring of Academic and Professional Identities: a Bernsteinian Analysis', *British Journal of Sociology of Education*, 2005, Vol. 26, No. 2, April, 183–97.

principles require that, even in the absence of a professional obligation to whistleblow, wider moral considerations may give rise to a personal duty.[10] Deontological theory leads to the conclusion that the obligation to whistleblow is independent of personal consequences.[11]

## Whistleblowing and Professional Self-Regulation

As previously discussed, the GMC has tended to adopt a reactive stance towards unacceptable behaviour – responding to complaints but generally taking few or no steps to pre-empt them. This adds importance to the need for effective whistleblowing procedures. However, as Becher notes, '...individual members of the profession appear obdurately to echo the reaction of schoolchildren to the cognate practice of "sneaking" or "telling tales"'.[12] Freidson makes a similar point:

> [O]ne should be reluctant to judge the work of a colleague when one lacks direct experience with the case and its circumstances. 'There, but for the grace of God, go I'...may...explain the suspension of condemnatory judgement...This etiquette expresses an important part of the ideal-typical spirit of professionalism – namely, collegiality...But because it tends to prevent the use of adequate regulatory procedures which protect the public, it violates the profession's implicit contract with the state and the public.[13]

This is unsurprising given the traditional hierarchies prevalent within medical practice. Trainee and junior doctors have been trained by consultants and as a result are strongly influenced by the dominant role models perpetrated by these senior colleagues. Deference was the norm, and it would be a brave or reckless junior doctor who challenged a senior colleague.[14] In the Kerr/Haslam case, one junior doctor explained to that Inquiry that she neither recorded accusations made to her about a consultant nor took any action, because of the prevailing culture which required loyalty to a fellow doctor, coupled with the awareness that she relied on references from consultants to progress in her career. This was in 1983. Another medically qualified commentator, discussing the same period, neatly summed up the attitudes which tended to prevail within the profession at the time:

---

10 Chambers, Andrew, 'Whistleblowing and the Internal Auditor', *Business Ethics: A European Review*, October 1995, 192–8. Cited by Southwood, Peter, 'Whistleblowing in Accountancy', in Lewis, David B. (ed.), *Whistleblowing at Work*, 2000, The Athlone Press, London, 53.

11 For further discussion in the context of other professions, see Southwood, P., 'Whistleblowing in Accountancy', in Lewis, D.B., (ed.), *Whistleblowing at Work*, 2000, The Athlone Press, London, 39–56.

12 Becher, T., *Professional Practices*, 1999, Transaction Publishers, New Brunswick, New Jersey, 215.

13 Freidson, E., *Professionalism Reborn*, 1994, Polity Press, Cambridge, 203—204.

14 See discussion by Irvine, D., *The Doctors' Tale*, 2003, Radcliffe Medical Press, Oxford, 30.

> When I joined St Thomas's in 1984, paternalism and patronage were so powerful that you didn't dare upset the establishment for fear of mucking up your reference. Thus club rules were deeply embedded at an early age. Never criticise your boss, have unswerving loyalty to your hospital and when the going gets tough, keep your head down…[15]

The Kerr/Haslam Inquiry Report expressed concern that little had changed in this respect, even by the mid 2000s.[16] Hammond, writing in 2002, commented that 'fear of reprisal and recrimination for owning up to anything in the NHS is still rife'.[17]

The Kerr/Haslam Inquiry also observed that GPs, who were not hierarchically dependent on consultants, were also reluctant to report concerns. For instance, a GP informed by a patient of an inappropriate sexual relationship with her consultant psychiatrist, responded as follows:

> It seemed to me that Haslam had been very foolish. It was…possibly professional misconduct, but not a crime. I was probably not in favour of reporting the matter…because I probably did have concerns [that]…[r]eporting the matter…was likely to do more harm than good as far as Patient B1 was concerned.
>
> …I do not believe that I discussed Patient B1's affair with Dr Haslam with my partners…As to why I did not report what I had learnt to the authorities, I have a feeling that it was probably not part of the culture at the time to report another doctor to the GMC…[18]

The general impression was that in the perception of many GPs, consultants occupied a higher status within the medical hierarchy. Any questioning of their behaviour was problematic. It was only to be contemplated in extreme circumstances where proof of inappropriate behaviour could be backed up by detailed and usually written corroboration.[19] Such a situation is particularly problematic in the closed environment which constitutes many areas of clinical practice. It has been suggested that the era of god-like consultants is at an end, with the rise in the number of consultants from more varied backgrounds and more open, less deferential attitudes.[20] However, cases which have come to light relatively recently demonstrate that the traditional power and status of consultants remains strong.

Not only were GPs wary of challenging consultants, but the converse was also true. For example, a consultant orthopaedic surgeon and later a Medical Director, told the Shipman Inquiry that he knew of no occasion when a hospital doctor had officially criticized the conduct or behaviour of a GP.[21]

---

15 Hammond, P., 'Bristol Inquiry: Medical Training Means Learning how to be Callous; a Physician's View', *Independent on Sunday*, 22 July 2001, 6.

16 *The Kerr/Haslam Inquiry Report*, July 2005, Cm 6640-1, 184.

17 Hammond, P. and Mosley, M., *Trust Me I'm A Doctor*, 2002, Metro Publishing, London, 212.

18 *The Kerr/Haslam Inquiry Report*, July 2005, Cm 6640-1, 298.

19 *The Kerr/Haslam Inquiry Report*, July 2005, Cm 6640-1, 429.

20 See discussion by Irvine, D., *The Doctors' Tale*, 2003, Radcliffe Medical Press, Oxford, 312.

21 The Fifth Report of the Shipman Inquiry, *Safeguarding Patients: Lessons from the Past – Proposals for the Future*, para 10.37 (www.the-shipman-inquiry.org.uk).

Stacey observed that only a minority of doctors who came before the discipline committee of the GMC worked in hospital. She questioned whether this was really because hospital doctors were less likely to misbehave, or if they did, whether this was more likely to be caught early and addressed, or whether colleagues were covering up for each other.[22] Misplaced loyalty and collegiality has, historically, also been found within general practice. For example, Irvine reports the late James Cameron, a former chairman of the BMA General Medical Services Committee, as frequently saying that there was no such thing as a bad GP. This, Irvine suggests, was part of the means used to maintain professional solidarity amongst GPs and to keep the BMA committee together.[23] The Ayling Inquiry heard that even challenging a fellow doctor or raising issues outside of the peer group was seen as 'letting the side down'. General practice was also seen as being extremely parochial. Within its tight-knit community, a GP would have concerns that he or she would have to work amongst colleagues, sometimes for a number of decades – not an environment conducive to telling tales.[24]

It has been suggested that Primary Care Trusts should provide more practical help, supporting employees who need to find alternative employment if their relationship with a practice has broken down following the need to whistleblow. As a fallback, for extreme situations where local procedures may have been compromised, a non-local point of reporting should be available.[25] For such occasions, there could be a member of staff at the PCT designated to receive such communications. Ideally, this person would take a proactive stance in terms both of making his or her presence known and helping to ensure that staff understand the importance of reporting concerns.[26]

The reluctance of doctors to criticize each other occurs for a number of reasons. One, for example, relates to the uncertainty of medical practice and from a sense of shared vulnerability, the feeling that 'there but for the grace of God go I'. Similar sentiments were expressed in Rosenthal's 'The Incompetent Doctor': 'If we criticise, we'll be criticised', 'If we all complained about each other all the time, we're all vulnerable'. Forgiveness, not confrontation, was the usual approach.[27]

Examples of doctors who have been courageous enough to report colleagues demonstrate that the price they have paid may be so high that few will be willing to follow in their footsteps. For example, Dr Bolsin in the Bristol case said:

---

22 Stacey, M., *Regulating British Medicine: the General Medical Council*, 1992, Wiley, Chichester, 149.

23 Irvine, D., *The Doctors' Tale*, 2003, Radcliffe Medical Press, Oxford, 54.

24 The Honourable Mrs Justice Pauffley, Committee of Inquiry – Independent Investigation into how the NHS Handled Allegations about the Conduct of Clifford Ayling, 15 July 2004, Cm 6298, para 4.34.

25 See the Fifth Report of the Shipman Inquiry, *Safeguarding Patients: Lessons from the Past – Proposals for the Future*, paras 9.117–9.137 (www.the-shipman-inquiry.org.uk).

26 See the Fifth Report of the Shipman Inquiry, *Safeguarding Patients: Lessons from the Past – Proposals for the Future*, paras 27.139–27.141 (www.the-shipman-inquiry.org.uk).

27 The Honourable Mrs Justice Pauffley, Committee of Inquiry – Independent Investigation into how the NHS Handled Allegations about the Conduct of Clifford Ayling, 15 July 2004, Cm 6298, paras 4.37–4.40.

> I and my family are living and working in Australia as a direct result of the treatment I received in Bristol after criticising the conduct of paediatric cardiac surgery at the infirmary. No medical or non-medical professional in the NHS should have to endure the threats and discrimination that I was subjected to in Bristol.
>
> …I felt a bit like a Russian dissident who was being accused of psychiatric disease for not thinking the right thoughts…The events in Bristol have left both [my wife] and I with a deep dislike of secrecy and a deep distrust of systems of patronage, both of which flourish in the current NHS.[28]

In another case a consultant in charge of an A&E department blew the whistle on a colleague. She went through the appropriate procedures, but at one point was told 'You don't welsh on colleagues'. She summarized the experience as follows:

> From the moment I let management know of my fears, I found I was in the firing line. I was accused of bullying, and even though they could find absolutely nothing wrong with my clinical competence, they said I should take early retirement.
>
> …There is absolutely no way I would ever now comment, report or deal in any way with anybody's poor performance. I would just ignore it. I have had to completely change my career.[29]

This was at the height of the Bristol scandal. The unnecessary deaths of babies at Bristol appeared to have done little to prick the collective conscience of the medical profession.

The GP in the Shipman case who did eventually raise concerns had been fearful of the possible consequences, in particular the potential of a financially ruinous defamation action. It was said that she would have valued a central body to which she could have reported concerns, leaving it to that body to decide how or whether to proceed.[30] This raises the obvious question, how do doctors perceive the GMC if it does not spring to mind as a body which already offers this prospect?

If doctors are reluctant to report colleagues, the problem is likely to be even more acute for nurses. For example, a consultant rheumatologist was convicted of attempted murder after giving potassium chloride to a patient. The nurse who blew

---

28 Boseley Heath, S., 'Whistle-blower Accuses NHS: On Eve of Report into Baby Cardiac Surgery Deaths, Consultant says He was Forced Out for Sounding Alarm', *The Guardian,* 18 July 2001, 2.

29 Bestic, L., 'Sidelined and Shamed without Trial', *Evening Standard*, 8 December 2003, 2.

30 In reality, it is unlikely that Dr Reynolds was actually at risk of a successful defamation action being brought against her, as long as she had acted within the limits of qualified privilege and/or restricted her disclosure to information she actually had, for example, the number of cremation certificates she and her colleagues had signed on behalf of Shipman. This illustrates a further absence of knowledge within the medical profession of important legal principles which are relevant to disclosures by doctors. The Fifth Report of the Shipman Inquiry, *Safeguarding Patients: Lessons from the Past – Proposals for the Future*, paras 8.98 and 11.121 (www.the-shipman-inquiry.org.uk).

the whistle was said to have received hate mail and to have been subjected to other abuse.[31]

Having established its dominant position with regard to the state, the medical profession has sought and achieved dominance over other healthcare workers. Writing initially in 1970, Freidson identified all non-doctor healthcare workers as 'paramedical' professions which stand in a subservient position to doctors.[32] Such dominance is not absolute, but nevertheless paramedical groups generally remain in the shadow of medical colleagues.[33] It has been suggested by some commentators that the development of team-working between doctors and nurses has reduced the impact of traditional hierarchies.[34] However, others have observed that reference to teamwork are more linguistic than real, with little change to underlying behaviour.[35]

Whilst relations between doctors and nurses have moved on significantly since the days when 'the nurse must be the person who pays blind obedience to [doctors'] orders',[36] a number of the cases discussed in this work illustrate that hierarchical issues continue to inhibit speaking out by nurses. The Ayling Inquiry also noted that 'reporting' guidance to nurses and midwives by their professional body was even less clear than that for doctors. The first code of professional conduct for nurses did not appear until the early 1980s and did not anticipate the need to report fellow health workers. Only in 1992 did the code begin to reflect this possibility, requiring nurses to: '…report to an appropriate person or authority where it appears that the health or safety of colleagues is at risk, as such circumstances may compromise standards of practice or care.'[37]

Burrows, in a study of community nurses, found that during the course of their careers, almost one third had encountered situations where they felt that a GP's performance placed patients at risk. Only 41 per cent had reported these concerns

---

31 (1993) 33 *Med Sci Law* 89, 18 September 1992, Winchester Crown Court. See also Samuels, A., 'Can a Doctor "Blow the Whistle" Or "Grass" on a Colleague?', *MLJ*, 2002, 70(135), 5 September.

32 Freidson, E., *Profession of Medicine: A Study in the Sociology of Applied Knowledge*, 1970, Dodd, Mead and Co., New York; and Freidson, E., *Professional Dominance*, 1970, Atherton Press, New York.

33 See, for example, Larkin G.V., *Occupational Monopoly and Modern Medicine*, 1983, Tavistock, London.

34 See, for example, Dingwall, R., 'Problems of Teamwork in Primary Care', in Lonsdale, S., Webb, A. and Briggs, T.L. (eds), *Teamwork in the Personal Social Services and Healthcare*, 1980, Croom Helm, London; Snelgrove, S. and Hughes, D., 'Perceptions of Teamwork in Acute Medical Wards', in Allen, D. and Hughes, D., *Nursing and the Division of Labour in Healthcare*, 2002, Palgrave Macmillan, Basingstoke.

35 Allen, D. and Hughes, D., *Nursing and the Division of Labour in Healthcare*, 2002, Palgrave Macmillan, Basingstoke, 55.

36 See Godlee, F., 'Editor's Choice – Cure or Care?', *BMJ*, 2005, 9 December, recounting an editorial published in 1880.

37 The Honourable Mrs Justice Pauffley, Committee of Inquiry – Independent Investigation into how the NHS Handled Allegations about the Conduct of Clifford Ayling, 15 July 2004, Cm 6298, para 4.58.

and in less than half of these cases was any action taken with regard to the GP. Only 61 per cent of nurses said that they would report future concerns about a GP, but even amongst this group many of these respondents had little idea about how they would go about this.[38]

A doctor may also be reluctant to comment adversely on a colleague's performance, for example, during a clinical audit, because of the harm this may inflict on continuing working relationships, or because the reporting doctor's workload might increase if the colleague is suspended.[39] In some other situations there may also be financial prohibitions to whistleblowing. For instance, it was noted by the Shipman Inquiry that had a district nurse been concerned about a GP's behaviour, reporting this could have severe personal financial consequences.[40] Also, unlike hospital nurses employed by the NHS Trust or hospital authorities, those in GP practices are employed by the practice. Expressing concerns or challenging a doctor in the practice could directly jeopardize the nurse's employment. In a small practice, there is also the added risk that close working relationships may blind colleagues to faults. For example, the Shipman Inquiry found that Shipman's practice nurse remained convinced of his innocence long after suspicions had arisen elsewhere.[41] Some doctors have also expressed concerns that if they go out on a limb to report a colleague, based upon concerns raised by a patient, they may be left in a vulnerable position if the patient subsequently declines to formalize their position and, if necessary, to give evidence in public.[42]

## The GMC and Whistleblowing

Professional bodies may reinforce their members' natural reluctance to whistleblow by producing disciplinary codes which present additional obstacles. Common provisions relate to maintaining professional solidarity, by regulating the professional interaction of members. In order to preserve stability, rules seek to minimize internal competition – which is seen as being highly divisive.[43] In the case of the medical profession in the UK, this attitude has continued to prevail even though the vast majority of doctors are employed by the NHS and are generally not in competition

---

38 Burrows, J., 'Telling Tales and Saving Lives: Whistleblowing – The Role of Professional Colleagues in Protecting Patients from Dangerous Doctors', *Medical Law Review*, Summer 2001, 9, 110–29.

39 For further discussion, see Davies, A.C.L., 'Don't Trust Me, I'm a Doctor – Medical Regulation and the 1999 NHS Reforms', *OJLS*, 2000, 20(437).

40 The Fifth Report of the Shipman Inquiry, *Safeguarding Patients: Lessons from the Past – Proposals for the Future*, para 9.70 (www.the-shipman-inquiry.org.uk).

41 The Fifth Report of the Shipman Inquiry, *Safeguarding Patients: Lessons from the Past – Proposals for the Future*, para 9.100 (www.the-shipman-inquiry.org.uk).

42 *The Kerr/Haslam Inquiry Report*, July 2005, Cm 6640-1, 488.

43 For further discussion in the context of lawyers, see Disney, J., Basten, J., Redmond, P., Ross, S. and Bell, K., *Lawyers*, 2nd ed, 1986, The Law Book Co., Melbourne, 82–3; and Parry, N. and Parry, J., *The Rise of the Medical Profession*, 1976, Croom Helm, London, 135.

with their colleagues for work. The history of the GMC's approach can be traced through various editions of the Blue Book and *Good Medical Practice*.

In the 1970s the Blue Book provided that 'the depreciation by a doctor of the professional skill, knowledge, qualifications or services of another doctor' could amount to serious professional misconduct. In the 1987 edition of the 'Blue Book', 'depreciation' was replaced with 'disparagement'. Doctors were given permission to express an opinion which differed from that of colleagues if, after careful consideration of the advice and treatment offered to a patient by the colleague, they expressed in good faith a different view and assisted the patient to seek an alternative source of medical care.[44] Such action had always to be justifiable as being in the patient's best medical interests. Doctors were also under a duty to disclose to an appropriate body concerns about the behaviour of colleagues which may have raised an issue of serious professional misconduct or serious impairment of fitness to practise.[45]

In its 1990 Annual Report, the GMC Standards Committee acknowledged that the way in which the term 'disparagement' had been used in previous editions of the Blue Book may have discouraged necessary reporting of concerns.[46] Therefore, by 1991, 'disparagement' had gone, and whereas previously the focus had been on serious professional misconduct or serious impairment of fitness to practise, it extended to include an obligation to report a doctor whose performance appeared 'deficient'.[47] In the section entitled 'Comment about professional colleagues', the guidance stated:

> Doctors are frequently called upon to express a view about a colleague's professional practice. This may...happen in the course of a medical audit or peer review procedure... It may also occur in a less direct and explicit way when a patient seeks a second opinion, specialist advice or an alternative form of treatment. Honest comment is entirely acceptable in such circumstances, provided that it is carefully considered and can be justified, that it is offered in good faith and that it is intended to promote the best interests of patients. Further, it is any doctor's duty where the circumstances so warrant, to inform an appropriate person or body about a colleague whose professional conduct or fitness to practise may be called into question or whose professional performance appears in some way deficient. Arrangements exist to deal with such problems and they must be used...

44 Robinson notes that this latter provision was omitted from later editions of the codes of conduct for doctors. Robinson, J., 'Thou Shalt Not Disparage Another Doctor', *healthmatters*, Spring 1998, Issue 33, 12–14.

45 See Robinson, J., 'Thou Shalt Not Disparage Another Doctor', *healthmatters*, Spring 1998, Issue 33, 12–14.

46 In practical terms the risk of a doctor being disciplined for 'disparagement' appears to have been very low, with only a handful of such cases being brought over a period of 120 years. See Smith, R., *Medical Discipline: The Professional Conduct of the GMC 1858-1990*, 1994, Oxford University Press, Oxford. However, these figures have to be viewed in the context of the awareness and significance many in the profession appear to have given the provision. In this respect, the number of doctors actually risking breaching these provisions might be expected to be low if awareness was high within the profession.

47 See the Fifth Report of the Shipman Inquiry, *Safeguarding Patients: Lessons from the Past – Proposals for the Future*, paras 10.21–10.22 (www.the-shipman-inquiry.org.uk).

> However, gratuitous and unsustainable comment which...sets out to undermine trust in a professional colleague's knowledge or skills is unethical.[48]

This guidance lacked specificity with regard to exactly when a disclosure should be made, and to whom, presumably to retain flexibility. However, it should have focused doctors' minds on the importance of reporting colleagues who were giving cause for concern. By 1994 the message should have been absolutely clear. In July of 1993 the GMC had issued a press release following the case of two doctors. The first had been found guilty of SPM after a patient had suffered brain damage whilst the doctor had been engaged as a locum consultant anaesthetist. The second doctor was Chairman of the Anaesthetics Division of the NHS Trust. He had failed to act upon earlier reports expressing concern about the first doctor and went on to provide a favourable reference. In March 1994 the second doctor was found guilty of SPM, the GMC concluding that: 'At all times patient safety must take precedence over all other concerns, including understandable reticence to bring a colleague's career into question.'[49]

At first sight, the approach of the GMC appears to conform to the theory that professional codes are public statements of the aspirations and ideals of the profession.[50] Over time, the wording regarding the reporting of colleagues appears to have been strengthened. However, Robinson sees this as little more than a PR exercise on the part of the GMC, with wording which does little to genuinely protect the public. She noted that whilst honest comment to patients was acceptable, the doctor had to be absolutely sure that it could be defended, and only if the patient asked for a second opinion. In, for example, the Bristol case, this was of little help as the parents of the harmed children had no idea they needed a second opinion. The 1985 Blue Book which allowed doctors to 'advise and assist' patients to go elsewhere might have provided better protection, had doctors chosen to follow it.[51] Reservations were also echoed by the Shipman Inquiry, which heard that even by 1994, the GMC's published guidance had been ineffective in altering attitudes within the profession.[52] The Communications and Policy Director at the Medical Protection Society told the Shipman Inquiry that on the whole members of the medical profession were neither familiar with nor interested in issues relating to medical ethics. The latter were not appropriately taught at either the undergraduate or postgraduate stages of medical education. Young doctors have been more likely to rely on these 'handed-down values' than to spend time scrutinizing formal guidance.

---

48 See General Medical Council, *Professional Conduct and Discipline: Fitness to Practise*, 1991, GMC, London, cited by Robinson, J., 'Thou Shalt Not Disparage Another Doctor', *healthmatters*, Spring 1998, Issue 33, 12–14.

49 See the Fifth Report of the Shipman Inquiry, *Safeguarding Patients: Lessons from the Past – Proposals for the Future*, paras 10.26–10.27 (www.the-shipman-inquiry.org.uk).

50 Nicolson, D., 'Mapping Professional Legal Ethics: The Form and Focus of the Codes', *Legal Ethics*, 1998, Vol. 1, Part 1, 51–69.

51 Robinson, J., 'Thou Shalt Not Disparage Another Doctor', *healthmatters*, Spring 1998, Issue 33, 12–14.

52 The Fifth Report of the Shipman Inquiry, *Safeguarding Patients: Lessons from the Past – Proposals for the Future*, para 10.39 (www.the-shipman-inquiry.org.uk).

They are likely to encounter their senior colleagues discussing ethical issues, but might well hear attitudes which themselves were incorrect.[53]

In the 1995 move to *Good Medical Practice*, under the heading 'Working with colleagues', doctors were told that they 'must not make any patient doubt a colleague's knowledge or skills by making unnecessary or unsustainable comments about them'. Robinson described the 'crime' as 'not disparaging as such, but sharing the knowledge with patients – letting it be known outside the club…Even the permission to make honest comment to patients in stringently controlled circumstances has vanished'.[54]

Direction regarding incompetent colleagues was addressed separately and provided that a doctor must protect patients when he or she believed that a colleague's conduct, performance or health constituted a threat. Before taking action, the doctor was required to do his or her best to establish the facts. If concerns persisted, someone from the employing authority or a regulatory body should be informed. The final sentence of the guidance emphasized that the 'safety of patients must come first at all times'. The 1998 version of *Good Medical Practice* repeated these provisions and extended the directions to doctors about what they can do if they suspect that a colleague presents a danger. These directions provided that doctors must follow their employer's procedure or inform an appropriate person from the employing authority, for example, the Medical Director or Chief Executive.

The May 2001 edition of *Good Medical Practice* said:

> Conduct or performance of colleagues
>
> 26. You must protect patients from risk of harm posed by another doctor's, or other healthcare professional's, conduct, performance or health, including problems arising from alcohol or other substance abuse. The safety of patients must come first at all times. Where there are serious concerns about a colleague's performance, health or conduct, it is essential that steps are taken without delay to investigate the concerns, to establish whether they are well-founded, and to protect patients.
>
> 27. If you have grounds to believe that a doctor or other healthcare professional may be putting patients at risk, you must give an honest explanation of your concerns to an appropriate person from the employing authority, such as the medical director, nursing director or chief executive, or the director of public health, or an officer of your local medical committee, following any procedures set by the employer. If there are no appropriate local systems, or local systems cannot resolve the problem, and you remain concerned about the safety of patients, you should inform the relevant regulatory body. If you are not sure what to do, discuss your concerns with an impartial colleague or contact your defence body, a professional organisation or the GMC for advice.
>
> 28. If you have management responsibilities you should ensure that mechanisms are in place through which colleagues can raise concerns about risks to patients.

---

53 The Fifth Report of the Shipman Inquiry, *Safeguarding Patients: Lessons from the Past – Proposals for the Future*, para 10.38 (www.the-shipman-inquiry.org.uk).

54 Robinson, J., 'Thou Shalt Not Disparage Another Doctor', *healthmatters*, Spring 1998, Issue 33, 12–14.

It is of note that the permitted action is entirely internal – to the employing body or a regulator. As Robinson notes, even in the later version when doctors are given a greater choice of places to make their disclosure, 'the information is [still] kept within the discreet knowledge of those who can be trusted not to frighten the horses – or rather the patients'. The implicit assumption within the GMC's choice of words is that when a disclosure is made, prompt and appropriate action will be taken. As the Bristol case illustrates, Dr Bolsin took steps which precisely matched these requirements, yet to no avail.[55]

In the 1980s, the BBC television programme *That's Life* featured patients who had been scarred when tattoos were removed by incompetent laser treatment. Other doctors were aware of the problems, but claimed their failure to report these resulted from the depreciation' clause.[56] In 1989, Duncan Campbell, an investigatory journalist, exposed on television two doctors who were selling overly hyped 'cures' for a number of serious illnesses. Campbell showed that many other doctors knew of this, but did nothing. The failure by colleagues to act was also attributed to the GMC guidance warning doctors against disparaging the professional skill, knowledge, qualifications or services of any other doctor.[57] This is the section of the Blue Book which seemed to stick in doctors' minds, at the expense of the section which required doctors to report colleagues whose professional behaviour might have raised issues of SPM. Robinson observed that doctors and medical students appeared to be more aware of these provisions than any others in the Blue Book, often citing them when challenged for failing to take steps to report incompetent colleagues.[58] In Stacey's opinion, this interpretation amongst rank and file doctors was unsurprising. She suggests that the GMC was quick to emphasize section 65 rather than the competing provisions. When, in 1990, it was proposed that the GMC should remove section 65, this was not initially taken forward. Stacey attributes this to a desire on the part of the Council to 'keep the club together and to impose a duty so to do'.[59]

The Shipman Inquiry was told that 'doctors were terrified of being involved with the GMC and were wary of possible criticism…[A] doctor would need solid evidence which would stand up in court before going to the GMC.' Even when gross negligence was suspected, 'it was exceptionally unusual' for doctors to report each other to the GMC, unless acting in an official capacity such as that of Medical Director of an NHS Trust. Furthermore, doctors often took it upon themselves to conclude that a 'genuine one-off accident' was something which could happen to any doctor – 'there but for the grace of God' – and so, not a matter to be reported. There are obvious risks with an attitude of this type. These risks are magnified when

---

55 Robinson, J., 'Thou Shalt Not Disparage Another Doctor', *healthmatters*, Spring 1998, Issue 33, 12–14.

56 See Robinson, J., 'Thou Shalt Not Disparage Another Doctor', *healthmatters*, Spring 1998, Issue 33, 12–14.

57 Section 65 of the Blue Book.

58 Robinson, J., 'Thou Shalt Not Disparage Another Doctor', *healthmatters*, Spring 1998, Issue 33, 12–14.

59 Stacey, M., *Regulating British Medicine: the General Medical Council*, 1992, Wiley, Chichester, 188–9.

it is individual doctors who take it upon themselves, often with inadequate evidence, to determine when a colleague falls into this category.[60]

The restrictive approach has gradually changed in recent years, but the folk memory within the profession has retained the idea that reporting colleagues without the clearest of evidence is itself an act of professional misconduct. An example of this attitude was displayed by the evidence from a GP to the Kerr/Haslam Inquiry: 'The reluctance to complain was explained in part, said [Dr KH1], by the stern warnings received when he was training to become a doctor that: "*You would never criticise a colleague, whether they be a GP or a consultant.*"'[61]

Fear of being criticized by the GMC for 'disparagement' was the reason given by Dr S3 to the Shipman Inquiry for failing to raise concerns following Mrs Overton's admission to hospital. As the Inquiry noted: 'As recently as 1999, [Dr S3] was hesitant about criticising a fellow practitioner, even one who had been arrested for murder.'[62]

The GMC, however, has been far from proactive in promoting the changed message about whistleblowing. Ideally, the GMC's regulatory provisions should help to instil within doctors the moral presumption that colleagues who give rise to concerns will be reported. Only this stance can maximize public protection. Alternatively, as previously discussed, there should be a real fear of the regulatory consequences if a doctor fails to report in circumstances where reporting was appropriate. This, it would appear, is the best means to counter the strong disincentives to report noted above. To date, the GMC has tended towards the opposite approach. This is illustrated by the recent case of *Cream v GMC*.[63] The PCC found two consultants guilty of serious professional misconduct for making allegations that a member of an appointment committee might be biased. The basis of the GMC decision was that the consultants had failed to do their best to find out the facts before taking action, as required by paragraph 24 of the 1998 Guide. When the decision was challenged by means of judicial review,[64] Turner J decided that the approach of the PCC was irrational, commenting that: '…the finding made by the PCC can…only properly be described as "perverse". It is known that the claimant had sought the views of his own Chief Executive as well as the MDU and the BMA before he made any revelations…'[65]

For the GMC to still adopt this approach after Shipman, Ledward, the Bristol Royal Infirmary case and other scandals where lack of reporting have been key factors, suggests that the presumption *against* whistleblowing is still very strongly

60 For full discussion, see the Fifth Report of the Shipman Inquiry, *Safeguarding Patients: Lessons from the Past – Proposals for the Future*, paras 10.2–10.8 and 10.48–10.52 (www.the-shipman-inquiry.org.uk).

61 *The Kerr/Haslam Inquiry Report*, July 2005, Cm 6640-1, 434.

62 The Fifth Report of the Shipman Inquiry, *Safeguarding Patients: Lessons from the Past – Proposals for the Future*, paras 2.53 and 10.9 (www.the-shipman-inquiry.org.uk).

63 [2002] EWHC 436.

64 The consultants had been reprimanded by the GMC, a penalty not affecting their registration. Because of this, the usual route of appeal to the Privy Council, in accordance with s40 Medical Act 1983, was not available.

65 Similar reasoning was adopted by Forbes J. in *Dowd v GMC* (2003), Professor Dowd being the other 'whistleblowing' consultant alongside Dr Cream.

ingrained within medical self-regulation. The message which *Cream* sends is that the regulations pay lip service to the importance of reporting concerns, but a doctor putting this into practice risks having to traverse the minefield of the disciplinary procedures.

*Pal v GMC*[66] originated from events in spring 2000 when Dr Pal had raised a number a complaints to the GMC, primarily involving the alleged mistreatment of elderly patients.[67] Dr Pal corresponded with the GMC's solicitors, but was reluctant to meet with the solicitors simply to repeat evidence she had already given in writing. She did express a willingness to meet with them once they had progressed their investigations. She was also reported as indicating in this correspondence that she did not trust the GMC or its solicitors.[68] A stalemate appears to have been reached: Dr Pal refused to continue to correspond with the GMC's solicitors, emphasizing that she had nothing to add and that they should progress their own investigations. The complaint was closed in October 2000.[69] Shortly afterwards, it was said that internal correspondence within the GMC, between a case worker, deputy to GMC Chief Executive and Registrar and a GMC screener, began to cast doubt on Dr Pal's mental health: 'Those of us who have dealt with the case in Conduct are concerned that the correspondence on file suggests that Dr Pal may have an underlying health problem.'[70] A screener suggested that: 'I do think that she could have a health problem. She is certainly intemperate and possibly paranoid. But at the present time I do not think we have sufficient evidence of ill health to proceed.'[71]

An extract from the court proceedings in *Pal* is illustrative:

> JUDGE HARRIS: For myself I don't really see why somebody complaining about the behaviour of doctors or the GMC, if that is what they are doing, why that should raise a question about their mental stability, unless anybody who wishes to criticise 'the party' is automatically showing themselves to be mentally unstable because they don't agree with the point of view put forward on behalf of the GMC or the party.
>
> ...It is like a totalitarian regime: anybody who criticises it is said to be prima facie mentally ill – what used to happen in Russia.[72]

In one respect, a proactive stance on the part of the GMC to appropriately consider the potential risk posed to the public by any doctor – however the information giving rise to suspicion comes to its attention – is to be commended. However, the more concerning aspect of this case is the apparent focus of the GMC on the mental health status of the complainant, apparently at the expense of fully investigating the

---

66 *Pal v GMC and others* [2004] EWHC 1485 (QB) Lawtel transcript.

67 Dr Pal's concerns had been aired in the media. See, for example, Macaskill, M. and Ungoed-Thomas, J., 'Elderly are Helped to Die to Clear Beds, Claims Doctor', *Sunday Times*, 2 April 2000.

68 *Pal v GMC and others*, Paragraphs 13–17.

69 Paragraphs 17–18.

70 Paragraph 19.

71 Paragraph 25.

72 *Pal v GMC and others* [2004] EWHC 1485 (QB), Transcript from Proceedings – Day 2, page 20.

substance of the original complaint. This case suggests the continuation of echoes within the GMC of the belief that 'disparagement' by doctors of their colleagues is somehow inherently unsavoury, and that a doctor making a complaint becomes prone to suspicion. Dr Pal's own reported response to these matters was as follows:

> There has been no complaint against me by any patients and my GP verifies that I have not been mentally ill and the judge agreed…The entire point centres on whistleblowing…If whistleblowers are to be treated with such contempt, then there will be no-one who will prevent the next Dr Harold Shipman.[73]

Recent high profile cases which demonstrate some progress by the GMC arise from the Bristol and Shipman cases. As discussed in Chapter 7, Roylance was found guilty of serious professional misconduct and erased from the medical register for failing in his managerial role, as chief executive of the trust, to protect patients. Following this case, a medically qualified manager should fear professional censure if she or he fails to act either as a whistleblower or as a recipient of whistleblowing disclosures.[74]

Two doctors in particular were involved in the treatment of one of Shipman's patients. Mrs Renate Overton was admitted to Tameside General Hospital in February 1994, following Shipman's administration of an overdose of diamorphine. She remained in a coma until her death in April 1995. Shipman indicated in her medical notes that he had injected her with 20mg of morphine, even though this was totally inappropriate for an asthmatic patient such as Mrs Overton. The hospital doctors responsible for Mrs Overton's care, a consultant cardiologist and a consultant anaesthetist, failed to report Shipman's actions either locally or to the GMC. In October 2005 both doctors were found guilty of serious professional misconduct by the GMC for failing to report concerns at the time of the incident and for misleading the Shipman Inquiry. The fitness to practise panel concluded that the findings against the anaesthetist constituted a serious breach of professional conduct principles. To comply with its essential role of protecting patients and maintaining public confidence in the profession, the panel would often erase a doctor following a finding of dishonesty. However, in the present case the dishonesty was considered to be limited to a single set of circumstances, outside of the clinical setting and did not directly cause harm to any patients. A 12-month suspension was therefore considered appropriate. In the absence of dishonesty and the circumstances of the cardiologist's (limited) attempts to raise concerns, a reprimand was considered to be appropriate.

---

73 Wells, T., 'How GMC Turned on Brave NHS Whistleblower', *Sunday Mercury*, 6 February 2005.

74 Robinson notes that the GMC was slow in its development of this principle, compared with, for example, the regulatory body for nurses which had for many years charged nurses when they failed in a managerial capacity to protect patients. Robinson, J., 'Thou Shalt Not Disparage Another Doctor', *healthmatters*, Spring 1998, Issue 33, 12–14.

**Bullying in the Medical Workplace – How Realistic is the Call to Whistleblow?**

In one survey of UK doctors, 37 per cent said they had been bullied during the past year.[75] In a subsequent survey, 18 per cent of respondents, ranging from house officers and senior house officers to specialist registrars, reported being bullied. Of these, only a minority (32 per cent) had complained.[76] Most of the negative behaviour came from other, more senior doctors. Consultants were the source of bullying in 27 per cent of cases.[77] A significant majority of medical students have also reported experiencing teaching by humiliation.[78] These statistics support the idea that within a structured power-based hierarchy, whistleblowing is likely to be more of an ideal than a reality. Only if the structure itself is changed is self-policing within the profession likely to be advanced. This takes on particular relevance when it is considered that doctors of similar levels of seniority, especially consultants, are far less likely to observe each other's work than they are to be observed by more junior colleagues.

As the Ayling case illustrates, the vast majority of staff who were in a position to judge Ayling's hospital practice and to report concerns were nurses and midwives. Yet, the dominant professional hierarchy prevented them from feeling able to challenge doctors or to question their judgement. Doctors were in a position to make the working lives of nurses and midwives very difficult. As complaints frequently appeared to result in no action being taken, nursing staff had little incentive to make their concerns known, and ample disincentives to do so. As well as nursing staff, trainee and junior doctors also felt themselves restricted within the medical hierarchy. For instance, a medical student who had worked with Ayling gave evidence to the Inquiry that she would not have considered reporting his behaviour. She also observed that she would not have been asked her opinion of Ayling's approach to patients. Even if they were fortunate enough to be listened to, junior doctors were often self-censoring because they depended on senior colleagues for references.[79]

A future direction suggested by Kultgen would see doctors cultivating a role distance, giving rise to the greater ability to question in individual circumstances whether they should always do what their peers and superiors expect. This would be supported by practical skills in moral reasoning. Leadership for scientific and

75 Quine, L., 'Workplace Bullying in Junior Doctors: Questionnaire Survey', *BMJ*, 2002, 324: 878–9.

76 Paice, E., Aitken, M., Houghton, A. and Firth-Cozens, J., 'Bullying Among Doctors in Training: Cross Sectional Questionnaire Survey', *BMJ*, 2004, Vol. 18, 658–9, September.

77 Paice, E., Aitken, M., Houghton, A. and Firth-Cozens, J., 'Bullying Among Doctors in Training: Cross Sectional Questionnaire Survey', *BMJ*, 2004, Vol. 18, 658–9, September.

78 Lempp, H. and Seale, C., 'The Hidden Curriculum in Undergraduate Medical Education: Qualitative Study of Medical Students' Perceptions of Teaching', *BMJ*, 2004, 329: 770–73, 2 October.

79 The Honourable Mrs Justice Pauffley, Committee of Inquiry – Independent Investigation into how the NHS Handled Allegations about the Conduct of Clifford Ayling, 15 July 2004, Cm 6298, paras 4.42 and 4.48–4.49.

technical practice is well established within the medical profession and similar leadership is needed for ethical and regulatory matters.[80]

## Whistleblowing and the NHS

In June 1993 the Department of Health published guidance[81] stating that all NHS staff had a duty to inform managers about any matter which might be detrimental to the interests of patients. Managers had a corresponding duty to facilitate an easy mechanism for raising such concerns. Emphasis was also placed on ensuring that employees were not penalized for acting in accordance with this guidance. The Ledward Inquiry, however, expressed concern that the title of the document – *Guidance for Staff on Relations with Public and Media* – may have misled some staff.[82] In the same period, the DoH also published guidance designed to ensure that adverse incidents were reported promptly.[83] As illustrated by a number of cases which post-date this guidance, it clearly had no dramatic impact on the position. New whistleblowing policies were introduced as mandatory for NHS Trusts in 1999, following the enactment of the Public Interest Disclosure Act. Such policies required employees disclosing information to have an honest and 'reasonable belief' that one or more of a number of specified offences had been committed. These included the commission or likely commission of a criminal offence; endangering health and safety; malpractice or ill-treatment of a patient. The whistleblowing employee will be protected as long as the disclosure is made in good faith. The Kerr/Haslam Inquiry noted that even though awareness has increased about whistleblowing, this has not prevented a continued tendency to 'turn a blind eye' or to give colleagues the benefit of the doubt. The challenge remains to change the culture, so that those who work most closely with wrongdoers, and so are in the best position to spot problems, are willing to raise concerns. The challenge is particularly acute within small teams and geographically isolated practices.[84] The culture should change to ensure that investigation is welcome within the NHS. This should extend to include the willingness to investigate 'mere' gossip and rumour if this relates to serious matters such as sexual misconduct, and early investigation would help to protect patients.[85]

## Public Interest Disclosure Act 1998

The Public Interest Disclosure Act 1998 provides legal protection for whistle-blowers. The PIDA takes effect as Part 4A of the Employment Rights Act 1996,

---

80 Kultgen, J., 'The Ideological Use of Professional Codes', in Callahan, J.C. (ed.), *Ethical Issues in Professional Life*, 1988, Oxford University Press, Oxford, 420.

81 EL(93)13.

82 *The Ledward Report*, Part V, paras 24.3.1.–24.3.3.

83 HSG(93)15. See *The Ledward Report*, Part V, para 24.4

84 *The Kerr/Haslam Inquiry Report*, July 2005, Cm 6640-1, 664–5.

85 See, for example, *The Kerr/Haslam Inquiry Report*, July 2005, Cm 6640-1, 682–3.

coming into force in July 1999. The purpose of the Act is to protect individuals who make certain disclosures in the public interest, offering employment protection to workers who raise appropriate concerns about malpractice in the workplace. The idea was to shift the focus from the messenger to the message, discouraging employers from covering up malpractice.[86] The Act applies to all health professionals who act in good faith, with reasonable belief and not for personal gain. In August 1999 the NHS Executive published a circular to help Trusts implement PIDA 1998.[87] This required all health authorities to have local procedures and to designate a senior manager or non-executive director to receive concerns outside of the usual management process. The circular also stated that ministers expect a climate and culture in the NHS which encourages staff to feel able to raise concerns without fear of victimization.[88] Concerns must first be raised in the appropriate way internally. The Bristol Inquiry concluded that Stephen Bolsin, the whistleblowing anaesthetist, would not have been protected by the Act because, in releasing information to *Private Eye*, he did not make his disclosure in the manner prescribed by the Act.[89] He would only have been protected if, in good faith, he had made a 'qualifying disclosure' to his employer, his legal adviser or the Minister of State or a prescribed official.[90] As already discussed, attempts by Dr Bolsin to report concerns internally fell on deaf ears.

In the fifth Shipman Inquiry Report, Dame Janet Smith considered the degree of protection offered by the PIDA. The report argued that the use of the word 'disclosure' caused difficulties because it implied that the information being disclosed was true. The word 'report' was considered to be a better alternative.[91] The requirement that those making disclosures have a 'reasonable belief' that their information fell into one or more of the statutory categories of wrongdoing was also considered to be a possible impediment to important disclosures. 'Suspicion' was seen as a better word than 'belief': 'I am concerned that, in order to make a disclosure even to his/her employer, a worker has to be in the position where s/he could say, for example, "I believe that this disclosure tends to show that a crime has been committed and my belief is reasonable".'[92]

Also, the requirement that disclosure be made in 'good faith' was questioned as possibly discouraging legitimate and valuable disclosures. There should also be

86 For further discussion, see the Fifth Report of the Shipman Inquiry, *Safeguarding Patients: Lessons from the Past – Proposals for the Future*, paras 11.23–11.24 (www.the-shipman-inquiry.org.uk).

87 *The Public Interest Disclosure Act 1998: Whistleblowing in the NHS*, HSC 1999/198, 27 August 1999.

88 Vickers, L., 'Whistleblowing in the Health Service', in Lewis, David B. (ed.), *Whistleblowing at Work*, 2000, The Athlone Press, London.

89 For further discussion, see Samuels, A., 'Can a Doctor "Blow the Whistle" or "Grass" on a Colleague?', *MLJ*, 2002, 70(135), 5 September.

90 The Bristol Report, para 162.

91 The Fifth Report of the Shipman Inquiry, *Safeguarding Patients: Lessons from the Past – Proposals for the Future*, paras 11.23–11.49 and 11.90–11.93 (www.the-shipman-inquiry.org.uk).

92 The Fifth Report of the Shipman Inquiry, *Safeguarding Patients: Lessons from the Past – Proposals for the Future*, paras 11.109–11.111 (www.the-shipman-inquiry.org.uk).

provision to enable employees of small organizations, for example, nurses in small GP practices, to make disclosures directly to an appropriate external body, because of the difficulties associated with internal reporting.[93]

In terms of the impact of the new provisions, the findings are mixed. A survey of NHS staff undertaken in 2000 demonstrated this. On the positive side, 90 per cent of respondents said that they had made a report when they had concerns about patient safety. Fifty per cent of these said that their concern was dealt with reasonably (this rose to approximately 66 per cent of those whose employer had a formal whistleblowing policy), and 33 per cent said that their employer would want them to blow the whistle even if it resulted in bad publicity. On the negative side, 30 per cent of respondents said that their employer would not want to be told about a major problem, and of those who had reported a concern, approximately 33 per cent said that they had experienced some personal retaliation (although not from those whose employer had a formal whistleblowing policy).[94]

## Oversight of Doctors by Other Healthcare Workers

The medical profession has devoted many decades to establishing a dominant position over other healthcare occupations. It is therefore optimistic, even unrealistic, to assume that members of historically subordinate occupations will have the confidence to whistleblow against doctors. This reticence is supported by comments of nursing staff from various Inquiries relating to the medical scandals in recent years. For example:

> Nursing staff simply did not raise issues...If you attempted to raise issues, it was not looked upon favourably by your colleagues. The advice given to staff was to report anything untoward up through line management. However, it seemed that if you reported anything up the line you were quickly moved on to a different position. There was a culture amongst staff that you did not complain about colleagues. Anyone who had attempted to make a complaint would have felt very vulnerable.[95]

It has also been noted that if a nurse reports a doctor, the doctor may refuse to work with the nurse, or even demand the nurse's transfer. Nurses may also be reluctant to complain for fear that the doctor will attempt to implicate him/her as a participant in the wrongdoing.[96] In recent years, some progress has been made in challenging traditional medical hierarchies. One positive example was given in the Fifth Report of the Shipman Inquiry. The case involved a locum senior house

---

93 The Fifth Report of the Shipman Inquiry, *Safeguarding Patients: Lessons from the Past – Proposals for the Future*, paras 11.94–11.114. For further discussion of these points, see Lewis, D., 'Shipman's Legacy: Whistleblowing Procedures for All?', *NLJ*, 2005, 155.7158(14), 7 January.

94 Ayling Inquiry Report, 15 July 2004, paras 6.91–6.93 and 6.87.

95 *The Kerr/Haslam Inquiry Report,* July 2005, Cm 6640-1, evidence from a community psychiatric nurse, 244.

96 See the Fifth Report of the Shipman Inquiry, *Safeguarding Patients: Lessons from the Past – Proposals for the Future*, para 11.83 (www.the-shipman-inquiry.org.uk).

officer who appeared to be using pethidine for patients where this was not the usual treatment. A nurse became suspicious that the doctor was abusing the drug and, having observed him switching a syringe, sent the remaining contents for analysis. It transpired that the doctor had injected the patient with water, keeping the pethidine for himself.[97] The willingness of the nurse to pursue her concerns was vital, as she may have been the only colleague in a position to observe the doctor's behaviour.

## Future Developments

There are some potential grounds for optimism. For example, the European Working Time Directive has required re-assessment of the traditional long working hours culture within medicine. One effect of this may be a reduction in the number of medical teams with fixed members. Junior doctors are likely to find themselves working with a number of different consultants, rather than just one. This pattern may have disadvantages in terms of consistency of training and personal commitment to patients,[98] but should have advantages with regard to whistleblowing. The reliance and personal commitment which junior doctors have had in the past to a single consultant should be significantly reduced.

Recent examples can also be found of doctors who are willing to report colleagues. For instance, in 2004, two privately practising doctors were found guilty of serious professional misconduct by the GMC for recommending alternative, scientifically unproven, therapies rather than conventional treatment for a patient with cancer. The important point from the perspective of whistleblowing was that no patient ever complained about the relevant behaviour of either of the two doctors. Instead, the complaint came from a surgeon who was concerned about his patient's refusal to have surgery.[99] Of course, this was not a case of a surgeon reporting working colleagues, with associated risks of being ostracized. Equally, it may have been less problematic to report doctors who were 'outsiders' to conventional medical practice.

An efficient system of clinical governance, including incident reporting and audit, should in principle minimize the need to whistleblow. However, the opportunity must remain to report, should these formal systems prove ineffective.[100] The Ledward Inquiry recommended the creation of a confidential hotline in every NHS Trust, which should facilitate reporting concerns. The person charged with receiving such calls must possess appropriate seniority and interpersonal qualities which ensure that complainants are not deterred inappropriately. This person should be answerable to a non-executive Director of the NHS Trust, who in turn will be responsible for ensuring that concerns are properly followed up. Both the GMC and the United Kingdom Central Council for Nursing, Midwifery and Health Visiting (UKCC) should be prescribed bodies under S.43 of the Employment Rights Act

97 The Fifth Report of the Shipman Inquiry, *Safeguarding Patients: Lessons from the Past – Proposals for the Future*, para 23.15 (www.the-shipman-inquiry.org.uk).

98 See Tallis, R., *Hippocratic Oaths*, 2004, Atlantic, London, 250.

99 Edzard, E., 'The GMC is Right to Come Down Hard on Doctors who Wrongly Prescribe Complementary Medicine', *The Guardian*, 16 November 2004.

100 *The Ledward Report*, Part VII, paras 2–4.

1996, as amended by the Public Interest Disclosure Act 1998, to whom an employee may disclose information without incurring disciplinary measures by the employing Trust.[101]

The Ayling Inquiry also heard differing opinions from medical staff about how much views had changed. A midwife described doctors as being 'the Gods of the hospital' 20 years ago and beyond challenge; the position now was that:

> The whole culture of the NHS is changing. It possibly isn't quite there yet, but it's certainly getting there, so that there is a lot more respect between the medical staff and the nursing staff now, and opinions on both sides are now valued. If you've got any – if you had any cause for concern, then you can – you would feel – I would feel happy to go to the consultants or to the lead consultants and speak about the problem.[102]

In contrast, Professor Malcolm Forsythe said:

> [T]here still is not that culture of openness. There is still a huge defensiveness on the part of professionals about being criticised, which affects people's willingness to be open and you have to try and deal with both those aspects, because if you raise a problem and all you get is antagonism and then revenge, if you see that happening somewhere else in your organisation you are going to be pretty loath to do it yourself.[103]

---

101 *The Ledward Report*, Part VII, paras (i)–(vi). The Fifth Shipman Inquiry Report made the same recommendation.

102 Ayling Inquiry Report, 15 July 2004, para 6.89.

103 Ayling Inquiry Report, 15 July 2004, paras 6.90 and 6.95.

# Chapter 14

# Lay Participation in the Regulatory Process

## Introduction

This chapter considers the role and importance of lay participation within the GMC's regulatory process.[1] It is beyond the scope of this book and the research which underpins it to investigate in detail the adjudicatory practice of particular lay members in individual hearings.[2] Rather, wider observations are drawn from the case studies previously discussed and from elsewhere, about the overall importance of lay participation and the types of lay membership which might be desirable.

Concern that a professionally dominated regulatory body will lack fairness has long roots. For instance, in the context of the legal profession in Australia it was said:

> If the function of policing and disciplining the profession are given to a body elected by members of the profession to look after their interests, the possibilities of conflict are obvious. Indeed they are so obvious that they arouse in many people a cynical attitude from the start, frequently expressed in the form that it is useless to complain to a professional body about one of its members. Even if an investigation or decision by such a body is thorough and fair, it is likely to lack credibility if the result favours members against the outside complainant…An investigator closely and sympathetically identified with the profession may be unduly sceptical of complainants, insufficiently interested in elucidating their complaints, unduly credulous of lawyers' explanations, and reluctant to impute misconduct to a lawyer.[3]

Irvine recalls a time in medical practice when lay opinions were viewed with near disdain by the medical profession. There has been little recognition that, whilst patients may not understand the technicalities of medicine, they are generally readily capable of judging the process; for instance, whether a doctor's manner and the nature of examination seemed appropriate and, ultimately, whether a condition

---

1 'Lay' is used in the usual dictionary definition sense of 'non-professional' or 'amateur'.

2 For an example of this type of research, see Smith, R., *Medical Discipline: The Professional Conduct of the GMC 1858-1990*, 1994, Oxford University Press, Oxford.

3 New South Wales Law Reform Commission, *Discussion Paper*, 1979, in Disney, J., Basten, J., Redmond, P., Ross, S. and Bell, K., *Lawyers*, 2nd ed, 1986, The Law Book Co., Melbourne, 346–7.

was correctly diagnosed with appropriate speed. Indeed, informal categorization of doctors by the public in a locality is common.[4]

With a dominant scientific model of medicine, clinicians have been able to define medical 'reality'. There has been little recognition that the patient voice can provide an important lay perspective on the provision of medical care, an alternative means of knowing.[5] This absence has resulted in the development of healthcare provision without reference to those using the service.[6] Approaches in recent years have focused upon managerial solutions to excessive professional power. However, cases such as Bristol and Ledward demonstrate that managerial authority is often not up to the task, or even that managers may identify themselves more with the professions they are supposed to control than with the patients they are there to serve.[7]

The historical attitude of the medical profession to the 'place' it considered the public should occupy in the regulatory process is neatly summed up by the approach to requests for copies of the regulatory guidance used by the profession. It was long considered that the Blue Book was suitable reading for doctors only, and GMC staff were discouraged from sending copies to members of the public, for fear they would use it to identify misconduct which a doctor might have committed. This position only changed when the Blue Book was replaced with *Good Medical Practice*.[8]

The Shipman case provides illustrations of lay voices which were either ignored, or never heard because the concerned party assumed that they would not be believed. For example, Mrs S4 was resident manager of a sheltered housing development in Shipman's practice area between 1987 and 2002. During this time a number of residents died in Shipman's presence or were found dead shortly after Shipman had visited. Mrs S4 gradually became suspicious that these deaths were unusual, for instance, with respect to the physical positions in which some residents were found, and the fact that there was not the gradual decline in health seen when other residents died. In one case, in February 1997, Mrs S4 reported the death to the police because she was unable to contact Shipman. However, Shipman attended at around the same time as the police and diverted their involvement by issuing a death certificate. The police accepted Shipman's explanation and, in these circumstances, Mrs S4 lacked the confidence to press her concerns. Mrs S4 also found herself further hindered in raising her concerns because of incredulity on the part of others. For instance, her

---

4 Irvine, D., *The Doctors' Tale*, 2003, Radcliffe Medical Press, Oxford, 15.

5 It has been suggested that doctor and patient do not share a reality regarding the perception of illness. Instead, doctor and patient perspectives represent two distinct realities. See Cornwall, J., *Hard Earned Lives*, 1984, Tavistock, London; Arksey, H., 'Expert and Lay Participation in the Construction of Medical Knowledge', *Sociology of Health and Illness*, 1994, 16(4), 448–68; Toombs, K., *The Meaning of Illness – A Phenomenological Account of the Different Perspectives of Physician and Patient*, 1992, Kluwer Academic Publishers, Norwell, MA; Mulcahy, L., *Disputing Doctors*, 2003, Open University Press, Maidenhead, 88.

6 See Mulcahy, L., *Disputing Doctors*, 2003, Open University Press, Maidenhead, 11 and 83. See also Oakley, A., 'Doctor Knows Best', in Robinson, M., (ed.), *Women Confined*, 1980, Blackwell, Oxford.

7 See Mulcahy, L., *Disputing Doctors*, 2003, Open University Press, Maidenhead, 11.

8 See the Fifth Report of the Shipman Inquiry, *Safeguarding Patients: Lessons from the Past – Proposals for the Future*, para 17.18 (www.the-shipman-inquiry.org.uk).

husband felt that she must be mistaken, and a trusted friend who worked in a medical practice advised her 'to say nothing about her suspicions because people would say she was mad'.[9] Other lay people – from home helps to a taxi driver – had suspicions but felt unable to voice them. Of particular note was the evidence of funeral directors, Mr and Mrs S5. In dealing with the funerals of Shipman's patients, Mr and Mrs S5 became aware of odd features about the deaths – notably that Shipman's patients often died alone, while sitting up, dressed in their day clothes with no obvious signs that they had been ill. This contrasted with the more usual position, that elderly patients died in bed, obviously ill and with family and friends around. The S5s also became aware that Shipman had often been present shortly before, or at, the time of death. The S5s did eventually mention their concerns to another GP, but this came late, in 1998. Had the funeral directors been valued more highly in the regulatory process, it is likely that they would have felt more confident in expressing their concerns sooner.[10]

Evidence of a lack of respect for, or even recognition of, patients' rights to be full participants in the regulatory system is illustrated by the operation of other aspects of that process. For example, it has been unclear whether patients treated by doctors whose performance has been found to be seriously deficient are provided with full, or even any, disclosure. The Shipman Inquiry noted that in 1999, the Performance Issues Working Group recommended that in cases where the doctor was undergoing remedial training following a performance assessment, patients should have enough information to ensure that informed consent is given to treatment by a doctor undergoing retraining. In November 1999, the GMC acknowledged the need for further consideration of these issues, but little of substance appeared to have been done.[11]

For example, a survey in July 2005 found that only 36 per cent of general practitioners considered that feedback from patients was important. Similarly, with regard to the assessment of doctors, only around one third of practitioners supported lay input.[12]

## Lay Involvement in the Professional Regulatory Process

Effective lay participation is important to the professional self-regulatory process.[13] Lay members can aid the profession's understanding of the needs of the community

9 See the Fifth Report of the Shipman Inquiry, *Safeguarding Patients: Lessons from the Past – Proposals for the Future*, paras 8.33–8.42 (www.the-shipman-inquiry.org.uk).

10 The Fifth Report of the Shipman Inquiry, *Safeguarding Patients: Lessons from the Past – Proposals for the Future*, paras 8.93–8.97 (www.the-shipman-inquiry.org.uk).

11 The Fifth Report of the Shipman Inquiry, *Safeguarding Patients: Lessons from the Past – Proposals for the Future*, para 24.151 (www.the-shipman-inquiry.org.uk).

12 See Department of Health, *Good Doctors, Safer Patients – Proposals to Strengthen the System to Assure and Improve the Performance of Doctors and to Protect the Safety of Patients: A Report by the Chief Medical Officer*, July 2006, Chapter 8, paragraphs 2, 8 and 9.

13 Although how this is to be achieved is the subject of debate. Smith, for example, writing in the 1990s, considered that lay membership of the GMC's disciplinary committee

and can also add legitimacy to the regulatory process. As the President of the Washington D.C. Bar Association is reported as saying:

> [Lay members] help us look at matters from another perspective, and make us aware of the needs and concerns of the public…The citizens make us aware of how laymen view our profession and what they expect from us. They call attention to our shortcomings, they make us engage in critical self-examination, and they step on some sensitive toes…[and] put us on our toes to improve the profession and our service to the community.[14]

Assessment of the public interest is difficult and complex for anyone, but the difficulties increase when a group of people with the same limited experience reinforce each other in their narrow judgement. This is exacerbated amongst groups of professionals who, in terms of socio-economic status and other background factors, differ from the wider community they are serving.[15] Traditional arguments that professional practice is so complex as to be beyond lay understanding have been refuted by successful examples of lay oversight, for example, in the case of the legal profession, by the Legal Services Ombudsman. My starting point, therefore, is that lay involvement should be a central and dominant feature of the GMC's activities, including membership of key committees and disciplinary panels.

Selection of lay members is also important. If the profession takes responsibility for this, they may pack the regulatory body with lay members who support the professional cause and lack true independence. For this reason an appointment body independent of the profession is desirable. However, the latter approach will not always guarantee transparency and fairness. For example, the historical appointment of GMC lay members by the Privy Council has been described as 'obscure and poorly understood'.[16] Lay members themselves should represent the wide public interest, but must also be sufficiently confident and articulate to stand up to the professional participants in the regulatory process.[17]

---

was more problematic than beneficial. Instead, public accountability was better achieved by other means – such as legal assessors, rights of appeal and the right of public and press admission to regulatory hearings. Smith, R., *Medical Discipline: The Professional Conduct of the GMC 1858-1990*, 1994, Oxford University Press, Oxford.

14 Pickering, J., 'The Bar and the Community', 1980, 4 *District Lawyer* 6, in Disney, J., Basten, J., Redmond, P., Ross, S. and Bell, K., *Lawyers*, 2nd ed, 1986, The Law Book Co., Melbourne, 213.

15 New South Wales Law Reform Commission, *Discussion Paper*, 1979, 119–20, in Disney, J., Basten, J., Redmond, P., Ross, S. and Bell, K., *Lawyers*, 2nd ed, 1986, The Law Book Co., Melbourne, 217–18.

16 GMC, *Effective, Inclusive and Accountable Reform of the GMC's Structure, Constitution and Governance*, March 2001, 18.

17 It has been suggested, for example, that the councils of regulatory bodies should be independently appointed. Such appointments should reflect a wide range of interested parties, and dominance by any single group should be avoided. Lay members should be genuinely 'lay', and therefore not connected with other healthcare professions or other aspects of healthcare. Potential for conflicts of interest should be explicitly recognized and, for instance, medical members who hold positions in organizations that are involved in representing the profession

There are significant differences between the rhetoric and reality of lay involvement in the regulation of doctors. Rhetorically, the perception within the GMC appears to be that lay participation is strong and effective. For instance, Sir Graeme Catto, speaking in March 2003, as President of the GMC, described the core function of the Council as follows:

> [F]irst and foremost we set the standards expected of doctors. We don't do that simply by going into a closed room and thinking these clever thoughts, we do it in discussion with patient organisations, with the public and with the profession…So there has been a general acceptance both by the profession and by the informed lay public and patients in this country that what the GMC is trying to do by way of standard setting is more or less appropriate.[18]

However, others within the profession have criticized lay participation. Tallis, for example, considers that the value of lay input has never been properly assessed. In terms of knowledge, lay participants are likely to be at the bottom of the learning curve. Meetings dealing with complex issues will be significantly slowed. Nor will they have the relevant background of clinicians or managers to facilitate continual improvement, including the opportunity to reflect upon and learn from mistakes.[19] Tallis's view presupposes a singular approach to medical issues. There is no recognition that the greatest strength which lay participants may bring is their ignorance of pre-existing systems and approaches – allowing for free thinking and novelty of approach. Nor does Tallis acknowledge that lay members of the GMC have often come from working environments closely associated with medicine. This latter approach brings its own concerns regarding levels of objectivity, but it does address some of the issues raised by Tallis.

Tallis also argues that moves by the GMC to ensure that patient expectations are met, and that doctors comply with the patients' right to be fully involved in decisions about their care, place unrealistic demands on doctors. This, in turn, raises serious issues about the attempts by the GMC to become more patient-focused. Time constraints on doctors and the lack or relative inaccessibility of information relating to issues such as risk–benefit analysis prevent the practical application of these requirements. It is, therefore, of little genuine value to the wider community if the GMC issues requirements which look good on paper but do not lead to real improvements in practice.

Formal lay involvement in the medical self-regulatory process dates back to 1926, from which time the Privy Council adopted the practice of including one lay person among the five people it nominated to the GMC.[20] The role of lay members was to provide a degree of critical vigilance over the Council, especially

---

would be excluded. Walshe, K. and Benson, L., 'GMC and the Future of Revalidation – Time for Radical Reform', *BMJ*, 2005, 330: 1504–1506, 25 June.

18 Sir Graeme Catto, 'The GMC – Revalidation – What Are We Trying to Measure?', *Medico-Legal Journal*, 2003, 71(106), 2 October.

19 Tallis, R., *Hippocratic Oaths*, 2004, Atlantic, London, 95.

20 Pyke-Lees, W., *Centenary of the GMC 1858-1958: The History and Present Work of the Council*, 1958, GMC, London.

with regard to matters of discipline. They were representatives of the consumer interest.[21] In subsequent years lay representation on the Council increased, but has always remained a minority. Statutory provision for lay members of the Council did not emerge until the Medical Act of 1950. This Act provided for eight of the 50 members to be Crown nominees, three of whom were to be lay.[22] For some commentators, nothing less than dominant lay oversight of the profession is enough. Perhaps most famously, George Bernard Shaw expressed the position as follows: 'Until the General Medical Council is composed of hard-working representatives of the suffering public, with doctors who live by private practice rigidly excluded except as assessors, we shall still be decimated by the vested interest of the private side of the profession in disease.'[23]

Opportunities in recent years to move to a lay-dominated Council have not been taken. A radical proposal from within the profession itself, a submission to the Merrison Committee from the Medical Practitioners Union, recommended replacing the GMC with a consumer body. The MPU members at this time were content to see themselves as technicians offering a technical service, rather than as professionals with rights to special privileges or as suppliers selling their wares in a market place.[24] The Merrison Committee concluded that the GMC should remain under professional control. The Committee also considered it preferable that members elected by the rank and file profession should occupy the dominant position. Similarly, fitness to practise panels should be dominated by doctors. The PCC would have some lay members, but not the Health Committee – Merrison seeing decisions of this committee as entirely professional or technical.[25]

The issue came to prominence again in the 1980s, with the Thatcher government's ideological opposition to the monopoly power of professions. For instance, Green, reflecting this approach, once again proposed the replacement of the GMC by a lay body. This would be coupled with market control of healthcare. The lay regulatory body would be responsible for reviewing training requirements, including the content of training. Green's view was that the register maintained by the GMC was not a register of competent doctors.[26] In the same decade, the Association of Community Health Councils of England and Wales also strongly questioned the capacity of

21 Irvine, D., *The Doctors' Tale*, 2003, Radcliffe Medical Press, Oxford, 46.

22 Stacey, M., *Regulating British Medicine: the General Medical Council*, 1992, Wiley, Chichester, 23 and 83. Stacey also notes that the GMC has been unusual, compared with medical bodies in other countries, in involving even a small proportion of lay members.

23 Shaw, G.B., *Preface to the Doctor's Dilemma*, 1957, Penguin, London.

24 Both the radical right and the radical left opposed the principle of professional self-regulation. The right would replace this with lay control through the market, the left with a lay-controlled regulatory body. Stacey, M., *Regulating British Medicine: the General Medical Council*, 1992, Wiley, Chichester, 247.

25 See Stacey, M., *Regulating British Medicine: the General Medical Council*, 1992, Wiley, Chichester, 59—60..

26 Green, D., *Which Doctor? A Critical Analysis of the Professional Barriers to Competition in Health Care*, 1985, Institute of Economic Affairs, London. See also Stacey, M., *Regulating British Medicine: the General Medical Council*, 1992, Wiley, Chichester, 189–90.

self-regulatory bodies to provide appropriate control and safeguards. In 1988, the Association proposed an independent complaints investigation service. This would be lay-controlled but have access to medical expertise for advice.[27] None of these proposals was taken forward.

Other initiatives attempted to bring a lay voice into other aspects of medicine. For example, in the 1980s the Royal College of General Practitioners, as part of a *Quality Initiative,* established the 'Patients' Liaison Group' which was intended to bring a lay perspective into the central workings of the College. However, these and associated initiatives remained voluntary and so limited in their effect.[28]

In more recent years, lay member numbers on the GMC have increased. In 1996, the number was increased to 25 out of a 104-member Council, but still remained a small minority. Clearly such a minority presence is likely to inhibit the potential effectiveness and power of the lay voice. A lay member will need strong resolve, even courage, to speak out against the medical majority on issues sensitive to the profession. In her Fifth Shipman Inquiry Report, Dame Janet Smith called for a lay majority on the GMC and greater lay involvement in disciplinary hearings.

## GMC Lay Members – Who are They?

Prior to the 1978 Medical Act, the Privy Council customarily nominated two politicians and a lay member of a university to the lay posts on the GMC. The 1978 Medical Act changed the composition of the lay membership, although Irvine notes that in the early 1990s three of the lay members were still MPs.[29] The pattern has therefore tended to be of lay participants in the GMC process being drawn from the great and the good. Even in recent years, professionals from other walks of life, often closely associated with healthcare provision, are far more likely than other members of the public to be admitted to the process. This elitist approach was also reflected in members of GMC disciplinary committees. For instance, a (presumably typical) sitting of the Professional Proceedings Committee discussed in the case of *Richards*[30] consisted of five practising or retired medical members, including two general practitioners, two consultants and a former president of a Royal College. The one lay member, who chaired the committee, had 'extensive experience in NHS management'. This experience included a Non-Executive Directorship of the parent company of a medical deputizing service.[31] Unlike a lay jury or even a bench of magistrates, this approach brings no true lay or grass roots voice to the process. Stacey, during her time as a lay member of the GMC, recalls that she suggested that 'truly lay' members, those whose only experience of the medical process was as a patient, should be distinguished from lay members who have professional or

---

27 Stacey, M., *Regulating British Medicine: the General Medical Council*, 1992, Wiley, Chichester, 248.

28 See Irvine, D., *The Doctors' Tale*, 2003, Radcliffe Medical Press, Oxford, 70—71.

29 Irvine, D., *The Doctors' Tale*, 2003, Radcliffe Medical Press, Oxford, 92.

30 (2000) QBD, Lawtel transcript.

31 This information was provided in evidence to the Shipman Inquiry.

occupational links with the medical profession. She notes that this suggestion did not find favour.[32]

This attitude continued within the GMC as recently as 2001, with its self-review of governance and regulatory structures. The suggested starting requirement for members of the new Council and Board would include 'a demonstrable involvement or interest in healthcare issues' and the free time to cope with a demanding workload. It was also emphasized that healthcare managers and non-doctor healthcare professionals should have the opportunity to be active within the GMC as part of its lay component.[33] This latter point is not without merit; those who work alongside doctors can play an important role in their governance. However, what is problematic is the implication that these other occupational and professional groups should fill some of the limited number of lay places within the GMC. In this respect, the GMC has singularly failed to 'think out of the box' with respect to genuinely radical reform. Healthcare managers and other healthcare professionals worked alongside all of the doctors who were subjects of the scandals referred to in this book. The lack of early detection or other intervention was in part facilitated by inaction on their part. This evidence, of the risks associated with an unhealthy cosiness within the healthcare system, is such that lay participation within the governance and regulation of the medical profession should be wholly detached.

Whilst highly educated non-doctors bring confidence and expertise from other walks of professional life, they may lack a fundamental difference in vision. In essence the GMC is a club run by middle class professionals, even if some of these are non-medics. It has been observed in another context that as highly educated, highly paid professionals, doctors may be poorly placed to understand the reality of life for many patients, especially those who are old, non-working or living with long-term illness. These patients may not share doctors' implicit views about medicine.[34] Furthermore, doctors tend to encounter the lay public when they are vulnerable, as patients. Again, an unlikely setting to encounter challenging lay voices. The GMC has done little or nothing to bring these alternative voices into either the regulatory or the general GMC process. A similar critique has been applied to previous proposals to replace a medical-dominated GMC disciplinary process with one run by lawyers. In the strict sense of the word, lawyers would be a 'lay' force in this context, but nevertheless would bring the rarefied view of an alternative professional group.[35]

---

32 Stacey, M., *Regulating British Medicine: the General Medical Council*, 1992, Wiley, Chichester, 84. The position is not entirely clear cut as there is evidence from elsewhere that experts may dominate lay members of a panel. Confident lay members who are used to senior status may be better equipped to resist this. See Peay, J., 'Tribunals on Trial: a Study of Decision Making under the MHA 1983', cited by Davies, A.C.L., 'Don't Trust Me, I'm a Doctor – Medical Regulation and the 1999 NHS Reforms', *OJLS*, 2000, 20(3), 437–56, 453.

33 GMC, *Effective, Inclusive and Accountable Reform of the GMC's Structure, Constitution and Governance*, March 2001, 18.

34 Shaw, J., '"Expert Patient" – Dream or Nightmare?', *BMJ*, 2004, Vol. 328, 723–4, 27 March.

35 Stacey, M., *Regulating British Medicine: the General Medical Council*, 1992, Wiley, Chichester, 266.

Recent expansion of the disciplinary aspects of the GMC's work has seen a need to increase the number of lay participants available for fitness to practise panels. It is of note that advertised job specifications for these positions have emphasized the need for the appointees to be available for sufficient periods during the year, including in some cases block sittings of a week or more at a time.[36] This illustrates a clash of priorities. The GMC has identified the need to deal speedily with cases and has focused on recruiting lay members who have time. However, this is likely to be at the cost of diversity. The GMC's stated requirements are likely to favour the retired or others with time on their hands.[37] In terms of more radical thinking on the part of the GMC, consideration should be given to appointing lay participants on a basis which facilitates flexibility for the lay membership rather than for the GMC, in order to maximize diversity. Taking this a stage further, greater local sitting of FTPs, again facilitating flexibility for lay members, and also the doctor and witnesses, would be a step forwards.

## Alternative Lay Voices and Empowered Patients

In addition to formal lay involvement in the regulatory process, highly committed individuals who are victims or otherwise connected with particular cases of misconduct may come together to form pressure groups. Examples of this can be seen in the wake of the Bristol, Shipman and Ledward cases. Pressure groups of this type may be instrumental in both drawing attention to the particular misconduct and bringing pressure to bear on various instruments of regulation. They can also be instrumental in pushing for change aimed at preventing the recurrence of similar misconduct. However, lay voices of this type are by their very nature limited. They are necessarily reactive, usually to flaws in the systems which have gone unchanged for long periods. Once pressure groups have achieved their aims, they are also likely to dissipate, leaving the modified systems prone to falling back into similar patterns of complacency which allowed the original failings to arise.

Today's consumers of medical services have the potential to be more informed than ever before. The rise in popularity of medical books aimed at the lay reader, together with the internet and other media sources, provide ample scope for patients to investigate and even challenge what their doctors have to say. It has been argued that 'This change in the balance will result in a more adult relationship between patient and doctor, public and profession'.[38] The GMC has also stated the need for patients' views to be listened to and respected by their doctors. Respect includes acknowledging the patient's expertise when it comes to an appreciation of how the medical problem is affecting them. These sentiments have some merit when a

36 Initial requirements were a time commitment of up to 40 days per year to reduce the backlog of cases, reducing to 20 days annually thereafter.

37 Even though lay members are paid on a daily basis, with no guaranteed sitting period, it is unlikely that many potential applicants in full-time employment will be willing and able to make themselves available in the manner required by the GMC.

38 Irvine, D., *The Doctors' Tale*, 2003, Radcliffe Medical Press, Oxford, 202.

competent, considerate doctor treats her patient, but break down when the doctor is incompetent or intentionally sets out to do harm. When patients are feeling ill, let alone suffering from debilitating symptoms, their capacity to challenge doctors when it really matters is likely to be much reduced or even entirely absent. As Ingelfinger expressed the position whilst terminally ill:

> I do not want to be in the position of the shopper at the Casbah who negotiates and haggles with the physician about what is best. I want to believe that my physician is acting under a higher moral principle than a used car dealer. I'll go further than that. A physician who merely spreads an array of vendibles in front of his patient and then says 'Go ahead, you choose, it's your life' is guilty of shirking his duty, if not malpractice.[39]

It has also been argued from within the GMC that patient complaints are not necessarily a robust way of identifying poorly performing or poorly behaved doctors. 'Patients often accept the amiably incompetent and it does take colleagues and people who know about the system to identify such people.'[40] For example, very few complaints were made against Shipman during his murderous career. In the Bristol case, only two formal complaints were received during the period under investigation.[41]

Notwithstanding the limitations of complaints by patients, both Dame Janet Smith in the Shipman Inquiry and more recently the GMC have identified a willingness to learn from mistakes, including those which have given rise to patient complaints, as being of central importance to reflective medical practice. To this end, the GMC has acknowledged:

> [T]he need for regulation to develop a more creative approach to engaging with patients and the public so that regulation properly reflects the needs of those in whose interests it is intended to operate. Principles of good practice must continue to be developed, maintained and enforced in partnership with society as a whole. The GMC will strive to improve this partnership and make it more effective so that, increasingly, regulation becomes patient-led.[42]

One step in this direction was the requirement that doctors' revalidation[43] folders should include information to show that they have attempted to obtain the views of patients which have then been used to reflect upon their practice. Folders were also to contain information about any patient complaints during the revalidation period, along with an account of how complaints were responded to and subsequent modifications made to practice. Doctors who do not work within the NHS or other

---

39 Ingelfinger, F.G., 'Arrogance', 304 *New England Journal of Medicine*, 1980, 1507–11.

40 Sir Graeme Catto, 'The GMC – Revalidation – What Are We Trying to Measure?', *Medico-Legal Journal*, 2003, 71(106), 2 October.

41 The Bristol Report, para 248.

42 *Developing Medical Regulation: a Vision for the Future – the GMC's Response to the Call for Ideas by the Review of Clinical Performance and Medical Regulation*, April 2005.

43 Revalidation is discussed in greater detail later.

GMC-approved environment will be required to produce the results of validated questionnaires which show that neither patients nor colleagues have identified any concerns about their practice.[44] However, these responses are rather limited in scope in terms of ensuring rigorous patient and other lay oversight of the GMC regulatory process.

## The Wider Perspective – Reporting of Disciplinary Cases

Public access to and the reporting of judicial proceedings have been seen as important to the proper administration of justice. The media are 'the eyes and ears of the general public'.[45] This approach has not always found favour in the context of GMC disciplinary proceedings. The GMC itself excluded the press and public during the very early years of its history. In the 1970s, the Merrison Committee heard arguments that extensive publicity would deter potential complainants to the GMC. It might also cause distress to witnesses who, at the extreme, may even refuse to give evidence as a result.[46] However, for many years GMC disciplinary proceedings were well reported, at least within the specialist medical press. Prior to the 1970s, both the *British Medical Journal* and the *Lancet* regularly reported, in significant detail, GMC disciplinary decisions.[47] More recently, these professional journals have been far more selective, tending to report only matters towards the higher end of the scale of seriousness, or which otherwise are seen as newsworthy. This is also the situation with the wider local and national press, which tend only to report the particularly newsworthy high profile cases or those with specific local relevance.[48] This has important implications. Not only are the public poorly informed about the day-to-day operation of the self-regulatory process, but members of the profession also have a limited picture of the work of the GMC and the types of behaviour which give rise to disciplinary proceedings. The Shipman Inquiry found that the public were of the opinion that some doctors who are incompetent or inappropriately behaved have been allowed to remain in practice by the 'powers that be'. Patients need to know that the doctor treating them does not fall into this category. They want to know if their doctor has been subject to criminal or regulatory sanctions. Such information is routinely available in other jurisdictions, for instance the US

---

44 See *Developing Medical Regulation: a Vision for the Future – the GMC's Response to the Call for Ideas by the Review of Clinical Performance and Medical Regulation*, April 2005, para 65.

45 *AG v The Observer Ltd* (1988) Times 11 February.

46 For further discussion, see Smith R.G., 'Reporting Medical Disciplinary Proceedings', *Media Law and Practice*, 1991, Vol. 12, Part 4, 110–14.

47 Stacey, M., *Regulating British Medicine: the General Medical Council*, 1992, Wiley, Chichester, 35.

48 For example, between March 1987 and June 1987 under 30 per cent of GMC proceedings were reported in *The Guardian* or *The Times*. Those cases which were reported were the more newsworthy ones, typically involving matters such as sexual misconduct, rather than representing a representative cross section of cases. See Smith R.G., 'Reporting Medical Disciplinary Proceedings', *Media Law and Practice*, 1991, Vol. 12, Part 4, 110–14.

and Canada. Even though some doctors complain about the loss of privacy and the potential for rehabilitation, Dame Janet Smith's view was that doctors should be expected to demonstrate that they have nothing in their past which might call into question the trust patients place in them.[49]

Whilst the GMC may legitimately argue that it cannot dictate the extent to which its activities are reported, a possible solution is offered by the rise of the internet. The GMC recently began including reports of disciplinary hearings on its website.[50] The opportunity exists, if the GMC has the willingness to grasp it, to create an open database which the public and profession alike could search for wide-ranging information about disciplinary decisions. Such a database would, ideally, have sophisticated search and cross-referencing facilities, for example, on the basis of name, part of a name, locality and the type of misconduct.[51] Prior to July 2005, doctors who were suspended from the register, or who were subject to conditional registration or undertakings, were not included in the online search. From July 2005, this was changed, for conditions or undertakings (both current and, in time, those relating to past behaviour) other than those relating to a doctor's health. The giving of a formal warning under the post-November 2004 reformed fitness to practise procedures will also be included as part of a search.[52] At the time of writing, the GMC's development of online searchable databases which are genuinely intuitive and user friendly still had some way to go. For example, my own attempts to use the system for what should have been the relatively simple task of identifying whether a particular name was on the medical register was often far from straightforward. Rigorous testing of the system by the GMC, utilizing a cross section of the likely user population, should allow such problems to be resolved.

Historically, even dissemination of information within the GMC has been limited. Both Robinson and Stacey, as past lay members of the GMC, expressed frustration at obstacles placed in their way. One important example was the withdrawal of PCC transcripts relating to previous hearings, and no transcribing of cases where the doctor was found not guilty.[53] This type of approach has negative implications in terms of learning and developing expertise from previous cases, and for consistency. In the 1970s, the Merrison Committee had recognized the potential value of a body of case law as preferable to rigid codes as a means of educating doctors about behaviour which might result in disciplinary sanctions.[54] Such an

49 The Fifth Report of the Shipman Inquiry, *Safeguarding Patients: Lessons from the Past – Proposals for the Future*, para 1.21 (www.the-shipman-inquiry.org.uk).

50 At the time of writing, this was found at http://www.gmc-uk.org/register/.

51 Legal databases such as Lawtel, Lexis and Westlaw provide useful models of the types of search sophistication which could be aimed for, although the task facing the GMC would be on a much smaller scale.

52 See GMC Online Update, July 2005.

53 See Robinson, J., *A Patient Voice at the GMC: a Lay Member's View of the GMC*, Report 1, Health Rights, London; and Stacey, M., *Regulating British Medicine: the General Medical Council*, 1992, Wiley, Chichester, 196. Robinson describes her work on the PCC as, in the end, merely an instrument for the occasional ritual sacrifice.

54 For further discussion, see Stacey, M., *Regulating British Medicine: the General Medical Council*, 1992, Wiley, Chichester, 57.

approach would also inform both medical and lay members of GMC regulatory panels. The GMC has resisted such moves.

## Lay Participation within the NHS

The Bristol Inquiry Report identified the need for public involvement in all aspects of NHS services, if they are to be truly patient-centred. Public involvement must be embedded in the NHS structures, and the views of patients and the public sought and considered whenever decisions affecting the provision of healthcare are made.[55] In particular, they should be involved in processes 'designed to secure the competence of healthcare professionals', in particular the setting of standards for education, training and continuing professional development. Lay participants should be drawn from a wide range of individuals and groups, and be trained and funded to facilitate full participation in the process.[56] Historically, the technical expertise of clinicians has prevailed, with an associated tendency for the patient to become objectified, 'merely' an ill body to be cured.[57] In contrast, Kennedy envisioned the provision of quality care as being dependent upon the development of relationships between professional and patient, based upon honesty, openness and mutual respect. The government, in its response to Bristol, noted the importance of changing the culture within the NHS to facilitate public involvement.[58] The government, in its *NHS Plan*, also acknowledged the need for greater public participation and proposed that all NHS Trusts and Primary Care Trusts in England should have a Patient Advocacy and Liaison Service.[59] The NHS Reform and Health Care Professions Act 2002 provided for the establishment of the Commission for Patient and Public Involvement in Health. The Act also made provision for the creation of Patients' Forums to promote the interests of patients and to represent them to NHS and Primary Care Trusts.[60]

---

55 'Report of the Public Inquiry into Children's Heart Surgery at the Bristol Royal Infirmary 1984–1995', Learning from Bristol, CM5207(I ), July 2001, Recommendations 157 and 105.

56 *BRI Inquiry Final Report Summary*, paras 98–102.

57 The debate within the medical profession about technical skill versus the interpersonal and human elements of practice is ongoing. An illustrative example is provided in the moves by some medical schools to replace the dissection of cadavers as a means of teaching anatomy with techniques involving medical-imaging technology using live subjects and sophisticated mannequins. There are various practical reasons for these moves, but proponents also point out that requiring medical students to dissect cadavers early in their careers can be emotionally challenging and sets the scene for the objectification of patients. For further discussion, see Sander, C., 'Why Low Body Count is Fatal for Anatomy', *The Times Higher*, 6 June 2003, 11.

58 *Learning from Bristol: The DH Response to the Report of the Public Inquiry into Children's Heart Surgery at the Bristol Royal Infirmary 1984-1995*, para 9.2.

59 Department of Health, *The NHS Plan: A Plan for Investment, A Plan for Reform*, Cm 4818-I, July 2000, Chapter 10, para 17.

60 National Health Service Reform and Health Care Professions Act 2002, sections 15 and 20.

## Conclusions

Appropriate lay input into the self-regulatory process should provide an important check both on the power of doctors and the risk that those involved in regulation will become detached from public sentiment. The history of lay involvement in the GMC demonstrates the continued insistence on a minority input, often with further obstacles placed in the way of lay members who wish to challenge entrenched values. Some lay participants, notably Robinson and Stacey, have sought to challenge the GMC from within and subsequently written about their experiences. However, both have acknowledged that even their willingness to vocally challenge outdated or otherwise inappropriate practices met with limited success against the influential medical interest groups on the Council. Other lay participants, however, have had close background experience with medical practice and may have experienced difficulties bringing a genuinely fresh view to the process. More recent attempts to expand lay input into all aspects of NHS provision are welcome, but are unlikely to provide more than an additional viewpoint into debates about aspects of healthcare provision. These developments should not detract from the importance of a strong, dominant, independent lay voice within the GMC to meet the needs of modern consumers of healthcare.

Chapter 15

# Self-Regulation in a 'No Fault' Culture

## Introduction

The procedures for accident reporting within medicine have developed largely within a confidential environment, where openness with the patient has been discouraged.[1] The fault-based approach has been described as reactive to those who make complaints and then seeking to individualize blame by finding an individual to pin it upon. This model disadvantages the complainant by limiting the scope of legitimate complaints to those issues where an individual, rather than the organization, can be shown to be at fault. In addition, because individual reputations and livelihoods are at stake, a fault-based system inevitably adopts a lengthy and expensive investigatory process.[2] 'Disasters' in medical practice tend to evolve rather than simply occur. A series of failures coincide to create a disaster and the doctor is usually just part of the chain of events.[3] Errors are described as an 'inevitable concomitant of the powerful cognitive processes that have permitted us to extend the limits of human achievement'.[4] Gawande recounts a number of examples of mistakes confided to him by respected surgeons:

> Consider some other surgical mishaps. In one, a general surgeon left a large metal instrument in a patient's abdomen, where it tore through the bowel and the wall of the bladder…A cardiac surgeon skipped a small but key step during a heart valve operation, thereby killing the patient. A general surgeon saw a man racked with abdominal pain in the emergency room and, without taking a CT scan, assumed that the man had a kidney stone; eighteen hours later, a scan showed a rupturing abdominal aortic aneurysm, and the patient died not long afterward.
>
> …all doctors make terrible mistakes. Consider the cases I've just described. I gathered them simply by asking respected surgeons I know – surgeons at top medical schools – to tell me about mistakes they had made just in the past year.[5]

---

1 See, for example, *The Ledward Report*, Part III, para 2.4.

2 Mulcahy, L., *Disputing Doctors*, 2003, Open University Press, Maidenhead, 75.

3 Gawande, A., *Complications*, 2003, Profile Books, London, 64.

4 Merry, A. and McCall Smith, A., *Errors, Medicine and the Law*, 2001, Cambridge University Press, Cambridge, 41, building upon the idea of a 'normal accident' discussed in Perrow, C., *Normal Accidents: Living with High Risk Technologies*, 1984, Basic Books, New York.

5 Gawande, A., *Complications*, 2003, Profile Books, London, 55–6.

From this point of view, the important question is not how to prevent bad doctors from harming patients but how to prevent the good doctors from doing so.[6] However, ideas from cognitive science, which seek to explain the processes which precede many errors, have yet to find favour within legal processes.[7]

'Negotiated compliance' is seen by some commentators as the most appropriate approach to professional regulation. Regulators should seek to ensure compliance by means of close collaboration with the regulated, reason and persuasion being the primary mechanism, with sanctions held in reserve only as a very last resort. A regulator who ignores this strategy risks losing the cooperation of the regulated who, in turn, may cheat or simply attempt to ignore the regulatory framework. Ratcheting up the sanctions in such circumstances may serve only to encourage more creative methods of cheating or circumventing the regulatory structure. Offering education rather than punishment, it is said, increases the likelihood of cooperation and compliance, although not all members of the profession will necessarily make the distinction.[8]

In recent years, there have been increasing calls, from within academic circles and elsewhere, for moves towards a no blame culture. Merry and McCall Smith, for example, argue that 'life in a blame obsessed system will be very different from life in a supportive and appropriately forgiving system'. Advances in the understanding of error and the complexity of 'blame' have not been adequately reflected in the response of the law and regulatory process. A continued emphasis on individual accountability, the search for a scapegoat, is inappropriate, with much of importance being missed by focusing all attention on the person holding the 'smoking gun'.[9] From this perspective, a system of regulation based on deterrence – identifying and punishing wrongdoing – is seen as inevitably prescriptive, rule-bound and reactive. Furthermore, such an approach tends to foster mistrust on the part of those being regulated. As the GMC has expressed it: 'individuals may have an incentive to do things right, but they will not necessarily be encouraged to do the right thing'.[10]

In similar vein, Berwick suggests that the majority of committed competent professionals need to be encouraged to improve, rather than being threatened with sanctions. Attempts to control rather than 'respect, trust, and inspire' will result in strained relationships, encourage underperformance and even sabotage.[11] A blame culture may also be of very limited use in aiding understanding of the complex

6 Gawande, A., *Complications*, 2003, Profile Books, London, 56–7.

7 Merry, A. and McCall Smith, A., *Errors, Medicine and the Law*, 2001, Cambridge University Press, Cambridge, 41, building upon the idea of a 'normal accident' discussed in Perrow, C., *Normal Accidents: Living with High Risk Technologies*, 1984, Basic Books, New York.

8 For further discussion, see Davies, A.C.L., 'Don't Trust Me, I'm a Doctor – Medical Regulation and the 1999 NHS Reforms', *OJLS*, 2000, 20(437).

9 Merry, A. and McCall Smith, A., *Errors, Medicine and the Law*, 2001, Cambridge University Press, Cambridge, 2.

10 *Developing Medical Regulation: a Vision for the Future – the GMC's Response to the Call for Ideas by the Review of Clinical Performance and Medical Regulation*, April 2005.

11 See Solomon, R.C. and Flores, F., *Building Trust*, 2001, Oxford University Press, Oxford, 29.

multi-faceted causes of many medical mishaps or in identifying appropriate remedial measures.[12] Advocates of a no blame approach have a strong preference for education and continuous improvement. This they see as far more effective than an attempt to improve behaviour through disciplinary measures.[13]

As part of the no fault debate, Merry and McCall Smith draw a distinction between deliberate wrongdoing and non-deliberate harm – the contrast between violations and errors. The latter are rarely intentional, whereas the former relate to deliberate deviations from accepted rules, norms or principles. The key difference between the two is choice. In making this distinction, five levels of blame emerge:

1. Pure causal blame, where the actor has behaved entirely reasonably
2. Errors with no moral culpability, but the actor has fallen below the expected standard of behaviour
3. Prior awareness that behaviour fell short of what could be expected
4. Recklessness
5. Deliberate wrongdoing[14]

An example of item 1 would be a patient's unforeseeable reaction to a drug. Item 2 can be illustrated by the example of a doctor making a momentary lapse leading to a drug administration error. An example of recklessness would be the behaviour of those surgeons at Bristol who carried on operating after they became aware of their failures and the risks present.[15] Shipman would be a classic example of level five.

The analogy is drawn with corporate wrongdoing. An individual actor may have done wrong, but to fully understand the position, the wider picture must be considered. Is, for instance, the actor under pressure to meet targets or otherwise to perform? The Bristol Inquiry emphasized that a culture of blame is no substitute for clear systems of responsibility and accountability.[16]

Proponents of a no fault approach often begin by noting the contrast between the inclination to find someone to blame when a medical mishap occurs and research findings which suggest that the majority of such mishaps are caused by systems failures.[17] Vilifying individual doctors will encourage concealment of errors, and therefore restricts exploration of the causes of such errors.[18] Systems can be devised

12 For further discussion, see, for example, Vincent, C., *Medical Accidents*, 1993, Oxford Medical Publications, Oxford.

13 Berwick, D.M., 'Continuous Improvement as an Ideal in Health Care', *New England Journal of Medicine*, 1989, 320, 1, 53–6; see also Becher, T., *Professional Practices*, 1999, Transaction Publishers, New Brunswick, New Jersey, 217–18. See also Phillips, A.F., *Medical Negligence Law: Seeking a Balance*, 1997, Dartmouth, Aldershot.

14 Merry, A. and McCall Smith, A., *Errors, Medicine and the Law*, 2001, Cambridge University Press, Cambridge, 242–5.

15 Merry, A. and McCall Smith, A., *Errors, Medicine and the Law*, 2001, Cambridge University Press, Cambridge, 149.

16 Kennedy, I.M., *The Inquiry into the Management of Care of Children Receiving Complex Heart Surgery at The Bristol Royal Infirmary*, section 2, Recommendations, at 435. (www.bristol-inquiry.org.uk).

17 See, for example, Mulcahy, L., *Disputing Doctors*, 2003, Open University Press, Maidenhead, 16.

18 See, for example, Tallis, R., *Hippocratic Oaths*, 2004, Atlantic, London, 172.

which should significantly reduce human error, for instance, computer-based approaches which prevent inappropriate drug dosages appearing on prescriptions.[19]

Kennedy considers that both patients and health professionals need to be 'more grown up about errors and mistakes'. Accountability is not the same as blame, the latter being 'a serendipitous weapon used to pillory someone who happens to be caught in its sights'.[20] From within the medical profession, objection is taken to the presumption that only 'complaints, threats and menaces' can ensure improvements in standards.[21] The Bristol Inquiry Report concludes that the culture of blame is a major barrier to the openness required if untoward events – 'sentinel events' – are to be reported and lessons drawn from them. Mechanisms to encourage the reporting of sentinel events should be implemented, providing immunity from disciplinary action if a report is made within a specified period. Failure to comply with reporting requirements could result in disciplinary action.

Tallis argues that increases in the blame culture within medicine have actually coincided with significant increases in performance by doctors:

> In short, blame becomes prevalent as surgeons become less and less blameworthy. Tolerance of error by those who take responsibility for other people's lives is approaching zero.
>
> ...The almost miraculous work of today's paediatric cardiac surgeons in deftly correcting errors in hearts the size of acorns in tiny babies...is less appreciated than that of the butchers of the past, who hacked crudely at their unanaesthetized patients with commonly disastrous results. The occasional tragic death nowadays of a patient from a routine operation is seen as a greater scandal than the routine death of patients from pretty well all but the simplest operation in the past. Success redefines what counts as failure: today's miracle cure is tomorrow's routine treatment.[22]

It is also argued that insufficient account is taken of the very low proportion of errors arising from the millions of doctor–patient interactions each year. For instance, Tallis is concerned that a consultant was found guilty of serious professional misconduct by the GMC, following the removal of the wrong kidney during surgery. Subsequent investigation revealed that three incorrect kidneys had been removed over a ten-year period, from a total of around 75,000 operations in the same period. An error rate of 1 in 25,000, it is argued, did not justify the extensive media coverage the case generated.[23] Of course, an equally logical explanation for improved performance alongside increasing blame is that a blame culture works, to a degree at least.

The government has also been persuaded of the benefits of a no fault approach in some circumstances. *The NHS Plan, A Plan for Investment, a Plan for Reform*, published in July 2000, considered ways in which the system for dealing with clinical negligence claims might be improved. The existing system was said to be, inter alia,

---

19 See, for other examples, Gawande, A., *Complications*, 2003, Profile Books, London.
20 Cited by Tallis, R., *Hippocratic Oaths*, 2004, Atlantic, London, 166–7.
21 Tallis, R., *Hippocratic Oaths*, 2004, Atlantic, London, 172.
22 Tallis, R., *Hippocratic Oaths*, 2004, Atlantic, London, 167–8 and 174.
23 Tallis, R., *Hippocratic Oaths*, 2004, Atlantic, London, 169–70.

complex, unfair, slow, costly and damaging to the morale of medical staff. It also encouraged defensiveness and secrecy in the NHS, which in turn was an obstacle to learning from mistakes. Following this, in his *Making Amends* paper of June 2003, the Chief Medical Officer recommended a move towards a no fault approach in certain situations. These recommendations were taken forwards by the NHS Redress Bill 2006. The Bill proposed the introduction of an NHS Redress Scheme, to allow for the resolution of certain claims without the need for court action. The scheme would cater for investigations, remedial treatment, care and rehabilitation, explanations and apologies, and potentially financial compensation.

## Distinctions between Misconduct and Error

Bosk makes the distinction between technical errors and moral failures. Technical errors involve the incorrect application of the professional body of knowledge, whilst moral errors involve the failure to follow professional codes of conduct. A technical error involves conscientious performance on the part of the doctor, but in the circumstances his or her skills fall short of those necessary. During the course of a career, all doctors are likely to experience technical errors, although the occurrence should be rare. To remain technical, the error must be reported speedily within the professional environment. Traditionally, moral errors have given rise to greater regulatory efforts.[24] Formal and informal responses to the different types of error tend to differ significantly. Restitutive sanctions – the error providing an opportunity to learn – are often seen as being the most appropriate response to technical errors, whilst repressive sanctions are more likely to result from moral errors. Within the medical community, senior colleagues usually 'support' those who make technical errors but 'degrade' those who make moral ones.[25] One justification for prioritzsing the control of moral errors stems from the uncertainty of much medical practice – doctors frequently cannot guarantee success. The best assurance they can give is to do their best. In this environment, it is essential that there is no doubt about the doctor's motivation. As Bosk puts it:

> It is not the patient dying but the patient dying when the doctor on call fails to answer his pager that makes it impossible to sustain a case of acting in the patient's interest…Moral error breaches a professional's contract with his client. He has not acted in good faith.[26]

In this respect, moral errors undercut the core of the doctor–patient relationship. Moral standards should be the organizing principle of the medical community. Without an overarching moral system, the technical system is not amenable to

24 Bosk, C.L., 'Forgive and Remember: Managing Medical Failure', in Dowie, J. and Elstein, A., *Professional Judgment*, 1988, Cambridge University Press, Cambridge, 522–3.

25 Bosk, C.L., 'Forgive and Remember: Managing Medical Failure', in Dowie, J. and Elstein, A., *Professional Judgment*, 1988, Cambridge University Press, Cambridge, 525 and 529.

26 Bosk, C.L., 'Forgive and Remember: Managing Medical Failure', in Dowie, J. and Elstein, A., *Professional Judgment*, 1988, Cambridge University Press, Cambridge, 525–6.

control.[27] This latter point is of particular importance. Potential problems with a no fault approach are discussed below, but even if these are overcome with respect to technical errors, the need for a robust regulatory system to deal with moral errors will remain.

Forgiveness of technical errors and punishment for moral errors can both be used as mechanisms for control. Forgiveness of technical errors places on the subordinate who is forgiven an obligation to his or her superiors, as well as the expectation that he or she will take greater care in future. Self-criticism, confession and forgiveness all allow a technical offender to re-enter the professional group, thus enhancing group cohesion.[28] The problem with this approach is that it applies only to superordinates discovering breaches of subordinates. Superordinates do not seek to identify breaches by each other. The principle that senior doctors do not interfere in each other's work is firmly embedded in medical culture:

> Just as it is inappropriate for parents to meddle in the lives of their grown children, surgeons view meddling in inappropriate surveillance of the performance of those released from training…The corporate responsibility of the profession is not seen to extend beyond raising one generation of surgeons after another from professional infancy to professional adulthood…A complete professional self is one that has earned the right to organise its work in a manner that it sees fit.[29]

As discussed elsewhere in this work, there is little evidence to suggest that this prevailing culture has changed significantly since Bosk was writing in 1988. It is this culture which remains one of the principal obstacles to the effective implementation of regulatory reform.

In the recent case of *Gregg v Scott*[30] Baroness Hale reiterated the longstanding principle that one of the objects of the law of negligence is to maintain proper standards in a range of situations, including professional conduct. If a professional person has taken less care than she or he should have taken, then damages become payable. Citing Lord Hope in *Chester v Afshar*: 'The function of the law is to enable rights to be vindicated and to provide remedies when duties have been breached.'[31] However, it is also recognized that doctors and other healthcare professionals are not solely, or even mainly, motivated by the fear of legal consequences. Rather, most are motivated by a desire and a professional duty to do their best for patients. This latter point regarding 'professional duty' is of particular relevance to the current discussion. Even if a no fault system were to be introduced to replace the current fault-based approach in negligence, the 'professional duty' suggested as a key motivator for ensuring appropriate behaviour by doctors would need to be maintained, through

---

27 Bosk, C.L., 'Forgive and Remember: Managing Medical Failure', in Dowie, J. and Elstein, A., *Professional Judgment*, 1988, Cambridge University Press, Cambridge, 527.

28 Bosk, C.L., 'Forgive and Remember: Managing Medical Failure', in Dowie, J. and Elstein, A., *Professional Judgment*, 1988, Cambridge University Press, Cambridge, 532.

29 Bosk, C.L., 'Forgive and Remember: Managing Medical Failure', in Dowie, J. and Elstein, A., *Professional Judgment*, 1988, Cambridge University Press, Cambridge, 535–7.

30 [2005] UKHL 2, paras 216–17.

31 [2005] 1 AC 134, [2004] 4 All ER 587, Para 87.

the mechanism of the GMC. Indeed, the role of self-regulation becomes even more important if the deterrent effect (however minor) of a fault-based negligence system were to be lost.

Proponents of an enhanced no fault culture within medicine often cite in support trends within the aviation industry, which has long utilized no fault reporting of adverse incidents. Airlines, it is said, have significantly improved their safety records by developing open and fair cultures, standardizing approaches and constantly reviewing incidents and making changes as a result. Engineering equipment to minimize the effect of human error, coupled with crisis simulation, has been used to reduce the incidence of untoward events. Staff are also trained in such a way that they should have confidence to speak out, allowing for open rather than confidential reporting systems.[32] Such a culture does have its merits in offering a means for encouraging disclosure of sensitive information. However, aviation and medicine differ in many respects. Not least, those in the front line in aviation, pilots and aircrew, have a vested interest in ensuring that safety systems and mechanisms for learning from adverse incidents are as effective as possible. Failures in this regard place pilots and aircrew in as much danger as the passengers under their charge.

Doctors, in contrast, have far more complex motives when interpreting and taking risks. These may include the search for self-advancement – being the first to perfect a new technique – which may require patient guinea pigs. The doctor may delude him/herself into the belief that his/her actions are in the patient's and society's best interests and hence a subsequent death is not actually an 'adverse' outcome. This is reflected in the mentality underlying the Bristol case. Bristol was also unusual in reaching the public stage. A serious aviation accident is inevitably a public event, whilst problems in the medical field are far less likely to come to public notice. For example, the Institute of Medicine has estimated that 44,000–98,000 patients are killed every year in US hospitals by preventable medical errors and misadventure[33] (roughly equivalent to 90–180 large plane crashes each year), yet figures of this magnitude rarely seem to enter the public consciousness. Research from the UK found that, on average, 2.2 per cent of all treatment episodes (276,000 per year) included an adverse event.[34] Whilst this was an average, some Trusts reported figures as high as 15 per cent and others none. The latter, accident-free, zones have been described as 'too miraculous to be credible'.[35] Similarly, society would not accept 'test' flights being undertaken as part of normal commercial aviation. This is not a criticism of medical practice; it is difficult to conceive an alternative system other than eventually using new techniques on patients. However, what can be criticized

---

32 See National Audit Office, *A Safer Place for Patients: Learning to Improve Patient Safety*, 31 October 2005, page 64, www.nao.org.uk; and Gawande, A., *Complications*, 2003, Profile Books, London, 66–8.

33 Gigerenzer, G., *Reckoning with Risk*, 2002, Penguin, London, 17.

34 See 'Doctor Foster's Case Notes', *British Medical Journal*, 2004, 369, 14 August (electronic edition). See also Woolcock, N. and Henderson, M., 'Blundering Hospitals are "Killing 40,000 Patients a Year"', *The Times*, 13 August 2004, 1. Figures from an earlier period are discussed in Phillips, A.F., *Medical Negligence Law: Seeking a Balance*, 1997, Dartmouth, Aldershot, 170.

35 'Deadly Mistakes', *The Times*, 13 August 2004, 25.

is the misleading of patients (as at Bristol) and the assumption that individual practitioners are capable of honestly and consciously assessing their own risk. External monitoring remains vital[36]

## Problems with 'No Fault' Reasoning

The difficulty with the reasoning put forward by commentators such as Tallis is that it can be applied to any area which is subject to advances in practice. The aviation industry, for instance, has advanced such that safety risks which were the norm a few decades ago are unacceptable today. Even the solicitors' profession, not traditionally closely associated with technological advances, is expected to adapt its practices to meet those advances which do apply to it. In an age of near instantaneous communication, a solicitor could no longer convincingly argue that speed of practice suitable to the age of the quill pen was acceptable; similarly, that in 74,997 procedures when the correct kidney is operated upon, suggest that in the three where this did not occur there is legitimate, and possibly serious, cause for concern. A rebuttal may also be addressed to the argument that the excessive expansion of the blame culture accounts for the increase in numbers of prosecutions against doctors for gross negligence manslaughter since the 1970s.[37] Rather than reflecting inappropriate blame, this increase may simply be attributable to greater societal willingness to test and challenge the actions of doctors using the rigorous legal mechanisms applicable to society as a whole. Doctors are entrusted with power which, if misused, is likely to have devastating consequences. Society rightly demands that such holders of power should be subject to full legal scrutiny. A comparator is the distinction between driving which is 'merely' negligent, and that which crosses into the criminal law to be classed as careless or dangerous. Society acknowledges that sufficiently serious lapses on the part of those who choose to drive motor vehicles can result in criminal sanctions, including imprisonment. As with doctors, the vast majority of motorists whose lapses cause harm to others bear no ill intent. The systemic arguments of the no fault proponents may even be applied – the accident could have been avoided, or at least the damage reduced, if better road safety systems had been in place or if the maximum speed capability of all cars was limited. However, in the absence of perfect safety systems, the law places responsibility on the individual – if I choose to drive, I am ultimately required to accept responsibility for the safety of others. Viewed in this comparative way, the protestations of doctors reduce in persuasiveness and begin to sound like yet more calls for special, privileged status.

Inappropriate blame may be undesirable, but the risk of blame, especially where failure has a significant, even irreversible, outcome, provides incentives to take

36 For further discussion regarding issues of monitoring and risk, see Gigerenzer, G., *Reckoning with Risk*, 2002, Penguin, London, chapter 2.

37 Tallis, R., *Hippocratic Oaths*, 2004, Atlantic, London, 170. Some of the increase from the early part of this period may be attributed to changes in the judicial definition of manslaughter. However, such explanation does not fit the alleged continuing rate of increase from the 1990s into the 2000s.

greater care. For instance, as an academic undertaking a simple task such as entering examination marks into a mark grid, there is a risk that I may become complacent or careless. However, such complacency can have significant consequences – a wrongly entered mark could have a disastrous impact upon a student's degree classification. Following the proponents of no blame, a better solution than apportioning blame would be to devise systems which minimize or remove the risk. However, without the risk of blame, who will devise such systems? By knowing that I have responsibility and risk blame, I have an incentive to take steps or push for changes or to implement them into my working practices. An effective blame culture should hardly ever need to be used, because empowered professionals anticipate risk and act to reduce it, motivated, at least in part, by self-preservation. The problems Kennedy et al should address are not actually with a blame culture per se, but with a blame culture which operates poorly. Not all within the medical profession favour a move away from a blame culture. For instance, Irvine cautions against a move too far in the direction of placing responsibility on systems and taking blame away from individuals. 'I think the term "no blame" is actually unhelpful. It can become so easily associated with the abrogation of responsibility.' Ultimately, systems are devised and run by individuals and where these individuals are doctors, they should expect to be individually accountable.[38]

One of the difficulties with the Merry and McCall Smith approach is that it tends towards excessive sympathy for the medical establishment. For instance, in questioning the criticism directed at the GMC following the Shipman case, they suggest that it will be 'extremely difficult to identify the homicidal practitioner'.[39] As is discussed elsewhere in this work, Shipman was a mass murderer who made numerous, clumsy errors. A self-regulatory process with an adequate system of monitoring should have detected him reasonably promptly. There is also the significant hurdle to overcome of a closed culture from within the profession itself. Irvine, for example, describes the medical profession as demonstrating 'tribal characteristics'. These derive from the intensive training undertaken by medical students and the intense socialization imbued by senior members of the profession. Part of this socialization includes the reinforcement of a culture of self-protection in which the group defends transgressors against external criticism, unless the professional group itself acknowledges the particular behaviour as unacceptable. The latter, it is suggested, occurs infrequently and only in exceptional circumstances. This professional culture does not encourage admission of error, nor are apologies the norm.[40]

It has also been suggested that doctors are treated unfairly compared with other professions. Advocates of a no blame approach point to the apparent inequity in treating doctors differently, when their culpability in making an error is the same as that of other professions.[41] However, this situation is not unusual in English law. The

38 Irvine, D., *The Doctors' Tale*, 2003, Radcliffe Medical Press, Oxford, 135.

39 Merry, A. and McCall Smith, A., *Errors, Medicine and the Law*, 2001, Cambridge University Press, Cambridge, 234.

40 Irvine, D., *The Doctors' Tale*, 2003, Radcliffe Medical Press, Oxford, 24–5.

41 See, for example, Mulcahy, L., *Disputing Doctors*, 2003, Open University Press, Maidenhead, 146.

driver of a car who drives dangerously faces a harsher penalty if someone happens to be killed as a result. A hunter who fires his gun without care is likely to face far greater legal consequences if someone is hit and killed, than if the bullet lands harmlessly. Some professions, such as medicine, bear greater risk of causing serious irreversible damage. Because of this, society is entitled to expect greater levels of care and to seek harsher penalties if the requisite standards are not met. In return, the medical profession might legitimately seek to retain the privilege, respect and financial rewards it has negotiated from society. What is unacceptable is the retention of privilege, power and high reward without the associated responsibility.

## Appropriate Blame rather than No Blame

Two examples cited by Hammond and Mosley can be used to draw the distinction between no blame and appropriate blame. The first example involves one of the authors, who recounts an occasion during his final year as a medical student when he agreed to fill in as a locum for a house officer:

> I bluffed my way through a night on call until…I was called to re-site a drip. The more senior doctors were in bed and I was too frightened to wake anyone. So I experimented with the drip and, thinking I'd got it in the vein, flushed it through with saline. The patient screamed…I'd injected potassium, which came in an identical bottle to the saline; at five in the morning in a dim light it was an easy mistake to make. Had the drip been properly in the vein, the patient would have had a cardiac arrest. Fortunately, it wasn't and she suffered a swollen, painful hand instead. I apologised and lied, telling her she must be allergic to saline.

The second example involved another student filling in for a house officer. During a very busy period he was left alone with a man who suffered a burst aortic aneurysm. The student made heroic resuscitation attempts but forgot to put in an airway. The patient vomited, aspirated into his lungs and died.[42]

How does 'no blame' apply here? In both examples, few would want the unfortunate medical students punished – both were doing their best in circumstances beyond their control and capability. But what about the broader implications in these examples of medical students being allowed to occupy positions beyond their competence. If no one is personally responsible for adverse outcomes in circumstances such as these, will lessons really be learned and appropriately acted upon? There must remain a serious temptation to continue to allow junior staff to stand in for more senior colleagues, if those senior members of the profession benefit from the practice and face no disciplinary consequences. Concerns about the inappropriate application of systems failure were also voiced to the Kerr/Haslam Inquiry by counsel for some of the patients:

> 'System failure' is a relatively modern expression…But, and I speak here on behalf of all the patients – I would not wish for the focus of blame to be shifted from those individuals

42 Hammond, P. and Mosley, M., *Trust Me I'm A Doctor*, 2002, Metro Publishing, London, 17.

on to a system where it is truly the fault of the individuals that this conduct continued unabated.

That doctors who knew of the reputations of Kerr and/or Haslam and nevertheless took no action and continued to refer patients to them:

> Those, for the main part, we do not say are system failures, they are personality failures which can be righted or corrected, if attention is paid in the first place to instruction and to awareness in the medical community of the burden that necessarily flows from administering health care…the system could have worked if individual doctors, GPs, had taken extra steps.[43]

## Professional Attitudes and Motivation

One line of reasoning used to support the argument against blame is that doctors by and large enter the profession to help patients rather than to further their own selfish interests. From this perspective, doctors are their own greatest critics and can be trusted – if given the appropriate supportive environment – to learn from their own and others' mistakes, and move forwards in the best interests of society.[44] This is a rather one-dimensional viewpoint. No doubt most doctors do have the best interests of patients as one of the central commitments. However, it is naïve to assume that they do not also have selfish motives. Recent moves by GPs to negotiate contractual arrangements which increase earnings, whilst simultaneously reducing obligations to provide support to patients out of normal working hours, is one example. That GPs, in some regions at least, are willing to see their patients deprived of effective out of hours care, unless they can make the trip to a hospital accident and emergency department, does not support the image of a selfless professional that some wish to promote. It is unnecessary to enter the debate about the reasonableness or otherwise of doctors' remuneration or working hours. Rather, the focus is upon the fact that if the profession, or at least key parts of it, seeks to move to resemble any other provider of goods or services, they cannot simultaneously expect to be assumed to have the attributes of selflessness associated with a risk-free, no fault climate.

Similarly, as previously discussed, how many doctors have failed to disinfect their hands between patients during hospital ward rounds, long after the threat posed by antibiotic-resistant infections was well publicized both inside and outside of medical circles? Thousands of patients have potentially been harmed by this behaviour, yet in the absence of fear of detection or punishment, some (perhaps many) in the profession have simply neglected to take such a simple precautionary step as washing their hands or using an appropriate alternative disinfectant measure.

Other studies also give rise to concerns about the likely effectiveness of a no blame approach. For example, it has been found that doctors use a variety of devices to externalize and deflect responsibility when complaints are made against them. One device sees the doctor describe the complainant's perspective as irrational,

---

43 *The Kerr/Haslam Inquiry Report*, July 2005, Cm 6640-1, 802.

44 See Tallis, R., *Hippocratic Oaths*, 2004, Atlantic, London, 172.

compared with the rational doctor. Others include uncertainty of the disease process; character failure on the part of the complainant; the shortcomings of others and external factors. Sociological studies have identified that doctors would frequently redefine untoward events as 'non-mistakes', but simply part of the uncertainty of medical practice. Others blamed the lack of resources and the difficult choices of risking treating patients badly, as opposed to not at all.[45] Negative responses from doctors to complaints included: irritation (52 per cent), annoyance (37 per cent), anger (33 per cent), distress (32 per cent) and anxiety (28 per cent). Concern was expressed that professional reputation was being questioned and feelings could arise to the effect that the expected norms – of moral authority and technical superiority on the part of the doctor – were being usurped. Seventy-five per cent of GPs surveyed and 88 per cent of consultants reacted by arguing that complaints were unjustified.[46] Almost all doctors (98 per cent) formally denied responsibility when a complaint was made. Following Giddens'[47] reasoning, intense socialization resulting, inter alia, from long training, patronage in career development and collegiate practice combine to make professional identity the dominant identity for doctors. Criticism of their work therefore becomes criticism of them.[48] Mulcahy points out that criticism of a doctor's work may be viewed as a challenge to the whole profession's knowledge base and standards. This in turn may give rise to a crisis of legitimacy within the profession, calling into question their technical and moral authority over specialized medical knowledge. In these circumstances, doctors tend to turn inwards, to their professional colleagues, for support and confirmation. This may go as far as members of the profession pushing themselves towards intellectual dishonesty, preferring to cover up mistakes rather than admit them. Defensive reactions to error may be seen as a reasonable reaction by doctors who still work in an environment where responsibility for clinical decisions rests with individuals. Rationalization and personal denial of the truth may occur when things go wrong. This may in turn lead to collective denials – 'there but for the grace of God'.[49] Recounting the words of a non-medic manager: 'Medics never, never accept that anything has ever gone wrong…'. This, it has been suggested, occurs because doctors subject to complaints

45 Allsop, J. and Mulcahy, L., 'Maintaining Professional Identity: Doctors' Responses to Complaints', *Sociology of Health & Illness*, 1998, Vol. 20, No. 6, 802–24, 811. See also Mizrahi, T., 'Managing Medical Mistakes: Ideology, Insularity and Accountability among Internists in Training', *Social Science and Medicine*, 1984, 19, 135–46.

46 Mulcahy, L. and Tritter, J., 'Pathways, Pyramids and Icebergs: Mapping the Links between Dissatisfaction and Complaints', *Sociology of Health & Illness*, 1998, Vol. 20, No. 6, 823–45.

47 Giddens, A., *Modernity and Self-Identity: Self and Society in the Late Modern Age*, 1991, Polity Press, Cambridge.

48 See Allsop, J. and Mulcahy, L., 'Maintaining Professional Identity: Doctors' Responses to Complaints', *Sociology of Health & Illness*, 1998, Vol. 20, No. 6, 802–24, 809; Mulcahy, L., *Disputing Doctors*, 2003, Open University Press, Maidenhead, 110 and 115–17. See also Rosethal, D., Marshall, V., Macpherson, A. and French, S., *Nurses, Patients and Families*, 1980, Croom Helm, London; Richman, J., *Medicine and Health*, 1987, Longman, Harlow; and Habermas, J., *Legitimation Crisis*, 1976, Heinemann, London.

49 Irvine, D., *The Doctors' Tale*, 2003, Radcliffe Medical Press, Oxford, 24.

fear censure from their professional colleagues and being labelled incompetent.[50] It has also been found that in a majority of cases (60 per cent) doctors did not follow requisite procedures to ensure that complaints were independently and appropriately handled. Instead of referring complaints to managers, the doctors in these cases kept the complaint to themselves. The reasons for this included competitiveness within the profession, resulting in an unwillingness to take the risk that colleagues might find out about the complaint.[51]

## Theoretical Principles of Regulation and 'No Fault'

Regulatory theory may also be used to raise questions about the desirability of a no fault approach. Lessig, for example, divides modes of regulation into four categories: law; the market; social norms; and structural design (architecture). The first three approaches engage with the regulated group, whilst the fourth does not. Using a simple example, a government decision that drivers should wear seatbelts. Regulatory choices include: passing a law; subsidizing insurance companies to offer reduced premiums to seatbelt wearers; promoting through advertising and public education the need to wear seatbelts; and stigmatizing failure in this respect; or, requiring manufacturers to design in systems which prevent driving unless the seatbelt is in use.[52] As Garland puts it:

> Instead of addressing human beings and their moral attitudes or psychological dispositions, the new criminologists address the component parts of social systems…They consider how different situations might be redesigned so as to give rise to fewer opportunities for crime…It is a problem of ensuring co-ordination…not of building normative consensus.
>
> The criminologies of everyday life thus offer an approach to social order that is, for the most part, amoral and technological. They bypass the realm of values and concentrate on the routine ways in which people are brought together in time and space. Their conception of social order is a matter not of shared values but of smart arrangements that minimize the opportunities for disruption and deviance. This…flies in the face of traditionalist ideas that see order as emerging out of moral discipline and obedience to authority.[53]

Regulation by structural design removes the moral focus from the regulated, who become totally dependent on the regulator for moral leadership. When regulators

---

50 Mulcahy, L., *Disputing Doctors*, 2003, Open University Press, Maidenhead, 110, 115–17 and 130.

See also Rosethal, D., Marshall, V., Macpherson, A. and French, S., *Nurses, Patients and Families*, 1980, Croom Helm, London; Richman, J., *Medicine and Health*, 1987, Longman, Harlow; and Habermas, J., *Legitimation Crisis*, 1976, Heinemann, London.

51 Allsop, J. and Mulcahy, L., 'Maintaining Professional Identity: Doctors' Responses to Complaints', *Sociology of Health & Illness*, 1998, Vol. 20, No. 6, 802–24, 818.

52 Lessig, L., *Code and Other Laws of Cyberspace*, 1999, Basic Books, New York, 93–4. Cited by Brownsword, R., 'Code, Control, and Choice: why East is East and West is West', *Legal Studies*, March 2005, 25(1), 6–7.

53 Garland, D., *The Culture of Control*, 2001, Oxford University Press, Oxford, 183.

design out choice on the part of the regulated, it becomes meaningless to consider them to be morally responsible agents, to be credited with appropriate acts and to be blamed where they fall short of moral requirements. Furthermore, by being denied autonomy, the regulated are likely to perceive that moral responsibility rests entirely with the system and lose sight of any personal obligations.[54]

Thus, by modifying systems to remove choice and discretion from doctors, the incidence of adverse events should decrease, but at the expense of the degree of professional autonomy and professional responsibility. A short-term gain in terms of adverse outcomes may therefore be at the cost of new generations of doctors perceiving themselves to be no more than technicians in a highly regulated system. Such doctors will lack the motivation and mindset required for the innovative streak needed to move medical practice forwards. A strategically clever regulator will therefore aim for the ideal mix of approaches.

## Initial Steps towards a No Blame Culture

In 2000, the Chief Medical Officer, in his report *An Organisation with a Memory*,[55] identified as obstacles to increasing patient safety a culture which inhibited reporting within NHS bodies and the lack of an effective system for learning from incidents and sharing these lessons. The report advocated a move from a culture primarily based on blame and fear to one which encouraged openness and reporting. From this, the NHS should become a far more effective learning organization. The recommended mechanism was a direct, confidential (but not anonymous) national reporting system. In the following year, the Department of Health published *Building a Safer NHS for Patients*.[56] This advocated patient safety and reducing risk as the central focus for improving the quality of care and protecting the public from poorly performing practitioners. Key to the DoH plans was the creation of a National Patient Safety Agency. A mandatory national reporting system for patient safety incidents and near misses would increase the collection and sharing of information. The Agency would collect and analyse information, and assimilate information from other reporting systems.

On 24 February 2004, the Health Minister, Lord Norman Warner, announced the launch of what he described as a 'world first…pioneering national reporting system' aimed at helping the NHS to improve patient safety. The new system, to be operated by the National Patient Safety Agency,[57] aimed to bring together reports of errors and

---

54 Brownsword, R., 'Code, Control, and Choice: why East is East and West is West', *Legal Studies*, March 2005, 25(1), 18–19. See also von Hirsch, A., Garland, D. and Wakefield, A. (eds), *Ethical and Social Perspectives on Situational Crime Prevention*, 2000, Hart Publishing, Oxford.

55 Department of Health, *An Organisation with a Memory*, Report of an Expert Group on Learning from Adverse Events in the NHS, Chaired by the Chief Medical Officer, 2000.

56 Department of Health, *Building a Safer NHS for Patients – Implementing An Organisation with a Memory*, April 2001.

57 The National Patient Safety Agency (NPSA) was established in July 2001 following the recommendations of the Chief Medical Officer's report on patient safety, *An Organisation*

systems failures affecting patient safety from health professionals across England and Wales. The National Reporting and Learning System, it was said, should aid the NHS in understanding the underlying causes of problems and errors and to act quickly to introduce reforms to prevent future mistakes.[58] The NRLS is premised on the belief that most problems affecting patient safety occur as a result of weaknesses in systems and processes, rather than the acts of individuals. Drawing from the experiences of, amongst others, the aviation industry, the new system aimed to make the reporting of adverse events the norm and to give the NHS a collective memory from which to learn. Local reporting, investigation and analysis were to be the norm, with the NRLS maintaining a national overview, identifying recurring patterns and developing solutions to ensure local consistency.

To avoid creating additional burdens, the NRLS was designed to extract information from existing local risk management systems. Reports previously only collected locally could therefore be used to track national trends. The NPSA has also developed an electronic reporting form – the eForm – for organizations without a local risk management system or for those staff who are only willing to report independently of their organization. However, the NPSA does encourage NHS staff to share their reports with their local organization, to enable learning to take place at both a local and national level. To encourage reporting, the NRLS will retain information only in an anonymous form. The NPSA does not investigate individual incidents or become involved in disciplinary proceedings. The NPSA will publish statistics on trends and issues identified through the NRLS, to promote a learning culture in the NHS. The data should also enable the NPSA to prioritize the development of safety solutions from improved patient safety.

Early indicators, based upon the statistics noted above, indicate significant under-disclosure of adverse events. The 276,000 reported events constitute less than one third of the 900,000 annual mistakes estimated by the NPSA. A cultural problem remains in that doctors perceive the issue very differently from the wider public. Edwin Borman, Deputy Chairman of the British Medical Association Consultants' Committee, is reported as saying that the findings are not a surprise, and that the lack of reporting may be attributed to the absence of a true no blame culture.[59] An alternative explanation, however, is that the language and culture adopted by doctors normalizes, even trivializes, mistakes.[60]

---

*with a Memory*. The role of the NPSA is to improve the safety of NHS patients by promoting a culture of learning and reporting from patient safety incidents, and to manage the national reporting and learning system to support this function.

58 The NRLS system was tested by the National Patient Safety Agency in partnership with 39 NHS organizations across England and Wales, and development work was completed in November 2003.

59 See Woolcock, N. and Henderson, M., 'Blundering Hospitals are "Killing 40,000 Patients a Year"', *The Times*, 13 August 2004, 1.

60 Quick, O., 'Outing Medical Errors: Questions of Trust and Responsibility', *Medical Law Review*, Spring 2006, 14, 22–43.

## Conclusion

Overall, there is little to suggest that the medical profession is ready for the responsibilities necessary for an effective no fault system. The failures by the GMC and the profession to ensure that self-regulation works in the public interest leave little room for confidence that doctors will universally live up to the trust necessary for an effective no fault environment. This has been demonstrated time and again by the case studies considered in this book. There are numerous examples of doctors who were, or should have been, aware of problems with a colleague. These doctors failed to act, thereby failing to take responsibility for their colleague's behaviour. To the extent that early developments of a no fault environment are to continue, these should be limited to 'technical errors'. Should these developments be successful, it may be possible to maintain a dual system, with a compliance approach for technical errors and a deterrent-based one for moral errors.

# Chapter 16

# Crisis and Change

## Key Aspects of the Crisis Facing Medical Self-Regulation

As detailed in this book, self-regulation by the medical profession has been subject to numerous challenges in recent years. This in turn has led to various government initiatives. For example, in its 1999 publication, *Supporting Doctors, Protecting Patients*, the Department of Health identified the need for a fundamental review of medical self-regulation. The Health Act 1999 empowered the government to reform professional regulation without the need for primary legislation. The NHS Plan of 2000 set out proposals for a Regulatory Council to coordinate professional regulatory bodies, as did the 2001 Bristol Inquiry Report.

The NHS Reform and Health Care Professions Act 2002 created the Council for the Regulation of Health Professions, now the Council for Health Regulatory Excellence. In response to its critics, the GMC had identified revalidation as its key proposal for reform. The Medical Act (Amendment) Order 2002 allowed for the introduction of revalidation, along with other governance and procedural changes within the GMC. However, by 2004 the Shipman Inquiry had been highly critical of the GMC's actual proposals for revalidation. In response to this, in 2005 the Department of Health suspended the GMC's planned timetable for the introduction of revalidation procedures and also announced a review of medical professional regulation.

In many respects, this raft of initiatives was long overdue – the GMC had been allowed one last chance after another for at least a decade longer than should have been the case. For example, writing from within the profession in 1993, Smith commented: 'Not with a bang but with a whimper, the GMC is slipping into history… The government is sidelining the GMC and with it the self-regulation the profession has enjoyed since 1858.'[1]

Similarly, Irvine identified deep-seated cultural flaws such as 'excessive paternalism, lack of respect for patients and their right to make decisions about their care, and secrecy and complacency about poor practice'. Self-regulation has proved unresponsive to these aspects of practice, preferring a reactive regulatory stance which has tended to show interest only in the most flagrant misconduct.[2] As demonstrated by the case examples discussed in this work, even 'flagrant misconduct' has not resulted in timely action by the GMC.

1 Smith, R., 'The End of the GMC? The Government, Not the GMC, is Looking at Under-performing Doctors', *British Medical Journal*, 1993, 307: 954.

2 Irvine, D., 'The Changing Relationship Between the Public and Medical Profession', The Lloyd Roberts Lecture – Royal Society of Medicine, 16 January 2001.

In 2000, the BMA annual conference passed a motion of no confidence in the GMC. The Council was criticized for failing to act quickly enough against poorly performing doctors, for its antiquated structure and for its failure to maintain public confidence, and the plans for revalidation were also treated with scepticism.[3] One BMA delegate described the GMC as 'dysfunctional, arrogant and inefficient'.[4] At the 2001 BMA conference the chairman of the BMA's working party on GMC reforms was reported as saying: 'Somehow, the GMC has got to get the confidence of the profession and the public back…Doctors feel as if the GMC is disconnected from the profession.' One GP described the GMC as a 'parochial, tinpot oligarchy', whilst another said it was a 'gargantuan organisation which is an archaic dinosaur'.[5]

Whilst the GMC Council reforms saw the retention of a medical majority, the BMA had proposed equal numbers of medical and lay members. The BMA had also reported grass roots members as wanting the complete separation of prosecutory and adjudication roles within the disciplinary process.[6]

Team-based medical practice has also added an additional dimension to the need for effective regulation. Multi-disciplinary and multi-professional teams on the one hand improve the opportunities for the mutual oversight needed for effective regulation. On the other hand, close-knit teams may increase even further the risk that problems and even blatant misconduct will be kept within the confines of the team. This was one of the disturbing features of the Bristol case, that both at team level and within the wider hospital infrastructure, there was failure to police the conduct of senior doctors.

Sentiments of this type were still present in 2005. Esmail, for example, says:

> In my view, the GMC has nowhere to go but down. This decline has two phases. The GMC realises that the modern world is running away from it, and it hopes that by reasserting its views it can re-create the time when its orthodoxy was accepted by all. Even its critics admire its refusal to compromise with reality. However, the pretence can't last forever, and the gulf between what it says and what everyone else thinks will become so preposterous that it will be forced into the second stage of decline when it must reform or die.[7]

Whilst the GMC must take primary responsibility for its failings, successive governments have also been complicit in permitting for far too long the continuation of ineffective self-regulation. An early demonstration of this can be found in the terms of reference of the Merrison Committee, appointed by the Conservative government in 1972. The Committee was charged with considering the future constitution and

3 See 'Doctors Declare No Confidence in GMC', *The Guardian*, 29 June 2000 (web edition); and Boseley, S. and Hartley-Brewer, J., 'Doctors Plunge into New Crisis', *The Guardian*, 30 June 2000 (web edition).

4 Beecham, L., 'Consultants Attack "Arrogant" GMC', *BMJ*, 2000, 320, 1557, 10 June.

5 BMA, 'Doctors Savage GMC "Dinosaur"', Press Release, Thursday, 5 July 2001, 16:08 GMT 17:08 UK.

6 BMA, 'Doctors Savage GMC "Dinosaur"', Press Release, Thursday, 5 July 2001, 16:08 GMT 17:08 UK.

7 Esmail, A., 'GMC and the Future of Revalidation – Failure to Act on Good Intentions', *BMJ*, 2005, Vol. 330, 14 May. Aneez Esmail was medical advisor to the Shipman Inquiry.

functions of the body responsible for the regulation of the medical profession, but it was emphasized by the Secretary of State for Health that removal of self-regulation was not contemplated: 'The General Medical Council is a body with a notable record of service to the public and to the profession. It is not contemplated that the profession should be regulated otherwise than by a predominantly professional body…'[8]

This was also reflected in the deliberations and findings of the Committee itself, which, early in its report, said:

> We take the view that the medical profession should be largely self-regulated. The principle reason for our view is that we have no doubt that the most effective safeguard of the public is the self-respect of the profession itself and that we should do everything to foster this self-respect.[9]

And later in the report: 'the medical profession has been regulated by a predominantly professional body for well over a century…a lay regulating body would labour under substantial disadvantage.'[10] Merrison, therefore, concluded that no fundamental change was necessary and that the self-respect of the profession was the best safeguard for the public.

Despite these and other votes of confidence, the GMC has been described as an organization which 'has been incapable of devising and operating its procedures and policies from the viewpoint of patients and patient protection'.[11] The Council failed over many years to take steps to put its house in order. It has sought to blame gaps in the legislative framework for a number of failings, but cannot explain away matters which were readily within its grasp. An example of this was the continued unsatisfactory practice of rejecting complaints which had not exhausted local procedures, some 15 years after one of its own lay members had been strongly critical of this practice. The power yielded by elected doctors on the Council, and the unwillingness of the profession as a whole to adequately fund the regulatory process, has strongly influenced the GMC's attitude towards regulation. This attitude has also been shaped by the confusion amongst some within the profession about whether the GMC, as a partially elected body paid for by the profession, should be a representative body which supports rather than challenges doctors. A constitutional change which sees a significant reduction in the number of elected GMC members is needed to help change the culture. Appointed medical members should be in a much

8 Sir Keith Joseph, *Hansard*, House of Commons, 23 November 1972, cited by Stacey, M., *Regulating British Medicine: the General Medical Council*, 1992, Wiley, Chichester, 51. See also Irvine, D., *The Doctors' Tale*, 2003, Radcliffe Medical Press, Oxford, 58.

9 *Report of the Committee of Inquiry into the Regulation of the Medical Profession*, 1975, Cmnd 6018, HMSO, London, Paragraph 11.

10 *Report of the Committee of Inquiry into the Regulation of the Medical Profession*, 1975, Cmnd 6018, HMSO, London, Paragraph 378.

11 The Fifth Report of the Shipman Inquiry, *Safeguarding Patients: Lessons from the Past – Proposals for the Future*, para 18.230 (www.the-shipman-inquiry.org.uk).

stronger position to view themselves as servants of the public interest, rather than as servants of a medical electorate.[12]

These weaknesses have also manifested in the codes produced by the GMC, as guidance to members of the profession and the Council's own regulatory committees. Key examples of this include an historically weak stance with respect to behaviour which falls short of serious professional misconduct, and confused guidance regarding reporting suspicions about the behaviour of fellow doctors. These observations correspond with those theoretical comments which suggest that professional discipline is undermined by the tendency of professional codes to limit their coverage to minimum levels acceptable within the profession. Rhode has described this as 'socialization to the lowest common denominator of conduct that a highly self-interested constituency will publicly brand as deviant'. Professional bodies may even take the view that if rules set their moral sights too high they will be routinely violated and so the whole regulatory structure undermined.[13] This may have been of less significance historically, when smaller cohesive professional communities were able to maintain informal sanctions. However, this tends to be lost with increased size and diversity of professional groups. Indeed, the increasing incidence of doctors working within large bureaucratic organizations enhances the importance of professional virtue.[14] Large organizations are able to wield significant power, including the capacity to cover up mistakes by their employees. External monitoring and oversight is therefore difficult unless professional employees work within a climate of effective and overarching professional guidance. The GMC's proposals to place greater reliance upon local, employer-based, procedures demonstrate little awareness of these considerations.

An ethically rigorous code should function to sensitize members of the profession to the wider consequences of their activities and collectively affirm an internally agreed statement of professional values and behaviour.[15] A rigorous code should also provide support for members of the profession who need to act in a manner which might place them out of step with their professional colleagues.[16] Had the GMC addressed this latter point, fellow doctors should have been far more willing

---

12 See the Fifth Report of the Shipman Inquiry, *Safeguarding Patients: Lessons from the Past – Proposals for the Future*, paras 18.231–18.234 and 27.309–27.310 (www.the-shipman-inquiry.org.uk).

13 Rhode, D.L., 'Ethical Perspectives on Legal Practice', *Stanford Law Review*, 1985, Vol. 37: 589, 641 and 647. Luban, D. (ed.), *The Ethics of Lawyers*, 1994, Dartmouth, Aldershot. See also White, J., 'Machiavelli and the Bar: Ethical Limitations on Lying in Negotiation', *American Bar Foundation Research Journal*, 1980, Vol. 15, No. 4, 926–38. Cited by Rhode, D.L., 'Ethical Perspectives on Legal Practice', *Stanford Law Review*, 1985, Vol. 37: 589, 647. Luban, D. (ed.), *The Ethics of Lawyers*, 1994, Dartmouth, Aldershot, 455.

14 For wider discussion, see May, W.F., 'Professional Virtue and Self-Regulation', in Callahan, J.C. (ed.), *Ethical Issues in Professional Life*, 1988, Oxford University Press, Oxford.

15 For further discussion, see Heijder, A. and van Geuns, H., *Professional Codes of Ethics*, 1976, Amnesty International Press, London, 10.

16 Rhode, D.L., 'Ethical Perspectives on Legal Practice', *Stanford Law Review*, 1985, Vol. 37: 589, 648. Luban, D. (ed.), *The Ethics of Lawyers*, 1994, Dartmouth, Aldershot, 456.

to report misbehaviour by colleagues than was actually the case. Once a code meets these standards, the recommendations from the Bristol case – that the codes of professional conduct should be included in the contracts of employment of doctors – carry greater force. Employers would be able to deal with breaches independently of actions by the GMC, thereby bringing rigorous codes into the day-to-day working environment.[17] The government response to the Bristol Report noted that the new consultant contract would include the headings in *Good Medical Practice*, so that compliance could be considered during appraisal.[18]

More recent consideration of professional codes has drawn into question whether these are appropriate means of ensuring appropriate levels of morality. At the extreme end of this scale, some postmodern theorists argue that codes are the very antithesis of morality.[19] It has also been suggested that the threat of punishment does not provide a sufficiently strong incentive towards particular behaviour.[20] With respect to the medical profession, however, the evidence strongly suggests that reliance upon the personal morality of each member of the profession has not worked either. Whilst codes do not offer a panacea for all potential ethical dilemmas, the lack of a rigorous and clear statement with regards to core matters such as whistleblowing did allow some doctors to avoid what should have been their moral responsibility. Indeed in contradiction to the above suggestions, the GMC's code with regard to reporting colleagues was clearly remembered by many doctors from their time at medical school. Unfortunately, the strict adherence to this code was based upon these doctors' interpretation that it forbade the making of negative assertions about colleagues.

Whilst important, professional codes alone are not sufficient to ensure appropriate behaviour. The wider aim must be to encourage reflective practice in the interests of the public. All members of the profession must be fully committed to patient-centred values. These must underpin all medical practice, and members of the profession must perceive ownership of them to ensure that they are not viewed with suspicion.[21]

As the Bristol case illustrates, there was a general belief until at least the late 1980s that as long as enough doctors were trained, they could be relied upon to provide high quality services throughout their working lives. Responsibility for the quality of clinical care was seen to lie with each individual doctor, acting in accordance

17 Recommendation 45.

18 See also *Learning from Bristol: The DH Response to the Report of the Public Inquiry into Children's Heart Surgery at the Bristol Royal Infirmary 1984-1995*, para 7.25.

19 See, for example, Bauman, Z., *Postmodern Ethics*, 1993, Blackwell, Oxford; and Dawson, A.J., 'Professional Codes of Practice and Ethical Conduct', 11 *Journal of Applied Philosophy*, 1994, 146. Both are discussed in the context of lawyers' ethics in Nicolson, D., 'Making Lawyers Moral? Ethical Codes and Moral Character, *Legal Studies*, November 2005, 24(4), 601–26, 608.

20 See Coady, M., 'The Moral Domain of Professionals', in Coady, M. and Bloch, C. (eds), *Codes of Ethics and the Professions*, 1996, Melbourne University Press, Carlton South, 49. Discussed in Nicolson, D., 'Making Lawyers Moral? Ethical Codes and Moral Character, *Legal Studies*, November 2005, 24(4) 601–26, 610.

21 See further *Developing Medical Regulation: a Vision for the Future – the GMC's Response to the Call for Ideas by the Review of Clinical Performance and Medical Regulation*, April 2005, paras 15–19.

with professional standards. The problem was that the GMC had neither properly articulated nor enforced such standards. A further difficulty was that clinicians did not see clinical practice as a concern of the 'client'.[22] This is in notable contrast to professions, such as solicitors, who have had to adapt to a market environment such that the client has become king. Kennedy neatly summed up the position:

> The adequacy of the care provided to patients could not…be effectively addressed through regulatory or employment mechanisms. It is out of this state of affairs and a series of much publicised examples of incompetence and bad professional behaviour, that the current pressure for appraisal and revalidation has grown.[23]

The GMC should have been aware of the need to act long before the Bristol case drew attention to the problem. For example, a 1991 study found that too many adverse incidents were occurring when inexperienced doctors performed operations with inadequate senior supervision.[24]

There were also situations where one doctor inappropriately protected another. An example of this saw a patient of Clifford Ayling who was considering bringing a negligence action against him being dissuaded from doing so by a report from Rodney Ledward, saying that there had been no negligence.[25] A subsequent example, involving inadvertent protection by a fellow doctor, occurred when Ayling was subject to criminal proceedings. He was able to merge his practice with that of other GPs, and thereby continued to assault women in his surgery up until his trial.[26]

One of the conclusions Stacey draws from her experience with the GMC was that it consisted of people whose ethical standards were high, but who were self-deluded as to the approach and actions needed to protect the public. That most GMC members were well meaning could only lead her to the conclusion that they had no real idea about what they were doing. This, in part, was due to doctors on the Council clinging to an outdated model of professional practice. The myth of a one-to-one doctor–patient relationship continued in the Council long after it had ceased to be the predominant model outside. As Stacey argued, the GMC's de facto powers are restricted by the need to maintain professional unity, in order to self-regulate, and the desirability of loyalty to the concept of the greater profession, over and above sectional medical interests.[27] The GMC's unfocused, even amateurish, approach has continued. Even when, in recent years, it has made positive changes, this has always

---

22 Kennedy, I.M., *The Inquiry into the Management of Care of Children Receiving Complex Heart Surgery at The Bristol Royal Infirmary* – www.bristol-inquiry.org.uk, 74 and 85.

23 Kennedy, I.M., *The Inquiry into the Management of Care of Children Receiving Complex Heart Surgery at The Bristol Royal Infirmary* – www.bristol-inquiry.org.uk, 193.

24 *Report of the National Confidential Enquiry into Postoperative Deaths*, 1991/1992, cited by Phillips, A.F., *Medical Negligence Law: Seeking a Balance*, 1997, Dartmouth, Aldershot, 170.

25 *Howard and Wright-Hogeland v Secretary of State for Health* [2002] EWHC 396, para 5.

26 *Howard and Wright-Hogeland v Secretary of State for Health* [2002] EWHC 396, para 11.

27 Stacey, M., *Regulating British Medicine: the General Medical Council*, 1992, Wiley, Chichester, 227 and 250.

been by way of reaction to external pressures. As Dame Janet Smith put it: 'None of [the changes] appears to have been made because the GMC realised for itself that it was not acting in the best interests of patients and the public. Those changes do not demonstrate that there has been much of a change of culture within the GMC.'[28]

Watkins has drawn attention to an apparent contradiction. Medicine as a profession has retained a powerful and dominant position, notwithstanding the attacks sometimes made against it. In contrast, individual practitioners often feel embattled and disempowered. Blame for this can be attributed to the exclusiveness and arrogance of the profession, and its unwillingness to share power with other professionals or patients' groups. It appears that few doctors understand that they, collectively, have created the opposition they fear and find oppressive.[29]

## Change

Changes to the medical self-regulatory process have variously been described as being required to: reduce harm to patients; recognize and address problems with conduct, competence or ill health at an early stage; provide a strong system which does not retreat from difficult cases; provide clear and well-publicized statements on standards of conduct and ethics; and provide a strong partnership between the professional body and the NHS.[30]

The Kerr/Haslam Inquiry asked whether, even by 2005, the GMC had both the means and the will to ensure that it did not repeat its past failings of missing opportunities to investigate allegations of misconduct.[31] Finlay Scott, Chief Executive and Registrar of the GMC, told the Inquiry that the Council would explore the full range of regulatory possibilities, including entering into discussion with the doctor's employer to seek local action. In the words of Scott:

> We recognise that the GMC is simply part of a much wider regulatory framework…We seek to engage the doctor's employer and any other relevant NHS organisation…at an early stage. This enables us to enter into a dialogue regarding the best method of handling the complaint and/or whether there may be wider causes for concern about the doctor's fitness to practise.[32]

This is an improvement on the previous approach, although the words 'simply part of a much wider regulatory framework' tend to downplay the unique power which the GMC possesses to control doctors' registration. The implication is that the GMC is attempting to water down its responsibilities by emphasizing that regulatory responsibilities are shared. Effective regulation must be concerned with

28 The Fifth Report of the Shipman Inquiry, *Safeguarding Patients: Lessons from the Past – Proposals for the Future*, para 27.292 (www.the-shipman-inquiry.org.uk).

29 Watkins, S., *Medicine and Labour: the Politics of a Profession*, 1987, Lawrence and Wishart, London; and Stacey, M., *Regulating British Medicine: the General Medical Council*, 1992, Wiley, Chichester, 228.

30 See *Supporting Doctors, Protecting Patients*, NHS Consultation Paper, 1999.

31 *The Kerr/Haslam Inquiry Report*, July 2005, Cm 6640-1, 740–41.

32 *The Kerr/Haslam Inquiry Report*, July 2005, Cm 6640-1, 742–43.

all elements which combine to ensure the competence of healthcare professionals. These include initial education and training, continuing professional development and revalidation.[33] These are principally within the remit of the GMC and, as such, cannot simply be displaced by seeking partnership with employers and others. A proactive, sufficiently funded GMC, committed and able to keep all unsuitable persons out of the profession, is still a long way off.

The Kerr/Haslam Report recommended common standards within the NHS and GMC to ensure that information is retained from complainants who are unwilling or too unwell to immediately pursue a complaint. In this way, complaints can be reactivated and patterns of discontent observed. Psychiatric patients gave evidence to the Inquiry that only some time, years in some instances, after their initial disclosure had they recovered enough to give evidence. By this time evidence of the original disclosure and contemporaneous documents had been lost or destroyed. A reliable and accessible national database detailing offences by doctors against patients was recommended.[34] There is no obvious reason why the GMC had not taken the initiative to compile a database of this type long before the recent crises.

## Rhetoric or Reality

It has been suggested that the medical profession was looking in the direction of reform, towards a new professionalism, prior to the Bristol and Shipman scandals.[35] It is impossible to be sure whether significant reforms would have actually been implemented without the pressure from these scandals. Some theories of regulatory behaviour suggest that significant reform would have been unlikely without the position reaching crisis point. Such theories assert that when faced with challenge or uncertainty, organizations tend to respond by creating visible symbols of compliance such as responsive policies or structural changes, as a means to minimize external intrusion.[36] Without these challenges, progress tends to stall or to proceed very slowly. For example, as early as 1980, Kennedy criticized the secrecy, lack of transparency and unaccountability which marked out the GMC. He also highlighted the fact that resources rather than public protection dictated the extent to which the Council took action.[37] These criticisms led to little in the way of effective change.

---

33 The Bristol Report, para 332.

34 The Kerr/Haslam Inquiry noted the value of allegations and similar information in terms of identifying patterns of behaviour, even when no criminal or disciplinary conviction results. *The Kerr/Haslam Inquiry Report*, July 2005, Cm 6640-1, 618, 654 and 744.

35 Stacey, M., *Regulating British Medicine: the General Medical Council*, 1992, Wiley, Chichester. See also Irvine, D., *The Doctors' Tale*, 2003, Radcliffe Medical Press, Oxford, 11.

36 See Edelman, L.B., Abraham, S.E. and Erlanger, H.S., 'Professional Construction of Law: The Inflated Threat of Wrongful Discharge', 26 *Law & Society Review*, 1992, 47; and, in the context of the legal profession, Chambliss, E., 'MDPs: Toward an Institutional Strategy for Entity Regulation', *Legal Ethics*, Summer 2001, Vol. 4, No. 1, 45–65, 57–58.

37 Kennedy, I., *The Unmasking of Medicine*, 1981, Allen & Unwin, London. See also Department of Health, *Good Doctors, Safer Patients – Proposals to Strengthen the System*

Irvine sees the way forward as deriving from the combination of three elements: well-informed patients able to make appropriate choices; high quality clinical governance; and rigorous regulation. The GMC's stated priorities included: adopting an ethos which puts the interests of patients at the heart of everything it does; providing, through *Good Medical Practice*, an explicit code of duties and basic standards; providing sufficiently robust standards to ensure that those admitted to the register and who subsequently remain there have the qualities needed. The remodelled GMC should be a role model, the conscience of the profession and steward of professional standards. Irvine sees this as starting with rigorous educational standards and the requirements in *Good Medical Practice.* Control of registration remains the core means by which the GMC can ensure that those admitted to and allowed to remain in the profession are fit to be there. Clarity regarding what constitutes competence and fitness is vital.[38] In 2000, a Governance Working Group of the GMC noted that the aim of the Council should be to develop a coherent framework of regulation incorporating undergraduate and postgraduate education, registration, continuing professional development, revalidation and fitness to practise procedures.[39]

In 2004, the President of the GMC, Professor Sir Graeme Catto, once again added his voice to those seeking to persuade the sceptics that this time the reforms would genuinely change things for the better.

> …medicine is far too important a subject simply to be left to doctors. Self-regulation, without public involvement, has been shown in the past to be a flawed model, which can lead to professions becoming increasingly isolated and losing touch with society. I know that self-regulation contributes to a loss of the public's trust in professions.
>
> I do not believe at all in self-regulating professions but I do believe very strongly in independent partnership with the public. Regulation should protect patients by fostering that professionalism in doctors, and by involving patients and the public.[40]

Catto went on to emphasize that medicine cannot be effectively regulated without doctors committing themselves fully to the values underpinning the practice of medicine. These values must be informed by patients' views and wants, and must be fully embraced.

## The New Publicly Focused GMC

The GMC has made some efforts to demonstrate that it is serious about protecting the public. For instance, between 1997 and 2000 the number of doctors removed from practice by means of suspension had quadrupled compared with the previous ten years or so.[41] However, the actual number of cases, around 300 (from 130,000

---

*to Assure and Improve the Performance of Doctors and to Protect the Safety of Patients: A Report by the Chief Medical Officer*, July 2006, Chapter 4, paragraph 25.

38 Irvine, D., *The Doctors' Tale*, 2003, Radcliffe Medical Press, Oxford, 207–9.

39 GMC, *The Draft Report of the Governance Working Group*, 18 September 2000, A5.

40 Catto, G., 'Public Opinion', *The Times, Public Agenda*, 19 October 2004, 3.

41 *BMJ*, 17 June 2000, Vol. 320, 1676.

practising doctors), referred annually to the GMC's fitness to practise panels remains exceedingly low. In turn, very few doctors, 46 in 2005, are permanently removed from practice.[42] Some of the issues raised in the Neale case should be less likely to be repeated now that the GMC seeks 'certificates of good standing' from the medical regulator in the jurisdiction from which the doctor is coming. Evidence from other regulators can now be treated for the GMC's purposes as evidence of impairment without the need to prove the facts again.[43]

The GMC has also attempted to more clearly outline the duties of doctors, the key duties being to:

- make the care of patients the primary concern;
- treat patients politely and considerately;
- respect patients' dignity and privacy;
- listen to patients and respect their views;
- give patients information in a way they can understand;
- respect the right of patients to be fully involved in decisions about their care;
- keep professional knowledge and skills up to date;
- recognize the limits of own professional competence;
- be honest and trustworthy;
- respect and protect confidential information;
- make sure that personal beliefs do not prejudice patient care;
- act quickly to protect patients from risk if have good reason to believe that 'you or a colleague' may not be fit to practise;
- avoid abusing position as a doctor;
- work with colleagues in the ways that best serve patients' interests.

These duties present the image of a caring profession, but do raise questions about the priorities of the new image. The requirement that doctors keep their professional skills and knowledge up to date comes some way down the list, after what have been described as a number of 'touchy-feely' qualities.[44]

The GMC has also argued that a coherent vision for regulation is now needed, linking all layers, from the individual practitioner, the clinical team, the employer, tonational bodies such as the GMC itself. The GMC also highlights that its disciplinary powers are predominantly concerned with taking action on concerns which call into question doctors' fitness to remain on the medical register, without

42 In the four years between January 2001 and October 2004, 545 doctors appeared before the PCC, 86 before the performance procedures and 526 before the Health Committee. These cases resulted in 460 doctors being removed from practice – 129 erasures and 331 suspensions. See Department of Health, *Good Doctors, Safer Patients – Proposals to Strengthen the System to Assure and Improve the Performance of Doctors and to Protect the Safety of Patients: A Report by the Chief Medical Officer*, July 2006, Chapter 5.

43 See Department of Health, *Good Doctors, Safer Patients – Proposals to Strengthen the System to Assure and Improve the Performance of Doctors and to Protect the Safety of Patients: A Report by the Chief Medical Officer*, July 2006, Chapter 3.

44 Toynbee, P., 'Between Aspiration and Reality', *British Medical Journal*, 2002, 325: 718–19.

restriction or at all. However, the Council points out that significant numbers of the complaints (in 2003, Catto put this figure at 50 per cent) it receives fall short of this level of seriousness and would be better dealt with through local procedures.[45] The level of generality of this statement limits its value. From 2004, the GMC sought to provide additional guidance to fitness to practise panels regarding the types of behaviour which constituted SPM or SDP. However, insistence on anonymizing case examples and an unwillingness to provide specific guidance severely limited these developments. The case study examples have been described as 'so brief as to be almost useless'. They were also potentially contradictory. For instance, of the five cases initially published, two involved dishonesty by the doctors. In one, the doctor's name was erased but in the other a suspension was imposed. Commentary in both cases emphasizes the reprehensible nature of dishonesty, but there is no basis on which an outside observer can understand why the penalties were different.[46]

As previously discussed, it is important that the GMC does not seek to alleviate its own shortcomings by shifting responsibility elsewhere. If the GMC fulfils its purpose with regard to control of the medical register, no unfit doctor should be in practice.

## The Human Rights Act and the Self-Regulatory Process

In the run up to and after coming into force of the Human Rights Act 1998 there was some concern within a number of professional regulatory bodies that aspects of their procedures would not be compliant. In particular, section 6(1) of the Act provides that it is unlawful for a public authority to act in a way which is incompatible with a Convention right.[47] Article 6(1) of the European Convention of Human Rights provides that: 'In the determination of his civil rights and obligations or of any criminal charge against him, everyone is entitled to a fair and public hearing within a reasonable time by an independent and impartial tribunal established by law.'

In *Le Compte, Van Leuven and De Meyere v Belgium*,[48] the European Court of Human Rights considered whether or not professional disciplinary matters fell

45 The categories which the GMC identify as automatically falling within their remit include: cases where immediate action to restrict a doctor's registration is needed to protect the public; cases involving police caution or court conviction; coroner referrals; cases involving locum doctors and cases involving doctors practising exclusively privately. Beyond these categories, the presumption should be that local resolution is most appropriate. *Developing Medical Regulation: a Vision for the Future – the GMC's Response to the Call for Ideas by the Review of Clinical Performance and Medical Regulation*, April 2005, paras 76—86.

46 See the Fifth Report of the Shipman Inquiry, *Safeguarding Patients: Lessons from the Past – Proposals for the Future*, paras 21.147–21.158 (www.the-shipman-inquiry.org.uk).

47 The question of whether self-regulatory bodies undertake public acts and thereby constitute public authorities has presented the courts with few difficulties. In *Tehrani v UK Central Council for Nursing, Midwifery and Health Visiting* [2001] IRLR 208, Lord Mackay considered that the defendant Council, as a statutory body, endowed with statutory regulatory powers, was, when exercising its disciplinary function, within the definition of public body contained in section 6(3)(b).

48 [1981] 4 EHRR 1.

within the definition of 'civil rights and obligations'. It was said that disciplinary proceedings did not usually give rise to a dispute over civil rights and obligations, but where the disciplinary body was interfering with the right to professional practice, this had affected civil rights and obligations. This approach was also adopted in *Albert and Le Compte v Belgium*,[49] the ECHR stressing that the right to continue to exercise a profession to which the applicants had earned admission was a private right and thus a 'civil right' when disciplinary sanctions threatened removal of professional status. In turn, the English courts have accepted that Article 6 applied to disciplinary proceedings, in that they determined 'civil rights and obligations'.[50] A different approach has been taken to sanctions which do not affect the right to practise. These do not breach Article 6 because the civil right in question is the right to practise the chosen profession.

The ECHR has said that in order to establish whether a tribunal can be considered 'independent', factors to be taken into account include the manner of appointment of its members and their term of office, the existence of guarantees against outside pressures and the appearance of independence.[51] To achieve 'impartiality', the tribunal must be both objectively and subjectively free from personal prejudice or bias.[52] Overall, the domestic courts have concluded that since the decisions of self-regulatory bodies such as the GMC can be appealed to an Article 6 compliant court, this ensures HRA compliance even if the body itself is not entirely independent and impartial. This is supported by a line of ECHR decisions, which establish that it was not necessary for every stage of a regulatory process to satisfy the requirements of Article 6. For example, in *Le Compte, Van Leuven and De Meyere v Belgium*[53] it was said that:

> Whilst Article 6(1) embodies the 'right to a court'…it nevertheless does not oblige the Contracting States to submit 'contestations' (disputes) over 'civil rights and obligations' to a procedure conducted at each of its stages before 'tribunals' meeting the Article's various requirements. Demands of flexibility and efficiency, which are fully compatible with the protection of human rights, may justify the prior intervention of administrative or professional bodies and, a fortiori, of judicial bodies which do not satisfy the said requirements in every respect...'

Therefore, in *Ghosh v General Medical Council*,[54] the Judicial Committee of the Privy Council did not find it necessary to consider whether the Professional Conduct Committee of the GMC was itself Convention compliant because the appellate jurisdiction was sufficient to remedy any deficiency. The opportunity for

---

49 [1983] 5 EHRR 533.

50 See, for example, *R v Securities and Futures Authority, ex parte Fleurose* [2002] EWCA Civ 2015.

51 See *Findlay v United Kingdom* (1997) 24 EHRR 221; *Langborger v Sweden* 12 EHRR 416, 425.

52 *Tehrani v UK Central Council for Nursing, Midwifery and Health Visiting* [2001] IRLR 208.

53 [1981] 4 EHRR 1, at para 51.

54 [2001] UKPC 29, [2001] 1 WLR 1915.

appeal to a court of full jurisdiction prevents a breach from occurring, rather than purging it.[55] This approach does give rise to both practical and theoretical difficulties with regard to the appropriate interconnection between first instance and appellate jurisdictions,[56] in particular, when considered alongside the preferred approach of appellate courts, to resist interfering with the decisions of professional disciplinary tribunals.[57] As illustrated by *Evans v General Medical Council:*[58]

> It has been said time and again that a disciplinary committee are the best possible people for weighing the seriousness of professional misconduct, and that the Board will be very slow to interfere with the exercise of the discretion of such a committee...The committee are familiar with the whole gradation of seriousness of the cases of various types which come before them, and are peculiarly well qualified to say at what point on that gradation erasure becomes the appropriate sentence. This Board does not have that advantage nor can it have the same capacity for judging what measures are from time to time required for the purpose of maintaining professional standards.

To properly meet the expectations of the HRA, the appellate body needs to ensure that they are willing to fully scrutinize decisions from the GMC, to fully utilize the capacity to reconsider the matter afresh.

## GMC Structural Reforms

### *GMC Governance*

In 2001, the GMC published a consultation document, *Effective, Inclusive and Accountable Reform of the GMC's Structure, Constitution and Governance.* Three alternative approaches were suggested. The first, favoured by government but not the GMC, was the move to a small executive board in which all statutory functions would be vested. The GMC's concern was that this would not be sufficiently inclusive. The second approach would have seen statutory functions vested in a smaller Council. A small executive committee would undertake key delegated functions, especially between Council meetings. The third approach would resemble the second approach with respect to the Council, but with powers to discharge the functions vested in – rather than merely delegated to – a smaller executive Board. Unlike the Council, the latter would meet frequently and be the strategic decision making body. This third approach was preferred by the GMC. The GMC's proposal was for a Council with a membership of 50–80, equally shared between medical and lay but chaired by a lay member. The executive Board would be elected by and from the Council and would comprise 20–25 members, with a medical majority (60 per cent) and a medical

55 See, for example, the approach of Lord Mackay in *Tehrani v United Kingdom Central Council for Nursing, Midwifery and Health Visiting* [2001] IRLR 208.

56 For further discussion, see Davies, M., 'Professional Self-Regulation and the Human Rights Act', *Professional Negligence*, 2003, Vol. 19, No. 1, 278–96.

57 For an early example of this, see *Libman v GMC* [1972] AC 217 at 221.

58 (1984) unreported, cited in *Ghosh v GMC*, at paragraph 34 and repeated by Lord Hoffman in *Bijl v GMC* [2001] UKPC 42, 65 BMLR 10, at paragraph 2.

President. The latter, it was argued, would demonstrate the essential importance of professional ownership of standards. Key functions of the President would be to lead the medical profession and act as guardian of the public interest.[59] The GMC's preference was for the continuation of the process that some medical members were appointed and some elected. Justifications for appointment included the value of doctors who were selected for their particular expertise, for instance, in medical education. Whilst the overall proposals retained a medical majority, for the first time elected medical members of the GMC would be in an overall minority.[60]

## Models for Regulatory Reform

The GMC had received additions to its regulatory powers prior to more recent, wider reaching reforms. For example, additional legislative powers were gained in August 2000 to allow recruitment of additional medical and lay members to serve on the PCC. This would allow the GMC's outstanding disciplinary case load to be dealt with more quickly. By November of that year, 73 additional panel members had been appointed. This allowed the GMC to plan almost 600 hearing days in 2001, twice the total for 2000 and four times that for 1995. This was needed to keep pace with the rising tide of complaints – from 1,500 in 1995 to almost 4,500 in 2000;[61] although, as previously noted, in prioritizing the need to clear outstanding cases, the GMC's appointment criteria were unlikely to lead to an increase in diversity of panel members. Following Shipman's conviction, the GMC had also sought clearer powers to impose interim suspension on a doctor pending prosecution or other investigation, and to remove any expectation on the part of doctors whose names were erased from the register that restoration would occur in anything other than exceptional circumstances. The GMC also sought additional investigatory powers and greater powers to disclose information to employers when the public interest required it. Greater collaborative links between the GMC and other interested organizations – notably NHS and other employers, the police and the Crown Prosecution Service – were also mooted.[62]

However, at the same time that it was seeking piecemeal changes, the GMC also looked to more radical reform. In November 1999, the Council embarked upon what it described as a 'fundamental review' of the fitness to practise procedures. With regard to doctors who pose a risk to the public, 'nothing short of a radical

---

59 GMC, *Effective, Inclusive and Accountable Reform of the GMC's Structure, Constitution and Governance*, March 2001, 6–7 and 12.

60 For further discussion, see GMC, *Effective, Inclusive and Accountable Reform of the GMC's Structure, Constitution and Governance*, March 2001, 21. In the fifth Shipman Report, Dame Janet Smith also recommended that the GMC should cease to have an elected medical majority. Rather the medical majority, in common with the lay membership, should be selected by the Public Appointments Commission on the basis of open competition.

61 See GMC, *Acting Fairly to Protect Patients: Reform of the GMC's Fitness to Practise Procedures*, March 2001, 5.

62 For further discussion, see GMC, *Acting Fairly to Protect Patients: Reform of the GMC's Fitness to Practise Procedures*, March 2001, 5–6.

overhaul of the current arrangements', it was said, would deliver the fair, timely and effective action which was expected by the public.[63] However, despite these strong words, the GMC ruled out the creation of a whole new disciplinary system, arguing that the creation of new structures would cause major disruption. Furthermore, it considered it to be far from certain that such new structures would be effective or an improvement on the old model. Improvements to the existing systems to maximize their efficacy was seen as the best way forwards.[64]

The GMC mooted four potential regulatory models. Model A envisaged the GMC retaining both investigatory and adjudication functions, but these would be entirely separate from each other in terms of membership and support structures. Separation would go some way to removing the accusation that the GMC has in the past blurred its investigatory, prosecutorial and adjudication roles, without losing the advantage of being able to derive the benefits of allowing lessons from all aspects of the regulatory process to feed back into education and standard setting.[65] Model B envisaged the GMC retaining the investigatory role, whilst adjudication would be divested to an entirely independent organization. This would have insulated the GMC from damage to its reputation from controversial decisions. The risk was that the public perception of such a move would have been that the GMC was shirking its responsibility with respect to a core aspect of the 'self'-regulatory process.[66] Model C was a mirror image of Model B, investigation and the initial sifting being undertaken by an independent external agency. The GMC would retain the adjudicatory role. A key disadvantage with this model is that the GMC loses control of who is prosecuted, possibly exacerbating previous criticism that too many cases were screened out at an early stage. Model D was the most radical, envisaging that both investigatory and adjudication functions would be delegated to separate external organizations. The Law Society was held up as the model for this approach. The GMC did not consider that the loss of all regulatory functions would be appropriate. The GMC's preferred model was A, retention of both investigation and adjudication being the only way in which it could take, and be seen to take, appropriate responsibility for the medical register.[67]

In the fifth report of the Shipman Inquiry, Dame Janet Smith recommended that adjudication in disciplinary cases should be undertaken by a body independent of the GMC, the existing structures offering insufficient division between investigation and adjudication. The GMC responded by arguing that it had long experience and significant expertise in the adjudication process and undertook comprehensive

63 See GMC, *Acting Fairly to Protect Patients: Reform of the GMC's Fitness to Practise Procedures*, March 2001, 6.

64 See, further, *Developing Medical Regulation: a Vision for the Future – the GMC's Response to the Call for Ideas by the Review of Clinical Performance and Medical Regulation*, April 2005, para 25.

65 See GMC, *Acting Fairly to Protect Patients: Reform of the GMC's Fitness to Practise Procedures*, March 2001, 27–28.

66 See GMC, *Acting Fairly to Protect Patients: Reform of the GMC's Fitness to Practise Procedures*, March 2001, 28–29.

67 GMC, *Acting Fairly to Protect Patients: Reform of the GMC's Fitness to Practise Procedures*, March 2001, 29–30.

audit of decisions to ensure a continuing learning process. Panellists were said to be independent in outlook, notwithstanding their place within the organization. Also, they were provided with judicially supported Indicative Sanctions Guidance, to aid consistency of decision making. Specialist legal advice was provided by legal assessors, experienced barristers or solicitors appointed (since 2002) through open competition. In support of its stance, the Council cited the very low rate of successful appeals against its decisions – only 0.7 per cent in 2004.[68] This line of argument illustrates an absence of critical self-reflection within the GMC, with little recognition that few other judicial bodies were so lacking in independence.

## GMC Rule Changes

On 1 November 2004, the rules governing the GMC disciplinary procedures underwent significant changes.[69] The new approach of the GMC is to consider the doctor's fitness to practise in all contexts, rather than having separate routes for conduct, health and performance. The concept of 'serious professional misconduct' also went and a new test was introduced – the question of whether a doctor's 'impaired fitness to practise' makes continued registration inappropriate. 'Impaired fitness to practise' might include: inappropriate behaviour; inadequate performance; being convicted or cautioned with respect to a criminal offence; impairment due to physical or mental ill health. Separate screening and preliminary proceedings stages were replaced with a single investigation stage, to be undertaken by specifically selected and appointed personnel – known as case examiners. Two case examiners, one medical and one lay, will be involved in every decision. In the absence of agreement between the two, a formal GMC committee, the Investigation Committee, will determine the matter. One notable omission from these new procedures (as was also the case with the old procedures) is a mechanism to ensure the identification of less serious acts which individually do not draw into question a doctor's registration but collectively may be indicative of a wider problem.[70]

The GMC had given some thought to the issues raised by Robinson and others, that letters of advice were insufficient to deal with conduct which gave rise to concerns, but not to such a degree that it calls into question a doctor's registration. The GMC had treated letters of advice as confidential communications between itself and the doctor, rather than as matters in the public domain or to be notified to the doctor's employer. The Council recognized that this did not command public confidence, although there were concerns about the possible floodgates implications from mechanisms designed to deal with complaints which fell short of serious professional misconduct.[71] The GMC also emphasized the need to distinguish clearly

68 *Developing Medical Regulation: a Vision for the Future – the GMC's Response to the Call for Ideas by the Review of Clinical Performance and Medical Regulation*, April 2005, paras 170–73 and Appendix E, paras 4–5.

69 The General Medical Council (Fitness to Practise) Rules (SI 2004 No. 2608).

70 See *The Kerr/Haslam Inquiry Report*, July 2005, Cm 6640-1, 758.

71 See GMC, *Acting Fairly to Protect Patients: Reform of the GMC's Fitness to Practise Procedures*, March 2001, 13.

between issues of fitness to practise and the resolving of complaints. It saw only the former as being within the scope of its role as regulator.[72]

Even though the new fitness to practise procedures dispense with the tests of SPM and SDP, the new approach does little or nothing to address the definitional problems previously encountered with SPM. Determining whether the doctor's fitness to practise is impaired to a degree which requires action on registration is likely to be as problematic as previous definitional issues. No benchmarks or objective standards are provided, so the degree of seriousness required remains subjective. For instance, there is likely to be no consensus about whether a doctor who commits an act of dishonesty unconnected with his medical practice is 'impaired' with respect to his fitness to practise medicine.[73]

## The New Screening Stages

The three 'screening' stages were replaced in November 2004 by a single investigation stage, with professional case examiners recruited for this purpose. Case examiners have greater potential for independence than their predecessors, as they are no longer nominated by the GMC President. An additional advantage of the new approach is that all cases which progress beyond the initial administrative stages will be considered by two case examiners, one medical and one lay. This was an advance on the previous system, where lay screeners only became involved if the medical screener was proposing to dismiss the case. The problem of the screener's decision being critical in deciding whether a case should go to conduct, performance or health was also removed by the new system, with the replacement of three separate panels with a single generic panel which will consider in the round the doctor's fitness to practise. The screening test adopted by the GMC (in the absence of any statutory provision) was whether there is a realistic prospect of establishing that the doctors fitness to practise is impaired to such an extent to require action against his or her registration. GMC Guidance in September 2004 provided that certain categories of conduct – sexual assault or indecency, violence, dishonesty and improper sexual/emotional relationships – should be referred unless there are 'exceptional reasons' for not doing this. With respect to other categories of case, this test does give rise to difficulties. In terms of construction, it could mean that the decision maker has to weigh up the evidence and reach a conclusion, based upon his or her own opinion. Alternatively, the decision maker could be required to consider whether the FTP panel would itself consider that the evidence leads to this conclusion. The test as originally drafted did not address this distinction.[74] In any event, both possibilities

72 *Developing Medical Regulation: a Vision for the Future – the GMC's Response to the Call for Ideas by the Review of Clinical Performance and Medical Regulation*, April 2005.

73 The Fifth Report of the Shipman Inquiry, *Safeguarding Patients: Lessons from the Past – Proposals for the Future*, paras 17.39, 25.43–25.45 and 25.61 (www.the-shipman-inquiry.org.uk).

74 See the Fifth Report of the Shipman Inquiry, *Safeguarding Patients: Lessons from the Past – Proposals for the Future*, paras 25.59–25.60 and 25.161 (www.the-shipman-inquiry.org.uk).

move against the approach eventually developed in relation to the previous screening process, that screening should be a filter only.

As an alternative, Dame Janet Smith proposed a two-stage approach to screening. The first stage would require the decision maker to consider whether the allegation, if proved, might show that the doctor's fitness to practise is impaired. This decision would be based on specific reasons: that the doctor presents a risk to patients; that he or she has brought the profession into disrepute; that he or she has breached one of the fundamental tenets of the profession or that the doctor's integrity cannot be relied upon. These concepts should be easier to recognize than 'impairment of fitness to practise'. The second stage would involve the decision maker considering the adequacy of the evidence. It is also important that case examiners do not mix evidence with mitigation. Unfortunately, the GMC has been inconsistent in clearly expressing this point. For instance, guidance to case examiners from June 2004 advised that they should not 'normally' consider mitigation. This advice was, however, absent from guidance issued in September 2004.[75]

'Investigation' retained its limited – previously criticized – role of determining whether a case should progress, rather involving the gathering of evidence. In this respect, the name originally proposed by the GMC – the 'prosecution' stage – would have been more descriptively accurate. GMC guidance issued in September 2004 did state that cases would be allocated to investigation teams and would be a 'lawyer-led process'. The General Medical Council (Fitness to Practise) Rules 2004 provide for the appointment of legally qualified case managers to give directions to secure the just, expeditious and effective running of proceedings before a fitness to practise panel. Case managers will act independently of the parties to a case and will be experienced barristers, advocates or solicitors with relevant judicial or adjudicatory experience. The main responsibilities of a case manager will be to chair case review meetings – either face to face with the parties or by telephone.

However, as observed by the Shipman Inquiry, it remains to be seen whether, in contrast to the old approach, the GMC develops a culture of proactive investigation: 'carried out with real determination and inquisitiveness – rather than by following a set protocol, at the end of which the investigation is regarded as complete, regardless of whether the issues have been "bottomed"'.[76]

If at the investigation stage it is decided that the matter should not proceed to a fitness to practise panel, the GMC may simply close the case or may issue a warning. If the case involves issues of health or performance, these may be dealt with by means of voluntary undertaking on the part of the doctor. It is of concern that in its 2004 Rules the GMC determined that decisions to seek health or performance assessments would rest with the Registrar (in practice, administrative staff) rather than case examiners. This, it seems, was a financially driven decision rather than one based on the needs of high quality regulation. In particular, it has the potential

---

75 The Fifth Report of the Shipman Inquiry, *Safeguarding Patients: Lessons from the Past – Proposals for the Future*, paras 25.63 and 25.163 (www.the-shipman-inquiry.org.uk).

76 See the Fifth Report of the Shipman Inquiry, *Safeguarding Patients: Lessons from the Past – Proposals for the Future*, paras 19.260, 25.19, 25.25 and 25.153–25.154 (www.the-shipman-inquiry.org.uk).

to undermine the benefits of screeners no longer having to determine at a very early stage which route a case should follow. In contrast, one positive advance was the move from largely ignoring convictions associated with a health problem – simply approaching the case on a rehabilitative basis – to referring most convictions to an FTP panel. This will not bar reference to the health procedures, but should ensure that a public hearing takes place.[77]

Cases which are referred to the adjudication stage will be heard by an FTP panel, which is empowered to remove or restrict a doctor's registration. An interim orders panel will determine whether a doctor's right to practise should be restricted pending final determination of a case. FTP panels will consist of selected and trained panellists, rather than members of the GMC. The changes still fail to adequately address the problem of a doctor who negligently commits an isolated serious error or a small number of less serious errors, which put patients at risk but do no reach the threshold for deficient performance.[78] Both the Ledward and Shipman Inquiries favoured a move towards FTP panels having a legally qualified and judicially experienced chair – probably a circuit judge or recorder. The aim would be to bring greater legal rigour to the decision making than could be guaranteed by the existing approach of having a legal assessor to provide advice, but not to engage in the decision making process. This recommendation did not find favour with the GMC.

The GMC has considered attempting to increase public protection by introducing restrictive registration, which would recognize the specialist nature of much medical practice and limit each doctor to particular areas of practice and specialities. However, the GMC's conclusion was that practical difficulties would be such as to make this system impractical and, furthermore, the Council said that a public consultation on the matter revealed little enthusiasm.[79]

## Criminal Convictions

A number of changes have been made in recent years regarding the GMC's approach to criminal convictions. One is that doctors charged with or convicted of a criminal offence are required to report it to the GMC, with failure to do so itself a disciplinary matter.[80] The GMC's draft 2003 rules provided that in cases where a doctor had been convicted and sentenced to immediate imprisonment, the Registrar was required to refer the matter directly to an FTP panel where he 'considers it in the public interest to

77 The Fifth Report of the Shipman Inquiry, *Safeguarding Patients: Lessons from the Past – Proposals for the Future*, paras 22.189–22.200, 25.21 and 25.219–25.239 (www.the-shipman-inquiry.org.uk).

78 See the Fifth Report of the Shipman Inquiry, *Safeguarding Patients: Lessons from the Past – Proposals for the Future*, paras 25.22–25.23 and 25.71 (www.the-shipman-inquiry.org.uk).

79 *Developing Medical Regulation: a Vision for the Future – the GMC's Response to the Call for Ideas by the Review of Clinical Performance and Medical Regulation*, April 2005, para 68.

80 See the Fifth Report of the Shipman Inquiry, *Safeguarding Patients: Lessons from the Past – Proposals for the Future*, para 27.291 (www.the-shipman-inquiry.org.uk).

do so'. This latter element adds an extra hurdle to the post-November 2002 position, that all convictions where immediate custody had been imposed would be referred to an FTP panel. By May 2004, this reversal had itself been reversed and expanded upon, with the Registrar being required to refer directly to an FTP panel any case where a doctor has been given a custodial sentence, immediate or suspended. In other conviction cases, the Registrar is required to refer them directly to an FTP panel 'unless he is of the opinion that it ought to be referred to a medical and a lay Case Examiner for consideration'. Subsequent GMC guidance indicates that these non-custody cases should be referred directly to an FTP panel when the offence was one which, inter alia, involved dishonesty, drugs or child pornography. In contrast, there was a presumption in favour of closing cases which involved minor motoring matters. Non-custody convictions between these extremes should be referred for consideration by case examiners. In determining what should happen to such cases, the examiner should consider all aspects of the doctor's fitness to practise, for instance whether there are health issues, whether voluntary arrangements would be sufficient or whether an FTP panel needs to be involved. The latter is required if there is a prospect that erasure will be considered.[81]

## Keeping Track of Misconduct

Guidance from the Department of Health in the early 1980s was provided in HC (77) 2.[82] Prospective employers were required to check the identity and registration of the doctor. Furthermore, it was recommended that a full curriculum vitae should be obtained, with references covering several years and several employers, including an explanation for any gaps in employment. In August 1992 the guidance was updated.[83] Emphasis was placed on the importance of confirming the accuracy of qualifications. Only in 2000[84] were doctors required to declare any fitness to practise proceedings in the UK or abroad. Similarly, notification was required of any convictions or current police investigation. By 2002[85] failure of an employee to disclose such information constituted a disciplinary matter. These requirements addressed issues raised by the Neale Inquiry, Neale having obtained locum posts some time after problems had arisen.[86] Following the recommendations of the Bichard Inquiry,[87] complaints about

---

81 See the Fifth Report of the Shipman Inquiry, *Safeguarding Patients: Lessons from the Past – Proposals for the Future*, paras 25.142–25.146 (www.the-shipman-inquiry.org.uk).

82 *Checks on Doctors' and Dentists' Registration, Identity and References.*

83 By means of Executive Letter EL (92) 53, *Recruitment Procedures – Validation of Certificates/Qualifications.*

84 With the Department of Health circular HSC 2000/19, *Appointment Procedures for Hospital and Community Medical and Dental Staff.*

85 With HSC 2002/08, *Pre and Post Appointment Checks for all Persons Working in the NHS in England.*

86 For further discussion, see Matthews, J., *Committee of Inquiry to Investigate how the NHS Handled Allegations about the Performance and Conduct of Richard Neale*, August 2004, Cm 6315, para 4.3.

87 *The Bichard Inquiry Report*, 2004, HC 653, HMSO.

an NHS employee which are made to the police will be recorded on the individual's Criminal Records Bureau file. This will be the case whether the allegation is proven or not.

Guidance for the writing of references was also tightened up. Prior to 1995 there was little guidance available from the Department of Health. The GMC did issue guidelines, which in the October 1995 version of *Good Medical Practice* required the reference writer to be honest and supportable. By 2001 this guidance was more precise: 'You must provide only honest and justifiable comments when giving references for, or writing reports about colleagues. When providing references you must include all relevant information which has any bearing on your colleagues' competence, performance and conduct.'

Historically within the NHS, a lax approach was taken with regard to doctors with criminal or disciplinary records who applied for employment. It took the Shipman case to change this. In February 2000, almost immediately after the conviction of Shipman, the National Health Service (General Medical Services) Regulations 1992 were amended so that applicants wishing to be included on health authority GP lists were required to declare criminal convictions, cautions and professional disciplinary findings. The regulations also contained provisions to ensure that similar information was obtained from practitioners already on the list. In turn, HAs were required to check the accuracy of this declaration, along with the applicant's qualifications and references. HAs were required to refuse to admit a doctor who had been convicted of murder or other criminal offence and sentenced to a term of imprisonment over six months.[88] Initially, individual PCTs had discretion whether or not to undertake a Criminal Records Bureau check. Since April 2004, all GPs applying to join a PCT list have had to submit an enhanced criminal record certificate. However, as noted by the Shipman Inquiry, the system is far from foolproof, as the accuracy and completeness of this certificate depends upon the applicant providing correct name(s) and a full address history.[89]

Only in 2000 was the Medical Act 1983 amended to require the GMC to disclose to a doctor's employer the fact that he or she was being investigated with respect to fitness to practise.[90] Not only was the GMC very slow to take this initiative, but even when it obtained the power it did not interpret the provision to require a GP's partners to be informed.[91] With respect to performance, it was originally proposed by the GMC in its draft rules of May 2004 that a copy of the report of an assessment of a doctor's performance would be sent to the doctor's employer at the same time as a copy was sent to the doctor him or herself. The previous absence of this had been observed by the Performance Procedures Review Group, which noted that performance assessment reports could not 'be regarded as a private document

88 National Health Service (General Medical Services) Amendment (No. 4) Regulations 2001.

89 See the Fifth Report of the Shipman Inquiry, *Safeguarding Patients: Lessons from the Past – Proposals for the Future*, paras 5.41–5.58 (www.the-shipman-inquiry.org.uk).

90 Section 35(B), Medical Act 1983.

91 See the Fifth Report of the Shipman Inquiry, *Safeguarding Patients: Lessons from the Past – Proposals for the Future*, para 26.61 (www.the-shipman-inquiry.org.uk).

between the GMC and the doctor'. However, this admirable advance was omitted from the July and November 2004 versions of these rules.[92]

Until 2002, independent Community Health Councils provided support to patients who wished to complain. In what has been described as a less than smooth transition, two replacement services were introduced – the Patient Advice and Liaison Services and the Independent Complaints Advocacy Services. PALS were intended to provide users of the NHS with an identifiable person to whom they could raise problems. In turn, PALS were expected to have direct access to the chief executive of their NHS Trust. The PALS approach is better suited to the larger environment of a hospital setting than to GP practices. Whilst PALS officers support patients at the early stages of raising informal concerns, they are expected to withdraw if a formal complaint is made. Support for formal complaints is intended to be provided by ICAS. This support applies to all aspects of the complaints processes, including external regulators such as the GMC.[93]

## A Decade of Government Intervention

It has been suggested that the regulation of the medical profession is facing a 'revolution'.[94] The Health Act 1999 introduced a new regulatory regime which placed more control of regulation in the hands of government, rather than the profession and promised to be more interventionist than previous approaches. The Act allowed the government to reform professional regulation without the need for primary legislation, heralding 'a new era of managerial intervention by government, moving away from the traditional paradigm of professional autonomy and self-regulation'.[95] Section 18 of the Act imposes a duty on each health authority, Primary Care Trust and NHS Trust to make arrangements for monitoring and improving the quality of healthcare which it provides to individuals. Doctors will continue to be involved, being required to have their performance reviewed by colleagues by means of participation in clinical audit. Power, however, is also shifted to managers who are assigned far greater involvement in clinical quality issues. The prospect of criticism for clinical failure should ensure that managers take an active interest in clinical governance. Ultimate responsibility for quality assurance lies with the chief executive of the relevant body.[96] It is suggested that some Primary Care Trust chief

92 See the Fifth Report of the Shipman Inquiry, *Safeguarding Patients: Lessons from the Past – Proposals for the Future*, paras 25.240–25.241 (www.the-shipman-inquiry.org.uk).

93 For further discussion, see The Honourable Mrs Justice Pauffley, Committee of Inquiry – Independent Investigation into how the NHS Handled Allegations about the Conduct of Clifford Ayling, 15 July 2004, Cm 6298, paras 5.44–5.49.

94 Davies, A.C.L., 'Don't Trust Me, I'm a Doctor – Medical Regulation and the 1999 NHS Reforms', *OJLS*, 2000, 20(437).

95 Davies, A.C.L., 'Don't Trust Me, I'm a Doctor – Medical Regulation and the 1999 NHS Reforms', *OJLS*, 2000, 20(437).

96 The Commission for Health Improvement (CHI), discussed below, has the role of periodically reviewing NHS Trusts and Primary Care Trusts, to ensure that adequate arrangements for monitoring clinical standards are in place.

executives still find the procedures 'daunting, inflexible and bureaucratic'. In these circumstances, PCTs may prefer to rely upon the GMC, even though they know that the high, criminal, standard of proof may mean that the doctor will not actually be disciplined.[97]

Two national mechanisms for setting clinical standards have also been introduced. One is the development of National Service Frameworks to determine standards for individual areas of care.[98] The other derives from the creation of the National Institute for Clinical Excellence.

In April 1999, NICE was introduced to provide health professionals and the public with guidance on 'best practice' with regard to health interventions and technologies. NICE was constituted as a Special Health Authority, responsible for advising NHS health professionals on means to maximize the standards of care provided to patients. Its remit includes advising health professionals on the appropriate use of specific health technologies (including pharmaceuticals) and in so doing it considers both clinical and cost factors. It also advises health professionals on the appropriate management of specific medical conditions. The aim is to ensure that decisions about which treatments should be provided by the NHS are taken at the national level, rather than by individual doctors or health authorities, in order to standardize treatments across the NHS. NICE also has a research and development role to improve the evidence base for its appraisals and reviews.[99] NICE was also given responsibility for developing audit criteria and audit tools to support local procedures. This would include providing individual clinicians and clinical teams with a framework to monitor their own performance. In April 2005, NICE joined with the Health Development Agency to become the National Institute for Health and Clinical Excellence (also to be known as NICE). The role of the new NICE was set out in the government's 2004 White Paper, *Choosing Health: Making Healthier Choices Easier*. This set out key principles for helping the public make more informed choices about their health. One clear implication of NICE is that it illustrates an unwillingness on the part of government to continue to trust individual doctors or the profession as a whole with choices about the scientific merit and effectiveness of particular treatments. This presents an attack upon one of the fundamental defining characteristics identified by many sociologists of the professions – that professions are the sole possessors and guardians of their esoteric specialist knowledge.

In November 1999, the Commission for Health Improvement was established, with the aim to ensure high standards and consistency within NHS care. This would be achieved by, inter alia, periodic clinical governance reviews of NHS bodies and monitoring of the implementation of NICE guidance. A majority of CHI members

---

97 Department of Health, *Good Doctors, Safer Patients – Proposals to Strengthen the System to Assure and Improve the Performance of Doctors and to Protect the Safety of Patients: A Report by the Chief Medical Officer*, July 2006, Chapter 2, paragraphs 59–60.

98 Department of Health, *National Service Frameworks* (HSC 1998/074).

99 NICE announced in 2003 that this element of its role was to be expanded. See White, C., 'NICE Expands Research and Development Role', *British Medical Journal*, 2003, 326: 1056, 17 May.

were drawn from outside of the field of healthcare employment.[100] The CHI was empowered to visit NHS Trusts and Primary Care Trusts to review arrangements for monitoring clinical standards. It also had extensive powers of entry to premises and to inspect and seize documents.[101] The CHI did not have enforcement powers, but its recommendations were to be implemented through NHS management structures. The remit of the CHI was extended in 2002 to encompass private hospitals. Ultimately, the Secretary of State was empowered to remove the Board of a Trust which did not respond to CHI criticisms. Again, this shifted power and influence away from the profession in the direction of managerial and structural power. The CHI ceased operating on 31 March 2004,[102] the Commission for Healthcare Audit and Inspection (the Healthcare Commission) taking over its functions. The Healthcare Commission promotes improvement in the quality of NHS and private healthcare. Its principal duties include: assessing the management, provision and quality of NHS healthcare and awarding annual performance ratings; regulating the private healthcare sector through registration, annual inspection, monitoring complaints and enforcement; and undertaking investigations of serious failures in the provision of healthcare. The Healthcare Commission is responsible for the second stage of the NHS complaints procedure, undertaking independent reviews of NHS complaints.[103]

The potential impact of the new regime on doctors has been described as 'striking'. Accountability for clinical matters has traditionally been of a reactive nature, following a mistake or other misconduct. Managers have not been involved in the monitoring of clinical care. Davies concludes that the Health Act 'heralds a new era of managerialist intervention by government, moving away from the traditional paradigm of professional autonomy and self-regulation'.[104]

In April 2001, the NHS Modernisation Agency was introduced as part of the Department of Health to support the national planning of NHS improvement strategies. It was superseded on 1 July 2005 by the NHS Institute for Innovation and Improvement. Established as a Special Health Authority in England, the role of the NHS Institute was described as supporting the NHS and its employees in accelerating the delivery of world-class healthcare by encouraging innovation and developing frontline capabilities.

After the publication of a Department of Health report in 1997, health authorities established Poorly Performing Doctors' Committees. Membership included the HA Medical Director and the LMC Chair. The committees aimed to act on information

---

100 The Commission for Health Improvement (Membership and Procedure) Regulations 1999, SI 1999 No 2801, reg 2.

101 Section 23, Health Act 1999.

102 Abolished by the Health and Social Care (Community Health and Standards) Act 2003.

103 A complaint can only be reviewed once it has been raised with the organization or practitioner concerned, and the complainant is not satisfied with their formal written response, or if the complaint has been with the healthcare provider for six months and has not been resolved.

104 For further discussion, see Davies, A.C.L., 'Don't Trust Me, I'm a Doctor – Medical Regulation and the 1999 NHS Reforms', *Oxford Journal of Legal Studies*, September 2000, 20(437).

which suggested there were concerns about a GP's performance, with patient protection as the core purpose. The committees adopted a supportive stance, seeking remedial and educational action. If, in extreme circumstances, this was not thought appropriate, the doctor could be referred to the GMC, but such a decision would require health authority ratification. The subsequent creation of the National Clinical Assessment Authority (discussed below) provided additional expertise on which to draw.

In April 2001, the National Clinical Assessment Authority was established, following recommendations made in the Chief Medical Officer's report, *Supporting Doctors, Protecting Patients*, published in November 1999, and *Assuring the Quality of Medical Practice: Implementing Supporting Doctors, Protecting Patients*, in January 2001. The NCAA subsequently became the National Clinical Assessment Service and in April 2005 became part of the National Patient Safety Agency. NCAS aims to promote public confidence in doctors by providing confidential advice and support to the NHS on how to manage doctors whose performance gives cause for concern. If an employer is considering excluding a doctor it must contact NCAS to discuss the situation before any move to 'formal exclusion'. NCAS undertakes targeted assessments where necessary and advises upon follow-up action. NCAS does not subsume the role of an employer, nor does it function as a regulator. It has no powers of enforcement. The NHS employer therefore remains responsible for resolving the problem once the NCAS has produced its assessment. NCAS only receives referrals from employers, not directly from the public. NCAS maintains contact with the GMC, to allow for fast-track referrals where appropriate, and also works closely with, inter alia, the medical Royal Colleges. NCAS involvement is normally confidential to the referred practitioners and his or her employer, although where patient safety is at issue, there may be discussion with or referral to the GMC. Unlike the GMC, NCAS will act on anonymous information in order to ensure patient safety. NCAS also has a whistleblowers policy for use when information is received from a concerned colleague. Since 2001, failure by a GP to cooperate with a request for an assessment has been a breach of the terms of service. Similarly, a hospital doctor is likely to face disciplinary action for a failure to cooperate. Assessments are intended to be formative, rather than to determine whether a doctor is fit to practise (that is still seen to be the role of the GMC).[105]

In many respects, NCAS appears to have very quickly stolen a lead over the GMC. However, it has been noted that educational models rely upon the doctor concerned being willing and able to acknowledge the need for remedial action. Intentional misconduct or simply a lack of insight is unlikely to fit well within this system. There is also a risk that a system which seeks to help and support may be vulnerable to misuse by a doctor if he or she is able to use it to delay more appropriate action.[106]

In June 2000, the government accepted the recommendations made in the Chief Medical Officer's report, *An Organisation with a Memory*. This acknowledged that there had been little systematic learning from patient safety incidents and

105 Ayling Inquiry Report, 15 July 2004, paras 6.41–6.43 and 6.46–6.49.

106 Ayling Inquiry Report, 15 July 2004, para 6.52.

service failure in the NHS that resulted in harm to patients. *An Organisation with a Memory* proposed the development of a culture of openness, reporting and safety consciousness within NHS organizations. In July 2001, the National Patient Safety Agency, a Special Health Authority, was created to coordinate the efforts of all those involved in healthcare, and more importantly to learn from patient safety incidents occurring in the NHS. The NPSA began to collect and analyse information on the estimated 900,000 annual adverse events in the NHS. This was to be used, in combination with appropriate safety information from elsewhere, to improve safety in the NHS and to provide leadership with regard to patient safety. A central role for the NPSA was the creation of a national system for reporting adverse events and near misses, the National Reporting and Learning System. In this respect, the NPSA's aim was to promote an open and fair culture in hospitals, encouraging doctors and other staff to report incidents and 'near misses' without fear of personal sanction. The change of emphasis has been described as more about the 'how' than the 'who'.[107] Reporting will have little direct impact in terms of dealing with individual doctors whose activities give cause for concern, because participation will be voluntary and all reports which are received by the NPSA will be anonymized. Individual cases will not be investigated and data will not be available for use in disciplinary actions. For example, the Shipman Inquiry noted that in 1994, the local PCT was not notified that Mrs Renate Overton had been admitted to hospital due, the doctors suspected, to Shipman's administering of morphine. Were such an event to occur today, an anonymous report may be made to the NPSA, but there would still be no guarantee that the matter would come to the attention of the PCT.[108]

## Advantages and Disadvantages of Multiple Regulators

These new agencies have little or no genuine independence from government and therefore represent significant challenges to the traditional model of self-regulation. They also represent something of a departure from previous attempts at government regulation, because the new regulatory bodies are primarily concerned with clinical quality, rather than with managerial and administrative issues. Ultimately, however, the new bodies have the potential to undermine medical self-regulation, not because they are imposed and override the GMC, but because the GMC has failed to ensure that their functions are unnecessary.

In more general terms, multiple regulators offer both advantages and disadvantages. A key disadvantage is the risk that some, potentially serious, problems will slip through gaps between regulatory bodies. In turn, these different regulatory bodies may seek to blame each other if there is a serious failure of the Shipman or Bristol type. Advantages include the possibility that an appropriately structured group of regulators may be encouraged to compete with each other, fearing that they will face public and government criticism if another regulator detects misconduct that

107 NPSA website, 15 December 2005.

108 For further discussion, see the Fifth Report of the Shipman Inquiry, *Safeguarding Patients: Lessons from the Past – Proposals for the Future*, paras 12.54–12.57 (www.the-shipman-inquiry.org.uk).

they have missed.[109] In this environment, competition has the potential to improve the overall quality of regulation. This contrasts with the position taken by Ogus, who considers the possibility that in a multi-regulator environment, consumers can choose the level of regulation they require and are willing to pay for. Assuming that sufficient numbers of consumers seek cheaper regulation, individual regulators may also compete to offer more lenient regulatory environments in order to attract greater numbers of the regulated community – the so called race to the bottom.[110] These issues have little relevance to the recent NHS reforms because the latter introduces multiple compulsory regulatory environments, rather than a choice of regulators. The greater risk is of creating a structure which is too complex for the public to understand and with which individual doctors become disillusioned if they feel that they are over-regulated, or even that different regulatory bodies are attempting to pull them in different directions.

The creation of the NPSA and subsequent developments sought to improve blame-free reporting within the NHS. By 2005, some progress had been made, with all Trusts having established local reporting systems and many having introduced open reporting cultures. All Trusts were linked to the National Reporting and Learning System by the end of 2004, two years later than the 2002 deadline set by the Department of Health (DoH), but by August 2005 at least 35 Trusts had still not submitted data.[111] Generally, progress at national level had been slower than the DoH had envisaged, with a national reporting system and effective sharing of 'lessons' some way off at the time of the National Audit Office (NAO) review in late 2005. Also, most Trusts remained predominantly reactive rather than proactive, and a blame culture still prevailed in some. A minority of nurses and other staff, 25 per cent, acknowledged that the environment within their Trust had moved away from a blame culture, but a third of employees still felt that their Trust would still not want to know about serious problems.[112] Under-reporting of adverse incidents and near misses also remained an issue, with estimates of 22 per cent of incidents and 39 per cent of near misses going unreported. Under-reporting was greater with regard to medication and other errors which could directly be attributed to individual staff, than to incidents such as patient falls which lacked such direct connection. Fear of repercussions continued to be an issue. The National Patient Safety Agency launched an e-Form in September 2004 as a safety net for those unwilling to report locally because of fear of reprisals.[113] Some Trusts had indicated that they would

109 For further discussion on this theme, see Davies, A.C.L., 'Don't Trust Me, I'm a Doctor – Medical Regulation and the 1999 NHS Reforms', *Oxford Journal of Legal Studies*, September 2000, 20(437).

110 Ogus, A., 'Rethinking Self-Regulation', *Oxford Journal of Legal Studies*, 1995, 15 (97).

111 See National Audit Office, *A Safer Place for Patients: Learning to Improve Patient Safety*, 31 October 2005, www.nao.org.uk.

112 See National Audit Office, *A Safer Place for Patients: Learning to Improve Patient Safety*, 31 October 2005, pages 13 and 23, www.nao.org.uk.

113 See National Patient Safety Agency, *Building a Memory: Preventing Harm, Reducing Risks and Improving Patient Safety. The First Report of the National Reporting and Learning System and the Patient Safety Observatory*, July 2005.

discourage use of the e-Form by their staff. They did not want an anonymous system, which they saw as undermining local reporting.[114]

Under-reporting by doctors was significantly greater than that by nurses.[115] A survey in 2004 of over 3,000 doctors revealed that 78 per cent had been involved in an incident which influenced patient care, yet only 19 per cent had reported this. Cultural barriers within the medical profession remained the major obstacle to reporting.[116] There was evidence of continued arrogance amongst doctors regarding their obligations to report adverse events. A survey of junior doctors aimed at eliciting reasons why incidents might not be reported revealed, inter alia, that they did not have time, did not think it would make any difference or were generally undecided as to whether the National Patient Safety Agency would improve patient safety. Patient partnership in the supposed new open culture also remained limited, with only 24 per cent of Trusts routinely informing patients when they had been involved in an adverse incident. Only 6 per cent of patients surveyed reported that they were consulted about how the adverse incident which they had experienced might be prevented in future.[117]

The NAO found that 41 per cent of Trusts had not undertaken detailed analysis of incidents. Of the 59 per cent which had, there was no systematic mechanism for determining which reports warranted detailed investigation. Idiosyncrasies and subjective aspects of approach were common. It was also found that only eight strategic health authorities reported intervening following serious incidents involving the competence of health professionals. Strategic health authorities lacked appropriate systems to learn from serious incidents. Nor did they monitor the implementation of good practice by Trusts. Other ongoing problems included the continuation of a complex variety of bodies to which reports might need to be made. Even after some rationalization by the National Patient Safety Agency, around 30 reporting routes remained.[118]

## Other Grounds for Optimism?

There has been a move in recent years to expand the roles undertaken by non-doctor healthcare professionals, notably nurses, into areas traditionally considered to be the preserve of doctors. Recognition that nurses have specific skills and associated professional accountability, rather than being merely relatively unskilled assistants

---

114 See National Audit Office, *A Safer Place for Patients: Learning to Improve Patient Safety*, 31 October 2005, para 18, www.nao.org.uk.

115 See National Audit Office, *A Safer Place for Patients: Learning to Improve Patient Safety*, 31 October 2005, page 27, www.nao.org.uk.

116 See *Mistakes and Near Misses in the NHS*, Survey June 2004, Doctors.net.uk; and National Audit Office, *A Safer Place for Patients: Learning to Improve Patient Safety*, 31 October 2005, pages 27–8, www.nao.org.uk.

117 See National Audit Office, *A Safer Place for Patients: Learning to Improve Patient Safety*, 31 October 2005, paras 10 and 24 and pages 27–8 www.nao.org.uk.

118 See National Audit Office, *A Safer Place for Patients: Learning to Improve Patient Safety*, 31 October 2005, pages 40, 51 and paragraphs 2.29–2.30, www.nao.org.uk.

to doctors, gives rise to greater optimism that they may in future be far more willing to challenge miscreant doctors. Practice based upon inter-disciplinary teams and a healthy degree of inter-professional competition offers the potential for better patient care and better systems of inter and intra-professional oversight.

In November 2003, the GMC agreed that when early indicators revealed concerns about a doctor's fitness to practise, this information should be disclosed to the doctor's employer and fed into their clinical governance systems.[119] In July 2004, the Council considered issues relating to the disclosure of a doctor's fitness to practise history. The following procedures were agreed:

- Generally, the GMC should disclose to inquirers all information already in the public domain.
- Information not already in the public domain will only be disclosed in limited circumstances.
- Sanctions imposed on a doctor's registration should remain a matter of public record indefinitely and be disclosed on request.
- Findings of serious professional misconduct, whether or not sanctions were imposed, should remain a matter of public record indefinitely and be disclosed on request.
- Even when serious professional misconduct or impaired fitness to practise has not been established, findings of relevant fact associated with the allegations should remain a matter of public record indefinitely and be disclosed on request.
- A doctor's appearances before the Professional Conduct Committee or a fitness to practise panel should generally be disclosed on request, even when no adverse finding was established.
- A warning issued to a doctor should be disclosed to prospective employers and to any enquirer during its five-year life.[120]

As previously noted, in the past the GMC have not gone out of their way to help identify a doctor when an enquiry is made. The above, largely positive, steps will only be meaningful if attitudes within the GMC are such that there is a positive will to disclose information in the public interest. The GMC have stated the intention to enhance the information about a doctor's disciplinary history and registration status available on its internet site. Also, and perhaps most importantly, the stated aim is to make all of this information available by way of a straightforward search against

119 *Developing Medical Regulation: a Vision for the Future – the GMC's Response to the Call for Ideas by the Review of Clinical Performance and Medical Regulation*, April 2005, Appendix B, paras 3–4.

120 *Developing Medical Regulation: a Vision for the Future – the GMC's Response to the Call for Ideas by the Review of Clinical Performance and Medical Regulation*, April 2005, Appendix B, paras 6–8. Dame Janet Smith, in her fifth Shipman Inquiry Report, had indicated that all regulatory information about a doctor which was already in the public domain should be disclosable.

the doctor's name.[121] In addition, as already noted, the GMC should also ensure that its online information is available via multiple search routes. Furthermore, the Council should make available electronically full details of disciplinary and other proceedings in a generic way, that is without the need to search by name of each individual doctor. This should enhance public confidence by enabling interested members of the public to readily obtain an overview of the regulatory work of the GMC and an insight into the penalties imposed for particular types of behaviour. It would also facilitate more systematic academic work in this field.

## Council for Health Regulatory Excellence

Historically, subject to limited rights of appeal by the doctor, decisions by GMC fitness to practise panels, and their predecessors, have been final. Concerns were expressed about this limitation and in 2000 the NHS Plan set out proposals for a Regulatory Council to coordinate professional regulatory bodies. The Bristol Royal Infirmary Inquiry Report in 2001 also recommended the creation of a coordinating body to oversee professional self-regulation. In August 2001, the government, in its consultation document, *Modernising Regulation in the Health Professions*, outlined proposals for the creation of the Council for the Regulation of Health Care Professionals. This idea was not new. For instance, in 1973, Rudolph Klein had proposed a Council for the Professions. Viewing the GMC as part of a larger complaints structure, in Klein's opinion collective accountability was the best way to ensure individual accountability. Klein's proposed council would have allowed information to be exchanged between self-regulating professions and review of the quality of service each was providing.[122]

The body, called the Council for the Regulation of Health Professions, was eventually created by the NHS Reform and Health Care Professions Act 2002. The Council subsequently changed its name to the Council for Health Regulatory Excellence. The general functions of the Council were described as, inter alia: to promote the interests of patients and other members of the public in relation to the performance of the functions of professional regulatory bodies;[123] to promote best practice in the performance of those functions; to formulate principles relating to good professional self-regulation; and to encourage regulatory bodies to conform to them.[124] The CHRE was empowered to do anything necessary or expedient for the purpose of the performance of its functions. For example, it could investigate

121 *Developing Medical Regulation: a Vision for the Future – the GMC's Response to the Call for Ideas by the Review of Clinical Performance and Medical Regulation*, April 2005, Appendix B, paras 12–15.

122 Klein, R., *Complaints against Doctors: a Study in Professional Accountability*, 1973, Charles Knight, London, 63 and 163.

123 Section 25(3) provides that the professional bodies in question include: the General Medical Council, the General Dental Council, the General Optical Council, the General Osteopathic Council the United Kingdom Central Council for Nursing, Midwifery and Health Visiting, and each of the National Boards for Nursing, Midwifery and Health Visiting.

124 Sections 25(1) and (2).

the performance of a regulatory body and could compare the performance of one regulatory body with another. It recommended changes to the way in which a regulatory body performs any of its functions.[125]

Restrictions of the powers of the CHRE were specified in section 26 of the 2002 Act:

> 26(3) The Council may not do anything in relation to the case of any individual in relation to whom–
> (a) there are, are to be, or have been proceedings before a committee of a regulatory body, or the regulatory body itself or any officer of the body, or
> (b) an allegation has been made to the regulatory body, or one of its committees or officers, which could result in such proceedings.
> (4) Subsection (3) does not prevent the Council from taking action under section 28 or 29, but action under section 29 may be taken only after the regulatory body's proceedings have ended.
> (11) In subsections (3) and (4), 'proceedings', in relation to a regulatory body, or one of its committees or officers, includes a process of decision-making by which a decision could be made affecting the registration of the individual in question.

If the Council considers it desirable for the protection of members of the public, it may give directions requiring a regulatory body to make rules (under any power the regulatory body has to do so) to achieve an effect specified in the directions.[126]

If the CHRE considers that a decision of the General Medical Council has been unduly lenient, whether as to a finding of professional misconduct or fitness to practise, or lack of such a finding, or as to any penalty imposed, or both, and that it would be desirable for the protection of the public for the CHRE to take action, it may refer the case to the relevant court.[127] This power also applies to a decision by the GMC not to take any disciplinary action and a decision to restore a person to the medical register. The court may quash the original decision, substitute for the decision any other decision which could have been made by the professional body, or remit the case to the professional body to dispose of the case in accordance with the directions of the court.

The approach adopted by the courts to appeals brought by the CHRE is that used by the Court of Appeal when determining whether a criminal court sentence is unduly lenient, that is, whether the sanction is outside of the reasonable range of sanctions available to the sentencing court in the particular circumstances of the case. Alteration of the sentence should also be desirable for the purposes of public protection.[128]

---

125 Section 26.

126 Section 27(1). Section 27(3) provides that the Council may give such directions, inter alia, only in relation to rules which must be approved by the Privy Council (whether by order or not) or by the Department of Health, Social Services. 'Making' rules includes amending or revoking rules, and 'rules' includes regulations, bye-laws and schemes.

127 Section 29(4). The relevant court is the High Court of Justice in England and Wales, the High Court of Justice in Northern Ireland and the Court of Session in Scotland.

128 See, for example, *Council for the Regulation of Healthcare Professionals v GMC and Solanke* [2004] 944 (Admin).

The *Council for the Regulation of Health Care Professionals v General Medical Council*[129] was the first case to consider the extent of the new powers to refer decisions of the GMC to the High Court. Levenson J concluded that the intention of Parliament was to provide the CHHE with the widest powers to oversee the activities of the regulatory bodies brought within its remit. Other than the exception in section 26, no aspect of the work of these bodies is exempt from investigation, recommendation or report. The section 26 exception is present to ensure that during the course of any disciplinary investigation or proceedings, the self-regulatory process is free from interference. However, once such proceedings are concluded, the CHRE was free to act. Both an unduly lenient finding by the professional regulator and a finding that there was no serious professional misconduct at all could trigger the power to refer. Considering the approach of the Court of Appeal in references by the Attorney General of unduly lenient sentences pursuant to section 36 of the Criminal Justice Act 1988, Levenson J noted that intervention should not occur unless there has been some error of principle so that public confidence would be damaged if the sentence were not altered.[130] With regard to section 26(3), which prohibits the Council from referring the case of any individual to the court while that case is being considered or, if disciplinary proceedings have been undertaken, until a 'relevant decision' has been taken by the appropriate regulatory body in that case, the CHRE was only prohibited from doing anything in relation to 'the case' of an individual; the prohibition does not relate to the individual him or herself. Section 26(4) therefore permits action to be taken after 'the regulatory body's proceedings' have ended, not after *any* proceedings of the body. That this was the appropriate interpretation of the statutory wording is reinforced by the very strict time limit imposed on the CHRE for making a referral to court, four weeks beginning with the last date on which the practitioner concerned has a right of appeal. Without this interpretation, the existence of some entirely different complaint under investigation could prevent a reference to the court ever being made.

## Are the Powers of the CHRE Likely to Impact Significantly on Medical Self-Regulation?

The creation of the CHRE presents a potentially significant challenge to the independence of the GMC and should add further pressure to the Council to ensure that its misconduct procedures are effective. How much pressure is actually brought to bear will depend upon the degree to which the CHRE exercises this power and, most importantly, the willingness of the courts to interfere with decisions of the GMC. As discussed above, in the small number of cases heard to date, the courts

129 [2004] EWHC 527 (Admin). For more recent discussion by the Court of Appeal, see *Council for the Regulation of Healthcare Professionals v General Medical Council, Council for the Regulation of Healthcare Professionals v Nursing and Midwifery Council* [2004] EWCA Civ 1356, [2004] All ER (D) 272 (Oct), which approved the first instance decision of Levenson J.

130 Attorney General's Reference (No 4 of 1989) 90 Cr App Rep 366 and Attorney General's Reference (No 5 of 1989), Reg. v. Hill-Trevor 90 Cr App Rep 358.

have adopted a broad interpretation of the CHRE's powers to refer cases to them. However, it is too early to determine how often the courts will actually overturn decisions by the GMC and other professional bodies. In other contexts where a significant body of case authority is available, notably in appeals from the PCC, both the Privy Council and the High Court have demonstrated a tendency to defer to the expertise of the professional bodies themselves. A modification to this approach will be needed if the powers of the CHRE are to be used to full effect.

# Chapter 17

# Revalidation – the GMC's Big Idea

## Introduction

As already discussed, in recent years the GMC has changed and developed aspects of its regulatory role. However, none of these changes could be described as groundbreaking. The GMC has sought to tackle this previously lacklustre approach with one big idea – revalidation.[1] The GMC was empowered to introduce revalidation from 2002.[2] The effectiveness of the revalidation process is likely to be of great importance to the future credibility of the GMC. The successful implementation of revalidation has the potential to significantly enhance the GMC's reputation, but unsuccessful implementation could seriously erode this reputation and undermine the progress already made.

The medical register was introduced in 1858 to provide a definitive list of those people who were qualified to practise medicine. Once a doctor's name was on the register it stayed there for life, unless the doctor chose voluntary removal or committed misconduct considered sufficiently serious to have it removed. Historically, therefore, once a doctor was admitted to the profession, the role of the GMC was negative. As Klein put it, the GMC had no interest in a doctor against whom no complaint had been made, or who was not physically or mentally ill, who did not abuse drink or drugs or had not broken the law. It had no involvement with the doctor who had simply lost interest and become an underperforming practitioner.[3] In short, the role of the GMC was to 'drum convicted sinners out of the profession, not to ensure continued professional virtue'.[4] This approach compares very badly against some other potentially high risk occupations. For example, whilst a doctor could remain in practice for 40 years or more with no check or intervention, an

---

1 It has been suggested that the GMC was already following an international trend towards revalidation of doctors, although the term 'revalidation' was not in widespread use. Recent scandals may have focused attention and speeded up the process, but were not the driving force. See Buckley, G., 'Revalidation is the Answer', *BMJ*, 1999, 319: 1145–6, 30 October; and Department of Health, *Good Doctors, Safer Patients – Proposals to Strengthen the System to Assure and Improve the Performance of Doctors and to Protect the Safety of Patients: A Report by the Chief Medical Officer*, July 2006.

2 Medical Act (Amendment) Order 2002, which defines revalidation as 'the evaluation of a medical practitioner's fitness to practise'.

3 Klein was writing before the introduction of the performance procedures. However, as these procedures had very limited impact in practice, his comments remain relevant.

4 Klein, R., *The Politics of the National Health Service*, 1983, Longman, London.

airline pilot would typically be subject to around 100 formal assessments in the course of his or her career. In these and many other high risk industries, the onus is upon the professionals to periodically prove their competence. To such professionals it 'was considered quite extraordinary' that within the medical profession the onus had been placed on the regulator to disprove a practitioner's competence.[5]

The core principle behind revalidation is that instead of the right to practise being conferred for life, registered doctors will have to satisfy the GMC on a periodic basis that they remain fit to practise. This follows the reasoning that if the profession is to warrant the privilege of self-regulation, it must do more than just police misconduct. Members must also put greater effort into ensuring continuing competence.[6] The performance of doctors has been found to decline over time. Older doctors and more 'experienced' practitioners have been found to have less factual knowledge, to be less likely to adhere to current standards and protocols and to achieve poorer patient outcomes.[7] Historically, doctors have not even been required by the GMC to undertake even minimum levels of continuing professional training.[8] Moves in the direction of revalidation in the USA and Canada are ahead of those in the UK.[9] In these other jurisdictions, a distinction is made between compulsory relicensure, designed to get the dangerous out of practice, and voluntary continuing improvement. In Quebec, the College des Medecins requires that all doctors provide annually information about their practice, including the details of work they undertake outside of their specialty. In Victoria, Australia, doctors seeking annual renewal of their licence may be required to supply information about matters such as the principal areas of practice undertaken and intended to be undertaken, plus any CPD.[10] Far earlier than recent moves in the UK, the Ontario medical system adopted

---

5 See, for example, Department of Health, *Good Doctors, Safer Patients – Proposals to Strengthen the System to Assure and Improve the Performance of Doctors and to Protect the Safety of Patients: A Report by the Chief Medical Officer*, July 2006, Chapter 10.

6 See, for example, Abel, R., 'Taking Professionalism Seriously', *Annual Review of American Law*, 1989, 41.

7 Choudhry, N.K., Fletcher, R.H. and Soumerai, S.B., 'Systematic Review: The Relationship between Clinical Experience and Quality of Health Care', *Ann Int Med*, 2005, 142: 260–73. Cited by Norcini, J.J., 'Where Next with Revalidation?', *BMJ*, 2005, 330: 1458–9, 25 June.

8 The Bristol Report, para 338.

9 See, for example, Finocchio, L.J. et al, *Reforming Health Care Workforce Regulation: Policy Considerations for the 21st Century*, Health Professions Commission, 1995; Cain, F.E., Benjamin, R.M. and Thompson, J.N., 'Obstacles to Maintaining Licensure in the United States, *BMJ*, 2005, 330: 1443–5, 18 June. The latter note that licensing authorities typically use hospital reports, disciplinary data, patient complaints and malpractice reports, although together these do not necessarily constitute a comprehensive assessment of fitness to practise. It is also noted that medical boards in the US lack the resources and capability to take sole responsibility for evaluating all areas of a doctor's competence. Work alongside other regulatory authorities and medical societies is necessary to achieve this. Cain et al also note that in 2004 the Federation of State Medical Boards adopted a policy which required individual state boards to ensure that physicians seeking to be re-licensed were competent.

10 GMC Paper, 20 September 2005, 'Developing Risk-based Regulation: Progress Report', para 39.

a joint Peer Assessment Program, involving half-day visits by two unknown peers, and a Physician Enhancement Program resulting in evaluation and assessment.[11] A 2003 survey from the US found that 80 per cent of respondents thought that doctors should periodically be retested regarding their knowledge and abilities; should be able to demonstrate and appropriate success rate from treatment; and receive good satisfaction ratings from their patients.[12]

Revalidation may be seen as an attempt by the medical profession to renegotiate its regulatory bargain with the state – promising that its members will once again be brought under proper scrutiny and control. This may be seen as a bold move on the part of the GMC to genuinely address the issues raised in recent scandals. Alternatively, it may be the latest instalment of what Macdonald has referred to as the GMC's historical success in developing tactics to manipulate and control its relationship with the state.[13] The GMC has faced a difficult political balancing act with revalidation. It has used the proposals to assure the government and public that unfit doctors will no longer be able to escape detection. Simultaneously, the GMC has sought to reassure doctors that they have nothing to fear from revalidation.[14] Described by the president of the GMC, responding to concerns after the Neale case, in the following way: '…the real lesson is…an urgent need to implement the systematic review of all doctor's practices through effective clinical governance locally, underpinned nationally by the regular revalidation of doctors' registration with the GMC.'[15]

In political terms, the GMC's proposals may be seen as being directed at those politicians and senior civil servants who are attracted to the proposition that weeding out incompetent members of a profession will dramatically increase quality.[16] Even if the GMC's proposals could actually achieve this, there is a lack of definitive knowledge about the proportion of doctors who might need to be weeded out. Best estimates seem to range around 5 per cent, but these figures are not necessarily based upon strong background information or an agreed definition of incompetence.[17]

---

11 Davis, D.A. et al. 'Attempting to Ensure Physician Competence', *Journal of the American Medical Association*, 1990, 263, 15, 2041–2, cited by Becher, T., *Professional Practices*, 1999, Transaction Publishers, New Brunswick, New Jersey, 224.

12 Brennan, T.A., Horwitz, R.A., Duffy, F.D., Cassel, C.K., Goode, L.D. and Lipner, R.S., 'The Role of Physician Specialty Board Certification Status in the Quality Movement', *JAMA*, 2004, 292: 1038–43. Cited by **Norcini,** J.J., 'Where Next with Revalidation?', *BMJ*, 2005, 330: 1458–9,. 25 June.

13 Macdonald, K.M., *The Sociology of the Professions*, 1995, Sage, London, 106. This follows the wider theory that professions deploy cognitive and narrative mechanisms in an attempt to define social reality and establish their social status.

14 See, for example, GMC, *Report of the Revalidation Steering Group*, February 1999.

15 Press statement issued after Neale was removed from the medical register on 25 July 2000.

16 For further discussion of this principle, see Becher, T., *Professional Practices*, 1999, Transaction Publishers, New Brunswick, New Jersey, 213.

17 See, for example, Rosenthal, M., *The Incompetent Doctor*, 1995, Open University Press, Buckingham; and Becher, T., *Professional Practices*, 1999, Transaction Publishers, New Brunswick, New Jersey, 214.

## The Historical Background to Revalidation

The concept of renewal of registration can be traced back at least to the 1970s. In 1975 the Merrison Committee had rejected re-certification as being too difficult. A year later the Alment Committee[18] (established by the BMA and consisting of medically qualified members), also considered the question of re-licensure. This committee recognized the value of participating in medical audit, but the emphasis was on a voluntary process. Re-licensure was rejected, the reasoning being that there was insufficient evidence to require this. Re-licensure would also result in trust in systems and institutions, replacing what the committee considered to be more valuable trust in individuals.

More recently, in 1992, Stacey was more enthusiastic, suggesting that re-licensure was a means to ensure that the medical register truly reflected only those competent to practise.[19] Catto identifies the term 'revalidation' as first appearing within the GMC in 1998. Developments in thinking about the process led the Council to conclude that it could not introduce revalidation as an isolated initiative. Rather, revalidation would need to be one component within a complex system of quality assurance. This, it was said, would end the perceived isolation of the GMC:

> So what does revalidation actually mean? It is a package in which the doctor demonstrates that he or she is up to date and fit to practise medicine and the GMC issues a licence. It is not primarily about identifying poorly performing doctors. Clinical governance and other mechanisms exist for that purpose. It is a system for promoting public confidence in the profession and ensuring the quality of the Register.
>
> It will promote confidence in the medical profession, help modernise professionally led regulation along the lines that is happening in other countries and I think it will make the medical Register far more relevant than it currently is.[20]

At its core, revalidation should ensure that unfit doctors are removed from practice and that others are encouraged to continually improve their standards. '[R]evalidation should be a new beginning…allow[ing] the medical profession to review its culture, allow[ing] doctors to practise in a supportive environment where they can give and receive feedback openly, allow[ing] them to learn from their mistakes, and…be reassured that they are doing a good job.'[21]

The GMC has identified three broad policy aims for revalidation:

1. To encourage all doctors to reflect meaningfully on their practice, using evidence obtained from audit and elsewhere.
2. To shift the emphasis away from qualifications alone, to being up to date and fit to practise as the defining characteristic of being qualified and registered.

---

18 Report of a Committee of Enquiry set up for the Medical Profession in the United Kingdom, *Competence to Practice*, 1976.

19 Stacey, M., *Regulating British Medicine: the General Medical Council*, 1992, Wiley, Chichester, 267.

20 Sir Graeme Catto, 'The GMC – Revalidation – What Are We Trying to Measure?', *Medico-Legal Journal*, 2003, 71(106), 2 October.

21 du Boulay, C., 'Revalidation for Doctors in the United Kingdom, the End or the Beginning?', *BMJ*, 2000, Vol. 320, 3 June.

Revalidation would be based on performance as well as competence.

3. To move from the 'management by exception' approach that had existed since 1858, by ensuring that all doctors had to regularly confirm that they are up to date and fit to practise.[22]

By explicitly linking professional standards with registration, the GMC's stated aim was to be able to hold individual doctors to account for their performance and conduct. Revalidation should therefore make the medical register fit for purpose.[23]

It has been observed from within the profession that revalidation may offer a means to embed peer review within day-to-day medical practice. Assessment, both formative and summative, would be part of medical practice from the time a prospective doctor enters medical school until the qualified doctor retires.[24] The principle of ongoing summative assessment was not, however, favoured by the GMC in its revalidation proposals.

GMC members who spoke against moves towards revalidation expressed concerns about the linkage between standards of performance and the medical register. There was concern that one part of the profession policing another would lead to damaging rifts. Lay voices on the Council, notably Julia Neuberger, argued more forcefully that the public rightly expected registered medical practitioners to continue to maintain a minimum level of competence. However, the reality was that the GMC had no idea whether or not this was the position in the case of most doctors.[25] It would be embarrassing for the GMC and problematic for both it and the NHS if the introduction of revalidation revealed that more than a small percentage of registered doctors were unfit to practise. There are grounds for concern that some within the profession describe as 'rifts' activities which the profession, through the GMC, should have been doing since the nineteenth century.

The outcome of this debate was something of a non-committed compromise. It was agreed that a steering group would prepare for a full debate at the GMC conference. However, the Council also decided to leave in abeyance the principle of linking revalidation with registration.[26] Irvine describes strongest support as coming from the lay and appointed members of the GMC. Strongest opposition came from those elected by the profession.[27] The concerns were obvious; support of rank and file members of the profession was central to the success of revalidation, yet their representatives stood in the way. Reactions from outside of the GMC were mixed.

22 GMC, *The Policy Framework for Revalidation: A Position Paper*, July 2004.

23 GMC, *Effective, Inclusive and Accountable Reform of the GMC's Structure, Constitution and Governance*, March 2001, 4; and GMC, *Developing Medical Regulation: a Vision for the Future – the GMC's Response to the Call for Ideas by the Review of Clinical Performance and Medical Regulation*, April 2005.

24 A point advanced by Roddy MacSween, Chairman of the Academy of Medical Royal Colleges. Cited by Irvine, D., *The Doctors' Tale*, 2003, Radcliffe Medical Press, Oxford, 145–6.

25 For further discussion of this debate, see Irvine, D., *The Doctors' Tale*, 2003, Radcliffe Medical Press, Oxford, 149–50.

26 Irvine, D., *The Doctors' Tale*, 2003, Radcliffe Medical Press, Oxford, 150.

27 Irvine, D., *The Doctors' Tale*, 2003, Radcliffe Medical Press, Oxford, 152.

For example, the *Lancet* described the opponents of revalidation as out of date and impeding progress.[28]

Opposition voices, mainly BMA Council members, continued at the GMC conference. It was argued in 2000, by the vice-president of the GMC, that revalidation would put on the line the registration and careers of the 95 per cent of doctors who were competent and trustworthy, in order to detect the estimated 5 per cent who were not. The 'whole exercise is bureaucracy gone mad and a waste of time'.[29] The proposal for revalidation was nevertheless passed by a substantial majority. Irvine reported hearing doctors complaining that the GMC was not representing them any more. There was the feeling that the profession was being excessively punished as a whole for the failings of a few.[30] Again, this raises serious concerns about the awareness amongst members of the medical profession that the GMC should not be seen as some form of elected representative body, and that each individual doctor has a part to play in ensuring that self-regulation is effective.

## Initial Proposals

The GMC's initial plans for revalidation were outlined in the 2000 document, *Revalidating Doctors*. Revalidation, it was said: '...will allow the vast majority of doctors to demonstrate publicly that they are worthy of their patients' trust. And it will enable much earlier and quicker action against the registration of doctors who are no longer worthy of that trust.'[31]

The GMC's consultation exercise was launched in June 2000. It was directed at over 5,000 organizations, all registered doctors and the public. It is of note that attempts to involve the latter were rather limited, the Council distributing 10,000 leaflets and the consultation document being downloaded, in full or summary form, 2,400 times from the GMC website.[32] Responses from within the profession were mixed. The GMC was supported in its proposals by the Royal Colleges and the General Practitioners' Committee of the BMA. In contrast, the BMA committees representing specialists, consultants and junior doctors, as well as the Public Health Committee of the BMA, opposed the plans.[33]

The paper stated that patients would benefit from revalidation, inter alia, by being protected from poorly performing doctors, and by receiving a better quality of service from doctors who are successful in the process. Doctors would benefit from the increased confidence which revalidation encourages outsiders to place in them, being given greater opportunities to address weaknesses in their practice

---

28 Horton, R., 'UK Medicine: What Are We to Do?', *The Lancet*, 1998, 352: 1166.

29 See Boseley, S. and Hartley-Brewer, J., 'Doctors Plunge into New Crisis', *The Guardian*, 30 June 2000 (web edition).

30 Irvine, D., *The Doctors' Tale*, 2003, Radcliffe Medical Press, Oxford, 161 and 183.

31 General Medical Council, *Revalidating Doctors*, 2000, 3.

32 General Medical Council, *Revalidation: Report on the Outcome of the Consultation Exercise*, November 2000, Annex A.

33 Irvine, D., *The Doctors' Tale*, 2003, Radcliffe Medical Press, Oxford, 181.

and being protected from unfounded criticism.[34] Employers would benefit from the increased reassurance that doctors are fit to practise, and enjoy the added benefit of an additional mechanism to identify inadequately performing doctors. Revalidation and clinical governance would complement each other, together protecting patients to a far greater extent than either can alone. The GMC envisaged that the provisions of *Good Medical Practice*[35] would provide the template for revalidation.[36]

## Proposed Stages in the Revalidation Process

The GMC's initial proposals were for a three-stage revalidation process.

Stage 1 – every registered doctor would be required to maintain a revalidation folder, which should contain information from a range of sources to demonstrate how well the doctor was practising. The folder would contain information covering, as a minimum, a five-year period. Such information might include: audit results; a continuing professional development record – as evidence that the doctor has maintained up-to-date skills and knowledge; views from patients and colleagues; and performance behaviour. The latter might include objective benchmarks such as mortality data. Doctors would also be expected to include details of any critical incidents, including the learning opportunities these have provided. Similarly, details of patient complaints and evidence of changes in practice as a result should also be included. Responses were mixed to the consultation question regarding any limits to the type of complaint to be included. Some doctors argued that anonymous complaints should be excluded, on the basis that they were difficult to verify and could be malicious. Conversely, others suggested that some patients might fear retribution (for instance, being removed from a GP's list or receiving inadequate future treatment) if they were not allowed anonymity. Also, it was suggested that a number of anonymous complaints of a similar type would suggest a genuine problem with the doctor's practice.[37] Doctors were to include in their folders a statement confirming that their own probity and health was appropriate for practice. The case examples discussed in this work illustrate that such a requirement would do little or nothing to deter or detect doctors intent on misconduct. Even the fallback position – that in addition to the doctor's self-declaration, any external evidence of lack of probity should be included in the folder – appeared to rely largely upon the doctor's cooperation.

---

34 General Medical Council, *Revalidating Doctors*, 2000, 4.

35 Good clinical care, including: practising within the limits of competence; maintaining good medical practice, including up to date skills; developing and maintaining good relationships with patients; working effectively with colleagues; probity; and ensuring that a doctor does not allow his or her own health problems to endanger patients. In addition, doctors who undertake teaching or training must develop and maintain appropriate skills for this role.

36 General Medical Council, *Revalidating Doctors*, 2000, 8–10.

37 General Medical Council, *Revalidation: Report on the Outcome of the Consultation Exercise*, November 2000.

There were also no clear guidelines about the security and robustness of the folder process. For instance, what would prevent a doctor altering his or her folder between jobs, or removing unfavourable information? One partial solution, suggested in the responses to consultation, was to make folders accessible to those responsible for monitoring clinical practice, or even more widely on the internet.[38] The folder would be subject to annual review, with recommendations for improvement made. In the NHS, the latter would be achieved through the appraisal process.

There were some areas of uncertainty at the early stages of these proposals. For example, appraisal within the NHS workplace was insufficiently developed for the GMC to know how extensive and how reliable the information would be. Monitoring of GPs at the time was undertaken on a practice basis, so very little information was available regarding individual doctors. There were also concerns about the practicality of appraisal being both formative at the employment level, but summative for revalidation. It was also unclear how minimum standards for revalidation would compare with those previously used by the performance procedures, in particular, whether revalidation standards would be set at a higher level than the minimum which had caused concerns for the performance procedures.[39]

Stage 2 – periodically, usually every five years, each doctor's folder would be independently assessed by a 'revalidation group'. The group would work to standards set by the GMC, medical Royal Colleges and speciality associations. The revalidation group would report to the GMC and the process would ensure that each doctor was properly assessed, no matter how complex his or her employment situation. It was anticipated that for the majority of doctors working within the NHS and other managed organizations, potential shortcomings will have been dealt with as part of the appraisal process. The role of the revalidation group should therefore need to be minimal. More intensive assessment should only be needed for those doctors not subject to regular appraisal.

The GMC's initial proposals for revalidation groups was that they should consist of a minimum of three members, two doctors and one lay person. One option would have included a doctor with personal knowledge of the practice of the doctor applying for revalidation, for example, clinical director of the doctor's employing organization. The second doctor would not know the doctor to be assessed, but would be from the same field of practice. The GMC sought views about whether the lay members should be recruited from the general public or should have health sector experience. Whilst the expectation was that in most cases the group would reach consensus, if a minority member felt strongly that a doctor should be referred to the GMC, this should happen. Doctor members of the groups would themselves be subject to potential disciplinary sanctions by the GMC if they did not approach

38 These questions were raised by some respondents to the GMC consultation process. General Medical Council, *Revalidation: Report on the Outcome of the Consultation Exercise*, November 2000.

39 See the Fifth Report of the Shipman Inquiry, *Safeguarding Patients: Lessons from the Past – Proposals for the Future*, paras 26.45–26.46 (www.the-shipman-inquiry.org.uk).

the work with appropriate integrity.[40] It is open to question whether the GMC would actually have been able to cope if lack of consensus arose in all but a very small minority of cases.

In the case of locum doctors, the GMC sought views about whether they should make use of the procedures within the organization which the locum happens to be working for at the time their revalidation was due or, alternatively, should be allowed to choose from a list of accredited groups.[41] The small proportion of doctors who work outside of a managed environment would be required to keep a folder of information and to identify someone who could undertake appraisal. There is an obvious risk that doctors in this position may enter into mutually convenient relationships which facilitate the 'rubber stamping' of each other's revalidation records. Examples of this behaviour can be found in the solicitors' profession, from those instances where a solicitor is prohibited from practising alone. So called 'sham partnerships' may sometimes be created to side-step such restrictions and mislead the Law Society.[42]

The GMC also concluded that doctors should include within their revalidation folders details of any disciplinary findings. The majority of responses to the GMC's early consultation exercise considered that there should be no time limit regarding disciplinary matters to be included.[43]

Overall, there was significant cause for doubt about the rigour of the revalidation group process as it was first envisaged. The GMC's suggestion was that each region might typically have ten groups with a workload which would require an average of 20 folders to be considered per day of sitting. With a maximum of 20 to 25 minutes per folder and each folder covering a five-year period, there would be little scope for a rigorous critical evaluation.

Stage 3 – the GMC would decide whether the doctor's registration should be revalidated. The expectation was that the majority of cases would cause no problem, but a minority would require detailed investigation under the Council's fitness to practise procedures.

Where possible, revalidation would use local systems associated with the doctor's employment. Therefore, where local systems exist these should be used, to avoid the GMC duplicating effort. The GMC also expressed the wish to avoid becoming a repository of lots of pieces of minor information about doctors.[44] These systems, notably clinical governance, would be central to the process – although individual doctors would ultimately remain responsible for their own revalidation. Fitness to practise issues which arose between revalidation periods should be identified by

---

40 General Medical Council, *Revalidating Doctors*, 2000, 23–4.

41 General Medical Council, *Revalidating Doctors*, 2000, 25.

42 See Davies, M., 'The Regulation of Solicitors and the Role of the Solicitors Disciplinary Tribunal', *Professional Negligence*, 1998, Vol. 14, No. 3, 143–73.

43 See General Medical Council, *Revalidating Doctors*, 2000, 32; and General Medical Council, *Revalidation: Report on the Outcome of the Consultation Exercise*, November 2000.

44 Sir Graeme Catto, 'The GMC – Revalidation – What Are We Trying to Measure?', *Medico-Legal Journal*, 2003, 71(106), 2 October.

local procedures within the NHS and either dealt with at that level or, if patients were at risk, referred immediately to the GMC.[45] It is open to question whether such information will necessarily come to light. It is therefore questionable whether five-year revalidation cycles are sufficient to ensure that doctors who might pose a risk to patients are promptly identified and dealt with.

The GMC also acknowledged that the majority of doctors' practise in a team environment and so such teams would be expected to generate information needed for each member's revalidation.[46] In this respect, it is unclear how genuinely independent and objective assessment was to be guaranteed. There was an obvious risk that some team members might be tempted to 'rubber stamp' each other's revalidation documentation. The GMC initially suggested that quality assurance would be maintained by sampling 1 per cent of revalidation group recommendations. It was estimated that this would amount to around 200 cases per year. The sample proportion would increase to 10 per cent in the case of doctors working outside of the NHS or other appropriate managed environment.[47]

With regard to openness and transparency, there was a difference in view between medical and lay respondents to the GMC's consultation process. Of particular interest was whether a doctor's due date for revalidation should be made public. Only a minority of medical respondents felt that this should be the case, compared with a significant majority of lay respondents.[48] On the one hand, knowing that a doctor was nearing his or her revalidation point might unnecessarily worry some members of the public regarding the doctor's current competence. On the other hand, in an adult, knowledge-based consumer society, there is no reason why the public should be deprived of such information.

## Procedures Underpinning Revalidation

### *Audit*

In 1989 the Department of Health published a discussion paper on medical audit. Audit, it was said, was central to the provision of good quality care. The discussion paper proposed that medical audit should be professionally led and controlled. Confidentiality was seen as important. In July 1993, the Department of Health published a follow-up clinical audit document[49] which stated that: 'Clinical audit involves systematically looking at the procedures used for diagnosis, care and treatment, examining how associated resources are used and investigating the effect care has on outcome and quality of life for the patient.'

45 General Medical Council, *Revalidating Doctors*, 2000, 11.

46 General Medical Council, *Revalidating Doctors*, 2000, 15.

47 General Medical Council, *Revalidating Doctors*, 2000, 26.

48 General Medical Council, *Revalidation: Report on the Outcome of the Consultation Exercise*, November 2000.

49 EL 93(59). For more recent discussion, see *The Ledward Report*, Part V, para 24.5.1 and Part VII, paras 1–3.

The Ledward Inquiry recommended that longer term outcomes should form part of the audit procedure, following up patients after discharge. There should be lay involvement in this process, to ensure that consideration is given to patients' expectations against outcome.[50] In April 2001, the requirement that NHS doctors participate in audit programmes was made a contractual provision.[51]

Audit, therefore, calls for systematic information relevant to improving the standards of care. Approaches may include: a review of case notes; routinely collected data; population-based epidemiological studies; use of investigations and therapies. The choice of approaches is frequently under the control of the group being audited, with a lack of external influence.[52] A key problem with this approach to audit was demonstrated by the Ledward case. Some doctors most in need of scrutiny may hold positions of power which enable them to deflect such scrutiny away from themselves. For example, notwithstanding concerns about Ledward, he was variously both the Director of Medical Audit and Clinical Director of the Obstetric and Gynaecology Division. It has also been suggested that audit practices may be developed with such high levels of flexibility, so that doctors are unlikely to encounter genuine challenges to their working methods.[53] The view expressed to the Ledward Inquiry was that clinical audit was often seen as little more than doctors 'just looking at interesting cases'.[54]

The understanding of audit varies between commentators, as do the conclusions about its effectiveness. Lord and Littlejohns, for example, found that even after some years of use, many medical staff in community and hospital medicine remained sceptical about its value.[55] Becher comments that audit may often be an expensive means of achieving modest, even marginal, improvements in quality and it may produce results which have little impact on the alteration of practitioner behaviour.[56] US commentators, such as Wergin, have found that the review of patient notes was often ineffective as a means of evaluating practitioner behaviour. This resulted from inaccuracies and inconsistencies in data recording, lack of sensitivity to subtle changes in patient management and the limited scope of behaviours which can be recorded

---

50 *The Ledward Report*, Part VII, para v.

51 See *Learning from Bristol: The DH Response to the Report of the Public Inquiry into Children's Heart Surgery at the Bristol Royal Infirmary 1984-1995*, para 8.26.

52 See Kogan, M. and Redfern, S., *Making Use of Clinical Audit*, 1995, Open University Press, Buckingham; Rosenthal, M.M., *The Incompetent Doctor*, 1995, Open University Press, Buckingham; Becher, T., *Professional Practices*, 1999, Transaction Publishers, New Brunswick, New Jersey, 226.

53 Davies, A.C.L., 'Don't Trust Me, I'm a Doctor – Medical Regulation and the 1999 NHS Reforms', *OJLS*, 2000, 20(437).

54 *The Ledward Report*, Part V, paras 5.1, 6.4–6.5, 18.3.3, 18.3.1–18.3.2.

55 Lord, J. and Littlejohns, P., 'Impact of Hospital and Community Provider Based Clinical Audit Programmes', *International Journal for Quality in Health Care*, 1996, 8, 6, 527–35.

56 Becher, T., *Professional Practices*, 1999, Transaction Publishers, New Brunswick, New Jersey, 225. See also Horder, J., Bosanquet, N. and Stocking, B., 'Ways of Influencing the Behaviour of General Practitioners', *Journal of the Royal College of General Practitioners*, 1986, 36, 517–21.

effectively.[57] Audit may be more effective in the case of, say, straightforward surgical procedures with expected and generally predictable outcomes. However, in many areas of team-based practice, with overlapping responsibilities, or general practice, with many conditions being self-limiting irrespective of the chosen treatment, the value of audit will be far more restricted.[58] Other researchers, whilst questioning the routine value of audit, have suggested that it may be of some use in detecting those cases of extreme deficiency and deviation from accepted practice.[59]

### *Appraisal*

The Kennedy Report identified appraisal as an essential tool to review performance and a crucial element of reflective practice.[60] Bridgeman notes that whilst the emphasis by Kennedy is directed at the delivery of high quality care, the focus of the government response is to give patients confidence in medical self-regulation and the competence of health professionals.[61]

Catto acknowledged that the appraisal process lacked the robustness necessary to underpin revalidation. Appraisal across the country was being introduced in a very patchy manner. However, he did expect this to improve over time.[62] The GMC has also acknowledged that an appraisal process requires a summative element if it is to satisfy the needs of revalidation.[63] Attitudes from some within the medical profession also cast doubt on the appropriate motivation towards appraisal. For example, in the early years at least, not only was GP appraisal highly reliant on self-assessment, but individual GPs expected to be paid for the time they devoted to the process. As described by the Chief Medical Officer: 'This seemed anachronistic given the element of professional development.'[64]

The BMA considered that appraisal should be formative, helping continuous improvement by doctors. If the same evidence is to be used for revalidation, the two exercises should remain distinct, to preserve the educational and supportive

57 Wergin, F., 'CME and Change in Practice', *Journal of Continuing Education in the Health Professions*, 1988, 8, 147–59; Becher, T., *Professional Practices*, 1999, Transaction Publishers, New Brunswick, New Jersey, 227.

58 Becher, T., *Professional Practices*, 1999, Transaction Publishers, New Brunswick, New Jersey.

59 Lockyer, J. and Harrison, V., 'Performance Assessment', in Davis, D.A. and Fox, R.D. (eds), *The Physician as Learner*, 1994, American Medical Association, Chicago, 176.

60 *Supporting Doctors, Protecting Patients*, NHS Consultation Paper, 1999.

61 Bridgeman, J., 'The "Patient at the Centre": the Government Response to the Bristol Inquiry Report', *Journal of Social Welfare and Family Law*, 2002, 24(3), 347–61.

62 Sir Graeme Catto, 'The GMC – Revalidation – What Are We Trying to Measure?', *Medico-Legal Journal*, 2003, 71(106), 2 October.

63 GMC, *Developing Medical Regulation: a Vision for the Future – the GMC's Response to the Call for Ideas by the Review of Clinical Performance and Medical Regulation*, April 2005, para 98.

64 See Department of Health, *Good Doctors, Safer Patients – Proposals to Strengthen the System to Assure and Improve the Performance of Doctors and to Protect the Safety of Patients: A Report by the Chief Medical Officer*, July 2006, Chapter 5, paragraph 96.

elements of appraisal. Care should be taken to ensure that the appraisal model is not stretched beyond what can reasonably be expected of it. Moving from a primarily formative appraisal process to one with summative elements risks jeopardizing the cooperation of doctors, turning revalidation into a more threatening and intimidating experience.[65]

*Clinical Governance*

Clinical governance seeks continuous improvement of services, within an environment which aims to allow excellence to flourish. This plays a potentially important role in revalidation. Central to the concept is the principle that health professionals should routinely think: 'How could my care be better?' The Health Act 1999[66] imposed a 'duty of quality' on NHS bodies, both at primary and secondary levels. This required the development of systems for monitoring and improving the quality of care.[67] Whilst clinical governance aims to prevent poor performance from emerging, it is not regulatory in the sense of controlling poorly performing doctors.

Clinical governance brings together a range of activities – ranging from continuing professional development (CPD) to risk management. In general practice, for example, prescribing data might reveal that a doctor is using out-of-date treatments and so has potential problems with his or her clinical knowledge. This, in turn, requires sufficient sophistication of the monitoring process – ensuring that the prescribing of individual doctors (rather than practices) is monitored and that all GPs (including locums, trainees, and so on) have their own individual identification code. However, other potentially important problems with medical practice – for instance, poor communication, poor team-working and poor managerial skills – are very difficult to identify by means of routine data analysis.[68]

Clinical governance is also restricted by the fact that it is primarily about systems, producing little information about individual doctors and being especially limited with regard to medical knowledge and clinical skills. Clinical governance has also tended to be of relatively low priority within PCTs. The Shipman Inquiry suggested that, apart from the monitoring of mortality statistics and significant event reviews focusing on sudden deaths, clinical governance tools would probably not have detected Shipman's crimes. Overall, clinical governance was not favoured by the Inquiry as a means for identifying deliberate malpractice, as such doctors are likely to be able to seek out ways to hide their behaviour.[69]

---

65 The comments in the following sections are taken from the *BMA Response to the Chief Medical Officer Review on Maintaining High Standards of Professional Practice*, May 2005.

66 Section 18.

67 Ayling Inquiry Report, 15 July 2004, paras 6.17–6.20 and 6.24.

68 For further discussion, see the Fifth Report of the Shipman Inquiry, *Safeguarding Patients: Lessons from the Past – Proposals for the Future*, paras 12.4–12.28 (www.the-shipman-inquiry.org.uk).

69 The Fifth Report of the Shipman Inquiry, *Safeguarding Patients: Lessons from the Past – Proposals for the Future*, paras 12.138–12.143 (www.the-shipman-inquiry.org.uk).

## Problems with the Initial Revalidation Proposals

There were concerns that the practical aspects of this revalidation model would not work, placing undue reliance on a thorough and effective system of local clinical governance and appraisal, as well as cooperation from individual practitioners in submitting appropriate evidence of their continued competence. There was little explanation from the GMC regarding what it could do if substantial numbers of practitioners did not cooperate, or for other reasons the timetable of revalidation slipped.[70] Even in the case of practitioners who did cooperate, there was to be no effective investigatory arm to ensure that the revalidation folder was not highly selective, especially with regard to sensitive matters such as complaints and critical incidents. There was also little focus by the GMC on how it would ensure the necessary quality of local clinical governance. The risks are illustrated by the Neale and Ledward cases. Neale came to England in 1985, having been struck off the medical register in Canada for incompetence and professional misconduct. Despite this background, Neale held a post of Head of Clinical Risk Manager during some of his period of practice in the UK, enabling him to dismiss complaints about his own activities. As previously noted, Ledward was at times both the Director of Medical Audit and Clinical Director of his division.[71]

In addition to practical difficulties of revalidation, there is an important theoretical flaw with the concept. In seeking to monitor all doctors through revalidation, resources will be spread very thinly. Equivalent to the police attempting to detect crime by undertaking a periodic audit of the whole population, the GMC will use significant resources checking the majority of doctors who give no rise for concern. In this inevitably fast-paced mass production process, doctors such as Shipman would still be likely to evade detection. This risk is exacerbated by the five-yearly gaps between revalidation events. A useful comparison is with the monitoring by the Law Society of the handling of clients' money by solicitors. Even though this is undertaken on an annual basis, the monitoring of solicitors' accounts has in some cases proved insufficient to detect problems promptly.[72] On this basis, a five-yearly revalidation cycle, even if revalidation were to be effective in other respects, is likely to be very far from adequate in detecting serious problems sufficiently quickly.

---

70 The GMC's initial proposal was that a doctor's failure to participate in the revalidation process might result in erasure of the doctor's name from the register, after a fair hearing. GMC, *Revalidating Doctors – Ensuring Standards, Securing the Future*, Consultation Document, 2000, 34. However, such an approach could only work on a modest scale, with a small minority only of doctors failing to cooperate. Should the GMC find itself needing to erase significant numbers of doctors who fail to comply with the revalidation process, then the problem will simply be transferred to the NHS. The NHS would be faced with closing many of its services, or simply employing unregistered doctors.

71 *The Ledward Report*, Part V, paras 5.1, 6.4–6.5, 18.3.3, 18.3.1–18.3.2.

72 See Davies, M., 'The Solicitors Accounts Rules – How Safe is Clients' Money?', *Legal Ethics*, Summer 2000, Vol. 3, Part 1, 49–75.

**Revised Plans**

The GMC's Consultation Paper of 2000 has been described as a 'seminal document, setting out proposals that were manifestly designed to protect patients'.[73] However, having produced an innovative plan, the GMC then proceeded to backtrack. It had become clear that the task of evaluating every doctor on a five-yearly cycle would be challenging and expensive for the profession. Powerful medical interest groups also opposed the plans. In this environment, the culture within the GMC of protecting the interests of doctors was able to prevail.[74] Therefore, in its later stages of planning of revalidation, the GMC moved in the direction of relying substantially on audit within employment and the local certification of doctors' fitness to practise. By April 2003, it was clear that the GMC had moved away from its plans to use revalidation panels, and instead intended to revalidate, without further scrutiny, all doctors who had successfully completed an appropriate number of NHS appraisals. As the GMC subsequently explained this position:

> We believe that for doctors working within a GMC approved environment, revalidation will be secured through local certification, which will in turn rely on strong local systems. We believe that the most effective way of delivering revalidation for doctors will be to build on local systems where these are effective.[75]

It has been argued that all the GMC's subsequent problems with regard to revalidation relate to its 'fateful' decision in April 2003. 'It was at this point that they lost sight of their aspirational proposals to evaluate doctors' fitness to practise.'[76] It was also of concern that in retreating from its original plans, much of the discussion within the GMC took place in private. It has been suggested that it is difficult to avoid the view that the GMC was embarrassed about its change of stance and had not wished the public to be aware of this.[77]

The GMC had also retreated from one of the original key purposes of revalidation, the detection of poorly performing doctors, although the GMC attempted to argue that it had never suggested that revalidation aimed to identify poor performance.[78] The view of Dame Janet Smith was very different. She described the new position as one in which the GMC had moved away from the statutory requirement of undertaking an individual evaluation of every doctor. Having initially taken the view

---

73 The Fifth Report of the Shipman Inquiry, *Safeguarding Patients: Lessons from the Past – Proposals for the Future*, para 27.300 (www.the-shipman-inquiry.org.uk).

74 The Fifth Report of the Shipman Inquiry, *Safeguarding Patients: Lessons from the Past – Proposals for the Future*, para 27.300 (www.the-shipman-inquiry.org.uk).

75 GMC, *Developing Medical Regulation: a Vision for the Future – the GMC's Response to the Call for Ideas by the Review of Clinical Performance and Medical Regulation*, April 2005, Appendix A, para 1.

76 See Esmail, A., 'GMC and the Future of Revalidation – Failure to Act on Good Intentions', *BMJ*, 2005, Vol. 330, May 14.

77 Esmail, A., 'GMC and the Future of Revalidation – Failure to Act on Good Intentions', *BMJ*, 2005, Vol. 330, May 14.

78 See the Fifth Report of the Shipman Inquiry, *Safeguarding Patients: Lessons from the Past – Proposals for the Future*, para 26.115 (www.the-shipman-inquiry.org.uk).

that it could not delegate the role, not even to the Royal Colleges, it had undergone a significant about-face and determined that 'it can delegate everything other than the final decision to revalidate':

> Thus it appeared that, by early 2003, not only had the GMC rejected the idea that revalidation should, for most doctors, be based on evaluation by local revalidation groups, it had also moved to a position where, as it was put in the medical press at the time, for doctors working in the NHS, 'five satisfactory appraisals equals revalidation'. Indeed, in the early years, only one appraisal might equal revalidation.
>
> The implications of the change must be understood. The GMC had moved from evaluation by a revalidation group of an individual doctor's fitness to practise by means of examination of evidence (be it the contents of his/her folder or the completed set of appraisal forms) to a position where there was to be no individual evaluation at all but, instead, an assumption that, if the doctor had been through the appraisal process, s/he must be up to date and fit to practise.[79]

For this to have any chance of being effective, local systems must be subject to robust quality assurance processes and be willing to share information about dysfunctional practice. This is not easy to justify when it is considered that the medical profession have consistently argued that appraisal must be a formative process. The role of the appraiser was to encourage self-examination by the appraisee in a confidential, non-judgemental environment. This was the view taken in the Shipman report:

> It seemed to me that…the GMC had, in effect, delegated responsibility for revalidation of GPs to appraisers, who were not expected and were not equipped to carry out an evaluation of the doctor's fitness to practise. It appeared to me that, instead, the GMC was going to renew, virtually automatically, the licence to practise of any doctor seeking revalidation provided that his/her appraisal had not been stopped on account of serious concerns having arisen about his/her fitness to practise. I became concerned that such a system would offer no greater protection to patients than that afforded by existing systems and that, therefore, the public could not reasonably have confidence in revalidation as then proposed.[80]

By November 2003, it had become clear that the vast majority of doctors would be 'revalidated' without being subject to any process envisaged by the amendments to the Medical Act 1983. For these doctors, revalidation and the process of local clinical governance would be indistinguishable. As the latter would have occurred anyway, the principle of revalidation adds nothing of substance. Furthermore, a certificate confirming compliance with local clinical governance requirements would not be based upon the totality of data available about a doctor. Rather, it would be based upon a few discrete aspects of that data, and could not confirm with certainty that there were no concerns about the doctor.[81]

---

79 The Fifth Report of the Shipman Inquiry, *Safeguarding Patients: Lessons from the Past – Proposals for the Future*, paras 26.68–26.69 and 26.189 (www.the-shipman-inquiry.org.uk).

80 The Fifth Report of the Shipman Inquiry, *Safeguarding Patients: Lessons from the Past – Proposals for the Future*, para 26.76. For further discussion, see para 26.72 (www.the-shipman-inquiry.org.uk).

81 See the Fifth Report of the Shipman Inquiry, *Safeguarding Patients: Lessons from the Past – Proposals for the Future*, paras 26.121, 26.173 and 26.183 (www.the-shipman-inquiry.org.uk).

By July 2004, the GMC was emphasizing the importance of reflexivity in its proposals for revalidation. If reflective practice becomes embedded across the whole profession, this, the GMC said, should result in better healthcare for society as a whole. The GMC also considered that certification by the medical Royal Colleges, if they have a robust methodology for determining that their Members and Fellows are 'of good standing', would satisfy the revalidation criteria. The GMC continued to reject a compulsory test of knowledge and skills, but welcomed voluntary participation by doctors who wished to do this as part of their own reflective practice. This might be of particular value for some doctors who had not undertaken medical practice over their revalidation cycle, as it would provide valuable input for their revalidation folder.[82]

The GMC had sought to justify its change of approach on the basis that clinical governance had developed rapidly since its original 2000 consultation exercise. However, this conveniently ignored the Council's earlier conclusions, that both clinical governance and revalidation were separate processes, that both were necessary for patient protection and that neither would be sufficient without the other. It was also clear that at the time the GMC changed its stance, clinical governance and appraisal were not embedded within the healthcare system and could not be said to be working well everywhere.[83]

The GMC has been keen to emphasize that appraisal could not be undertaken if there were significant local concerns about the doctor. Initially, it was considered to be implicit that if a doctor had undergone successful appraisal, there were no such concerns. However, the GMC came to recognize that 'implied' recognition was not sufficient to allay public concerns. As a result, the Council came to favour explicit, rather than implicit, local certification. Such a certificate would confirm that the doctor had been appraised by a trained and experienced appraiser, that the appraisal was underpinned by verifiable data about the doctor's actual practice, and that the appraisal culminated with an agreed Personal Development Plan. The certificate would also confirm that there were no unresolved local concerns raising fitness to practise issues.[84] Specifically with respect to fitness to practise, local certification would confirm that there were no concerns about the doctor's health; there were no concerns about the doctor's probity; no disciplinary findings during the period in question and no disciplinary actions in progress; the local processes for appraisal and clinical governance are quality assured. Only in the case of doctors unable to obtain local certification would a more thorough review of their fitness to practise be needed.[85] The GMC is silent on what can be termed the 'Ledward effect' – what if the miscreant is in charge of the local procedures?

82 GMC, *The Policy Framework for Revalidation: A Position Paper*, July 2004.

83 See the Fifth Report of the Shipman Inquiry, *Safeguarding Patients: Lessons from the Past – Proposals for the Future*, paras 26.88–26.90 (www.the-shipman-inquiry.org.uk).

84 GMC, *Developing Medical Regulation: a Vision for the Future – the GMC's Response to the Call for Ideas by the Review of Clinical Performance and Medical Regulation*, April 2005, Appendix A, paras 2, 3 and 5.

85 GMC, *Developing Medical Regulation: a Vision for the Future – the GMC's Response to the Call for Ideas by the Review of Clinical Performance and Medical Regulation*, April 2005, Appendix A, paras 6 and 8.

The GMC has worked on the presumption that most doctors will sail through revalidation without problems. In the case of the expected small minority of doctors whose revalidation evidence is insufficient or raises a question about fitness to practise, the GMC considered that one or more of a number of actions might occur. The doctor could be asked to provide further evidence; further evidence might be obtained via secondary sources such as peer and patient questionnaires or observations of practice. Registration decisions panels, composed of medical and lay members, would review this and any other appropriate evidence.[86] As previously noted above, this approach was originally intended to be applied to *all* doctors, but the GMC have now backtracked significantly.

In seeking to justify its watered down proposals, the GMC drew comparisons with the process for ensuring that airline pilots remained competent and safe. However, it omitted to mention that pilots undergo competence tests as part of periodic assessments – an element notable by its absence in the plans for revalidating doctors. Similarly, revalidation has been compared with a car's MOT. The latter is an objective assessment of the vehicle's roadworthiness, with various requirements having to be satisfied, and if any one is not the whole test is failed. Unlike a vehicle MOT test, revalidation as remodelled did not include any detailed standards against which it was possible to pass or fail. Neither the comparison with pilots nor with the MOT can withstand scrutiny. The GMC had rejected a model for revalidation which would have involved doctors undergoing tests, either written, practical or possibly both. Such tests might have been supplemented by patient and peer satisfaction surveys. Whilst the public rated such an approach highly, the medical profession was unhappy with the idea of retesting. The GMC also considered it impractical to administer tests which would have needed to encompass the whole range of medical specialities.[87]

The British Medical Association, responding in 2005 to the Chief Medical Officer's consultation about the future of revalidation, expressed the view that the process should be about ensuring that doctors are fit to continue practising, with a supportive ethos for those who are not. Revalidation should be positive – about reflective practice and continuing development, not merely a process for identifying bad doctors. It was also considered to be important that revalidation take into consideration the systems within which individual doctors work. The BMA also favoured the GMC's approach, that revalidation should be an assessment of performance, not an examination of theoretical knowledge.[88] In setting the standards for revalidation, it was considered important to avoid attempts to excessively codify matters. Significant aspects of professional practice involve judgement, which is necessarily subjective and does

86 GMC, *Developing Medical Regulation: a Vision for the Future – the GMC's Response to the Call for Ideas by the Review of Clinical Performance and Medical Regulation*, April 2005, Appendix A, para 13.

87 See the Fifth Report of the Shipman Inquiry, *Safeguarding Patients: Lessons from the Past – Proposals for the Future*, paras 26.66, 26.105 and 26.185–26.187 (www.the-shipman-inquiry.org.uk).

88 The comments in the following sections are taken from the *BMA Response to the Chief Medical Officer Review on Maintaining High Standards of Professional Practice*, May 2005.

not lend itself to codification. Indeed, attempts to do so would weaken the practice and the benefit it brings to patients. The BMA recognized that for revalidation to command public respect, it should use and appropriate a range of methods, for example, analysis of a selection of anonymous patient consultation records and peer-observation of consultations. It was also considered that if a doctor constitutes an immediate danger to patients, suspension is necessary pending full investigation. However, where there is no danger, the matter should remain confidential until proven.[89] The BMA also considered that a 'no blame' culture should permeate the appraisal process and should extend to revalidation. Effective regulatory systems were said to work badly in a blame culture, discouraging self-reporting of performance or health problems, and reporting by colleagues if they do not consider the system to be fair and proportionate. Retraining, funded by the NHS, should be the outcome in most cases of adverse revalidation.[90] As the representative body for the medical profession, it is unsurprising that the BMA approaches revalidation with a primary focus upon doctors' interests. However, this approach is inadequate to ensure public protection. It is also open to question why the NHS, in effect the public purse, should pay for retraining, especially if the doctor has failed revalidation due to his or her own laxity or even misbehaviour.

Not all within the profession favoured the watered down approach. Mike Pringle, professor of general practice and elected member of the GMC, expressed the opinion that the Council's proposed system of revalidation was not good enough: 'I have no confidence that "five appraisals and a clinical governance sign off" will protect patients or support the profession of medicine.'[91]

Standards for both appraisal and clinical governance could vary from trust to trust and were inadequate for the purpose of revalidation. The approach was also unfair to doctors, who need to know what standards they are expected to reach. Revalidation evidence should be assessed openly by both lay and medical personnel, with the lay element being 'intimately involved in the approval of every doctor', as a means of ensuring public confidence in the process.[92]

Similarly, Irvine has repeated his opinion that doctors have both personal responsibility for their own continuing ability and collective responsibility for the appropriate standards and practice of colleagues. Revalidation should therefore be summative as well as formative, improving standards of all doctors whilst simultaneously weeding out those who are unfit to practise.[93]

---

89 The comments in the following sections are taken from the *BMA Response to the Chief Medical Officer Review on Maintaining High Standards of Professional Practice*, May 2005.

90 The comments in the following sections are taken from the *BMA Response to the Chief Medical Officer Review on Maintaining High Standards of Professional Practice*, May 2005.

91 Pringle, M., 'Making Revalidation Credible', *BMJ*, 2005, 330: 1515, 25 June.

92 Pringle, M., 'Making Revalidation Credible', *BMJ*, 2005, 330: 1515, 25 June.

93 See Irvine, D., 'GMC and the Future of Revalidation: Patients, Professionalism, and Revalidation', *BMJ*, 2005, 330: 1265—8; and Catto, G., 'GMC and the Future of Revalidation: Building on the GMC's Achievements', *BMJ*, 2005, 330: 1205–7.

## What Will Revalidation Measure?

Speaking in 2003, Sir Graeme Catto, President of the GMC, noted that it would be relatively easy to measure a doctor's knowledge, for instance, by using multiple-choice exams. However, he considered that this was probably not particularly important. Catto considered that the vast majority of doctors who were disciplined by the GMC did not lack the requisite knowledge and skills. Rather, revalidation should relate to and measure the way in which doctors perform in practice. Doctors showing, by examination or otherwise, that they knew in principle what they should do was not the core issue.

> [I]t is what do they do at half-past six on a Saturday evening, when they would rather be at home than answering the telephone? What do they do at three in the morning, when they are worried and there are other issues requiring their attention? Revalidation is not primarily about identifying poorly performing doctors. If that had been the aim we would not need to assess 120,000 doctors in order to identify the 3 or 4% that are apparently under-performing.[94]

The problem with this approach is that it is far from certain that in the past the GMC has been doing any more than scratching the surface in detecting, disciplining or otherwise dealing with problem doctors. Catto is therefore making assumptions when he suggests that inadequate up-to-date knowledge is not a problem faced by the medical profession. He also neglects to consider evidence from negligence claims. For example, Phillips adduces statistics which demonstrate that over 60 per cent of cases contained some degree of clinical fault which might have escaped clinical audit.[95]

Catto's assumption is also in stark contrast to the view of a previous lay member of the GMC, Jean Robinson. Robinson concluded that far too little was known about the causes of poor care and bad behaviour on the part of doctors. Some doctors displayed levels of medical knowledge and competence that was 'so low as to make one wonder how they ever got on the Register in the first place'. Others had become sloppy or cavalier in their attitude over time. Only by requiring such doctors to retake examinations could the public be properly protected. In some cases, retraining would not be appropriate. Those who were found to be temperamentally unsuited to practise medicine should be advised regarding alternative careers.[96]

## Burdens of Proof within the Revised Approach to Revalidation

The GMC's intended approach to revalidation splits, in broad terms, into two stages. The first stage places the burden upon the doctor to provide relevant information

---

94 Sir Graeme Catto, 'The GMC – Revalidation – What Are We Trying to Measure?', *Medico-Legal Journal*, 2003, 71(106), 2 October.

95 Phillips, A.F., *Medical Negligence Law: Seeking a Balance*, 1997, Dartmouth, Aldershot, 170.

96 Robinson, J., *A Patient Voice at the GMC: a Lay Member's View of the GMC*, Report 1, Health Rights, London.

to the GMC to support revalidation. If the doctor refuses or otherwise chooses not to participate, his or her licence may be withdrawn on that basis. The second stage comes into play if the doctor submits insufficient evidence. Catto notes that in those circumstances, the burden of proof switches to the GMC. If the Council suspects that the doctor is not fit to practise, it will have to prove this by putting the doctor through its fitness to practise procedures. These have been described by the GMC as 'robust but time-consuming and quite expensive'.[97] The likely robustness, however, has not necessarily been demonstrated by the standards applied by the GMC's performance procedures. Cases can be identified in which a doctor has been allowed to return to practice, even though he or she has scored well below the norm in competence assessments.[98] Whilst it has been suggested from within the GMC that the introduction of revalidation will result in the continuing monitoring of doctors from qualification to retirement, in reality there will be significant differences at the various stages. Prior to full qualification, the onus is squarely on the prospective doctor to establish suitability. If an examination or other assessment is failed, the usual situation will require the prospective doctor to retake and pass this assessment before he or she can progress to ultimate admission to the profession. In contrast, Catto's description of the revalidation process suggests that only doctors who fail entirely to participate will find themselves in this position. A doctor who submits some evidence will do enough to shift the burden to the GMC. This would be akin to a medical student turning up to an exam, writing a few lines and thereby shifting the burden to the medical school to prove that the student was incapable of passing.

## Criticism of the Revised Plans

The GMC's plans for revalidation were the subject of significant criticism in the fifth report of the Shipman Inquiry. The Council was accused of pandering to doctors' wants and needs at the expense and neglect of the interests of patients. It was doubted whether the proposals would offer any greater protection to patients than had previously been available.[99] Dame Janet Smith was especially concerned with the GMC plans to rely on annual appraisals to identify problem doctors, when appraisal was not designed for this task. Appraisal is a formative process, intended to allow doctors to develop in a confidential, non-threatening environment. As previously noted, it is not uncommon for appraisal to be based on material chosen by the appraisee and, often, the material is not readily verifiable. Appraisers are not trained to judge appraisees and may be encouraged by the appraisee to engage in little more than a cosy chat. Normally, it is not possible to fail an appraisal.[100]

---

97 Sir Graeme Catto, 'The GMC – Revalidation – What Are We Trying to Measure?', *Medico-Legal Journal*, 2003, 71(106), 2 October.

98 The Fifth Report of the Shipman Inquiry, *Safeguarding Patients: Lessons from the Past – Proposals for the Future*, paras 24.162–24.165 (www.the-shipman-inquiry.org.uk).

99 See Department of Health, *Revalidation to be Reviewed*, Press Release, 17 April 2004.

100 See the Fifth Report of the Shipman Inquiry, *Safeguarding Patients: Lessons from the Past – Proposals for the Future*, chapters 12 and 27 (www.the-shipman-inquiry.org.uk).

> Appraisal is a blunt instrument and as yet (despite being in operation for nearly three years) has probably not identified a single doctor whose performance is seriously deficient. Appraisal for all doctors is conducted by a peer. Is it right that a single doctor should have the responsibility to make that judgment about one of his or her peers?[101]

For GPs in England, each PCT has been allowed to make its own arrangements for appraisal. Usually, appraisal of a GP will be undertaken by another from the same PCT, in some cases the appraisees being allowed to choose their own appraisers. Also, there was significant variation in the quantity and quality of documentation provided by individual appraisees – at the extreme, some GPs providing 'virtually nothing'. Appraisers lack power of compulsion in these circumstances. The Shipman Inquiry also observed that some doctors were appraised by nurses or practice managers. There was no enforcement of recommendations arising from an appraisal, and even the very limited DoH guidance, that appraiser and appraisee should hold at least one review meeting during the 12 months after the appraisal, tended to be ignored.[102] Problems may be exacerbated if, by directly linking appraisal with revalidation, some appraisers are reluctant to provide information which could result in a colleague losing his or her licence to practise.[103]

Similarly, the GMC was placing significant trust in clinical governance at local level, when this was still a poorly developed and established system. Dame Janet Smith considered that the primary platform for revalidation should still be the production of a folder of evidence by each doctor, demonstrating what he or she had been doing over the five-year revalidation period; in essence, a modified return to the GMC's original proposal. Key contents would be prescribed and include as a minimum: clinical governance data such as prescribing information; appraisal information; a patient satisfaction questionnaire; results of clinical audit and significant audit events; and a video record of the doctor in consultation with patients. She also noted that doctors could not function appropriately without an up-to-date knowledge base, and so satisfactory completion of a knowledge test should also form part of the process. The GMC's proposals contained no clear standards by which a doctor's fitness to practise could be determined, no objective test, and no independent scrutiny of that test.[104] Only at the extreme, when a doctor was found unfit to practise, would action be taken in this direction. Even then, the mechanisms proposed to reach this conclusion were inadequate. As Dame Janet Smith observed:

> I have mentioned more than once in this Report the fact that the standards applied within the GMC's performance procedures have been very low…There is no indication of an intention to raise them under the new FTP procedures. This low standard will, to a very

---

101 Esmail, A., 'GMC and the Future of Revalidation – Failure to Act on Good Intentions', *BMJ*, 2005, Vol. 330, May 14.

102 See the Fifth Report of the Shipman Inquiry, *Safeguarding Patients: Lessons from the Past – Proposals for the Future*, paras 12.80–12.94 (www.the-shipman-inquiry.org.uk).

103 See the Fifth Report of the Shipman Inquiry, *Safeguarding Patients: Lessons from the Past – Proposals for the Future*, para 12.116 (www.the-shipman-inquiry.org.uk).

104 See Esmail, A., 'GMC and the Future of Revalidation – Failure to Act on Good Intentions', *BMJ*, 2005, Vol. 330, May 14.

large extent, underpin revalidation. In my view, for reasons of patient protection, there is an urgent need for this standard to be raised. There can be no justification for judging the performance of an experienced GP by a standard lower than the equivalent of the standard set for admission to general practice.'[105]

Whilst appropriate knowledge in itself does not guarantee a doctor's competence or suitability to practise, no doctor can function well without an adequate knowledge base. Public protection, it was said, is far too important to allow doctors' opposition to retesting to prevail. 'If a doctor cannot bring his/her knowledge base up to standard within five years, surely s/he should not be practising.'[106]

Doctors need not fear some ritualized humiliation of returning to the equivalent of the school exam hall. Knowledge tests could be devised in such a way that doctors could undertake them in private, probably online.[107]

The Shipman Inquiry favoured a model of revalidation of the type originally proposed by the GMC. As a first stage, scrutiny of the revalidation folder would be undertaken by a local group, including an independent lay member and an appropriately accredited doctor from outside of the area. If possible, the doctor under consideration for revalidation would attend a meeting of the panel to discuss his or her folder. For those folders with which the local group was satisfied, revalidation of the doctor would be recommended to the GMC. Only if a doctor did not satisfy this first stage, progression to the second stage would see the GMC taking over. It would be essential that this stage was both rigorous and transparent, with sufficient lay input.[108]

Unless the GMC improved its fitness to practise procedures and plans for revalidation, the Shipman Inquiry recommended that it should lose its regulatory powers.[109] This resulted in the Council suspending the planned 2005 introduction of revalidation.[110] Also in response to the criticisms from the Shipman Inquiry, the Chief Medical Officer of England was instructed by the government to undertake a review of the GMC's proposals for revalidation.[111]

## Lay Views of Revalidation

It has been argued that it is the absence of the strong lay voice in the regulation of medicine which is a key factor in explaining why a robust programme of revalidation

105 See the Fifth Report of the Shipman Inquiry, *Safeguarding Patients: Lessons from the Past – Proposals for the Future*, para 27.231 (www.the-shipman-inquiry.org.uk).

106 See the Fifth Report of the Shipman Inquiry, *Safeguarding Patients: Lessons from the Past – Proposals for the Future*, para 26.197 (www.the-shipman-inquiry.org.uk).

107 See the Fifth Report of the Shipman Inquiry, *Safeguarding Patients: Lessons from the Past – Proposals for the Future*, para 26.197 (www.the-shipman-inquiry.org.uk).

108 See the Fifth Report of the Shipman Inquiry, *Safeguarding Patients: Lessons from the Past – Proposals for the Future*, paras 26.191–26.196 (www.the-shipman-inquiry.org.uk).

109 The Fifth Report of the Shipman Inquiry, *Safeguarding Patients: Lessons from the Past – Proposals for the Future* (www.the-shipman-inquiry.org.uk).

110 See also *BMJ*, 2005, 330: 9, 1 January; and *BMJ*, 2005, 330: 10, 1 January.

111 For further discussion, see Chapter 18.

was not put in place a significant time ago. In the absence of strong external pressure, the profession has historically been able to resist the imposition of ongoing universal scrutiny, with the associated risk of the loss of livelihood for some in the profession.[112] Now that revalidation has been proposed, lay involvement has been described as 'critically important'. However, perhaps in an effort to reassure the rank and file within the profession, it has also been emphasized that the structured questionnaires for patients to complete are not complicated and that it will not be necessary to get a sample of hundreds or even tens of patients. It has been suggested that a 'consistent point, identified by 15 patients or colleagues, has validity and reliability'.[113] What is of greatest concern is not the validity of this statement in statistical terms, but the ease with which a doctor who is required only to obtain a few questionnaires might skew the sample by selecting only patients who will provide positive feedback.

Consumer groups and patient representatives favoured revalidation with a strong public involvement, underpinned by a restructured GMC with a lay majority.[114] From within the GMC, it was also recognized that public involvement was an essential component: '[revalidation] cannot be done by some kind of magic circle of doctors agreeing that other doctors are fit for practice.'[115]

> The real test of the trustworthiness of the new GMC will be the credibility of the standards of competence, care and conduct it sets for revalidation and the robustness of the evidence it is prepared to accept from doctors to demonstrate their compliance. Public involvement in the process will be essential. In fact, most doctors will offer evidence derived from local clinical governance and appraisal. This could be highly variable. Consequently public and professional confidence will be determined largely by the effectiveness of the regular quality checks that the GMC will use to show that revalidation is sound, reliable and consistent.[116]

However, despite consumer groups and some within the GMC and the profession expressing similar sentiments, the degree of effective lay input is highly questionable. The GMC's initial revalidation proposals were more favourable towards the consumer view, with revalidation panels having lay members. However, during their period of development, the revalidation procedures have become watered down in terms of lay involvement.

The BMA,[117] whilst denying that it was reluctant to see patients involved in revalidation, questioned the extent to which patients are able to assess a doctor's

112 Norcini, J.J., 'Where Next with Revalidation?', *BMJ*, 2005, 330: 1458–9, 25 June. See also Dauphinee, W.D., 'GMC and the Future of Revalidation: Revalidation in 2005: Progress and Maybe Some Lessons Learned?' *BMJ*, 2005, 330: 1385–7.

113 Sir Graeme Catto, 'The GMC – Revalidation – What Are We Trying to Measure?', *Medico-Legal Journal*, 2003, 71(106), 2 October.

114 See Irvine, D., *The Doctors' Tale*, 2003, Radcliffe Medical Press, Oxford, 188.

115 Sir Graeme Catto, 'The GMC – Revalidation – What Are We Trying to Measure?', *Medico-Legal Journal*, 2003, 71(106), 2 October.

116 Irvine, D., *The Doctors' Tale*, 2003, Radcliffe Medical Press, Oxford, 210.

117 The comments in the following sections are taken from the *BMA Response to the Chief Medical Officer Review on Maintaining High Standards of Professional Practice*, May 2005.

fitness to practise. Reiterating the primary importance of peer assessment, the BMA's view is that:

> Ultimately, we believe it is very difficult for a patient to judge the competence of a doctor. Indeed, it is difficult for an untrained observer to ascertain much beyond the manner and demeanour of an individual.
>
> ...Clearly, an individual's ability to communicate effectively is important and the views of patients on the level of information they receive, whether they were helped to understand their post-operative care, for example, can help, but it is doubtful that patients could play a fuller part in assessment.

Whilst members of the public cannot be expected to compete with doctors in terms of medical knowledge, the BMA's comments still smack of the professional arrogance traditionally associated with the medical profession. Patients and other interested lay parties may often have well-informed views about aspects of illness and medical practice (in recent times supported by significantly increased levels of information available from the internet). Furthermore, appropriate questioning of doctors by lay participants should offer the potential to challenge (possibly erroneous) professional assumptions and, at the very least, ensure that doctors practise communicating effectively outside of professional circles.

**How Likely is Revalidation to be Effective?**

Catto describes revalidation as 'a beguilingly simple concept'. However, some of the practical details can also be described as so simple that they are inadequate.[118] An example from the Ledward case illustrates the challenges faced in creating an effective revalidation process. One consultant gave evidence to the Ledward Inquiry that he had been asked to find examples of cases which showed problems with Ledward's practice. Even though Ledward's misconduct had, by then, been ongoing for some time, the consultant said that it was very time-consuming to go through notes 'with nothing to guide you as to where to look'. It had taken him a couple of years to find three or four cases.[119]

In the case of a seriously dysfunctional, criminal, doctor such as Shipman, it might be expected that a well-designed system of revalidation would have no difficulties with early detection. However, it is far from certain that this will be the case. Revalidation should be able to pick up underperforming doctors, in part because such doctors are often unaware of their limitations, so make no attempt to hide them. In contrast, Shipman exhibited deviousness in hiding his crimes, whilst at the same time maintaining the image of a competent and caring doctor. Appraisal, in its current form, would have caused him few, if any, problems. Indeed, the Shipman Inquiry concluded that: 'There is no possibility that [Shipman] could have "failed"

118 Sir Graeme Catto, 'The GMC – Revalidation – What Are We Trying to Measure?', *Medico-Legal Journal*, 2003, 71(106), 2 October.

119 *The Ledward Report*, Part V, para 14.2.2.

at appraisal. In fact, it is quite likely that he would have volunteered (and been accepted) as an appraiser.'[120]

He would also have experienced little difficulty in obtaining a clinical governance certificate and, from there, progressing to revalidation. For there to have been any realistic chance of routine detection, revalidation would have needed to include elements such as an analysis of mortality rates or the submission of patient records for independent review. These would have needed to be selected without interference from Shipman, and in sufficient numbers to present a realistic prospect that selected records would include those of patients he had killed.[121]

Whilst not the panacea for all the GMC's ills, revalidation does offer an important way forwards. However, the revolt by doctors in 1969 against the imposition of the annual fee to fund the GMC illustrates the power that the profession can wield if it objects to a change. If, for example, sufficient numbers of doctors refused to cooperate with revalidation, there would be little prospect of mass erasure without many thousands, even tens of thousands, of NHS patients suffering as a result. This experience strongly suggests that for revalidation to work, the rank and file members of the profession have to support it, or at the very least not be actively against it. The GMC appears to have been unwilling to take this risk. The GMC's early proposals for revalidation had the potential, if properly funded, to provide a meaningful and reasonably effective revalidation process. However, the move by the Council to a watered down version does little to offer the public protection necessary. There are potential ways forward which at the time of writing had not been considered fully, or at all, by the GMC. For example, sub-registers relating to particular areas of expertise, whilst presenting a challenge to set up and being potentially unpopular within the profession, could lead to a far more focused and effective revalidation process. Similarly, significant effort on the part of the GMC to devise a revalidation system which incorporates risk-based regulation should strengthen its effectiveness. The latter, discussed further in the next chapter, could be developed by the GMC systematizing and drawing upon the information it has or could obtain from its investigatory and disciplinary activities.

---

120 The Fifth Report of the Shipman Inquiry, *Safeguarding Patients: Lessons from the Past – Proposals for the Future*, paras 26.199–26.200 (www.the-shipman-inquiry.org.uk).

121 See the Fifth Report of the Shipman Inquiry, *Safeguarding Patients: Lessons from the Past – Proposals for the Future*, para 26.201–26.202 (www.the-shipman-inquiry.org.uk).

# Chapter 18

# Conclusions and Future Directions

## Introduction

It has not been my intention to mount a wholesale attack on modern healthcare provision. I am content to support those proponents of scientific medicine who point to the many advances in the last century or so, and the dramatic impact these have had on core issues such as infant mortality, life expectancy and diseases which in the past were major causes of disability and death.[1] Also, I do not seek to attack the whole medical profession as cynical manipulators of society, harbouring ill-will towards their patients.[2] Patient satisfaction and other surveys indicate that of the many millions of individual encounters with medical practice annually, satisfaction in doctors as dedicated career professionals remains high.

However, throughout this book, evidence has been presented repeatedly that doctors have lost sight of their obligation to self-regulate. The core of my argument is that medical self-regulation has failed because of a significant lack of proactivity on the part of individual practitioners and the General Medical Council. That only a handful of doctors were found guilty of serious professional misconduct each year suggests that the GMC were hardly scratching the surface of the problem.[3] The failure over lengthy periods to detect serious misconduct on the part of doctors such as Ledward, Ayling, Neale, Shipman and other high profile cases all lends support to this conclusion. There is little evidence that the GMC sees itself as a regulatory organization whose role is to seek out serious misconduct amongst practitioners. As previously noted, the GMC has been constrained by budgetary and statutory constraints, but has done too little to attempt to address and rectify this.

---

1 For instance, between 1901 and 1999, deaths of 0–4-year-olds fell as a proportion of all deaths from 37 to 0.8 per cent. Tallis, R., *Hippocratic Oaths*, 2004, Atlantic, London, 226.

2 Not all commentators agree that the majority of doctors are necessarily always concerned with the best interests of their patients. Wootton, for example, argues that the history of Western medicine is peppered with examples of the medical profession holding up progress to further its own material self-interest. Wootton, D., *Bad Medicine: Doctors Doing Harm Since Hippocrates*, 2006, Oxford University Press, Oxford.

3 For example, in 1998 the Professional Conduct Committee of the GMC found only 31 doctors guilty of serious professional misconduct and dealt with a further five convicted of criminal offences. From a base of well over 100,000 practising doctors, these figures are extremely low. See *Supporting Doctors, Protecting Patients*, NHS Consultation Paper, 2.4.

It is depressing that the historical concerns with the process of medical self-regulation discussed at the beginning of this work still remain pertinent. As expressed by the Shipman Inquiry:

> The process of change has been tortuous and piecemeal. It is discouraging…that, even now, at the start of the new era, there is no real commitment to the underlying principles of good regulation. In short, I am not convinced that the leopard has changed its spots or ever will.[4]

Problems of regulatory capture by the targets of regulation, inadequate staffing and a lethargic and passive approach to investigation are all evident in the work of the GMC. The limited resources which are committed to regulation still tend to be focused in a manner which is likely to minimize the risk of provoking serious resistance from the profession.[5] For example, even after the numerous high profile cases which have demonstrated a widespread failure within the profession to report concerns about colleagues, the GMC has shown very limited willingness to tackle the issue. Therefore, whilst reforms in recent years are, on the whole, to be welcomed, they only scratch the surface of what urgently needs to be addressed. Notwithstanding its rhetoric and recent buzz words – such as 'effectiveness', 'inclusiveness' and 'accountability'[6] – the GMC has consistently failed to think truly radically. It described the introduction of *Good Medical Practice*, a strengthened education function and the linking of professional standards with regulation as 'far reaching changes',[7] yet in practice these have done little to stem the flow of problems, or to significantly enhance confidence that the GMC is truly committed to dealing with problem doctors. Above all, the GMC has failed to instil within individual members of the medical profession the understanding that modern professionals should 'only have duties – they do not have privileges. They have duties over and above the duties of being a citizen.'[8] Whilst Kennedy's sentiments have considerable force, the medical profession does continue to enjoy the privilege of high status, relatively high incomes (especially when compared with other professionals in the public sector) and the privilege of self-regulation, albeit within a wider regulatory framework. In reality, therefore, the duties owed continue to constitute one half of the bi-partite contract between profession and state.

4 The Fifth Report of the Shipman Inquiry, *Safeguarding Patients: Lessons from the Past – Proposals for the Future*, para 25.357 (www.the-shipman-inquiry.org.uk).

5 For discussion of these ideas in the context of the legal profession, see Arthurs, H.W., 'A Global Code of Legal Ethics for the Transnational Legal Field', *Legal Ethics*, Summer 1999, Vol. 2, No. 1, 60—69.

6 See GMC, *Effective, Inclusive and Accountable Reform of the GMC's Structure, Constitution and Governance*, March 2001, 5.

7 GMC, *Effective, Inclusive and Accountable Reform of the GMC's Structure, Constitution and Governance*, March 2001, 4.

8 Professor Sir Ian Kennedy giving evidence to a working party of the Royal College of Physicians of London, 20 May 2005. Cited in Department of Health, *Good Doctors, Safer Patients – Proposals to Strengthen the System to Assure and Improve the Performance of Doctors and to Protect the Safety of Patients: A Report by the Chief Medical Officer*, July 2006.

Voices from within the profession have continued to assert the importance of the GMC. For example: 'The General Medical Council is the crucible of our professionalism and without it, doctors in this country would become mere technicians. Any alteration to professionally-led regulation is unthinkable.'[9]

However, the GMC itself has sought to place its role as just one of a number of regulators within a complex framework, thereby minimizing the significance of its weaknesses or failings. However, whilst the medical profession retains the status and power which accompanies self-regulation, the GMC remains at the forefront, as the only body which combines the power to erase a doctor's name from the medical register, suspend the doctor from practice or ensure that the doctor can only practise subject to conditions. Regulatory systems common to some other areas of employment, for example, close surveillance and a requirement that employees adhere to detailed rules, are unlikely to be effective for professional work involving complexity and high task uncertainty.[10] The GMC is also the only regulator which can act against a registered medical practitioner irrespective of employment or other organizational boundaries. This was illustrated by the Alder Hey case. The actions of the doctor at the centre of this case went unchecked, in part because he had dual academic and clinical roles and neither of his line managers accepted responsibility for ensuring that concerns were followed up.[11] As Dame Janet Smith put it: 'The GMC's powers are the "teeth" by which all other monitoring processes can ultimately be enforced.'[12]

Even on the GMC's own terms, recent changes and proposals for change do not clearly locate it within the wider system. It remains unclear exactly how appraisal, clinical governance, complaints handling and revalidation will work together and how protection of the public will be guaranteed by this multitude of complex systems. Within this complexity, the GMC has bounced between the competing demands of its varying stakeholders at the expense of adopting a clear public-centred focus.[13]

## Future Directions

Command and control models of regulation have been subject to significant criticism. Rigid and inappropriately targeted rules and under- or over-rigorous enforcement are often ineffective. Regulation cannot assume that the behaviour of the regulated is

9 Dr Brian Keighley, elected member of the General Medical Council, cited in Department of Health, *Good Doctors, Safer Patients – Proposals to Strengthen the System to Assure and Improve the Performance of Doctors and to Protect the Safety of Patients: A Report by the Chief Medical Officer*, July 2006, Chapter 8.

10 For further discussion, see Degeling, P., 'Reconsidering Clinical Accountability', *International Journal of Health Planning Management*, 2000, 15, 3–16.

11 This was one of the conclusions of the PPC when complaints arising from the Alder Hey case were considered by the GMC. See comments of Burton J in *Woods v General Medical Council* [2002] EWHC 1484.

12 The Fifth Report of the Shipman Inquiry, *Safeguarding Patients: Lessons from the Past – Proposals for the Future* (www.the-shipman-inquiry.org.uk).

13 'Reforming the GMC', *BMJ*, 2001, Vol. 322, 689–90, 21 March.

constant. When government adopts the role of 'commander' and 'controller', an additional problem results from insufficient knowledge of actual problems, likely solutions and the means to identify non-compliance.[14] O'Neill suggests an approach based upon 'intelligent accountability'. This envisages that good governance will only be achieved when institutions are allowed an appropriate margin for self-governance. This recognizes that attempts at excessively standardized or relentlessly detailed regulatory requirements are inevitably flawed, and that much that 'has to be accounted for is not easily measured, it cannot be boiled down to a set of stock performance indicators'.[15] The GMC has been allowed a significant margin with respect to self-governance of the medical profession, but has not utilized this appropriately in the interests of the public. This problem is potentially exacerbated by recent discussion both within the medical profession and within academia, focusing on the suggested need for greater moves towards a no blame culture. The focus of my argument is that the failings of medical self-regulation in recent years have arisen not from too much blame, but from too little. Individual members of the medical profession must face the constant challenge of seeing themselves as having a central role in their colleagues' careers, as well as themselves being overseen and regulated by their colleagues. The importance of this is underpinned by theoretical arguments. For example, it has been suggested by Dunsire that the maintenance of effective self-regulation depends upon constant opposition between alternative states. Manipulation of these alternative states can lead to appropriate developments to ensure the continued effectiveness of regulation. The common feature of opposing or alternative states is that they cannot be made routine, but rather must be custom decided to appropriately affect the regulatory process.[16] It has also been suggested that duplication of functions in different forms are desirable, to ensure that if one fails, others remain effective.[17] Within the profession, such opposition may be created between different types of doctor, or between doctors and other health professionals. The potential for this was seen in the Bristol case, with anaesthetists and nurses being concerned about the performance and success rates of cardiac surgeons. What was missing were the systemic mechanisms to make use of this. Instead, the emphasis was upon persuading or cajoling those with concerns to keep quiet and rejoin the professional fold.

In practice, many medical practitioners have demonstrated an unwillingness to regulate each other, with loyalty to colleagues taking precedence over obligations

14 Black, J., 'Decentring Regulation: Understanding the Role of Regulation and Self-Regulation in a "Post-Regulatory" World', in Freeman, M.D.A. (ed.), *Current Legal Problems*, 2001, Vol. 54, Oxford University Press, Oxford, 103–146, 106 and 108.

15 O'Neill, O., *Reith Lectures 2002*, Radio 4, http://www.bbc.co.uk/radio4/reith2002/ONora O'Neill.

16 Dunsire, A., 'Modes of Governance', in Kooiman, J. (ed.), *Modern Governance: New Government-Society Interactions*, 1993, Sage, London.

17 Landau, M., 'Redundancy, Rationality and the Problem of Duplication and Overlap', *Public Administration Review*, 1969, 39. Cited by Black, J., 'Decentring Regulation: Understanding the Role of Regulation and Self-Regulation in a "Post-Regulatory" World', in Freeman, M.D.A., (ed.), *Current Legal Problems*, 2001, Vol. 54, Oxford University Press, Oxford, 103–146, 128.

to the wider public.[18] The importance of changing this is illustrated by the Shipman case. The fact that patients, their relatives and even the police held Shipman in high esteem and were reluctant to challenge him illustrates the trust and high moral status which the medical profession still receives from the public. When at their most vulnerable, physically and mentally, patients have to convince themselves that their doctors command a moral position which puts them beyond reproach. Practitioners themselves know that not all of their colleagues deserve this status and trust, and that patients are not always in the best position to recognize this.[19] This is illustrated succinctly by the reported comment of a relative of one of Shipman's victims: 'I remember the time Shipman gave to my Dad. He would come around at the drop of a hat. He was a marvellous GP apart from the fact that he killed my father.'[20]

It has to be a primary responsibility of each member of the medical profession to protect the public from their professional colleagues, should the need arise. An enormous change in the professional culture of doctors is required to instil a genuine commitment to this. Historically, the medical profession has itself striven to achieve a position of privileged social status by presenting a unified front of near infallibility and ethical superiority. Colleagues who have breached these professional norms may find themselves isolated and ostracized by colleagues, victimized and subjected to personal abuse. Whistleblowing may be viewed as an act of betrayal against both the individual colleague and wider notions of collegial loyalty which underpin professional practice.[21] Not only do members of a hospital, or other practice unit, who whistleblow have to be protected from reprisals from colleagues, they also have to believe genuinely that an open dialogue about regulatory matters will be welcomed as part of a positive and healthy self-regulatory environment.

The strength of the ingrained culture of professional loyalty is well illustrated by the Bristol Royal Infirmary case. The anaesthetist, Stephen Bolsin, who made repeated efforts to report the activities at Bristol, emigrated to Australia soon afterwards, blaming a high degree of ostracization by colleagues. If fellow doctors were willing to accept that the, potentially avoidable, deaths of young children were preferable to reporting colleagues, then the challenge to change this dominant culture is enormous. Similar cultural obstacles were identified in the case of Rodney Ledward. The Inquiry into the activities of Ledward identified a culture of fear and intimidation and noted that the processes operated by the GMC did little or nothing

18 May, W.F., *Professional Virtue and Self-Regulation*. Cited by Parker, J., 'Moral Philosophy – Another Disabling Profession?', Chapter 3, in Allsop, J. and Mulcaly, L., *Maintaining Professional Identity: Doctors' Responses to Complaints*, 1998, Blackwell, Oxford.

19 Some may even be attracted to the profession because of the power it allows them to wield over others. Neither Shipman's trial nor the subsequent Public Inquiry were able to provide an explanation for his crimes. One possible explanation is the perverted sense of satisfaction he derived from exercising the power of life or death.

20 Christopher Rudol, quoted in Barkham, P., 'The Shipman Report', *The Times*, 20 July 2002, 15.

21 Burrows, J., 'Telling Tales and Saving Lives: Whistleblowing – The Role of Professional Colleagues in Protecting Patients from Dangerous Doctors', *Medical Law Review*, Summer 2001, 9, 110–29, 112.

to protect members of the profession from the fear of whistleblowing.[22] Even consultants who gave evidence against Ledward said that they felt themselves to be at risk of being ostracized.

## Government Role in Regulation

Arguments favouring greater government involvement in professional regulation focus upon the idea that government is more in touch with the democratic process and the wider needs of society than professional bodies. Even if regulatory powers are delegated to the profession, the government should retain oversight and ensure that the profession remains accountable.[23] However, ministers and senior civil servants face a high level of competing demands on their time and lack of specialist expertise. They are therefore likely to be reluctant to engage closely with the regulation of individual professions. One feature of the contemporary neo-liberal state has been described as the capacity to implement regulatory structures which facilitate natural tendencies towards regulation. As Parker describes this so-called 'new regulatory state':

> [T]he purpose of the new regulatory state [is] to 'deregulate' by pushing legal values so far down into organisational everyday life that it no longer becomes a technocratic system of command and control rules which governments find hard to enforce, and with which businesses only grudgingly comply, but a part of the everyday reflexes of the company, its management and work.[24]

In the context of her discussion about the regulation of lawyers, Parker suggests that penalties for failing to comply and incentives for voluntary adoption of regulatory strategies may both be used. Market incentives and risk management may be used to influence conduct without the appearance of direct interference with institutional autonomy.[25] Self-regulation would seem to already have a natural place within this regulatory environment.[26] At first sight, the new regulatory state model may be seen as a boost to the maintenance of the status quo for established self-regulating professions such as law and medicine. However, these professions are used to wielding significant control over their regulatory activities. The new regulatory state

22 *An Inquiry into Quality and Practice within the National Health Service Arising from the Actions of Rodney Ledward*, 1 June 2000. Chaired by Jean Ritchie QC.

23 Disney, J., Basten, J., Redmond, P., Ross, S. and Bell, K., *Lawyers*, 2[nd] ed, 1986, The Law Book Co., Melbourne, 216–17.

24 Parker, Christine, 'Lawyer Deregulation via Business Deregulation: Compliance Professionalism and Legal Professionalism', *International Journal of the Legal Profession*, 1999, Vol. 6, No. 2, 175–96, 186.

25 Parker, Christine, 'Lawyer Deregulation via Business Deregulation: Compliance Professionalism and Legal Professionalism', *International Journal of the Legal Profession*, 1999, Vol. 6, No. 2, 175–96, 179.

26 Black, J., 'Decentring Regulation: Understanding the Role of Regulation and Self-Regulation in a "Post-Regulatory" World', in Freeman, M.D.A. (ed.), *Current Legal Problems*, 2001, Vol. 54, Oxford University Press, Oxford, 103–146, 113.

is likely to impose a model very much on its own terms. For those areas of activity which have experienced significant bureaucratic external command and control, 'new' regulation may be welcomed and embraced purely for the relative freedom it brings. However, for established professions there may be a significant loss of freedom.

One approach which may be applied to professional regulation is the appointment of a lay person or committee consisting of independent, committed and forthright members who could undertake oversight on behalf of the government.[27] The self-regulatory processes of the legal professions in England and Wales have been overseen since the early 1990s by the Legal Services Ombudsman.[28] The LSO, who cannot be a member of the regulated professions she is responsible for, plays an oversight role with regard to complaints handling and other aspects of the self-regulatory process. Whilst this does not offer a panacea solution to the problems of professional self-regulation, a powerful overseer should ensure that the front-line regulator is kept constantly on its toes. Furthermore, if the overseer has to frequently criticize the operation of the self-regulatory process, then this provides evidence which can be used to challenge the continuation of self-regulation. This has recently been demonstrated by the part the LSO has played in challenges to self-regulation by the legal professions, and the subsequent reforms recommended by the Clementi Review.[29]

Paradoxically, zealous adherence to regulatory and ethical principles may be to the public detriment if the costs outweigh the benefits. In the case of free market professions, such as law, such costs are felt directly by the client in the form of increased fees.[30] In the case of public provision, such as NHS medicine, the costs may manifest in the form of delay and longer waiting lists. The GMC, therefore, faces a potential dilemma. Too lax, and unfit doctors remain in practice. As the Merrison Committee observed in the 1970s, significant numbers of overseas doctors whose skills fell below acceptable standards were admitted to the register to meet manpower requirements of the NHS.[31] Too harsh, and doctors who are fit to practise may find themselves unnecessarily suspended or otherwise restricted from maximizing the services they can provide to patients.

The GMC came into being at a time when the medical profession was far smaller and its members were far more likely to practise alone, or at least not for a large, well-structured employer. In these circumstances the GMC was the only body which could with any degree of certainty control the behaviour of the doctor. Today,

---

27 For discussion in the context of lawyers, see Disney, J., Basten, J., Redmond, P., Ross, S. and Bell, K., *Lawyers*, 2nd ed, 1986, The Law Book Co., Melbourne, 217.

28 The position of Ombudsman was created by the Courts and Legal Services Act 1990.

29 For further discussion, see Davies, M., 'Solicitors – The Last Twenty Years of Self-regulation?', *Professional Negligence*, 2005, Vol. 21, No. 1, 3—26.

30 For discussion with respect to lawyers, see Tur, R.H.S., 'Accountability and Lawyers', in Chadwick, R.F. (ed.), *Ethics and the Professions*, 1994, Avebury, Aldershot.

31 *Report of the Committee of Inquiry into the Regulation of the Medical Profession*, 1975, Cmnd 6018, HMSO, London, Paragraphs 185–7, in Stacey, M., *Regulating British Medicine: the General Medical Council*, 1992, Wiley, Chichester, 54.

the picture is very different. The majority of doctors work for the NHS and often do so within complex organizations. This leaves the GMC with a choice. Either it positions itself as a 'higher regulator', concerned only with complaints which other organizations (whether NHS or private) refer to it because local sanctions are inadequate given the seriousness of the matter. Alternatively, it continues as it has done in the past, expressing a willingness, in principle at least, to look at all complaints. As the Shipman Inquiry observes: 'it is not acceptable…for the GMC to seek to keep a foot in both camps: offering to receive all complaints and then selecting for investigation only those which raise the most obvious concerns about the safety of patients.'[32]

Whichever route the GMC chooses, it must commit itself to investing appropriate resources to undertake the role well. A limited 'higher regulator' role should be the cheaper option, but at the expense of the loss of genuine self-regulation with regard to all but the most serious cases. The alternative, continuing an all-encompassing regulatory stance, retains self-regulation to a much greater extent, but will be expensive and will require each member of the profession to pay a relatively high price to invest the necessary resources. Above all, the GMC must avoid underestimating the scope of this task. In this respect, lessons can be learned from the solicitors' profession. Historically, the Law Society has dealt with virtually all concerns about solicitors, from low level complaints about service to matters so serious that they warrant removal from practice.[33] In recent years, the Law Society has struggled to meet the demands placed upon it by such an extensive role. The resulting criticism led to a review, by Sir David Clementi, of the whole complaints handling process. The recommendations of this review have seriously challenged the Law Society's role as independent self-regulator of the profession.[34]

## Risk-Based Regulation

In March 2005, the GMC began to ask whether a risk-based approach would improve its performance in regulating doctors.[35] Flexibility based upon risk should allow for a light-touch approach where the regulatory risk is low, and more proactive scrutiny where it is higher. The starting point was to consider whether the past, 'complaints-driven', reactive approach was still appropriate. In particular, it was observed that there was no straightforward correlation between complaints and fitness to practise. Furthermore, a reactive approach may often miss opportunities to act before harm

32 See the Fifth Report of the Shipman Inquiry, *Safeguarding Patients: Lessons from the Past – Proposals for the Future*, para 18.105 (www.the-shipman-inquiry.org.uk).

33 The latter are handled by an autonomous adjudicatory body, the Solicitors Disciplinary Tribunal.

34 For further discussion, see Davies, M., 'Solicitors – The Last Twenty Years of Self-regulation?', *Professional Negligence*, 2005, Vol. 21, No. 1, 3—26.

35 See GMC, *Developing a Risk-Based Approach to Regulation: the Early Identification of Impairment*, 17 March 2005.

occurs, or at least to minimize the resulting degree of harm.[36] A risk-based approach could also improve the performance of the GMC by targeting resources towards areas of particular risk.[37]

The GMC expressed its commitment to the five principles of good regulation developed by the Better Regulation Task Force – in particular the final one, targeting[38] – and also drew upon the findings of the Hampton review of risk-based regulation in business.[39] Key differences between medical regulation and business regulation were recognized, in particular the importance of maintaining public confidence in the medical profession. This may need a greater regulatory response than indicated on a strict risk-based assessment.[40]

Broad notions of a risk basis have already been recognized in the GMC's approach to revalidation. Notably the plan for a 'lighter touch' for doctors working within NHS or other environments which have appropriate quality assured clinical governance arrangements. [41] This broad approach could be extended to include a focus on actual indicators of serious impairment. Key amongst these are research into antecedent factors possibly predisposing doctors to future serious impairment; identification of the indicators warning of existing serious impairment; the use of complaints and other data from various parts of the regulatory framework to identify areas of high risk.[42]

A risk-based approach might go some way to assuaging those critics of the GMC who question the absence of knowledge and skills testing from the proposals for revalidation. The GMC would defer to local procedures but, in developing indicators for risk assessment, it would also involve the medical Royal Colleges as well as NHS employers. The GMC would limit its role to that of 'co-ordinator and facilitator'.[43]

---

36 GMC, *Developing a Risk-Based Approach to Regulation: the Early Identification of Impairment*, 17 March 2005, paragraphs 5–6.

37 In reaching this position, the GMC has expressed commitment to the principles of good regulation developed by the Better Regulation Task Force: proportionality, accountability, consistency, transparency and targeting, and also the target-based approach favoured by the Healthcare Commission. See GMC, *Developing Medical Regulation: a Vision for the Future – the GMC's Response to the Call for Ideas by the Review of Clinical Performance and Medical Regulation*, April 2005, paras 69–71 and 134.

38 The others being: proportionality; accountability; consistency; and transparency.

39 Hampton, P., *Reducing Administrative Burdens: Effective Inspection and Enforcement*, December 2004.

40 GMC Paper, *Developing Risk-based Regulation: Progress Report*, 20 September 2005, para 11.

41 GMC, *Developing a Risk-Based Approach to Regulation: the Early Identification of Impairment*, 17 March 2005, paragraph 21.

42 GMC, *Developing Medical Regulation: a Vision for the Future – the GMC's Response to the Call for Ideas by the Review of Clinical Performance and Medical Regulation*, April 2005, para 71.

43 GMC, *Developing a Risk-Based Approach to Regulation: the Early Identification of Impairment*, 17 March 2005, paragraphs 30–33.

One key potential weakness derives from the GMC's intended reliance on local systems to identify existing or emerging dysfunctional practice.[44] The Council continues to express optimism that new clinical governance procedures will facilitate more doctors resolving their difficulties at local level, without the need for referral to the GMC. In turn, a higher proportion of doctors who are referred should be ones who represent a 'clear and present danger to patients'; or are presented with 'a well-documented and properly investigated history of less serious impairment that it has not been possible to remedy locally...' and which requires consideration of the removal or restriction of registration.[45] Lessons from the past continue to cast doubt on the rigour and consistency of local procedures. Even assuming that the GMC's confidence in local procedures is now well founded, an obvious gap in the intended approach is the controlling of doctors who fit the 'history of less serious impairment that it has not been possible to remedy locally' category, but not to the degree that the GMC would recognize the need to limit or remove registration. Furthermore, the GMC accepts that it has little information about the possible extent of impairment within the profession. The Chief Medical Officer for England is cited as estimating the figure to be 5–6 per cent. It has also been suggested that 10 per cent or more of doctors are addicted to drugs or alcohol.[46] The GMC has demonstrated little enthusiasm for finding out the actual scale of these problems.

Identifying and codifying factors which are likely to predict future serious impairment presents a significant challenge. The NCAA has suggested factors such as poor availability;[47] inappropriate anger; rigidity;[48] professional avoidance by colleagues; unwillingness to accept constructive criticism and general defensiveness. Further research may provide insight into the correlation between certain career and life events – 'sentinel events' – and serious impairment. More could be done to utilize data already received relating to complaints and similar events, to identify patterns which might inform risk-based regulation.[49] An obvious starting point would be to use previous fitness to practise findings as events giving rise to greater

44 See GMC, *Developing Medical Regulation: a Vision for the Future – the GMC's Response to the Call for Ideas by the Review of Clinical Performance and Medical Regulation*, April 2005, paras 69–71.

45 GMC, *Developing a Risk-Based Approach to Regulation: the Early Identification of Impairment*, 17 March 2005, paragraphs 11–12.

46 See GMC, *Developing a Risk-Based Approach to Regulation: the Early Identification of Impairment*, 17 March 2005, paragraph 13; and Department of Health, *Good Doctors, Safer Patients – Proposals to Strengthen the System to Assure and Improve the Performance of Doctors and to Protect the Safety of Patients: A Report by the Chief Medical Officer*, July 2006.

47 For example, not responding to bleeps, poor attendance or poor punctuality.

48 Often identified by factors such an inability to compromise and difficulties with prioritizing.

49 National Clinical Assessment Authority, *Understanding Performance Difficulties in Doctors*, November 2004. See also GMC, *Developing a Risk-Based Approach to Regulation: the Early Identification of Impairment*, 17 March 2005, paragraphs 36—40.

risk. Similarly, a higher risk profile may be attached to doctors who have frequently changed employers in the recent past.[50]

By way of illustration, risk-based regulation has been used for a number of years by the Financial Services Authority. In late 2001, the FSA became the sole regulator of the financial services industry and fundamentally changed the approach to regulation. The new risk-based approach was described as one of trying to work smarter, aiming at a more analytical and thinking regulatory regime.[51] With a steer towards reflexivity, the focus of the new regime was on the effectiveness of controls and management systems rather than compliance with intricate rules.[52]

The regulatory tools adopted by the FSA were directed towards those designed to monitor and influence the behaviour of consumers, groups of regulated firms and the financial services industry as a whole.[53] In practice, these regulatory tools include consumer education programmes, consumer alerts, industry training and even working to bring financial literacy education into schools.[54] Industry-wide activities focus upon training and competence regimes and essential regulatory rules.[55] The aim was to raise standards and thus reduce the need for firm specific regulation.

The FSA approach to individual firm monitoring involved a two-stage process: first, identifying and classifying risks;[56] and second, estimating the probability that the risk will crystallize. To achieve this, intelligence is utilized from a range of sources including consumer research, liaison with practitioners, economic analysis and 'mystery shopping'.[57] By focusing resources on areas of greatest risk, the FSA seeks early intervention before significant damage can be caused. A key focus of the approach is to ensure that firms have incentives to maintain standards and seek improvements in practices. Key amongst these is the promise of a less intensive

---

50 See GMC Paper, *Developing Risk-based Regulation: Progress Report*, 20 September 2005,

51 Davies, H., Chairman FSA, *Proceedings of Financial Services Authority Conference – A Radical New Approach to Regulation.* Keynote Speech, *A New Regulator for the New Millennium*, www.fsa,gov.uk.

52 Spilka, I., 'Risk-Based Compliance Monitoring', *Compliance Monitor*, November 2001, 14.4(6) (Lexis transcript).

53 FSA, *A New Regulator for the New Millennium*, January 2000, 21.

54 The FSA has categorized its regulatory tools under four headings: diagnostic; monitoring; preventative; and remedial. Diagnosis will aim to identify, assess and measure risk by means, for example, of inspection visits. Monitoring will track the development of identified risks, for example, by reviewing information provided by institutions. Preventative measures will aim to limit or reduce identified risks, for example, by presenting comparative information to consumers. Remedial measures will involve responding after risks have crystallized, for example, by providing compensation. FSA, *Building the New Regulator, Progress Report 1*, December 2000, 19.

55 The rule-making agenda will aim to avoid an excess of rules, which can lead to an overly bureaucratic system and give rise to unnecessary compliance costs for firms and monitoring costs for the FSA.

56 In December 2000, the FSA reported that it had drawn up preliminary risk profiles of regulated institutions and allocated these institutions to a spectrum of regulatory categories. FSA, *Building the New Regulator, Progress Report 1*, December 2000, 5.

57 FSA, *A New Regulator for the New Millennium*, January 2000, 10–15.

regulatory relationship for those firms which take prompt and effective remedial action to meet FSA requirements.[58] Different risk categories – from high to low impact[59] – allow for varying regulatory relationships. At one end of this spectrum, high impact firms are subjected to a continuous regulatory relationship with the FSA.[60] At the other end, low impact firms can be remotely monitored. This was in contrast with previous practice of regular routine monitoring visits for all firms.

Whilst the regulatory challenges facing the GMC differ in many respects from those faced by the FSA, lessons can still be learned from the latter's approach, in particular, the division of the regulated population into risk categories. As previously discussed, the GMC's revised plans for revalidation have been severely criticized because of the intention to rely upon local procedures. If the GMC returns to its original model of revalidation folders and adequately resourced revalidation panels, and adds to this appropriate mechanisms for regular retesting, then it will have a potential model on which to build a thorough system of risk-based regulation. In light of the recent scandals, at least the first couple of revalidation cycles should be extremely thorough and applied to all doctors. However, after this the GMC should have amassed sufficient information about doctors in different working environments to undertake meaningful risk evaluation and risk ranking. In this way, doctors and their employers who have put in the time and effort to create local procedures which are demonstrably thorough and robust can be rewarded with a lighter touch from the GMC. Those who have not will continue to face regular, thorough and intrusive inspection from the Council. Public education is also a valuable idea which can be adopted from the FSA. The GMC should push to ensure that from school onwards, the public are encouraged to acquire medical information which, inter alia, will better equip them to enter into a more effective partnership with their doctors.[61] As part of this process, the public could also be introduced to the workings of the

58 FSA, *Building the New Regulator, Progress report 1*, December 2000, 26.

59 Initial categorization placed 80 per cent of institutions in the low impact category, 15 per cent medium low, 4 per cent medium high and less than 1 per cent in the high category. FSA, *Building the New Regulator, Progress Report 1*, December 2000, 11. Low impact institutions are numerically important but have a very low aggregate market share, usually less than 3 per cent and often less than 1 per cent. The small number of high impact firms account for roughly 65 per cent of total market share, the 4 per cent of firms categorized as medium high impact account for approximately 24 per cent of market share and the 15 per cent categorized as medium low account for around 8 per cent of total market share. Foot, M., Managing Director and Head of Financial Supervision, FSA, *Our New Approach to Risk-Based Regulation – What Will be Different for Firms*, www.fsa.gov.uk.

60 FSA, *A New Regulator for the New Millennium*, January 2000, 19. The FSA will carry out a formal interim assessment of high impact firms once a year to review the risk mitigation programme and risk profile. This is likely to include some site visits. FSA, *Building the New Regulator, Progress Report 2*, February 2002, 23.

61 It is obviously impractical for the average member of the public to be equipped with detailed medical knowledge, but it should be possible to provide sufficient knowledge and vocabulary to encourage people to engage in meaningful discussion with their doctors. At school level, such education could be combined with associated matters, for example, information regarding nutrition and other health-related information.

healthcare system and be encouraged to view doctors as servants of the state funded by the taxpayer and, therefore, to be respected for their medical knowledge but not afforded undue respect simply because of a title.

## An Independent Regulator

If self-regulation has proved to be ineffective, then ultimately removal of this privilege may be the only solution. An independent body can bring to regulation the greater guarantee that it will genuinely focus on the public interest. It can also ensure lay involvement with less risk that lay members will be daunted or dominated by professionals, as may be the case with self-regulatory professional bodies.[62] An independent inspectorate for medical regulation, to monitor complaints and investigate poor clinical practice, was suggested in evidence to the Shipman Inquiry. This idea received little support from the medical profession, in particular because this was likely to require significant reorganization and possible abolition of existing bodies such as the GMC and the Healthcare Commission. A compromise approach was the development of the Healthcare Commission's inspectorate role to provide an expert, independent investigatory function.[63]

Lessons may be learned from the recent history of the regulation of the legal professions. A Department for Constitutional Affairs report,[64] published in July 2003, concluded that the regulatory framework governing lawyers was 'outdated, inflexible, over-complex and insufficiently accountable or transparent'. In the same month, Sir David Clementi was appointed to undertake a review of the regulation of legal services. Clementi issu*ed a consultation paper in March 2004.* The paper proposed two distinct models for regulation. Model A would remove all regulatory functions from the professional bodies and place these in the hands of a new unified regulator, the Legal Services Authority. The LSA's functions were likely to include: setting and enforcing rules and codes; providing general policy guidance; and exercising investigative, enforcement and disciplinary powers. The rule-making arm of the regulator could be sub-divided to facilitate the development of specialist provisions for distinct areas of practice. A key argument in favour of Model A was the complete independence of the regulator from the regulated. This model was preferred by the Legal Services Ombudsman, who considered that those benefits which might be derived from professionally controlled regulation had been overridden by an almost total loss of public faith in professional-led regulation.[65] In contrast, Model B would see the professional bodies retaining their regulatory responsibilities, but with oversight from a new overarching regulator – the Legal

62 For further discussion in the context of the legal profession, see New South Wales Law Reform Commission Discussion Paper, 1979, 119–20, in Disney, J., Basten, J., Redmond, P., Ross, S. and Bell, K., *Lawyers*, 2nd ed, 1986, The Law Book Co., Melbourne, 218.

63 See the Fifth Report of the Shipman Inquiry, *Safeguarding Patients: Lessons from the Past – Proposals for the Future*, para 27.76 (www.the-shipman-inquiry.org.uk).

64 *Competition and Regulation in the Legal Services Market*, July 2003.

65 *In Whose Interest – Annual Report of the Legal Services Ombudsman for England and Wales 2003/2004*, HC 729, 10.

Services Board. Model B offered the advantage of keeping regulation close to the profession, with the possible benefit that members retained a sense of ownership and an interest in maintaining the standards necessary to sustain public confidence. The two regulatory models were polarized constructs, with the potential for a number of variants.[66]

The final Clementi Report[67] favoured a hybrid solution, Model B+, which would build upon the existing systems. This model was considered preferable to Model A, in part because the latter would be costly for the government and would contradict the government's preference for moving away from direct regulatory control.[68]

Professional bodies would be required to separate regulatory and representative functions (much as the medical profession has already done, with the division between the GMC and the BMA) and would be subject to an oversight regulator, the Legal Services Board.[69] The LSB would hold the regulatory powers, but would be empowered to delegate functions to front-line regulators if satisfied that they have the competence and commitment to deal properly with this role. The structure of the LSB would consist of a board of between 12 and 16 members. The majority of members would be non-lawyers, including the senior positions of Chairman and Chief Executive.[70]

Overall, the Clementi proposals presented an uncertain future for self-regulation by lawyers, threatening the loss of self-regulatory control possessed, in the case of solicitors, since the mid nineteenth century. The government is now taking forward some of the Clementi recommendations.[71] Whilst the medical profession is not currently facing an immediate threat to its self-regulatory status, the Clementi experience demonstrates that this can change very quickly if the profession itself fails to put its own house in order. It is also of note that whilst the medical profession has for a long time had separate representative and regulatory bodies, a key element of the thesis of this book draws into question whether the GMC has drifted towards being, and being seen by individual members of the profession as, another representative body, alongside the BMA, rather than as a robust regulator.

---

66 Sir David Clementi, *Review of the Regulatory Framework for Legal Services in England and Wales – Final Report*, December 2004, 25.

67 Sir David Clementi, *Review of the Regulatory Framework for Legal Services in England and Wales – Final Report*, December 2004.

68 See Better Regulation Task Force, *Alternatives to State Regulation*, 2000, Cabinet Office, London; and Better Regulation Task Force, *Alternatives to Regulation*, 2004, Cabinet Office, London.

69 Sir David Clementi, *Review of the Regulatory Framework for Legal Services in England and Wales – Final Report*, December 2004, 49.

70 Sir David Clementi, *Review of the Regulatory Framework for Legal Services in England and Wales – Final Report*, December 2004, 82–5. It is proposed that the appointment of the Chairman and Chief Executive should be made by the Secretary of State in consultation with a senior member of the judiciary, probably the Master of the Rolls. All other appointments to the Board should be made by a Nominations Committee, operating in accordance with 'Nolan' principles.

71 Department for Constitutional Affairs, *The Future of Legal Services: Putting the Consumer First*, October 2005, Cm 6679.

## A Single Point for Complaints

The plethora of bodies within the healthcare system, to which complaints and concerns might be addressed, has caused confusion amongst lay and even medical complainants. As previously discussed, those complainants who approached the GMC would find the matter rejected if it did not fall within the Council's definitions of misconduct, performance or health issues. Complaints would also frequently be returned if they had not been subjected to the available local procedures. Inevitably, some complainants will have been deterred from taking their concerns further if it appeared that the GMC were uninterested. The GMC's updated fitness to practise procedures, with the removal of the distinct misconduct, performance and health elements, should make it a little easier for an outsider to understand the process but does not remove the other complicating and inhibiting factors. One suggested solution is the creation of a single 'portal' or 'gateway' for complaints – to maximize the likelihood that they quickly reach the appropriate organization. This portal could make maximum use of technology, with web- and email-based support. However, for potential complainants who lack internet access or the confidence to use this resource, a 'human' element should also play a core role.[72]

A single complaints portal would be strengthened by the creation of a centralized database, in which could be recorded a range of information about the performance of individual doctors. The various bodies which might acquire information about a doctor's disciplinary history should be under a duty to share this. This should include information about unsubstantiated complaints, unproven allegations and informal concerns.[73]

## References

References play an important role in ensuring that problem doctors cannot simply move from employer to employer. A number of cases discussed in this work illustrate a range of problems with references in practice. Inappropriate loyalty to colleagues may, once again, come into play. For instance, concerns about a doctor's practice may be omitted from a reference; inappropriate positive assumptions may be made about a doctor's clinical competence because he or she is socially charming; references may be provided by colleagues who have no knowledge of the doctor's clinical skills or whose knowledge may be historical only in nature. The Ledward Inquiry recommended the establishment of a central system for recording the employment history of every doctor. Potentially, this could be combined with the centralized conduct database discussed above. The GMC would be an appropriate central repository for such a system, although this would be a significant undertaking to ensure that it was done well and sufficiently rigorously.

---

72 For further discussion, see the Fifth Report of the Shipman Inquiry, *Safeguarding Patients: Lessons from the Past – Proposals for the Future*, paras 27.83–27.88 (www.the-shipman-inquiry.org.uk).

73 This was recommended by both the Shipman and Kerr/Haslam Inquiries. See, for example, *The Kerr/Haslam Inquiry Report*, July 2005, Cm 6640-1, 32–4.

## Inter-Professional Rivalry

A number of the cases discussed in this book illustrate that the historical inequalities of power between doctors and other health workers has meant the latter were reluctant to report concerns about the former. For instance, in the Bristol and Ledward cases, nurses were reluctant to challenge or even question the actions of doctors, especially consultants. In the Shipman case, the local pharmacist proved reluctant to question the prescribing and associated activities of a well-respected GP.

Empowerment of other healthcare professionals and the encouragement of intra-professional monitoring have the potential to significantly enhance the regulatory process. It was suggested some time ago that nurses have been developing their power base and increasingly taking on senior management roles, and that they had begun to challenge some of the traditional clinical roles of doctors.[74] These developments are to be welcomed, although the speed with which they have progressed and are progressing remains a cause for concern.

## Competitive Self-Regulation

In some areas of professional practice, multi-regulator models have been proposed or even implemented. Consumers can then choose the level of regulation they require and are willing to pay for.[75] In particular, this has the potential to be effective with those professions which operate in the free market. For instance, providing they have adequate information, consumers may prefer to instruct a solicitor rather than a licensed conveyancer, or vice versa, in part on the basis of the level of regulatory protection each offers. This model has scope for further development, for instance, particular solicitors could offer more rigorous regulation to give themselves a competitive advantage.[76] However, within the monopolistic environment of the NHS, there is far less scope for doctors to adopt or to have imposed upon them a multi-regulator model. Unlike the example of solicitors and licensed conveyancers, the public have lacked any genuine degree of choice within the NHS. Particular areas of specialism, for example, general practitioners and different specialists within hospitals, could, conceivably, be regulated separately. However, not only would this add to the regulatory complexity which already presents problems, but it offers uncertain public benefit. The most obvious potential benefits are the return to smaller scale regulated groups – allowing for greater intimacy in the regulatory process – and the creation of intra-group competition. The latter may encourage regulators to compete to demonstrate the highest standards – a race to the top.

74 See, for example, Dingwall, R., Rafferty, A.M. and Webster, C., *An Introduction to the Social History of Nursing*, 1988, Routledge, London.

75 See Ogus, A., 'Rethinking Self-Regulation', *Oxford Journal of Legal Studies*, 1995, Vol. 15, No. 1, 97–108, 103–105.

76 It may be argued that this already occurs informally with large commercial firms of solicitors which may offer ex gratia compensation to valued clients and otherwise deal rigorously with misconduct, if this threatens their reputation and commercial interests.

## Monitoring

In the context of GPs, the Shipman Inquiry considered how the monitoring of drug prescribing could be improved to be of greater value to clinical governance. Key recommendations included the tightening up of the use of prescription pads, so that the prescribing habits of individual doctors could be more accurately monitored. Additional safeguards would be built into this system for the monitoring of the prescribing of controlled drugs. In this latter respect, particularly close scrutiny should be applied to doctors who have been found to have drug abuse or associated problems in the past. The creation of a controlled drugs inspectorate would, inter alia, monitor controlled drugs registers for abnormal prescribing patterns or other issues of concern.[77]

The Shipman Inquiry also highlighted the absence of a system for collecting and analysing information about the circumstances of deaths. No organization was professionally interested in the unusually high numbers of Shipman's patients who had died unexpectedly at home, or whilst Shipman was present. The Inquiry proposed a new approach, with all deaths being reported to the coroner and in much greater detail. The coroner would be in a position to detect, monitor and investigate unusual patterns. This could be combined with the introduction of a national system to monitor GP mortality rates, preferably coupled with reform of the death certification system. This could also be combined with the inspection of medical records of deceased patients.[78] As previously discussed, each of these reforms has its own limitations. For instance, the routine inspection of patient records may not reveal problems, especially if the doctor takes greater care than Shipman did to cover his or her tracks.

## Information and Choice

There is much information about individual doctors which is in the public domain, yet is often not readily available. This might include a doctor's disciplinary history and any criminal convictions. Some organizations, for example the BMA, have argued that it is for the GMC, PCTs or a doctor's employer to weigh up the seriousness of particular behaviour and to deal with the doctor appropriately. There should be no need for patients to have further information about the doctor's history. This attitude is not restricted to doctors' organizations. Giving evidence to the Shipman Inquiry, the Chairman of the Patients' Association suggested that patients presented with such information about their doctor might be caused unnecessary stress and worry. However, as Irvine argues, not only does this approach tend to ignore the fact that this history is already publicly available – just not made adequately available – but

77 See the Fifth Report of the Shipman Inquiry, *Safeguarding Patients: Lessons from the Past – Proposals for the Future*, para 27.103–27.104 for a summary of these recommendations and the fourth report for fuller discussion (www.the-shipman-inquiry.org.uk).

78 See the Fifth Report of the Shipman Inquiry, *Safeguarding Patients: Lessons from the Past – Proposals for the Future*, paras 4.44–4.45 and 27.105–27.109 (www.the-shipman-inquiry.org.uk).

patients may, justifiably, be very angry if, having placed their trust in a doctor, they subsequently discover that they have been denied important information about his or her background. Dame Janet Smith reinforced this argument by pointing out that it was not only about giving patients the prospect of choosing an alternative doctor, but also about allowing more subtle choices. For instance, if a patient knew that her doctor had a conviction for indecent assault, she could choose always to attend with a chaperone.[79]

There are international precedents for the greater availability of information. For example, the College of Physicians and Surgeons of Ontario operates a website which includes a doctor's disciplinary history and practising restrictions. Serious matters, for instance, cases relating to sexual abuse, would remain on this record for the whole of the doctor's career. Less serious matters would be removed after a period of time. In the US, similar information about doctors is published electronically.[80]

In contrast, the GMC has shown reluctance to make information about doctors' regulatory past readily available. Inquirers could write or phone for information about a particular doctor, but my own experience has been that this approach left a lot to be desired, especially if the Council had records relating to more than one doctor with the same name. Whilst the latter will cause understandable difficulties for the GMC, there was no evidence of a genuine interest to find out more from the enquirer to track down the correct doctor's details.[81] This relative lack of helpfulness was supported by the findings of the Shipman Inquiry. It found that an enquirer would only be told the status of the doctor's registration (full, limited or provisional). Only if enquirers specifically asked would they be told whether the doctor had been suspended or subject to conditions.[82] Even then, as my own experience has shown, significant determination and persistence was needed to obtain what should have been readily available public information. Furthermore, 25 per cent of doctors against whom complaints had been made had never been identified by the GMC. Overall, the position was neatly encapsulated by the following extract from the Shipman Inquiry determinations:

79 See the Fifth Report of the Shipman Inquiry, *Safeguarding Patients: Lessons from the Past – Proposals for the Future*, paras 27.156–27.162 (www.the-shipman-inquiry.org.uk).

80 See the Fifth Report of the Shipman Inquiry, *Safeguarding Patients: Lessons from the Past – Proposals for the Future*, paras 27.171–27.173 (www.the-shipman-inquiry.org.uk).

81 Historically, the GMC identified registered doctors by means of name and registered address. In May 2006, it acknowledged that this could cause problems and the system was changed so that each doctor would be identified by name and unique registration number. Whilst the GMC also announced that doctors should make this information available to patients, this is unlikely to work well in practice. At best, most patients are unlikely to request a doctor's registration number as a matter of routine. At worst, a doctor deliberately misbehaving may simply give an incorrect number in response to a request. If a doctor in this position wishes to divert suspicion further, he or she may give a number close to the correct one but, for example, with one or more numbers transposed. If challenged later, this is more likely to appear as an innocent example of miscommunication.

82 The Fifth Report of the Shipman Inquiry, *Safeguarding Patients: Lessons from the Past – Proposals for the Future*, para 27.291 (www.the-shipman-inquiry.org.uk).

> The experience of a member of the Inquiry staff who made a registration enquiry…about a doctor whose registration was subject to conditions was that she was kept waiting and that it was necessary for her to be quite persistent in order to obtain the information requested. Indeed, it appeared doubtful that she would ever have been given the information at all if she had not been able to quote the doctor's GMC number. Initially, when she gave the doctor's (correct) name, she was told that no doctor of that name was registered.[83]

In 2004, rather late in the day, the GMC did recognize and consult on these concerns. As a general principle, it was agreed that all information in the public domain, even fitness to practise acquittals, should be disclosed. However, the GMC's discussions appear not to have addressed the practical issues regarding disclosure when the enquirer does not ask the 'correct' specific questions. As the Shipman Inquiry concluded:

> Mr Finlay Scott, Chief Executive and Registrar of the GMC, told the meeting that the GMC received about 1000 registration enquiries each day but that 999 of them went no further than finding out whether the doctor was currently registered. It does not appear to have occurred to the Council that this suggests that many prospective employers (or PCOs) are not finding out whether the doctor whose application they are considering has a FTP history, or even whether s/he is subject to current conditions.[84]

The Shipman Inquiry went even further and recommended that when a patient was to be operated upon in hospital, he or she should be told about any conditions on the doctor's registration and the arrangements to ensure that these are being complied with. Disclosure should be at a sufficiently early stage to provide the patient with genuine choice with regard to consenting to treatment.[85]

To its credit, the GMC has gradually been improving the availability of fitness to practise findings on its website. However, at the time of writing there was still scope for further improvement – especially where a doctor has a relatively common surname, and so further help may be required to ensure that the correct information has been found.

## Independent Adjudication

As previously noted, in reforming its fitness to practise structures, the GMC resisted the creation of a genuinely independent adjudicator body. The Council continues to select, train, appraise and dismiss FTP panellists. A move towards independently appointed professionalized panels, with full-time or virtually full-time panellists and a legally qualified chair would ensure a clear independence from the GMC, as well

83 The Fifth Report of the Shipman Inquiry, *Safeguarding Patients: Lessons from the Past – Proposals for the Future*, para 27.176 (www.the-shipman-inquiry.org.uk).

84 See the Fifth Report of the Shipman Inquiry, *Safeguarding Patients: Lessons from the Past – Proposals for the Future*, paras 27.179–27.183 (www.the-shipman-inquiry.org.uk).

85 The Fifth Report of the Shipman Inquiry, *Safeguarding Patients: Lessons from the Past – Proposals for the Future*, para 27.199 (www.the-shipman-inquiry.org.uk).

as the benefit of greater expertise.[86] As discussed in the context of lay involvement in the regulatory process generally, it would further distance fitness to practise adjudication from genuinely representative lay involvement. Unless, perhaps, lay participants were drawn from all walks of life and appointed full-time, but for a fixed period to avoid long-term socialization and associated loss of 'lay' characteristics. To be workable, such an approach would require panellists to be very generously rewarded if a good mix of people were to be tempted to leave other occupations on a temporary basis.

Along with greater independence, panels should move away from a 'beyond reasonable doubt' adversarial approach, towards a greater inquisitorial stance with the focus upon proof on the balance of probabilities in most cases.[87] With respect to this point, the Shipman Inquiry concluded that the criminal standard of proof remained appropriate where allegations of misconduct constituted a criminal offence. However, this argument becomes difficult to sustain if public protection is genuinely to be given centre stage. Doctors hold a special position in society, with a 'peculiar ability, not only to help and cure, but also to harm those who are in their care'.[88] From this viewpoint, the public interest may demand that a doctor who has probably (but not certainly) seriously harmed or risked harming a patient, should not be allowed to remain in unrestricted practice. Historically, both the GMC and the courts have placed great store on members of the medical profession not being improperly deprived of their professional status and livelihood. There is clearly an appropriate issue of fairness in this approach but this should not take precedence over the public interest and public protection.

### Return to Practice after Disciplinary Sanction

Historically, when the GMC has erased or suspended a doctor, or imposed conditional registration, there has been no consistent approach to ensuring that the doctor is fit if allowed to return to practice. It has been far from unusual for a doctor to be allowed to return to unrestricted practice without any objective assessment aimed at checking that the problems which originally led to the sanction have been remedied. For example, in *Prasad v GMC*[89] the doctor had his name erased from the register. He later successfully applied for restoration, went on to re-offend and was admonished, and subsequently offended again to a degree that his name was once again erased. In another case, the doctor was convicted of indecent assault of a patient, sentenced to nine months' imprisonment in 1997 and subsequently had his name erased from the medical register. He was restored to the register only four years later and allowed to practise free of conditions approximately a year after that. In a third example,

86 See the Fifth Report of the Shipman Inquiry, *Safeguarding Patients: Lessons from the Past – Proposals for the Future*, paras 27.206–27.209 (www.the-shipman-inquiry.org.uk).

87 For further discussion of these suggestions, see the Fifth Report of the Shipman Inquiry, *Safeguarding Patients: Lessons from the Past – Proposals for the Future*, paras 27.255–27.256 (www.the-shipman-inquiry.org.uk).

88 *The Kerr/Haslam Inquiry Report*, July 2005, Cm 6640-1, 759.

89 [1987] 1 WLR 1697.

the doctor was suspended after a number of incidents of sexual misconduct. The suspension was lifted after 18 months and the doctor allowed to practise without conditions.[90] This approach does not offer sufficient protection for the public. A more appropriate system would require doctors in this position to satisfy an objective assessment of their fitness to practise. In addition, there should be a limited number of opportunities for doctors to fail and 'retake' such objective assessment, before the GMC acts in the interests of public protection and removes the doctor's name permanently from the medical register or suspends him or her indefinitely.[91]

## Chaperones

In a number of the cases discussed in this book, the doctor was able to commit misconduct, in part because of an under-developed approach to chaperoning. The Ayling Inquiry considered the role of chaperones in medical encounters involving intimate examinations. A distinction was made between the passive and active chaperones. A passive chaperone is a 'mere' observer and so, in principle, the role could be undertaken virtually using appropriate technology. A 'virtual' chaperone could offer a relatively cheap solution, but it would lack the element of personal support and the capacity to intervene if necessary. In contrast, an active chaperone is part of the clinical team and has a defined role in the examination and treatment of the patient. The Inquiry concluded that the active chaperone model was preferred, with chaperones having appropriate training and sufficient status to challenge a doctor when necessary. Untrained chaperones, family or friends of the patient, should not be expected to undertake the role. The use of chaperones should be underpinned by appropriate disciplinary sanctions if the requirements are breached.[92]

Whilst suitably trained 'live' chaperones are preferred, their provision in all situations where they may be of value will be expensive, and if insufficient numbers are available, additional delays are likely to result. As discussed above, technology, in the form of virtual chaperones, may offer an alternative in some situations. Digital recording could offer a relatively cheap alternative to human chaperones, and also play an important evidentiary role with respect to allegations of a disciplinary or negligence nature.[93] This would constitute an advance on the recommendation from

90 *The Kerr/Haslam Inquiry Report*, July 2005, Cm 6640-1, 625–6.

91 See the Fifth Report of the Shipman Inquiry, *Safeguarding Patients: Lessons from the Past – Proposals for the Future*, paras 27.269–27.274 (www.the-shipman-inquiry.org.uk).

92 The Honourable Mrs Justice Pauffley, Committee of Inquiry – Independent Investigation into how the NHS Handled Allegations about the Conduct of Clifford Ayling, 15 July 2004, Cm 6298, para 2.54–2.60.

93 The potential for 'virtual chaperones' was also addressed in the Kerr/Haslam Report, subject to appropriate testing and monitoring. The Inquiry envisages the technology comprising of a digital video camera and microphone with the capacity to produce an encrypted record on DVD. See *The Kerr/Haslam Inquiry Report*, July 2005, Cm 6640-1, 635–9.

the Bristol Inquiry, that the NHS should provide tape recording facilities to enable patients who wish it to record consultations with healthcare professionals.[94]

Technology does have its limitations, for instance, it can only provide evidence after the event, whereas a human chaperone can intervene immediately. However, as was illustrated in the Ayling and Ledward cases, human chaperones may be reluctant to intervene and may convince themselves, or be convinced, that they are not actually witnessing inappropriate behaviour. They may also feel intimidated by the seniority of the doctor they are observing. In contrast, a digital recording can be kept by the patient and examined at leisure by experts of his or her choosing. Virtual chaperones and the recording, where practical, of all doctor–patient encounters, could provide reassurance to the public and further enhance moves towards the greater empowerment of patients.

## Criminal Activities

There have been problems in establishing lines of responsibility when a doctor is suspected of criminal activity. The Ayling Inquiry found a lack of clarity regarding the respective investigatory responsibilities between the criminal justice system, the NHS and the GMC. In the Ayling case itself, priority was given to the criminal investigation. As any NHS and GMC actions were likely to share witnesses with the criminal investigation, there was concern that the latter might be prejudiced if the NHS and GMC were to take action first. The Inquiry recommended that a Memorandum of Understanding should be agreed between the NHS, professional regulatory bodies and the Crown Prosecution Service, setting out the responsibilities of each in the event of an investigation into potential criminal activity by a doctor or other healthcare professional.[95] The findings in this work suggest that more is required. Procedurally, it is important that the various routes of regulation appropriately interact. However, it is also important that the GMC respects the decisions of the criminal courts when cases subsequently come before FTP panels. Public trust in self-regulation will continue to be undermined if GMC disciplinary panels continue to treat leniently doctors who have been convicted of serious criminal offences. This is especially the case when the court has accepted in mitigation the argument that the doctor's professional life is in ruins and has taken this into account when imposing the criminal sanction.

## Supporting Dissatisfied Patients from Within

The Kerr/Haslam report expressed concern that a number of GPs sought to distance themselves from complaints about other doctors, rather than helping their patients

94 Kennedy, I.M., *The Inquiry into the Management of Care of Children Receiving Complex Heart Surgery at the Bristol Royal Infirmary* (www.bristol-inquiry.org.uk) at 439.

95 The Honourable Mrs Justice Pauffley, Committee of Inquiry – Independent Investigation into how the NHS Handled Allegations about the Conduct of Clifford Ayling, 15 July 2004, Cm 6298, paras 2.65, 2.67 and 2.71.

to pursue them. In this regard, there was little evidence that GPs saw their medical role of helping patients negotiate their way through the complexities of the NHS as extending to include help with complaints against other doctors. In the Kerr/Haslam situation, at a time when distressed psychiatric patients needed a 'champion' to help them ensure that their voices were heard, none was forthcoming. Evidence from some NHS personnel was that the idea of being a champion for a complaining patient was frowned upon, even criticized, within the culture of the medical profession. This approach is unacceptable. The primary concern of all NHS staff should be the well-being of patients, including patient safety. Doctors and others to whom complaints are made should be as anxious as the complainant to expose unacceptable practice and performance.[96] As previously discussed, the necessary awareness that this should be an important element of genuine self-regulation appears to have passed many individual doctors by. When it has suited them in recent years, many GPs have emphasized the importance of their role with regard to continuity of care, yet in regulatory terms they have backed away from this responsibility. This has to change if self-regulation is to be retained and is to work effectively.

## Medical Education

Most of the cases discussed in this book would probably have arisen irrespective of the system of medical education in place. For example, Shipman, Ayling, Kerr and Haslam can have been in no doubt that what they were doing was wrong. Whilst education cannot be guaranteed to turn the non-virtuous into the virtuous, it can be valuable in concentrating the minds of other doctors who need to both recognize and act upon inappropriate behaviour by their colleagues. In short, medical education has the potential to help to focus attention on ethical issues, and on the position of the vulnerable patient. It can also help doctors to determine when and how to respond to issues of concern which come to their attention. Such ethical, legal and regulatory education should be central to both the initial training of doctors and to continuing professional development. Whilst there have been some advances in the humanities and social science aspects of medical education in recent years, there was concern from the Ledward, Shipman and Kerr/Haslam Inquiries that law and ethics were still not given sufficient priority in the education of doctors. It was noted that a number of doctors were unfamiliar with the GMC's regulatory requirements and guidance. Ethics and legal issues should be central to training, from the very start of undergraduate study. Doctors cannot simply be expected to pick it up as they go along.[97] This concern was expressed as follows by the Kerr/Haslam Inquiry:

> It is regrettable that there appears to be a continuing failure to teach our medical students to understand their fundamental ethical responsibilities. We consider it to be important that very careful thought is given to how ethical issues are taught…If the issues are not addressed, and monitored centrally, there is a real danger that ethical training can

96 *The Kerr/Haslam Inquiry Report*, July 2005, Cm 6640-1, 700–701.

97 For further discussion, see *The Kerr/Haslam Inquiry Report*, July 2005, Cm 6640-1, 738 and 785.

> be delivered in a way that reinforces existing (self-protective and unhelpful) attitudes, including disbelieving patients, and attitudes generally towards patients who raise complaints. We keep well in mind that Michael Haslam was responsible for teaching medical ethics.[98]

Findings from research in the United States suggest a correlation between problematic medical school records and subsequent post-qualification professional discipline. Over 25 per cent of the risk of disciplinary action during the career of a doctor, it was found, could be attributed to previous unprofessional conduct at medical school.[99] The earlier discussion of cheating by medical students in the UK suggests that medical schools have failed to address the possibility that such a finding might apply in the UK also.

The GMC has responsibility for monitoring the content of medical school curricula, yet there has been a longstanding absence from the education process of guidance on how to manage complaints about fellow professionals.[100] Detailed consideration of reforms to the educational process is beyond the scope of this book, but such reforms should be considered fully alongside considerations for changes to the wider regulatory process.

## Putting the Patient at the Centre

The Bristol Inquiry identified a patient-centred focus and a 'holistic' approach as being necessary to ensure high quality healthcare. A professional team should support the patient throughout the 'treatment journey', with honesty and openness being paramount. Overall, the way forwards was seen as moving towards a patient-centred health service built around an 'ethic of care'. In the case of hospital medicine, this would involve multi-disciplinary teams working in collaboration, but willing to give priority to the patient's best interests, should this conflict with that of colleagues.[101] As Bridgeman describes the past failings:

> [F]eatures of the [health] service which are no longer acceptable include organizations structured around the needs of doctors and upon inter and intra professional hierarchies and protective of clinical freedom; the patient treated as a passive recipient of care, given little information and discouraged from asking questions; and doctors paternalistically making decisions as to what is best for the patient without reference to their wishes.[102]

---

98 *The Kerr/Haslam Inquiry Report*, July 2005, Cm 6640-1, 787.

99 Papadakis, M. et al, 'Disciplinary Action by Medical Boards and Prior Behaviour in Medical School', *N Engl J Med*, 2005, 353: 2673–82. Cited in Department of Health, *Good Doctors, Safer Patients – Proposals to Strengthen the System to Assure and Improve the Performance of Doctors and to Protect the Safety of Patients: A Report by the Chief Medical Officer*, July 2006, Chapter 10.

100 *The Kerr/Haslam Inquiry Report*, July 2005, Cm 6640-1, 793.

101 See Bridgeman, J., 'Learning from Bristol: Healthcare in the 21st Century', *MLR*, 2002, 65(2), 241–52, 244.

102 Bridgeman, J., 'The "Patient at the Centre": the Government Response to the Bristol Inquiry Report', *Journal of Social Welfare and Family Law*, 2002, 24(3): 347–61.

In turn, professional bodies should support their members in bringing openness and reflexivity to their practice, including openness about the limitations and risks of the treatment they can provide.[103]

Whilst not so readily applied to the more individualistic style of general practice, it is conceivable that structures could be devised to provide multi-practitioner groupings, which could better ensure that the well-being of patients was not solely under the control of one (possibly rogue or incompetent) doctor.[104] Recent changes to the NHS contract for primary care have moved from the position where each doctor in a practice had his or her own list of patients, to one where each patient is registered with the practice as a whole. The Shipman Inquiry saw this as a positive move. When Shipman was in partnership, his partners had little or no reason (from a contractual or business standpoint) to take an interest in the patients on *his* list. With the new arrangements, all of the partners should be interested in all of the patients registered with the practice.[105] However, the reality may be very different. The likely size of the patient list of medium to large GP practices will be such that continuing to assign each patient to a named doctor will be the only practical means of ensuring continuity of care. It will be very easy, therefore, for the old approaches and attitudes to continue. In this respect, only those changes which are specifically introduced for the express purposes of monitoring and regulation are likely to be effective.

The government response to the Bristol Report also talks about patients in partnership with healthcare professionals with a relationship based upon honesty, openness and respect.[106] However, unlike the patient envisioned by Kennedy, someone whose life is disrupted by their healthcare needs and who may require

103 See Bridgeman, J., 'The "Patient at the Centre": the Government Response to the Bristol Inquiry Report', *Journal of Social Welfare and Family Law*, 2002, 24(3): 347–61.

104 A basic model could involve each patient having two general practitioners, independent of each other. The 'primary practitioner' would undertake medical care as today. The 'secondary practitioner' would have a much more low-key role. This would be a doctor to whom the patient could turn, in confidence, if they had any concerns about the care they were receiving from their primary practitioner. In addition, the secondary practitioner would have a much more proactive oversight role when patients died or were taken seriously ill, that role being to ensure that appropriate primary care had been provided. There would, of course, be resource implications – each general practitioner taking on a workload as primary practitioner to some patients and secondary practitioner to others. It would also be important to safeguard against abuse; for example, the structures would have to be such as to avoid general practitioners simply entering into cosy mutual relationships which satisfy the letter of the provisions but not the spirit. For example, in the context of the solicitors' profession, there is evidence of this type of abuse when de facto sole practitioners enter into partnerships of convenience to evade the minimum qualification period before practising alone is allowed or to bypass a Disciplinary Tribunal ruling forbidding sole practice. See, for example, Davies, M.R., 'The Regulation of Solicitors and the Role of the Solicitors Disciplinary Tribunal', *Professional Negligence*, 1998, Vol. 14, No. 3, 143–73.

105 The Fifth Report of the Shipman Inquiry, *Safeguarding Patients: Lessons from the Past – Proposals for the Future*, paras 8.4–8.16 (www.the-shipman-inquiry.org.uk).

106 Department of Health, *Learning from Bristol: The Department of Health's Response to the Report of the Public Inquiry into Children's Heart Surgery at the Bristol Royal Infirmary 1984–1995*, Cm 5363, January 2002, Chapter 1, para 10.

caring support and counseling, the government response focuses upon patient choice, the redesign of services to meet the 'needs and convenience' of the patient as an informed consumer. The patient envisioned by the government is autonomous, assertive and able to interpret data, statistics and performance indicators in order to make rational choices.[107] This ignores the issues of information asymmetry, which have long provided an argument in favour of self-regulation. The complexity of both medical knowledge and of the healthcare system make the 'production' of informed patients problematic.

Even though recent developments in the wider field of consumer protection focus upon addressing asymmetries of information between trader and consumer,[108] patients cannot be equated with the typical consumer of other goods or services. Information also has little or no value if viable alternatives are not available. This will frequently be the position within the NHS. It has also been suggested that even in the context of more straightforward consumer goods and services, the majority of consumers ignore the information presented to them, and that even fewer take the opportunity to seek out information.[109] When the 'consumer' is ill, or concerned for the health of a loved one, it is likely that these observations will be even more pertinent. Asymmetric information, deriving from specialized knowledge possessed by the doctor, means that a patient has little choice but to enter into an agency relationship with the doctor. In economic terms, the doctor identifies the treatment required (the necessary level of production) and simultaneously specifies to the patient the amount of consumption needed to improve his or her health status. Imperfections in the ability of doctors to determine these factors require the doctor to become a part bearer of the risk associated with the outcome of the production process.[110] Partnership between doctor and patient is therefore essential. For this partnership to benefit patients, appropriate systems, professional attitudes, trust relationships and underpinning regulatory processes are essential. Once again, the role of the GMC takes on far greater significance than merely disciplining the occasional aberrant doctor. Greater proactivity on the part of the GMC would aid the effectiveness of this partnership.

## Reforms Following the Shipman Inquiry

At the time of writing the government had instigated two key initiatives following the recommendations by the Shipman Inquiry. First, in March 2005 the Chief Medical Officer was instructed to undertake a review of the difficulties identified in the fifth

107 Bridgeman, J., 'The "Patient at the Centre": the Government Response to the Bristol Inquiry Report', *Journal of Social Welfare and Family Law*, 2002, 24(3): 347–61.

108 See Howells, G., 'The Potential and Limits of Consumer Empowerment by Information', *Journal of Law and Society*, September 2005, 32(3), 349–70.

109 See Howells, G., 'The Potential and Limits of Consumer Empowerment by Information', *Journal of Law and Society*, September 2005, 32(3), 356–7 and 359–60.

110 McGuire, A., 'Ethics and Resource Allocation: An Economist's View', in Dowie, J. and Elstein, A., *Professional Judgment*, 1988, Cambridge University Press, Cambridge, 492–507, 498.

Shipman Inquiry report.[111] As noted in Chapter 16, in consequence the planned start date of April 2005 for the GMC's revalidation scheme was postponed. The focus of the CMO's review was to concentrate on the steps needed to: 'Strengthen procedures for assuring the safety of patients in situations where a doctor's performance or conduct pose a risk to patient safety or the effective functioning of services; Ensure the operation of an effective system of revalidation; Modify the role, structure and functions of the General Medical Council.'[112]

The review had a comprehensive brief, including consideration of what the future regulation of the medical profession should look like. However, the implication was that the future of the GMC per se was not under threat, as consultation questions included ones regarding the future structure and membership of the Council. The questions did not seek to determine alternatives to the GMC.

With respect to the future of revalidation, key questions were whether the system should have as its focus the detection of impairment and other measures required to secure public trust. Or, should it concentrate on promoting continuing professional development and other standards raising measures? If a combination of these aims was appropriate, how should these be combined?[113]

In terms of the structure of revalidation, likely choices were between a screening process aimed at identifying practitioners at risk of having a fitness to practise problem; alternatively, aimed at the actual identification of dysfunctional practitioners; or, focused upon evaluating fitness to practise.

In July 2006 the CMO published the findings of his review. Key recommendations included:[114]

- The introduction of a system of 'recorded concerns', those falling short of formal disciplinary action. These would remain on the doctor's file with the General Medical Council. A national committee, with a lay majority, would review all such records and take action where appropriate.
- A move by the GMC to using the civil standard of proof in its fitness to practise decisions.
- The extension of the GMC's activities to local level by the creation of a system of 'affiliates'. These would be senior doctors who would command the respect and cooperation of other doctors, patients and managers. Affiliates would handle at local level less serious fitness to practise cases, thereby reducing the workload of the central GMC and also bringing together some FTP decisions with corresponding employer responses. Medical schools would also have affiliates, to ensure that medical students become familiar with regulatory issues at an early stage of their careers. To avoid isolation within the medical organization, each affiliate would be teamed with an appropriately trained lay

111 *CMO Review of Medical Revalidation: A Call for Ideas*, 3 March 2005. The consultation period closed on 13 May 2005.

112 *CMO Review of Medical Revalidation: A Call for Ideas*, 3 March 2005.

113 *CMO Review of Medical Revalidation: A Call for Ideas*, 3 March 2005.

114 For full discussion, see Department of Health, *Good Doctors, Safer Patients – Proposals to Strengthen the System to Assure and Improve the Performance of Doctors and to Protect the Safety of Patients: A Report by the Chief Medical Officer*, July 2006, Chapter 10.

person, complaints management and administrative support. Affiliates would aim to bring a personal touch to the activities of the GMC, and so part of the role would include face to face meetings with complainants.

- The GMC nationally would continue to be responsible for serious cases, but only from the investigatory perspective. The adjudicatory function would be removed from the GMC and vested in an independent tribunal. The aim of the GMC should be to provide measures to seek rehabilitation of doctors who come to its attention, with referral to the independent tribunal as very much the last resort. The GMC should develop a clear set of standards, leading for the first time to a definition/description of a 'good doctor'. Such standards should be incorporated into doctors' contracts of employment.
- Responsibility for setting the content of the undergraduate curriculum and inspecting medical schools should be removed from the GMC and transferred to an appropriately renamed Postgraduate Medical Education and Training Board.
- The GMC should be restructured and the medical profession should cease to elect members, all members instead being independently appointed. In turn, the membership would elect one of their number as president.
- With particular respect to general practitioners, PCTs would have enhanced powers to ensure personal accountability and such powers should include full access to patient records. PCTs should also seek to interview patients who transfer between GPs without a geographical move requiring such a change.
- NHS appraisal, albeit revised, would remain central to the process of revalidation and GMC affiliates would have a part to play. In addition to general revalidation, specialist certification would also be subject to renewal periodically. A risk-based approach would be applied, the period of renewal and other factors depending upon the nature of the doctor's specialism. A failure by a doctor to satisfy the requirements of revalidation would result in the requirement to undertake supervised practice or to cease practising until a 'tailored plan of remediation and rehabilitation' was implemented. However, the assumption remains that only a very small proportion of doctors would need to be subjected to these remedial measures.[115]

Given the potential scope of the CMO review, it is disappointing that the recommendations contain relatively little which is new or radical. The proposals for revalidation are particularly disappointing. Whilst subtly different from those watered down proposals from the GMC which were so roundly criticized by the Shipman Inquiry, the CMO's proposals neither return to the rigour of the initial GMC plans nor introduce any blue skies thinking in this area. A few of the recommendations do have the potential to lead to effective reform. In particular, local affiliates could remedy some of the significant detection and investigatory failings by the GMC, but only if the scheme is properly funded and individual affiliates adopt a suitably rigorous

---

115 See Department of Health, *Good Doctors, Safer Patients – Proposals to Strengthen the System to Assure and Improve the Performance of Doctors and to Protect the Safety of Patients: A Report by the Chief Medical Officer*, July 2006, Chapter 10.

regulatory stance. It should be feasible for the GMC to raise additional funds from the profession to ensure that it has the resources to properly pursue these and other regulatory activities. The annual retention fee of around £300[116] required from each doctor is significantly less than that paid by some other health professionals. Whilst increasing fees would not be popular within the profession, it should be a small price to pay to retain self-regulation. However, any increased resources must be used effectively. The GMC's budget has already doubled in the period 2001–2006, yet effective regulation remains elusive.[117]

The second initiative emerged in June 2006, with the publication of the Coroners Bill. This aimed to address some of the problems of the coronial system identified by the Shipman Inquiry. However, some areas of potential reform were notable by their absence. For example, the first draft of the bill rejected the recommendation that all death certificates should be independently verified and that all deaths should be subject to investigation. It would be possible for a second opinion to be requested regarding a death certificate, but this fell far short of the routine verification called for by the Shipman Inquiry. In an apparently cost-limiting exercise, the government rejected the complete break with the past which the Inquiry had called for. Dame Janet Smith's evidence to the Commons Constitutional Affairs Committee in February 2006 was that the government's plans would not prevent a future 'Shipman': 'If these reforms go through there could still be a Shipman out there, still killing patients, still certifying their deaths, handing the medical certificate of cause of death to a member of the family, who takes it to the registrar's office, who registers the death…Nothing will have changed.'[118]

The government response was that the proposals for change being considered by the Chief Medical Officer were more appropriate to address the regulatory issues raised by the Shipman case. Michael Wilks, chairman of the BMA's committee on medical ethics, responded to this by commenting that: 'It isn't the GMC's role to spot people like Shipman. So, for [the Minister] to suggest that proposed changes to the GMC that Sir Liam Donaldson hasn't even published will protect the public is not really relevant.'[119]

It remains of concern that influential commentators from within the medical profession continue to deny that the GMC should be central to detecting doctors such as Shipman. It appears that there are some within the profession who still insist that Shipman was a mass murderer who just happened to be a doctor. However, as previously discussed, the reality is that Shipman was only able to commit his crimes because he was a doctor. His professional status and the associated access

116 See Department of Health, *Good Doctors, Safer Patients – Proposals to Strengthen the System to Assure and Improve the Performance of Doctors and to Protect the Safety of Patients: A Report by the Chief Medical Officer*, July 2006, Chapter 4, paragraph 41.

117 See Department of Health, *Good Doctors, Safer Patients – Proposals to Strengthen the System to Assure and Improve the Performance of Doctors and to Protect the Safety of Patients: A Report by the Chief Medical Officer*, July 2006, Chapter 4, paragraph 43.

118 See Rozenberg, J., 'Shipman Inquiry Findings Rejected in Coroners Bill', Daily Telegraph, 12 June 2006 (online edition).

119 See Day, M., 'Government Rejects Independent Verification of All Death Certificates', *BMJ*, 2006, 332: 1409 (online edition).

and privilege it conferred upon him were central and essential to his criminal behaviour.

## Reflexivity as the Way Forwards?

Instead of detailed formal rules, reflexive law focuses upon those procedural norms which regulate processes and the distribution of rights and competencies.[120] The aim is to achieve desirable regulatory outcomes by concentrating upon the design and implementation of self-regulatory mechanisms.[121] Legal control is indirect, with the legal system limiting itself to the establishment of the organizational and procedural foundations.[122] The legal system escapes the need to directly regulate complex social areas, but instead actively controls the self-regulatory structures and processes. It is vital, therefore, that these structures and processes are fit for their purpose. Once appropriate structures are in place, reflexive law aims to mobilize the self-referential capacities of institutions to enable them to best shape their own response to complex problems.[123] Reflexive self-regulation should encompass those aspects of the public interest which are most in need of protection. To engage in sufficiently objective self-examination and learning, self-regulating organizations must break free from competing pressures. In the case of doctors, these pressures are likely to derive from misplaced loyalty to colleagues, excessive professional arrogance and the side effects of NHS bureaucracy. The latter has insulated doctors from market pressures, which when present offer the potential to ensure that the patient's needs, wants and satisfaction remain central to the doctor's attention.[124] A reflexive, more ethically rigorous, regulatory approach should aim to sensitize doctors to the wider consequences of their activities. Such an approach should also provide support for those members of the profession who feel the need to speak out against a dominant clique within their work environment.[125] This would have been of particular value to Dr Stephen Bolsin, at Bristol, and other 'witnesses' to misconduct discussed in this book.

In the case of legal practice, it has been suggested that an alternative to the centralized command and control model of regulation would see compliance

---

120 Teubner, G., 'Substantive and Reflexive Elements in Modern Law', 17 *Law & Society Review*, 1983, 239, 254–5.

121 For further discussion, in the context of environmental law, see Fiorini, D., 'Rethinking Environmental Regulation', 23 *Harvard Environmental Law Review*, 1999, 447.

122 Teubner, G., 'Substantive and Reflexive Elements in Modern Law', 17 *Law & Society Review*, 1983, 239, 254–5.

123 See Orts, E., 'Reflexive Environmental Law', 89 *Northwestern University Law Review*, 1995, 1227.

124 Excessive moves to the market can be counterproductive. It has been argued that the increased marketization of legal services has undermined some of the traditional ethical values of lawyers. See, for example, Davies, M., 'Regulatory Crisis in the Solicitors' Profession', *Legal Ethics*, 2003, Vol. 6, No. 2, 185–216.

125 For further discussion in the context of lawyers, see Rhode, D.L., 'Ethical Perspectives on Legal Practice', *Stanford Law Review*, 1985, Vol. 37: 589, 648. Luban, D. (ed.), *The Ethics of Lawyers*, 1994, Dartmouth, Aldershot, 456.

delegated down to the level of the individual firm, allowing greater freedom for performance and conduct objectives to be decided at this level. Reflexivity would require management structures and procedures which keep conduct and competence issues continually high on the agenda within the practice. Arguments in favour of delegating regulation down to law firm level paralleled some of those originally used in the nineteenth century to persuade the state to grant self-regulatory powers to professional bodies. Arguments that the complexity of professional expertise was such that the state could not directly regulate the medical profession could now be applied to the professional bodies themselves. In the case of medicine, a significantly larger profession and far more complex knowledge base means that the GMC has increasingly become subject to problems posed by information complexity and limits in analytical capacity. In the case of solicitors, the Law Society would focus upon creating robust and effective structures and procedures through which would be implemented a reflexive self-regulatory structure at the level of the firm. These would provide support, but also severe sanctions for firms which failed to respond. All firms, however large, would have to believe that they were not immune from severe penalties and even exclusion from the profession. In the case of medical regulation, the GMC may seek to argue that they have begun to move in the direction discussed above, with the proposals for greater interaction with local regulatory structures. However, there is little in the GMC's proposals to suggest that it can ensure that these procedures are appropriately robust and that they meet the key requirements for reflexivity. The GMC has no power to close down the organizations within which doctors work if these organizations fail to comply. It is likely, therefore, that if the GMC is to adopt a reflexive approach, this will be limited to instilling an appropriate ethical awareness within members of the medical profession and encouraging reflexivity when considering self-regulation. In this way, groups of doctors within their employment units should become highly ethically focused and mutual monitors of each other. If this is achieved, the problems observed at Bristol – that career progression was dependent on someone's 'fit' within the 'club', rather than performance, and that any challenge was perceived as disloyalty – should be more readily avoidable. As the Bristol Inquiry noted 'this approach was neither conducive to self-assessment or reflective criticism'. [126] Whilst these changes are important to ensure that a more appropriate attitude prevails within the profession, regulatory power and mechanisms to enforce this change need to remain with a committed and effective GMC.

## Further Reforms

I have argued that revalidation as currently modelled by the GMC will be insufficient to avoid future crises in medical regulation. Three key requirements must be addressed if self-regulation is to be effective. These are:

1. Individual members of the profession must take responsibility for their own

126 Kennedy, I.M., *The Inquiry into the Management of Care of Children Receiving Complex Heart Surgery at The Bristol Royal Infirmary* (www.bristol-inquiry.org.uk) 198 and 201.

behaviour and competence and that of colleagues.

2. Key to achieving this is a move from dominance of professional loyalty to the ideal that patient and public interest must always come first.
3. Overseeing this grass roots self-regulation, a strong regulatory body with effective surveillance, investigatory and adjudicatory mechanisms.

The challenge is to embed these values within the medical mindset and to make the appropriate modifications to the formal regulatory system. Instilling appropriate professional values should begin at the earliest stages of medical education and training by involving lawyers, philosophers and other non-medics whose approaches can add a range of perspectives. If such non-medics play a central part in the medical school curriculum, they can also go some way towards weakening the insular nature of medical education and positively undermining the socialization of students into the medical 'club'. More difficult is ensuring that qualified doctors are exposed to such influences. At the very least, compulsory continuing professional development, with a focus upon the ethical and regulatory aspects of medical practice, should be introduced. Altering the formal regulatory structure presents a greater challenge because of the greater range of views which are adopted in this respect. Recent trends have supported a move away from detailed rules, close regulatory surveillance and punitive sanctions in favour of a no blame culture.[127] Support for this approach is provided by the need to ensure greater openness, and thus the opportunity to learn from mistakes. It also recognizes that a punitive command and control model is likely to be counterproductive in a complex field such as medicine, where the achievement of goals requires high levels of individual professional commitment and initiative. There is intellectual force in this line of argument, but ultimately it allows the retention of significant power in the hands of individual members of the medical profession with limited provision for genuine regulatory oversight. It may even be argued that in the regulatory sense a form of 'no blame' approach has by default been tried by the GMC and has failed. The GMC has taken a reactive background role, allowing doctors to operate largely in a de facto blame-free environment.[128] It was this environment which allowed doctors such as Shipman, Ledward, Ayling and those involved in the Bristol case to behave as they did. Command and control is necessary, but it is still possible for this to come from within the profession – reasserting what should be the true values of self-regulation.

---

127 See, for example, Degeling, P., 'Reconsidering Clinical Accountability', *International Journal of Health Planning Management*, 2000, 15, 3–16, 6; and *The Report of the Public Inquiry into Children's Heart Surgery at the Bristol Royal Infirmary 1984-1995: Learning from Bristol*, CM5207(I), July 2001.

128 This statement is, of course, simplistic in ignoring other systematic aspects whereby 'blame' may be assigned to a doctor, for example, litigation for negligence or breach of contract. However, these also have restrictions on their effectiveness, for example, the cost of bringing proceedings and the likelihood that a doctor found liable will be indemnified for any award of damages and costs. It cannot even be said to be the case that a doctor's reputation will always be affected by an unfavourable civil litigation action in negligence, given that the cast majority are settled before trial and therefore remain outside of the public arena.

## Compliance Officers

It is increasingly common amongst other professions to find compliance officers, often members of the profession, who specialize in monitoring colleagues' adherence to professional standards. Such a role does not remove the need for all members of the profession to maintain a primary duty to report misconduct or incompetence, but it does ensure that resources are committed in a specialist and focused way. Compliance officers should typically have a proactive monitoring and investigatory role, rather than simply being the first port of call for complaints. In other professions compliance officers often operate at firm level or, in the case of very large firms, departmental level. Within medicine, similar levels of coverage could be adopted within hospitals and amongst groups of general practitioners.[129] The Chief Medical Officer's proposals for more localized involvement in the GMC process could be modified to incorporate some of the elements of a compliance officer model used by or proposed for other professions.

## Whistleblower Hotline

To encourage reporting without the fear of reprisals or of being ignored, a confidential hotline direct to the GMC could be established. A confidential hotline was one of the recommendations of the report of the Inquiry into the Ledward case,[130] but this was not a new idea. The regulatory arm of the Law Society has had such a hotline since 1992, and has reported it to be a considerable success. This confidential 'red alert line' allowed other solicitors and employees to report suspicions. This has proved to be an important source of information. For example, calls to the red alert line about suspected dishonesty on the part of solicitors rose by 300 per cent in the first two years after its introduction.[131] During the first three years of operation, calls to the line led to 32 per cent of all inspections of solicitors' accounts and the discovery of 43 per cent of all shortages of client funds. Unlike the GMC, the solicitors' profession did close the loop by having an investigatory arm (at least in the context of financial irregularity). There would be little point in the GMC seeking further disclosure of potential misconduct without the investigatory infrastructure to pursue the information received.

The Ledward Report also recommended a clinical incident reporting system to identify untoward events – anything unusual, for example, an intimate examination

---

129 For discussion in the context of the legal profession, see Davies, M., 'Regulatory Crisis in the Solicitors' Profession', *Legal Ethics*, 2003, Vol. 6, No. 2, 185–216.

130 The Ledward Report recommended that this be based in individual NHS trusts, with a non-executive director having responsibility for ensuring that reports are followed up. *An Inquiry into Quality and Practice within the National Health Service Arising from the Actions of Rodney Ledward – The Report*, 1 June 2000, 303. The Law Society model, with the hotline being direct to a proactive central regulator, is preferable as it better ensures consistency of response and avoids the risk of local inaction.

131 See *The Supervision of Solicitors – The Next Decade*, The Law Society, 4; and the *Solicitors Complaints Bureau Final Annual Report, 1 January–31 August 1996*, 9.

without a chaperone. Anyone aware of the event would be required to fill in a form. If a culture of openness can be instilled in medical professionals, this approach to reporting should become second nature.[132] This approach may have some chance of success in the multi-professional environment of hospital medicine, where most incidents may be expected to be witnessed, but it would not translate as well into the more isolated environment of general practice.

## The Continuing Importance of Self-Regulation

Various procedures now exist to discipline doctors, and it has been suggested that the recent creation of additional supervisory and regulatory bodies should be reassuring to the public.[133] I depart from this view, concerned that the proliferation of regulation will create greater capacity for confusion amongst patients and may even open more cracks in the regulatory framework. The GMC is still the only body which has the ultimate authority to remove a doctor's registration. Notwithstanding reforms external to the profession, if self-regulation is to continue, primary responsibility for detection and discipline should remain with the GMC. The commonly cited justifications for self-regulation, in particular the technical knowledge and expertise a profession can bring to its own regulation, remain valid. The GMC claims that the safe care of patients by doctors is at the heart of everything that it does, and that this includes setting standards which reflect the expectations of the public.[134] However, there is little advantage to the public if this rhetoric is not actively translated into effective regulation – including the effective investigation and detection of misconduct. Self-regulation by the medical profession has been shown by Shipman, Ledward, Bristol et al to have become hopelessly inadequate. Each of these scandals illustrates that this failure permeates the whole professional structure – from the sole practising GP through to consultants in specialist departments within large hospitals. The GMC has proposed some reforms, notably revalidation, and has sought certain statutory enhancements to its powers. However, this only scratches the surface. More frequent routine monitoring, specialist proactive investigation, grass roots compliance monitoring and a commitment from all members of the medical profession to monitor and detect misconduct amongst colleagues should be the GMC's more ambitious aim. If the profession is unwilling the deliver this, if self-regulation is to remain largely a paper exercise in which the GMC is merely the body which imposes sanctions at the end of a complaints process, then the public are not receiving the promised return for granting the privilege of self-regulating professional status. If this is the case, then the honest approach is to remove self-regulation from the profession and to impose an entirely external process – controlling admission to the profession, as well as policing, prosecutorial and judicial functions when things

132 *An Inquiry into Quality and Practice within the National Health Service Arising from the Actions of Rodney Ledward – The Report*, 1 June 2000, 277.

133 Newdick, C., 'NHS Governance after Bristol: Holding On or Letting Go?', *Medical Law Review*, Summer 2002, 10, 111–31, 130.

134 GMC, *Acting Fairly to Protect Patients: Reform of the GMC's Fitness to Practice Procedures*, March 2001, 7.

go wrong. The trend for the GMC to become less and less relevant can already be observed. A decade ago virtually all fitness to practise decisions would have been made within the GMC procedures. More recently the shift has been towards greater local handling of complaints, to the extent that the GMC could now be described as a minority regulator.[135]

**A Recognition within the Profession of What Needs to be Done?**

Recent evidence suggests that there are still notable differences of opinion about necessary reforms. Whilst many external voices consider that there is still much to be done, some within the profession express the view that regulatory initiatives have already gone too far. For example, writing in 2004, one GP comments with concern and a sense of loss, that trust in the medical profession has been lost:

> Despite my previous knowledge of a female patient, I now offer to bring in a chaperone if I need to do a breast or gynaecological examination. When I make that offer it is received quizzically and I see doubt crossing the lady's eyes where before there was trust. When the offer of chaperone is turned down, as it invariably is, what do I do?...I see patients in terrible pain for whom I am wary of administering morphine by injection…We work in a climate of fear. There is no longer the trust there was between the caring professions. Every decision I make as a doctor is scrutinised by nurses, pharmacists, physiotherapists, fellow doctors and heaven knows how many others. It may sound paranoid, but each is evaluating my actions from their own knowledge base and perspective…I cannot rely on my professional governing body, the General Medical Council, because it chooses repeatedly to sacrifice the individual to preserve the corporate mass…I was led to write this article by the recent case of a long-established GP…by all accounts well-loved and respected by his patients, who was accused of killing one of their number and arrested. The deceased was an elderly person with multiple pathology, including recently diagnosed terminal cancer, which was causing debilitating pain. The doctor administered morphine to alleviate the pain. The patient died. Ten months later the doctor was arrested following a police tip-off…During the arrest itself, five police officers ransacked his surgery, removing records, computers and equipment. While he was being questioned at the police station, a further 15 officers undertook a thorough search of his house…This seems a disproportionate, almost hysterical, response more apt in dealing with a terrorist than a country GP…[136]

The BMA has expressed concerns that the profession may become over-regulated, intimidating doctors and discouraging innovation. Excessive demands of regulation are also likely to detract from clinical care.[137] Fox suggests that trust may spiral

135 See Department of Health, *Good Doctors, Safer Patients – Proposals to Strengthen the System to Assure and Improve the Performance of Doctors and to Protect the Safety of Patients: A Report by the Chief Medical Officer*, July 2006, Chapter 10.

136 Sherifi, J., 'We Doctors Work in a Climate of Fear', *The Times*, 29 December 2004.

137 BMA *Response to the Chief Medical Officer Review on Maintaining High Standards of Professional Practice*, May 2005.

downwards as regulatory activity continues to increase.[138] The more the regulator attempts to control the regulated, the more the relationship of trust between the two breaks down, leading in turn to yet more detailed regulation.[139]

Above all, this type of attitude from within the profession illustrates the ongoing misunderstanding by doctors of the costs of complacency. Most professionals will sympathize with the distress caused by a loss of trust and autonomy, let alone with the experience of being accused of a serious crime. However, for a very long time doctors have been willing to accept the privilege of their status without an associated commitment to genuine self-regulation. The basis for Sherifi's concerns, quoted above, have arisen to a significant extent because fellow doctors who worked around Shipman, Ayling, Ledward et al did not promptly identify and report concerns. That the GMC should finally begin to make clear that public protection constitutes its primary focus appears to many doctors to be an affront to their expectations. In reality, however, this is merely the price to be paid for many years of regulatory complacency by individuals within the profession.

138 Fox, A., 'Beyond Contract: Work, Power, and Trust Relations', 1974, cited by Davies, A.C.L., 'Don't Trust Me, I'm a Doctor – Medical Regulation and the 1999 NHS Reforms', *OJLS*, 2000, 20(437).

139 Davies, A.C.L., 'Don't Trust Me, I'm a Doctor – Medical Regulation and the 1999 NHS Reforms', *OJLS*, 2000, 20(437).

# Bibliography

## Journal Articles and Book Chapters


Abel, R., 'The Politics of the Market for Legal Services', 1982, in Disney, J., Basten, J., Redmond, P., Ross, S. and Bell, K., *Lawyers*, 2nd ed, 1986, The Law Book Co., Melbourne, 89.

Abel, R., 'Taking Professionalism Seriously', *Annual Review of American Law*, 1989, 41.

Abraham, A., 'Legal Ethics and the Legal Services Ombudsman', *Legal Ethics*, Summer 1998, Vol. 1, Part 1, 23–4.

Airaksinen, T., 'Service and Science in Professional Life', in Chadwick, R.F. (ed.), *Ethics and the Professions*, 1994, Avebury, Aldershot.

Akerlof, G.A., 'The Market for Lemons: Quality Uncertainty and the Market Mechanism', 1970, 84 *Quarterly Journal of Economics* 488.

Allsop, J., 'Two Sides to Every Story: Complainants' and Doctors' Perspectives in Disputes about Medical Care in a General Practice Setting', *Law & Policy*, April 1994, Vol. 16, No. 2, 149–83.

Allsop, J. and Mulcahy, L., 'Maintaining Professional Identity: Doctors' Responses to Complaints', *Sociology of Health & Illness*, 1998, Vol. 20, No. 6, 802–24.

Annandale, E. and Hunt, K., 'Accounts of Disagreements with Doctors', *Social Science and Medicine*, 1998, 1, 119–29.

Arksey, H., 'Expert and Lay Participation in the Construction of Medical Knowledge', *Sociology of Health and Illness*, 1994, 16(4), 448–68.

Arthurs, H.W., 'A Global Code of Legal Ethics for the Transnational Legal Field', *Legal Ethics*, Summer 1999, Vol. 2, No. 1, 60–69.

Aylin, P., Alves, B., Best, N. et al., 'Comparison of UK Paediatric Cardiac Surgical Performance by Analysis of Routinely Collected Data 1984–86: Was Bristol an Outlier?', *The Lancet*, 2001, 358: 181–7.

Aylin, P., Best, N., Bottle, A. and Marshall, C., 'Following Shipman: a Pilot System for Monitoring Mortality Rates in Primary Care', *The Lancet*, 2003, Vol 362: 485–91.

Baker R., Jones D. and Goldblatt P., 'Monitoring Mortality Rates in General Practice after Shipman', *British Medical Journal*, 2003, 326: 274–6.

Bauchner, H. and Vinci, R., 'What Have We Learnt from the Alder Hey Affair?', *British Medical Journal*, 2001, 322: 309–10.

Beck, J. and Young, M.F.D., 'The Assault on the Professions and the Restructuring of Academic and Professional Identities: a Bernsteinian Analysis', *British Journal of Sociology of Education*, April 2005, Vol. 26, No. 2, 183–97.

Beecham, L., 'GMC Wants a Tougher Restoration Procedure', *British Medical Journal*, 1999, 319, 1319, 20 November.

Beecham, L., 'Consultants Attack "Arrogant" GMC', *British Medical Journal*, 2000, 320, 1557, 10 June.

Berwick, D.M., 'Continuous Improvement as an Ideal in Health Care', *New England Journal of Medicine*, 1989, 320, 1.

Black, J., 'Decentring Regulation: Understanding the Role of Regulation and Self-Regulation in a "Post-Regulatory" World', in Freeman, M.D.A. (ed.), *Current Legal Problems*, 2001, Vol. 54, Oxford University Press, Oxford, 103–46.

Bolt, D., 'Dealing with Errors of Clinical Judgment', 54 *Medico-Legal Journal*, 1986, 220.

Bosk, C.L., 'Forgive and Remember: Managing Medical Failure', in Dowie, J. and Elstein, A., *Professional Judgment*, 1988, Cambridge University Press, Cambridge, 525.

Brazier, M., 'Organ Retention and Return: Problems of Consent', 29 *Journal of Medical Ethics*, 2002, 30–33.

Brennan, T.A., Horwitz, R.A., Duffy, F.D., Cassel, C.K., Goode, L.D. and Lipner, R.S., 'The Role of Physician Specialty Board Certification Status in the Quality Movement', *Journal of the American Medical Association*, 2004, 292: 1038–43.

Bridgeman, J., 'Learning from Bristol: Healthcare in the 21st Century', *Modern Law Review*, 2002, 65(2), 241–52, 244.

Bridgeman, J., 'The "Patient at the Centre": the Government Response to the Bristol Inquiry Report', *Journal of Social Welfare and Family Law*, 2002, 24(3), 347–61.

Brownsword, R., 'Code, Control, and Choice: why East is East and West is West', *Legal Studies*, March 2005, 25(1).

Buckley, G., 'Revalidation is the Answer', *British Medical Journal*, 1999, 319: 1145–6, 30 October.

Burke, K., 'Trust Chiefs Cause Flood of Serious Cases to GMC', *British Medical Journal*, 2002, Vol. 321, 1177, 18 May.

Burrows, J., 'Telling Tales and Saving Lives: Whistleblowing – The Role of Professional Colleagues in Protecting Patients from Dangerous Doctors', *Medical Law Review*, Summer 2001, 9, 110–29.

Cain, F.E., Benjamin, R.M. and Thompson, J.N., 'Obstacles to Maintaining Licensure in the United States', *British Medical Journal*, 2005, 330: 1443–5, 18 June.

Cane, P., 'Tort Law as Regulation', *Common Law World Review*, 2002, Vol 31, 305–31.

Catto, G., 'The GMC – Revalidation – What Are We Trying to Measure?', *Medico-Legal Journal*, 2003, 71(106), 2 October.

Catto G., 'GMC and the Future of Revalidation: Building on the GMC's Achievements', *British Medical Journal*, 2005, 330: 1205–7.

Chambers, Andrew, 'Whistleblowing and the Internal Auditor', *Business Ethics: A European Review*, October 1995, 192–8.

Chambliss, E., 'MDPs: Toward an Institutional Strategy for Entity Regulation', *Legal Ethics*, Summer 2001, Vol. 4, No. 1, 45–65.

Choudhry, N.K., Fletcher, R.H. and Soumerai, S.B., 'Systematic Review: The Relationship between Clinical Experience and Quality of Health Care', *Annals of Internal Medicine*, 2005, 142: 260–73.

Coady, M., 'The Moral Domain of Professionals', in Coady, M. and Bloch, C. (eds), *Codes of Ethics and the Professions*, 1996, Melbourne University Press, Carlton South.

Cohen, D., 'Medical Students should be Added to GMC Register, Says Judge', *British Medical Journal*, 2005, 330: 1104, 14 May.

Cornwall, J., *Hard Earned Lives*, 1984, Tavistock, London.

Cruess R.L., Cruess S.R. and Johnston, S.E., 'Professionalism: an Ideal to be Sustained', *The Lancet*, 2000, 356: 156–9.

Dauphinee, W.D., 'GMC and the Future of Revalidation: Revalidation in 2005: Progress and Maybe Some Lessons Learned?' *BMJ*, 2005, 330: 1385–7.

Davies, A.C.L., 'Don't Trust Me, I'm a Doctor – Medical Regulation and the 1999 NHS Reforms', Oxford Journal of Legal Studies, September 2000, 20(437).

Davies, M., 'The Regulation of Solicitors and the Role of the Solicitors Disciplinary Tribunal', *Professional Negligence*, 1998, Vol. 14, No. 3, 143–73.

Davies, M., 'The Solicitors Accounts Rules – How Safe is Clients' Money?', *Legal Ethics*, Summer 2000, Vol. 3, Part 1, 49–75.

Davies, M., 'Regulatory Crisis in the Solicitors' Profession', *Legal Ethics*, 2003, Vol. 6, No. 2, 185–216.

Davies, M., 'Professional Self-Regulation and the Human Rights Act', *Professional Negligence*, 2003, Vol. 19, No. 1, 278–96.

Davies, M., 'Solicitors – The Last Twenty Years of Self-regulation?', *Professional Negligence*, 2005, Vol. 21, No. 1, 3–26.

Davis, D.A. et al. 'Attempting to Ensure Physician Competence, *Journal of the American Medical Association*, 1990, 263, 15, 2041–2.

Dawson, A.J., 'Professional Codes of Practice and Ethical Conduct', 11 *Journal of Applied Philosophy*, 1994, 146.

Day, M., 'Government Rejects Independent Verification of All Death Certificates', *BMJ*, 2006, 332: 1409 (online edition).

Degeling, P., 'Reconsidering Clinical Accountability', *International Journal of Health Planning Management*, 2000, 15, 3–16.

Dingwall, R., 'Problems of Teamwork in Primary Care', in Lonsdale, S., Webb, A. and Briggs, T. L. (eds), *Teamwork in the Personal Social Services and Healthcare*, 1980, Croom Helm, London.

'Doctor Foster's Case Notes', *British Medical Journal*, 2004, 369, 14 August (electronic edition).

Donaldson, L. and Cavanagh, J., 'Clinical Complaints and their Handling: a Time for Change?, *Quality and Regulation in Healthcare*, 1992, 1(1), 21–5.

du Boulay, C., 'Revalidation for Doctors in the United Kingdom, the End or the Beginning?', *British Medical Journal*, 2000, Vol. 320, 3 June.

Dunsire, A., 'Modes of Governance', in Kooiman, J. (ed.), *Modern Governance: New Government-Society Interactions*, 1993, Sage, London.

Dyer, C., 'GMC Member Forced to Stand Down from Disciplinary Panel', *British Medical Journal*, 2000, 320: 822, 25 March.

Dyer, C., 'Professor Reprimanded for Failing to Act over Fraud', *British Medical Journal*, 2001, 322: 573, 10 March.

Dyer, C., 'Seven Doctors to Face GMC over Shipman Inquiry Findings', *British Medical Journal*, 2004, 329: 591, 11 September.

Dyer, O., 'GMC Regrets Failure to Act on Police Warning about Gynaecologist', *British Medical Journal*, 2004, 328: 1035, 1 May.

Dyer, O., 'GMC Censures Professor for Not Disclosing Conflict of Interest', *British Medical Journal*, 2005, 331: 1358, 10 December.

Eaton, L., 'Hand Washing is More Important than Cleaner Wards in Controlling MRSA', *British Medical Journal*, 2005, 330: 922, 23 April.

Edelman, L.B., Abraham, S.E. and Erlanger, H.S., 'Professional Construction of Law: The Inflated Threat of Wrongful Discharge', 26 *Law & Society Review*, 1992, 47.

Esmail, A., 'GMC and the Future of Revalidation – Failure to Act on Good Intentions', *British Medical Journal*, 2005, Vol. 330, May 14.

Ferriman, A., 'Consultant Suspended for Research Fraud', *British Medical Journal*, 2000, 321: 1429, 9 December.

Ferriman, A., 'Professor Faces GMC for Failure to Prevent and Report Fraud', *British Medical Journal*, 2001, 322: 508, 3 March.

Fiorini, D., 'Rethinking Environmental Regulation', 23 *Harvard Environmental Law Review*, 1999.

Flood, J., 'Doing Business: The Management of Uncertainty in Lawyers' Work', *Law & Society Review*, 1991, 25.

Frankel, S., Sterne, J. and Smith, C.D., 'Mortality Variations as a Measure of General Practitioner Performance: Implications of the Shipman Case', *British Medical Journal*, 2000, 320: 489, 19 February.

Freidson, E., 'A Theory of Professions: State of the Art', in Dingwall, R. and Lewis, P. (eds), *The Sociology of the Professions: Lawyers, Doctors and Others*, 1983, London, Macmillan.

Gibbs, J.P., 'Deterrence Theory and Research', in Melton, G.B. (ed.), *The Law as a Behavioural Instrument*, 1985, University of Nebraska Press, Lincoln, 87–130.

Gobert, J. and Punch, M., 'Whistleblowers, the Public Interest, and the Public Interest Disclosure Act 1998', 63 *Medical Law Review*, 2000, 1.

Godlee, F., 'The GMC: Out of its Depth?', *British Medical Journal*, 2005, 331, 30 July.

Godlee, F., 'Editor's Choice – Cure or Care?', *British Medical Journal*, 2005, 9 December.

Good, B.J. and Good, M.D., '"Learning Medicine" – The Construction of Medical Knowledge at Harvard Medical School', in Lindenbaum, S. and Lock, M., *Knowledge, Power and Practice – The Anthropology of Medicine and Everyday Life*, 1993, University of California Press, Berkeley.

Groundwater-Smith, S. and Sachs, J., 'The Activist Professional and the Reinstatement of Trust', *Cambridge Journal of Education*, 2002, Vol. 32, No. 3.

Hammond, P., 'The Death of the Autopsy', *NHS Magazine*, June 2002 (online edition).

Harre, R., 'Trust and its Surrogates', in Warren, M. (ed.), *Democracy and Trust*, 1999, Cambridge University Press, Cambridge, 249–72.

Hope, B., 'Half the Deaths of Young Infants may be Avoidable', *British Medical Journal*, 1997, 315: 143–8, 19 July.

Horder, J., Bosanquet, N. and Stocking, B., 'Ways of Influencing the Behaviour of General Practitioners', *Journal of the Royal College of General Practitioners*, 1986, 36, 517–21.

Horton, R., 'UK Medicine: What Are We to Do?', *The Lancet*, 1998, 352: 1166.

Howells, G., 'The Potential and Limits of Consumer Empowerment by Information', *Journal of Law and Society*, September 2005, 32(3), 349–70.

Hughes, E.C., 'Professions', in Callahan, J.C. (ed.), *Ethical Issues in Professional Life*, 1988, Oxford University Press, Oxford, 31.

Hunter, M., 'Alder Hey Condemns Doctors, Management, and Coroner', *British Medical Journal*, 2001, 322: 255.

Ingelfinger, F.G., 'Arrogance', 304 *New England Journal of Medicine*, 1980, 1507–11.

Irvine, D., 'The Performance of Doctors I: Professionalism and Self-Regulation in a Changing World', *British Medical Journal*, 1997, 314: 1540–42.

Irvine, D., 'The Performance of Doctors II: Maintaining Good Practice, Protecting Patients from Poor Performance', *British Medical Journal*, 1997, 314: 1613–15.

Irvine, D., 'The Performance of Doctors: the New Professionalism', *The Lancet*, 1999, 353: 1174–7.

Irvine, D., 'The Changing Relationship between the Public and the Medical Profession', *Journal of the Royal Society of Medicine*, 2001, 94: 162–9.

Irvine, D., 'Doctors in the UK: their New Professionalism and its Regulatory Framework', *The Lancet*, 2001, Vol. 358, November 24.

Irvine, D., 'GMC and the Future of Revalidation: Patients, Professionalism, and Revalidation', *British Medical Journal*, 2005, 330: 1265–8.

Jonsen, A.R. and Hellegers, A.E., 'Conceptual Foundations for an Ethics of Medical Care', in Tancredi, L.R. (ed.), *Ethics of Medical Care*, 1974, Institute of Medicine, Washington.

Kinnell, H.G., 'Serial Homicide by Doctors: Shipman in Perspective', *British Medical Journal*, 2000, Vol. 321, 1594, 30 December.

Kirwin, S., 'First Doctor Suspended under GMC Performance Procedures', *British Medical Journal*, 1999, 318:10, 2 January.

Kmietowicz, Z., 'Trusts to Handle Minor Complaints against Doctors, Says GMC', *British Medical Journal*, 2005, 331: 178, 23 July.

Kultgen, J., 'The Ideological Use of Professional Codes', in Callahan, J.C. (ed.), *Ethical Issues in Professional Life*, 1988, Oxford University Press, Oxford.

Landau, M., 'Redundancy, Rationality and the Problem of Duplication and Overlap', *Public Administration Review*, 1969, 39.

Lempp, H. and Seale, C., 'The Hidden Curriculum in Undergraduate Medical Education: Qualitative Study of Medical Students' Perceptions of Teaching', *BMJ*, 2004, 329: 770–73, 2 October.

Lewis, D., 'Shipman's Legacy: Whistleblowing Procedures for All?', *NLJ*, 2005, 155.7158(14), 7 January.

Liddell, K. and Hall, A., 'Beyond Bristol and Alder Hey: The Future Regulation of Human Tissue', *Medical Law Review*, Summer 2005, 13, 170–223.

Lloyd-Bostock, S., 'Attributions and Apologies in Letters of Complaint to Hospitals and Letters of Response', in Harvey, J.H., Orbuch, T.L. and Weber, A.L. (eds), *Attributions, Accounts and Close Relationships*, 1992, Springer-Verlag, New York.

Lock, S., 'Regulating Doctors: a Good Case for the Profession to Set Up New Inquiry', *British Medical Journal*, 1989, 299: 137–8.

Lockyer, J. and Harrison, V., 'Performance Assessment', in Davis, D.A. and Fox, R.D. (eds), *The Physician as Learner*, 1994, American Medical Association, Chicago, 176.

Longley, D., 'Complaints after Wilson; Another Case of Too Little Too Late?', *Medical Law Review*, Summer 1997, 5, 172–92.

Lord, J. and Littlejohns, P., 'Impact of Hospital and Community Provider Based Clinical Audit Programmes', *International Journal for Quality in Health Care*, 1996, 8, 6, 527–35.

Luhmann, N., 'Familiarity, Confidence, Trust: Problems and Alternatives', in Gambetta, D. (ed.), *Trust: Making and Breaking Cooperative Relations*, 1988, Blackwell, Oxford.

Maclean, M., 'Doctors, Parents and the Law – Organ Retention after Paediatric Cardiac Surgery at the Bristol Royal Infirmary', *Child and Family Law Quarterly*, December 2001,13.4 (399).

Mahendra, B., 'Bristol and Beyond', *New Law Journal*, 2001, Vol. 151, No. 6995, 1149.

Maiman, R.J., McEwen, C.A. and Mather, L., 'The Future of Legal Professionalism in Practice', *Legal Ethics*, 1999, Vol. 2, No. 1, 71–85.

Marco, C.A. and Bessman, E.S. et al, 'Ethical Issues of Cardiopulmonary Resuscitation: Current Practice among Emergency Physicians', *Academic Emergency Medicine*, 1997, 4: 898–904.

Maxwell, J.W., Lyon, T.P. and Hackett, S.C., 'Self-Regulation and Social Welfare: the Political Economy of Corporate Environmentalism', *Journal of Law & Economics*, October 2000, Vol. XLIII, 613–14.

May, W.F., 'Professional Virtue and Self-regulation', in Callahan, J.C. (ed.), *Ethical Issues in Professional Life*, 1988, Oxford University Press, Oxford.

McCall Smith, A., 'Criminal Negligence and the Incompetent Doctor', 1 *Medical Law Review* 336, 1993.

McComick, K., 'Professional Conduct and the Law Society', *Law Society Journal (N.S.W.)* 17, in Disney, J., Basten, J., Redmond, P., Ross, S. and Bell, K., *Lawyers*, 2nd ed, 1986, The Law Book Co., Melbourne.

McGuire, A., 'Ethics and Resource Allocation: An Economist's View', in Dowie, J. and Elstein, A., *Professional Judgment*, 1988, Cambridge University Press, Cambridge, 492–507.

McHale J., 'Whistleblowing in the United States, in Hunt G. (ed) *Whistleblowing in the Health Services*, 1994, Edward Arnold, London 116-133

McHale, J., 'Medical Malpractice in England: Current Trends', 2003, 2 *European Journal of Health Law* 135-151

McHale J, and Hervey, T., 'Law, Health and the European Union', 2005, 25(2) *Legal Studies* 228-259

McLean, M., 'Letting Go…Parents, Professionals and the Law in the Retention of Human Material after Post Mortem', in Bainham, A., Day Sclater, S. and Richards, M. (eds), *Body Lore and Laws*, 2002, Hart Publishing, Oxford.

Mizrahi, T., 'Managing Medical Mistakes: Ideology, Insularity and Accountability Among Internists-in-Training', *Social Science and Medicine*, 1984, 19, 135–46.

Mohammed, M.A., Cheng, K.K., Rouse, A. and Marshall, T., 'Bristol, Shipman and Clinical Governance: Shewhart's Forgotten Lessons', *The Lancet*, 2001, 357: 463–7.

Montgomery, J., 'Medicine, Accountability and Professionalism', *Journal of Law and Society*, Autumn 1989, Vol. 16, 319–39.

Mulcahy, L. and Tritter, J., 'Pathways, Pyramids and Icebergs: Mapping the Links between Dissatisfaction and Complaints', *Sociology of Health & Illness*, 1998, Vol. 20, No. 6, 823–45.

New South Wales Law Reform Commission, *Discussion Paper*, 1979, in Disney, J., Basten, J., Redmond, P., Ross, S. and Bell, K., *Lawyers*, 2nd ed, 1986, The Law Book Co., Melbourne.

New South Wales Law Reform Commission, *Second Report on the Legal Profession*, 1982, in Disney, J., Basten, J., Redmond, P., Ross, S. and Bell, K., *Lawyers*, 2nd ed, 1986, The Law Book Co., Melbourne.

Newdick, C., 'NHS Governance after Bristol: Holding On or Letting Go?, *Medical Law Review*, Summer 2002, 10, 111–31.

News, *Health Service Journal*, August 2000, Vol. 110, No. 5667.

Nicolson, D., 'Mapping Professional Legal Ethics: The Form and Focus of the Codes', *Legal Ethics*, 1998, Vol. 1, Part 1, 51–69.

Nicolson, D., 'Making Lawyers Moral? Ethical Codes and Moral Character', *Legal Studies*, November 2005, 24(4), 601–26.

Norcini, J.J., 'Where Next with Revalidation?', *British Medical Journal*, 2005, 330: 1458–9, 25 June.

Oakley, A., 'Doctor Knows Best', in Robinson, M. (ed.), *Women Confined*, 1980, Blackwell, Oxford.

Ogus, A., 'Rethinking Self-Regulation', *Oxford Journal of Legal Studies*, 1995, 15 (97).

Orts, E., 'Reflexive Environmental Law', 89 *Northwestern University Law Review*, 1995.

Paice, E., Aitken, M., Houghton, A. and Firth-Cozens, J., 'Bullying Among Doctors in Training: Cross Sectional Questionnaire Survey', *British Medical Journal*, 2004, Vol. 18, 658–9, September.

Papadakis, M. et al, 'Disciplinary Action by Medical Boards and Prior Behaviour in Medical School', *New England Journal of Medicine*, 2005, 353: 2673–82.

Parker, Christine, 'Lawyer Deregulation via Business Deregulation: Compliance Professionalism and Legal Professionalism', *International Journal of the Legal Profession*, 1999, Vol. 6, No. 2, 175–96.

Parker, J., 'Moral Philosophy – Another Disabling Profession?', Chapter 3, in Allsop, J. and Mulcaly, L., *Maintaining Professional Identity: Doctors' Responses to Complaints*, 1998, Blackwell, Oxford.

Parsons, T., 'The Professions and the Social Structure', in *Essays in Sociological Theory*, 1954, Free Press, Glencoe, Illinois.

Paterson, A., 'Professionalism and the Legal Services Market', 3 *International Journal of the Legal Profession*, 1996, 137–68.

Pickering, J., 'The Bar and the Community', 1980, 4 *District Lawyer* 6, in Disney, J., Basten, J., Redmond, P., Ross, S. and Bell, K., *Lawyers*, 2nd ed, 1986, The Law Book Co., Melbourne.

Pringle, M., 'Making Revalidation Credible', *British Medical Journal*, 2005, 330: 1515, 25 June.

Quick, O., 'Outing Medical Errors: Questions of Trust and Responsibility', *Medical Law Review*, Spring 2006, 14, 22–43.

Quine, L., 'Workplace Bullying in Junior Doctors: Questionnaire Survey', *British Medical Journal*, 2002, 324: 878–9.

'Reforming the GMC', *BMJ*, 2001, Vol. 322, 689–90, 21 March.

Rennie, S.C. and Crosby, J.R., 'Are "Tomorrow's Doctors" Honest? Questionnaire Study Exploring Medical Students' Attitudes and Reported Behaviour on Academic Misconduct', *British Medical Journal*, 2001, 322: 274–5, 3 February.

Rhode, D.L., 'Ethical Perspectives on Legal Practice', *Stanford Law Review*, 1985, Vol. 37: 589.

Robinson, J., 'Thou Shalt Not Disparage Another Doctor', *healthmatters*, Spring 1998, Issue 33, 12–14.

Samuels, A., 'Can a Doctor "Blow the Whistle" Or "Grass" on a Colleague?', *The Medico-Legal Journal*, 2002, 70(135), 5 September.

Scally, G., 'Tackling Deficient Doctors', *British Medical Journal*, 1997, 314:1568, 31 May.

Shaw, J., '"Expert Patient" – dDream or Nightmare?', *British Medical Journal*, 2004, Vol. 328, 723–4, 27 March.

'Shipman: the NHS's Response', *Health Service Journal*, 2000, Vol. 110, No. 5460, 3 February.

Smith, R., 'The Day of Judgement Comes Closer', *British Medical Journal*, 1989, 298, 1241–4.

Smith, R., 'The End of the GMC? The Government, not the GMC, is Looking at Under-performing Doctors', *British Medical Journal*, 1993, 307: 954, October 16.

Smith, R., 'Cheating at Medical School', *British Medical Journal*, 2000, Vol. 321, 398, 12 August.

Smith, R., 'The GMC: Where Now?', *British Medical Journal*, 2000, 320: 1356, 20 May.

Smith, R., 'Doctors Mangled by "Justice", *British Medical Journal*, 2004, Volume 328, 17 January.

Smith R.G., 'Reporting Medical Disciplinary Proceedings', *Media Law and Practice*, 1991, Vol. 12, Part 4, 110–14.

Snelgrove, S. and Hughes, D., 'Perceptions of Teamwork in Acute Medical Wards', in Allen, D. and Hughes, D., *Nursing and the Division of Labour in Healthcare*, 2002, Palgrave Macmillan, Basingstoke.

Southgate, L., Campbell, M., Cox, J., Foulkes, J., Jolly, B., McCrorie, P. and Tombleson, P., 'The General Medical Council's Performance Procedures: the Development and Implementation of Tests of Competence with Examples from General Practice', *Medical Education*, 2001, Vol 35 (Suppl. 1): 20–28.

Southwood, P., 'Whistleblowing in Accountancy', in Lewis, David B. (ed.), *Whistleblowing at Work*, 2000, The Athlone Press, London.

Spiegelhalter, D.J., Kinsman, R., Grigg, O. and Treasure, T., 'Risk-adjusted Sequential Probability Ratio Tests: Applications to Bristol, Shipman and Adult Cardiac Survey', *International Journal for Quality in Health Care*, 2003, 15: 7–13.

Hon J J Spigelman AC, 'Are Lawyers Lemons?: Competition Principles and Professional Regulation', 2003, 77 *Australian Law Journal* 44–61.

Spilka, I., 'Risk-Based Compliance Monitoring', *Compliance Monitor*, November 2001, 14.4(6) (Lexis transcript).

Stacey, M., 'The General Medical Council and Self-regulation', in Gladstone, D. (ed.), *Regulating Doctors*, 2000, Institute for the Study of Civil Society, London.

Stiglitz, J.E., 'Contributions of the Economics of Information to Twentieth Century Economics', 2000, 115 *Quarterly Journal of Economics* 1441.

Sztompka, P., 'Trust, Distrust and Two Paradoxes of Democracy', *European Journal of Social Theory*, 1998.

Teubner, G., 'Substantive and Reflexive Elements in Modern Law', 17 *Law & Society Review*, 1983, 239, 254–5.

Teubner, G., 'After Legal Instrumentalism: Strategic Models of Post-Regulatory Law', in Teubner, G. (ed.), *Dilemma of Law in the Welfare State*, 1986, Berlin.

Toynbee, P., 'Between Aspiration and Reality', *British Medical Journal*, 2002, 325: 718–19.

Trebilock, M.J., Tuohy, C.J. and Wolfson, A.D., 'Professional Regulation', 1979, 40–43, in Disney, J., Basten, J., Redmond, P., Ross, S. and Bell, K., *Lawyers*, 2nd ed, 1986, The Law Book Co., Melbourne, 209.

Tur, R.H.S., 'Accountability and Lawyers', in Chadwick, R.F. (ed.), *Ethics and the Professions*, 1994, Avebury, Aldershot.

Vickers, L., 'Whistleblowing in the Health Service', in Lewis, David B. (ed.), 'Whistleblowing at Work', 2000, The Athlone Press, London.

Walshe, K. and Benson, L., 'GMC and the Future of Revalidation – Time for Radical Reform', *British Medical Journal*, 2005, 330: 1504–1506, 25 June.

Wasserstrom, R.A., 'Lawyers as Professionals: Some Moral Issues', in Callahan, J.C. (ed.), *Ethical Issues in Professional Life*, 1988, Oxford University Press, Oxford, 65.

Webb, J. and Nicolson, D., 'Institutionalising Trust: Ethics and the Responsive Regulation of the Legal Profession', *Legal Ethics*, Winter 1999, Vol. 2, No. 2, 148–68.

Wergin, F., 'CME and Change in Practice, *Journal of Continuing Education in the Health Professions*, 1988, 8, 147–59.

White, C., 'NICE Expands Research and Development Role', *British Medical Journal*, 2003, 326: 1056, 17 May.

Wilmshurst, P., 'The GMC is Too Lenient', *British Medical Journal*, 2002, 325: 397, 17 August.

**Books**

Abel, R.L., *American Lawyers*, 1989, Oxford University Press, New York.

Alderson, P., *Choosing for Children: Parent's Consent to Surgery*, 1989, Oxford University Press, Oxford.

Allen, D. and Hughes, D., *Nursing and the Division of Labour in Healthcare*, 2002, Palgrave Macmillan, Basingstoke.

Allsop, J., *Health Policy and the NHS: Towards 2000*, 1995, Longman, London.

Allsop, J. and Mulcaly, L., *Maintaining Professional Identity: Doctors' Responses to Complaints*, 1998, Blackwell, Oxford.

Bainham, A., Day Sclater, S. and Richards, S.M. (eds), *Body Lore and Laws*, 2002, Hart Publishing, Oxford.

Baldwin, R. and Cave, M., *Understanding Regulation*, 1999, Oxford University Press, Oxford.

Barber, B., *The Logic and Limits of Trust*, 1983, Rutgers, New York.

Bauman, Z., *Postmodern Ethics*, 1993, Blackwell, Oxford.

Bauman, Z., *Alone Again: Ethics After Certainty*, 1994, Demos, London.

Becher, T., *Professional Practices*, 1999, Transaction Publishers, New Brunswick, New Jersey.

Becher, T., Eraut, M. and Knight, J., *Policies for Educational Accountability*, 1981, Heineman, London.

Black, D., *The Behavior of Law*, 1976, Academic Press, New York.

Blau, P., *Exchange and Power in Social Life*, 1964, Wiley, New York.

Bosk, C., *Forgive and Remember: Managing Medical Failure*, 2nd ed., 1982, Chicago University Press, Chicago.

Brazier, M., *Medicine, Patients and the Law*, 1992, Penguin, London.

Bull, A., *Risk and Trust in the NHS*, Foxwood, H. (ed.), 2002, The Smith Institute, London.

Callahan, J.C. (ed.), *Ethical Issues in Professional Life*, 1988, Oxford University Press, Oxford.

Carrier, J. and Kendall, I., *Medical Negligence: Complaints and Compensation*, 1990, Avebury, Aldershot.

Chadwick, R.F. (ed.), *Ethics and the Professions*, 1994, Avebury, Aldershot.

Coady, M. and Bloch, C. (eds), *Codes of Ethics and the Professions*, 1996, Melbourne University Press, Carlton South.

Davis, D.A. and Fox, R.D. (eds), *The Physician as Learner*, 1994, American Medical Association, Chicago, 176.

De Cruz, P., *Comparative Healthcare Law*, 2001, Cavendish, London.

Diamond, J., *Snake Oil*, 2001, Vintage, London.

Dingwall, R. and Lewis, P. (eds), *The Sociology of the Professions: Lawyers, Doctors and Others*, 1983, Macmillan, London.

Dingwall, R., Rafferty, A.M. and Webster, C., *An Introduction to the Social History of Nursing*, 1988, Routledge, London.

Disney, J., Basten, J., Redmond, P., Ross, S. and Bell, K., *Lawyers*, 2nd ed, 1986, The Law Book Co., Melbourne.

Dowie, J. and Elstein, A., *Professional Judgment*, 1988, Cambridge University Press, Cambridge.

Earle, T.C. and Cvetkovich, G.T., *Social Trust: Toward a Cosmopolitan Society*, 1995, Praeger, Westport, CT.

Freeman, M.D.A. (ed.), *Current Legal Problems*, 2001, Vol. 54, Oxford University Press, Oxford.

Freidson, E., *Professional Dominance: The Social Structure of Medical Care*, 1970, Atherton Press, New York.

Freidson, E., *Profession of Medicine: A Study of the Sociology of Applied Knowledge*, 1970, Dodd, Mead and Co., New York.

Freidson, E., *Doctoring Together*, 1975, Elsevier, New York.

Freidson, E., *Professionalism Reborn*, 1994, Polity Press, Cambridge.

Freidson, E., *Professionalism: The Third Logic*, 2001, Polity Press, Cambridge.

Gambetta, D. (ed.), *Trust: Making and Breaking Cooperative Relations*, 1988, Blackwell, Oxford.

Garland, D., *The Culture of Control*, 2001, Oxford University Press, Oxford.

Gawande, A., *Complications*, 2003, Profile Books, London.

Giddens, A., *The Consequences of Modernity*, 1990, Polity Press, Cambridge.

Giddens, A., *Modernity and Self Identity: Self and Society in the Late Modern Age*, 1991, Polity Press, Cambridge.

Gigerenzer, G., *Reckoning with Risk*, 2002, Penguin, London.

Gladstone, D. (ed.), *Regulating Doctors*, 2000, Institute for the Study of Civil Society, London.

Gould, D., *Examining Doctors*, 1991, Faber and Faber, London.

Green, D., *Which Doctor? A Critical Analysis of the Professional Barriers to Competition in Health Care*, 1985, Institute of Economic Affairs, London.

Habermas, J., *Legitimation Crisis*, 1976, Heinemann, London.

Hammond, P. and Mosley, M., *Trust Me I'm A Doctor*, 2002, Metro Publishing, London.

Handy, C., *The Hungry Spirit*, 1998, Arrow, London.

Harvey, J.H., Orbuch, T.L. and Weber, A.L. (eds), *Attributions, Accounts and Close Relationships*, 1992, Springer-Verlag, New York.

Heijder, A. and van Geuns, H., *Professional Codes of Ethics*, 1976, Amnesty International Press, London.

Hervey, T. and McHale, J., *Health Law in the European Union*, 2004, Cambridge University Press, Cambridge.

Hirsch, F., *Social Limits to Growth*, 1978, Harvard University Press, Cambridge, Mass.

Irvine, D., *The Doctors' Tale*, 2003, Radcliffe Medical Press, Oxford.

Kennedy, I., *The Unmasking of Medicine*, 1981, Allen & Unwin, London.

Kennedy, I. and Grubb, A., *Medical Law*, 2000, Butterworths, London.

Klein, R., *Complaints against Doctors: a Study in Professional Accountability*, 1973, Charles Knight, London.

Klein, R., *The Politics of the National Health Service*, 1983, Longman, London.

Knight, B., *Legal Aspects of Medical Practice*, 1992, Churchill Livingstone, London.

Kogan, M. and Redfern, S., *Making Use of Clinical Audit*, 1995, Open University Press, Buckingham.

Kooiman, J. (ed.), *Modern Governance: New Government-Society Interactions*, 1993, Sage, London.

Larkin G.V., *Occupational Monopoly and Modern Medicine*, 1983, Tavistock, London.

Larson, M.S., *The Rise of Professionalism*, 1977, University of California Press, Berkeley, CA.

Lewis, D.B. (ed.), *Whistleblowing at Work*, 2000, The Athlone Press, London.

Lindenbaum, S. and Lock, M., *Knowledge, Power and Practice – The Anthropology of Medicine and Everyday Life*, 1993, University of California Press, Berkeley, CA.

Lonsdale, S., Webb, A. and Briggs, T.L. (eds), *Teamwork in the Personal Social Services and Healthcare*, 1980, Croom Helm, London.

Luban, D., *Lawyers and Justice: An Ethical Study*, 1988, Princeton University Press, Princeton, NJ.

Luban, D. (ed.), *The Ethics of Lawyers*, 1994, Dartmouth, Aldershot.

Luhmann, N., *Trust and Power*, 1980, Wiley, New York.

Macdonald, K.M., *The Sociology of the Professions*, 1995, Sage, London.

Mason, J.K., McCall Smith, R.A. and Laurie, G.T., *Law and Medical Ethics*, 2002, Butterworths, London.

McHale J, and Hervey, T., Health Law and the European Union, 2004, Cambridge University Press, Cambridge

Melton, G.B. (ed.), *The Law as a Behavioural Instrument*, 1985, University of Nebraska Press, Lincoln.

Merry, A. and McCall Smith, A., *Errors, Medicine and the Law*, 2001, Cambridge University Press, Cambridge.

Mulcahy, L., *Disputing Doctors*, 2003, Open University Press, Maidenhead.

Newman, C., *The Evolution of Medical Education in the 19th Century*, 1957, Oxford University Press, Oxford.

Parry, N. and Parry, J., *The Rise of the Medical Profession*, 1976, Croom Helm, London.

Perkin, E., *The Rise of Professional Society – England Since 1880*, 1996, Routledge, London.

Perrow, C., *Normal Accidents: Living with High Risk Technologies*, 1984, Basic Books, New York.

Phillips, A.F., *Medical Negligence Law: Seeking a Balance*, 1997, Dartmouth, Aldershot.

Porter, R., *Quacks*, 2000, Tempus Publishing Inc., Charleston, SC.

Porter, R., *Blood and Guts: A Short History of Medicine*, 2002, Penguin, London.

Power, M., *The Audit Society: Rituals of Verification*, 1999, Oxford University Press, Oxford.

Pyke-Lees, W., *Centenary of the GMC 1858-1958: The History and Present Work of the Council*, 1958, GMC, London.

Richman, J., *Medicine and Health*, 1987, Longman, Harlow.

Robinson, M. (ed.), *Women Confined*, 1980, Blackwell, Oxford.

Rosethal, D., Marshall, V., Macpherson, A. and French, S., *Nurses, Patients and Families*, 1980, Croom Helm, London.

Rosenthal, M., *The Incompetent Doctor*, 1995, Open University Press, Buckingham.

Rueschemeyer, D., *Lawyers and their Society: A Comparative Study of the Legal Profession in Germany and the United States*, 1973, Harvard University Press, Cambridge, Mass.

Sharpe, V. and Faden, A., *Medical Harm: Historical, Conceptual and Ethical Dimensions of Iatrogenic Illness*, 1998, Cambridge University Press, Cambridge.

Shaw, G.B., *Preface to the Doctor's Dilemma*, 1957, Penguin, London.

Smith, R., *Medical Discipline: The Professional Conduct of the GMC 1858-1990*, 1994, Oxford University Press, Oxford.

Solomon, R.C. and Flores, F., *Building Trust*, 2001, Oxford University Press, Oxford.

Stacey, M., *Regulating British Medicine: the General Medical Council*, 1992, Wiley, Chichester.

Stevens, R., *Medical Practice in Modern England: the Impact of Specialisation and State Medicine*, 1966, Yale University Press, London.

Stimson, G. and Webb, B., *Going to See the Doctor: The Consultation Process in General Practice*, 1975, Routledge & Kegan Paul, London.

Tallis, R., *Hippocratic Oaths*, 2004, Atlantic, London.

Tancredi, L.R. (ed.), *Ethics of Medical Care*, 1974, Institute of Medicine, Washington.

Tassano, F., *The Power of Life of Death*, 1995, Duckworth, London.

Teff, H. (ed.), *Medical Practice and Malpractice*, 2001, Ashgate, Aldershot.

Teubner, G., (ed.), *Dilemma of Law in the Welfare State*, 1986, Berlin.

Toombs, K., *The Meaning of Illness – A Phenomenological Account of the Different Perspectives of Physician and Patient*, 1992, Kluwer Academic Publishers, Norwell, MA.

Vincent, C., *Medical Accidents*, 1993, Oxford Medical Publications, Oxford.

von Hirsch, A., Garland, D. and Wakefield, A. (eds), *Ethical and Social Perspectives on Situational Crime Prevention*, 2000, Hart Publishing, Oxford.

Walshe, K., *Regulating Healthcare: a Prescription for Improvement?*, 2003, Open University Press, Buckingham.

Watkins, S., *Medicine and Labour: the Politics of a Profession*, 1987, Lawrence and Wishart, London.

Wootton, D., *Bad Medicine: Doctors Doing Harm Since Hippocrates*, 2006, Oxford University Press, Oxford.

## Other Sources


Davies, H., Chairman FSA, *Proceedings of Financial Services Authority Conference – A Radical New Approach to Regulation.* Keynote Speech, *A New Regulator for the New Millennium*, www.fsa,gov.uk.

GMC, *The Conduct Procedures of the General Medical Council*, 2000.

Irvine, D., 'The Changing Relationship Between the Public and Medical Profession', The Lloyd Roberts Lecture – Royal Society of Medicine, 16 January 2001.

O'Neill, O., *Reith Lectures 2002*, radio 4 http://www.bbc.co.uk/radio4/reith2002/ ONora O'Neill.

*Real Story*, broadcast on BBC 1, 7.30pm, 8 November 2004.

Royal College of Physicians, 'Response to the Human Tissue Bill', 14 May 2004.


## Reports and Consultation Papers


*A Statement on Behalf of the Government, the Medical Profession and the NHS: A Commitment to Quality; a Quest for Excellence*, 2001, Department of Health, London.

Ackroyd, E., 'The Patient's Complaint', *British Journal of Hospital Medicine*, December 1986.

Allen, I., *The Handling of Complaints by the GMC: a Study of Decision-making and Outcomes*, 2000, Policy Studies Institute, London.

Allen, I., Perkins, E. and Witherspoon, S., *The Handling of Complaints Against Doctors*, 1996, Policy Studies Institute for the Racial Equality Group of the GMC, London.

*An Inquiry into Quality and Practice within the National Health Service Arising from the Actions of Rodney Ledward – The Report*, 1 June 2000.

Association of Community Health Councils for England and Wales, *The NHS Complaint Procedure: ACHCEW's Memorandum to the Public Administration Committee*, 1990.

Better Regulation Task Force, *Alternatives to Regulation*, 2004, Cabinet Office, London.

BMA, 'Doctors Savage GMC "Dinosaur"', Press Release, Thursday, 5 July 2001.

*BMA Response to the Chief Medical Officer Review on Maintaining High Standards of Professional Practice*, May 2005.

Clementi, D., *Review of the Regulatory Framework for Legal Services in England and Wales – Final Report*, December 2004.

*CMO Review of Medical Revalidation: A Call for Ideas*, 3 March 2005.

Committee of Inquiry – Independent Investigation into how the NHS handled Allegations about the Conduct of Richard Neale, Cm 6315, 2004.

*Competition and Regulation in the Legal Services Market*, July 2003.

Department for Constitutional Affairs, *The Future of Legal Services: Putting the Consumer First*, October 2005, Cm 6679.

Department of Health, *A First Class Service*, 1998, HSC 1998/113.

Department of Health, *Guidance for Staff on Relations with Public and Media*, EL(93)13.

Department of Health and Social Security, *Report of the Committee on Hospital Complaints Procedure*, HMSO, London.

Department of Health, *Harold Shipman's Clinical Practice 1974-1998* (http://www.doh.gov.uk/hshipmanpractice/shipman.pdf).

Department of Health, *An Organisation with a Memory*, Report of an Expert Group on Learning from Adverse Events in the NHS Chaired by the Chief Medical Officer, 2000.

Department of Health, *The NHS Plan: A Plan for Investment, A Plan for Reform*, Cm 4818-I, July 2000.

Department of Health, *Building a Safer NHS for Patients – Implementing an Organisation with a Memory*, April 2001.

Department of Health, *Revalidation to be Reviewed*, Press Release, 17 April 2004.

Department of Health, *Maintaining High Professional Standards in the Modern NHS:Directions on Disciplinary Procedures*, Department of Health, Crown, London, 2005.

Department of Health, *Good Doctors, Safer Patients – Proposals to Strengthen the System to Assure and Improve the Performance of Doctors and to Protect the Safety of Patients: A Report by the Chief Medical Officer*, July 2006.

*Developing Medical Regulation: a Vision for the Future – the GMC's Response to the Call for Ideas by the Review of Clinical Performance and Medical Regulation*, April 2005.

Finocchio, L.J. et al, *Reforming Health Care Workforce Regulation: Policy Considerations for the 21st Century*, Health Professions Commission, 1995.

FSA, *Building the New Regulator, Progress Report 1*, December 2000.

GMC, *Professional Conduct and Discipline: Fitness to Practise*, 1987.

GMC, *Tomorrow's Doctors*. London, 1993.

GMC, *Performance Procedures Position Paper No 2*, June 1996.

GMC, *A Problem With Your Doctor*, 1997.

GMC, *Report of the Revalidation Steering Group*, February 1999.

GMC, *Revalidating Doctors*, 2000.

GMC, *The Draft Report of the Governance Working Group*, 18 September 2000.

GMC, *Revalidation: Report on the Outcome of the Consultation Exercise*, November 2000.

GMC, *Acting Fairly to Protect Patients: Reform of the GMC's Fitness to Practise Procedures*, March 2001.

GMC, *Effective, Inclusive and Accountable Reform of the GMC's Structure, Constitution and Governance*, March 2001.

GMC, *The Policy Framework for Revalidation: A Position Paper*, July 2004.

GMC, *Developing a Risk-Based Approach to Regulation: the Early Identification of Impairment*, 17 March 2005.

GMC, *Developing Medical Regulation: a Vision for the Future – the GMC's Response to the Call for Ideas by the Review of Clinical Performance and Medical Regulation*, April 2005.

GMC, *Developing Risk-based Regulation: Progress Report*, 20 September 2005.

Hampton, P., *Reducing Administrative Burdens: Effective Inspection and Enforcement*, December 2004.

Kennedy, I.M., *The Inquiry into the Management of Care of Children Receiving Complex Heart Surgery at The Bristol Royal Infirmary* (www.bristol-inquiry.org.uk).

*Learning from Bristol: The DH Response to the Report of the Public Inquiry into Children's Heart Surgery at the Bristol Royal Infirmary 1984-1995.*

Legal Services Ombudsman, *In Whose Interest – Annual Report of the Legal Services Ombudsman for England and Wales 2003/2004*, HC 729.

Matthews, J., *Committee of Inquiry to Investigate how the NHS Handled Allegations about the Performance and Conduct of Richard Neale*, August 2004, Cm 6315.

National Audit Office, *A Safer Place for Patients: Learning to Improve Patient Safety*, 31 October 2005, www.nao.org.uk.

National Clinical Assessment Authority, *Understanding Performance Difficulties in Doctors*, November 2004.

National Patient Safety Agency, *Building a Memory: Preventing Harm, Reducing Risks and Improving Patient Safety. The First Report of the National Reporting and Learning System and the Patient Safety Observatory*, July 2005.

NHS Executive, *Being Heard: Report of the Review Committee on NHS Complaint Procedures*, 1994.

NHS Executive, *Modernising Medical Regulation: Interim Strengthening of the GMC's Fitness to Practise Procedures*, March 2000.

Pauffley, Honourable Mrs Justice, Committee of Inquiry – Independent Investigation into how the NHS Handled Allegations about the Conduct of Clifford Ayling, 15 July 2004, Cm 6298.

Report of a Committee of Enquiry set up for the Medical Profession in the United Kingdom, *Competence to Practice*, 1976.

'Report of the Public Inquiry into Children's Heart Surgery at the Bristol Royal Infirmary 1984–1995', Learning from Bristol, CM5207(I ), July 2001.

Richardson, Lord, *The Council Transformed*, GMC Annual Report 1983, GMC, London.

Robinson, J., *A Patient Voice at the GMC: a Lay Member's View of the GMC*, Report 1, Health Rights, London.

Royal Liverpool Children's Inquiry, *Report*, 2001, Stationery Office, London (www.rlcinquiry.org.uk/).

Secretary of State for Social Services, *Report of the Committee of Inquiry into the Regulation of the Medical Profession,* 1975, Cmnd 6018, HMSO, London.

Smith, J., *The Shipman Inquiry*, First Report, Volume One, Death Disguised, July 2002, HMSO.

Smith, J., The Second Report of the Shipman Inquiry, *The Police Investigation of March 1998*, 14 July 2003, Cm 5853.

Smith, J., The Third Report of the Shipman Inquiry, *Death Certification and the Investigation of Deaths by Coroners*, 14 July 2003, Cm 5854.

Smith, J., The Fourth Report of the Shipman Inquiry, *The Regulation of Controlled Drugs in the Community*, 15 July 2004, Cm 6249.

Smith, J., The Fifth Report of the Shipman Inquiry, *Safeguarding Patients: Lessons from the Past – Proposals for the Future* (www.the-shipman-inquiry.org.uk).

Smith, J., The Sixth Report of the Shipman Inquiry, *The Final Report*, 27 January 2005.

*Solicitors Complaints Bureau Final Annual Report, 1 January–31 August 1996.*

*Supporting Doctors, Protecting Patients*, NHS Consultation Paper, 1999.

*The Bichard Inquiry Report*, 2004, HC 653, HMSO.

*The Future of Professionally Led Regulation for General Practice – a Discussion Document Issued in Conjunction with and on Behalf of The Royal College of General Practitioners, The General Practitioners Committee of the British Medical Association and the Joint Committee on Postgraduate Training for General Practice.*

*The Kerr/Haslam Inquiry Report*, July 2005, Cm 6640-1.

*The Supervision of Solicitors – The Next Decade*, The Law Society, 4.

**Newspaper Articles**

Armstrong, S., 'Dad Fights for Death Case Doc to be Fired', *Newcastle Evening Chronicle*, 6 January 2004, 2 (Lexis transcript).

Barkham, P., 'The Shipman Report', *The Times*, 20 July 2002, 15.

Bestic, L., 'Sidelined and Shamed without Trial', *Evening Standard*, 8 December 2003.

Boseley, S., 'Doctors' Caring Image Struggles to Survive', *The Guardian*, 13 May 2000.

Boseley, S., 'Doctors Failing 3m Patients', *The Guardian*, 18 December 2004, 1.

Boseley, S. and Hartley-Brewer, J., 'Doctors Plunge into New Crisis', *The Guardian*, 30 June 2000 (web edition).

Boseley, S. and Wintour, P., 'New Checks will Rule Out "Dodgy Doctors", *The Guardian*, 23 June 2000 (web edition).

Boseley Heath, S., 'Whistle-blower Accuses NHS: On Eve of Report into Baby Cardiac Surgery Deaths, Consultant says He was Forced Out for Sounding Alarm', *The Guardian,* 18 July 2001, 2.

Bruce, D., 'Vinall Faced 4 Previous Complaints', *Yorkshire Evening Post*, 11 March 2002 (Lexis transcript).

Catto, G., 'Public Opinion', *The Times, Public Agenda*, 19 October 2004, 3.

Dalrymple, T., 'Useful Scapegoat Struck Off', *The Times*, 21 July 2005.

'Deadly Mistakes', *The Times*, 13 August 2004, 25.

'Doctors Accused', *The Times*, 1 June 2006, 4.

'Doctors Declare No Confidence in GMC', *The Guardian*, 29 June 2000 (web edition).

Edzard, E., 'The GMC is Right to Come Down Hard on Doctors who Wrongly Prescribe Complementary Medicine', *The Guardian*, 16 November 2004.

'Five Years for GP in Sex Assaults', *Daily Mail*, 20 March 2004, 5.

Hall, C., 'NHS at Fault for Failing to Stop Sex Assault GP', *The Daily Telegraph*, 31 August 2001, 9.

Hammond, P., 'Bristol Inquiry: Medical Training Means Learning How to be Callous; a Physician's View', *Independent on Sunday*, 22 July 2001, 6.

'Inquiry into Blunders by Doctor, 78', *The Guardian*, 13 June 2000 (web edition).

Jenkins, R., 'Doctor Jailed for Indecent Acts on Women Patients', *The Times*, 20 March 2004, 9.

Laurance, J., 'GPs Face Inquiry for Failing to Stop Colleague Abusing Patients', *The Independent*, 31 August 2001.

Lawrence, L., 'Sex Predator Doctor Had Been Struck Off Twice Before I Was Victim No. 3; Patient's Fury over GMC Scandal', *Sunday Mirror*, 14 July 2002, 27.

Lister, S., 'How a Fake Doctor Took £1½m and Helped 1,000 People to get Asylum', *The Times*, 18 January 2005, 3.

Macaskill, M. and Ungoed-Thomas, J., 'Elderly are Helped to Die to Clear Beds, Claims Doctor', *Sunday Times*, 2 April 2000.

McLeod, N., 'Sickening. This Bungling Doctor was Convicted of Killing a Patient. 8 Months Later He's Back at Work', *News of the World*, 4 January 2004 (Lexis transcript).

Rozenberg, J., 'Shipman Inquiry Findings Rejected in Coroners Bill', *Daily Telegraph*, 12 June 2006 (online edition).

Sander, C., 'Why Low Body Count is Fatal for Anatomy', *The Times Higher*, 6 June 2003, 11.

Sherifi, J., 'We Doctors Work in a Climate of Fear', *The Times*, 29 December 2004.

'Struck Off; Dr Kolathur Unni', *The Times*, 12 July 1989.

Templeton, S., 'Doctors Face Charges after 12-year Fight', *The Sunday Herald*, 25 August 2002 (Lexis transcript).

Templeton, S., 'Babies Fall Sick aş Doctors Ignore Superbug Hygiene', *The Sunday Times*, 16 October 2005, 2.

'The Bristol Report Must Mark the End of Doctors' Lack of Accountability – Incompetence and Arrogance Make a Lethal Combination', *The Independent*, 19 July 2001, 3.

Waterston, C., 'Dirty Docs Carry on Working; Perverts a Danger to Women Patients', *The People*, 5 December 2004.

Wells, T., 'How GMC Turned on Brave NHS Whistleblower', *Sunday Mercury*, 6 February 2005.

Woolcock, N. and Henderson, M., 'Blundering Hospitals are "Killing 40,000 Patients a Year"', *The Times*, 13 August 2004, 1.

# Index